Praise for *George VI and Elizabeth*

'*George VI and Elizabeth* is a vivid history that captures the courage of a
couple whose actions saved a monarchy. It is also a largely unknown love story.
Sally Bedell Smith's reputation rests on her commitment to scholarship and
access to previously undiscovered information. But it's not enough to find it – you
have to bring wisdom to it. This book is a deeply moving marvel'
Peggy Noonan, columnist for *The Wall Street Journal*

'Sally Bedell Smith takes us into the inner sanctum of the Windsors,
giving us an intimate and gripping portrait of a royal marriage
that survived betrayal, tragedy and war. The product of meticulous
research, *George VI and Elizabeth* is an unputdownable book'
Amanda Foreman, bestselling author of *Georgiana:
Duchess of Devonshire*

'Sally Bedell Smith has written a richly textured and deeply
moving paean to the power of duty, honor and courage
in Britain's darkest – and finest – hour'
Evan Thomas, author of *First: Sandra Day O'Connor*

'With a marvelous combination of sympathy and perception,
Sally Bedell Smith has created a memorable and touching portrait
of two decent people who took on a job they never wanted
and did it with dedication, courage and success'
Margaret MacMillan, author of *War:
How Conflict Shaped Us*

Praise for *Prince Charles*

'[Smith] understands the British upper classes and aristocracy
(including the royals) very well indeed . . . Smith makes many telling, shrewd
points in pursuit of realigning the popular image of Prince Charles'
William Boyd, *New York Times Book Review*

Praise for *Elizabeth the Queen*

'Smith breaks new ground, [with the cooperation of] the Queen's
relatives and friends . . . [A] smart and satisfying book'
Los Angeles Times

ABOUT THE AUTHOR

Sally Bedell Smith is the *New York Times* bestselling author of *Elizabeth the Queen* and *Prince Charles*, as well as biographies of William S. Paley; Pamela Harriman; Diana, Princess of Wales; John and Jacqueline Kennedy; and Bill and Hillary Clinton. An on-air contributor for CNN since 2017, she was a contributing editor at *Vanity Fair* from 1996 to 2018 and previously worked at *Time* and *The New York Times*, where she was a cultural news reporter. In 2012, Smith was the recipient of the Washington Irving Medal for Literary Excellence. She is the mother of three children and lives in Washington, D.C., with her husband, Stephen G. Smith.

King George VI and Queen Elizabeth with Princesses Elizabeth and Margaret in coronation robes and crowns.

GEORGE VI
and
ELIZABETH

*The Marriage That
Shaped the Monarchy*

SALLY BEDELL SMITH

MICHAEL JOSEPH

PENGUIN MICHAEL JOSEPH

UK | USA | Canada | Ireland | Australia
India | New Zealand | South Africa

Penguin Michael Joseph is part of the Penguin Random House group of companies
whose addresses can be found at global.penguinrandomhouse.com

First published in the United States of America by Random House,
an imprint and division of Penguin Random House LLC 2023
First published in Great Britain by Penguin Michael Joseph 2023
001

Book design by Susan Turner
Printed and bound in Great Britain by Clays Ltd, Elcograf S.p.A.

The authorized representative in the EEA is Penguin Random House Ireland,
Morrison Chambers, 32 Nassau Street, Dublin D02 YH68

A CIP catalogue record for this book is available from the British Library

HARDBACK ISBN: 978–0–241–63821–7
TRADE PAPERBACK ISBN: 978–0–241–63822–4

www.greenpenguin.co.uk

Penguin Random House is committed to a
sustainable future for our business, our readers
and our planet. This book is made from Forest
Stewardship Council® certified paper.

For Amanda Urban

CONTENTS

A NOTE ON ROYAL NAMES

Names in the royal family are inconsistent and often puzzling, partly due to habitual nicknaming, but more because of the inevitable changes that come with the progression of titles, especially among those first in line to the throne.

For the purposes of this book, King George VI will be variously known as Prince Albert (his given name); Albert; Bertie, his nickname in the family throughout his life; the Duke of York—the title his father gave him in 1920; George VI, the name he chose from among his four Christian names when he ascended the throne in 1936; and the King.

Queen Elizabeth will be referred to as Lady Elizabeth Bowes Lyon; Elizabeth; the Duchess of York—her title on marrying Albert, the Duke of York, in 1923; Queen Elizabeth, the title she took on her husband's accession in 1936; the Queen; and the Queen Mother after the death of her husband in 1952.

Princess Elizabeth, the future Queen Elizabeth II, will be referred to as Princess Elizabeth, her name from birth; Lilibet, the nickname from childhood she gave herself; Queen Elizabeth II on taking the throne in February 1952; and the Queen.

Princess Margaret, the younger daughter of George VI and Queen Elizabeth, will be called Princess Margaret, her birth name, and Margaret.

King George V will be called first Prince George, then George V.

Queen Mary will be referred to initially as Princess May, as she was known from the time of her birth, and Queen Mary after her husband, George V, took the throne in 1910.

King Edward VIII, the older brother of King George VI, will be called Prince Edward or Edward, as well as David, his name within the family; the Prince of Wales—his title from 1910 until he became king in January 1936 on the death of George V; and the Duke of Windsor—the title his brother gave him after the abdication in December 1936.

Wallis Warfield Simpson, the Duke of Windsor's wife, will be called Mrs. Simpson, Wallis, and the Duchess of Windsor following her marriage to the duke in 1937.

Prince Henry, a younger brother of George VI, will be called Henry rather than Harry, his family nickname (to avoid confusion with his sister Mary's husband, also nicknamed Harry), and the Duke of Gloucester, the title given him in 1928 by his father, George V.

Princess Alice, Duchess of Gloucester, will be called the Duchess of Gloucester and Alice. (It was not until the death of her husband in 1974 that Queen Elizabeth II designated her aunt as a princess.)

Prince George, another younger brother of George VI, will be called Prince George, but also Georgie, his family nickname; he will also be referred to as the Duke of Kent, the title given him by King George V in 1934.

Princess Marina, the wife of Prince George, will be called Princess Marina, the Duchess of Kent, and Marina.

Princess Mary, the younger sister of George VI, will be called Princess Mary.

Henry Lascelles, the sixth Earl of Harewood (pronounced "Hahrwood"), Princess Mary's husband, will be called Harry Lascelles and later Harry Harewood, when he inherited the earldom in 1929 on his father's death.

Prince John, the youngest brother of George VI, will be called

Prince John and Johnnie, as he was known in the family until his death at age thirteen in 1919 from a major epileptic seizure.

Other historical and collateral members of the royal family will be known by their given titles: for example, King Edward VII or Edward VII and Queen Alexandra or Alexandra, the grandparents of King George VI.

In the interests of simplicity, the terms His or Her Royal Highness and His or Her Majesty will be avoided except in specific circumstances or when mentioned in a direct quotation.

*"They were more resilient and strong-minded
than they appeared to be."*

King George VI and Queen Elizabeth on their twenty-fifth wedding anniversary,
April 26, 1948.

PROLOGUE

IT IS A BIG CLAIM TO SAY THAT A SINGLE ROYAL COUPLE SAVED THE centuries-old British monarchy. But King George VI and Queen Elizabeth, later known as the Queen Mother (or "Queen Mum" in affectionate slang), did exactly that, by an accident of history and through personal qualities that earned the admiration and support of the British public. They imparted their values and sense of duty to their daughter Elizabeth, who succeeded her father in 1952. As Queen Elizabeth II, she became the longest-reigning monarch in British history and arguably the most popular.

The accident of history was the constitutional crisis provoked by George VI's older brother, King Edward VIII, who abdicated in 1936 because of religious, official, and popular opposition to his intended marriage to the American socialite Wallis Simpson. She had already divorced one husband and was divorcing her second. Because the monarch is the nominal head of the Church of England, which forbade divorced people to remarry in the church, she was considered an untenable choice to be queen. When Edward defied the advice of Prime Minister Stanley Baldwin and insisted on Queen Wallis,

Baldwin and his cabinet threatened to resign en masse. In the end, Edward VIII chose Mrs. Simpson over the Crown.

Shocked by his older brother's decision, George VI nevertheless embraced his destiny. He transformed himself into an exceptional leader, through grit and determination. During his fifteen-year reign, his wife, Queen Elizabeth, was at his side every step of the way, providing support, encouragement, and wise counsel.

Their remarkable partnership lasted until George VI's death at age fifty-six. Elizabeth was just fifty-one and would live to be nearly 102. Her fifty years as a widow—the merry Queen Mum beloved by the British people and throughout the world—have overshadowed the nearly three decades of a successful and happy marriage that is the scope of this book. The British actor Colin Firth said he had no idea that the Queen Mother had been George VI's wife until he made the Oscar-winning film *The King's Speech,* about the monarch's struggle to overcome a crippling stammer.

Crucial to the marriage of King George VI and Queen Elizabeth were the qualities of duty and service they exemplified, especially during Britain's ordeal in World War II. From the earliest days of the war, Adolf Hitler targeted the King and Queen. His bombers hit Buckingham Palace nine times. On one occasion they nearly succeeded in killing the monarch and his queen consort.

As I began my research into the lives of George and Elizabeth, I soon realized that her life was more deeply entwined with that of the King than is generally known. Not only is theirs a touching love story—with surprising dramatic twists—it is a story of inspiration in the most challenging circumstances: repeated personal tragedies and ailments, the ravages of two world wars, and a terminal illness. It's equally a story of resilience and shared joy.

With the centenary of the marriage of King George VI and Queen Elizabeth being celebrated in 2023, it seems a good time to reflect on who they were, what accounted for their strong marriage, and how they made a difference in the world. How did he grow into his job? How did this inherently withdrawn man gain confidence in his judgments and his interactions with others? How did she mature from a fundamentally unserious aristocrat into a public-spirited source of strength for her husband, her family, and her nation? How did she balance her work as consort with her role as a mother?

Their indelible legacy was their daughter Queen Elizabeth II, who would be widely admired not only for her unflagging service but also for her wisdom and her modesty. Their second daughter, Margaret, caused heartache for both her mother and her sister, starting in the years after her father's death. Insecure and spoiled, she never found an appropriate role despite her many advantages.

With the permission of Her Majesty Queen Elizabeth II, I was able to spend three months in the Royal Archives at Windsor Castle and several days at Glamis Castle, the ancestral home of her mother's Bowes Lyon family—the earldom of Strathmore. The extent of this access was noteworthy for someone who was not designated an official biographer.

Reaching the archives at Windsor posed a challenge each day. It required climbing with a backpack up a staircase of more than one hundred medieval stone steps—the equivalent of ten stories—with my lunch in tow so I wouldn't have to climb them again. The reward was a research room atop the Round Tower that is cozy, hushed, and efficient. Getting to Glamis (pronounced Glahms) involved a flight from London to Edinburgh, a ninety-minute drive, and a comparable climb to the top of a tower. This aerie was cluttered and minimally heated, but it offered an illuminating trove of letters and other documents, mostly handwritten.

My research also included reminiscences from elderly friends and family who shared helpful insights. But King George VI and Queen Elizabeth revealed themselves most fully in their diaries and letters. Elizabeth's correspondence was vivid and often entertaining, but thoughtful—and even poignant—when the moment demanded. Her adult diaries, kept intermittently during her twenties, were less mature than her husband's detailed chronicle from 1939 to 1947, but similarly telling.

The story that unfolded in leather-bound books and on monogram-engraved writing paper showed their strengths as well as their frailties, their complicated family dynamics, and the crosscurrents of intrigue and secrets within the royal court. Amid the wartime terrors of air raids and invasion threats came unexpected pleasures: shooting weekends, movies, plays, golf, bicycle and horse riding, and dances. These papers also revealed the perspective of the King and Queen on their relationship with Winston Churchill, who became prime minister in May 1940. Their dealings encompassed lunches, dinners, and other occasions that went far beyond the typical weekly formal audiences of a monarch and the first minister.

Supplementing these documents, additional previously unexplored archives shed light on the royal couple's relationships with an array of political and military leaders, and show how others saw them working as a mutually supportive duo. George VI's and Elizabeth's "special relationship" with key Americans, from President Franklin D. Roosevelt on down, emerges from these documents in surprising ways, revealing both admiration and annoyance.

The British royal family is by definition insular and wrapped in mythology, much of it self-created. It wasn't until the late twentieth century that the press dropped its deference, and the tabloids filled their pages with a mixture of fact and speculation. In the twenty-first century, the Netflix series *The Crown* upped the ante by presenting a beautifully produced but largely fictitious account of the monarchy that most viewers believed to be factual. It was a long leap from the time of George VI and Queen Elizabeth, when Buckingham Palace tightly managed all information about the royal family.

The men in control were the top-echelon advisers to the King and Queen, the "courtiers." Aristocratic and well-educated, they held military rank, and many fought heroically in the First World War. They had impressive connections throughout British society and in Parliament and at Whitehall. They had the inside track, and through their letters and diaries, combined with those of royal family members, a modern biographer can better understand the story of George VI and Elizabeth and their family.

First among these courtiers was Sir Alan Lascelles, an erudite and commanding figure who worked for the royal family for twenty-seven years. During eighteen of those years, he served as private secretary to King George V, King Edward VIII, King George VI, and Queen Elizabeth II. He was the most influential of royal insiders—and the most problematic.

When he was a boy, his father likened his large head and skinny body to "Tommy Tadpole." Everyone thereafter called him "Tommy" except Winston Churchill, who always referred to him as Alan. Over the decades, Tommy Lascelles melded into the blur of the "grey men" (as Diana, Princess of Wales, derisively called them) in the royal court. But his razor-sharp depiction by the actor Pip Torrens in *The Crown* made him an unforgettable figure—something of a twenty-first-century star with his intense dark eyes, basso profundo voice, bristling mustache, punctilious manner, and severe opinions. His words may have been invented for the television show, but his personality was true to life.

Lascelles embodied rectitude and stern moral judgment. He scrupulously kept government and royal secrets, but behind his puritanical demeanor he hid the biggest secret of all: a clandestine life concealed from the royal family he served. Tommy was bisexual, a fact known only to a select few close friends. This private side of Lascelles is not raised casually, but rather because it is germane to a more nuanced understanding of his role as a trusted counselor and confidant to both George VI and Elizabeth as well as their nemesis, the Duke of Windsor.

During Tommy's days in Buckingham Palace, male homosexuality was a crime in Britain. Prominent people such as the actor John Gielgud and the mathematician and wartime code breaker Alan Turing were prosecuted for being gay. For a high-level courtier like Alan Lascelles, the potential for scandal or blackmail was real.

Equally important was his unique position as the guiding force behind the official biographies of King George VI and of his parents, King George V and Queen Mary, written by John Wheeler-Bennett,

Harold Nicolson, and James Pope-Hennessy, respectively. Published in the 1950s, these books shaped the public perception of two monarchs and a queen consort.

Working closely with all three biographers, Tommy nudged angles to pursue, shared indiscreet views and vignettes, applied his "sharpest blue-pencil" to their words, and smoothed the way with royal family members who accepted his judgment without question and gave their approval. He deftly coaxed the authors to obfuscate when he deemed necessary; at other times he loosened traditional restraints and permitted language close to mockery. His influence was as impressive as it had been for his sixteen years as a senior adviser to King George VI. What complicated Tommy's role was that two of the royal biographers, Harold Nicolson and James Pope-Hennessy, were at various times his lovers.

George VI and Elizabeth were each tested in their formative years. Her life as the second youngest of the Earl and Countess of Strathmore's ten children has been portrayed as sunlit and carefree—having the run of beautiful estates, playing games, singing, and dancing reels. Glamis Castle in Scotland had the magical aura of Brigadoon. Until 1929, the castle was illuminated only by candles and gas lighting.

In many ways it was an idyllic upbringing, devoid of stuffiness and cushioned by wealth, but Lady Elizabeth Bowes Lyon and her family stoically endured great suffering, too. Her parents' firstborn, a daughter named Violet Hyacinth, died of diphtheria at age eleven, seven years before the birth of Elizabeth in 1900. When Elizabeth was eleven, an older brother named Alec died from a brain tumor. He was just twenty-four.

During World War I, Elizabeth lost her brother Fergus, who died at age twenty-six at the Battle of Loos in 1915. Two other brothers, Patrick and Michael, were damaged psychologically in the trenches. Michael went missing in 1917 and was feared dead. After three weeks of agonizing, the family learned he was alive but imprisoned by the

Germans. He finally came home in early 1919, two months after the armistice. Although he maintained a veneer of bonhomie, his wartime traumas permanently scarred him. Yet another brother, Jock, was wounded and had a finger amputated.

Both Glamis and the family's home at St. Paul's Walden Bury in Hertfordshire, some thirty miles from London, served as convalescent hospitals for wounded soldiers throughout the war. Day after day at Glamis, Elizabeth and her mother comforted men with severe mental and physical injuries (crushed chests, shattered spines, and punctured lungs, among them). The teenager showed compassion and understanding, amplified by unrelenting cheerfulness—qualities that would help buoy her future husband. She also learned to avert her eyes from trouble, and to bury gloomy thoughts beneath her effervescent exterior.

Elizabeth's world revolved around her parents and her siblings. Her letters to "my darling sweetest Mother" overflowed with adoration and solicitude, often masking anxiety over illnesses and surgeries that kept her mother bedridden for weeks on end. Elizabeth saw her as "an angel of goodness and fun."

When she was well, Lady Strathmore presided at Glamis as a sparkling chatelaine who played Scottish ballads on the piano after dinner, and instilled a deep Christian faith in her children. She also taught Elizabeth to favor the bright side of life. "Now darling, you must look at these two houses," she said, pointing to an ugly one and a beautiful one. "This is the beautiful one, you see, and bypass the ugly one."

Elizabeth's father, Lord Strathmore, was more distant—and decidedly eccentric. He thought eggs were poisonous, ate plum pudding every day for lunch, and diluted his wine with water. He was known for quoting at length from Lewis Carroll's *Through the Looking-Glass*.

Marked by formality and severe emotional restraint, the childhood of King George VI was 180 degrees removed from that of Elizabeth, but no less touched by adversity. Born as Prince Albert in 1895 during the waning days of the Victorian era, he was the second son and second child of Prince George and Princess May—the future King George

V and Queen Mary. He seldom saw his formidable great-grandmother Queen Victoria, who died in 1901 when he was five. Despite his tender age, he was pressed into solemn duty, joining the mourners on a frigid February day for his "Gangan's" funeral at St. George's Chapel in Windsor Castle, and burial at nearby Frogmore.

His father, King George V, dominated everything and everyone, with his demands for proper comportment and his sharp criticisms, brusque manner, and hair-trigger temper. When he wasn't shooting pheasant, duck, or partridge, he retreated to his small and dark corner library on the ground floor of York Cottage, the royal family's home on the Sandringham estate in Norfolk for thirty-three years. There he would read his official papers and work on his vast stamp collection. A summons to the library invariably meant a tongue-lashing.

Queen Mary was inherently shy, yet spirited in her own way. But she lived to obey her husband, and above all to revere him, suppressing emotion and maintaining a starchy façade. She could defend her children from her husband's barbs and rebukes only up to a point. George and Mary were tenderly dependent, and they loved their children. But they felt most comfortable expressing those feelings in writing.

As the "spare" to Prince Edward, the eldest son and heir, young Albert (known as "Bertie" among family and friends) was diffident and often ill. Subjected to ceaseless comparisons with his cosseted older brother (who went by "David" within the family), Albert lacked confidence and was prone to dark moods as well as angry eruptions.

Worst of all, this sensitive boy developed a stutter around the age of eight. "Get it out!" his father demanded, making the stammer worse. Albert often withdrew into silence, which allowed him to observe and absorb. He noticed more than anyone realized, and he became a good listener—traits that would serve him well as king.

That he would become king was something that neither Bertie nor his family imagined. He never aspired to be monarch, nor was he groomed for the role. When it was thrust upon him, he wept on his mother's shoulder.

———

PRINCE ALBERT FELL IN LOVE with Lady Elizabeth Bowes Lyon when they first danced at the Royal Air Force Ball in the Ritz hotel on July 8, 1920. She was vivacious and pretty, the "it girl" of her aristocratic set. She had already rebuffed proposals of marriage, some of them rash, some more serious. Albert joined the queue. That September, he invited himself to Glamis for a boisterous weekend with Elizabeth and her friends. He was drawn as much to her family as he was to her, exhilarated by their informality and open affection.

For more than two years, Albert courted Elizabeth. She turned down his marriage proposals twice, kindly offering instead to be "good friends." It took the intervention of nearly a half dozen people to embolden him to try a third time.

The thought that he would one day become king never occurred to Elizabeth and certainly didn't affect how she regarded Bertie as a prospective husband. Whatever their personal chemistry, the best she could expect was life as a hardworking member of the royal family, dutifully carrying out countless public engagements that required strong legs and a constant smile.

After numerous maneuvers by friends and family members, including the timely removal of a rival to a job in America, Elizabeth accepted Bertie's hand in January 1923. They were married four months later, to the immense pleasure of both families and their many friends, and she came to love him unreservedly. "Such a sweet little couple and so fond of one another," Duff Cooper, a diplomat and politician, wrote to his wife, Lady Diana. He had watched them at the theater "having private jokes . . . standing together in a dark corner of the passage talking happily."

Her mischievous and teasing manner was infectious. She loved to laugh, and her high spirits bubbled through her letters to family and friends, which she sprinkled with expressions like "tinkety-tonk" and "what ho" from P. G. Wodehouse, one of her favorite authors. "I write to the accompaniment of the squeaking of rats, melodious and soothing to a degree," she told her brother Jock from St. Paul's Walden Bury, "and the patter of their little feet in the walls calm my troubled brain—the little darlings. Bless them."

Albert was as timid as Elizabeth was exuberant, as awkward and doubting as she was effortlessly confident, as formal as she was spontaneous and relaxed. Yet they turned out to be ideally matched. They both had what the British call "bottom": integrity, honesty, and loyalty, bound up in an ingrained sense of duty.

Elizabeth's parents, the Earl and Countess of Strathmore, may have been technically "commoners," a category that included anyone not from a European royal family, but they lived near the pinnacle of the British aristocracy just below the monarchy: the hierarchy, in descending order, of dukes and duchesses, marquesses and marchionesses, earls and countesses, viscounts and viscountesses, and barons and baronesses. The Strathmores' traditions and trappings—the shooting parties, elegant entertaining with liveried servants, even bagpipers circling the table after dinner at Glamis—matched those of the royal family. Elizabeth easily adjusted to the constraints of the court, blending into it rather than being grafted onto it. Decades later, Princess Margaret confided to a friend that having come "from a home where nobody quarreled," her mother "was appalled by the family storms that swept over York Cottage—and did much to relieve the tension of those cramped rooms."

Elizabeth's gentle and encouraging manner helped soothe Albert's temper and allay his frustrations. It was at her urging that he enlisted Lionel Logue, the Australian speech therapist who raised his self-esteem and tamed his stammer. Twenty-five years on, in a letter urging her older daughter to make the most of married life on the island of Malta with Prince Philip, Elizabeth wrote: "Papa & I were so lucky, because we have tried so many different ways of life—We did night club life madly for a few years, but also mixed with dinners & country house visits, & big game shooting in Africa, & visits to Paris & Oslo & Belgrade & Rome and Brussels & Australia and MALTA, and out of the welter, one gradually found one's feet & head. You are so young, & you are also 'finding out.'"

Albert and Elizabeth were—in different ways—more resilient and strong-minded than they appeared to be. When dealing with her husband's adversaries, Elizabeth could be steely: "a marshmallow made on a welding machine," in the words of photographer Cecil Beaton.

Toughness was essential in dealing with Albert's bête noire, the pampered and careless Edward, Prince of Wales. The two brothers had enjoyed a reasonably congenial relationship growing up and had socialized during the fizzy 1920s. Elizabeth initially took pleasure in Edward's company and wrote him breezy and affectionate letters. But his carousing and womanizing, and his deficiencies of character—selfishness, narcissism, duplicity, and disloyalty among them—pulled Albert and Elizabeth away from him.

The Prince of Wales knew how to turn on the charm and carry out his duties. Behind the smiles, he was bored and bitter about his fate, emotionally stunted and self-absorbed. In letters to his married lover Freda Dudley Ward he poured out his self-loathing and complained about his advisers and the people he met, not to mention those who entertained him. He expressed contempt for his family, especially his father, George V, whom he considered outdated and narrow-minded. At times he said he wished the monarchy would be overturned, calling himself a "bolshie." Frequently depressed, he even spoke of suicide.

The public knew none of this, but over time Edward's family and members of the court became aware of his flaws. Their biggest concern was his poor choice of women. While there were many flings, his main attraction was to married women: first Freda, then Thelma Furness, and, beginning in January 1933, Wallis Warfield Simpson.

Edward was obsessive and submissive with all three women—once writing to Freda that he was "the kind of man who needs a certain amount of cruelty"—but especially so with Wallis, whose dominance disturbed those who witnessed it. Once when he was on all fours releasing the hem of her dress from the leg of a chair, she berated him mercilessly.

On December 28, 1935, King George V and Queen Mary invited some friends who lived on their Sandringham estate, Sir John and

Lady Maffey and their daughter Penelope, to dinner. As they walked into the entrance hall, the Maffeys witnessed an altercation between the King and his eldest son, standing on the staircase as his father shouted from below: "You've got to get rid of that woman!"

Three weeks later, George V was dead, and the prince took the throne as King Edward VIII at age forty-one. He was a terrible monarch, inattentive and cavalier; his behavior and attitudes corroded the very center of the monarchy. He was determined to marry "that woman" once she had divorced her second husband. During the complicated and painful abdication crisis of December 1936, Edward marginalized his brother Albert as well as his own advisers. When the British government rejected his effort to make Wallis his queen and he renounced the throne, Albert became the king, and he honored his late father by calling himself George VI. He was three days shy of his forty-first birthday. The new queen, his wife Elizabeth, was thirty-six. Edward VIII became the Duke of Windsor and Wallis his duchess.

The day of his accession, one of his cousins asked George VI what he was going to do. "I don't know," he replied. "But I am going to do my best." And so he did, despite a rocky beginning amid concerns that his stammer would prevent him from carrying out his duties effectively. With the support of Elizabeth and unrelenting practice with Lionel Logue, the new king mastered his coronation oath and muscled through crucial speeches, delivered slowly and sometimes haltingly.

George VI applied himself diligently to his job as a constitutional monarch. As head of state, he represented his government at home and overseas, studied the official documents delivered daily in red leather boxes—memos from the Foreign Office, the Treasury, and other departments; secret intelligence reports; laws, regulations, and appointments requiring his signature—and received his prime minister and a stream of other functionaries in confidential audiences.

The fundamental nature of his role had been defined by the nineteenth-century constitutional expert Walter Bagehot: "the right to be consulted, the right to encourage, and the right to warn." The monarch was expected to remain apart from party politics and to serve as a unifying force. Together, Bertie and Elizabeth also symbolized the "domestic virtues" essential for a successful king and queen. They exercised positive influence rather than actual power.

George VI and Elizabeth found their footing during the jittery pre-war years between 1937 and 1939. They made triumphal visits to France, Canada, and the United States, winning hearts and minds everywhere. Over hot dogs at Franklin D. Roosevelt's home in Hyde Park, the royal couple famously bonded with the president and first lady. Their mutual respect for one another's character and temperament proved vital in the war years ahead.

When Britain declared war on Germany on September 3, 1939, George VI began keeping the diary that he would continue for more than seven years. The privilege of reading these pages in their entirety at the Royal Archives gave me an extraordinary lens on the momentous events of World War II and the leaders of the military and the coalition government. I could also appreciate in full the King's intellect and common sense that were all too often underestimated.

George VI's daily jottings show his trusting and friendly relationship with Winston Churchill, his wartime prime minister. He understood Churchill's overpowering personality and could detect his shifting moods. When the prime minister made a decision, the King observed, "personal feelings are nothing to him, though he has a very sentimental side."

The King's diary pages reveal an inquisitive mind keen to absorb every detail. He could be unexpectedly assertive (telling Labourite minister of supply Herbert Morrison in 1940 that his party was "partly to blame" for armament shortages), and was often farsighted. From the war's earliest days, for example, he urged government officials to begin postwar planning "to keep the spirit of the class mixing going." He also perceptively read character: Soviet foreign minister Vyacheslav Molotov, he noted, "looks a small quiet man with a feeble voice but is really a tyrant."

To an unusual degree, George VI shared his wartime responsibilities with Elizabeth. An "unprecedented" feature of the lunches

Winston Churchill had with the King at Buckingham Palace each Tuesday "was the presence of the Queen at these private conversations," according to Elizabeth's official biographer, William Shawcross. The mutually supportive trio met at Buckingham Palace in a dimly lit dining room with boarded-up windows, or in the "immense catacomb" of the Palace air raid shelter. George VI described many of these encounters in his diary. Elizabeth, who considered herself "very much a part of the team with the King," said virtually nothing about them.

The King traveled more than fifty thousand miles around Britain during the war, often straining his fragile constitution. The Queen accompanied him on most of these journeys in their heavily armored train and automobiles. They were constantly moving targets. Visiting bombed-out neighborhoods in London, they frequently defied air raid warnings. They spent nights on the train adjacent to tunnels where they could find protection if danger arose.

When they weren't out inspecting military bases, factories, hospitals, ships, and damaged cities and towns, they risked their lives by spending their working days at Buckingham Palace. For three of the nine Palace bombings, they were present. In September 1940, government officials advised them to sleep at Windsor Castle, either in an underground shelter or in reinforced ground-floor bedrooms. There they endured regular air raid "Red Warnings" and heard the drone of enemy aircraft, the explosions of bombs landing nearby, and booming antiaircraft weapons.

George VI and Queen Elizabeth were effective during World War II not only because of their sympathy and thoughtfulness but also because of their innate feel for the soul of Britain. The King noted in his diary that "one of my main jobs in life" was "to help others when I can be useful to them." That job took a terrible toll on his health, aggravated by his two-packs-a-day smoking habit and constant anxiety over making speeches.

Winston Churchill sensibly dispatched King George VI's brother, the Duke of Windsor, to Nassau from 1940 to 1945. His job as governor was a "war expediency" to remove him from Europe. Edward VIII would have been a disastrous wartime leader, because of both his temperament and his well-known admiration for Germany and its Nazi leadership.

George VI and Queen Elizabeth redoubled their discipline to navigate the bleak postwar terrain after the election defeat of Winston Churchill and his Conservative Party. They knew most of the Labour leaders from their wartime jobs, and they worried about the pace and consequences of the new government's radical policy to nationalize industries. George VI spoke in private to Churchill and other prominent Conservatives while being scrupulously correct with his Labour ministers. Elizabeth regarded Clement Attlee, the Labour leader who became prime minister in 1945, as a "practical little man." To the King, he was "shriveled & small" as well as reticent. "I find I have to tell him things," George VI recorded a week after Attlee took office, although in time the two men developed a mutually respectful relationship.

The King and Queen found happiness in the marriage of their eldest daughter—their "Lilibet"—to Prince Philip, followed by the birth of their grandson, Prince Charles, and granddaughter, Princess Anne. They restored Royal Lodge, their war-damaged country house in Windsor, and they enjoyed meals in the gardens there when they needed to escape the formality of the castle. They entertained more, with dinner parties and dances for their friends. They had months-long holidays at Sandringham and in the Scottish Highlands at the monarch's Balmoral estate.

But their life couldn't return to normal. During the last three years of his reign, George VI was frequently bedridden with cardiovascular disease and lung cancer. It was customary then for doctors to withhold a cancer diagnosis to spare the patient needless anxiety. Neither the King nor the Queen discussed the disease, even after his malignant left lung was removed. The doctors said the surgery was done to address "structural changes" in the lung.

George VI and Elizabeth took comfort in the illusion that he was getting stronger, even when his weakness was all too evident. Yet on his last day, he was out in the Norfolk countryside shooting rabbits—the sport he enjoyed after the pheasant season had ended—with neighbors, tenant farmers, and estate workers, and in the evening, he dined quietly with his family. In his tribute following the King's death, Winston Churchill marveled that he had remained "cheerful and undaunted—stricken in body but quite undisturbed and even unaffected in spirit."

For a highly conventional couple, George VI and Elizabeth's twenty-eight years together were filled with unanticipated and unwanted drama. First came the fraternal betrayal by his brother the Duke of Windsor. The immense ordeals of World War II strained the King to the breaking point and drew deeply from his wife's reserves of strength. They rose again to the challenges of postwar deprivations and jarring social change, adjusting to a socialist government that cut against much that they stood for. In her five decades of widowhood, Elizabeth solidified the late king's legacy. She spanned the twentieth century and deservedly earned the love of the people as Britain's grandmother.

Their fifteen years as king and queen began with trepidation and uncertainty and ended with stoic suffering and premature death. They rescued and rebuilt a monarchy battered by the abdication crisis. In their wartime leadership, they showed the world their personal courage and capacity to inspire. And through example and instruction, they prepared their elder daughter for her eventual succession to the throne, setting the stage for a new Elizabethan age that would secure the foundation of the monarchy through the twentieth century and well into the twenty-first.

The Duke and Duchess of York with their dog, Glen, at Glamis Castle in 1925.

PART ONE

Loss and Love

"It was a great thing to be loved."

*"Decided to wait a little. . . . I hope
I am not behaving badly."*

Lady Elizabeth Bowes Lyon and Prince Albert in the garden at St. Paul's
Walden Bury in Hertfordshire.

ONE

Twelve Days

Prince Albert's quest for the hand of Elizabeth Bowes Lyon was less a courtship than a campaign. He conducted it for thirty months. He used spontaneous charges, tactical retreats, and evidently well-considered feints. From time to time he called in reinforcements. He often despaired, but he persisted with single-minded determination, taking even the most ambivalent responses as signs of encouragement.

If Elizabeth had been as enamored as Bertie was, they would have had a textbook romance. Within months of his first flash of interest in the summer of 1920, she would have accepted his inevitable proposal. But her heart was with another man, James Stuart, the third son of the seventeenth Earl of Moray, and, as irony would have it, Bertie's equerry, an aide-de-camp who arranged his logistics and assisted him at events.

Stuart was a tall, fine-featured, and mustachioed Scotsman with a lady-killer reputation. He and Elizabeth had met at a house party hosted by her family at Glamis Castle in September 1919, when James was twenty-two and she was nineteen. Something must have clicked because Bertie knew he had a formidable rival. Lured by the prospect of a financial windfall, Stuart left Bertie's employ and went to the United States—a move rumored to have been arranged by Bertie's mother, Queen Mary. In any event, the field had been cleared for Bertie.

The denouement of Bertie's campaign played out over twelve days in January 1923. On the evening of Wednesday, the third, Elizabeth was invited to an intimate dinner hosted by Bertie at Claridge's, the rosy-hued Victorian hotel known as "the Palace of Mayfair," a magnet for aristocrats, bright young things, and British royalty since the late nineteenth century.

Intriguingly, Francis Doune, James's older brother, came to visit Elizabeth at five-thirty that day and stayed an hour. She made no record in her diary about what they discussed. Although she was suffering from a "heavy cold," she was ready when Bertie and his equerry, Captain Giles Sebright, arrived to pick her up an hour later. They were joined by Lady Anne Cameron, Sebright's girlfriend.

After dinner, the foursome attended a performance of *The Co-Optimists,* a popular revue in the West End featuring numbers by Irving Berlin and Arthur Schwartz, among others. It was fast-paced topical entertainment, with ten performers switching from character to character as they sang and danced across the stage. One subversive song by Noël Coward, "Down with the Whole Damn Lot," poked fun at "the idle rich" and "the bloated upper classes." To Elizabeth, it was all "great fun."

Back at Claridge's, Bertie took Elizabeth to the dance floor in the stately foyer, with its crystal chandeliers and fluted columns. (They both loved dancing and were equally graceful and accomplished.) There he asked for her hand in marriage for the third and final time. On leaving Claridge's, they went to Anne Cameron's house, and Elizabeth didn't arrive home until two A.M. before falling asleep at three A.M. As Bertie recounted later in a letter to his mother, he "had a long talk with her & told her how I had always felt towards her & she told me that she looked upon me as more than an ordinary friend & asked me to give her time to think over what I had said."

During the following eleven days, Elizabeth vacillated as she confided in friends and family and sent reassuring letters to lovestruck Bertie. She alternated between giddy activity—teas, luncheons, dinners, theater, being photographed for a fashion magazine, trying on clothes, playing cards, tramping across fields on a shooting weekend, dancing all night at two country house balls—and quiet moments riven with worry: fretful, morose, confused, guilt-stricken, and exhausted.

Based on the entries in her diary, she devoted more than twenty hours to discussing the proposal with Bertie and a selection of confidantes. Over fifteen of those hours were one-on-one talks with her persistent suitor.

A century later, it is difficult to divine what was running through her mind, especially her motivations. She was drawn to Bertie's sweet and humble simplicity—a rare trait in the British royal family—and to the vulnerability betrayed by his stammer. But she was frustratingly hazy when finally, at age ninety-four, she tried to explain her thinking to her friend Eric Anderson, the head master of Eton College. He had asked whether she took advice from anyone about "the serious proposal" or "did you know at once?"

She admitted it had gone on for "a year or two," adding, "You know you are not sure about anything, and then one of my brothers said to me, 'Look here, you know, you must either say yes or no. It's not fair.' I think he was right. Because one is rather inclined to dither along if somebody's fond of you, you know. I suppose when one is young and busy and things. No, he was quite right. . . . It's a good thing, having brothers." The sibling in question was likely her older brother Michael or younger brother David, both of whom had been friendly with the prince since September 1921, when he stayed at Glamis to shoot partridges.

Others who knew Elizabeth well offered their own explanations, most hinging on her unwillingness to give up her freedom for a lifetime of duty inside the royal family. "She was so uncertain with Bertie because she had been brought up in such a closed world of a large family and small circle of close friends," her great-niece Lady Elizabeth Anson told me. "She was smart and grounded and understood what being a member of the royal family would mean. She was not eager to have a public life. That was the crux of it."

The twelve days in January 1923 from proposal to acceptance encompassed a drama of Elizabeth's own making, if not her explicit design. Behind the scenes, family and friends had been working for a full year to ensure that the third time would be the charm. Principal among them were Bertie's mother, Queen Mary; her trusted friend and lady-in-waiting Mabell, the Countess of Airlie; Elizabeth's mother, Cecilia Strathmore; Louis Greig, the comptroller and head of Bertie's household; even, perhaps unwittingly, Bertie's younger sister, Princess Mary. Other peripheral characters were involved as well. Neither Bertie nor Elizabeth was fully aware of stratagems that included subterfuge and misdirection plays. But well before they took to the dance floor at Claridge's, she sensed a proposal could be imminent.

Amid all her activity and emotions that January, two pivotal events nudged her toward becoming Bertie's wife: a nearly two-hour conversation with Mabell Airlie, and a false gossip item in a newspaper that embarrassed and alarmed her.

In the late afternoon of Thursday, January 4, 1923, Elizabeth sat down for tea in Lady Airlie's small flat in a Victorian-era apartment building in London's Westminster neighborhood. Elizabeth arrived in an agitated state because her mother had forbidden her to attend the popular Pytchley Hunt Ball that night in the Northampton Town Hall. She and Bertie had been invited to a house party at nearby Pitsford Hall, a grand eighteenth-century estate owned by Captain George Henry Drummond, and they had both planned to go to the hunt ball.

It had been ten days since Lady Strathmore had squelched her daughter's plans, and Elizabeth was still upset. In no uncertain terms, her mother had said she "must not go." This was a thoroughly uncharacteristic action by Cecilia Strathmore, who enjoyed an open and trusting relationship with her daughter. It turned out that her prohibition had followed an urgent letter from none other than Lady Airlie, who was acting in the belief that Elizabeth was stringing Bertie along.

"My dearest Cecilia," Mabell had written on December 23, noting that Elizabeth doubtless had many invitations for the winter season. "I don't suppose there is any likelihood of her accepting one to Pitsford for the Northampton Ball," she wrote, adding that she "had been asked to hint" that "perhaps you could announce" that Elizabeth "should not accept it as it is perhaps wiser for the young man [Bertie] . . . that nothing further could come of the friendship."

Although no record exists of what precisely Lady Strathmore said to her daughter, the source of the "hint" was undeniably Queen Mary. On what must have been a ruined Christmas Day, Elizabeth said as much in an overwrought letter to Bertie, who was spending the holidays with his family at their Sandringham estate. "Perhaps you know already," she wrote, that the idea of her joining him at the Drummonds' house party "is very unpopular in some quarters?" She added, "I quite understand your family's point of view," which she knew was "for the good," and they were "probably quite right."

She emphasized—as she had many times previously—that he and she were the best of friends, and she fretted that he might think she had "behaved badly" toward him. She confessed to feeling "very sad" about missing the dance. She had been "thinking deeply" about the situation all day, even during the Christmas church service.

Bertie and Elizabeth met just three days later, on December 28 at the West Norfolk Hunt Ball at Holkham Hall, the magnificent Palladian country house of the Earl and Countess of Leicester near Sandringham. Elizabeth and her brother David had been invited to stay with the Leicesters, who were friends of the Strathmores.

Accompanying Bertie to the ball were two of his brothers, Prince Edward and Prince George. With some four hundred other guests in evening dress, they proceeded through Holkham's pink Marble Hall under the coffered and gilded fifty-foot-high ceiling modeled on the Pantheon's in Rome. They climbed the wide marble staircase to the Saloon lined with ornate crimson caffoy fabric. Adorning the walls were huge paintings by Rubens and Van Dyck. The Clifford Essex Band played, but neither Bertie nor Elizabeth was interested in dancing.

Instead, they were eager to discuss busybodies who were clucking over Bertie's tortuous courtship, which was well known among their circle of friends. As the speculation intensified, Elizabeth had become increasingly discomfited, and she also shared her upset over Lady Strathmore's anti-Pitsford edict.

On returning to Sandringham at three-thirty A.M., Bertie picked up his pen and set out his thoughts for Elizabeth in his sturdy and precise handwriting. He spoke to some extent in code. "It is the limit the way other people mix themselves in things which do not concern them," he fumed. He urged Elizabeth to see Mabell Airlie as soon as possible "to tell her exactly what great friends we are & I will do the same."

Now it was his turn to say he hoped *she* didn't think badly of *him*. He seemed determined to brace his mother for interfering, and he announced his intention to decline the Pytchley ball.

From 17 Bruton Street, her family's London townhouse, Elizabeth replied the next day, December 30, to say she had tried to reach Lady Airlie by phone, but she had gone to the country. Elizabeth reassured Bertie that she had sent a note and asked to see the countess the following week. In the meantime, she counseled him that it would be "much wiser if you did nothing about it" until she had talked to Lady Airlie: "There is no hurry—the thing is done"—probably a reference to her forced absence from the Pytchley ball.

MABELL AIRLIE HAD BEEN A crucial player in the romance since late 1920, offering encouragement for a match she believed was desirable. Her advantage was having known Bertie and Elizabeth since they were young children, and admiring both of them greatly. Although Bertie didn't refer to it in his December 29 letter to Elizabeth, Lady Airlie had sent him a message addressed to both of them shortly after Christmas that he later said had been an "inspiration" to him.

In her memoirs, Lady Airlie wrote that she felt her "final effort" to persuade Elizabeth to marry Bertie had failed when they had tea on January 4, 1923. She regretted that most of the conversation revolved around the early years of her own marriage to cavalry officer David

Ogilvy, the eleventh Earl of Airlie, who had died at age forty-four in the Second Boer War. She said that her love for him had been "the cornerstone" of her life.

When Elizabeth revealed that Bertie had proposed the previous night, Mabell tried to draw a parallel between her initial "hatred" of army life and Elizabeth's reservations about life in the royal family. Mabell said she had eventually "grown to love" being married to an army officer. After Elizabeth left her flat, Mabell feared she had bored her and wished she had focused more on Bertie's merits. But her underlying message of doing one's duty was significant.

Elizabeth reported on her teatime tête-à-tête in a letter to Bertie that night. She and the countess had "talked it all over," and she believed Mabell would be discreet and keep their conversation to herself. Intriguingly, Elizabeth said Mabell had assured her that the message in the December 23 letter to her mother "did <u>not</u> come" from anyone in the royal family. Rather, Lady Airlie said she had been told "by a lot of people" that Elizabeth and Bertie were planning to stay at Pitsford.

Mabell said she had written preemptively to Lady Strathmore because, Elizabeth recounted to Bertie, "she thought the Queen might be very annoyed with me for going there as the Queen thinks it is all off for ever, and Lady Airlie was afraid I might get into trouble." It was, Elizabeth wrote, "a little private hint to my mother," adding "I don't think your family need know—do you?"

Lady Airlie was fibbing by laying the blame on unnamed gossips. Five days later, on January 9, Queen Mary wrote to her expressing gratitude "for yr <u>kind help</u> in that tiresome matter." She and King George V understood the situation. "I confess now we hope nothing will come of it as we feel ruffled at E's behaviour!" wrote the Queen.

Unaware of how acutely she had irritated the King and Queen, Elizabeth in her January 4 letter to Bertie thanked him for being "so angelic" in giving her time to seriously consider his proposal. "I really do need it," she wrote, "as it takes so long to ponder those things, & this is so <u>very</u> [underlined twice] important for us both."

If she were to conclude that "it will be all right, well and good, but Prince Bertie, if I feel that I can't (& I will not marry you unless I am quite certain for your own sake) then I shall go away & try not to see you again. . . . I am determined not to spoil your life by just drifting on like this."

"I do want to do what is right for you," she wrote. And then, a hopeful intimation: "I have thought of nothing else all today—last night seems like a dream. Was it? It seems so now." Again she asked him to "not say anything just yet to <u>anybody</u>."

Elizabeth's peregrinations that Thursday before her meeting with Lady Airlie showed no sign of such preoccupation. Over lunch at Bruton Street, she entertained the sixth Viscount Gage, her friend since the age of fourteen. Sir Henry "George" Gage, who was five years older and very rich, had harbored a crush on her for several years.

She had met Gage through her brother Michael when the two were Oxford undergraduates. Henry "Chips" Channon, a rich American-born Conservative member of Parliament who kept a diary by turns catty and astute, viewed Gage as "desperately fond" of Elizabeth, "in vain, for he is far too heavy, too Tudor and squirearchal for so rare and patrician a creature." Still, she valued Gage's friendship—and would continue to do so for the rest of his life.

The main outcome of their lunch together on January 4, 1923, was that Gage invited her to Firle Place, his family's home in Sussex, to attend the Southdown Hunt Ball in Lewes the next evening. Otherwise, Elizabeth spent the day after Bertie's proposal visiting the dentist and having a "very amusing" tea with friends, before her sit-down with the Countess of Airlie.

For the first time in her diary, Elizabeth used "mirror writing," a technique "to conceal her thoughts," according to William Shawcross—although it was easy enough to decipher on the page by reading the words backward. After a two-sentence description of her colloquy with Mabell Airlie, she wrote, "*I ma tsom dexelprep*": "*I am most perplexed.*"

On Friday, January 5, she confided to her diary, in mirror writing: "*Am I thinking too much? I wish I knew.*" She took the train to Lewes, where the house party at Firle was off to a jolly start until the arrival of Chips Channon.

He had in hand an evening newspaper, the *Daily Star,* with a brief item announcing that Bertie's older brother Edward, the twenty-eight-year-old Prince of Wales, was planning to marry the daughter of a "well-known Scottish peer," the owner of "castles both north and south of the Tweed." The official engagement announcement, according to the report, was "imminent." Only one "Scottish lady of noble birth" fit this description: Lady Elizabeth Bowes Lyon, whose family had, until recently, owned Streatlam Castle in county Durham, "south of the Tweed," as well as Glamis.

"Not mentioning my name," Elizabeth wrote in her diary, "but quite obvious enough. Too stupid & unfounded." The item provoked much merriment at Firle. "We all bowed and bobbed and teased her, calling her 'Ma'am,'" recorded Chips Channon. "I am not sure that she enjoyed it. It couldn't be true, but how delighted everyone would be! But she certainly has something on her mind. . . . I thought her unhappy and distraite."

Channon was well aware of Bertie's pursuit, which he had witnessed firsthand during a shooting party at Glamis the previous autumn. "One rainy afternoon we were sitting about," he had written in his diary, "and I pretended that I could read cards, and I told Elizabeth Lyon's fortune and predicted a great and glamorous royal future. She laughed, for it was obvious that the Duke of York was much in love with her."

THE IDEA OF ELIZABETH IN a romance with the dashing and promiscuous Prince of Wales was laughable. She scarcely knew Prince Edward, who had been deeply involved with Freda Dudley Ward, a married socialite, since they met in February 1918 when he was twenty-three. All of London had known of the affair almost immediately. That March, when Elizabeth was eighteen, she had danced with the Prince of Wales at a ball in London given by the future Earl of Leicester. She wrote to her mother that she found it "very amusing." Prince Edward probably didn't give it a second thought.

In May 1921, Elizabeth and the Prince of Wales were guests at a house party at Bicton, the home of Lord and Lady Clinton in Devon. In a letter to her former governess and trusted confidante, Beryl Poignand, Elizabeth listed her friends who were staying, along with "Our Prince" and some "old gargoyles whom I can't remember." They all played tennis and "lazed about & occasionally did a few official Prince of Wales things and had great fun."

After arriving by train, the prince had begun a packed ten-day schedule of engagements in Devon and Cornwall that included giving speeches, laying foundation stones and wreaths, inspecting ex-servicemen, calling on tenant farmers, visiting agricultural shows, meeting mayors and lord lieutenants, and chatting with patients in hospital wards.

He stopped at Bicton for two nights, squeezing in a round of golf at the Budleigh Salterton links. It's unclear which of the "official Prince of Wales things" Elizabeth witnessed, but she surely took in the atmosphere of a typical royal tour: the cheering crowds in towns and villages festooned with flags and streamers. Before the prince left Bicton for his next stop, five hundred tenants and residents on the Clinton estate watched him plant a white beam tree. As he departed, they all gathered outside the house and gave him a "great send-off."

At age twenty-one, Elizabeth had observed routine royal rounds up close for the first time. She was unimpressed. In her letter to Beryl, she noted that Edward "was away all day working hard, & only got back at tea-time—he does have a hellish life—that's the only word for it."

She and the Prince of Wales did not encounter each other again until October 1922 at Wilton House in Salisbury for a debutante ball. If they danced that evening, it was unremarkable. In a letter to "Prince Bertie," she only said that "Wilton was great fun."

So how to account for such a glaringly false report in the *Daily Star* two days after Bertie's proposal? Might it have been planted by someone close to the royal family to apply pressure on Elizabeth? Palace courtiers were not averse to slipping information to sympathetic and willing journalists. Whatever the means and motivation, the article hit a nerve.

ELIZABETH NEVERTHELESS MANAGED TO PUT on a good show at the Southdown Ball that Friday night, dancing with "nice old friends" until "nearly 4." Back at Firle, she ate biscuits and drank sherry before going to bed at five A.M. Chips Channon "watched her unseen" from his window as Elizabeth left "at almost dawn" on Saturday, January 6. She spent the weekend at St. Paul's Walden Bury in Hertfordshire with her parents. Both her mother and her older brother Jock were unwell, and the weather was cold and rainy.

One can imagine her rattling around the cozy rooms of "St. Paully Walden," an eighteenth-century brick home in the Queen Anne style. It was elegant yet unpretentious, lacking the grandeur of Glamis but equaling its informality. There was "no extravagance or luxury, no attempt to be modern or up to date," wrote Cynthia Asquith, an aristocratic contemporary of Elizabeth who published two authorized books about her. In the two downstairs drawing rooms, one with red silk walls, the other paneled in green, both embellished with fine plasterwork, Elizabeth read, knitted, and played her favorite records on the gramophone.

Monday, January 8, 1923, brought yet another sheaf of newspaper articles "about my rumoured engagement to the Prince of Wales." Exasperated, she wrote in her diary: "Too silly." After a rainy morning, she escaped for an afternoon walk and cheered herself by making cocktails with her brother Jock's wife, Fenella.

That evening she anxiously wrote to Bertie asking if he had seen the Prince of Wales story that had gotten under her skin. "It's too extraordinary," she wrote. "Why can't they leave one alone? And in this case, it was so utterly absurd." She also hinted encouragement, once again saying the evening at Claridge's seemed like a dream. "I think the great thing is to be <u>with</u> the person, or it all seems too unreal—do you feel that at all?" She thanked him profusely for writing to her and ended, "God Bless you, yours Elizabeth."

They had already arranged to meet for tea at Bruton Street on Thursday, January 11. In the meantime, Elizabeth was on the move—all in a rush, as if she could feel the clock ticking. She and Lady Strathmore motored to London in the rain on Tuesday the ninth, and after lunch took a train from Paddington station to Longleat, a magnificent sixteenth-century stately home in Wiltshire owned by the Marquess of Bath. They were among some twenty guests staying in the vast Elizabethan pile, where they had dinner and a quiet evening of card games.

The next night the Marquess and Marchioness of Bath were giving a dance in honor of their youngest daughter, Lady Mary Thynne, who was one of Elizabeth's good friends. The mothers and daughters spent the morning arranging chairs while the men went out shooting on a bitterly cold day. The ladies joined the "guns" for a luncheon outdoors and followed them on their afternoon drives. Back at the house, everyone had tea and played games.

Guests dined at Longleat and a dozen other houses in Wiltshire and Somerset before the ball began in the drawing room and long saloon—the first time those rooms were used for entertaining since before World War I. Elizabeth's dance card was typically full, and the ball lasted until three-thirty A.M.

Elizabeth left early on Thursday morning the eleventh and was back in London in time for lunch with her close friend Doris Gordon-Lennox. The two young women talked until midafternoon, then diverted themselves by buying gramophone records on Bond Street. Nevertheless, Elizabeth was "feeling very ill with vaccilation [sic] & worried, too," as her teatime with Bertie approached.

BACK IN HIS APARTMENT AT Buckingham Palace, Bertie had been occupying himself with planning an official two-day visit to Glasgow at the end of January—a prospect that filled him with dread. He was scheduled to give two speeches, always a challenge for his untamed stutter.

That week his name popped up several times in *The Times'* "Court Circular"—the detailed chronicle of the activities of the royal family and the aristocracy. One evening he attended a boxing tournament, and one afternoon he saw the film *Robin Hood* at the London Pavilion.

Bertie turned up promptly at Elizabeth's house for tea in the late afternoon on the eleventh. Their conversation ran until seven-thirty— more than three hours. He left without an answer to his proposal. "*I am very worried too,*" she recorded in mirror writing.

In the evening Elizabeth had dinner with Doris, Fenella, and several young men, including James Stuart's brother Francis. They all went to the West End for a performance of *The Nine O'Clock Revue,* a musical ensemble in the same vein as *The Co-Optimists.* Their spirits buoyed, the friends were treated by Francis to a late supper at the Savoy Hotel's lavish Edwardian dining room. Elizabeth arrived home at one A.M. "very tired, but enjoyed it awfully."

She was still exhausted when she awakened at eleven A.M. on Friday, January 12. Doris dropped by for a long chat, after which Elizabeth "sat before the fire in a stupor" for an hour. She "dashed off" to be photographed for *Vogue* magazine—"The pretty Strathmore girl" had already appeared in the pages of *Tatler* magazine—followed by tea with a friend.

While Elizabeth was dashing about that Friday, Bertie decided to unburden himself in a letter to "my darling Mama" to be sent by messenger to Sandringham. He began apologetically by saying he hoped she and "Papa" wouldn't think ill of him for not telling them about "my relations with Elizabeth." He knew they were both under the impression "that it was all over between us, with regard to marriage." But he assured his mother that "in the last two months a distinct change has come over Elizabeth, & I have been able to see a good deal of her in a quiet way, & she has always been very charming to me in every way."

He told Queen Mary that he had proposed nine days earlier, and that Elizabeth had encouraged him even as she postponed her reply. He had seen her the previous afternoon "& she was very nice." He revealed that she had invited him to St. Paul's Walden Bury for the weekend and had said "she is going to give me a definite answer one way or the other on Saturday."

In his earnest, heartfelt way, he confessed, "This is all very difficult to write to you darling Mama, but I know that you & Papa will give me your blessing if this all comes right & I shall be very very happy." He admitted that "this has all taken a very long time to adjust itself, but I am certain now that it was ever so much better to play the waiting game & give Elizabeth plenty of time to think things over, as I did not want to rush her into anything, & I know she would have said no, had I pressed her for an answer before now."

Elizabeth had refused Bertie's two previous proposals "quite stead-fastly," in the words of her mother. Each time, he had withdrawn with profuse apologies. "I never really had the opportunity of seeing any-thing of her at a stretch," he wrote to Queen Mary, "& we were never able to have any long talks together, but lately everything has come my way & we have not missed opportunities."

Now, feeling more optimistic about his third proposal, he wrote, "I will send you a telegram at once, if her answer is as I hope it will be, in 3 words 'All right. Bertie.' Not another soul will know what has hap-pened until I hear from you & I will let you know where I am." He asked her to wish him luck and closed by saying, "I am very very excited about it all. Best love to you darling Mama, I remain Ever Your very devoted boy Bertie."

Fifteen minutes after Elizabeth returned home at the end of her frenetic day, Bertie arrived at Bruton Street at six P.M., and they drove for an hour and a half to St. Paul's Walden Bury. He joined the Strath-more family for dinner at eight-thirty and presumably retired for the evening.

At that point, Elizabeth did something unexpected. She and Fenella (whose husband, Jock, had been laid up with a cold all week) went together to a dance hosted by some Hertfordshire neighbors. Not only did Elizabeth dance with a number of partners (her diary count stopped at four), she also stayed for supper and did not arrive at home until one-thirty A.M. Her behavior had the whiff of a last burst of freedom before making her decision.

The marathon discussions resumed on Saturday, January 13, when Elizabeth and Bertie had a long walk before lunch. In the afternoon the young couple sawed wood with Elizabeth's father. "Prince Bertie sawed <u>hard</u>!" Elizabeth noted in her diary. The quirky earl was famous for going into the woods on his estates at all hours with his valet, cutting off branches, dragging them back to the house, and chopping them up for kindling. During one visit to Glamis, Elizabeth's friend Diamond Hardinge was told "not to be disturbed if she heard a knocking or thumping through the night as it was only Lord Strathmore 'chopping wood.'"

After tea, Bertie and Elizabeth talked again "for hours." By dinnertime at eight-thirty, Fenella had left for London. The couple then talked until nearly midnight before they parted for bedtime as the promised deadline passed. She recorded in mirror writing that night: *"decided to wait a little. . . . I hope I am not behaving badly."*

On Sunday, January 14, 1923, Elizabeth's diary entry consisted of five sentences. "Woke at 9. Breakie at 10:30. Sat and talked till 12:30 & then went for a walk in the enchanted wood ["the haunt of fairies" for Elizabeth since childhood]. Long walk after lunch & long talks after tea and dinner. Jock went up to London at 5."

It was only after their final extended nighttime conversation that Elizabeth accepted Bertie's proposal. Her failing to mention the historic moment in her diary is confounding, given the buildup. She didn't even use mirror writing to record *"dias sey."* Nor did she mention what time she went to sleep.

We must turn to Lady Strathmore to learn what happened that night. In a letter two days later to her daughter May Elphinstone, she wrote that Bertie "came down to St. P.W. suddenly on Friday and proposed continuously until Sunday night when she said Yes at 11:30!! My head is completely bewildered, as all these days E was hesitating & miserable, but now she is absolutely happy—& he is <u>radiant</u>."

What changed, after so many hours of deep conversation? Did the "enchanted wood" work its magic? Writing to Beryl Poignand a week later, Elizabeth offered no clue: "I am so happy, & most surprised, as I never thought I'd marry him!!!"

According to Helen Hardinge, Elizabeth's friend since childhood and wife of Alexander Hardinge, an assistant private secretary to George V, Prince Albert dispatched the "ALL RIGHT—BERTIE" telegram to Sandringham as promised. "The excitement was great," she wrote, "for this was a code which he had arranged with his mother previously."

On Monday, January 15, the prince traveled to Sandringham with Louis Greig, his trusted longtime adviser, to share the details with his parents. Queen Mary—who of course had been briefed by her son the previous Friday—wrote a letter of welcome and congratulations to Elizabeth that afternoon. "Bertie has just appeared looking beaming, to inform us of his engagement to you," she said. "The news has come as a great surprise and we feel very much excited!"

Writing to his mother the following day, Bertie admitted uncertainty about Elizabeth's state of mind. "I am very very happy," he said, "& I can only hope that Elizabeth feels the same as I do. I know I am very lucky to have won her over at last." Without her actually saying it, Elizabeth seemed to believe that even if she wasn't "in love" with Bertie, she could learn to love him. Her constant use of the word "friend" underlined her conviction that love was essentially a passionate companionship. Once Elizabeth made her commitment on Sunday, January 14, 1923, she never looked at anyone else, and she remained unwaveringly devoted to the man who would be her husband for nearly three decades.

"George V remained a distant figure inspiring reverence, reserved affection, and sometimes genuine fear."

King George V circa 1902 with four of his children. Left to right: Prince Albert, Princess Mary, Prince Edward, and Prince Henry.

TWO

An Honorable Boy

THE FUTURE KING GEORGE VI WAS BORN ON AN INAUSPICIOUS DATE. December 14, 1895, was the thirty-fourth anniversary of the death of his revered great-grandfather, Queen Victoria's husband, Prince Albert. The little boy's mother and father were known as Prince George and Princess May, and fifteen years later became King George V and Queen Mary. They sent word to seventy-six-year-old Victoria that they would honor the late prince consort's memory by naming their son Albert Frederick Arthur George. They nicknamed their son "Bertie" after his grandfather, the future King Edward VII. In a letter to "darling Georgie," Queen Victoria praised the "dear name of Albert."

Bertie had entered the world at 3:40 A.M. in his mother's claustrophobic bedroom at York Cottage on the Sandringham estate. At eighteen and a half feet by ten and a half feet, the room was uncomfortably narrow and confining, even with a bow window overlooking the adjacent pond. Its small size would have been more appropriate for a servant's quarters in nearby Sandringham House (nicknamed the "Big House"), owned by Bertie's grandparents.

Albert's older brother, Prince Edward, had been born eighteen months earlier in White Lodge, the home of Princess May's parents, the Duke and Duchess of Teck. Set in Richmond Park on the outskirts of southwest London, the eighteenth-century Palladian villa built by King George II was far grander than York Cottage. The twenty-seven-year-old princess had her first child in the room where she had lived from age three until her marriage. Its sweeping view of the Queen's Ride, a greensward lined with ancient oaks, seemed fitting for the future King Edward VIII.

The arrival of the heir to the throne—Edward Albert Christian George Andrew Patrick David—on June 23, 1894, had caused great celebration. His grandfather announced the news at a ball in the middle of the Ascot racing week. Congratulatory telegrams poured in from royal palaces across Europe, and thousands of members of the public flocked to a marquee on the White Lodge lawn to sign a commemorative book for the infant boy who would come to be known in his family as David.

By contrast, Bertie's birth was a quiet affair. The rest of the family was with Queen Victoria marking "Mausoleum Day" at the annual service honoring the Prince Consort in the Frogmore Mausoleum near Windsor Castle. Writing in her diary, the elderly Queen set aside any feeling of "regret" on the timing of the boy's birth, adding that "it may be a blessing for the dear little boy and may be looked upon as a gift from God."

Two months later, on February 17, 1896, Prince Albert met his great-grandmother at his christening in the Church of St. Mary Magdalene, Sandringham, presided over by the Bishop of Norwich. In addition to Victoria, his godparents were all relations: Victoria's daughter "Vicky," the mother of Kaiser Wilhelm II; Princess Augusta, the beloved aunt of Princess May; her aunt's husband, a German grand duke; the Crown Prince of Denmark (brother of the infant's grandmother Queen Alexandra); Prince George's uncle Arthur, the Duke of Connaught; and Princess May's brother, Prince Adolphus. As a token of her approval, Queen Victoria presented the infant with a bust of his esteemed namesake.

IN 1897, QUEEN VICTORIA'S DIAMOND Jubilee year marking her sixty years on the throne, Albert's only sister arrived. George and May pleased the Queen by naming their daughter Victoria Alexandra Alice Mary, to be known as Princess Mary. In the following years came Prince Henry in 1900, Prince George in 1902, and Prince John in 1905. All were born at York Cottage in their mother's cluttered bedroom and were destined to grow up in the eccentric atmosphere of the royal family's most unusual and uncomfortable residence.

York Cottage was a rambling house with wings and bays, mock-Tudor beams, gables, miniature balconies, and turrets. In the eyes of ordinary people, it probably looked large enough. But it was more like a home in the suburbs. While it could sleep forty, it was inadequate as a royal residence for a family with dozens of staff and servants.

The hallways were narrow and twisting, the ceilings low, the bedrooms tiny. (Princess May once compared York Cottage to a doll's house.) The smells from the basement kitchen pervaded every room. Prince George's private secretary—his most senior adviser—was forced to work out of his bedroom, lacking a suitable office. The bathrooms used by George and May had toilets with special lids that doubled as tables.

When the monarch's household traveled to the royal estate at Balmoral in Scotland and to Windsor Castle, George and May and their family trailed behind them. They spent time in London, first at York House in St. James's Palace and later Marlborough House down the street on Pall Mall. Although their London homes were substantially larger than York Cottage (seventy-five rooms at York House), there was "no proper space for growing children," according to Charlotte "Lalla" Bill, their nurse. Prince George disliked socializing and the sort of holiday travel to the Continent favored by his father, so he stayed mainly at Sandringham, living the life of a country squire.

At York Cottage, he occupied himself with shooting pheasants and partridges, and tending to his game books and his guns (displayed in a glass case along one wall of his library). Seated at the large desk in this little room where the windows were darkened by laurel leaves, and the walls were covered with the scarlet serge used for French military uniforms, he devoted hours to his enormous stamp collection or reading the newspaper. May engaged in self-improvement by immersing her-self in books or stitching needlepoint—a passion so great, it was said, that she worked on her canvases even while dozing.

George and May professed devotion to their children, but they had little comprehension of the juvenile mind, much less the basics of child development. Alexander Hardinge, who served both George VI and his father as a loyal courtier, told royal biographer Harold Nicolson he was baffled that George V, "who was one of the most kind-hearted people in the world, could have been such a brute to his children."

John Wheeler-Bennett put his best spin on the situation. In his official biography, *King George VI,* he wrote that when his children were young, George V showed his devotion by "bathing them in turn, weighing them, playing with them on occasion," and teaching them to ride horses and shoot. At age twelve, Bertie had his first day shooting at Sandringham, bagging three rabbits. Four years later, he shot his first stag at Balmoral, and proudly recorded in his Sandringham game book, "My first woodcock." These milestones met with his father's approval, but George V "remained a distant figure inspiring reverence, reserved affection, and sometimes genuine fear."

So where did they go wrong as parents? George V had a booming voice—the result, in part, from impaired hearing in his right ear—that particularly intimidated children. He was irritable, impatient, and intolerant. Reverential toward her husband, Princess May yielded too often to his bellicose strictness. The daughter of George V's longtime private secretary, Lord Stamfordham, said that May "would never stand up to him over his shouting at the children."

His sons were his primary targets, since he doted on his only daughter, Princess Mary, and seldom scolded her. As the boys grew older, their father alternated between harshly criticizing them and mocking them with his "chaff"—leg-pulling banter that he liberally used among family and friends who could laugh it off. The children usually didn't get the joke and felt humiliated.

Princess May also endured tirades from Prince George during meals when staff were not present. He was "foully rude to my mother," the Duke of Windsor told James Pope-Hennessy, his mother's biographer, adding that he had "often seen her leave the table because he was so rude to her, and we children would all follow her out."

Only when outside her husband's overbearing orbit did May unbend somewhat. When Prince George visited country estates for weeks of shooting or thoroughbred races, the children would have their mother to themselves. Before dinner at York Cottage, she would gather the children in her boudoir.

This "cozy room overflowing with personal treasures," as her son David later described it, served as a haven of sorts. During their golden hour together, Princess May would recline in a negligee on her chaise as the children sat in little chairs. She talked to them softly, sharing knowledge from her "cultivated mind" and playing card games featuring the counties of England. Since their father had neither intellectual curiosity nor interest in the arts, this was the sole source of culture for Albert and his siblings. May also taught them needlework, an unlikely skill that Bertie and David embraced to relax their restless minds. During World War I on the Western Front, Prince Edward would crochet comforters for charity "as a means of killing time." In later years, Prince Albert would embroider in petit point a dozen chair covers for his home with Elizabeth near Windsor Castle.

George made little effort to properly educate his heir and second son, who spent their days in the care of nurses, nannies, and ineffective tutors. Dressed alike in sailor suits or tartan kilts and tweed jackets, David and Bertie were chubby-cheeked towheads who could have passed for twins. But there the resemblance stopped. David was the shining star, and Bertie the fragile laggard.

They both suffered at the hands of a mentally unstable nurse who abused David—pinching his arms to make him cry before formal evening visits with his parents—and ignored Albert. She even denied Bertie food, which may have led to later stomach upsets that began plaguing him as a teenager. When he was two, Lalla Bill, then the under-nurse, reported the sadistic treatment. The head nurse was dismissed, and for the next four years, Lalla managed her young charges with finesse and firmness.

Despite their attachment to Lalla, their father decided the boys needed "masculine discipline." When Bertie was six, Lalla was supplanted by a thirty-year-old former royal footman named Frederick Finch, who oversaw their care for nearly a decade as an early twentieth-century version of a "manny." "Handsome, stalwart, and muscular," Finch not only supervised their hygiene and wardrobe but also nursed the princes when they were ill, listened to their morning and evening prayers, and put them to bed.

In 1902, shortly after Prince Albert's sixth birthday, Prince George hired Henry Peter Hansell as the brothers' principal tutor. The thirty-nine-year-old Oxford graduate had taught at a couple of boarding schools, but his main credential in George's eyes was his genteel Norfolk background, along with his skill as a yachtsman and golfer.

Hansell set up a mock classroom on the second floor at York Cottage with two desks, a blackboard, and bookcases. A pipe-smoking bachelor, Hansell was humorless and straitlaced, although the boys grew fond of him. He oversaw a daily schedule of classes, supplemented by other tutors who taught French, German, and mathematics. But he was a poor teacher and lax disciplinarian when faced with inattentive and often disobedient pupils. His downbeat reports on David and Bertie's lack of progress provoked furious reprimands from their father when he summoned the boys to his gloomy library.

It was in Hansell's first year of instruction, between Bertie's seventh and eighth birthdays, that the prince began to stutter—a condition aggravated by his father's anger, which reduced him to incoherence. One theory is that the stutter originated with Hansell's efforts to force left-handed Bertie to use his right hand. Whatever the cause, it soon became a crippling affliction. Bertie couldn't participate in oral lessons, either in English or in foreign languages. He fell mute amid noisy family banter, unable to muster a quick riposte. The only slender upside was his development of sharp powers of observation.

Bertie's nightmare was a ritual on family birthdays. Each child was commanded to recite a poem from memory in front of a glamorous gathering of guests in the Big House at Sandringham. One can only imagine Bertie's terror while struggling red-faced to recite passages from Tennyson and Shakespeare, and even worse, La Fontaine in French and Goethe in German. Two of the most troublesome words were "king" and "queen." Not surprisingly, Bertie's verbal inadequacy led his family and teachers to conclude he was slow-witted.

Bertie was also judged physically handicapped by his knock-knees. On the orders of one of the royal doctors, Bertie was fitted with splints to straighten the deformity. He was forced to wear them at night, which disrupted his sleep, and during the day, which prevented him from concentrating in the schoolroom. This inhumane treatment was as painful as it was humiliating. After more than a year, the remedy was deemed effective. Albert would eventually develop graceful athletic ability. But the psychological damage was done.

The essence of Prince Albert's character was evident by then. He was innately high-strung, easily wounded, and prone to panic attacks. He was so timid that he could not even bring himself to ask servants to light the lamps as darkness fell. Frustration often overwhelmed him in his studies, driving him to tears when he couldn't master mathematical concepts.

Most alarming were his bouts of depression and sudden eruptions of anger that intensified with the onset of his stutter. John Wheeler-Bennett, who had the same affliction, wrote compassionately about the "tragedies of the stammerer . . . infuriating inhibitions and frustrations, bitter humiliation and anguish of the spirit; the orgies of self pity; and the utter exhaustion, mental and physical; perhaps, above all the sense of being *different* from others and the shrinking from help prompted by pity."

But Bertie was also developing sterling qualities such as determination, reliability, bravery, and modesty. In its embryonic form, he was showing the trait that his daughter Queen Elizabeth II most admired in him: steadfastness. When Bertie was just six years old, Mabell Airlie saw through his moody silences and sometimes defiant naughtiness when he shyly approached her with an Easter card he had made with cut-out pictures of flowers pasted on cardboard. She drew him out with tact and understanding, and he spoke to her without his usual hesitations. "I found that far from being backward he was an intelligent child," she recalled, "with more force of character than anyone suspected in those days."

At York Cottage, the children were under the eyes of liveried servants and ladies-in-waiting. But on the twenty-thousand-acre Sandringham estate, Bertie and David, along with their younger sister, Mary, were free to roam the woodlands, fields, and salt marshes, and to bicycle to the seven villages scattered around the monarch's property. They caught fish in the lake in front of the cottage, where they skated in the winter.

On the sixty acres around the Big House, they could wander through the gardens, the greenhouses, carriage houses, Alexandra's carving school where master craftsmen made furniture, and kennels filled with her collection of dogs, numbering as many as fifty at one time. The children might stop by the estate's own train station at Wolferton or see thoroughbreds at the royal stud farm. The boys also picked up the game of golf, which they played on Sandringham's nine-hole course. These rambles inculcated in Albert a love of Sandringham that matched his father's.

QUEEN VICTORIA DIED IN JANUARY 1901. Bertie and his brothers were in quarantine for measles at York Cottage when their eighty-one-year-old "Gangan" suffered a series of strokes at her Osborne House residence on the Isle of Wight. "It has come too late," said King Edward VII, Bertie's grandfather and Victoria's successor. He was already fifty-nine.

Prince George rushed to Osborne House, but also succumbed to the measles, which he had caught from his children. Unable to attend Queen Victoria's funeral on the second of February, he sent Princes Edward and Albert, aged six and five, in his stead. The mourning was intense for the queen who had reigned for nearly sixty-four years. The two boys saw their grandfather on horseback in a white-plumed helmet behind Victoria's caisson in the impressive cortege. There were thirty-three thousand soldiers and massed bands, along with one of the largest gatherings of European royalty in history. The two princes attended the funeral service in St. George's Chapel, followed by the Queen's burial at the Frogmore mausoleum on February 4.

In August of the following year, their grandfather, Edward VII, was crowned in Westminster Abbey. Princes Edward and Albert, wearing costumes of royal tartan kilts and dress tunics, sat in the royal box with their minders, Finch and Hansell. Then aged eight and seven, the boys "fidgeted and whispered incessantly but watched with awe their father do homage to the newly crowned king."

The world outside the bubble of royal childhood at the end of the nineteenth and beginning of the twentieth centuries was of no consequence to Prince Albert. Britain was riding a wave of industrial strength powered by a global empire that stretched across eleven million square miles and encompassed four hundred million people. In its South African colony, war broke out with rebellious Dutch settlers that ended in British victory. Otherwise, its relations were peaceful with a European continent ruled by twenty monarchs.

Whenever Bertie and his siblings joined their parents in London, he took dancing classes—with emphasis on Highland reels, waltzes, and polkas—and singing lessons at Marlborough House, where they moved in April 1903 when Edward VII and Alexandra relocated to Buckingham Palace. At the Bath Club, an elegant gentlemen's club in Mayfair, he and Prince Edward learned to swim and play racquet sports. Hansell did his best to enrich their dry curriculum with sightseeing trips to the Tower of London and museum exhibitions, as well as cricket matches at Lord's and the Oval.

Albert plodded through five years of Hansell's tedious lessons until he reached the age of thirteen in December 1908. As the second son, he was destined to follow George V's career in the Royal Navy. Was he ready for naval training? Not particularly, either by temperament or by experience. That didn't matter to his dictatorial father. In his final report on Bertie's academic achievement, Hansell vaguely pegged him as a "scatter-brain" in need of "a shove." But he was unequivocal in sizing up Bertie's character: As "a very straight and honourable boy, very kind hearted and generous," he was "sure to be popular with other boys."

"When he felt at ease in the company of others, his stutter diminished."

Prince Albert at the Royal Naval College, Dartmouth, in 1911.

THREE

※

Stuck in Sick Bay

BERTIE SHOWED ADMIRABLE PLUCK WHEN HE SUCCESSFULLY TACKLED the entrance examinations for the fledgling junior Royal Naval College on the grounds of Osborne House. He enrolled in January 1909, two years after his brother David, who was destined to be king, not a naval officer.

It was a shock to the system for both brothers, but less so for the confident and gregarious Prince Edward. Neither of them had competed with peers, and most of the other boys had already spent four years at boarding schools. Albert was acutely homesick. His stammer was aggravated by heightened anxiety and the inevitable taunting of the other cadets, who nicknamed him "Sardine" for his scrawny physique.

But within months, Bertie's essential goodness and "never say I'm beaten" spirit won them over, as Hansell had predicted. He compensated for his inadequacy in team sports with his speed as a cross-country runner. His royal pedigree notwithstanding, he was appealingly down-to-earth. As Mabell Airlie had discovered, when he felt at ease in the company of others, his stutter diminished.

The cadets slept in unheated dormitories with iron beds and small chests for their belongings, and they followed a strict daily schedule that began with a plunge in a frigid pool. Albert was discomfited by living cheek by jowl in these conditions. The education was technical rather than classically academic: navigation, knot-tying, engineering, and the mathematics that had always bedeviled Bertie.

Infected with whooping cough at the end of the summer term in 1909, Albert missed the state visit of the czar of Russia, his father's first cousin. But he was fortunate to be treated by a dynamic Scottish doctor, twenty-eight-year-old Lieutenant Louis Greig, who also happened to be an international sports legend for his prowess on the rugby pitch. Bertie took instantly to Greig's cheerful encouragement. It was the beginning of a lifelong friendship in which Greig would serve for six crucial years as a mentor and father figure. Tall and rugged, Greig would not only instill confidence in the timorous young prince but also rescue him from chronic illness and play a pivotal role in Bertie's courtship of Elizabeth Bowes Lyon.

Nine months later, King Edward VII was dead at age sixty-eight from emphysema and heart failure, a victim of his chronic smoking. Alexandra smoked discreetly, as did Princess May, while Prince George inherited his father's nicotine dependence and was constantly wreathed in smoke. It's no wonder that starting as a teenager, Prince Albert would smoke one cigarette after another to tame his nerves. On his eighteenth birthday, his mother gave her blessing to his habit with a gift of a silver cigarette case. His daily intake was routinely around forty "gaspers."

Bertie and David stood at attention atop the garden wall at Marlborough House as they watched their father proclaimed King George V in Friary Court at St. James's Palace on May 9, 1910. They participated in an elaborate state funeral eleven days later. On an unusually hot day they wore their naval cadet uniforms and marched slowly behind their grandfather's coffin up the hill at Windsor Castle to St. George's Chapel. A month afterward, David, the next in line to the throne, was made Prince of Wales.

They witnessed the coronation of their father and mother in Westminster Abbey a year later, on June 22, 1911. On the King's crowning, the Prince of Wales, who would turn seventeen the next day, lifted a coronet onto his own head and knelt before the throne to pay his homage. From the royal box, dressed in his naval cadet's uniform, Prince Albert observed this ancient ritual, followed by emotional kisses on young Edward's cheeks from George V.

The two princes were now handsome boys with delicately sculpted faces. The Prince of Wales was generally regarded as the better looking of the two. Each had an attractively turned-up nose and narrow blue eyes above high cheekbones. Albert's mouth was more generous than Edward's, with a hint of warmth that his brother lacked despite his charm. Edward's eyes were steely, while Albert's betrayed his sensitivity. Edward claimed to be five foot seven, but he was easily two inches shorter than Albert, who was five foot six at most.

Bertie had completed his studies at Osborne in December 1910, ranking sixty-eighth out of his class of sixty-eight. He was nevertheless admitted to the new Royal Naval College at Dartmouth, where David was in his final year when Bertie arrived in January 1911. Bertie's progress through Dartmouth over the following two years was no more distinguished than at Osborne. His final result after six terms was a disappointing sixty-first out of sixty-seven. George V reacted with equanimity to his second son's setbacks, and his attitude generally softened as he witnessed his progress in other ways.

Bertie was developing into a fine shot on the grouse moors at Balmoral and the fields and woodlands at Sandringham, and he showed considerable skill at tennis. He also took seriously his preparation to be confirmed in the Church of England. He asked searching questions and developed a depth of faith that would be integral to his character. He regarded his confirmation on April 18, 1912, as a day "on which I took a great step in life."

Prince Albert finished his naval training with a six-month cruise to the West Indies and Canada. For the first time in his life, he was on his own, without having to measure up to the magnetic and debonair brother who preceded him. Edward had already been sent to Magdalen College at Oxford, where he spent two years and hardly opened a book.

George V had taken a liking to Louis Greig, and he shrewdly arranged to have Bertie assigned to HMS *Cumberland,* where the Scotsman was the ship's surgeon. Bertie was chronically seasick and gripped with insecurities, but he was determined to show his father he could succeed. He passed the exams to qualify as a midshipman, and he took on whatever task was asked of him, even lugging heavy bags of coal to the engine room.

Thirty-three-year-old Greig and eighteen-year-old Bertie solidified their friendship during these months on shipboard as well as ashore, where they went riding and played tennis. Bertie toured banana, cocoa, and sugar plantations, listened to talks on the science of irrigation, and saw oil wells in Trinidad. In Toronto and Quebec, he endured mandatory social functions. He was timorous around girls, finding refuge in corners so he wouldn't be compelled to dance with strangers. He even touched down briefly in the United States for a tour of Niagara Falls. He groused that the Americans had "no manners at all and tried to take photographs all the time."

Sir Martin Charteris, one of Queen Elizabeth II's private secretaries, later likened Greig to a psychiatrist, saying, "he listened, he encouraged, he helped. He allowed Albert to help himself. He was the doctor who thought that he could set him right after a childhood with its own peculiarities. Louis was the right man in the right place to help him reach his potential."

Prince Albert optimistically embarked on his naval career aboard HMS *Collingwood* in September 1913, while Louis Greig transferred to medical duty with the Royal Marines. As one of the midshipmen, also known as "snotties," Bertie held the lowest rank on his ship. He learned to obey orders and perform all manner of menial tasks during a thirteen-thousand-mile cruise around the Mediterranean that took him to Gibraltar, Malta, Italy, Egypt, and Greece. When he came home to Sandringham at the end of December after his eighteenth birthday, he showed greater maturity behind his natural reserve.

Six months later, on June 28, 1914, Bertie was back on *Collingwood* off the isle of Portland in the English Channel when some disquieting news came through. The heir to the Austrian throne, Archduke Franz Ferdinand, and his wife, Sophie, had been killed in Sarajevo, the capital of Bosnia—a province of Austria-Hungary. The assassin was a fanatical member of a Serbian nationalist group that believed Bosnia actually belonged to Serbia. The Austrians had been fiercely at odds with the Serbs, who were actively trying to annex Bosnian territory on the southern border of the Austria-Hungarian empire. Franz Ferdinand was unpopular in Sarajevo, so his visit was especially ill-advised.

The assassination of his heir gave the Austrian emperor Franz Joseph the pretext to invade and dismember the small nation of Serbia, triggering a cascade of violent reactions among a complicated web of European alliances. The Germans, led by George V's first cousin, the volatile and aggressively nationalistic Kaiser Wilhelm II, sided with Austria. The Russians, led by another first cousin of George V, Czar Nicholas II, backed their ally Serbia and tumbled into war with Germany and Austria. Having significantly built up its army and navy, Germany then seized the opportunity to launch an assault on France, which was aligned by treaty with Russia. Among other motivations, Germany was eager to encroach on the French and British colonial empires.

The German invasion of France first blazed through Belgium—a meticulously premeditated plan that the high command had been preparing for years. At that point, Britain honored its treaties with Belgium and France and went to war on their behalf against Germany and Austria-Hungary on August 4. What had begun as a bilateral skirmish between Austria and Serbia exploded into a world war that would drag on for four years and claim the lives of more than nine million combatants and thirteen million civilians. As military men and materiel flooded across Europe, it was hard to imagine that only fourteen years earlier, Kaiser Wilhelm had held his grandmother, Queen Victoria, as she lay dying.

Britain reacted to the onset of war with giddy excitement. Crowds surged to Buckingham Palace in a show of support for King George V and Queen Mary, who came to the Palace balcony three times. The cause seemed honorable, and nearly everyone assumed the war would be short; some said it could be over by Christmas.

The men rushing to enlist included the Prince of Wales, who escaped Oxford to train with the Grenadier Guards. The army waived the minimum height of six feet in the Grenadiers' King's Company, making the prince "a pygmy among giants." In November 1914, he reported for staff duty at the headquarters of the British Expeditionary Force in France.

At first, George V failed to grasp the implications of events escalating rapidly across the Channel. Writing to Bertie a week before Britain declared war, he lamented that he had to give up the Goodwood races, and that his annual yachting at Cowes might be canceled. By August 4, the gravity of the situation had sunk in. King George V wrote in his diary, "Please God it may soon be over & that he will protect dear Bertie's life."

That month marked the onset of a more personal battle for Prince Albert that would persist throughout the war, bringing recurrent physical agony and mental anguish. His incessant seasickness was the least of it. He was now seized regularly with what were described as "gastric attacks."

Bertie described his initial illness as a "violent pain in the stomach" so severe he could scarcely breathe. After being transferred to a hospital ship on a stretcher, he was hoisted by a crane to shore in his hospital bed. Two weeks later, he underwent an appendectomy at a hospital in Aberdeen, Scotland. He returned to London in October 1914 and shuttled between Buckingham Palace and Sandringham. Waves of pain returned the following month, and his doctors judged him unfit for service at sea.

That autumn was particularly harrowing for Britain. Its forces suffered more than fifty thousand casualties at the First Battle of Ypres over a three-week stretch, and Turkey entered the war as Germany's ally, putting the Ottoman Empire in direct conflict with the British Empire. Feeling guilty for "not doing his bit," Bertie took a staff job at the Admiralty where Winston Churchill was First Lord.

Churchill invited Prince Albert for lunch, and over the next two months the young prince had his first opportunity to see in action the man who would serve as his prime minister some twenty-five years later. The prince was given access to the top-secret War Room, where he was responsible for charts that mapped the locations of British and enemy warships. From time to time he would proudly tip off his father about naval maneuvers before they were officially relayed to the monarch.

But Bertie was restless and despondent. "Nothing to do as usual," he often peevishly wrote in his diary. When he turned nineteen in mid-December 1914, he was keenly aware that everybody he knew was on active service, especially David. Although his older brother was safely installed thirty miles from the Western Front, he was agitating to get into the action. Louis Greig had not only seen combat but also had been captured during the fall of Antwerp, Belgium, and was a prisoner of war in Germany.

Bertie pressed to return to his ship, and the Admiralty finally granted his request. He rejoined *Collingwood* on February 12, 1915. Three months later, his illness struck again. By late June, his superior officer reported that Bertie "is sick every time he swallows any food and is very mouldy. In fact wasting away."

In mid-July 1915, his doctors fastened on what turned out to be a misdiagnosis: "the weakening of the muscular wall of the stomach and a consequent catarrhal condition." His treatment consisted of rest, "careful dieting," and nightly enemas. The confounded medical experts fell back on recommending a "change of scene and air."

That meant a month in Scotland at Abergeldie Castle, three miles down the River Dee from Balmoral Castle, which was closed for the duration of the war. Bertie had enjoyed eight contented child-hood summers with his family in the fourteenth-century castle with a medieval stone tower. Abergeldie was a reminder of an unrestrained time when he and his siblings had been alone with their mother. They had thrived in the wildness of the surroundings—the endless pine forests, the hills dappled with wildflowers, the shimmering lochs and the gurgling burns. Bertie loved it there, but cooped up with his doctor, he took little pleasure from Abergeldie during his recuperation.

Several weeks after he returned to York Cottage that October, his father had a horrific accident while on horseback reviewing troops on the front lines in France. Startled by the sound of a military band, the king's horse reared and fell backward, pinning George V underneath in the mud. He suffered a fractured pelvis in at least two places, and he was in agonizing pain. His broken bones never properly knitted and would plague him for the rest of his life, increasing his general irrita-bility and limiting his mobility. "He was never quite the same man again," wrote Harold Nicolson.

George V returned to Buckingham Palace, where he was con-fined to his bed for six weeks. A greatly distressed Bertie rushed to London and fell ill again—exacerbated by his "emotional excite-ment." The King's recovery was prolonged and difficult; it took four weeks before he could walk with two canes, and he "lost seriously in weight."

These weeks when father and son were convalescing together brought them closer. George V and Albert discussed political issues as well as news from the battlefields and the high seas. For Bertie, it was an invaluable opportunity to observe how a wartime monarch con-ducted himself—lessons he would revisit when faced with compara-ble challenges during World War II.

Once again, Prince Albert was assigned to the Admiralty for "light duty" that was unsatisfying. He broke the monotony of his London life with a trip to the Western Front to see David at the end of January 1916. Under tight security, the brothers visited scenes of fighting the previous autumn—La Bassée, Hulluch, and Loos. The two princes also witnessed a British bombardment and German counterattack.

Back in England, the high points of his dreary existence were visits to Sandringham for shooting with his father. He was in touch with Louis Greig, who had been released from German captivity in July 1915 in an exchange for a German doctor. Louis was married the following February, but Bertie was unable to leave his sickbed to attend the wedding in Norfolk. From late August 1914 to early May 1916, he was on sick leave for sixteen months and served on his ship for a mere four months.

LADY ELIZABETH BOWES LYON WAS feeling downhearted as well. She had come to London in the spring of 1916 for a respite from caring for wounded soldiers at Glamis Castle and to take examinations for a certificate of academic achievement. She had been through one of the hardest years of her young life as the horrors of the battlefield hit home.

Her older brother Patrick, the scion of the Bowes Lyon family, had been sent to Glamis from the front in February 1915 with an injured foot and such severe shell shock (now known as post-traumatic stress disorder) that he didn't recover and had to leave active service. Three months later, Michael Bowes Lyon had returned to Scotland after being hospitalized in France for a head wound as well as shell shock.

Then in early October 1915 came the crushing news that Fergus Bowes Lyon had been killed in action at the Battle of Loos. His right leg was blown off by a German bomb, and he was shot several times in the chest and shoulder. He was twenty-six years old, married for just over a year, the father of a two-month-old girl named Rosemary.

Elizabeth and her family were devastated, especially after they learned the gruesome details of his death. Among those who consoled

Elizabeth was her good friend Lady Lavinia Spencer, who sent a letter expressing her sympathy. "It really is all so ghastly and terrible," she wrote. "It does seem wicked that the best men should all be killed." She praised Elizabeth for being "so brave."

Lavinia was the sixteen-year-old daughter of the sixth Earl Spencer, one of the foremost noblemen in Britain and the great-grandfather of Diana, Princess of Wales. She was the perfect friend for a downcast Elizabeth. The two girls exchanged letters filled with private jokes, even sending up the royal family: Lavinia addressed letters to "Mary" and signed them "George R." Elizabeth played the nom de plume game in reply as Queen Mary. They shared crushes on actors and dreams of marrying sailors.

When Elizabeth failed her exams that March and her mood turned melancholy, Lavinia wrote to invite her to tea on Sunday, April 2, 1916, to meet Prince Albert and Princess Mary. The twenty-year-old midshipman and fifteen-year-old pre-debutante met as planned at Spencer House, one of the most beautiful neoclassical homes in London.

Neither Bertie nor Elizabeth was in a particularly sociable frame of mind. Writing to her mother two days later, Elizabeth said the tea party was "rather frightening, in fact very"—although it's unclear why that was so. She described the small group Lavinia had assembled to meet the royal siblings: a duchess (Sutherland: "rather pretty"), and the daughters of two marquesses and one duke. There were several men Elizabeth hadn't previously met, including Arthur Penn, a Grenadier Guards officer she found "entrancing" and who would become a lifelong friend.

Elizabeth passed no judgment on Princess Mary, and all she could muster about Bertie, sitting at the next table, was "he's rather nice." Elizabeth gave a few additional details about Lavinia's party to her governess and confidante, Beryl Poignand. Bertie and Mary were known to be shy, but they had proved to be unexpectedly lively, "staying and staying—they played games after tea."

If Elizabeth Bowes Lyon made an impression on Prince Albert that Sunday afternoon, he kept it to himself. Her assessment of him could charitably be called tepid. She was worried about her return to Glamis Castle, where her parents and brother Michael and wounded soldiers awaited. He could think of little else but a hoped-for return to *Collingwood*. She had no notion of Bertie's combination of fortitude and sweetness that would draw her into his life seven years later. And he had no idea of Elizabeth's qualities of affection, imagination, kindness, vitality, and serenity that would be the making of him.

"You feel very safe in a big family."

Lord and Lady Strathmore with their nine children circa 1906–07.

FOUR

The Rent You Pay for Life

ELIZABETH'S ARISTOCRATIC STRATHMORE LINEAGE HAD ITS ORIGINS IN the fourteenth century when her earliest noteworthy ancestor, John Lyon, married Princess Joanna, the daughter of Robert II, the first Stewart king of Scots. Lyon received a knighthood as well as a hunting lodge in the Vale of Strathmore, which was replaced by the current pink sandstone castle in the fifteenth century, when Sir John's grandson became the first Lord of Glamis.

By the late seventeenth century, the Lord of Glamis had acquired the additional titles of Earl of Strathmore and Kinghorne. The ninth earl enhanced the family further by marrying an English woman, Mary Eleanor Bowes, who inherited a large fortune from her parents. In the mid-nineteenth century, after an Act of Parliament approved the change, the family name became Bowes Lyon.

The Bowes Lyons not only presided over Glamis Castle and its sixty-five thousand acres but also owned Streatlam Castle in England's county Durham, as well as St. Paul's Walden Bury in Hertfordshire. Elizabeth's grandfather Claude, the thirteenth Earl of Strathmore and Kinghorne, married a devout woman named Frances

Dora Smith, who produced eleven children—seven sons and four daughters.

The eldest son, Claude George (known in the family as Claudie), was Elizabeth's father. Born in 1855, he attended Eton College and was an officer in the Life Guards of the Household Cavalry. Trim and erect, he sported a luxuriant handlebar mustache under his long nose; before planting a kiss, he would first carefully part the profusion of hair at the center and push it aside. In 1881, when he was twenty-six, he married nineteen-year-old Nina Cecilia Cavendish-Bentinck. She was the daughter of an Oxford-educated clergyman and the great-granddaughter of the third Duke of Portland, who served twice as prime minister during the reign of King George III.

Cecilia was a handsome woman, with an aquiline nose and warm blue-gray eyes. She pulled her dark hair into a demure topknot, softened by tendrils on her forehead. Decidedly stout by middle age, she wore long, flowing dresses, usually black, a sign of her frequent state of mourning for deceased family members. In February 1904, after the death of his father, Claude inherited the castles and estates and became the fourteenth Earl of Strathmore and Kinghorne.

Lord Strathmore oversaw his tenant farmers and carried out official duties as a lord-lieutenant, the monarch's official representative in the county of Forfarshire surrounding Glamis. Between organizing regular cricket matches with his sons against a village team, he shot game birds and waterfowl.

Cecilia hosted house parties, tended to her gardens and needle-work, and brought food to ailing villagers. Her primary role was as a hands-on mother, in contrast to her aristocratic counterparts. Unlike most of them, Cecilia rejected the practice of wet nurses and breast-fed her babies. In the twenty years following her marriage, Cecilia bore ten children—eight of them during the first eleven years. Her final two, Elizabeth and David, arrived when she was thirty-seven and thirty-nine, and Lord Strathmore was forty-six and forty-eight. Claude, who looked considerably older than his years, was often mistaken for Elizabeth's grandfather.

By the time Cecilia turned fifty-three, she had lost three of her large brood. Such sorrows were common for that generation, between incurable diseases and the toll of battle, but they were no less devastating. In 1893, only two weeks after Cecilia gave birth to her eighth child, Michael, her daughter Violet Hyacinth contracted typhoid fever and died of heart failure at age eleven. The death of her firstborn child, by all accounts a beautiful girl, was a terrible shock at a time when Cecilia was already weakened by childbirth. A friend of hers later wrote that Violet's death "left wounds which never healed," adding that the lingering sadness gave Cecilia "an unusual power of sympathy and a rare understanding of other people."

Seven years elapsed before the birth of Elizabeth Angela Marguerite on August 4, 1900. Her mother would keep her baby girl's cradle by her bedside for eighteen months. David followed in 1902. Cecilia taught her two youngest children reading, writing, drawing, and music. At Glamis, a local fiddler instructed them in the intricate steps of Scottish reels, and they took conventional ballroom dancing lessons during the months the family stayed in London.

As the product of a lively and informal home atmosphere, Elizabeth—nicknamed Buffy by her family—was "an elfin creature swift of movement, quick of intelligence, alive with humour," said a friend of her brother Patrick. Lord David Cecil, the noted biographer, was one year older than Elizabeth when they met as children. Later in life he remarked that "the personality which I see now was there already."

She wasn't advanced intellectually or artistically, but she was outgoing and confident. Her sister Mary (known as May in the family) was old enough to be a surrogate mother, and her older brothers were by turns protective and playful. "You feel very safe in a big family," Elizabeth said when she was in her midnineties. "It was a great thing to be loved."

Elizabeth spent most of her childhood at St. Paul's Walden Bury, which was a children's paradise. Though considerably smaller than Glamis, its wide grassy avenues were lined with hornbeam hedges; the woodland gardens burst with rhododendrons, lilies, cowslips, and bluebells; and verdant fields sloped out to the horizon.

Elizabeth and David were an inseparable pair, rising at dawn and crawling around haylofts in the farm buildings, digging up nuts, rowing on the ponds, catching rabbits, riding ponies, and feeding the multicolored chickens before and after morning lessons. Elizabeth knew the names of all the wildflowers in the wood with its crisscrossing paths, its follies and statues with fanciful nicknames such as "the Bounding Butler." Biographer Cynthia Asquith observed that nowhere at St. Paul's Walden Bury "can there ever have been very strict rules as to the shutting of doors, the wiping of boots or the putting away of toys."

Elizabeth called Glamis her "holiday place." It was ancient and mysterious, a repository of legends and ghosts. A romantic turreted and crenellated castle of pink sandstone, it was dramatically set in the open, at the end of a long driveway, with the Grampian Mountains and Sidlaw Hills in the distance. Throughout its storied history, royal visitors stayed in the spacious rooms, some of which were said to be haunted by benign as well as malevolent ghosts. William Shakespeare used Glamis as the setting for *Macbeth*.

Elizabeth adored the castle's magic, starting with the spy hole in the guardroom, where a stuffed bear stood sentinel, and the historic crypt that was filled with suits of armor, battle axes, animal hides, breastplates, and swords. She excitedly showed visitors the trapdoor in a bedroom that led to the drawing room by a narrow stone staircase.

She also thrived outdoors, riding on her pony cart or her bicycle, her long brown hair flying, and playing with her numerous cousins as well as children in nearby Glamis village. From an early age, she accompanied her father and his shooting parties, riding astride a donkey.

When the house was full during the shooting season, as many as forty guests would sit at the mahogany table in the wood-paneled dining room. After two kilted bagpipers marched around the diners and the skirls faded into silence, Cecilia would organize a concert in the drawing room. While she played the piano, often joined by a visiting musician on the violin, Elizabeth and her cousins would eavesdrop, seated on cushions atop the stone steps of the secret stairway.

The pivot of the Strathmore family was Cecilia, an outgoing and sympathetic presence with a soft and melodious voice, swishing down the hallways at Glamis in her ample silk skirts. "She was a great force in a very dignified, gentle way," said her granddaughter Lady Mary Clayton. Cecilia was famous for her exquisitely designed Italian garden covering four acres on the east side of the castle. Its tall yew hedges were cut with alcoves holding statues of her ten children.

She had little regard for high society, although the comings and goings of the Strathmores surfaced from time to time among the upper-class chronicles in *The Times,* and they attended dinner parties and dances hosted by such prominent ducal families as the Buccleuchs and the Devonshires. She set an example with her thoughtfulness and shared maxims such as "Work is the rent you pay for life" and "Life is for living and working at; if anything or anyone bores you, then the fault is in yourself." Elizabeth took those sayings to heart and would impress them on her own elder daughter.

Cecilia kept a close eye on household accounts and supervised a large staff headed by longtime butler Arthur Barson, who had risen through the ranks from footman and valet. He was so beloved that Lord and Lady Strathmore "insisted he be included" in a 1909 portrait of the family that they hung at St. Paul's Walden Bury.

Along with a housekeeper, Barson managed a French chef, a half dozen maids, two footmen (dressed smartly in livery), a page, a coachman, and a groom who became the family chauffeur when Claude bought his first Daimler around 1908. The outdoor staff included gardeners and farmworkers. A half dozen washerwomen worked in the Glamis laundry, scrubbing and ironing table linens as well as sheets and towels for nearly thirty bedrooms during the seasons when the family hosted weeklong house parties.

Some of the staff traveled with the family from house to house for the annual Strathmore peregrinations. On the eve of the "Glorious Twelfth" each August, they would board the overnight Flying Scotsman in London destined for Glamis. They would stay through October for shooting holidays—first grouse, then partridge, then pheasant. They spent Christmas at St. Paul's Walden Bury and returned to Glamis for New Year's celebrations.

During the short winter social season in January and February, they stayed in London at their rented residence at 20 St. James's Square, a stately eighteenth-century townhome. They enjoyed the best of springtime at St. Paul's Walden Bury, followed by London for the full social season of balls and racing in June and July. Then it was time to resume the shooting season and "follow the birds" northward.

Spindly and nimble, Claude Strathmore hovered at the edges of the family, typically dressed in an ancient raincoat tied at the waist with twine. "He lived more of his own life," Elizabeth said many years later.

Besides his famous obsession with late-night excursions into the woodlands to saw branches off trees and chop them into kindling in his study, Claude occupied himself with menial labor. Once the local minister rebuked him for allowing an estate worker to dig a ditch on a Sunday, only to learn that Claude himself had done the digging. He thought nothing of drinking whisky at the homes of his tenant farmers, and he chain-smoked cigarettes.

Claude was such a fanatical cricketer that he practiced bowling along the Glamis corridors. Cecilia was a good sport, adroitly catching oranges when he rolled them down the dining room table. "She never muffed it," said Mary Clayton. "He used to come round and sit on the corner of her chair and put his arm round her."

Elizabeth's only escapes from the hermetic but happy life at St. Paul's Walden Bury, Glamis, and St. James's Square were trips to visit her widowed maternal grandmother, Caroline Scott, in Italy. Cecilia accompanied six-year-old Elizabeth on her first long journey by rail to San Remo. Subsequent trips took her to Bordighera and Florence, where she admired the "magnificent cypresses standing out against the blue distant mountains behind Fiesole." Italy widened Elizabeth's aperture to the beauty of paintings and classical architecture—passions she handed down to her favored grandson Prince Charles.

Lady Strathmore imbued all her children with her devout religious faith. Throughout her childhood, Elizabeth prayed every morning with her mother; they bowed their heads under lace caps in the private Anglican chapel at Glamis. Following her mother's example, Elizabeth began her lifelong practice of kneeling by her bedside to pray at night—a habit she in turn would pass on to her daughter, the future Queen Elizabeth II.

That faith was tested by the precarious health of the Strathmores' third eldest son, twenty-four-year-old Alexander. Like his father, he was an avid cricketer, and in the summer of 1910, he had been hit in the head by a ball during a match. He was plagued afterward by unceasing headaches that baffled the doctors.

Alexander tried to keep up with the shooting parties on the moors, but his headaches often forced him to return home early. On October 18, 1911, he was in too much pain to join the guns and remained in bed. He died in his sleep at three-thirty A.M. on the morning of the nineteenth. According to his death certificate discovered by biographer Hugo Vickers, the cause of death was "a tumour at the base of the cerebrum."

At age forty-nine, Cecilia had suffered the overwhelming loss of another child. There is no explicit record of Elizabeth's reaction to the family's second tragedy. She was eleven years old, the same age Violet had been at her death. Her relationship with her mother seemed to intensify, however. Whenever they were apart, she wrote effusively and often to "My darling preacious [sic] love" from "Your very very loving Elizabeth." Years later she confided to her friend Sir Arthur Penn, "It is a curious thing, but I have always been terrified of my mother dying, ever since I was a little child."

In September 1912, she lost the constant companionship of her younger brother David when he left home at age ten for St. Peter's Court preparatory school. Alone with her grieving parents, Elizabeth was miserable. When her mother traveled south from Scotland to visit him, Elizabeth sent her an apologetic letter: "Lovie I was so sorry to have cried when you went away. I couldn't help it though. . . . I hope David is all right."

Like his five older brothers, David was later educated at Eton, across the river from Windsor Castle—a standard of learning that excluded the Bowes Lyon sisters. Cecilia Strathmore followed the theories of a nineteenth-century German educator, Friedrich Froebel, who believed that "play is the highest expression of human development in childhood for it alone is the free expression of what is in the child's soul."

When Elizabeth was old enough, she was taught in a rather haphazard fashion by a series of governesses, interrupted by two brief spells in London schools. Her most rigorous governess was a twenty-one-year-old German woman named Kathe Kubler, who joined the family when Elizabeth was thirteen. Fräulein Kubler was appalled by how little had sunk in from previous instruction.

She set up a rigid schedule of lessons, and Elizabeth performed capably in all the customary subjects. Cecilia was "not a believer in very high mathematics for girls," but she put a premium on English literature as well as fluency in French and German, which Elizabeth achieved. Prodded by Kathe's intense drilling, Elizabeth passed her Oxford local preliminary examination early in 1914. But Fräulein Kubler lasted just over a year before she returned to Germany for a home visit only weeks before the outbreak of World War I.

Her successor, Beryl Poignand, arrived at Glamis in November 1914. With the war under way, the lessons became intermittent, and Beryl served primarily as a companion. She was thirteen years Elizabeth's senior, a gap that meant little in a family where her sisters Rosie and May were respectively ten and seventeen years older than their baby sister.

Teacher and pupil struck up an irreverent and affectionate friendship. Elizabeth wrote Beryl exuberant letters addressed to "my dearest Medusa," "dearest Pig," or "My dear silly ass." The letters brimmed with inside jokes, family news, frothy descriptions, nonsense ("Zut! I mean Phut or Fut or Futte"), and lighthearted patter.

The declaration of war on August 4, 1914, coincided with Elizabeth's fourteenth birthday, when she was watching a vaudeville revue at the London Coliseum with her family. "The streets were full of people shouting, roaring, yelling their heads off—little thinking what was going to happen," Elizabeth recalled many years later.

Patrick, Jock, Fergus, and Michael Bowes Lyon volunteered to fight in the Scots Guards, Black Watch, and Royal Scots regiments. Michael gave up his studies at Oxford to enlist. Fergus and Jock hurriedly married their sweethearts that September before reporting for duty.

By December 1914, the Glamis convalescent home was receiving wounded soldiers who had been treated at the Dundee Infirmary twelve miles away. Lady Strathmore turned the spacious dining room into a sixteen-bed ward. She designated the billiard room lined with seventeenth-century tapestries for storage and distribution of supplies. The ambulatory wounded ate their meals in the crypt, where the staff set up a large tree for the first Christmas holidays at Glamis in two decades. The soldiers gathered with the family in the stone chamber lit by hundreds of candles, with plenty of food, music, and dancing.

Elizabeth's job was to spread cheer among the physically disabled and mentally damaged men needing recuperation before many of them returned to the horrors of the front. Dressed in her white uniform with a long skirt, wide dark belt, black stockings, and white sunbonnet-style cap, Elizabeth played games with the men, helped them write letters, and bought tobacco and other supplies in the village.

These humble soldiers of modest backgrounds were awestruck by the castle and by what one convalescent described as "the essence of politeness, a smile and a word for everyone, and not an atom of assumption." More than fifteen hundred men would stay at Glamis during the First World War. Many of them would cherish their friendship with Elizabeth for years to come.

Lady Strathmore "appeared to sail through life, like a swan on a mirrored lake," according to one of her friends. But her serenity masked constant worry about her boys in France and Belgium. By the middle of 1915, she had tended to the psychological and physical distress of Patrick, Michael, and Jock when they were sent home from the front. It bothered Patrick to be declared unfit for duty due to shell shock, but both Michael and Jock were deemed well enough to return to the front lines.

That August brought the joy of Fergus's five-day leave at Glamis with his wife, Christian, and their month-old baby girl. All too quickly, he was back in France, David left for his first year at Eton, and the castle returned to its wartime routines. Elizabeth's anxieties were obvious to convalescent Corporal Ernest Pearce, who watched her daily vigil for the postman. "She always rose early," he remembered. "You would see this tiny dainty figure looking down the drive. She always stood in the same place. . . . With so many friends and relations at the front, she wanted to be the first to know so she could look after her mother."

The news about Fergus did not arrive until Friday, October 1, four days after his death in combat. Less than an hour later, Beryl Poignand wrote to her mother about the "awful blow." She said "poor darling" Elizabeth "cried dreadfully," and Beryl worried that the "shock of the bad news" would have a particularly damaging effect on Patrick's "nervous state."

The loss of her third child shattered Lady Strathmore. She was joined in her grieving by Michael and David, who had traveled all night by train, with her other children to follow. On Sunday the third, Beryl revealed to her mother that Cecilia "has all her meals taken either to her room or to her sitting room & they all go & sit with her there at different times." The rest of the family tried to make "ordinary conversation" at mealtimes. "They never speak about Fergus except Elizabeth does to me." The "poor child" clung to the futile hope that the report from the War Office had been mistaken.

Twenty-five-year-old Rose took over running the hospital and household, and the soldiers withdrew to avoid disturbing anyone. "They have hardly made a sound since the news came," Beryl wrote. The men sent Lady Strathmore a letter of sympathy, and she replied gratefully, assuring them that they should resume their usual activities.

It may have been during these years that Elizabeth first learned the technique of "ostriching" that would characterize her approach to all problems across her very long life. She would submerge them and cover them with merriment, primarily to spare others pain and embarrassment. Within her family, she avoided anything that she found disagreeable. Such was her approach in the months following Fergus's death, keeping up lighthearted correspondence with friends and her determined efforts to soothe the soldiers in her charge.

Soon after her first encounter with Prince Albert at Lavinia Spencer's London tea party in April 1916, Elizabeth returned to Scotland. Now defiant about failing to attain her academic certificate that spring, she wrote to Beryl, "All I can say is, DAMN THE EXAM!! . . . Oh hell . . . Yes, I am very disappointed, but I daresay I shall get over it." Fortunately, she had a new and cheering event on which to focus: Rosie's impending marriage to an aristocratic Scottish naval officer, William "Wisp" Leveson-Gower. The future fourth Earl Granville was a big and jolly man who would eventually become a vice admiral.

The ceremony on Wednesday, May 24, 1916, at St. James's Piccadilly in London was appropriately modest in the middle of a world war. The congregation comprised some fifty women and half as many men. Cecilia hosted a reception afterward at home in St. James's Square. Low-key it may have been, but it was the pinnacle of Elizabeth's otherwise grim year.

Prince Albert's mood lifted that month as well. He was finally permitted to rejoin *Collingwood* on May 5 after spending nine wretched months at home. His return to sea duty would soon bring the only note of triumph in his hapless naval career. He and Elizabeth would ply separate paths for the following four years until their next encounter, a kismet moment for Bertie if not Elizabeth. The ironic twist would be this: The man who would arrange their introduction had already stolen her heart.

*"He listened, he encouraged, he helped.
He allowed Albert to help himself."*

Prince Albert with Louis Greig after the First World War.

FIVE

Coolness and Courage

ON THE AFTERNOON OF WEDNESDAY, MAY 31, 1916, ACTING Sub-Lieutenant Prince Albert heard the call to "action stations" on *Collingwood*. It was the beginning of a colossal two-day engagement known as the Battle of Jutland. The clash in the North Sea ended in a draw, as the vastly outnumbered German fleet escaped during the night. But the toll for the British was far greater than for the Germans: Over 6,000 sailors died, more than twice the German losses of 2,551. It rankled Admiral Sir John Jellicoe that his fleet didn't vanquish the German enemy in the North Sea. Still, Britain held the strategic advantage by confining the entire German navy to port for the rest of the war.

Jutland was the only major conflict between the British Grand Fleet and its German adversaries, and Bertie was thrillingly in the thick of it. From the outset, he took his position on the fore turret mounted with a twelve-inch gun. It was a testing assignment for a twenty-year-old with a nervous temperament and no previous battle experience on the high seas. He began by observing from the top of the turret until a salvo from a German ship—previously hidden by fog—whizzed over his head and drove him inside.

Confined in the turret's claustrophobic steel pen, he spent many hours firing on command as he observed the surrounding carnage through a telescope. As noted in *The Times,* "the young prince was among the officers commended for their services in the Battle of Jutland," in Bertie's case for his "coolness and courage."

"I am pleased with my son," proclaimed George V after visiting the Grand Fleet. He showed his admiration for Prince Albert by investing him as a Knight in the Order of the Garter on his twenty-first birthday that December. Dating from the fourteenth century, the Garter Knighthood is the highest personal honor a monarch can confer.

With considerable pride, Bertie gave his father a detailed report of the battle, adding, "It was certainly a great experience to have been through." Even more revealing was Bertie's letter to the Prince of Wales, who had spent the first two years of the war constantly chafing at his staff duties in France well away from the front lines.

Bertie now had the bragging rights that David would always be denied. "When I was on top of the turret I never felt any fear of shells or anything else," he wrote to his older brother. "It seems curious but all sense of danger and everything else goes except the one longing of dealing death in every possible way to the enemy."

Bertie's exuberance was short-lived. In late August, the prince was stricken again with severe abdominal pain. This time the royal physicians agreed on their first correct diagnosis of his ailment: a duodenal ulcer. They dismissed surgery as an option, because they feared potential risks. Instead, they advised that he take a prolonged rest.

Once more Bertie endured vexing uncertainty for nearly a year. When he resumed sea duty in May 1917 on the battleship HMS *Malaya,* at his elbow was Louis Greig, recruited by George V to monitor the prince's health and keep up his spirits. Bertie's confidence was battered, his stutter more pronounced than ever. Greig's ministrations could do little to relieve the prince's immobilizing waves of nausea and cramps. That August, Prince Albert left his ship for the final time as a naval officer and was again admitted to a hospital.

In the eight years since his cadet training began, Bertie had seen just sixteen months of active service in the Royal Navy. His stellar performance at Jutland notwithstanding, he felt he was a complete failure and a disappointment to his seaman father. He was "deeply depressed" when he wrote to George V that July: "Personally I feel that I am not fit for service at sea, even when I recover." Wheeler-Bennett discreetly referred to the prince's most concerning trait, much in evidence in those days: "squalls of temper which, though of brief duration, left him exhausted in both mind and body."

With Bertie's support, Louis Greig persuaded George V that the only remedy was surgery on the duodenal ulcer. The dithering court doctors relented, and the successful operation on November 29, 1917, relieved Bertie of his misery at last. He had understandably indulged in self-pity throughout his ordeal, but he had also shown an inner strength and a touching appreciation for those who had helped him, Greig in particular.

The convalescing prince and his mentor spent Christmas with the royal family in York Cottage at Sandringham. Greig, like so many other first-time visitors, was astonished by the "small house" inhabited by King George V and his family. In his will, Edward VII had given Queen Alexandra a life tenancy in Sandringham House. There "Motherdear" continued to live in its 365 rooms with her spinster daughter, Princess Victoria ("Toria" within the family), along with some ancient retainers, amid moth-eaten upholstery and curtains resembling Miss Havisham's in *Great Expectations*. Meanwhile, the King and Queen endured endless inconvenience at York Cottage. Harold Nicolson wrote that "maternal tyranny" prevented Alexandra's eldest son from sensibly suggesting they swap homes.

Greig was equally taken aback that the royal family was "most simple & friendly and awfully easy." In wartime they had adjusted to unaccustomed austerity imposed by food shortages caused by submarine warfare. Each family member had a ration book, and dinners featured four courses rather than the ten or more before the war, with meat served only three times a week. It wasn't until later in the following year that the U-boat campaign was curtailed, and the food shortages eased.

In the billiard room at York Cottage (the largest in the house), members of the royal family showed their gratitude to Louis Greig for his care of Bertie by showering him with expensive gifts: signed photographs of the King and Queen in frames that were a foot and a half high; a monogrammed cigarette case from George V, and gold cuff links from Bertie. Greig viewed George V as alternately crotchety and "damned funny," with his use of "refreshing language" at mealtimes—no doubt chaffing everyone within range. Greig got on especially well with Queen Mary because he "treated her like a human being and she adored him for that," wrote his grandson Geordie Greig. He found the royal family "most frightfully anti-German." Their opinions on that score were "unrestrained & refreshing. . . . They are dying to bombard their towns & make reprisals etc."

IN 1918, PRINCE ALBERT AND Louis Greig switched from the Royal Navy to the newly formed Royal Air Force, which combined the separate flying corps of the navy and army. They spent much of the year at Cranwell, a temporary facility in Lincolnshire. Greig was now officially Bertie's equerry, and the prince had been promoted to lieutenant with an administrative job overseeing a large contingent of boys going through training.

Bertie's main challenge in the RAF was a fear of flying. He finally mustered the courage to take his first flight in early March 1918. In rainy and windy conditions, the plane flew only several hundred feet above the ground. He told his mother it was "a curious sensation" that he enjoyed, "but I don't think I should like flying as a pastime."

Twenty-two-year-old Bertie made no friends at Cranwell, relying entirely on Greig, now close to forty years old, for companionship. The two men rode together and went out with several local hunts. Greig coached him in tennis and taught him how to drive a car. Crucially, Bertie could confide in Greig as he could not to his mother and father.

Throughout Prince Albert's time at Cranwell, the momentum of World War I had begun shifting in the Allies' favor. The United States had entered the conflict in April 1917, and by summer of the following year, some ten thousand American soldiers were flooding into the Western Front every day. Allied forces led by France's General Ferdinand Foch broke through the formerly impregnable Hindenburg Line—a defensive position built by the Germans two years before—in late September 1918, and the German army began to collapse.

Eager to see the final stages of the war, Bertie and Greig were flown across the Channel to France on October 23 to join the RAF staff at its headquarters at Autigny. Three nights later, Bertie had an initiation into manhood that was so important he immediately shared it with Prince Edward, who was stationed in France with the Canadian Corps.

Bertie at that point had little experience with the opposite sex. As a worldly mentor, Greig had introduced him to friends in his London set, which revolved around the theatrical world. Bertie met glamorous actresses and became more confident in their company, but his relationships remained platonic. When the time came to lose his virginity, the place was Paris, under circumstances similar to those experienced by his older brother, who also had his sexual initiation at age twenty-two with a French prostitute.

Bertie's encounter was a one-night stand with an unnamed woman, presumably in a suitable setting. On October 26, 1918, the Prince of Wales breathlessly recounted to his mistress, Freda Dudley Ward, that he had been "amused" to receive a letter from his brother that very evening from Paris "where he spent a night with old Derby at the Embassy" en route to his posting in Autigny. The seventeenth Earl of Derby was a prominent Tory grandee, the British ambassador to France, and a man for whom King George V had respect and affection.

It is unknown whether Derby knew what his great friend's son was planning, but according to David, Bertie "didn't sleep at the Embassy as, in his own words, 'the deed was done,' though he gave me no details & perhaps just as well!!" David added slyly, "You see darling, 'C'etait le premier fois car il etait vierge' [*It was the first time because he was a virgin*], which is why it amuses & interests me so much!"

"What marvellous fun we 4 do have."

Prince Edward, Freda Dudley Ward, Prince Albert, and Sheila Loughborough at Lankhills, Sheila's country home, in 1919.

SIX

Do's and Don'ts

THE IMMEDIATE POSTWAR YEARS BROUGHT NEW MEANING TO PRINCE
Albert's life even as Prince Edward began his long but little-noticed
slide into dissipation and irresponsibility. For a time, the Prince of
Wales exerted a malign influence on his younger brother that was
eventually checked by George V. Louis Greig was instrumental in
keeping the second in line on a steady path.

Ten days after the official armistice, at eleven A.M. on November 11, 1918, Bertie proudly represented his father with the Belgian
royal family for a jubilant arrival in Brussels. A triumphant parade
down the Champs-Élysées in Paris with George V and the Prince of
Wales offered an even greater thrill. Prince Albert was deeply moved
by the gratitude of the French to the British. The Prince of Wales had
a more typically jaundiced view, complaining to Freda, "Gud [sic] how
I loathe all the official work. . . . It's rotten having to trot around with
the King, really, such a waste of time."

By George V's command, Albert remained on the Continent with
Greig. Bertie was appointed captain and attached to the Royal Air Force
headquarters staff, in Spa, Belgium, where the brothers spent Christ-

mas. Among those befriended by the prince was Alec Cunningham-Reid, a World War I flying ace who had been awarded the Distinguished Flying Cross. During long walks in the nearby hills, Bertie confided to Alec that to continue representing the RAF, he needed to "wear the wings" by actually learning to fly, although he was uncertain that he could "stand the strain." Bertie drilled the veteran pilot with questions about "practical flying," including casualty rates as well as do's and don'ts. Alec admired Bertie's "sheer determination and pluck."

BEFORE BERTIE COULD BEGIN HIS instruction, the royal family was hit in mid-January 1919 by the death of his brother, Prince John, just thirteen years old. It was a sudden although not unexpected tragedy that dramatically illuminated the increasingly divergent characters of Bertie and David—one kind and compassionate, the other selfish and stony-hearted.

"Johnnie"—as everyone called him—was the youngest of the six royal children. At the age of four in 1909, he had been diagnosed with epilepsy. The seizures were intermittent and relatively mild at first. He often kept company with his brother, Prince George, just two years older, until his episodes intensified to several alarming attacks a day. Some seizures lasted as long as ten minutes: "very painful to see, as he struggles so much poor child," George V reported to Queen Mary toward the end of 1912.

Queen Mary closely monitored Johnnie's condition and entrusted his care to the royal family's longtime nurse, Lalla Bill. Johnnie also failed to advance beyond the age of six in his mental development—severe learning disabilities that may have been a form of autism—which further relegated him to the periphery of royal life.

When Johnnie was eleven, the King and Queen moved him into his own home at Wood Farm on the Sandringham estate. The five-bedroom cottage was set in a secluded location with views over the marshland. Decades later, it would become a weekend retreat for

Queen Elizabeth II and the Duke of Edinburgh, and his home for several years after his retirement.

Johnnie lived as normal a life as possible, with Lalla as his devoted companion, along with a male orderly to help restrain his fits. He tended a garden plot, was driven to the Norfolk seaside, cared for his chickens, and played with local children. His mother and sister visited him periodically, but he received the most attention from his "Grannie," Queen Alexandra, and his aunt Toria.

At the end of December 1918, George V and Queen Mary traveled to Norfolk for a month of house parties and shooting. Their entourage included twenty-one-year-old Princess Mary; Prince Henry, who at eighteen was finishing at Eton; and sixteen-year-old Prince George, in training for the navy at Dartmouth.

Saturday, January 18, 1919, was a "lovely day" on the Sandringham estate, Queen Mary noted in her diary. In the morning she took a walk with her sister-in-law, Queen Maud of Norway, while Princess Mary walked with Johnnie. Back at Wood Farm in the afternoon, Johnnie suffered an especially violent seizure. Lalla held his hand as he fell asleep, and he died shortly afterward. Moments after Lalla's phone call, the King and Queen drove to Wood Farm, where they found Johnnie looking "very peaceful."

"I feel rather stunned," Queen Mary wrote to Bertie in Belgium. "Poor Mary and Georgie awfully upset. Their first *real* sorrow." Bertie responded tenderly, "It must have been a great shock to you coming at a time like this. I can see from your letter that it has upset you very much. I don't wonder either. When I received the telegram from Papa it upset me too, especially as I had not seen him since this time last year."

The Prince of Wales also wrote to his mother, but with "chilling insensitivity," in the words of his official biographer, Philip Ziegler. The specific contents of that letter remain unknown, but Edward made his feelings clear to Freda. He was upset—not by the loss of his brother, but by his father's order that he and Bertie remain on duty rather than

come home for the funeral or travel to Paris for fun, as Edward had
originally planned. He called Johnnie's death "the greatest relief imag-
inable . . . but to be plunged into mourning for this is the limit just as
the war is over which cuts parties etc right out!!" Johnnie, he wrote,
"had become more of an animal than anything else & was only a
brother in the flesh & nothing else!!!"

Queen Mary declined to reply to David. A week later he apologized, calling himself a "cold-hearted and unsympathetic swine," and
weakly explaining "how little poor Johnnie meant to me who hardly
knew him." He professed to "feel so much for you, darling Mama, who
was his mother." She accepted his apology and said she and the King
recognized his commonsense view that Johnnie had been released
from his suffering.

Still, she was more anguished than she revealed to her callous
eldest son. The funeral took place on Tuesday morning in St. Mary
Magdalene Church at Sandringham followed by burial in the church-
yard. She shared her sorrow with Bertie, knowing she could rely on his
empathetic nature. The little church was "crammed with our own
people, who love poor little Johnnie, who was so kind hearted, and
polite to them all," she wrote. In his reply, Bertie said, "It must have
been very trying for you, but at the same time a great relief to know
that all those present had known him all his life and had the same feelings as you."

PRINCE ALBERT AND LOUIS GREIG trained together for their pilot's
licenses. In July 1919, Bertie became the first—and for many years
the only—member of the royal family to qualify as a pilot. His achievement came with a caveat, however: The RAF medical board judged
him too high-strung to fly solo, a restriction that embarrassed the
twenty-three-year-old prince.

It had been a tradition since Edward VII for royal princes to receive a smattering of university education. The Prince of Wales had
endured Oxford until World War I gave him an excuse to bolt. For

Prince Albert and his brother Prince Henry, George V devised a postwar stint at Trinity College, Cambridge. Classes began in early October 1919 and wrapped up in July the following year.

As Bertie's equerry, Greig attended lectures with the two brothers and reported back to the King. Bertie's stutter frequently plagued him, and he enlisted an Italian speech therapist, with uneven results. He did manage on several occasions to minimize his hesitations by speaking off the cuff rather than from prepared remarks. Nevertheless, any public forum overwhelmed him with anxiety.

He diligently applied himself to his courses in economics, civics, and history, with particular emphasis on Walter Bagehot's book on the English constitution. But these studies were often interrupted by an increasing number of royal engagements around Britain.

Among Albert's new public duties, one enterprise stood above all others and proved essential training for his future role as monarch. The Boys' Welfare Association was founded in July 1918 by the Reverend Robert Hyde, an idealistic and energetic clergyman from London's East End. At a time of growing labor unrest, Hyde's aim was to improve working conditions in factories by enlisting industry leaders to provide resources such as healthcare facilities and canteens.

When Hyde sought a royal patron to raise the profile of the organization, George V recommended Bertie. The prince instantly recognized the opportunity to have a meaningful royal role—especially with the Prince of Wales being dispatched by Prime Minister Lloyd George on a series of tours around the empire to reinforce ties with Britain. "I'll do it," Bertie said, "provided that there's no damned red carpet about it."

He signed on as president of the association in March 1919 and presided over the first annual meeting in London two months later. To broaden its scope beyond "boys," the association renamed itself the Industrial Welfare Society (IWS). Prince Albert told the participants their work to promote "good will between all classes in industry" was "essential to the prosperity of the nation." In the months before he went to Cambridge, and for many years afterward, Bertie visited hundreds of factories and mines throughout Britain. He became known in the press as "the Industrial Prince," which pleased him. Bertie's brothers jokingly called him "the Foreman," but they failed to dent his earnestness.

Determined to learn at ground level, he literally got his hands dirty time and again—deep inside coal mines, climbing scaffolding at construction sites—as he vastly increased his knowledge of Britain's industrial life. His tours were often unannounced and invariably informal. Remarked one business manager after a visit from Prince Albert, "I never met one who asked more sensible questions or showed greater understanding of our fundamental problems. He does like getting to the bottom of things."

Louis Greig traveled with the prince as his equerry and mentor. His encouragement and sound guidance were vital in shaping the character of the second in line to the throne. But in Bertie's private life, Greig was no match for David's magnetic appeal. Bertie first kicked over the traces with his elder brother in the spring of 1919 when he became involved with Freda Dudley Ward's best friend, a beautiful Australian named Sheila Loughborough.

Freda, an Anglo-American unhappily married to well-connected aristocrat William Dudley Ward, was pretty and petite. The Prince of Wales had been besotted with her since their chance meeting early in 1918 during a London bombing raid. Shortly afterward, Freda had befriended Sheila, a kindred spirit locked in an equally bleak marriage.

Sheila had a classic oval face, sultry dark eyes, a delicate nose, a cupid's bow mouth, and wavy auburn hair. Serge Obolensky, an émigré Russian prince who had his own affair with Sheila, once observed, "Her entire appearance was languorous. Her every gesture was dreamlike."

Born Sheila Chisholm in 1895, she had spent her childhood in rural Australia where her father bred racehorses. She learned to ride and to hold her own among the rough ranch hands, even as she lived graciously in her parents' well-appointed homestead with a staff of five. She was educated by a series of governesses and finished at the

Anglican Kambala school for girls in Sydney, where her family moved when she was seventeen.

Two years later, in 1914, she and her mother left on an ocean liner for an extended European tour, but after the declaration of war, they sailed to Cairo to be near Sheila's brother Jack, who had joined the Australian Expeditionary Forces. It was there, after the Battle of Gallipoli, that she fell in love with a wounded English aristocrat, twenty-three-year-old Francis St. Clair-Erskine, the heir to the Earl of Rosslyn. He was titled Lord Loughborough—nicknamed "Loughie"—and he had a reputation as a compulsive gambler and alcoholic. But he pursued her ardently, and they were married in December 1915.

On arriving in England the following April, Lady Loughborough made a splash in aristocratic circles. But Loughie's reckless behavior made her miserable, even after the birth of two sons whom she adored. She had nannies to care for her boys, which allowed her to get out and about with complete freedom while Loughie indulged his gambling and drinking with friends. When the Prince of Wales introduced Sheila to his shy and gentle younger brother in May 1919, she was ready for a romance, and so was Bertie.

He had never known anyone as exotic and worldly as Sheila. They were both twenty-three when they began going out together, and they made a handsome pair. Freda abetted the affair by letting Bertie and Sheila use her house on Great Cumberland Place for assignations in London. In mid-May, Edward confided to Freda that Albert had left the Palace for Lankhills, the Loughboroughs' house near Winchester. "I don't expect to see him tonight!!!!"

Despite the high profile of the princes, the two couples blended into London's elite social scene—dancing at the balls, joining the glamorous crowds at the theater, in restaurants and nightclubs such as the Embassy on Old Bond Street in Mayfair. They named themselves "The 4 Do's." David was "Do No. 1" and Bertie was "Do No. 2." "What marvellous fun we 4 do have, don't we angel & f___ the rest of the world," David wrote to Freda.

It wasn't until April 1920 that King George V and Queen Mary fully realized the extent of their second son's involvement with a married mother of two children. By then Prince Edward was on an extended empire goodwill tour, spending six months in Australia and New Zealand from March until October. He only belatedly learned from his brother that their father had confronted Bertie about Sheila on April 7. As Bertie recounted to David the next day, "He is going to make me Duke of York on his birthday provided that he hears nothing more about Sheila & me!!!!"

After reading Albert's message in mid-May, Edward furiously wrote to Freda: "Christ! How I loathe & despise my bloody family as Bertie has written me 3 long sad letters in which he tells me he has been getting it in the neck about his friendship with poor little Sheilie & that TOI et MOI came in for it too!!" Three days later, Edward continued, "If he really loved Sheilie he wouldn't care a d___ about dukes or anything else."

Prince Albert did indeed care a great deal about being honored with what his father called the "fine old title" that he had himself borne "for more than 9 years & is the oldest Dukedom in this country." According to Sheila's biographer, Robert Wainwright, father and son had their final showdown over Sheila at Buckingham Palace on June 2, the eve of the King's fifty-fifth birthday. In a note written four days later, Bertie pledged, "I can tell you I fulfilled your conditions to the letter and nothing more will come of it."

George V's reply on June 7 underlined the gravity of what he had demanded of Bertie: "I know that you have behaved very well, in a difficult situation for a young man & that you have done what I asked you to do," he wrote. "I feel that this splendid old title will be safe in your hands & that you will never do anything which could in any way tarnish it." In accepting the dukedom, Bertie wrote, "I am very proud to bear the name that you did for many years, and I hope that I shall live up to it in every way."

How serious was Bertie about his dangerous liaison? In his letters to Freda, David dismissed his brother's feelings for Sheila as a poor imitation of his own ardor. But Robert Wainwright discovered that after World War II, a diplomat named Sir Charles Hepburn Johnston took Sheila to dine with George VI and Queen Elizabeth at Buckingham Palace. Johnston wrote in his diary that George VI and Sheila got to reminiscing about "what fun they all had" after World War I. Added Johnston, "Sheila saw the Q listening and thought it prudent to damp this a bit. She said 'And when you think, Sir, how innocent it all was.' K (red with fury): 'Innocent? I don't know what the devil you mean.'"

As the Sheila affair ended, so did David's influence. Greig was ascendant, having been named comptroller of the Duke of York's household. His next move arguably changed history when he recruited a handsome twenty-three-year-old Scotsman who had fought across France and Belgium and earned the Military Cross for bravery after the battle of the Somme.

Bertie and Greig met Captain James Stuart when they were in Brussels at the end of the war. Greig was impressed by his dash and his intelligence. Stuart went on to study law in Edinburgh, and on June 1, 1920, he joined the ranks of Buckingham Palace courtiers as equerry to none other than Bertie, his future rival for Elizabeth's hand.

James Stuart astutely sized up Prince Albert, admitting "he was not an easy man to know or to handle." He observed that Louis Greig was Bertie's only close friend. James noted that Bertie's temper, while intense, "did not last" and was usually the product of frustration. "He was never a strong man physically, and this doubtless affected his outlook on life," James recalled. He felt "desperately sorry" about Bertie's stammer, which he ascribed to a "nervous affliction, born of shyness."

While Bertie and James were superficially amicable, their differing temperaments caused unease that Greig could not have anticipated. Nor did Greig know the most important fact of all: that Stuart had often stayed at Glamis for house parties and had been romantically involved with Elizabeth since September 1919. In only a matter of weeks after James's arrival at Buckingham Palace, that relationship would open one door for Bertie and, eighteen months later—with the likely connivance of the Queen—shut another for his equerry.

"The biographer David Cecil recognized 'great sweetness and sense of fun, and a certain roguish quality.'"

Lady Elizabeth Bowes Lyon as a teenager.

❧

SEVEN

Radiant Vitality

W<small>HILE</small> B<small>ERTIE</small> <small>HAD MARKED THE ARMISTICE ON</small> N<small>OVEMBER</small> 11, 1918, with the RAF in France, Elizabeth had observed the milestone quietly at Glamis. The convalescents "went straight to the village to celebrate and I think they drank too much," she recalled. "Seats got broken up to make a bonfire and all that sort of thing. I can see them now, all going to enjoy this wonderful moment."

When Elizabeth was just fourteen, her mother had remarked that she was "very old for her age"—likely a result of her upbringing with considerably older siblings. Four years later, having witnessed great suffering and having cared for physically and mentally broken men, Elizabeth had deepened her empathy and broadened her scope.

Yet in other respects she led what one of her admirers, Victor Cochrane-Baillie, called "a gay and giddy life." Her coterie of friends came from the top tier of the hereditary aristocracy. During wartime, the upper-class social rituals of the summer "season" had been suspended, and in 1919 they resumed with garden parties at Buckingham Palace for the debutantes who had been waiting for five years. Each young woman was expected, after being introduced to society at court, to marry an equally highborn man.

Elizabeth had a lively and questing intelligence. She once recalled that as a child her elbows were "perpetually rough and red from excessive reading on the floor." Yet while she devoured books and showed an active imagination, neither her conversation nor her writing was remotely intellectual. Her lilting voice was a conspicuous asset, not only for singing, which she did with sweet enthusiasm, but also as a fetching instrument of engagement in conversation: "clear, rather high, silvery . . . curiously young," in Cynthia Asquith's description, and with impeccable enunciation. She had sharp powers of observation and could charm with witty remarks. Her postwar focus with her friends was finding as much fun as they could.

They called themselves the "Mad Hatters," tearing around England and Scotland from one house party and formal dance to another. They had silly crushes and innocent flirtations. Chaperones were required in London and at grand country balls. But when they reached the age of eighteen, the girls had more leeway to circulate on their own. Elizabeth and her aristocratic friends were by no means "fast" or modern in their looks and attitudes. They dressed conservatively in long skirts and modest blouses. Mabell Airlie considered Elizabeth the opposite of the "cocktail-drinking, chain-smoking girls" in the Prince of Wales's café society set.

Within her rarefied social group, Elizabeth Bowes Lyon stood out for what Mabell Airlie called her "radiant vitality and a blending of gaiety, kindness and sincerity" that "made her irresistible to men." Petite at five foot two, she no longer wore her dark brown hair loose around her shoulders or in a girlish braid. Instead, she parted her hair in the middle and pulled it into a demure knot, her forehead fringed with wispy bangs. Her dark brows and thick lashes contrasted vividly with her deep blue eyes and milky complexion. She had a round chin, a fine tip-tilted nose, and an elegantly thin mouth that effortlessly erupted into a radiant smile. Her expression in repose was winsome, her manner open and affectionate. The biographer David Cecil recognized "great sweetness and sense of fun, and a certain roguish quality."

Elizabeth played the coquette and savored the attention. Many young men misinterpreted what Chips Channon described as her "mildly flirtatious" manner as something more meaningful. "People were rather inclined to propose to you in those days," she told Eric Anderson. "You know, it was rather the sort of thing, I suppose. And you said, 'No thank you,' or whatever it was." She insisted that those she rejected weren't actually serious. "Oh, I thought you wouldn't," they would reply. "It was all very nice and light-hearted."

In addition to James Stuart, her wellborn suitors included her Scottish neighbor Major Bruce Ogilvy, Mabell Airlie's second son, and Prince Paul of Yugoslavia, a member of the Serbian royal family who shared a London flat with her brother Michael along with Lord Gage, another romantic hopeful. Scottish neighbor Christopher Glenconner would come along later, with no better result despite an exchange of "soulful correspondence" with Elizabeth: "<u>most</u> high brow—so funny," she told Beryl Poignand.

MONDAY, JULY 5, 1920, BEGAN the most eventful week of Elizabeth's young life—one month shy of her twentieth birthday. Because of the backlog of wartime debutantes, her formal court debut had been delayed for a year. George V and Queen Mary were staying at Holyroodhouse in Edinburgh for their annual week of garden parties, receptions, dinners, investitures, and engagements around the city.

Tuesday afternoon was Elizabeth's presentation to the King and Queen at a midafternoon court in the Throne Room. Before the First World War, these rituals had been elaborately formal. Each debutante wore a white or pastel evening dress with a long train and a veil or headpiece adorned with three ostrich feathers. They were heavily bejeweled and covered their arms with long white gloves. After the wartime interruption, traditional courts came back in 1920, but initially in a pared-down version without feathers and a full court train—both of which would be restored in 1922.

Among the 150 debutantes, Elizabeth hewed to the required form and wore a long gown. She was accompanied by Lady Strathmore, similarly dressed. Elizabeth's name was announced by the Lord Chamberlain, and she dropped a deep curtsey to the King and Queen in turn, followed by a respectful bow to them both, as well as to Princess Mary. She then withdrew from their presence, walking backward out of the room.

For the next ninety minutes, George V and Mary shook hands with 1,100 people. "It was all over at 4:30," Queen Mary noted in her diary in her customary succinct fashion. Wednesday brought Elizabeth's final obligation at court, a garden party on the Holyroodhouse grounds for 4,500 worthies that ran from 4:00 until 6:30 P.M. She and her mother hopped on the night train and were in London the next morning.

Bertie, meanwhile, had been miles away, traveling around with James Stuart and Louis Greig on official engagements and playing lawn tennis with Greig, his coach as well as his partner in doubles. While Elizabeth was strolling through the gardens of Holyroodhouse on Wednesday, Bertie won a singles match in the Royal Air Force championship at Queen's Club in London, and he and Greig won the semifinals in the Air Force Doubles.

The next day, Thursday, July 8, 1920, Bertie and Greig were back at Queen's Club. Together they won the RAF Doubles final—"a pretty match, productive of exciting rallies and brilliant strokes," said *The Times*. It was only fitting that in the evening, Prince Albert, accompanied by James Stuart, would be the guest of honor at a ball in the Ritz hotel in aid of the Royal Air Force Memorial Fund, of which Bertie was president. The money raised would support "the education of the children of officers and men of the flying services and to assist the disabled."

Before the ball, Bertie gave a small dinner party at the Berkeley

Hotel and walked over to the Ritz on Piccadilly with James Stuart. By then, the prince's new equerry had known Elizabeth Bowes Lyon for nearly a year and had become a Glamis regular. James's future daughter, Davina Ritchie, later told Grania Forbes, one of Elizabeth's biographers, that her father's battlefield memories had left him periodically depressed in the postwar years. "Lady Elizabeth managed to bring him out," she said, "and captured his heart. There is no doubt that they felt a great deal for each other."

The RAF Ball was huge, with six hundred guests taking the floor. "I was on duty so I saw the party settled in and sought out my own friends," James Stuart recalled. "Later in the evening HRH came over and asked who was the girl with whom I had just been dancing. I told him her name was Lady Elizabeth Bowes Lyon and he asked me if I would introduce him, which I did."

"It really was most amusing," Elizabeth wrote to Beryl Poignand about her evening at the Ritz. "There were some priceless people there. All the heroes of the Air too. I danced with Prince Albert who I hadn't known before, he is quite a nice youth." Her reaction to the Duke of York echoed almost word for word what she had expressed four years earlier—the damning-with-faint-praise adjective "nice."

This time, though, Bertie took notice. He told Mabell Airlie he had "fallen in love that evening, although he did not realize it until later." As James Stuart wrote in his memoir, "It was a more significant moment than it was possible to realise, but it is certainly true to say that from then on he never showed the slightest interest in any other young lady."

*"James is an angel, and I should
like you to see him."*

At a Glamis house party for the Forfar County Ball on September 9, 1920, James Stuart stands between Lord Gage and Prince Paul of Yugoslavia. Seated below James is his brother Francis Doune, who is next to Lady Elizabeth Bowes Lyon.

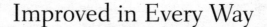

EIGHT

Improved in Every Way

AT FIRST ELIZABETH TREATED PRINCE ALBERT'S INTEREST AS A LARK. She was politely dismissive and remained as neutral as she could. The attention flattered her, but she grew concerned. Yet even as she resisted committing to Bertie, she declined to shut him out. Instead, she sent mixed signals and wavered, not just for weeks or months, but for more than two years. The pressure exerted on her and on her mother, Lady Strathmore—not only from Prince Albert but also from his equally determined mother, Queen Mary—was both intense and strategic.

Scarcely nine days after their first dance at the Royal Air Force Ball, Bertie and Elizabeth met again at a house party weekend on July 17, 1920. It was hosted by Lady Helena Balfour, a close friend of Cecilia Strathmore. Known by her nickname "Nina," she was also a confidante of Elizabeth. During the season, Nina rented Bisham Abbey, a spacious manor house on the Thames, and was known for lively gatherings.

Elizabeth was now officially "out" in society following her presentation in Edinburgh to the King and Queen. When Nina took her houseguests for a cruise on the Thames in her "famous electric launch," twenty-four-year-old Bertie made a sweetly tentative move.

He held Elizabeth's hand "under Nina's very nose," as their friend Helen Cecil recounted later. "Elizabeth says it was quite worth it just to see Nina's face."

Bertie frequently confided in his mother, and she may have known at this early date about his infatuation. Something may indeed have been afoot on the twenty-third of July, when the Duchess of Portland—kin to Cecilia Strathmore—hosted a small dinner dance in London for the Queen, Prince Albert, Princess Mary, and Prince Henry.

The list of thirty-six guests tucked into the pages of Queen Mary's 1920 diary—written in someone else's hand—named eight young single women and an equal number of eligible bachelors. It happened to include Elizabeth Bowes Lyon, but James Stuart was notably missing. Not only were the guests "invited to meet" the members of the royal family, they were also given ample opportunity to dance with the princes and the princess. This exercise in royal matchmaking went unnoticed in the wider world. The occasion merited just two sentences in the "Court Circular" of *The Times* the next day, which mentioned only Queen Mary and her daughter.

Elizabeth and Bertie then parted company, he to join the King and Queen at the Cowes sailing regatta and she to Glamis for shooting season house parties. Bertie and his new equerry, James Stuart, made their own grouse-shooting rounds in Scotland once the court had decamped to Balmoral in mid-August. Stuart had been on duty at the royal estate in the Highlands for a little over three weeks when Lord and Lady Strathmore invited him to join their house party for the Forfar County Ball, to be held near Glamis on Wednesday, September 8.

The ball took place in Reid Hall, a large Victorian building in the middle of the ancient town of Forfar. It was a picturesque assembly, with kilts and uniforms compulsory for the men. Elizabeth had a full dance card as she twirled around the floor doing foxtrots, waltzes, and one-steps. She danced two reels—one with James Stuart, the other with an ever-hopeful George Gage. Afterward, Elizabeth pronounced herself "completely exhausted."

James Stuart slipped back to Balmoral on September 11, just in time to accompany Bertie to Inverness for grouse shoots, regimental duties, Highland games, and two big balls. But before they left, Bertie initiated another excursion for the following weekend. "Prince Albert is coming to stay here on Saturday. Ghastly!" Elizabeth scrawled as a P.S. atop a letter she wrote to Beryl Poignand. Naturally, James Stuart would accompany him—setting up a potentially awkward situation.

Bertie actually had plausible cover for the visit. His sister Mary had been planning since mid-August to stay for three nights with Mabell Airlie at her home, Airlie Castle, down the road from Glamis. As the recently appointed honorary president of the Girl Guides—Britain's decade-old scouting organization for girls—Mary intended to spend Saturday the eighteenth reviewing troops in Dundee and Forfar. The following day she would attend a service in the chapel at Glamis with her new friend Elizabeth, and a luncheon hosted by Lord and Lady Strathmore.

Suddenly the young men and women gathering at Glamis faced the prospect of not one but two royal visitors. Elizabeth asked her friends Helen Cecil, Doris Gordon-Lennox, Katie Hamilton, and Diamond Hardinge to help amuse Bertie when he and James arrived in the afternoon on Saturday. "There is a <u>fearful</u> fuss over tonight & the week-end in general," Helen wrote to her fiancé, Captain Alexander "Alec" Hardinge, the brother of their friend Diamond. An assistant private secretary to King George V on duty at Balmoral, Alec was jealous of Bertie's new equerry. "You won't let James cut me out," he wrote to Helen. "He is so attractive that there would be every justification for it!"

On Saturday evening after dinner, Mabell Airlie arrived with Mary, who hadn't been expected at Glamis until Sunday. The twenty-three-year-old princess had been with the Girl Guides all day, and she was ready for some diversion. Everybody danced vigorously—even Cecilia, who did "sliding races" on the slippery stone floor.

With the exception of the church service on Sunday, the weekend carried on with the same exuberance. Bertie played tennis on the castle's new hard court, as well as hide-and-seek and other childhood games. That evening, after Mary returned to Airlie Castle, all the guests sang "the most appalling songs." The Duke of York "did it with more gusto" than anybody: "rather alarming," noted Helen Cecil.

From time to time, Elizabeth sent "signals of distress" to Helen when Bertie tried to steer her away for one-on-one conversation. James Stuart was the weekend's center of attention, overshadowing Bertie. "I wonder he isn't spoilt with all the women making such fools of themselves over his good looks," Helen told Alec.

Bertie seized his chance on Monday morning after breakfast when the guests took a long walk. Helen, Katie, and Doris tactfully slowed their pace while Bertie went ahead with Elizabeth and led her into the garden for a tête-à-tête. Bertie, Mary, and James returned to Balmoral that day, the prince now besotted not only with Elizabeth but with her family, her friends, and their ebullient way of life.

Both Albert and James dashed off thank-you notes to Cecilia, the former begging forgiveness "for the very abrupt way in which I proposed myself." James told Lady Strathmore that the weekend was a complete success for her royal guests, adding that "no other house in the United Kingdom could have done it so well."

Elizabeth, however, felt decidedly conflicted. Helen Cecil figured as much, writing that she was sure Prince Albert was grateful for Helen's "leaving him in peace with you . . . tho I'm not so certain about you!" In letters to Beryl Poignand and her sister May Elphinstone, Elizabeth used almost identical language. She called Bertie and Mary "babies," although the princess was "most awfully nice," and Bertie was "very nice . . . very much improved in every way." She observed to May that James Stuart "has worked wonders" on the prince, although "royalty staying is a nuisance."

The following month, James Stuart wriggled out of Balmoral duty again to shoot at Glamis for a week. During their time together, he and Elizabeth ventured off for an unchaperoned interlude with Doris Gordon-Lennox's family at Ballathie House near Perth. The gabled and turreted Victorian pile overlooking the River Tay was just thirty-five miles from Forfar, but Elizabeth felt apprehensive about appearances.

In a letter written after the pair had returned to Glamis, Doris sought to reassure Elizabeth. "Of course we didn't think anything of you & James coming!" she wrote. "No one thought it a bit funny." On the contrary, her family considered it "fashionable" for Elizabeth to "tour around Perthshire & Forfar" with James.

With James Stuart back at Albert's side in London, Elizabeth took on a new responsibility in Scotland inspired by Princess Mary's visit. "I have got to start <u>GIRL GUIDES</u>," she wrote to Beryl in October. "The beasts, the arses, the fools, <u>how</u> I hate them! <u>Don't laugh</u>!"

She made it to London by early November. Soon afterward, Prince Albert arrived at the Strathmores' house unannounced. "Our <u>Bert</u> stayed till 7, talking 100 to 20 or even 200 to a dozen," Elizabeth wrote to Beryl Poignand. "I do wish he hadn't come this evening, but I simply couldn't stop him." Elizabeth subsequently sent a cryptic note to Beryl, evidently after they had discussed Bertie's pursuit. "Don't say one word about what I told you please, as that sort of thing is too awful if it gets about & would make things very uncomfortable," Elizabeth wrote. "So do keep it strictly to yourself—it is very important."

In December 1920, Elizabeth received an invitation from Margaret "Maggie" Greville to a dinner dance on the fifteenth at her home on Charles Street in London to celebrate Bertie's twenty-fifth birthday. Plump and plain, fifty-seven-year-old Maggie had first ingratiated herself with the royal family during the reign of Edward VII through her marriage to his friend Captain Ronald Greville, the good-looking but dull grandson of a duke. The illegitimate daughter of a Scottish brewer named William McEwan, Maggie inherited her father's vast wealth and spent lavishly on entertaining the aristocracy in superb comfort and style.

Twelve years after the death of her husband in 1908, "Mrs. Ronnie Greville" had become adept at moving the levers of power and gaining favor—including coveted invitations to Buckingham Palace and Balmoral. Her new project was helping Bertie in his pursuit of Elizabeth Bowes Lyon by nudging them together at her Mayfair parties.

In her first known letter to Bertie, written on December 13, 1920—a reply to one from him—Elizabeth admitted she hadn't been to a dinner dance in months. The prospect of Mrs. Greville's party "terrifies me," she wrote. She had "quite forgotten how to behave," and she supposed the prince had been "dancing every night." He had actually been plowing through his duties, usually accompanied by James Stuart.

Maggie's dinner was a success, as was a dinner dance the following night hosted by another well-known socialite, Lady Evelyn Guinness. But Elizabeth missed a third dance the next week when her mother fell seriously ill. "I couldn't leave her," Elizabeth explained in a letter to Bertie on December 23 from St. Paul's Walden Bury. He had sent her a Christmas gift, and she thanked him profusely in two separate letters for the "darling" little blue box. It was the first of a number of gifts from the prince—nothing extravagant, but thoughtfully chosen.

Otherwise, Elizabeth gave no encouraging signals to Prince Albert. Over the holidays at Sandringham, Queen Mary told Mabell Airlie that Bertie was "always talking" about Elizabeth. But Elizabeth's mind was definitely elsewhere. On the evening of December 22, before she went to St. Paul's Walden Bury for Christmas, James Stuart unexpectedly came round for a visit. "I'm sure you would like James," she wrote to Beryl. "He is an angel, and I should like you to see him."

The early months of 1921 brought the first crisis in Bertie's campaign for Elizabeth. Mabell Airlie arranged to meet with each of them at her flat to take soundings. She found Elizabeth to be "frankly doubtful" and "uncertain," while Bertie, "so humble" and "touching," was "deeply in love." In her replies to his letters, Elizabeth kept up her carefree tone. She went to a week's worth of parties in Sussex and wrote to Bertie from Petworth, a massive seventeenth-century estate owned by the Wyndham family. The house party of thirty was "enormous," she told Bertie. "We danced till 3 last night, and I didn't go to sleep till 5."

Bertie at that moment was flat on his back, having fallen ill several days earlier after a day of "beagling" at Sandringham—running at full speed after a pack of beagles intent on killing hares. He replied to

Elizabeth's letter by inviting himself to lunch at St. Paul's Walden Bury on Monday, January 17. When he told her he had been sick, she was sympathetic even as she tried to downplay a luncheon date.

Her "very ill" mother would be with them, and it would be "a sort of picnic." She worried he would be "bored to tears." She apologized in advance for her small and "tumbledown old house," where a "tumbledown little person . . . which will be <u>ME</u>!" would greet him. He proceeded as planned, arriving in his new motorcar, an Armstrong Siddeley that he had shown off at Sandringham the day before.

They did not meet again until February 8 for the wedding of Helen Cecil and Alec Hardinge at St. Paul's Knightsbridge in London, with a reception at the home of Helen's aunt and uncle the Marquess and Marchioness of Salisbury. The guest list was headed by the King and Queen, Princess Mary, and Prince Albert, with James Stuart in attendance. Elizabeth was one of the five bridesmaids.

Little over a week later, Mabell Airlie had Bertie and Cecilia Strathmore to tea. There is no record of what transpired, but shortly afterward, Bertie invited himself for lunch at St. Paul's Walden Bury on Sunday, February 27. This time, he and Elizabeth would be alone.

Three days before their appointed meeting, Elizabeth tried to wave Bertie off in a hastily scribbled and "extremely ill expressed" letter to "just let you know about Sunday." She warned him that with the exception of the cook, there would be "nobody to wait on us! So if you have something more amusing to do, please don't worry to come." Bertie would not be dissuaded. He arrived as planned, proposed marriage to Elizabeth, and she turned him down.

One can scarcely imagine what was running through his mind the next day, when he attended a charity matinee with James Stuart. There has been speculation over the years that James had already asked Elizabeth to marry him. No proof exists, but his grandson Dominic, the third Viscount Stuart of Findhorn, wouldn't dismiss the notion. "The romance was on its way," he said. "He may have proposed, and she may have been thinking seriously about it when she rebuffed the Duke of York for the first time."

Elizabeth wrote to "Prince Bertie" on Monday, February 28, asking his forgiveness and saying how "dreadfully sorry" she was. She felt "miserable" about making him unhappy and appreciative that he was "so <u>very</u> nice" about her rejection. "We can be good friends can't we?" she wrote, and pledged she would keep his proposal secret. "Nobody need ever know."

But Lady Strathmore, Lady Airlie, and Queen Mary knew soon enough. On March 5, Cecilia informed Mabell that "I have written to the young man as you advised—& told him how truly grieved we are that this little romance has come to an end." She thanked Mabell for being "angelically kind" to Elizabeth "through this little episode in her life." She hoped Queen Mary was "not very much annoyed with E & me, altho' it would be quite natural that she shd be, but I wd be so unhappy to cause her (the Queen) any worry." She wished Bertie would "find a very nice wife, who will make him happy—so between you and me, I feel he will be 'made or marred' by his wife." She emphasized her "deep disappointment," but "I daresay it is all for the best."

Bertie had replied to Elizabeth's apologetic letter by then, but his words have been lost. Whatever he said "much relieved my mind," she wrote to him on March 7. "I feel just the same as you do about it and am <u>so</u> glad." After some chitchat, she closed by offering a glimmer of possibility. "I feel I know you so much better this last few weeks," she wrote. "I think it is much easier to get to know people in the country— even if it's only for an hour or two—don't you? One is more natural, I expect."

The most intriguing—and forever mysterious—twist came two days later, in a brief note to "Dearest Mabell" from Queen Mary: "Many grateful thanks. I will gladly see Ly E. at 3.30 Monday if you will arrange this. Privy Purse Entrance please—Gt haste. Yrs ever M.R." Elizabeth was being summoned for an audience with the Queen, at short notice, arranged by her lady-in-waiting. She was to come to the door on the extreme right side of Buckingham Palace's main East Front, the entrance designated for those on official business with the royal household.

Monday, March 14, 1921, was a typical day for the King and Queen at Buckingham Palace, as detailed in the "Court Circular" of *The Times.* Queen Mary noted in her diary that she walked in the Palace garden and packed for their departure two days later to stay with the Earl of Derby for the Grand National. She made no mention of a visit in midafternoon by Lady Elizabeth Bowes Lyon.

Perhaps the hush-hush appointment didn't materialize, which is unlikely, given Queen Mary's exactitude about such matters. Elizabeth had been to the Palace just once before, early in 1920 in the company of Scottish ladies, to present needlework chairs to the Queen. This solo visit would have been intimidating, to say the least.

Whatever happened, Elizabeth's attitude toward Bertie did not discernibly change. She went to Glamis for Easter as planned, and Bertie continued writing to her. She replied belatedly on March 25— Good Friday. Her tone was informal and self-deprecating. She complained about her boredom, guessed that Bertie was "very flourishing," and asked his forgiveness for "such a deadly letter."

These were busy months for Bertie, with numerous engagements, most attended by James Stuart. Since the beginning of 1920, Prince Albert had been called upon to give short speeches—many of them connected to his work on behalf of the Industrial Welfare Society. In early March 1921, he made remarks in Birmingham about "the spirit of enterprise" and in London to the IWS about the "human factor" in industry. At a moment of growing industrial tension, his call for "closer cooperation and good feeling between all sections of the industrial community" was well timed. In her letter to Bertie on March 7, 1921, Elizabeth commended him on the "excellent speeches" that she had read in the newspaper. "Many congratulations—Hope they went off well."

Such words surely warmed the prince, who had confided to his mother some months earlier that he was "longing to get over" a particular speech that he described as an "ordeal." Without the benefit of recordings, it is difficult to measure the extent of his speech impediment in those days. His stress was apparent to his audiences when the muscles around his mouth twitched and he repeatedly blinked his eyes as he struggled to speak.

Journalist Hector Bolitho watched Albert give a speech describing leadership as "the gift of vision, and the desire in his soul to leave things in the world a little better than he found them." Bolitho noted that "although in private conversation his voice was clear and vibrant," Albert's "inner trepidation made him hesitant on a platform. He stammered when he spoke at Croydon."

With the season winding down, there was one more big occasion before the aristocracy dispersed to various points on the country house compass: a state visit by the King and Queen of Belgium in early July. The capstone was the State Ball at Buckingham Palace on July 7. It was the first event of its kind since a ball in July 1914, held two weeks before the outbreak of World War I. Seven years later, the state rooms were filled with two thousand guests, who formed a double line for the passage of the royal party into the gilded ballroom. A quadrille led by George V and Queen Mary was followed by dancing into the small hours.

The crowd included Claude and Cecilia Strathmore among sixty-nine earls and eighty-five countesses. Elizabeth was there as well, along with her friends. James Stuart and Louis Greig attended in their official capacity as aides to Prince Albert. It was the first such royal occasion for Elizabeth and her parents at Buckingham Palace, a rare peek into what she could experience if she would only say "yes."

Elizabeth was with James Stuart several nights later at the Royal Caledonian Ball in London. To tunes played by bagpipers, they danced in one reel after another: the men in tartan kilts, scarlet and blue full-dress uniforms, pink hunt coats, and black velvet frock coats, and the women in white dresses with tartan sashes. Bertie was absent, but he did see Elizabeth at a Mayfair dance. They also played tennis and had tea at her sister May's home in Mayfair before she set off for Glamis.

That summer Bertie launched one of his proudest achievements as Duke of York: a weeklong camp for four hundred teenage boys, half from elite "public" schools such as Eton and Harrow, and half young factory workers. He had conceived the idea to encourage understanding between social classes, and to break down stereotypes and prejudice. On July 30, 1921, he treated the boys to lunch at Buckingham Palace before they proceeded to New Romney on the Channel coast in Kent.

They wore identical uniforms of shorts and shirts, ate and slept in the same quarters, and played games in teams—specifically excluding the cricket and football familiar to the "posh" boys. They were encouraged to "play the game for their side and not for themselves," as Prince Albert put it.

Dressed in the "camp kit," he visited the boys for several hours on August 3. He proudly observed the friendship and cooperation of the "welfare spirit" he wished labor and industry leaders would adopt more widely. Under Bertie's close supervision, the Duke of York's Camps would continue for seventeen more years with seven thousand participants, until World War II made them impossible to continue.

Elizabeth came of age with her twenty-first birthday on August 4. Bertie sent his best wishes to her at Glamis, along with a book of humorous verse. She quickly responded with a chipper thank-you note. "Your Boys Camp was a great success wasn't it?" she wrote. "I hope so anyway, as it is such an excellent idea, and a wonderful thing for the boys." She confirmed that he could come to Glamis for partridge shooting on Saturday, September 24. With a hint of caution, she also said she was glad "that we are such friends after what happened."

"I know I am very lucky to have won her over at last."

The Duke of York and Lady Elizabeth Bowes Lyon on the announcement of their engagement on January 16, 1923.

NINE

❧

More Than an Ordinary Friend

IN THE SUMMER OF 1921, QUEEN MARY DEVISED HER OWN PLAN TO further scrutinize Elizabeth and her family. She invited herself to stay with Mabell at Airlie Castle from September 5 to September 10 while the King was shooting at friends' estates. Her proposed itinerary of "expeditions" included a day at Glamis Castle on the ninth. She would be accompanied by Princess Mary and an entourage of eight attendants.

Several days before her departure, the Queen quizzed the Reverend John Stirton, the minister at Balmoral's Crathie Church, who had previously held the same post at Glamis. Stirton also spoke with Prince Albert about his own planned visit to Glamis at the end of September. "From the way he talked of Lady Elizabeth Lyon I felt he must have a 'penchant' for her," Stirton wrote in his diary. He also observed that Bertie's brother David teasingly "sang in an undertone" the popular song "I love a lassie, a bonnie Hieland [*sic*] lassie."

Cecilia was ailing again and unable to leave her bed when Queen Mary arrived at Glamis. Elizabeth gave the Queen a tour of the castle followed by luncheon. "Lady Elizabeth filled her mother's place as hostess so charmingly," wrote Mabell, "that the Queen was more than ever convinced that this was 'the one girl who could make Bertie happy.'" Queen Mary confided to Mabell that she would "say nothing to either of them," adding—disingenuously to say the least—"Mothers should never meddle in their children's love affairs." Mabell deduced that the Queen wanted to help Bertie in his quest, and that as her friend and lady-in-waiting, she should permit herself some "discreet meddling" by continuing to plead Bertie's case to Elizabeth.

When Bertie turned up at Glamis with James Stuart on Saturday, September 24, 1921, for a week of shooting, Cecilia Strathmore's condition had worsened, but the castle was nevertheless filled with guests. Elizabeth had to organize everything for the week, assisted by her older sister Rosie. Her friends Katie Hamilton and Doris Gordon-Lennox were also on hand. The men shot partridge for three days with Lord Strathmore, and bagged well over two hundred birds each day. Bertie was distressed by his own performance, writing later to Elizabeth that he "shot so badly," and "I did so want to have shot well."

The mood in the castle was subdued that week. Lady Strathmore faced exploratory surgery on Sunday, October 2, for a possible tumor, and Elizabeth did her best to conceal her intense worry. Cecilia stayed in bed the whole time, and Bertie visited her twice, the second time for a "good talk."

"Elizabeth is very kind to me," Bertie wrote to his mother. "The more I see of her the more I like her." But after the prince boarded the night train to London on Friday, James Stuart stayed at Glamis for three additional days to keep Elizabeth and her brothers company following their mother's operation. It appeared that he was no longer obliged to attend Bertie. Their last engagement together in the "Court Circular" had been on July 18, 1921, when they watched the Oxford and Cambridge Air Race at Hendon Aerodrome.

Mabell Airlie reported to the Queen her relief that the surgeons had found only a large gallstone that they had removed. But Cecilia's heart was so weakened that they thought they could lose her. Elizabeth described to her former governess Beryl Poignand the awful six days of suspense before her mother's pulse strengthened and she turned the corner.

Over the next weeks, Bertie wrote "my dear Elizabeth" a series of touching and sympathetic letters from Buckingham Palace on plain paper with no royal cypher. They were carefully crafted in his simple hand, the straight lines widely spaced. His words were unaffected, his sentiments heartfelt. Elizabeth's replies in her rounded and relaxed hand were more upbeat than what she shared with Beryl. The exchanges highlighted Bertie and Elizabeth's contrasting personalities—his earnestness and her breeziness.

In the first letter, written on the Sunday of Cecilia's surgery, he expressed gratitude for Elizabeth's hospitality, praising her "tremendous spirits" despite her anxieties. Elizabeth responded immediately to "Dear Prince Bertie," saying how "touched" she was by his concern about her mother. She gave a guarded progress report and told him it was "such a relief" to share her worries with him. "I hope you don't mind." This tone was new, and showed an appreciation for his compassion. She apologized for being a "lugubrious hostess" and sympathized with his discouragement over his shooting. "I'm sure next time you will be back in your old form," she said. Whether or not this meant he would be invited back to Glamis, it seemed encouraging.

Her next letter, on October 11, relayed "good progress" after a "ghastly week." "It was nice of you to take so much interest," she wrote. Her spirits restored, she reverted to jocularity. "Do you go to dozens of fast little parties?" she asked. "Don't have anything to do with FASTY [Doris Gordon-Lennox's nickname]—she's dangerous."

"I have been leading a very quiet life, with no fast little parties as you call them," Bertie replied. The weather was too hot, he had "nothing to do," and "everything was wrong" with his shooting. But he had heard from "Fasty," who sent him photographs from Glamis. And finally, a playful nod: "I will keep your warning about her in mind!!!!"

Elizabeth and her father had kept Queen Mary informed about Cecilia in the weeks after her surgery. The Queen wrote Elizabeth in mid-October that she had "felt so deeply" during the family's anxious time "and shared your feelings to the full." She added that she had become "much attached to your dearest Mother."

Sometime that month, Sir Sidney Greville, a royal courtier since 1898, got in touch with James Stuart with a proposition. The first Viscount Cowdray, a wealthy industrialist, wanted to offer him a well-paying job in one of the oil businesses he controlled. But if he was interested, James needed to go to America early in 1922—first to the corporate office in New York City, and then to the oil fields in Oklahoma.

It has been suggested that Queen Mary was behind this proposal. In his biography of the Queen Mother, Hugo Vickers wrote that three decades later, James Stuart told a friend, Sir Anthony Nutting, that Queen Mary caused the banishment, and "ruined my life," because she wanted Elizabeth for the Duke of York. Also according to Vickers, James's son David said Cecilia and James's mother, the Countess of Moray, deferred to the Queen's wish to get James out of the way.

Given Cecilia's serious incapacity—even in late November 1921, she was "still too weak to move an inch"—such a role for her seems improbable. But Queen Mary was in a uniquely influential position—and Sidney Greville had been staying at Balmoral that September. Yet the Queen Mother's official biographer, William Shawcross, found "no evidence" in the Royal Archives to prove such high-level intrigue regarding James.

As the second son of an earl, twenty-four-year-old James Stuart needed to earn a living, and a courtier's modest salary wouldn't suffice. "The point is, James didn't have any money, and he didn't have any prospect of an inheritance," said his grandson Dominic. "To marry Elizabeth Bowes Lyon or anyone, he needed to create financial security to give her the kind of lifestyle she was accustomed to."

Sidney Greville's offer was "the opportunity to make a quick fortune in the oil business and get an established income," said Dominic. "But that doesn't disprove the possibility of a conspiracy—that the women agreed it was a good idea, made it happen, and he leapt at it. He had no choice, really. Queen Mary was very keen for the relationship between Bertie and Elizabeth to prosper."

After she had been caring for her invalid mother for six weeks straight, the doctors ordered Elizabeth to have a respite in London. On November 18, the day she was returning to Glamis from London, James Stuart appeared unannounced at 17 Bruton Street, where the Strathmores had moved after leaving St. James's Square. He "insisted on taking me to Euston [station]," she wrote to Beryl. "He placed me in the train & stalked off."

On December 3, James officially resigned his court position in an audience with George V, who recognized his eighteen months of royal service by appointing him an MVO, a Member of the Royal Victorian Order, a personal gift of the monarch. A month later, over the New Year's holiday, James traveled to Glamis to say goodbye to Elizabeth and her family.

On January 28, 1922, he set sail for New York as a first-class passenger on the *Aquitania*. More than seventy years later, Elizabeth recalled that James had been "a very serious" suitor. "He used to go away to America or something, you know," she added, rather vaguely. George VI was more pointed, telling his daughter Princess Margaret that "her mother had almost married James Stuart but that he had gone abroad."

WITH BERTIE'S MARITAL STATUS STILL hanging in the balance, his twenty-four-year-old sister Princess Mary got engaged. It happened in late November at York Cottage when she accepted a proposal from thirty-nine-year-old Henry, Viscount Lascelles—known as "Harry" to the royal family. As the heir to the Earl of Harewood, he had been cultivated by Queen Mary since the middle of 1920 as a suitable husband for her only daughter. George V's children were no longer required, as had been the case during previous reigns, to marry someone of European royal blood. Instead, they could choose wives and husbands from the families of the first three ranks of the nobility— dukes, marquesses, and earls. Harry Lascelles would be the first.

Mary could be described as handsome rather than pretty. She had a heavy chin and wavy hair, with blue eyes like her brothers Edward and Albert, and a lovely complexion. She had always been extremely shy in public, although in private she was natural and easy, with a dry sense of humor. Tommy Lascelles, Harry's first cousin, regarded her as "solid and endearing," with a "fresh and jolly" manner. "She wrinkles up her nose when she smiles," he wrote after meeting her for the first time.

Harry Lascelles was tall and lean, with a long face, pale blue eyes, prominent nose, full mustache covering his upper lip, and sleek dark hair crisply parted. He had fought on the Western Front in the First World War as a captain in the Grenadier Guards, was wounded three times and gassed once, and was decorated for bravery.

His father was stupendously wealthy, with vast estates in Yorkshire as well as the West Indies. Harewood House, the earl's eighteenth-century Palladian mansion on twenty-two thousand acres near Leeds, was designed by Robert Adam, with landscaping by Lancelot "Capability" Brown.

Through an inheritance of some £2.5 million from an eccentric great-uncle (£130 million today, or $176 million), Harry Lascelles was also very rich in his own right. Chesterfield House, his huge eighteenth-century home in Mayfair, featured paintings by Titian and Rubens in its rococo rooms. He owned and raced thoroughbreds, on which he placed substantial bets.

Prince Edward wrote to Freda from India that he was thrilled the "poor girl is going to be free and let out of Buckhouse prison. Of course Lascelles is too old for her and not attractive. . . . But anyway he's rich, and I'm afraid that is a very important thing for poor Mary. I hope to God he'll make her happy." As it turned out, Mary and Harry were actually well matched, with a shared love of foxhunting and thoroughbred racing and a preference for country living. Elizabeth thought Harry was "rather dull," but "they like each other which is all that matters."

Elizabeth continued to send Bertie conflicting signals. In late November she seemed to encourage him by writing to ask his advice on new dresses she wanted to buy in London. "What colours do you like?" she inquired. But she missed his twenty-sixth birthday on December 14. In a belated letter, she wrote, "I should have bought a large and magnificent offering," adding that all she could find were bull's-eye candies—"very sticky, and they won't travel."

Was she stringing him along? Elizabeth was a sensitive soul who had known suffering. Perhaps she was simply oblivious to his feeling bruised or puzzled. Or perhaps she was coping with the imminent departure of James Stuart. Bertie pressed ahead and sent a Christmas present as well as a photograph of himself. Writing from her sickbed "with a chill or something," she thanked him extravagantly for the "darling little clock." She was "enchanted" with it and thought the picture "excellent." Yet again, she apologized for failing to reciprocate by sending him a gift.

Early in January 1922, Elizabeth received a letter from Princess Mary asking her to be a bridesmaid in her wedding to Harry Lascelles at Westminster Abbey on February 28. This was a command performance, as the headline in *The Times* on January 16 made clear: "Princess Mary's Bridesmaids: The Chosen Eight." Three of Elizabeth's close friends—Rachel Cavendish, Mary Thynne, and Doris Gordon-Lennox—were among the group.

Only days before that news broke, Bertie and Elizabeth were together in Warwickshire for a house party hosted by her godmother, Venetia James, a cousin of Cecilia Strathmore. In a letter to his mother on January 19, Bertie said Elizabeth had been among the guests. His mother's reply three days later showed how enmeshed she had become in Bertie's romantic efforts. She was "longing to hear" how "Elizabeth had behaved & whether she is beginning to thaw or not! Your letter does not enlighten me on this point so I must have patience till we meet." She reminded Bertie, "Don't forget that my Ly [Lady] Airlie is in town in case she can in any way be a help."

Queen Mary's pointed comments flushed out Bertie's feelings about the house party. In a January 25 letter, he confessed that "I was rather depressed" by Elizabeth's behavior. The weather had been foul, forcing the guests to be "cooped up" with "nothing to do," despite Venetia having "kept things going more or less in her master-ful way."

But Bertie sensed something else afoot with Elizabeth. They had danced "a lot" for two nights running, and he "thought things were going better," but "I don't think she was very well there, as she lost her good spirits after the first evening." He asked if his mother could set aside some time to discuss the situation. "I am sure Lady Airlie could help a lot now," he wrote.

Elizabeth arrived in London in time for the wedding rehearsal. "I am beginning to feel rather nervous," she confided to Bertie. She discovered "it is very difficult to walk slowly & steadily on high heels. I am so afraid I shall appear intoxicated, which would be awful."

Day after day the newspapers reported every detail of the forth-coming nuptials. There were three receptions at Buckingham Palace and St. James's Palace for thousands of guests who ogled the wedding gifts on display. It was the first wedding in Westminster Abbey of a monarch's child since the thirteenth century, and Mary was George V and Queen Mary's only daughter, which heightened the fervor.

The sun shone on the morning of February 28, 1922. Spectators stood fifteen deep along the route of the processional from Bucking-ham Palace to the Abbey, where the guardsmen discarded their gray greatcoats and formed a "living ribbon of vivid red." *The Times* expressed its approval that Princess Mary would marry "a man of her own country."

There was one noteworthy moment following the service. The gilded horse-drawn state coach carrying Harry and Mary back to the Palace paused unexpectedly by the Cenotaph, the Portland stone memorial to those who had died in the First World War. After the car-riage stopped, the crowd fell silent as Princess Mary summoned one of the guardsmen and gave him a piece of her bouquet to place among the flowers at the base of the Cenotaph. The bride and groom then observed a moment of silence—a fitting tribute in light of Harry's courageous wartime service. As the coach proceeded, the crowd let out a cheer.

Queen Mary and the King were depressed for days after the

newlyweds left for a honeymoon on the Continent. "Dreadful saying good bye," she wrote in her diary. Bertie, however, was on high alert, doubtless mindful of an exhortation in *The Times* on his sister's wedding day: "The whole nation hopes that it may be followed before long by another auspicious event of the same character." Exactly a week later, on Tuesday, March 7, 1922, Bertie proposed for the second time to Elizabeth, and for the second time, she turned him down.

Presumably he made his move at 17 Bruton Street, for it was from there the next day that Elizabeth wrote a brief letter: "I am so terribly sorry for what happened yesterday, & feel it is all my fault, as I ought to have known." She felt doubly miserable because he had been "so nice" to her. She called him her "most faithful friend" and said she would readily listen any time he wanted to "talk about things in general." But she ended by saying, "I do wish this hadn't happened."

Bertie sent his anguished reply the same day. Her letter, he wrote, "somewhat depressed me." He had spent "all today" going over what had passed between them. "I feel that you must think so badly of me," he wrote. "For my sake please do not make yourself miserable or worried about it, as I should never forgive myself."

He faulted himself for proposing "without giving you any warning as to my intentions." He poignantly told her that "ever since last year I have always been hoping to get to know you better & to let you know my thoughts, but I see that I failed to enlighten you. How were you to guess what they were when we never really had any good talks like we did yesterday? I see it all now & blame myself entirely for what happened."

He thanked her for being "a wonderful friend through it all." He clung to the tiny grain of encouragement in her letter: "Now you say that you want me to come & see you when I want to have a talk." He thanked her for the offer and asked forgiveness "for making you miserable." He implored her to see him again. What seemed final to Elizabeth appeared to Bertie as an "uncertain state . . . so bad & unsettling for us both. . . . I am so very sorry. Yours, Albert."

Before her return to Glamis the following week, Elizabeth said she hoped he had stopped worrying about what happened. "Please do try & forget about this," she wrote. She told him they could not meet for some time: "Au revoir—till I don't know when."

In his reply, he expressed dismay that she had bolted to Glamis on his account, which "would be too sad for me." He grasped that she did "not wish me to discuss" her feelings anymore. "But I feel I must tell you that I have always cared for you & had the hope that you would one day care for me." Perhaps in an allusion to James Stuart, he admitted that "things were difficult for both of us" at the beginning. "I understand from your letter that you want me to forget it." He promised to "try."

He asked her to tell her mother what had happened, as "she has a right to know." But he implored her to keep it a secret "from everyone else in this world as I shall." More touchingly than ever, he asked Elizabeth "to look upon me as more than an ordinary friend."

She responded at greater length several days later to say that she had informed her mother, but "nobody else in the world" would know. Most of all, Elizabeth wanted to remain friends, "as it would be too sad if a happening like this should come between our friendship." She reiterated that he was welcome to drop by for tea and a talk.

"I wish I could put into words what I feel about it all," she wrote. "I think it is wonderful of you to have gone on caring—oh <u>why</u> didn't I guess. How silly I have been. . . . Of course, I shall look on you as more than an ordinary friend." Between that letter and Bertie's reply a week later, Lady Strathmore wrote to the wounded prince, apparently with kindness. He later told Elizabeth he hoped her mother "was not very upset."

But someone else was very upset: James Stuart. He and Elizabeth had been corresponding since his early February arrival in New York. He had been jolted by a letter she had written before her return to Glamis in mid-March, and he sent a reply ten days later. "The most extraordinary things have happened to me the last 3 weeks," she had written, although the specific details she shared with James are unknown.

He was surely aware of Mary's wedding, but he did not appear to know about Bertie's continuing pursuit. Yet something Elizabeth wrote—likely in her typically devil-may-care way—stirred up intense jealousy. Not only had James been brooding about her words all day, he had also heard from a friend that she was keeping company with another man—either Christopher Glenconner or someone named Michael.

In her correspondence with her former governess Beryl Poignand, Elizabeth had played down her friendship with Glenconner. But in his diary some months later, Chips Channon would call Christopher Glenconner Elizabeth's "tragic" victim.

"Not that it's any of my business but you know what a fool I am," James wrote to Elizabeth on March 24, 1922. "I hope he's very nice. . . . I am just about to destroy your letter as that paragraph upsets me too much, if I should read it again. Jealousy is a very bad trait, and I have always tried to get rid of it." James was so distraught that he broke away for ten minutes to smoke a cigarette and calm down.

Continuing his letter, he said he needed to recognize that he was "luckier than most people" to be given a potentially lucrative job opportunity. "'It's fair enough by me,' as they say here—or I'm going to think so anyway." He apologized for sending a "waily" letter and signed off, "Yours, James." The tone of his letter seemed remarkable to his grandson Dominic. "The fact that he displayed such emotion was very unusual," he said. "They must have had a certain degree of intimacy for him to have expressed himself so strongly."

Two days later, Bertie wrote to tell Elizabeth he felt more cheerful. He reverted to quotidian patter about foxhunting and race going and said he was now convinced she was not angry with him: "So long as we can still be great friends that is all I was worrying about."

For whatever reason, Queen Mary took it upon herself to write to Cecilia Strathmore in early May 1922. She was sorry to hear that Cecilia was "still so far from well," but said her piece anyway. She and King George V were "much disappointed" that the "little romance" had ended. "We should so much have liked the connection with your family." Bertie felt "very sad" although he was content to "remain friends" with Elizabeth.

But the Queen couldn't resist playing the guilt card: "I hope you and E. will not reproach yourselves in any way," she wrote. "No one can help their feelings & it was far better to be honest." She signed, "with my love to you and E. and <u>many</u> regrets." Elizabeth tactfully told Bertie it had been a "most charming letter . . . so kind of her."

The day after Queen Mary wrote her letter, Cecilia had another operation at Glamis, this time to drain an abscess that had been causing chronic pain and fever. While her mother convalesced, Elizabeth was herself bedridden with tonsillitis and a high fever for a week. In a letter to Beryl in mid-May, she mentioned she had heard from James Stuart, by then working in the oil fields.

"He says it's exactly like books there," she wrote. "Everybody packs a gun & the sheriff has got nine nicks on his for the g men he's killed." James also sent a flattering photo of himself in his work clothes, shorn of his mustache. According to author Grania Forbes, Elizabeth kept it "in her private collection ever after."

Elizabeth finally made it to London after an absence of more than two months, in time to see Bertie at a dinner dance on May 23 hosted by Lady Evelyn Guinness. Over the following weeks, Elizabeth and Bertie each popped up at various London social events, but rarely in each other's company. The "little romance" did appear to have ended. As Elizabeth wrote to her sister May, "Yes, I did put an end to that affair you mentioned . . . but did not tell anyone except Mother."

Bertie felt profoundly discouraged. Louis Greig, who had remained close to Prince Albert throughout this stressful period, was still his key adviser. He remembered that a Scottish friend named John Colin Campbell Davidson, a new member of Parliament, had recently married a woman who had repeatedly turned down his proposals. He thought Davidson might be able to offer advice to help Bertie persevere with Elizabeth.

Greig surreptitiously called Davidson and asked if he could join a parliamentary delegation traveling with Prince Albert to Dunkirk to lay the foundation stone for a First World War memorial on July 25. At thirty-three, Davidson was seven years Bertie's senior and could be counted on to speak discreetly during the return trip across the English Channel.

In the wardroom on a Royal Navy destroyer, Greig introduced the two men. As they sat together, Bertie unburdened himself during a conversation that lasted nearly three hours. The prince was at a "crisis" point, Davidson recalled in a memorandum written many years later. He got some of the facts about Bertie's courtship wrong, but the import of the discussion was correct.

Bertie said he was "desperately in love," but "in despair for it seemed quite certain that he had lost the only woman he would ever marry." Davidson told him "however black the situation looked he must not give up hope; that my wife had refused me consistently before she finally said yes, and that like him, if she had persisted in her refusal, I would never have married anyone else." He urged Bertie to try again. The prince's mood "was much brighter and more buoyant" when they parted.

Bertie had no idea about Greig's motivation behind the introduction to Davidson, but Greig could see "a new spring to his step." The very next day, Elizabeth sent a short note to Bertie from Bruton Street to inquire when he wished to come to Glamis for shooting. Keeping it light, she said she needed advance warning "so that I can collect a few charmers and Society Beauties for the same week." Bertie replied two days later to say the last week of September would suit his schedule.

Elizabeth didn't reply to Bertie's letter until the middle of September. "I do hope you won't be terribly bored here," she wrote, bemoaning that heavy rainfall had diminished the partridge population by drowning the youngest birds. "I noticed some old chickens flying quite high down at the farm," she added. "We might have a chicken drive to vary the monotony."

On September 26, 1922, the day Prince Albert left for Glamis, John Stirton, the Balmoral minister, wrote in his diary that Elizabeth "refuses to accept him as a husband. An understanding therefore has been made that he must not speak again on the subject. I am very sorry for him as Lady Elizabeth is the only girl the duke wishes to marry." Stirton thought it unwise for Albert to have gone to Glamis. He claimed to have encouraged Bertie to pursue the romance two years earlier: "I therefore feel a little sore upon the subject."

Elizabeth fulfilled her promise to cast her house party with lively company, including Doris Gordon-Lennox, Rachel Cavendish and her cousin Mary Cavendish, as well as Arthur Penn, Prince Paul, and Chips Channon. It was on that occasion that Channon observed Bertie's obvious love for Elizabeth. Writing in his diary, he recalled "the pipers playing in the candlelit-dining room, and the whole castle heavy with atmosphere."

For the first three days the weather was "horrid," until Friday the twenty-ninth, when the sun finally emerged. In his game book Bertie described two days of partridge shooting with Michael Lyon, David Lyon, and Arthur Penn. He reported to Queen Mary that Cecilia was "much stronger." It was "a large party," and a "happy one." Bertie's affection for Elizabeth's family had deepened: "They were all so kind to me," he told his mother.

Something in the dynamic between Elizabeth and Bertie seemed to shift after those days at Glamis. The tone in her letters turned more beguiling, even welcoming. After he sent her the latest gramophone records from London, she thanked him "ten million times. . . . It was very angelic of you to take the trouble." She jokingly enclosed "two crackly sovereigns" as payment. A photograph of James Stuart on an oil rig had evidently appeared in the press, which prompted her to write, "James looks very thin, doesn't he? I suppose it is pretty dirty work too—he looks covered in oil & grease."

She wrote Bertie again a month later to say, "I play the records you gave me. . . . Do come around one day." Shortly afterward, Claude Strathmore invited him to shoot at St. Paul's Walden Bury.

The prince's day in Hertfordshire on Saturday, November 25, 1922, surpassed his expectations. He shot with Elizabeth's father and brothers in perfect conditions. To Elizabeth he wrote, "Wonderful day wonderful shoot & wonderful time. . . . I hope I have redeemed myself as a shot after those dreadful exhibitions at Glamis in your eyes." Equally meaningful were the hours he spent alone with Elizabeth.

Bertie and Elizabeth had been invited to a number of pre-Christmas dinner dances in London. She expressed her apprehension about potential gossiping, and Bertie replied that he did "not think really that people will start talking about us again as they must know by now what friends we are."

This was not a trivial concern in 1922, when a young woman's reputation could be ruined by gossip. The romance had gone on long enough, and was sufficiently well known in elite circles—with Chips Channon's antennae as a leading indicator—to invite criticism, not to mention mockery. The Queen herself had told Cecilia that Elizabeth had hurt Bertie, and it was best that they had parted company. If Elizabeth was playing a game, it was fraught with risk.

In early December both Bertie and Elizabeth received their invitations to stay at Pitsford Hall at the beginning of 1923 for the Pytchley Hunt Ball. "I should love to go," Elizabeth wrote Bertie on December 6. "Do you think it will start all these horrible people talking again? . . . They have left us in peace lately." She was keen to accept "if you think it will be alright." The next day Elizabeth told Bertie she intended to accept "at once!"

They appeared together at Mrs. Greville's and several other London dinner dances publicized in the "Court Circular," which inevitably set tongues wagging. Maggie's party was the night before Bertie's twenty-seventh birthday on the fourteenth, which he celebrated with his family at Buckingham Palace.

He saw Elizabeth the next day at Bruton Street, where she gave him a complete set of the works of Stephen Leacock, a celebrated British-born humorist who wrote bestselling satires and parodies "unmasking and highlighting cracks in the human veneer." This was an imaginative and knowing present. She had failed to give Bertie anything the previous two years, but now Elizabeth showed that she was savvy enough to tickle his understated sense of humor. "I cannot thank you enough for them," he wrote the next day.

He was equally delighted by their evening at Maggie Greville's. "You were very kind to me . . . in giving me so many dances & all the rest of it," he wrote. "I have never enjoyed an evening more, & I rather think, at least I hope that you did, too."

Emboldened by his success, he invited Elizabeth to dinner the next week at Claridge's with her brother David and sister-in-law Fenella, followed by "whatever you want to see" in the West End. One can sense his growing confidence as he steered toward the moment he would follow John Davidson's advice and ask Lady Elizabeth Bowes Lyon for her hand a third time after the Christmas and New Year's holidays.

He could not have anticipated that the invitation to Pitsford Hall would trigger Queen Mary, Mabell Airlie, and Cecilia Strathmore to intervene and prevent Elizabeth from joining him. After confiding in his mother for many months, Bertie had kept her in the dark about Elizabeth's warmer attitude since his September visit to Glamis. The Queen had heard the rumors about them and felt exasperated by what she viewed as Elizabeth's leading Bertie on yet again.

Nor did Elizabeth's mother recognize that the Duke of York's romance with her daughter seemed to be making genuine headway. She remained under the impression, as she said some years later, that Elizabeth "was torn between her longing to make Bertie happy and her reluctance to take on the responsibilities which this marriage must bring." As the eleven days between Bertie's January 3, 1923, proposal and Elizabeth's acceptance would show, her continued qualms and misgivings weighed more heavily than anyone could have predicted. When they finally collapsed after more than fifteen hours of intense conversations, there was as much surprise as relief, not least for Elizabeth herself.

Wedding portrait of the Duke and Duchess of York, with King George V, Queen Mary, and the Earl and Countess of Strathmore, April 26, 1923.

PART TWO

Halcyon Days

"A blessing not only to yourselves but to others."

"Gild the lily as you may she <u>will</u> be royal now."

York Cottage on the Sandringham estate, the home of King George V and Queen Mary, where Elizabeth and her parents visited for the first time at the end of January 1923.

TEN

Don't Forget Your Honey Lamb

FOR ALL HER EXPERIENCE IN THE UPPER REACHES OF THE BRITISH aristocracy, royal life introduced twenty-two-year-old Elizabeth to a new level of dazzle and ritual and, for the first time, massive public exposure. She may have appeared in the pages of *Tatler* and *Vogue*, but as *The Times* freely admitted on her wedding day, "In the public mind Lady Elizabeth Bowes Lyon is probably all the more welcome an addition to the Royal Family because the public knows practically nothing about her."

When the engagement was announced in the newspapers on Tuesday, January 16, 1923, *The Times* resorted to a "character sketch" by "a friend" who noted "little that is modern in her appearance," and observed that she showed a "touch of the picturesque" in her selection of clothing. She had an "unselfish nature, simple and affectionate; a mind and character incapable of unkindness . . . a complete lack of affectation or pose; a candid sincerity, and an ingrained gentleness." Much of that was true, as was her enjoyment of lawn tennis, her "exceptionally beautiful" dancing, and her "fondness for reading and music." But the "friend" ventured on shakier ground by saying, "she rides and goes well to hounds."

Elizabeth was nonplussed by the crowds, including reporters and photographers. "Great headlines & lots of rot!" she wrote in her diary. The pressmen were "Awful!" and "too appalling"—a lifelong judgment that would be reinforced by her encounters that day with two "Scotch reporters," as she described them, along with Charles Graves of the London *Evening News,* who inveigled Claude Strathmore into writing a letter of introduction to his daughter.

The gushing front-page articles were predictably innocuous, but they revealed Elizabeth's nascent efforts to create a narrative about herself and her relationship with Bertie. Seated at her desk piled with congratulatory letters and telegrams, she admitted she played golf "badly" and was "fond of lawn tennis." Her engagement ring, she said, "is to be made of sapphires." This was actual news, as she had earlier been to Buckingham Palace to select a ring from an array offered by Bert jewelers of Vigo Street: a large Kashmir sapphire with two diamonds set in platinum.

She accurately said that Bertie had "proposed in the garden" at St. Paul's Walden Bury on Sunday—leaving out the many imploring hours before and after. But her friends and family must have chuckled when she insisted that "the story that he proposed or had to propose three times—well it amused me, and it was news to me."

She was equally disingenuous when asked if she was fond of hunting. "Oh yes, but I have done little lately," she said. She had not, in truth, ridden on horseback for many years. In his letter of congratulations, her brother-in-law Wisp Leveson-Gower, Rosie's husband, couldn't resist playfully calling out Elizabeth. "I had no idea that you were (vide today's press) such a distinguished person in the hunting field," he wrote.

"How tiresome the newspaper people have been interviewing poor E—such a shame," Queen Mary wrote to Bertie the next day. In her long life, Elizabeth never again sat for an on-the-record conversation with a journalist. But within a few years, she would begin to play an astute image-making game, not only with her beaming smile and mesmerizing eye contact but also through authorized accounts of her life, and later of the early lives of her two daughters. She would choose the authors—all women—carefully from the ranks of the aristocracy and her own household, and just as carefully mold their narratives. She would speak to them selectively and privately. The results would set the perception of her as a model wife and mother for decades.

BERTIE AND ELIZABETH WERE RARELY apart during the more than three months between their betrothal and the April 26, 1923, wedding at Westminster Abbey. Bertie was a constant presence at Bruton Street, popping in for luncheon, tea, and dinner. Their life was a whirl of shopping, visits with royal relatives, formal presentations of wedding gifts, writing hundreds of thank-you notes, preparing their new home, and many evenings out with friends and siblings at restaurants, night-clubs, and grand dinners. Bertie and Elizabeth stayed up until well past midnight on more than a dozen occasions. Their sole refuge for quiet time together was her family's home in Hertfordshire, where they took long walks in the woods, read, danced to the gramophone (or "grammy," as she called it), and baked potatoes over a small fire.

After more than two pent-up years of polite and periodically anguished correspondence, Bertie wrote passionately to "my own little darling one" on the few occasions he was separated from her. "I think I must have always loved you darling but could never make you realise it without telling you actually that I did & thank God I told you at the right moment," he wrote ten days after the announcement of their engagement. Several weeks later, he recalled, "just a month tonight isn't it darling when you told me you loved me. What a day that was for me!!!! & for you too." Unlike the letters from Prince Edward to Freda Dudley Ward, which were whiny, cynical, and histrionic, Bertie's endearments were sweet and simple, marked by sincere devotion.

The tone of Elizabeth's letters to "my dear darling" Bertie also shifted, with new expressions of love intermingled with reassurance. "I do love you Bertie & feel certain that I shall more and more," she wrote on January 25. But her sense of mischief and irreverence

remained intact: "What HO, & happy Easter little P.A. (pink Angel),"
and "s'long Bertie, don't forget your Honey Lamb, will you?"

Her light touch liberated Bertie's sense of fun after twenty-seven
years of constraint at home. She knew how to boost his fragile confidence without pushing too hard. "Bertie, do you know you have got a
most changeable face?" she wrote a few weeks before their wedding.
"It is too odd, sometimes you look a completely different person,
always nice though, but I must not flatter you because your head will
swell, & you will have to buy new hats. That would be very sad,
wouldn't it?" At last Bertie knew he could spend his life with someone
who understood him and didn't take him—or herself—too seriously.

King George V and Queen Mary's view of Elizabeth flipped overnight from irritation to adoration, although privately they remained
slightly irked by her behavior in the preceding weeks and months. "I
think they have rather the usual parental feeling that she needn't have
kept him so long," Joan Verney, a lady-in-waiting to the Queen, confided to Mabell Airlie. Lady Joan, the daughter of an earl and a first
cousin of both Harry and Tommy Lascelles, knew royal nuances inti-
mately; her husband, Harry Verney, had been the Queen's private secretary since 1919.

Queen Mary wrote to Elizabeth the day after the betrothal to
invite her parents to Sandringham the following weekend, when they
would receive "a very warm welcome. I hope you will look upon me as
a 'second mother' and that we shall become great friends." George V
also conveyed his delight, writing to Elizabeth, "I know you will do all
you can to help him in his many duties."

She swiftly expressed her thanks for their kind words, addressing them as "Sir" and "Madam," and signing off "your humble &
obedient servant." (Once they were married, she would call the
King and Queen "Papa" and "Mama"—less formal than her use of
"Father" and "Mother" for her own parents—and she would sign
her letters "from your loving daughter-in-law.") To the King, she
pledged to support Bertie to the utmost. To the Queen, she promised to do all she could to make Bertie "very happy, as he deserves

to be." She added that her "greatest wish" was to be a "<u>real</u> daughter to Your Majesty."

ELIZABETH HAD BEEN TO BUCKINGHAM Palace and Holyroodhouse in Edinburgh, but never to the other royal residences at Sandringham, Windsor Castle, and Balmoral. Her first command performance for the royal family took place at Sandringham in Norfolk on the weekend of January 20 with her parents. Her brother Mike teasingly wrote that their father had better behave himself.

Bertie and the Strathmores traveled in a private carriage attached to the steam train from London to Wolferton station adjacent to the Sandringham estate. After alighting in the porte cochere at the Big House, they passed by the weighing machine and stuffed baboon holding a tray for visiting cards and walked directly into the high-ceilinged saloon where the royal circle had assembled for an elaborate fireside tea. Bertie's grandmother Queen Alexandra was a very old seventy-eight—just three years from her death—and only marginally communicative. One of her relations likened Alexandra's deafness to "railway trains in her head." "Motherdear" was also nearly blind, and her maquillage was so thick she could scarcely move her lips.

Joining Alexandra were two of George V's sisters, Queen Maud of Norway and the widowed Princess Louise, Duchess of Fife. George V's unmarried sister Toria had been ailing with a respiratory infection for nearly three weeks, so Elizabeth went upstairs with Bertie to the suite that Toria shared with her mother. "They were all so charming," Elizabeth wrote in her diary, "but it was rather an ordeal for me!" Meeting "<u>all</u> the old ladies" was "ghastly," although they were "angelic," she told her sister May. The experience left her "utterly exhausted," she wrote to Beryl Poignand, not least because Queen Alexandra was "stone deaf." Years later she marveled to Prince Charles at the way Alexandra "managed with those Danish gestures to convey quite a lot!"

At York Cottage, Elizabeth and her parents experienced what many described as the "terrible squash" of everyone on top of each other in close quarters amid the pervasive odors of food preparation and tobacco—not a problem for habitual smoker Claude, but less pleasant for his daughter and wife, who never took up the tobacco habit. Dinner meant ankle-length gowns, tiaras, and profusions of diamonds for the ladies. The men wore white-tie and tails, with "orders and decorations" on their formal jackets.

While Elizabeth found the King and Queen "terrifying" at first, she charmed them both. "We got on," she said years later of her relationship with George V. "He was a bit gruff . . . but essentially kind underneath." She rolled with his chaff and laughed at his jokes. "As he told his stories, he would bang you on the arm," she remembered. "By the end of a visit it would be black and blue."

Like everyone else, she humored his eccentricities: Charlotte, the gray and pink African parrot that the King carried on his wrist and fed scraps at breakfast and lunch, and "Sandringham Time," whereby all clocks were set a half hour ahead of everywhere else in Britain to extend the hours for shooting in the winter. The tradition was begun by Edward VII in the late nineteenth century, but it pleased George V, who was devoted to the sport.

Elizabeth shrewdly sensed that George V "rather enjoyed having somebody new and young." She subtly altered the atmosphere even as she observed all the court customs—the ritual curtsey to the King after dinner as the men withdrew to the Billiard Room for coffee and cigars while the women chatted in the drawing room, where Queen Mary typically lit a cigarette. At the King's summons, the women were free to watch the men play billiards. On her second night, Elizabeth and her longtime friend Helen Hardinge, now a helpful companion in the King's court, "sat on hot water pipes" and chatted as Bertie and his father played. Their casual seating arrangement signaled that Elizabeth had already cracked the crust of formality.

From her collection at York Cottage, Queen Mary gave Elizabeth a sunburst diamond brooch pendant—the first of many priceless jewels Elizabeth would receive from the royal family. The Queen would later give Elizabeth "some wonderful lace" in "the same room" at

Buckingham Palace "in which Queen Victoria gave me presents for my trousseau 2 days before I was married."

On Sunday they all attended the service at Sandringham's Church of St. Mary Magdalene, where the royal family was seated in the choir stalls on the right, facing the altar sideways. It was a peculiar place, cattily described by James Pope-Hennessy as a "minor mausoleum" filled with memorial plaques, tablets, and busts: "not, as the books say, an ordinary country church," but rather "the private chapel of ailing megalomaniacs: the shrine of a clique."

The King and Queen were pleased with the Strathmore visit. Queen Mary told Cecilia that seeing the "radiant faces" of "our children" had given her much joy. "We are simply enchanted with your darling little Elizabeth, and one and all back here rave about her." She wrote to Bertie that Cecilia and Claude were "dear people," and that she and the King had much enjoyed their company.

Lady-in-waiting Joan Verney witnessed something else that she described in a letter to Mabell Airlie: "I can't tell you how sorry I am for the parents," she wrote from York Cottage after the Strathmores had left. "I don't believe they had really the least realised before coming here how different things really are & that gild the lily as you may she <u>will</u> be royal now." But Cecilia Strathmore understood all too well, writing to her friend Lady Salisbury that same week, "When all is said and done, it is a strenuous life for a girl who has not been trained from her childhood for it—but Elizabeth has great tact & good judgment & a <u>very</u> kind little heart, so I hope she will pull through."

One source of mild friction was the Strathmores' initial assumption that they would be responsible for planning the wedding. The King's Lord Chamberlain soon disabused them and took over all the arrangements, which were controlled and financed by the Palace. Queen Mary even designated her favorite dress designer, Elizabeth Handley-Seymour, to create Elizabeth's wedding gown.

But Lady Strathmore oversaw everything else having to do with Elizabeth's preparation for her big day. Mother and daughter shopped together for clothing as well as personal items and jewelry. When

Elizabeth sat for miniature portraits by William Lee Hankey and his wife, Mabel, a bust by L. F. Roslyn, and two charcoal portraits by John Singer Sargent, Cecilia came along. Sargent completed his first sketch in two hours, and Elizabeth proclaimed it "simply marvelous." The legendary artist—who also did a sketch of Bertie—later told Cynthia Asquith that Elizabeth was "the only completely unself-conscious sitter I have ever had."

AT QUEEN MARY'S INVITATION, ELIZABETH accompanied Bertie for a weeklong return visit to York Cottage at the end of January. She clicked into all the Sandringham routines: strolling in the gardens, visiting Alexandra and her relatives ("Old as the hills!" she wrote in her diary), and inspecting the King's horses. Bertie went out twice with his father and several guests to shoot game.

Elizabeth and Queen Mary joined the men for luncheon in a small cottage on the first day. A typical menu at these rustic meals, described by Nora Wigram, the wife of Clive "Wiggy" Wigram, one of George V's private secretaries, consisted of "mulligatawny soup—a savoury stew of some sort—cold meats and salad" and "a rice pudding, followed . . . by cheese and a delicious selection of fruit."

After luncheon, Elizabeth and Helen Hardinge walked through the plowed fields with the men as they moved from one shooting stand to the next. The beaters who flushed out the game wore blue smocks and black felt hats, and shaggy ponies were available for those who tired of walking. A distant horn heralded each drive, followed by the simultaneous crack of the shotguns along the line of "pegs"—assigned spots for each man. The gun dogs scampered out for the picking-up, and when the bag had been collected, the shooting party moved on. As the light faded at the end of the final drive, cars arrived to ferry everyone back to York Cottage for tea.

The evenings were predictably subdued, in contrast to the gramophone music and dancing Bertie and Elizabeth enjoyed at St. Paul's Walden Bury. After dinner they mainly wrote letters and read. To match Queen Mary's example of industriousness, Elizabeth briefly took up knitting again. As a teenager at Glamis during the First World War, she had knitted sweaters for the local battalion of the Black Watch. But it wasn't a hobby in which she showed much pride or interest.

DURING THE PREMARITAL RUSH, ELIZABETH's excited friends swarmed around her as she swept through London gathering items for her trousseau ("to Zyrot & bought hats. Such fun! Also country suits!"). Her selections were inspected at Bruton Street by Queen Mary, Princess Mary, and Queen Alexandra before the press saw the trousseau on display: "very simple, as suits a woman of small stature," wrote *The Times,* which described a dozen representative day gowns, evening frocks, afternoon dresses, and tea gowns in meticulous detail: "a cyclamen moiré evening frock . . . made on straight picture lines with little trains at either side." With multiple changes of clothing required each day while staying at a royal residence, Elizabeth's wardrobe had to be extensive.

Elizabeth's siblings were a constant presence as well. She was forever ducking into May and Sidney Elphinstone's house on Upper Brook Street in Mayfair. At thirty-nine, May was the mother of four children aged twelve to five. Elizabeth chose her eldest, twelve-year-old Elizabeth Elphinstone, as one of her bridesmaids. Thirty-three-year-old Rosie Leveson-Gower was less in evidence, as her husband, Wisp, was a serving naval officer, and she had two children under six. After having lost their first daughter in infancy (Patricia, who died at eleven months), Jock and Fenella were expecting their fourth child. Elizabeth's older brother Patrick was living in the country and seldom seen. According to the Balmoral minister John Stirton, he "seems not to have recovered from his nervous breakdown in the war."

Elizabeth saw a lot of Mike and David, the two bachelor Bowes Lyon siblings at twenty-nine and twenty. David was at Oxford and came to Bruton Street or St. Paul's Walden Bury on as many weekends and term breaks as he could manage. Mike was equally omnipresent. Besides lunches and dinners at home, in chic restaurants and at glamorous private parties, the brothers accompanied Elizabeth and Bertie to comedy revues and on shooting weekends. With Mike in particular, Elizabeth had long discussions.

Shortly after her engagement, Elizabeth introduced the term "talked hard" to her diary. It was her euphemism for a serious and often difficult conversation. Notably on February 11, she wrote, "Mike, Mother & I talked hard." The likely proximate cause was the sudden and unexpected arrival in London five days earlier of James Stuart.

The first intimation of potential trouble had come in a letter from Mike to Elizabeth on January 20: "Have you written to James? I think you ought to. Poor James! He will be angry, won't he?" It's unclear if she did, but on February 1 she noted in her diary, "Cable of congratulations from James."

By then he had taken a leave from his job and had booked a first-class ticket on the *Berengaria,* the flagship of the Cunard line. He landed at Southampton on February 6 and took the special train to Waterloo station in London. "James rang up after lunch," Elizabeth wrote in her diary. "He has arrived this morning. Terribly depressing to find everybody engaged & scattered. He came round at 3 & stayed till nearly 4:30. He is just the same—very slow!"

It was an odd way to describe a ninety-minute conversation, obliquely hinting at James's upset over "everybody" getting engaged and calling him "very slow," when his transatlantic movements had been quite the opposite. Mike arrived at Bruton Street from Glamis two mornings later and went straight to Elizabeth's bedroom for a talk. James's brother Francis showed up the following afternoon, and he, Mike, and Elizabeth talked for about a half hour. James Stuart was doubtless on everyone's mind.

Elizabeth's diary entry the next day, Friday, February 9, was conflicted, to say the least. In the late morning, James and Francis arrived at Bruton Street, just like old times. "Mikie still dressing!" she wrote. Elizabeth and the three young men "started off at 11:30 for Oxford in the Vauxhall," pausing en route at Henley for some cherry brandy. They had lunch with David Bowes Lyon and walked around the Magdalen College grounds.

In the late afternoon they drove back to London, with a stop for tea at Skindles, the fashionable hotel on the Thames at Maidenhead. They reached Bruton Street shortly before seven P.M., and Francis and James stayed for a cocktail. Then, in her first mirror writing since the fraught Saturday night before she accepted Bertie's proposal: *"I feel rather depressed."* Bertie came to dinner at eight-thirty, and they talked for three hours. Elizabeth gave no hint—nor did others—that she had regrets about her decision to marry Prince Albert. But she and her family were trying to help James Stuart through his heartbreak.

The drama continued the next day. Elizabeth talked to Mike in her bedroom, and he had lunch with Francis and James. It was on the following day that Mike, Elizabeth, and their mother "talked hard." At that point, James Stuart disappeared for several weeks. He showed up again at Bruton Street one afternoon in early March, when he and Elizabeth "talked hard." Afterward, she went for a solitary walk.

In the weeks before the wedding, James visited Bruton Street a few times. One morning he came to see Mike, and Elizabeth walked to Berkeley Square with him. Another afternoon he stopped in for a cocktail before she and Bertie had dinner with her mother and her brother David.

Meanwhile, James had embarked on a lightning courtship of Elizabeth's beautiful and wealthy friend Lady Rachel Cavendish, a daughter of the Duke and Duchess of Devonshire. He had spent time with her at a house party in October 1921 at Chatsworth, the Devonshire family's vast Derbyshire estate. But James was then in love with Elizabeth Bowes Lyon, and three months later, he had sailed to America. In the interval, Rachel had been a bridesmaid at Princess Mary's wedding in 1922, but a year later, at age twenty-one, she was still unattached. How and where she reconnected with James is unknown, but "it all happened very quickly," said his grandson Dominic. "You could say that it was on the rebound."

Two days before Elizabeth and Bertie's wedding, James and Rachel revealed their engagement at a dinner James hosted in a private dining room at Claridge's. The party of fourteen included Bertie and Elizabeth, James's brother Francis, and the two Bowes Lyon bachelors. They all went to the Hippodrome for some comedy, "then to the Berkeley & danced," Elizabeth wrote. "I was in good form! Went home & talked to Bertie. Then talked to Mike for ages. Bed 3:30."

That evening appeared to be the last time Elizabeth saw James until midsummer. Rachel would attend the royal wedding with her parents, but neither James, nor Francis, nor their mother and father, the Earl and Countess of Moray, were among the 1,780 guests listed in *The Times*. James did send a wedding gift to Elizabeth, however: a diamond and emerald brooch in the shape of an arrow.

ON MARCH 22, ELIZABETH ANNOUNCED her bridesmaids. In addition to the daughters of her sister May and brother Patrick, she named four of her dearest friends: Katie Hamilton, Mary Thynne, Diamond Hardinge, and Betty Cator. The first three were daughters of well-known titled aristocrats (Abercorn, Bath, Hardinge), but Betty (who would marry Elizabeth's brother Mike five years later) was from a less visible family of Norfolk gentry. According to *The Times,* she was descended from "a prominent Quaker in the seventeenth century" as well as "another old English house," the Adeanes of Cambridgeshire.

"Of course do ask Betty Cator to be your bridesmaid," Bertie wrote Elizabeth in mid-March. "I will tell my mother about her & I know she will not mind who you ask, as they must all be who you wish." The Queen raised no objection, but she had her say over the remaining two bridesmaids: her nieces Lady Mary Cambridge, a daughter of Adolphus ("Dolly"), the Marquess of Cambridge, the eldest of the Queen's three younger brothers; and Lady May Cambridge, the daughter of the Queen's youngest brother, Alge, the Earl of Athlone.

Bertie chose two of his brothers, Edward and Henry, to be his "supporters" on his wedding day. "I hope you don't mind my calling you

just plain 'Elizabeth,'" the Prince of Wales wrote the day the engage-
ment was announced. She and Bertie kept convivial company with
Edward over tea, cocktails, dinner, and dancing into the small hours.
Bertie's younger brother George frequently tagged along.

Bertie and Elizabeth saw less of Princess Mary, who was heavily
pregnant and gave birth to a son on February 7 in London. Several
weeks later, they dropped in to see the baby. But they didn't attend the
christening in Yorkshire of the first royal grandchild, George Henry
Hubert, on March 25. Instead, they spent a leisurely weekend at St.
Paul's Walden Bury.

At Queen Mary's suggestion, the King gave Bertie and Elizabeth
White Lodge in Richmond Park on the outer reaches of London for
their marital home. The Queen regarded this royal residence where
she had grown up as a meaningful and generous gift. But even before
the young couple took possession in June, the house was causing friction. As lady-in-waiting Joan Verney wrote to Mabell Airlie, "I do hope
the Strathmores don't dislike it as much as I should!" Although the
house wasn't presented to Elizabeth as a fait accompli, the Queen
called most of the shots on the overall improvements and décor.

White Lodge was a highly impractical combination of elegant and
quirky. Despite Bertie and Elizabeth having it rent-free, the operating
expenses were onerous. All three of its prior occupants had gone bankrupt, starting with Queen Mary's parents, the Duke and Duchess of
Teck, who were able to live there for twenty-eight years only with a
generous royal subsidy.

Built in 1730, White Lodge epitomized the Palladian style of classical simplicity. The main central pavilion featured an impressive
arched and columned front hall and a dramatic curved staircase with
a filigreed iron banister. To the left of the front hall was a light and airy
dining room with a carved coffered ceiling.

Straight ahead through a large doorway was the two-story saloon,
a long rectangular room with an imposing chimneypiece six feet high

and nine feet wide. Its large Venetian window overlooked the White Lodge lawn and oak-lined Queen's Ride leading into Richmond Park's more than two thousand acres. On either side of the saloon were the future sitting rooms for Elizabeth and Bertie.

Elizabeth was impressed by White Lodge on her first visit with Bertie in late January 1923 when they walked around the Dutch garden, topiaries, and ornamental pond. Several days later they had a tour of all the rooms. "I was simply enchanted by it all," she told Queen Mary. "There is nowhere I should like to live more. I have fallen in love with it."

During Bertie and Elizabeth's subsequent seven visits before the wedding, Queen Mary accompanied them on two tiring afternoons. The first time they went over the house twice with architects and had a picnic before examining the basement, which contained the kitchen, servants' rooms, dairy, and storerooms. The second time they joined Queen Mary in one of her favorite activities: labeling furniture that she had gathered from royal collections.

Elizabeth brought her mother and sister May once to have a look around the house, and Cecilia helped select chintz fabrics as well as sofas and chairs. But the Queen asserted her proprietary interest, and her constant meddling irritated Bertie. "I am a hopeless person for worrying about things," he complained to Elizabeth in mid-March about his mother. "My patience was tried very high on one or two occasions, don't you think? All I want is that you should have what you want & that you should get the benefit & pleasure of going round & finding them for yourself & not having things thrust at you by other people. I am sure this is realized now at least by one lady who is kindness itself & is only too ready to help us all she can, but it was all being done in such a dreadfully hurried way when there was no need."

"Don't worry about White Lodge & furniture," Elizabeth replied in her usual upbeat fashion. "I am quite certain we shall make it enchanting—you & I; so please don't fuss yourself little darling. You are such an angel to me always, and I hate to think of you worrying about anything. 'Keep calm and don't be bullied—rest if you can' is my advice!!"

BERTIE AND ELIZABETH'S PRIMARY DUTIES before the wedding involved meeting deputations offering wedding gifts and congratulations in the form of "loyal addresses" at Buckingham Palace. Elizabeth had trouble taking these earnest occasions seriously. "Bertie & I had to stand with the King & Queen whilst 'privileged ladies' read addresses! Some very funny," she confided to her diary in early March. On another morning the Lord Mayor made a presentation from the City of London. "Very pompous," she observed.

After racing around London on too many days and dancing on too many late nights, Elizabeth was feeling exhausted by the middle of March. She had long been plagued by recurrent tonsillitis, which had flared up four days after the proposal weekend. Her physician, Dr. Irwin Moore, treated the condition by cauterizing her tonsils (in her words, having her "throat burnt"), which he did eight times in three months. In the middle of those painful treatments, she came down with a cold.

With Bertie's encouragement, she went to Glamis for three days of rest. "I thought so much of you last night darling," he wrote when she had arrived safely in Scotland early the next morning. "I wished I could have been with you away from this horrible London. . . . I do hope you are not feeling too terribly tired. . . . I think you are a perfect marvel the way you do it darling & always remaining cheerful."

Her reply limned "the morning sun just rising over the Sidlaw hills," which "made the snow on the Grampians look pink & heavenly. . . . It would be more delicious if you were here too. I hate to think of you in horrible London by yourself." Her cold had worsened, but she expected the fresh air at Glamis to cure it. One of her strong beliefs since childhood had been to keep windows open in the bedroom and take bracing walks in the wind to "blow the germs away."

"How I loved your little letter," Bertie wrote the next day. "It did cheer me up so, as I was feeling so lonely without you, & still do though your letter brought me heaps of comfort." They were planning to meet in Edinburgh to watch a rugby match between England and Scotland, tour two factories, and inspect the design for their wedding cake.

"Are you having a real rest at Glamis & not overdoing it writing letters of thanks?" he asked. Why, he wondered, "couldn't we be married first & do all the work afterwards." He wrote of missing her "terribly. . . . I am only existing now while you are away." He couldn't wait until Saturday when "I shall see your sweet little face again all radiant with smiles. And so will mine."

Elizabeth left Glamis on the afternoon of Friday, March 16, for Edinburgh, "very sad. I have loved my three days here," she wrote in her diary. She slept "very little" in her hotel, possibly from nerves. The next morning Bertie and Louis Greig arrived, and Elizabeth experienced the sort of day that would soon be central to her life.

They drove through the streets with Edinburgh's lord provost, surrounded by exuberant crowds. At the McVitie and Price bakery, they approved their four-tier wedding cake "rich with ornamentation." The bottom tier represented the union of the Windsor and Strathmore houses with their combined coats of arms, the second tier was decorated with the Strathmore arms, the third displayed the Duke of York's coat of arms, and the top tier symbolized love and peace.

Their second stop was the Blighty Works, where they met disabled workers trained to manufacture cloth. One worker who had lost a leg gave them tartan plaid traveling blankets that the men had woven and embroidered with Bertie's and Elizabeth's monograms. In thanking them, Bertie said their appreciation was even greater as the men had been "so grievously disabled in their country's service."

The prince had lunch with the rugby teams while Elizabeth dined with her mother at the hotel. The couple were driven down Princes Street to the football field, where thirty thousand fans "gave them a rousing cheer." England narrowly beat Scotland in "one of the most exciting and evenly contested games on record." Yet again the crowd "lustily cheered" as Bertie and Elizabeth left the stadium.

Elizabeth's last royal family ritual before joining their ranks was four days at Windsor Castle after Easter. "I shall always be thinking of you & shall miss you terribly during these days darling, & I do hope you will miss me too," Bertie wrote from Windsor Castle after she left for Easter weekend with her family in Hertfordshire. "Only 4 more weeks darling, & then we can take a rest away from everybody & everything. I wonder how you are looking forward to that time. I know I am very much indeed & I hope you are too. . . . This is the last time I shall be without you my little angel, & I think it is one too many."

In her cheery reply, she joked about Frogmore House in Windsor Home Park, where they would be spending part of their honeymoon. The eighteenth-century royal residence was situated near the family mausoleum designed for Queen Victoria and Prince Albert. "Having never seen Frogmore," she wrote, "I imagine it as a large white Tomb full of frogs!" She wished Bertie was with her: "Why haven't you got a small aeroplane, then you would fly over here for an hour or two."

On Easter Sunday, Bertie wrote, "Another 2 days to go before I shall see you & it seems like years to me. My mother wanted you to stay here till the Monday but I told her you had so much to do Saturday morning in London. Do say you have if she asks you & do let's go to St. Paul's Walden for the weekend as here there is no rest & the day is so marked out into minutes for this thing & the other, which is always such a bore. . . . My father & mother can never understand that we are young & want to get some more exercise than a mere walk in the grounds of the Castle every day."

The problem with his parents' court life, he continued, was that "there is never the question of being asked what you want to do; it is always orders. Life is not as easy as it should be but the change is coming & you my little darling I hope are going to help me with this change. You must take them in hand & teach them how they should do these things."

She arrived at Windsor, and as expected, the customs were more elaborate than at Sandringham. The dinners were similarly white-tie and tails, and diamond-dusted gowns and tiaras. Both the King and the Prince of Wales also wore the "Windsor uniform" dating to George

III: a dark blue tailcoat trimmed with red collar and cuffs, white waistcoat, and knee breeches.

A string orchestra played selections from popular musicals during
the meal, which ended on the dot after an hour. Queen Mary withdrew with the women to the ornate Green Drawing Room for conversation while the men remained at the table for twenty minutes of port
and cigars. Back together in the drawing room, everyone listened to
the gramophone but didn't dance. Promptly at eleven o'clock, the
company stood for the national anthem, then bowed and curtseyed to
the King and Queen, who retired for the evening.

Queen Mary and George V did their best to make Elizabeth feel
welcome. The Queen escorted her son and his fiancée all over the
castle and arranged a tour of the treasures in the Royal Library. As
Bertie had hoped, Elizabeth's blithe spirit leavened the mood, particularly around the King, who appeared quite smitten with her.

George V took special pride in showing Elizabeth around his apartment filled with photographs and lithographs of friends and relatives.
The King even played some gramophone records for his future
daughter-in-law. After dinner on the second night, there was "much
chaff," Elizabeth wrote approvingly of his famous teasing.

The clearest evidence of her position as the King's favorite was his
indulgence of her chronic tardiness. Queen Mary had painful memories of her father's fury over her mother's inattention to the clock, and
George V had watched his father seethe when Queen Alexandra kept
him waiting, often for spite. As a result, the King and Queen were
both sticklers for punctuality down to the minute.

Elizabeth meant no harm when she lingered too long in conversation or was otherwise occupied and lost track of the time. According
to legend, in the early days of her royal life, Elizabeth arrived two minutes late to luncheon. As she offered her apologies to the monarch, he
was said to have replied, "You are not late, my dear. I think we must
have sat down two minutes early."

Having run the Windsor gauntlet, the couple made their prearranged escape after staying only three nights. They stopped briefly

for lunch at Bruton Street before driving to St. Paul's Walden Bury for the weekend. There they "ragged about" and had a generally idle time with Mike and David Bowes Lyon.

In the last weeks before the wedding day, photographs and descriptions of the couple's thousands of gifts filled Britain's newspapers and magazines. *The Times* featured long lists in seven editions beginning on March 23. The presents ranged from small but precious objects—a dozen gold fruit knives from the King and Queen and Crown Prince of Norway, a gold cigarette case from the King and Queen of Spain—to furniture the couple requested to fill the many rooms and long corridors at White Lodge.

The most eye-catching of all was the jewelry presented to Elizabeth by George V and Queen Mary. The King gave her an exquisite diamond and turquoise tiara with matching bracelet, brooch, hair ornaments, earrings, and necklace. From Queen Mary she received an intricately wrought sapphire and diamond necklace with matching bracelet, ring, brooches, and pendant. In a fitting royal gesture, the King also gave his future daughter-in-law an ermine cape.

The Strathmores gave their daughter jewelry they had purchased at Catchpole and Williams. Claude's gifts were a diamond bandeau and a rope necklace of pearls and diamonds. From Cecilia, she received a long platinum chain of pearls and diamonds with a matching bracelet.

Bertie gave his bride-to-be a diamond and pearl necklace with a matching pendant, along with a Cartier diamond wristwatch. She gave him a platinum watch chain with pearls that they had selected together at Cartier.

On Saturday, April 21, Elizabeth motored to St. Paul's Walden Bury for two final nights as a single woman at her childhood home. Her parents were there, along with David, Mike, Jock, and Fenella. She took long walks all around the Bury Wood with her father and three brothers, and a separate stroll with her mother and David. "Feel very odd & sad leaving home," she wrote in her diary.

She arrived at Bruton Street that Monday to see a large crowd beginning to gather. There was a rehearsal in the Abbey in the late afternoon, followed by an evening party at Buckingham Palace—the first of three pre-wedding receptions. On Tuesday there would be a "servants' party," and on the wedding eve, an afternoon party for eight hundred "donors of presents and personal friends of the bride and bridegroom." Each party introduced Elizabeth to a ritual she would undertake regularly for the next eight decades: shaking hundreds of hands and making relentless small talk.

The Monday-night gathering was the most elaborate and formal. The band of the Irish Guards played, and refreshments were available at buffet tables in the State Dining Room. The main event was the display of gifts in the Picture Gallery lined with paintings by Holbein, Rembrandt, Rubens, and Canaletto. Some six hundred guests— members of the diplomatic corps and donors of wedding presents— thronged through all the state rooms. "Elizabeth looked so pretty in pink," the Queen noted in her diary.

The scene was captured by seventy-year-old Herbert Henry Asquith, who had served as the Liberal Party's prime minister for eight years before the war. Asquith arrived after dinner in his tailcoat, knee breeches, and medals, and made his way up the grand staircase with its gilded balustrade. He described "huge glass cases like you see in Bond Street shops, filled with jewels and every kind of gilt and silver ware: not a thing did I see that I would have cared to have or give."

Then the dyspeptic veteran politician spotted the "poor little bride," reputed to be "full of charm." On this night, she "stood in a row with the King and Queen and the bridegroom, and was completely overshadowed." Yet Elizabeth Bowes Lyon's apparent fragility was an illusion. She gave no evidence—yet—of the outsize force she would become, for the future King George VI, for the royal family, and for the British nation and its empire.

"Bertie smiled at me when I got up to him
& it all went off well."

The wedding of Prince Albert and Elizabeth Bowes Lyon in Westminster
Abbey, April 26, 1923: the bride and bridegroom at the chancel rails, with the
Archbishop of Canterbury officiating.

ELEVEN

A Gilded Carriage

ON HIS WEDDING EVE, PRINCE ALBERT AND HIS THREE BROTHERS DINED formally with their parents at Buckingham Palace, his last night in the rooms he had occupied for thirteen years. Over at Bruton Street, Lady Elizabeth Bowes Lyon "felt terribly moved" as she said good night to "the darling boys & Mother." She retired at eleven P.M., and slept more than nine hours.

She rose late on the momentous morning of Thursday, April 26, 1923, at eight-thirty, and she didn't begin dressing until ten. With its square neckline, her ethereal wedding gown intentionally harked to medieval times, suitable for a ceremony in a great abbey dating to the eleventh century. *The Times* proclaimed it "the simplest ever made for a Royal wedding."

Its chiffon moiré was tinted ivory to match the Flanders lace veil that Queen Mary had presented to Elizabeth at Buckingham Palace. A strip of Brussels lace, a Strathmore family heirloom, formed a panel down the front of the gown. The bodice featured silver lamé bands embroidered with pearls and pearl beads, threaded with silver. An accent of pale green tulle swept to the ground, pinned to the bodice by a silver thistle and white rose. One silk net train edged in lace flowed from Elizabeth's shoulders; a second, shorter train fell from her waist. Elizabeth's lace veil covered her hair like a gossamer prayer cap pulled down to her dark eyebrows. Instead of a tiara, she secured the veil with a wreath of myrtle leaves (symbolizing love and constancy), adorned with a white rose on either side of her temple.

Elizabeth was ready on the dot at 11:12 A.M., when she and her father stepped across the pavement at Bruton Street into a horse-drawn state coach decorated with the Strathmore arms. Two attendants in black greatcoats and plumed bicornes saluted smartly, and Elizabeth beamed a "frank smile of pleasure, and almost of surprise" at the welcoming crowds. Off they went, escorted by a detachment of four police officers on white horses, traveling at a rapid clip through Hyde Park Corner, down Constitution Hill, past the gates to Green Park, and down the Mall to appreciative roars.

Threatening weather compelled the soldiers from the Grenadier, Coldstream, Scots, and Welsh Guards lining the route to the Abbey to wear their gray overcoats, denying Elizabeth the sight of the "double line of vivid scarlet" that she had seen a year earlier as Princess Mary's bridesmaid. An estimated one million people crowded the sidewalks and parks and cheered loudly, undeterred by the morning's intermittent rain. Among them were numerous Americans who had booked most of London's hotel rooms. At a time of straitened economic conditions, George V had decided against decorating the Mall, although blue and white pylons erected outside Westminster Abbey were festooned with garlands of greenery. Stands were built nearby, with admission tickets sold to benefit two charities.

By the time sixty-eight-year-old Lord Strathmore and his twenty-two-year-old daughter pulled up to the Abbey shortly before eleven-thirty, everyone else had settled into their places. The King and Queen had arrived in a gilded carriage. He wore the uniform of Admiral of the Fleet festooned with epaulettes, aiguillettes, medals, and orders. She wore a layered creation of aquamarine and silver, ornamented with lace and showers of aquamarine crystals, and a matching turban. They were accompanied by the entire royal family, from Queen Alexandra down.

Sixty-year-old Cecilia Strathmore led her own extended family. Even for her youngest daughter's wedding, she wore her habitual somber attire: black marocain and georgette embroidered in jet and blue paillettes, with a cloak of black lace and morocain. Her only concessions to color were large blue fabric roses on her collar, and blue osprey feathers on her black hat.

The sun had broken through the thick clouds when Elizabeth and Claude Strathmore alighted from the coach and walked inside the Great West Door. She knew the path she would follow through the vast nave, having walked it three days earlier in the rehearsal. She also may have had in her mind's eye the most arresting moment on Princess Mary's wedding day: the impromptu pause by the Cenotaph when the new bride broke off a piece of her bouquet to be placed among the tributes to the war dead.

Within several minutes, two unexpected occurrences momentarily derailed the precision timings for Elizabeth's nuptials. A large beadle in a flowing red gown quietly approached the bride, proffering a dainty white object: a small bag, likely for her handkerchief, that she had left in the carriage. She accepted the bag with a grateful smile and then moved ahead of her father.

In front of her, some twenty steps from the door, was a black marble stone embedded in the floor and inscribed in gold. It marked the grave of the Unknown Warrior, representing "the many multitudes who during the Great War of 1914–1918 gave the most that man can give." The burial "among the Kings" at the Abbey had taken place on Armistice Day in 1920 in the presence of King George V after he had earlier unveiled the Cenotaph memorial.

Historical records have not revealed whether Elizabeth anticipated her next move, or whether she spontaneously thought of her brother Fergus's death at Loos, the soldiers at Glamis dispatched to the front who never returned, and so many other men she had known who had perished on the battlefields. She leaned over and gently placed her bridal bouquet of white roses on the tomb. Elizabeth already had a flair for the dramatic and meaningful gesture. This one would set a poignant precedent: Every royal bride married in Westminster Abbey—from Elizabeth's daughter the future Queen Elizabeth II, to Kate Middleton, the future Queen Catherine—would lay her bouquet on the tomb.

Elizabeth then took her father's arm for the procession. Ahead of them were the men's choir of the Abbey in red cassocks, and the boys of the Chapels Royal choir, wearing their seventeenth-century state uniform of red tunics banded with black and gold. They all sang "Lead us, Heavenly Father, lead us."

Father and daughter began their long walk through the nave, Lord Strathmore's scarlet uniform making "the white and green of the bride look all the fresher and sweeter." Behind them were the eight bridesmaids in sheer white chiffon floating over dresses of Nottingham lace. Their sashes were pale green tulle fastened with silver and white roses and sprays of white heather. Four strands of silver lamé leaves trailed from their waists to mid-calf. Across their foreheads were narrow bandeaux of myrtle leaves and heather with pink roses on either side. They all wore Bertie's special gift: a crystal and diamond brooch carved to resemble the "York Rose," and monogrammed with "E" and "A." In their arms they held large sheaves of white roses and heather.

In keeping with George V's efforts to avoid excessive display, there were nearly one thousand fewer people in the congregation than at Princess Mary's wedding. But the splendor of the scene that greeted Elizabeth was undeniable. Along with the dazzle of diamonds, rubies, emeralds, and sapphires removed by women from family vaults for these occasions, the sartorial arrangements of the men strikingly evoked the kingdom's history: the scarlet and gold military dress uniforms; the high-collar jackets of the dark blue court uniform—richly decorated with gold oak-leaf embroidery from collar to gauntlet cuff; the "gleaming Roman helmets and high white coque mounts"; the swords and pikes; the polished medals; the tightly curled wigs and capacious gowns of the law lords. The clergymen wore elaborate vestments: the Archbishop of Canterbury in a multicolored cope, the

Primus of Scotland in green, the Archbishop of York in white and red, the Bishop of London in yellow and pale green. The sunshine now streaming through the stained-glass windows gave it all an extra glow.

High up under the arches of the triforium stood fifty-two lucky boys with an eagle-eye view. Some of them had attended the Duke of York's summer camps. Twenty came from boys' clubs around London and thirty from industrial centers. All had been specially invited by Prince Albert to represent his interest in the Industrial Welfare Society. It was a hopeful modern gesture.

At the eastern end of the Abbey, the great and good were seated in the north and south transepts and into the crossing, up to the edge of the carpeted aisle where Elizabeth and her father would soon appear. The prominent Conservative politician Duff Cooper and his wife, Lady Diana, were pleased to have "very good seats," with Freda Dudley Ward and her husband immediately behind.

The families of the bride and bridegroom faced each other in the brightly illuminated sanctuary—the sacrarium—bounded by a wrought iron chancel rail at the top of five steps. They all sat in white and gold chairs, the King and Queen and their closest relatives on the south side, the Strathmores on the north. Behind them was the magnificent high altar, covered with richly embellished tapestries and arrayed with gold sacred vessels, gleaming plate, and flickering candles. Around them were ancient paintings and banners, as well as the throne of the Dean of Westminster. In that sumptuous sacred setting, flowers would have been superfluous.

Prince Albert, in his gray-blue uniform of a group captain in the Royal Air Force—a first for a royal wedding—stood near the rail with the Prince of Wales in his scarlet Grenadier Guards tunic and Prince Henry in a handsome deep blue uniform of the Tenth Royal Hussars. Queen Alexandra found the groom so irresistible that she rose up and kissed him. Bertie seemed unsettled for a moment as he noticed something askew with the cushions where he and Elizabeth would kneel. He had a word with his brother David, who chuckled and stepped forward to rearrange them.

The bride and her father passed through the ornate gilded screen of the choir and walked between the side-facing rows of pews filled with choirboys and men as well as members of the diplomatic corps in scarlet uniforms trimmed with gold lace, and government ministers in tailcoats or frock coats, breeches, silk stockings, and buckled shoes. The ailing Prime Minister Andrew Bonar Law attended, only weeks away from his resignation due to terminal throat cancer. Nearby in the stalls were his predecessors Asquith and Lloyd George, as well as his successor Stanley Baldwin, leaders of the Labour Party, and Winston Churchill, "in his best form and really amusing," according to Asquith.

Traversing the choir toward the crossing, Elizabeth finally saw Prince Albert, who faced her "with shining eyes and a look of happiness." "Did not feel very nervous," she wrote in her diary that evening. "Bertie smiled at me when I got up to him & it all went off well." As Bertie later confided to his mother, "I was very nervous about it until it was over." The Queen gazed at her son "very kindly and proudly," noted *The Times,* and "the King's eyes never left his second son, sending him silent messages."

The ceremony of marriage—"so brief, so momentous"—that unfolded in the sacrarium cast a spell of unusual intimacy. The bride and bridegroom stood by the rail at the top of the steps, facing the Archbishop of Canterbury, with Lord Strathmore to Elizabeth's left. The rest of the clergy were clustered behind the archbishop. The family tableaux had an enveloping air. "When you are at the top, it feels like a very small church," recalled Jock Bowes Lyon's granddaughter Lady Elizabeth Anson, who was married there five decades later. "It is lovely for the couple, the most extraordinary feeling that you are getting married with forty or so people in two rows of chairs."

After the couple said their vows, the Prince of Wales produced the simple ring for Bertie to slip on the fourth finger of Elizabeth's left hand: twenty-two-carat gold fashioned from a nugget mined in a tiny North Wales village. The archbishop blessed them both, and they went forward as man and wife to kneel at the altar for further prayers.

Once the choir had sung a psalm, the Archbishop of York, Cosmo Lang, delivered a short address of "homely sentiment and advice."

To the Duke of York, he said, "You, sir, have already given many proofs of your care for the welfare of our working people." To the new Duchess of York, he said, "Dear bride, in your old Scottish home, [you] have grown up from childhood among country folk, and friendship with them has been your native air." He urged them both to "resolve to make this wedded life of yours a blessing not only to yourselves but to others, not least to those who, in a world of toil and struggle, have most need of help and care."

Following the hymn, "Praise My Soul, the King of Heaven," the final prayers, the blessing, and the "Amen" of Orlando Gibbons, the service concluded with the congregation's full-throated first verse of "God Save the King." Bertie and Elizabeth, the King and Queen, the Strathmores, and several other family members disappeared through the door in the screen behind the altar to the tomb of King Edward the Confessor.

There, on an ancient oak table, they signed the wedding registers as well as the book that records all the births, marriages, and deaths of royal family members. One gold pen, designed as an old-fashioned quill, had been a gift to Bertie from the Institute of Chartered Secretaries. On presenting it to him a week earlier, they had asked him to use it for signing the register. And so he did.

The newlyweds and members of their respective families returned to the sacrarium as the last verse of the anthem "Beloved, Let Us Love One Another" was sung. Bertie and Elizabeth held hands and smiled at the Duchess of Strathmore, whose eyes were brimming with tears. She thought her daughter looked "so dignified & restful, just her own sweet little self as usual." As the couple turned to the King and Queen, Bertie bowed and Elizabeth dropped a tidy curtsey. Down the aisle they walked to Mendelssohn's classic "Wedding March," followed by the bridesmaids, the clergy, officers of the royal household, and the two newly joined families.

For their journey to Buckingham Palace, they rode in a scarlet and gold coach with a mounted escort of Life Guards in red tunics, the sunshine glinting off their white-plumed helmets. Elizabeth had traveled that road little over an hour earlier as an aristocratic commoner. Now she was Her Royal Highness the Duchess of York, with the status of a princess.

They crossed Parliament Square into Whitehall, where the coach paused for the duke's solemn salute at the Cenotaph, a complement to Elizabeth's earlier gesture in the Abbey. Through tumultuous crowds waving thousands of flags and white handkerchiefs, they rode along Horse Guards Parade into the Mall, turning right at Marlborough Gate. On St. James's Street, bunting decorated the stately gentlemen's clubs, and women made a rare appearance to cheer from the windows. The newlyweds drove down Piccadilly, where nearly every building was covered with flags and decorations. They bowed over and over to the immense roars at Hyde Park Corner and along Constitution Hill before they made their final turn into the forecourt of the Palace.

Some forty-five minutes later, the jubilant couple stepped onto the Palace balcony draped with crimson and gold cloth. It was the first time Elizabeth had seen such a multitude, stretching from the Palace railings all the way up the Mall, spilling into Green Park and St. James's Park. After the initial round of cheers, the King, the Queen, Queen Alexandra, her daughter, Princess Louise, and her granddaughter, Princess Maud, joined them for five minutes. When their elders stepped back inside, Elizabeth acknowledged the roaring throng by saying "Thank you, thank you, thank you," as Bertie gamely waved.

A party of sixty-six family members and intimate friends gathered in the State Dining Room for the wedding breakfast, with nearly sixty more seated in the Ball Supper Room. The menu comprised eight courses—a significant reduction from the standard royal fare of sixteen or eighteen courses two decades earlier. It included *consommé à la Windsor, supremes de saumon Reine Mary, cotelettes d'agneau Prince Albert, chapons à la Strathmore,* and *fraises Duchesse Elizabeth.* According to custom, there were no speeches. At the end of the meal, the King raised his glass for a simple toast:

"I ask you to drink to the health, long lives, and happiness of the bride and bridegroom."

In the Blue Drawing Room stood the nine-foot-high, nine-hundred-pound wedding cake, which Elizabeth ceremonially cut with a silver knife. She and Bertie then slipped away to change into their traveling clothes. Elizabeth was joined first by her mother, with Jock and Fenella's daughter Anne. Following them came Lord Strathmore, May and Rosie, Mike and David. "Awful saying goodbye," Elizabeth later wrote in her diary.

The families and their principal guests made their way to the inner quadrangle. On cue, an open landau drawn by four gray horses pulled up to the Grand Entrance, and the duke and duchess appeared at four-fifteen for the drive to Waterloo station. She wore a dress of embroidered gray crepe with a coat wrap in the same soft shade. Her small brown hat had an upturned brim to ensure the people could see her face.

The guests at the doorway bade them farewell while Princes Edward, George, and Henry waited with the bridesmaids by the archway into the forecourt. As the carriage passed, the Prince of Wales led a bombardment of confetti at the couple in the carriage, while the Queen, Princess Mary, and Princess Toria showered them with rose petals from the balcony above. Two top-hatted postilions stood at the back of the carriage, which was followed by an escort of Life Guards on horseback.

After several earlier waves of heavy showers, the weather broke favorably again. Bertie and Elizabeth drove through more cheering crowds and across Westminster Bridge. Potted palms, hydrangeas, and rhododendrons decorated the Waterloo platform where they boarded a special "saloon carriage" attached to an ordinary local train. The seats were upholstered in gold brocade, and there were arrangements of white roses, white heather, white carnations, and lilies of the valley. Before the train pulled away, one of the postilions hurriedly brought in an old pair of shoes that had been thrown into the carriage at the Palace.

Writing in his diary that evening, King George V judged the service "very fine," the arrangements "admirable," and the Archbishop of York's address "beautiful." Once the bride and bridegroom left the Palace, the King attended to that day's boxes of government documents. Queen Mary's assessment of the day was equally spare. The service was "beautiful," the address was "charming," and the departure of "the young people" was "a splendid send-off. G & I dined quietly at home."

On disembarking at Bookham in Surrey, Albert and Elizabeth faced more cheers, this time from villagers and officials. The chairman of the parish council made a short welcoming speech, and a little girl gave the bride a bouquet of heather and roses of York tied with a ribbon of tartan. With that, they disappeared in their car past the hedgerows and through the gates of Mrs. Ronnie Greville's Polesden Lacey estate, the first stop on their honeymoon.

"Above everything I love his really worshipping you."

Bertie and Elizabeth strolling in a woody glade on their honeymoon at Polesden Lacey, owned by hostess Maggie Greville.

TWELVE

A Splendid Partner

FOR THE THREE YEARS UNTIL THE ARRIVAL OF THEIR FIRST DAUGHTER IN
April 1926, the Duke and Duchess of York coasted through married
life at a leisurely pace that included a five-month safari holiday in East
Africa. Bertie carried out his duties representing his father and pursu-
ing his role as "the Industrial Prince." Elizabeth, who would later be
known as a paragon of dutifulness, showed little initial enthusiasm for
the traditional royal rounds. The spotlight invariably shone on the
Prince of Wales, who increasingly led a double life of public adulation
and private misbehavior that was already grating on the King and
Queen by the time of Bertie's marriage.

George V and Queen Mary were thrilled by Elizabeth, who
blended into the family even as she enlivened it. From Polesden Lacey,
Bertie wrote effusively to "my dearest Papa," thanking him for "all your
kindness," and for "allowing me to marry Elizabeth. . . . We are both so
glad we are married at last."

"I am quite certain that Elizabeth will be a splendid partner in
your work & share with you & help you in all you have to do," replied
the King. He praised his son for having "endeared yourself to the

people" by "your quiet useful work." He expressed his gratitude that Bertie had "always been so sensible & easy to work with." But he pressed the inevitable thumb by adding, "You have always been ready to listen to my advice & to agree with my opinions about people & things." Pointedly, and almost prophetically, he wrote, "I feel that we have always got on very well together (very different to dear David)."

Bertie was more expansive to his "darling Mama." Touchingly, he said, "I hope you will not miss me very much, though I believe you will as I have stayed with you so much longer really than the brothers. I am very very happy now with my little darling so perhaps our parting yesterday was made easier for me but still I did feel a pang at leaving my home."

The next day the Queen thanked Bertie "with all my heart" for his sweet letter. "<u>You</u> will of course be much missed by Papa and me. . . . You have always been such a good son that we shall miss you in so many ways, as we always turned to you in difficulties, knowing how reliable you always are." But she added that "the pang of parting with you my much beloved boy was much softened by the knowledge that your darling Elizabeth will make you such a perfect little wife."

Elizabeth wrote to Lady Strathmore, her "Darling Angel," in a flood of emotion: "I felt so worried about you," for fear that she would be exhausted by all the activity since January. "I could not <u>ever</u> have said it to you—but you know I love you more than anybody in the world, mother, and you do know it, don't you? Bertie adores you too, & he is being too marvellous to me, & so thoughtful. He really is a darling—I hope you all like him."

Lady Strathmore's reply was equally confessional: "I won't say what it means to me to give you up to Bertie—but I think you know that you are by <u>far</u> [underlined twice] the most precious of my children, & always will be. I do <u>love</u> Bertie—& think very highly of his <u>character</u>, but above everything I love his really worshipping you, & I go on telling myself that when I get low about you."

Bertie reassured his "darling" mother-in-law that he loved

Elizabeth and that he would "always take care of her. I do hope you will not look upon me as a thief in having taken her from you. I know only too well what Elizabeth is to you, & to me she is everything." Cecilia replied that she felt "at peace about you & my darling Elizth who I know is so very happy with you."

Behind Cecilia Strathmore's joy over her daughter's match with a son of the King, she felt genuinely stricken by her loss. "What shall I do without my darling little girl I cannot imagine," she told her friend Mollie Cazalet. "However Bertie is as dear & kind to me as if he was my own son." To Fergus's widow Christian, Cecilia wrote, "I cannot tell you what she has been to me—never once a cross word in her whole life & such a sympathetic & loving help to me."

It turned out that Cecilia's apprehensions were unwarranted. Elizabeth's sprawling family would remain firmly in her life, and she would keep her mother close. Elizabeth would spend far more time at Bruton Street than at Buckingham Palace, despite Queen Mary having assiduously prepared an apartment for the couple's use in London. "I hope you will remember that your 'suite' of rooms here will always be ready when you want to come to us," she wrote to Bertie two days after the wedding.

The Queen even spent time arranging pictures in the room she had set aside for the duchess and told Bertie she had made the décor "as nice as possible" for his new wife. But to Elizabeth, "Buck House" (royal sibling slang first noted in her diary shortly after her engagement) was for formal events and periodic lunches and dinners with the King and Queen. When they were living out in Richmond at White Lodge, and Elizabeth needed to have a cup of tea or change into a ball gown after a busy day in London, she returned to her family home.

The newlyweds spent six uninterrupted days at Polesden Lacey. In a letter to Louis Greig on the first night, Bertie reported on his conjugal success: "Everything was plain sailing, which was a relief," he wrote. "You know what I mean. I was very good!!" Bertie's comfort in sharing such an intimate moment revealed how close he remained to his friend and mentor.

Although the Yorks had frequently been entertained by Maggie Greville at her London mansion, this was Elizabeth's first visit to the Surrey estate where Albert had spent country weekends since 1919. Its opulent Edwardian interiors featured paintings by Raeburn, Lawrence, and Reynolds. The drawing room was "an ornately carved masterpiece in gilt, mirror, and velvet." Maggie's legendary collection of silver and porcelain filled every room.

Elizabeth saw through Mrs. Greville's assiduous social networking, but she didn't mind. Years later, she summed her up as "so shrewd, so kind and so amusingly <u>un</u>kind, so sharp, such fun, so naughty . . . altogether a real person, a character, utterly Mrs. Ronald Greville and no tinge of anything alien."

What mattered most to Maggie was the ultimate compliment Bertie sent straight to the top. "Mrs Greville has made us <u>so</u> comfortable," he wrote to King George V. They stayed in the "King's Suite," one of seven such guest accommodations that boasted the unusual luxury of en suite bathrooms. They had breakfast in bed and read the newspapers. In the afternoons they sat in the sunshine, took leisurely strolls through the fourteen hundred acres of gardens, lawns, and woodlands, and played golf on the estate's nine-hole course.

On the fourth day, a photographer from *The Illustrated London News* turned up to take pictures of them on the terrace, walking through a "woody glade," relaxing on a "rustic seat," and putting on the links. Bertie even posed as he played out of a bunker. In the evenings, they listened to the gramophone, wrote letters, and fell asleep before midnight.

The Yorks returned to London on Monday, May 7, for a turnaround visit before taking the night train to Scotland. They had Glamis to themselves, which was "delicious," Elizabeth told Beryl Poignand, despite the weather: "icy cold—snow—hail & sleet!" Whenever they could, they spent time outdoors shooting rabbits with rifles. From the first day in Scotland, Elizabeth felt unusually tired, and she soon developed a cough that progressed from "troublesome" to "worrying" to "beastly." After little more than a week, they were back in London. One doctor gave Elizabeth cough mixtures, and Louis Greig prescribed some pills.

Since White Lodge wasn't yet ready for occupancy, the King let them stay at Frogmore House near Windsor Castle for the next three weeks—longer than originally anticipated for the third leg of their honeymoon. Bertie had fond memories of Frogmore, where his mother would escape with her children while George V was away shooting or yachting or watching the races at Newmarket and Goodwood.

The three-story Georgian house features a creamy colonnaded façade and a row of arched French doors on the central pavilion. Its windows overlook the picturesque serpentine lake, a central feature of the romantic gardens laid out in the late eighteenth century with a network of paths winding through cedars and weeping willows. When Bertie and Elizabeth arrived in late May 1923, the purple lilac and yellow laburnum were in full, fragrant bloom. Elizabeth called it "a heavenly place."

Despite her persistent cough, they yielded to Prince Edward's temptation when he visited Frogmore on the fourth day. Up they went to London in David's car for dinner and a dance at the Embassy Club—described by P. G. Wodehouse as "the smartest, most exclusive supper place in London, posh to the eyebrows. . . . It was a very exceptional evening when you could throw a brick in it without beaning some member of the royal family."

Among the large party organized by Prince Paul were none other than David's mistress Freda Dudley Ward, and Sheila Loughborough, Bertie's former lover. They all "danced hard till 2:30," Elizabeth wrote in her diary. "David sent us back in his car. Very tired & enjoyed it awfully. Coughed a good deal."

Three days later, on May 25, a royal doctor diagnosed Elizabeth with whooping cough. "The cure for it is rest & quiet," Bertie wrote to his mother, begging off her fifty-sixth birthday luncheon with the family the next day at Buckingham Palace. "How she got it mystifies us . . .

as we had not seen anyone with it." He figured she might have caught it before the wedding when she was tired and run-down. "It is so unromantic to catch whooping cough on your honeymoon—!!"

On doctor's orders, Elizabeth was put under quarantine for three weeks. She would miss the annual Trooping the Colour parade in honor of the King's birthday on June 3, and she had the perfect excuse to finesse Royal Ascot, which she had long disliked.

White Lodge was ready for them on June 6, and together they "arranged things" around the house. The duke's ground-floor sitting room had a book-lined alcove, comfortable sofa, upholstered chairs, and desk as well as a gramophone and cumbersome "radio apparatus," showing his "interest in that latest wonder of science, broadcasting." Elizabeth's sitting room on the other side of the drawing room featured a Chippendale breakfront containing a collection of her objets d'art behind its glass doors. The elegant, airy, and uncluttered ambiance was the antithesis of York Cottage.

Elizabeth didn't see George V and Queen Mary again until the end of June, when the Yorks went to luncheon at Buckingham Palace. Two days later, on June 28, Bertie and Elizabeth apprehensively reciprocated at White Lodge. "I had better warn you that our cook is not very good," the duke wrote to his mother. "She can do the plain dishes well, & I know you like that sort." In typical Queen Mary fashion, she and the King "went all over the house." They agreed that White Lodge looked "so nice with all their presents."

ELIZABETH HAD HER FIRST ROYAL rite of passage that summer when the Yorks accompanied the King and Queen for their annual visit to Holyrood Palace in Edinburgh. Bertie and Elizabeth accompanied the monarch and consort on two busy rounds of engagements, with eight stops on one day and a half dozen on another. During their visit to a medical clinic in Dunfermline founded by philanthropist Andrew Carnegie, Elizabeth showed a glimmer of her talent for connecting with people in crowds. She spotted a military veteran she had known at Glamis during the war and approached him to shake hands and have a chat—an exchange captured by an alert reporter.

Back in England, Elizabeth had a light schedule of official duties. The expectations for her in those first years of marriage were fairly low. She inherited an assortment of health and welfare patronages and lent her name to highlight their work and raise money. She accompanied the duke on tours around London and further afield in Liverpool and Manchester, watching him cut ribbons, present prizes, and unveil plaques.

Her most meaningful show of support for Prince Albert was her visit with him in early August 1923 to the third Duke of York's Camp at New Romney. Dressed informally—he in a light gray suit and bareheaded, she in a simple beige dress and cloche hat—they arrived on the camp's fourth day after the four hundred boys aged seventeen to nineteen had finished their morning competitions. As the boys cheered their arrival, "smiles of real gratification were returned by the two chief visitors."

In the afternoon, they watched the campers play games for nearly three hours. As they left, Bertie praised the camp's continuing success, and Elizabeth received a large basket of white roses. She would not see the camp again until it convened at Balmoral only weeks before the outbreak of World War II.

Prince Albert would return to the camp for a day every year, "not only the founder and inspirer of it all, but an active member, following the same routine, and wearing the same clothes . . . playing the same games, yelling himself hoarse . . . throwing himself heart and soul into everything," recalled John Cornwell, one of the camp leaders. For the "Great Chief," as Bertie was known to the campers, "restraints, etiquette, the awful burden of Royalty, are laid aside," wrote another staff member. "He can really let himself go. We know him as a man."

THE FRILLS AND DUTIES AND flummery aside, Bertie and Elizabeth were mainly interested in settling in as a newly married couple. They were sociable but modest, having fun together and with friends and family. Elizabeth watched her husband play polo, and they took full advantage of the White Lodge lawn tennis court. Bertie usually played with Louis Greig, his coach and partner for nearly a decade.

White Lodge—nicknamed "Whiters" by Elizabeth soon after they moved in—initially offered some advantages to the young couple. They had more freedom to roam in the vastness of Richmond Park than they would in London. They were also able to entertain informally with small luncheons and tea parties. One of their visitors that first summer was a Russian artist named Savely Sorine, who painted in watercolor on paper.

Elizabeth did four sittings for Sorine, beginning on July 20. Her first portrait as Duchess of York shows her wearing a plain white dress with a small ruffled collar, a green-beribboned straw hat slung from her right arm. Her wrists are demurely crossed on her lap, her only adornments a long double strand of pearls and her large sapphire and diamond engagement ring. Her expression is winsome, her eyes hinting melancholy, her pale skin showing a slight blush on the cheeks.

The composition was well under way for her penultimate sitting on Saturday, August 4, Elizabeth's twenty-third birthday. Bertie was off playing polo, and Elizabeth spent an hour with Sorine in the morning, resuming after lunch until the late afternoon. "Felt depressed," she wrote in her diary.

Far north that day at the Duke and Duchess of Devonshire's Chatsworth estate, James Stuart and Rachel Cavendish were being married. Many of Elizabeth's friends were in the congregation, among them Arthur Penn, as well as her brother Michael. She and Bertie sent a set of six cut-glass decanters as a wedding gift, and the King and Queen gave Rachel a blue enamel brooch adorned with "G and M" in diamonds. Elizabeth's only comment about the marriage in her diary was "hope it will be alright."

Her absence from the nuptials by no means signaled an end to their friendship. She and Bertie continued to see James and Rachel socially, including visits to Balmoral after he took the throne. Elizabeth even became a godmother to James and Rachel's son John. But her apprehensions about the marriage were prescient, as he was openly unfaithful. Rachel remained loyal, even in the face of scandal, and they stayed married.

James went on to a highly successful career as a member of Parliament for nearly thirty-six years. He served as chief whip for Prime Minister Winston Churchill during World War II and as secretary of state for Scotland in the 1950s. In his memoir, James mentioned Elizabeth only once, recounting how he had introduced her to Bertie at the RAF Ball. "He had the ability to be close to important people," his grandson Dominic observed. "People trusted him. He was quite discreet."

Elizabeth's affection for James never dimmed. When he turned seventy in 1967, she invited him to Clarence House, her London home, to celebrate over a drink. She surprised him by inviting all his closest male friends as well. "She dispensed with her servants and served everyone herself," said Dominic Stuart. "He was touched. He was very fond of her and highly patriotic." James died four years later at age seventy-four, and Rachel died six years after that. Elizabeth would long outlive them both.

"Elizabeth I hope is not too bored here."

The Duke and Duchess of York with Queen Mary at Balmoral in September 1924.

THIRTEEN

Family Affairs

ELIZABETH MADE HER BALMORAL DEBUT ON SATURDAY, SEPTEMBER 1, 1923, for a stay of two weeks. She would eventually grow to adore the twenty-five-thousand-acre estate bounded by the River Dee—Royal Deeside, as it was known. But in the beginning, she fled when she could to the informality of Glamis.

With its riot of tartan on walls, upholstery, carpets, and even linoleum, Balmoral was more stoutly Scottish than her own family's castle. She knew that Bertie treasured Balmoral with the same intensity as Queen Victoria and her beloved consort, Prince Albert. After they bought the estate in 1848, the Prince Consort knocked down the "pretty little castle in the old Scottish style" and replaced it in 1855 with a white granite schloss (turned gray over time) of a Scots baronial design that featured turrets and an imposing tower. The castle's many large windows had stunning views of gardens, lawns, the silvery ribbon of the Dee snaking through the wide valley, the surrounding hills crowded with Caledonian pine trees, and the distant Cairngorm Mountains. The highest point within the estate was the craggy peak of Lochnagar.

Just inside the castle entrance, a full-sized statue of the Prince Consort stood in the front hall. Queen Mary had stripped the dark ginger varnish from the woodwork to reveal natural pine paneling, which lightened the interior. But otherwise, the surroundings were only slightly altered from Queen Victoria's day. The drawing room had a fine bow window, and its walls were covered with paintings of Queen Victoria, the Prince Consort, assorted children, and ghillies (the estate's hunting and fishing scouts), all by the Victorian artist Sir Edwin Landseer. Carefully positioned with its back to the window was a small tartan armchair reserved for Queen Victoria. Bertie would have warned his wife that nobody else was ever allowed to sit there, not even Victoria's successor monarchs.

King George V enjoyed his time at Balmoral, especially for the deer stalking, but he mainly shot grouse on his friends' estates around Britain. While Queen Mary put on a good show, "the truth was she didn't like Scotland," Elizabeth confided to James Pope-Hennessy. Asked about Balmoral specifically, Prince Henry told his mother's biographer that she "loathed it, hated it." After the death of George V in 1936, she never returned to the Highlands.

Balmoral allowed Bertie to recapture "tranquility of spirit" on the heather-clad hills, sometimes accompanied only by a ghillie. Elizabeth could readily appreciate the natural beauty while simultaneously sharing Bertie's dislike for the dull routines imposed by George V and Queen Mary, along with its unvarying cast of stuffy characters. "Elizabeth I hope is not too bored here," Bertie wrote to Lady Strathmore near the end of their first week. In fact, she found it all tiresome—to use one of Queen Mary's favorite words. A year later, Elizabeth told her mother, "It is so boring that I felt there was nothing to tell you!!"

The King forbade women from accompanying the "guns" who roamed Balmoral's moors and hills to shoot grouse and stalk stags. This was no sacrifice for Elizabeth, who confessed to Queen Mary that "even though I am the wife, daughter and sister of 'guns,' I fail to see what pleasure there can be in walking about all day in an icy wind and driving rain!!" Nor could the women fish—a disappointment to

Elizabeth, who had learned angling from her father and shared her fondness for the sport with Bertie. She and the other wives were compelled to march to Queen Mary's drum while the husbands were shooting, stalking, and wading for hours in the rivers. "When I first married," Elizabeth recalled, "it was nothing but expeditions, expeditions, expeditions every single day."

Balmoral rituals were akin to those at Glamis, but more elaborate. After the guns had returned from the hills in the late afternoon, an abundant tea was laid out on a table in the drawing room: sausage rolls, shrimps, scones, and special Scottish griddle cakes called baps and bannocks. Footmen served dinner, where the men wore their kilts with short jackets and jabots. The King usually wore the gray and red Balmoral tartan designed by Prince Albert during Queen Victoria's time. The menus invariably included grouse, along with such dishes as cream soup and toast, fish, cheese soufflé, iced cakes, peaches, coffee, champagne, port, and liqueurs. As many as a half dozen kilted bagpipers circled the table playing evocative airs.

The family filed into Crathie Church next to Balmoral the day after Bertie and Elizabeth's arrival that first summer, attracting the largest crowd ever for a Sunday service. Four days later, Elizabeth joined Bertie for her first Highland games at nearby Braemar.

They drove through the purple heather with the King and Queen in a carriage drawn by four grays, with scarlet-coated outriders on white horses. Against the mountain backdrop, the royal family and their guests sat in a pavilion and spent ninety minutes watching bagpipe competitions, obstacle races, Highland dancing, hammer throwing, and the tossing of the caber—a fifteen-foot tree trunk—by "colossal kilted men." To Queen Mary, this annual obligation attended by some twenty thousand people was "not amusing," and the King privately dismissed the games that day "as usual . . . not very exciting." But Bertie found fun in the spectacle, especially when something went awry—such as a hammer thrown the wrong way that fell inches from his feet, causing him to convulse with laughter.

The following week, Elizabeth attended her first Ghillies Ball, where the royal family danced reels with the ghillies and other estate workers and their wives in the castle ballroom. This was familiar territory for Elizabeth, who knew all the steps and turns from childhood and could pirouette with any partner. She sparkled in her diamond tiara and cream-colored evening gown. The men wore black dress tunics with their kilts and sporrans, knee socks, and black buckled shoes.

George V disliked dancing and preferred to watch from a platform atop the double staircase leading down to the ballroom. Some three hundred people swung into action at nine-thirty P.M. and kept going for two hours. Prince Albert danced nearly as vigorously as his mother, who insisted that English country numbers as well as foxtrots, tangos, and waltzes be on the program along with traditional Scottish dances.

At the King's signal around eleven-thirty, the royal family withdrew to the dining room for refreshments before retiring for the night. Everyone else was served in the steward's room and servants' hall. The band struck up anew, and the ordinary folk resumed their revels until as late as three A.M.

Elizabeth also got unexpectedly intimate glimpses of royal life at Balmoral. She saw Queen Mary's private sitting room, where one table was filled with photographs and knickknacks precisely as Queen Victoria had left them. Ten minutes before dinner, George V invited the duchess and other guests into his dressing room to watch him complete his evening rig. "He would put a little scent on his handkerchiefs and wind up all his watches," Elizabeth recalled with pleasure, marveling that "he had so many of them."

IN LATE SEPTEMBER 1923, BERTIE and Elizabeth moved on to Lord Strathmore's Holwick Hall shooting lodge in county Durham. As they settled in for their sixth week of sport and leisure, Bertie received a telegram from the King commanding them to travel to Belgrade at the end of October. Prince Albert and the Duchess of York had already agreed to be the godparents—"Koom" and "Koomitsa" in the Eastern

Orthodox Church—to Prince Peter, the newborn son of Serbian King Alexander, the ruler of the recently created kingdom of Yugoslavia. But the Yorks had not planned to attend the baptism.

Now, at the direction of the government, as relayed by the King, Bertie was expected to represent Britain to show support for the new kingdom uniting the Serbs, Croats, and Slovenes. The day after the baptism, the duke and duchess would also attend the wedding of their friend Prince Paul—a first cousin of King Alexander—who was marrying Princess Olga of Greece. Bertie was additionally asked to be Paul's best man. Only a year earlier, Bertie had been present in Belgrade at the marriage of King Alexander to Princess Marie (known as "Mignon"), a daughter of the King and Queen of Romania.

All the Greeks, Serbians, and Romanians were relatives of the British royals, so the celebrations were primarily a family affair. Still, Bertie was furious at his father for the peremptory summons. Not only was his shooting curtailed, now Elizabeth had to hurriedly prepare for a trip to the Balkans.

One unintended consequence of the abrupt change of plans was the ending of Louis Greig's role as Prince Albert's comptroller and chief adviser. For reasons that were never entirely clear, Bertie decided to enlist Lieutenant Colonel Ronald Waterhouse—James Stuart's replacement as private secretary and equerry—to run the visit. Waterhouse had accompanied the duke to Belgrade for King Alexander's wedding but had left soon afterward for a position in the government. Presumably Bertie reckoned that Waterhouse knew the territory and cast of characters and could manage the last-minute details, so he asked him to step in on a temporary basis—without first alerting Greig.

It was an uncharacteristically thoughtless move by Bertie. Greig was offended that he wouldn't be making the trip himself, and he overreacted by complaining to the King. George V's private secretary, Lord Stamfordham, tried to soothe Greig by telling him that Waterhouse was selected because he was "up to the ropes," but Greig felt wounded and threatened to resign. Clive Wigram, the King's assistant private secretary, wrote to reassure Greig that he and George V had "often discussed" how "indispensable" and "irreplaceable" he was. "I have a presentiment," he added, "that Prince Albert will some day be King."

Finally, George V himself intervened to suggest that both Greig and Waterhouse accompany the duke to the Balkans. Bertie rejected the idea, and after a tense meeting in London, Greig submitted his resignation. The King and Queen Mary were "miserable" about the outcome, Wigram reported to Greig, who stayed in his post until the following February, when he took a job at the stock brokerage firm owned by his wife's family. The duke and Greig remained tennis partners, and, more importantly, friends.

The suspected hidden hand in the Greig contretemps was the Duchess of York, who felt that she should now fulfill the role of confidante and chief adviser to her husband. As Cynthia Asquith observed in her authorized biography of Elizabeth published five years later, "The success with which she coped with serious domestic crises proved the iron determination which is to some extent camouflaged by her manner and smile."

On October 9, shortly after Greig's resignation, Bertie finally wrote to his parents to explain the situation. To his mother, he said, "I feel that now I am married it is better to have a change as things have not been working too smoothly, and we both feel the time has come. We have no row at all; it is quite mutual." Two days later, the duke and duchess went to Buckingham Palace for lunch with the King and Queen, who were still in high dudgeon. "Talked after lunch about L.G.," Elizabeth wrote in her diary that evening. "I don't care what the little duchess says, but he is not going to go," the King reportedly said to Clive Wigram.

But there was no turning back. "Greig is going you know, and is being rather silly," Elizabeth wrote to her mother. "They [the King and Queen and senior courtiers] were all furious about it but it was almost impossible. Especially as he resigned himself." The duchess took pains to write to Greig to express her gratitude for all he had done for the duke, and indeed said Louis had been responsible for "saving his life."

In the six months since Elizabeth's marriage to the duke, Louis had discovered, in the words of his grandson Geordie Greig, that she was "a force to be reckoned with." Louis wrote to her with surprising candor: "I have been trying to summon up courage to have a talk with you on the matter, but felt it might not be agreeable & might be difficult." He went on to say that he had been "bucked up" by her letter, which had "made a tremendous difference" in dispelling his concern that "Prince Bertie had been keeping me on against his will."

The King was not so easily mollified. During a Sandringham shooting weekend shortly after the resignation was announced, Bertie told Greig that his father wouldn't speak to him. "I am not going to say anything as I shall only have my head bitten off again," he wrote. The King and Queen calmed down, and Greig remained especially close to Queen Mary, who became a godmother to his son born two years later.

The Yorks treated the trip to Belgrade as a lark, finding more amusement than they could have anticipated. "We are off to Suburbia," Elizabeth joked to Beryl Poignand. On arriving at King Alexander's "Palais Royal," they were eager for hot baths after a ten-hour train journey. But when they turned on the taps, out flew a swarm of earwigs, followed by a splash of water, and more earwigs. "How we all lived in the Palace is a mystery," Bertie told his father.

At the christening, Prince Albert solemnly handed Prince Peter to the patriarch, Monsignor Dimitriye, for immersion in the baptismal font. The elderly prelate then lost his grip, and Bertie had to retrieve the sinking child from the water. Acting as "Koom," he carried his wailing godson on a cushion around the altar three times. The screaming was so loud that it "drowned the singing & the service altogether," Bertie recalled.

The luncheons, teas, and dinners with the Greek and Romanian royals were "like a musical comedy!" Elizabeth told her mother, "very unpunctual & very pompous!" But she and Bertie were touched by Prince Paul's wedding to Princess Olga. "He was enchanted at having us there," wrote Elizabeth. "Otherwise he had no real friends." Photographs of the baptism and wedding were splashed across five pages of

The Illustrated London News, underlining British support for the fledgling kingdom.

ELIZABETH'S FIRST CHRISTMAS AT YORK Cottage filled her with dread.
"<u>How</u> dull," she commented to her mother after their week of shooting
at Sandringham in November, with the "how" underlined three times.
"We have to go to Sandringham for Xmas, which I <u>loathe</u> & <u>hate</u>," she
wrote to her mother's sister, Violet Cavendish Bentinck ("Auntie
Vava") on the eve of their departure for Norfolk on December 22.

She had grown accustomed to the train journey to Wolferton station at the edge of the Sandringham property and the obligatory visit
to Queen Alexandra and the King's sisters at the Big House even
before settling in at the cottage. "Everybody looking even older!" Elizabeth wrote in her diary. But she was struck by the precision of the
royal rituals marked out by the King and Queen—unchanged from
Bertie's childhood during the reign of Edward VII—in sharp contrast
to her own rollicking Christmases at St. Paul's Walden Bury.

The first event on the day before Christmas was the family procession in midafternoon to the stables to watch George V distribute his
"treat" to "all our people," in Queen Mary's words. Hundreds of hefty
joints of Sandringham beef were arrayed on a long wooden table in the
stable yard and tagged with each estate worker's name. The King
handed them all out personally and wished each recipient a Happy
Christmas.

The royal family exchanged gifts German-style on Christmas Eve
in the ballroom at Sandringham House around a majestic (as tall as
twenty-five feet) candlelit and heavily tinseled tree that had been cut
from the nearby woodlands. At age seventy-nine, Queen Alexandra
had spent hours supervising the tree decoration as well as laying out
the presents on a trestle table covered in a white cloth that extended
the entire length of the room. The family, household, and guests were
allocated specific sections piled high with presents that took around
an hour to distribute in the early evening before dinner at York

Cottage. In her diary, Elizabeth noted only that the King and Queen gave her a "pretty bracelet & lots of little things." Queen Mary was irked that the Prince of Wales "arrived just before 8 o'clock, alas too late for the tree as he had been out hunting!"

Elizabeth walked with the King, Bertie, Prince Henry, and Prince Edward on Christmas morning to church for Holy Communion. She wore a red velvet gown to dinner at Sandringham House, where Queen Alexandra seated her next to Bertie's twenty-year-old first cousin Prince Olav, the son of George V's sister Maud, the Queen of Norway, and King Haakon. A sunny character with a robust laugh, Olav was attending the Norwegian Military Academy and would go on to study at Balliol College, Oxford.

He had been born at Appleton House, Maud's home on the Sandringham estate, and had been close to Bertie since childhood. He also had a shrewd appreciation of his English relatives. George V, he once said, "hated dawdling" and treated his children "as teenagers even when they were adults." Elizabeth had a lively night with Olav: "crackers & much laughter," she wrote in her diary.

AFTER JUST SEVEN MONTHS IN White Lodge, the Yorks concluded that the house was, in the words of Bertie's official biographer, John Wheeler-Bennett, "an incubus and a liability." The property was fourteen miles from central London, a shorter distance than the twenty-two miles between Buckingham Palace and Windsor Castle, but it still took more than an hour to drive each way—a journey that became dangerous in the winter fog. On some days they traveled to London and back three times, a source of major exasperation. As their profile in the press rose, they became such a focus of public curiosity that throngs of people gathered near the house on the weekends.

They also chafed at the burdensome running cost—by their estimate around £11,000 a year (some £708,000 at current values)—for a house that had inadequate heating and electric lighting, as well as substandard plumbing. Under the "Civil List"—the system of government-funded annuities to support members of the royal family—Bertie and Elizabeth received £25,000 annually (more than £1.6 million today). In a letter to her mother before their departure for Belgrade, Elizabeth pronounced her White Lodge bedroom to be "HIDEOUS." Louis Greig tried to help as they launched a quiet campaign for a house in London that would take three years to secure.

Queen Mary was displeased that Bertie and Elizabeth found her beloved childhood home unsuitable. "I went to White Lodge in the afternoon on business," she wrote in her diary on Saturday, January 12, 1924. "On business" was the Queen's code for a serious discussion, akin to Elizabeth's "talked hard." Elizabeth made no mention of the Queen's visit in her own diary, but the next day she used mirror writing to record that Louis Greig had telephoned after tea to say *he'd had a talk about White Lodge & that it had failed. Terrific disappointment.*

There the matter sat while Elizabeth and Bertie tried to spend as much time as they could away from White Lodge. Starting in the autumn of 1923, they rented the "Old House" at Guilsborough in Northamptonshire for Bertie's foxhunting weekends. They took it fully furnished, and Elizabeth was thrilled that its owner had "wonderful taste." "It is really tiny," Elizabeth told her mother, "but I think we can just do it."

Bertie shared his brother Edward's zeal for hunting, and they frequently rode to hounds together. As in nearly every other aspect of his life, the Prince of Wales was more reckless on horseback than his younger brother and had his share of spills resulting in broken bones and concussions—one of which knocked him out for a half hour and kept him bedridden for a month.

The relationship between the Yorks and the heir to the throne in those days was marked by genuine fondness. After returning from a six-week Canadian junket in the autumn of 1923, the Prince of Wales complained to Diana Cooper about "the gloom of Buckingham Palace, how he himself and all of them 'freeze up' the moment they get inside it. How bad-tempered his father is. How the Duchess of York is the one bright spot there. They all love her and the King is in a good temper whenever she is there."

Sometimes when Bertie had an official function, the Prince of Wales would take Elizabeth out to dinner at the exclusive Hurlingham Club along the banks of the Thames or to a fashionable London restaurant, followed by dancing long into the night. More often it was the three of them, surrounded by a clique of Prince Edward's friends, including a famous dancing duo, Fred Astaire and his sister Adele.

The King was perpetually vexed by Prince Edward, who just as consistently privately disparaged his father. "David ought to marry," George V wrote to Queen Alexandra in the autumn of 1923. "He is more than 29, but who is he to marry? It is not easy to find any one who is suitable & he is very obstinate & I don't think has any wish at all to marry & one can't force him, that is impossible."

By then Prince Edward had circled the globe several times on behalf of the King: nearly four months in Canada, a seven-month journey of forty-six thousand miles to Australia and New Zealand, and nearly eight months in India, Ceylon, and Japan. These prolonged absences, plus David's entrenched aversion to court life, deepened his gulf with his parents.

Bertie was sufficiently alarmed by the growing estrangement that he wrote to his mother asking her to show some appreciation for David: "I am sure it will come right again one day if he does not have to go on another tour for several years." Bertie explained that while the Prince of Wales was overseas, he was absorbed in himself and "other things are in the background." He hoped that if David stayed at home "for a good long time I feel he will get back to the home ties which will become strong again. We must all <u>help</u> him to get back to our way of thinking."

Despite their dismay over "selfish, ill-tempered and irresponsible behaviour," the Prince of Wales's advisers on his foreign trips—Admiral Lionel Halsey, his comptroller, and his equerry, Lieutenant Colonel Sir Piers "Joey" Legh—covered up his dissipations and sent home glowing reports on his impressive public performances. In one typical dispatch from India in 1922, Legh said the prince had "exceeded the most sanguine expectations," but cautioned that his manic exercise was causing his doctors to be in a "perpetual state of fear about his health. . . . Probably through sheer exhaustion he becomes fractious & unreasonable at times."

THE ONE MAN WITH THE potential to guide the Prince of Wales in the right direction was his assistant private secretary since November 1920, Alan Frederick "Tommy" Lascelles. Prince Edward's only requirements for the job had been "a chap younger than me & a cavalry man." He had hired Tommy sight unseen on the recommendation of his private secretary, Sir Godfrey Thomas. At thirty-three, Tommy was seven years older than the prince, but he was an accomplished cavalry man—likely the more important of the two criteria.

After meeting David for the first time at St. James's Palace, Tommy wrote in his diary, "He won me completely. He is the most attractive man I ever met." He was convinced that "the future of England is as much in his hands as in those of any individual." Tommy's main job was to write speeches that were typed onto rectangular cards the prince could easily remove from his breast pocket. "People began to remark on the excellence of the speeches the prince was giving," wrote Duff Hart-Davis, the editor of Lascelles's letters and journals. That turned out to be "rather dangerous, for it led many people to overestimate the Prince's intellectual capabilities."

Tommy Lascelles took seriously his mission to make Prince Edward fit for kingship, and he remained loyal even after he was beset by despair. He had a sense of duty, a strong streak of patriotism, and a high regard for the monarchy as an essential British institution. But he was not overawed by the royal family. His first cousin—the son of his father's older brother—was Princess Mary's husband, Harry Lascelles. His sister Blanche had been a maid of honor to Queen Alexandra since 1905. From an early age, Tommy had been a frequent guest in the great aristocratic houses of Britain and had dined at 10 Downing Street with Prime Minister Asquith.

Tommy had detested his boarding school, Marlborough College, whose students were the grandsons of "county cricketers," while his own aristocratic ancestors and those of the boys at Eton (where he wished he had gone) were masters of foxhounds. But he came into his own at Trinity College, Oxford. He earned his degree in ancient history and philosophy, wrote in Greek, and readily turned a Latin phrase.

At Oxford he found his "own tribe" of young men who sought "liberty from the dour conventionality." He had been "a lonely and damnably sentimental boy" with an "empty pedestal" that he filled with young men, but "never more than one at a time." "What is to most people merely a sensual adventure has always been to me an act of devotion," he wrote many years later to James Pope-Hennessy, the object of Tommy's affection in the 1950s when "Jamesy" was writing the official biography of Queen Mary.

The first of Tommy's lovers at Oxford had been Harold Nicolson, the future biographer of King George V. Even after Nicolson was supplanted on the pedestal, he and Tommy maintained an affectionate lifelong friendship. Nicolson went on to lead a discreet gay life within an unorthodox marriage to the writer Vita Sackville-West. "If their marriage is seen as a harbor," wrote their son Nigel, "their love affairs were mere ports of call."

During the First World War, Tommy served as a cavalry captain in Flanders and France, losing one friend after another in the trenches—including the celebrated war poet Julian Grenfell, another beloved "god" on his Oxford pedestal. Toward the end of 1916, Tommy was wounded and awarded the Military Cross for bravery. After the armistice he traveled to India, where at age thirty-two he fell in love with twenty-four-year-old Joan Thesiger, the eldest daughter of Britain's viceroy, Lord Chelmsford. He had a coup de foudre when he watched her kill a nine-foot tigress in one shot.

Tommy said Joan "looked best in boots and breeches," but what mattered most to him was the fine quality of her mind and her "natural and unaffected" manner. She also loved everything he loved, from books to music to shooting and riding fast on horseback. After their three-month courtship, they wed in New Delhi and honeymooned in Kashmir before returning to Britain.

Since the middle of the war, Tommy had envisioned "being a secretary to a Great Man," who "must have a sense of humour and enthusiasm for whatever he is Great at. . . . I must be able to make a hero out of him. I can't work for people I don't admire pretty blindly." Yet aside from hunting and steeplechasing, it is hard to imagine what Tommy Lascelles and the Prince of Wales had in common. And just as Prince Edward could not know the submerged experiences of Tommy's youth, neither could Tommy fathom the extent of the Prince of Wales's pathologies, especially with the women in his life.

What he could observe was Edward's philistinism, immaturity, and superficiality, which must have been galling for someone of Tommy's intellectual rigor and cultural refinement. But the Prince of Wales was a superlative charmer and a polished public performer—perhaps the full extent of his ability to be "great." Tommy devoted eight years trying to create a "hero" in that mold. Like Prince Edward's parents and siblings, he could for a time avert his eyes and excuse the character defects and bad behavior of the heir to the throne. Along the way, Tommy Lascelles accumulated unmatched knowledge of the royal family that would turn him into the monarchy's indispensable courtier. The unforeseen irony was that the "Great Man" he would ultimately serve was the stammering but steadfast Prince Albert.

"It is like a very large Scotland—especially in the soft evening light."

Bertie and Elizabeth on safari in East Africa, February 1925.

❧

FOURTEEN

Out of the Welter

A POLITICAL STORM HIT BRITAIN IN JANUARY 1924 WITH THE ARRIVAL OF Britain's first Labour government under the premiership of Ramsay MacDonald amid rising unemployment and workers' unrest. George V noted that the shift of power coincided with the anniversary of Queen Victoria's death twenty-three years earlier. Despite his private affinity for the Conservative Party, the King took the practical view that the Labour leader would be a moderating advocate for workers as a hedge against the greater threat of Russian-inspired Bolshevism. MacDonald had even promised the King that he wouldn't promote any extreme measures in Parliament.

Neither Prince Albert nor Elizabeth had shown much interest in the political scene. But on the advice of his father, Bertie joined David to watch the debate in the House of Commons that preceded the resignation of Conservative prime minister Stanley Baldwin. In so doing, he gained "first-hand knowledge of parliamentary procedures and personalities."

Through the Industrial Welfare Society, Prince Albert had good relations with labor leaders and workingmen, but he was as instinctively Conservative as his father. At age twenty-four, Elizabeth was even more implacably Tory. She believed that Labour's ambitions for a more egalitarian society posed a threat to the aristocratic way of life.

"I am extremely anti-Labour," Elizabeth wrote to her aristocratic friend D'Arcy Osborne in March 1924. A lifelong bachelor, Osborne was an erudite and witty diplomat with whom Elizabeth could be playfully indiscreet, and in the following years he would become one of her most trusted confidants. She told him that Labour was far removed from "fairies and owls and bluebells & Americans & all the things that I like. If they agree with me, I know they are pretending—in fact, I believe everything is a pretence to them. . . . I think the Labour Party is narrow minded and snobbish."

Scarcely a month later, on the Yorks' first wedding anniversary, Elizabeth met MacDonald, a handsome Scot with a Highland brogue, when she was seated next to him during the soccer FA Cup Final at Wembley Stadium. The last-minute two-goal win by Newcastle over Aston Villa caused "terrific excitement" for the crowd of over ninety thousand. Careful to cloak her Tory sympathies, she turned on her famous charm. MacDonald "talked a lot," she noted in her diary.

It was otherwise a desultory winter and spring for the young royal couple. Bertie tramped around the country inspecting factory conditions in his role as president of the IWS. Ever dutiful, he spoke at length to men making everything from shoes and sausages to beef bouillon cubes and margarine boxes. At the Rutland Works in Sheffield, he was fascinated by the "pyrotechnics" in the "handling of molten metal."

Elizabeth spent most of her time socializing with friends and family, as well as playing with their two new dogs, a golden retriever named Glen, and a Pekingese called Ping that had been given to her at the opening of the Ideal Homes Exhibition at Olympia. She was also laid up for several weeks in March with one of her periodic bouts of tonsillitis and flu.

That spring they had lunch with Princess Mary and Harry Lascelles at their opulent London home, Chesterfield House. Mary and Harry lived mainly at Goldsborough Hall on the Harewood estate in Yorkshire, and she was now pregnant with their second child, due in August. After lunch, the Yorks got a complete tour of the house, and Elizabeth exulted in mirror writing: *"They have offered it to us for the summer."*

Shortly after Bertie and Elizabeth began their summer stay at Chesterfield House, they hosted a dinner dance for seventy guests, including Fred and Adele Astaire. "They danced *a pas seul* with their usual genius for *savoir faire*," wrote Chips Channon. "The Yorks partnered them immediately after as a reward." "Stopped dancing 3:15. Bed 4!" Elizabeth wrote in her diary.

She went to her first Trooping the Colour, a military spectacle dating from the eighteenth century that celebrated the King's birthday on June 3. At age fifty-nine, wearing the red tunic of the Grenadier Guards, George V rode his dark brown charger from Buckingham Palace up the Mall in a mounted procession that included the Prince of Wales and the Duke of York.

On Horse Guards Parade, the King inspected the troops from the Household Cavalry and the five infantry regiments of the Brigade of Guards (Grenadier, Coldstream, Irish, Scots, and Welsh). He was then honored by bands marching in slow and quick time. The actual "trooping" of the "Colour" involved the crimson flag of the Grenadiers being carried aloft past the ranks of guardsmen. Watching from the window above the Horse Guards arch were the Queen and the Duchess of York, who proclaimed it "a very beautiful sight"—one that she would witness scores of times in the years ahead.

Two weeks later, Elizabeth joined the family for Royal Ascot, which she had dodged the previous year. Bertie and Elizabeth stayed at Windsor Castle from Monday, June 16, to the following Saturday, along with thirty-four other guests. For the first time Elizabeth rode onto the racecourse to the Royal Enclosure in "semi-state": a procession of six open landaus, each drawn by four horses with two postilions in Ascot livery, and outriders in scarlet.

David and Bertie rode in the first carriage with the King—in black top hat and morning dress with a white carnation—and the Queen in a white dress trimmed with ostrich feathers, wearing her signature toque and sitting erect under a white parasol. The duchess and Harry Lascelles followed in the second carriage. Luncheon at the racecourse was served by footmen in the dining room at the rear of the royal box, its balcony decorated with flowers and the coveted Gold Cup.

Elizabeth recorded only the final day of her first Ascot with the royal family. After "breakie in bed as usual," she wore her "pinky mauve chiffon" and walked in the paddock with Bertie. "We lost all our bets as usual!" The Prince of Wales bolted after tea, but the Yorks left with everybody else late Saturday morning.

They had a quick turnaround at Chesterfield House and headed to Polesden Lacey for one of Maggie Greville's lively house party weekends. They played tennis after lunch and poker after dinner. Elizabeth was pleased to have won on both nights. In later years, she would look back on those weekends as "delectable & idle and rich and careless."

Just five days later, on June 27, Bertie and Elizabeth were the guests of honor at a dinner for thirty-four hosted by the indefatigable Mrs. Greville in her Mayfair mansion at 16 Charles Street. Among the prominent names were Rothschild, Vanderbilt, Churchill, Northumberland, Sutherland, and Sassoon. For dancing afterward, Maggie had the Savoy Havana Band, along with entertainment by the Trix Sisters, a popular American vaudeville duo who danced, sang, and played the piano. The party lasted until two A.M.

Maggie gave Elizabeth an excellent seat next to forty-nine-year-old Winston Churchill. The well-connected politician and author was out of power at that moment, but he held Elizabeth spellbound as he recounted his travels in Africa seventeen years earlier. "Winston was extraordinary," Elizabeth recalled when she was in her nineties. "He said, 'Now look here, you're a young couple. You ought to go out and have a look at the world. I should go to East Africa. It's got a great future, that country.'"

With Bertie and Elizabeth's encouragement, Churchill proposed to the government that they travel to East Africa. Bertie raised the idea with his mother, and by July 14 they had the King's approval. "Marvellous," Elizabeth wrote in her diary. She later said she had "always been grateful" to Churchill. "I don't think we would have thought of going."

At Glamis that autumn—both before and after their mandatory two-week stint at Balmoral—Elizabeth practiced shooting to prepare for their trip to Africa. She bagged rabbits and grouse, and even stalked roe deer with Bertie, honing her skills with a rifle as well as a shotgun. Elizabeth griped that their time at Glamis was spoiled by the presence of some Strathmore relatives—"the most awful people," she wrote. "Mother nearly mad!!" She and Bertie mostly ignored them while dining with friends and playing cards. "The relations clustered coldly in corners," she wrote.

At Balmoral, the Reverend Stirton observed during the Ghillies Ball that "the Duchess of York looked so pretty and she is greatly improved in manner—so quietly purposeful now and filling her high position so well. She sent for me and asked me to dance with her—the Circassian Circle—which I did and enjoyed it so much."

Although the duke and duchess made their return to Glamis as planned in late September, the King summoned Bertie back to Balmoral at the end of the month for another week of stalking. "I am feeling very lonely, & am quite lost not seeing and hearing you in this room," Bertie wrote to Elizabeth on his arrival in Royal Deeside. "I do hope you will not miss me too much, tho' you will know I am always thinking of you. Don't get frightened at night sleeping all alone darling in that enormous bed."

Elizabeth replied, "I miss you dreadfully, and am longing for Monday, when I hope you will arrive here sunburnt, manly, & bronzed, bearing in your arms a haunch of *venaison roti* as a love offering to your spouse." She wished him a "fine stalk, not to mention a fine stag at good old Immoral." She ended by saying, "It seems all wrong that we shouldn't be together, doesn't it—from your <u>very very</u> loving E Xxxxxxxx kisses Ooooooooooo hugs." Bertie assured her he would be back at Glamis in time for lunch: "Two lunches of course. One from you I hope darling in xxxxx etc etc & then an ordinary culinary one. . . . Goodbye & bless you my sweet. Ever Your very very loving Bertie."

THE BIG EVENT IN THE autumn of 1924 was the general election in which the Tories defeated Labour, returning Stanley Baldwin to the premiership. "The election news wonderful, already great conservative majority," Elizabeth wrote in her diary on October 30. "Everybody relieved—hopes for a year or two of comparative peace." That night she even set aside time to read the lists of winning candidates in the newspaper.

Bertie and Elizabeth spent those months preparing for their African adventure—seeing doctors and dentists, getting vaccinated against typhoid fever and other diseases, and buying safari clothing. They both needed a break from their royal life, and Elizabeth especially wanted respite from the climate that aggravated her persistent tonsillitis.

She was also concerned about the strain on Bertie that was evident in his eruptions over small matters. His outbursts had much to do with his stammer, and the accompanying anxiety over public speaking. Louis Greig had noticed him "grinding his teeth in rage," which some courtiers referred to as his "gnashes." One of Elizabeth's strengths was her ability to defuse Bertie's temper with soothing words and affectionate gestures.

They left for their African journey on Monday, December 1. From Sandringham, the King cautioned his son "never to be without a Doctor & you are not to run unnecessary risks, either from the climate or wild beasts." In a farewell letter to his mother, Bertie said he felt "very sad having to say goodbye. . . . It is quite a long time to be away 5 months but I feel it will do us a lot of good."

Elizabeth admitted apprehension about their African journey in a letter to D'Arcy Osborne on the night before they sailed from Marseilles on Friday, December 5. "I am feeling slightly mingled in my feelings," she wrote. "I hate discomfort, and am so afraid that I shall not like the heat, or that mosquitoes will bite my eyelids & the tip of my nose, or that I shall not be able to have baths often enough, or that I shall hate the people." Still, she believed it would be rejuvenating to "see a little LIFE."

Elizabeth was overjoyed to greet her high-spirited friend Lavinia Annaly as they settled into the SS *Mulbera*. The duchess had designated the daughter of the sixth Earl Spencer as her lady-in-waiting for the trip. Lavinia was now married and the mother of one-year-old Patsy, who was Elizabeth's goddaughter. But she was as mischievous as ever and would be a steady source of amusement during their travels. Accompanying Bertie was his comptroller, Captain Basil Brooke, and equerry, Lieutenant Commander Colin Buist. A valet and lady's maid rounded out their small entourage.

They landed at the Indian Ocean port city of Mombasa in Kenya on December 22. The governor, Sir Robert Coryndon, introduced them to representatives of European and native communities. Bertie listened intently to what Sir Robert told him about Kenya's prospects. "The place is growing steadily," he told his father.

Their 325-mile train journey inland to Nairobi opened their eyes to the natural wonders of East Africa—"absolutely wild country; untouched as yet by man," Bertie wrote to the King. They spotted snow-clad Mount Kilimanjaro in the distance, and as they neared their destination, they sat on a special seat in the front of the engine to see exotic animals in the wild for the first time: zebra, hartebeests, ostrich, baboons, and wildebeest.

They slipped into the silky pleasures of the Muthaiga Club, a low-slung pink stucco haven set amid broad lawns and ficus trees, where they dined and danced with aristocratic English colonials. They enjoyed the civilized ambience of Nairobi's Government House for a brief Christmas holiday as their respective families were celebrating at St. Paul's Walden Bury and Sandringham. Bertie went horseback riding on Christmas Eve, and at church the next morning, the Duke and Duchess of York heard "God Save the King" sung in Swahili.

ON BOXING DAY THEY LEFT their comfort zone and set off for more than three months of living rough. It was an experience that opened their eyes, stretched the limits of their physical endurance, and imposed a new kind of rigor on their lives. Both of them—particularly Elizabeth—were surprised by what they could do when faced with challenges, and even outright fear. Their admiration for each other grew, along with their self-assurance.

They scattered their impressions across their diaries and their letters to friends and family. The daily chronicles revealed their contrasting personalities as well as affinities. Her writing was more emotive, with piquant character sketches and rapturous descriptions of flora and fauna. He offered a more matter-of-fact recitation—often in great detail—of his stalking and shooting. As with the quotidian diaries of his mother and father, the value of his chronicles could be found in snippets of self-awareness and sparks of liveliness around the dutiful tally of the big and small game he bagged.

Bertie and Elizabeth took three separate journeys through Kenya, Uganda, and the Sudan that more or less followed planned itineraries but allowed spontaneous excursions as well. For each leg they were assigned at least two "white hunters," experienced big-game experts originally from England. Elizabeth was especially intrigued by these romantic characters renowned for their bravery and marksmanship. She described English South African Pat Ayre, one of their white hunters in Kenya, as "charming . . . with an imagination, an accent & a sense of humour." The Yorks also had a doctor for each country, as well as game wardens and other functionaries. To transport their equipment and set up their camps, upward of six hundred native porters accompanied them in long processions.

For the first three weeks, they operated from a base camp at Siolo near the lower slopes of Mount Kenya. The setting on a huge plain seemed to Elizabeth "exactly like an English park, and on every side there are mountains." They slept in bandas—large mud huts with conical tops of woven rush—and could take hot baths before dinner. Bertie did serious stalking with the white hunters and bagged lions, rhinos, oryx, buffalo, eland, a leopard, and more. Elizabeth stayed nearer to camp, honing her new skills initially by shooting partridge, guinea fowl, and other wild birds with a small double-barreled .300 bore rifle. On some days Elizabeth was incongruously ferried about in an open-top Rolls-Royce belonging to Captain Keith Caldwell of the Kenya Game Department.

For a further fortnight they had what Bertie called "a proper safari," on the move, and sleeping under canvas. The Yorks rose well before dawn and walked together at least a dozen miles a day, pitching their tents wherever the big game seemed most promising. The hikes were arduous, taking them through thick bush and stony ground with lava rocks the size of soccer balls. Working with a .275 Rigby rifle, Elizabeth killed her first rhino, as well as an oryx, zebra, water buck, and giant gazelle.

"Don't tell your sweet father that I am shooting," she wrote to the Prince of Wales in mid-January. But Bertie was so pleased by her success that he boasted to George V that she was "a very good rifle shot," adding that she hadn't used a shotgun. "I know you don't approve of ladies shooting at home, but out here things are so different."

In early February they motored two hundred miles back to Government House in Nairobi for three days of rest and recreation: polo, thoroughbred racing, fine dining, duck shooting on Lake Naivasha, and dancing until three A.M. at Muthaiga with their host, fifty-three-year-old Lord Delamere, one of Kenya's first English settlers. For another two days they enjoyed the luxuries of Deloraine, a spacious two-story house built on the western edge of the Great Rift Valley by Lord Francis Scott. It was 250 miles from Nairobi, but Scott had created an island of British civilization reminiscent of the Scottish Highlands. Bertie played polo, and the Yorks had long and leisurely meals with their hosts.

They traveled by rail to the Ugandan border for their next three-week expedition. They crossed Lake Victoria overnight on the *Clement Hill* steamer, awakened to a misty dawn on the far shore, and visited Ripon Falls, the source of the White Nile. Shouting and singing natives in a hundred war canoes greeted them at Entebbe. They stayed at Government House (surprisingly primitive, with neither electricity nor running water), where they met the local dignitaries at a garden party.

On February 18, they were driven two hundred miles to Fort Portal in Captain Caldwell's Rolls. The start of their Ugandan safari took them eight miles into the Semliki Valley, a descent on an escarpment of some two thousand feet. At their base camp they slept in mud huts decorated by the natives with paintings of animals and hunting weapons.

From there, for the next week they fanned out at six each morning in search of big game, walking for hours, as many as twenty miles a day. Bertie and Elizabeth killed an assortment of animals, but the biggest prey were the elephants that they saw for the first time. Elizabeth watched Bertie shoot an "immense" elephant in the heart and the head, which fell with a great crash. The tusks, Bertie proudly reported to his father, weighed ninety pounds each.

They crossed Lake Albert on the *Samuel Baker,* a small paddle wheel steamer that took them down the White Nile until rapids prevented them from going further. They disembarked at Nimule on the Sudanese border and were driven nearly one hundred miles to Rejaf, where they boarded *Nasir,* a large and comfortable riverboat that served as their base for the next month. "It is rather nice having a bath etc after so long of camping," Elizabeth wrote. *Nasir* trailed three barges, one of which housed the white hunters and their native attendants, with a fleet of automobiles, ten donkeys, and wood for fuel on the other two.

As they steamed down the Nile, the Yorks either stalked along the shore or left the boat to camp inland. Bertie killed triang, white-eared kob, reedbuck, and red-fronted gazelle. Elizabeth brought down several gazelle and a roan antelope. Their trophies would be mounted by Rowland Ward taxidermists on Piccadilly for display back home.

The trip offered psychological and physical benefits as well. Writing to the Prince of Wales, Elizabeth expressed her relief that Bertie was "a different being, quite calm and losing all his nerviness . . .

enjoying every moment of safari life." Captain Roy Salmon, their white hunter in Uganda, observed that the Prince "speaks very slowly but has practically no stammer as a rule."

The duke showed courage in more than one tight situation. Early on the safari, a wounded rhino ran straight at him. It took additional shots from the white hunter and a gun bearer to bring down the beast. Nor did Bertie flinch when an elephant "made a terrible bellowing noise" as it fell, or when he shot a lion in the stomach, causing "a smell you don't easily forget." When sharp swamp grass cut his legs, Bertie kept trudging through it anyway. His closest call came in Uganda, when he and Salmon were chasing an elephant in a dry ravine. Salmon ran out of ammunition, and Bertie knew that if the elephant turned around and charged them, escape was impossible. The duke "calmly began firing and killed the bull," Salmon recounted.

Until those months, Elizabeth had observed field sports in Scotland and England, dressed demurely in a long skirt. In Africa she was a participant, wearing trousers for the first time. She initially worried that safari garb was unflattering, making her look "very small which annoys me." But Captain Salmon wrote admiringly of her "khaki shirt & slacks & red silk handkerchief." She took pride in her new shooting skill, telling her sister May, "I have become mad about shooting, and simply adore it."

Elizabeth was equally enchanted by the beauty of the wildlife. To D'Arcy Osborne, she described rhinos as "very funny, very fussy like old gentlemen, & very busy all the time, quite ridiculous, in fact. Giraffes I adore—they are utterly prehistoric and very gentle. Also they move like a slow motion movie."

When Roy Salmon took her to "a wonderful place, miles & miles of palms, simply crawling with elephants," it was almost a mystical experience. Walking among them "was simply wonderful," she told her sister Rosie, "and made one feel such a worm looking at those enormous creatures. One could watch for hours—they are too amusing and frightfully dangerous, but . . . we walked about among the herds quite easily."

The duke and duchess observed but only commented briefly on the native culture they witnessed—mainly displays of dancing at various stops. At the Nubian gathering in the Sudan, they watched ten thousand tribesmen armed with rifles march past their tent, followed by "very big men" wrestling, dancing, and catching spears on shields. Several days later, Elizabeth "changed into a crepe de chine" as they went ashore and watched tribal dancing by the Shilluks, a major ethnic group in the southern part of the Sudan. The performers had painted faces and wore leopard skins and huge bracelets. Elizabeth told her mother they sang "very well—rather like a violoncello."

The whole experience was liberating for the Yorks. "I never knew that I could like this sort of life so much," Elizabeth told D'Arcy Osborne. "Out all day long, and one never knows the day of the week. I feel it must be good for one. England seems so small & full & petty and unhappy in contrast to Africa." At one point she jotted, "I love meandering." Bertie, too, savored what he called "our own little world." "We shall have seen & learnt a great deal in different ways," he wrote to his father.

Out in the bush, they uncomplainingly relied on such basics as tinned tongue, and they had to filter muddy drinking water with alum to remove the sediment. Nothing seemed to faze either of them—not the growling lions and shrieking hyenas at night, nor the long and difficult walks, nor the mosquitoes and other pesky insects. They bathed in dirty water and poured with sweat. On one of their last days of shooting, Elizabeth spotted a nine-foot crocodile on a sandbank and confidently finished him off.

Bertie and Elizabeth dropped all formalities and spoke on familiar terms with the white hunters, especially over dinner and into the night. Elizabeth and Lavinia relaxed in silk dressing gowns, and the duke wore "a sort of Jaeger pyjama suit." "We are all so pally (!), and talk gaily on the most intimate subjects," she told D'Arcy Osborne. One of the white hunters introduced Elizabeth to the "shandy," a mixture of beer and lemon soda. In the evening, the preferred beverages were whisky and champagne.

In a conversation with Roy Salmon, Elizabeth even let slip the secret of her luminous skin: She never used soap on her face, only lots of water. She confided that overnight she applied cream (a special formula called Cold Cream of Roses) that rubbed off by the morning. She also revealed an awareness of how she worked her charm. "She used to say, 'Watch so & so while I catch his eye,' & proceed to startle some man with a glance & then laugh like a child," Salmon wrote in a letter to his mother.

On the sixth of April, they arrived at the Khartoum Palace "feeling too tattered and burnt and dirty for words." After so many weeks in the wild, it was almost surreal for Bertie to show up in a uniform and Elizabeth to wear a pearl tiara for a small reception in the palace gardens illuminated by colored lights. "We met a lot of Sheiks," Elizabeth noted. "Very fine old men." Following a railway journey to Port Sudan, they were homeward bound on April 10 aboard SS *Maloja*.

Elizabeth had mixed feelings as their trip wound down, but in a different way from her apprehensions at the outset. At the very least, she had overcome her fear of discomfort. As she would tell her elder daughter years later, she and Bertie had come "out of the welter" to find a more solid footing as the Duke and Duchess of York. "It is so difficult to write ones impressions," she wrote to her sister May. "I've had so many that everything has got blurred into a large whole. But Africa is not as African as one imagines, & very often it is like a very large Scotland—especially in the soft evening light." She regretted their having to leave but was eager to see her family. Nearly seventy years later, with the benefit of many points of comparison, she summarized the experience succinctly: "best bit of one's life."

"Bertie got through his speech all right, but there were some rather long pauses."

After introducing George V at Wembley Stadium on May 9, 1925, the Duke of York listens as his father officially opens the British Empire Exhibition.

FIFTEEN

My Heart Goes Pit-a-pat

"I AM ENCLOSING A COPY OF MY SPEECH TO YOU NEXT SATURDAY, WHICH I hope you will think is short enough," Prince Albert wrote to King George V on May 4, 1925. It had been scarcely two weeks since his return to England. He now faced a performance five days later that tormented him with anxiety.

A year earlier, in April 1924, the Prince of Wales had stood at a podium in Wembley Stadium before a vast crowd. His role, as president of the British Empire Exhibition, had been to deliver a welcoming address before the King officially opened the ambitious celebration of the empire spread across 216 acres around the stadium. Its overtly imperial purpose had been to reinforce Britain's ties with its far-flung territories, and to showcase their diverse cultures. There were pavilions representing fifty-six countries as well as "palaces" highlighting industry, horticulture, engineering, and the arts.

Bertie and Elizabeth had been present at the grand opening and had witnessed the historic moment when the King's remarks were amplified through loudspeakers and transmitted by radio—the "wireless" as it was then known—for the first time to listeners throughout

Britain. The exhibition had run for six months and had been such a success—drawing seventeen million visitors—that the organizers decided to offer it again with new attractions in 1925. Since the Prince of Wales was traveling overseas, Prince Albert was named president of the exhibition. The duty of introducing his father on May 9, as his older brother had done previously with evident ease, fell to him.

"I do hope I shall do well, but I shall be very frightened as you have never heard me speak & the loud speakers are apt to put one off as well," Bertie wrote to his father. "I hope you will understand that I am bound to be more nervous than I usually am." Bertie's remarks were brief—some four hundred words—and he practiced them relentlessly at White Lodge as well as in rehearsals at Wembley. His bugbear was the instrument suspended from the canopy above the dais. "His stammer was still a grievous burden to him," wrote his biographer and fellow stammerer, John Wheeler-Bennett. "He also suffered the normally shy man's dread of the microphone." To make matters worse, the speech was an obstacle course of run-on sentences and challenging consonants. No one thought to simplify the remarks to accommodate his stutter.

Bertie was so worked up that he spent several sleepless nights before Saturday the ninth—chosen as the fifteenth anniversary of the date George V was publicly proclaimed "King-Emperor" at St. James's Palace. That morning, the duke left for Wembley "very downhearted," Elizabeth wrote in her diary. When he arrived in the stadium, he saw that "banked from ground-level to roof, were massed 100,000 spectators." The "great oval of emerald turf" was filled with military bands and guards of honor in "khaki and dark blue, grey-blue, and scarlet."

He strode toward the royal dais decked in crimson and gold, flanked with yellow and white tulips and pink azaleas. Moments later, shortly before noon, the gilded state coach carrying the King, Queen, and Prince Henry arrived, and Prince Albert descended the steps to greet them. Both he and his father were in full-dress naval uniforms and cocked hats, each wearing his Garter Riband and Star.

The band played "God Save the King" when they reached their

places under the columned canopy. It started to rain, and out popped thousands of umbrellas. Everyone remained standing while a "deep hush fell upon the throng." The Duke of York began to speak, conscious of the "cloud of witnesses" in faraway places who could hear him but not see him. He was "nervous in the legs & not in my mouth or throat," he recalled.

At the beginning the duke struggled to articulate some words, but he muscled his way along, speaking for less than four minutes. He emphasized that the new exhibition would expand on the first, and "present its lessons of Empire in a new manner." He likened the 1925 version to "a complete University of Empire."

Bertie stood at attention several paces to the right of his father, who wore glasses as he read his remarks. Touching on his son's speech, the King noted the acuity of the educational metaphor. "I declare this British Empire Exhibition open," George V concluded, prompting a trumpet fanfare followed by volleys of gun salutes, flags unfurling on masts around the stadium (triggered by the King pressing a button), and a squadron of airplanes roaring overhead as the crowd cheered and cheered.

"It was an ordeal but I came out of it all right," the duke told his older brother. Glued to her wireless at White Lodge, Elizabeth felt relief. "It was marvelously clear & no hesitation," she concluded. "It all went off very well." Bertie thought so, too, telling David it was "easily the best I have ever done." His father "seemed pleased which was kind of him," he added. The King confided to Prince George, however, "Bertie got through his speech all right, but there were some rather long pauses."

THE DUKE AND DUCHESS OF York passed the summer, autumn, and winter in a kind of limbo, marking time until they transformed from a couple to a family. At first they were discontented to be back in England generally and at White Lodge in particular. "Horrible," Elizabeth had written in her diary after walking into their marital home late in the afternoon of April 19. "Between ourselves we were not very glad to get back from our travels, although it was very nice seeing our friends again," Bertie wrote to the Prince of Wales.

Bertie kept a light schedule of engagements, while Elizabeth resumed her late rising and mornings of writing letters and reading. Together, the duke and duchess spent a day visiting factories in the West Midlands and traveled to their eponymous city of York. Bertie dedicated a war memorial, and Elizabeth unveiled the newly restored six-hundred-year-old "Five Sisters" window of intricate glass patterns in the York Minster cathedral. In the briefest of remarks, she said the window—supposedly based on tapestry designs by five sister nuns— would honor "the lives and devotion of the 1,400 women of the Empire who died for their country in the war."

Perhaps it was the Africa journey, or feeling more settled in her position, but Elizabeth seemed more assertive. "I quickly saw she holds the leading strings," Chips Channon commented when he encountered the Yorks in the spring of 1925. In a letter to the Prince of Wales while on safari, she had described her "relief and freedom" in being away from the force field of George V. "I hate being always under the eye of a narrow minded autocrat," she wrote.

David advised her to "stand up to them a bit & do things to please them once in a while. . . . It's not much trouble really & then they don't mind bigger things so much." The following autumn, when Bertie was at Balmoral and Elizabeth was visiting her sister May, she urged him to "stick up for yourself . . . don't let anybody patronize you, especially one old fool," adding "for goodness sake <u>don't</u> [underlined twice] leave this letter around, you really mustn't please please." Replied Bertie, "I loved what you said about the old fool it is so true." The duke was well aware of the personality quirks among members of the royal family. He told Elizabeth he could "never fathom" his father's spinster sister Toria. "Sometimes she's nice, other times bitter," he wrote. "Odd family, mine, what?"

The two matters prominent in their minds turned out to be linked. Bertie and Elizabeth were desperate to extricate themselves from

White Lodge and find a permanent home in London. They equally yearned for Elizabeth to get pregnant. In a letter to the Prince of Wales that August, Bertie confided, "I still long for one thing which you can guess, & so does she."

That mission had likely already been accomplished by then. A month later, writing to Bertie at Balmoral, Elizabeth reported, "I am feeling much better now, tho' the sight of wine simply turns me up! Isn't it extraordinary? It will be a tragedy if I never recover my drinking powers."

In the middle of October, they shared the good news with the King and Queen and the Strathmores. Queen Mary conveyed their joy "that we may look forward to a direct descendent in the male line" and that "the country will be delighted when they are allowed to know."

With an April due date, Bertie and Elizabeth now had the leverage to persuade the King and Queen that they would be better off full-time in London. They found Curzon House on Curzon Street, only a mile from Buckingham Palace, a suitable rental. "It will be much better for Elizabeth," Bertie wrote to his mother on October 27, "as she will be able to see her friends & will not have to motor up and down from here each day; besides, she will not be lonely."

Other than headaches and fatigue, the duchess was faring well. But her still unannounced pregnancy enabled her to bow out of previously scheduled engagements. The Duke of York went alone to Sunderland, Leeds, and Norwich, explaining to his mother "they would have been tiring for Elizabeth & I am so glad she did not come." He told the disappointed crowd in Norwich that she was absent "owing to a cold."

She was, however, very much at the duke's side on Saturday, October 31, 1925, when he gave the speech at the closing ceremony of the British Empire Exhibition at Wembley.

When the Yorks arrived in midafternoon, the arena was once more filled to capacity. It was a less formal occasion without the King and Queen in attendance. After inspecting the guard of honor, Prince Albert took his place in front of the royal box and delivered his speech, again fewer than four hundred words, taking a little over three minutes.

As before, it was broadcast over loudspeakers, but this time not on the radio. And as before, it contained words bound to halt Bertie's flow: "King," "King-Emperor," "contributed," "capacity." *The Times* wrote that the duke spoke "very well" and that "every word" transmitted throughout the stadium was "clearly audible to everyone in the vast audience."

But one discerning listener, Australian speech therapist Lionel Logue, had a different reaction, according to Reginald Pound, the first writer to obtain access to Logue's private case notes for a book published in 1967. Logue was in the stadium with his son Laurie. "Hearing him speak, noting his hesitancies," wrote Pound, "Logue remarked to his son as the cheering died away: 'He's too old for me to manage a complete cure. But I could very nearly do it. I'm sure of that.'"

ON NOVEMBER 20, 1925, EIGHTY-YEAR-OLD Queen Alexandra died after suffering a heart attack. Bertie and David rushed to Sandringham and spent two days consoling their grieving father over the loss of his beloved "Motherdear." Elizabeth expressed to the King her "deepest & truest sympathy from the very bottom of my heart."

The Yorks took part in Alexandra's funeral at Westminster Abbey on Friday the twenty-seventh. It was a majestic service attended by kings and queens of Norway, Belgium, Denmark, and Spain—all relatives of the late dowager queen. They reassembled the next morning for a private committal in St. George's Chapel at Windsor Castle, where she was buried next to her husband, King Edward VII.

Bertie returned to York Cottage alone in early December for five days of shooting with his father. He wrote to "my own little darling" that he was glad she had stayed in London "as you would be so bored & Mama spends the whole day at the other house. Such a mistake as it is too quick. . . . But you know Mama's methods of going through things, very nice & all that but tactless." He expressed concern that

Elizabeth was "feeling wretched," but he hoped "as time goes on you will not find things such an effort."

She felt strong enough to accompany Bertie to York Cottage for Christmas. They did their best to enliven what Bertie described as "awful & deadly dull" evenings. "We brought down a cinema & a radio & a gramophone, which are all hard at work at different ends of the house, which is much the same here, as being in the same room!" she wrote to her sister May. On Christmas Eve, Bertie wrote to Elizabeth tenderly, recalling, "It is just 3 years since I wrote you that letter & what a lot has happened since then."

He didn't specify, but he was probably referring to his outpouring at three-thirty in the morning on December 29, 1922, after the Norfolk Hunt Ball, where they had anguished together about the busybodies gossiping about their romance. "My heart still goes pit-a-pat in the same way as it did then," he wrote, adding, "Why I have written these letters to you when you're in the room I don't know. But I just have, All my love darling. Always Your very loving HUBBY Bertie."

The Yorks faced another quandary about where to live when the lease on Curzon House expired shortly after the new year. They located a place on Grosvenor Square that the King and Queen approved—always a requirement. But the house rental fell through in March. With Elizabeth's due date imminent, they moved in with the Strathmores at Bruton Street. They would end up living there for another fifteen months.

"I am just sitting here waiting now," Elizabeth wrote on April 12 to the Queen, who had sent a parcel of "exquisite" baby clothes. "I don't think it will make an appearance for another two or three weeks." Her doctors were less patient. On the seventeenth, they decided that she should be induced, and on the twentieth, she endured many hours of difficult labor in her bedroom at 17 Bruton Street. With the fetus in the breech position, her doctors decided to perform a cesarean section. As they delicately phrased it, "a certain line of treatment was successfully adopted."

The four royal brothers in the 1930s: Prince George; Prince Edward, the Prince of Wales; Prince Albert, the Duke of York; and Prince Henry, the Duke of Gloucester.

PART THREE

The Road to the Crown

"God help us all to be calm & wise."

"We always wanted a child
to make our happiness complete."

The Duchess of York holding Princess Elizabeth Alexandra Mary as the Duke of York touches his daughter's hand, April 1926.

SIXTEEN

Tremendous Joy

THE FUTURE QUEEN ELIZABETH II WAS BORN AT 2:40 A.M. ON APRIL 21, 1926. Complying with the ancient custom of ensuring a bogus baby swap had not occurred, the home secretary, Sir William Joynson-Hicks, was present in the Strathmores' house at the time of the birth. At 4:00 A.M., a courtier awakened the King and Queen with the news. "Such relief and joy," Queen Mary wrote in her diary.

In an odd coincidence, the King and Queen gave a small luncheon that day for a group of royal relatives including Princess Alice of Battenberg—the mother of the infant's future husband, four-year-old Prince Philip. But it was Chips Channon—shrewdly applying his knowledge of the many flaws of the Prince of Wales, still unmarried and immature at age thirty-two—who won the prize for prescience. "I have a feeling the child will be Queen of England," he wrote in his diary.

Later in the afternoon, George V and Queen Mary visited Bruton Street to see Bertie and meet their granddaughter. The duke wrote to his mother the next day describing his "tremendous joy." He said he and Elizabeth "always wanted a child to make our happiness complete, & now that it has at last happened it seems so wonderful & so strange." He told the Queen and others how proud he was of his wife "after all she has gone through." To his father, Bertie confessed, "I was very worried and anxious before the baby was born."

They needed George V's consent for their choice of name: Elizabeth Alexandra Mary, which honored her mother as well as her paternal great-grandmother and grandmother. "I am sure there will be no muddle over two Elizabeths in the family," Bertie wrote six days after the birth. "We are so anxious for her first name to be Elizabeth as it is such a nice name & there has been no one of that name in your family for a long time. Elizabeth of York sounds so nice too."

The King replied to say, "I quite approve" of the name. He didn't think two Elizabeths would matter. As it turned out, the clever child eliminated any confusion in the family on her own. Shortly after her second birthday, the King noted for the first time in his diary that "Little 'Lilibet'" was coming for a visit. It was a nickname she had given herself, and soon everyone in the family used it.

BRITAIN WITHSTOOD A GENERAL STRIKE called on May 3 by the Trades Union Congress to protest an effort to reorganize the coal industry. Bertie's involvement in the Industrial Welfare Society heightened his interest in the crisis, and he listened to the debates in the House of Commons for five straight days. The public did not support the wide disruption of essential services, and the government carried out well-organized emergency measures. As a result, the TUC ended the strike "unconditionally," as George V noted, after nine days in which "4 million have been affected" and "not a shot has been fired & no one killed. . . . It shows what wonderful people we are."

Elizabeth's slow recovery from surgery prevented her from attending family luncheons at Buckingham Palace for the sixty-first and fifty-ninth birthdays of the King and Queen at the end of May and beginning of June. But she was front and center for the christening of Elizabeth of York in the private chapel at Buckingham Palace on May 29, 1926, a windy and rainy day.

The King and Queen were among the half dozen godparents for the infant, who was now third in the line of succession to the throne after Uncle David and her father. The small chapel—originally built by Queen Victoria—was adorned with scarlet and white flowers, and the golden font at the altar steps was filled with holy water from the River Jordan—where Jesus was baptized by John the Baptist. The baby wore the christening robe of Brussels lace used for the children of Queen Victoria, Edward VII, and George V. "Of course poor baby cried," noted Queen Mary in her typically laconic fashion.

Less than a month later, *The Illustrated London News* ran a portrait of the Duke of York on its cover, headlined "The First Member of the Royal Family to Enter for Wimbledon." The news that the thirty-year-old duke would play with Louis Greig in the first round of the men's doubles championship had "aroused the greatest interest." Bertie was described as "a strong left-handed player." Forty-five-year-old Greig, the duke's longtime partner and instructor, played at professional caliber. Bertie felt nervous about competing in front of the tournament's large crowds and asked to play on an outer court. But Wimbledon assigned them the Number Two court, visible from the royal box, on Friday, June 25. Their opponents, A. W. Gore and H. Roper Barrett, were multiple winners at Wimbledon.

Greig and Bertie had remained friendly despite their difficult parting two years earlier. One of the first letters the duke wrote after the birth of his daughter was to Greig, saying that he had learned about babies and children from his former adviser's family. "Now I know from the beginning what it is to be a father," he said. The two men spent hours "practicing and planning their Wimbledon debut," according to Louis's grandson, Geordie Greig.

Elizabeth sat in a chair at one end of the royal box, smartly attired in a cloche hat and a fur-trimmed jacket. She stoically watched as her husband and Greig went down to a humiliating defeat in straight sets: 1–6, 3–6, and 2–6. Bertie had been rattled from the start, overwhelmed by the noise and proximity of the crowd, "lashing out wildly with his racquet," in the words of one spectator. "Try the other hand, Sir," the spectators shouted, as his partner ran all over the court attempting to catch the shots Bertie was missing. The next day's edition of *The Times* ran a photograph of the Duke of York reaching for an overhead shot and noting the dismal score. Bertie never again played tennis in public.

That summer a far more consequential challenge arose for the duke and duchess when the King decided to send them to Australia as his representatives for the opening of the parliament in the new capital of Canberra. In 1900, the British colonies of Australia had become a federation of states, joined together as a commonwealth. The British monarch was the head of state, and the country was a large and important dominion in the empire. The Prince of Wales's visit to the antipodes in 1920 had been a huge success, and the King now wanted Prince Albert to undertake a "mission of first-rate imperial importance."

Australian prime minister Stanley Bruce had met the Yorks three years earlier during the Imperial Conference in London attended by the heads of the empire's dominions. At a Buckingham Palace banquet, he had been seated next to the duchess, beguiling in a tiara and satin gown embroidered with pearls. On hearing Prince Albert's stammering speeches, however, Bruce had been "appalled at the prospect of the King's representative being so gravely inhibited." But Bruce relented, and the visit was announced in July 1926. With no comparable reluctance, the government of New Zealand extended its own invitation, promising the couple "a hearty welcome." The King decided to send the Yorks across the Pacific, stopping first in New Zealand.

The tour would last six months, with a nearly seven-week outward journey and five weeks at sea for their return. The demands on the couple would be intense, especially the number of speeches the Duke of York would be called upon to make. His "secret dread," wrote Wheeler-Bennett, was that "the hidden root" of his stuttering affliction "lay in the mind rather than in the body." It was imperative that he try another speech therapist.

Late in the summer of 1926, the duke's new private secretary, Patrick Hodgson, first heard about Lionel Logue, the Australian speech therapist who had listened to Bertie's halting speech at Wembley nine months earlier. Since immigrating to England in 1924 and setting up shop on Harley Street—London's hub of medical practitioners—Logue had become known for his effective techniques to mitigate stuttering. He wasn't a trained doctor, but he had devised his own blend of motivation, breathing exercises, and language drills. After so much failed therapy, Bertie was skeptical until Elizabeth finally convinced him to make "just one more try."

Logue asked Prince Albert to visit him in his consulting room on the second floor of 146 Harley Street. "He must come here," said Logue. "That imposes an effort on him which is essential to success. If I see him at home we lose the value of that." The duke's first meeting took place in midafternoon on October 19, 1926. Logue was struck immediately by the "slim quiet man, with tired eyes and all the outward symptoms of the man upon whom habitual speech defect had begun to set the sign."

He sensed "an acute nervous tension which has been brought on by the defect," and he discovered a crucial traumatic memory from Bertie's days at Osborne: When queried by a mathematics teacher, he had been "struck dumb" and unable to utter the word "quarter." During their first ninety minutes together, Logue persuaded Bertie that his condition was curable, "but it will need a tremendous effort by you." When Bertie left, "you could see that there was hope once more in his heart," Logue wrote.

For the next two and a half months, Bertie visited Logue nearly every day—always "on equal terms" either at Harley Street or Logue's flat in South Kensington. Each hour-long session required breathing lessons to control and strengthen his diaphragm, gargling with warm water, repeating vowel sounds while standing by an open window, and practicing tongue-twisting phrases. Elizabeth frequently accompanied her husband so she could assist with the regimen at home, which he carried out conscientiously.

Nearly a century later, the bond between the sympathetic and straightforward therapist and his determined patient would form the plot of the award-winning film *The King's Speech*. Logue did not, however, call the duke "Bertie," as shown in the film. Nor did Prince Albert spout profanities as part of his regimen. But the mutual trust and admiration were genuinely portrayed.

The Yorks solved their housing problem when Elizabeth found a London property that would work for them. Number 145 Piccadilly near Hyde Park Corner had been vacant for five years and was in a state of disrepair. Elizabeth fell in love with the four-story gray stone house with twenty-five bedrooms including servants' quarters, as well as a conservatory, a ballroom, and an electric elevator. From the front it had a view of Green Park and Buckingham Palace, and it shared a large rear garden with adjacent townhouses.

Queen Mary insisted, "In spite of yr new house being dirty & untidy," that she and the King inspect it "before the improvements are commenced." The four of them took the tour on July 7. "There are possibilities in the house," Queen Mary wrote in her diary. In other words, she could see yet another project to supervise. It was perfect timing, actually, as the Queen was wrapping up her extensive alterations to the Big House at Sandringham so that she and the King could leave York Cottage in the autumn after thirty-three years.

Like White Lodge, the house in Piccadilly belonged to the Crown Estate—the vast property holdings owned by the monarch—so Bertie negotiated a favorable grace-and-favor lease requiring a "peppercorn" rent. The Yorks could then begin the renovation and redecoration financed by the Crown Estate.

Bertie assiduously applied himself to Logue's regimen. He allotted time during official engagements to take hour-long breaks, and he even cut short his foxhunting to squeeze in his therapist before dinner. He implored Logue to accompany him on the trip Down Under, but the therapist firmly but gently said no. The duke needed self-reliance, and Logue believed it would be a "psychological error" to travel with him.

The Yorks had been savoring their first eight months of parenthood, with holidays at Glamis and Balmoral. Elizabeth reveled in her baby girl. "She is going to be very wicked, and she is very quick I think," she wrote to her mother. They had their first Christmas at the Big House, which Elizabeth proclaimed "<u>a million</u> times better" than York Cottage. "Plenty of room and a much better atmosphere." At St. Paul's Walden Bury for the New Year's holiday, she "talked hard" with her mother. "We shall not see dear S.P.W. for a long time now," she wrote on January 2.

London was a whirl of preparation for what Elizabeth privately called "this horrible trip": packing, shopping, inoculations, and partings from family and friends, including James Stuart, who came to lunch at Bruton Street while Bertie was shooting at Windsor. The Prince of Wales threw a sparkling farewell party at York House, his apartment in St. James's Palace. Among the guests were the Astaires, the recently divorced Sheila Loughborough, and her future second husband, Sir John "Buffles" Milbanke. The Plantation Orchestra, a popular African American jazz ensemble, started playing at midnight. "I did the Charleston with David for nearly 20 minutes!!" Elizabeth wrote in her diary. "Home at 3:30. Bed 4. Oh Lord."

"His new confidence, he said, 'comes from being able to speak properly at last.'"

The Duke of York with the Duchess of York at the opening of the Federal Parliament in Canberra, Australia, on May 9, 1927.

SEVENTEEN

Eager to Do Well

ON JANUARY 6, 1927, THE DAY OF THEIR DEPARTURE FROM BRUTON Street for Victoria station, Elizabeth felt "very miserable at leaving the baby. Went up & played with her & she was so sweet. Lucky she doesn't realize anything. . . . I drank some champagne & tried not to weep." Parting from the baby gave Bertie a "terrible pang." He told his mother that she would be "so grown up when we return."

HMS *Renown,* a battle cruiser dating from the First World War, flew the Duke of York's standard, and the navigating bridge was painted with the white rose of York surmounted by the duke's coronet. A tidy officer's cabin was scarcely altered for the duke's quarters. The duchess had her own sleeping cabin and adjacent boudoir. The chairs and sofas in the sitting room were covered in a blue chintz selected by Elizabeth. Tucked into the stern was a small paneled chapel, and the dining saloon had a long table that seated thirty-four.

The duke and duchess had a retinue headed by the Earl of Cavan, a much-decorated First World War veteran and field marshal who was appointed by George V as the chief of staff. Among his duties was to send the King regular reports on the duke's performance. Lord Cavan's wife, Joan, a friend of Queen Mary, was designated as a lady-in-waiting for Elizabeth, who was twelve years younger.

"It is clear that both Their Royal Highnesses dislike the Cavans," Bertie's private secretary, Patrick Hodgson, reluctantly confided to the Queen. They saw Lord Cavan as "too punctilious and rather narrow," and the couple's "little mannerisms and ways" irritated the Yorks. But Cavan proved efficient in running the logistics of the tour, and Bertie and Elizabeth eventually warmed to them both.

A companionable contemporary, twenty-five-year-old Victoria "Tortor" Gilmour, was the twenty-six-year-old duchess's second lady-in-waiting. She was the mother of a three-year-old daughter and six-month-old son, so would be feeling the same pangs of interrupted motherhood. A blithe spirit like Elizabeth, she was also the second youngest in a large family, and had been a similarly favored child. Tortor's grandfather was the fifth Earl Cadogan, and her four older sisters were known as "the Cadogan Square." Hodgson reported to Queen Mary that Tortor was "much liked and keeps us all amused." She quickly became "the life and soul of the Staff, and both their Royal Highnesses are very fond of her."

Patrick Hodgson was a classic aristocratic courtier, descended from an earl and a marquess. He knew precisely how to serve as a back channel to Queen Mary during the lengthy trip, offering the sort of frank information she required. "I feel it is better to describe things just as I see them so that you may really know what is happening," he wrote.

The duke was also served by equerries Colin Buist and newcomer Major Terence Nugent, as well as the British government's representative, political secretary Harry Batterbee. The ship's company comprised 1,300 officers and men, along with the band of the Royal Naval School of Music, a drum and fife band, 16 marine buglers, and 150 Royal Marines to serve as guards of honor during ceremonies. The Yorks also hired an official chronicler, journalist Taylor Darbyshire, to write a book about the tour, as well as a photographer and two newsreel cameramen. As in Africa, they had a personal physician, Surgeon

Commander H.E.Y. White, in addition to the medical staff on the ship.

Bertie and Elizabeth amused themselves throughout the long voyage much as they would on a typical country house weekend. Elizabeth spent many hours chatting with Tortor and reading from a library stocked with popular titles by authors including P. G. Wodehouse, John Buchan, and Agatha Christie. Bertie sometimes read aloud to his wife, although more often he played deck tennis or shot clay pigeons. Every evening they had cocktails, and after dinner they played mahjongg, watched films, or danced to gramophone records.

During brief stops in Las Palmas, Jamaica, Panama, and Fiji, the Yorks ran through their official paces, but faced no particular challenges. Patrick Hodgson told Queen Mary that Bertie's "natural tendency to shyness is being overcome" and that he was talking to strangers "genially."

Bertie stuck with Lionel Logue's treatment regimen every day. After making three short speeches in Jamaica and Panama, he proudly reported to Logue, "I have not been held up for a word in conversation at any time," adding, "I don't think about the breathing anymore. . . . I try to open my mouth and it certainly feels more open than before. You remember my fear of 'The King.' I give it every day at dinner on board. This does not worry me anymore." Hodgson told Logue the speeches went well enough, "though perhaps there is a trifle more hesitancy than when you are near at hand." But he emphasized that Bertie was "full of confidence" and "much better than I expected he would be in your absence."

Bertie and Elizabeth yearned for news of their daughter, which came intermittently, like everything else posted across great distances. "I miss the baby all the time, & am always wondering what she is doing," Elizabeth wrote in her diary after a month at sea. Several days later she told Queen Mary, "I miss her quite terribly."

Dr. George F. Still, the princess's pediatrician, dispatched regular progress reports that were informative but dry: pulling herself to a standing position, saying her first words ("Yight!" when pointing to an electric light), waving, and cutting teeth. Queen Mary offered more satisfying descriptions. She told Bertie about the baby's "funny little noises & screams & shouts for fun." Princess Elizabeth uttered "shrieks of delight at each dog she saw." And at breakfast, Charlotte the parrot entertained her as she "watched the bird eating pips with an air of absorption."

The grandmothers engaged in a polite tug-of-war over possession of their little princess. Days after the Yorks' departure, Cecilia told Beryl Poignand that Elizabeth had "begged me to see all I could of her," so she planned to keep her granddaughter at St. Paul's Walden Bury "until the Queen appropriates" her. Elizabeth knew that her mother would be more hands-on and naturally affectionate than Queen Mary.

Princess Elizabeth stayed with the Strathmores for the first month while the King and Queen were at Sandringham. When they returned to London in early February, their granddaughter was whisked to Buckingham Palace and installed in an airy nursery in the north wing. Each day, dressed in a white gown with fringed sash, she would be presented to the King and Queen at teatime. "Here comes the Bambina!" Queen Mary would exclaim.

THE YORKS STEELED THEMSELVES FOR their landing in New Zealand on February 22. Hodgson reported to Queen Mary that the duke was "determined to make a success of it," and that the duchess, at first seemingly uninterested in the details of the arrangements, had grown "alive to all that is involved."

Still, fear of his father's censure lay heavily on Bertie. He had already received captious letters from the King, in one of which was enclosed a press photo showing the duke in the wrong place while inspecting a guard of honor. Lord Cavan sent a top-secret letter to Clive Wigram, reminding him that the Yorks were "both sensitive and frightfully anxious to do well," but they had been "plunged into depths of woe" by the King's criticism. An "approving word" from George V "wd work wonders." In particular, Cavan asked for a "short encouraging telegram" before the young couple began their "difficult & arduous work."

Two days prior to the Yorks' arrival in Auckland, they received the requested reassurance from the King and the Queen. They underlined the importance of Bertie and Elizabeth's "mission," which they would be following "with affectionate interest." They acknowledged that the program would be "strenuous" but expressed the belief that the duke and duchess could rise to the challenges. "I cannot thank you enough for His Majesty's splendidly timed message of encouragement," Cavan wrote to Wigram.

Once on shore, Bertie immediately wrote to his mother to say that "the New Zealand programme has filled us with awe, as it looks & I am sure will be very full & very tiring. Every day we are traveling except in the big cities, & at each place where we stop for a few minutes we do exactly the same thing."

For the next three months, the Yorks repeated all the familiar rituals of royal engagements, but at a level of intensity and duration they had never previously experienced. They saw natural wonders such as hot springs and geysers (Elizabeth "thinking every moment we would all disappear through a thin crust into the unknown!"), witnessed countless local customs, such as the fierce Maori haka dance, and formed strong impressions of individuals and groups. For the first time they watched massive pageants performed by thousands of children doing precision formations such as the "living" Union Jack and Cross of St. George.

On the North Island of New Zealand, from Auckland to Rotorua to Wellington and multiple towns along the way, they were hailed by cheering crowds in the tens of thousands. Bertie made a half dozen speeches. In his final remarks in Wellington, he took note of all the thriving children they had seen, and he memorably said, "Take care of the children and the country will take care of itself."

He reported to his mother that he was "really pleased . . . as I had perfect confidence in myself & I did not hesitate at all. Logue's teaching is still working well but of course if I get tired it still worries me."

Elizabeth had absorbed so much of Logue's techniques that she could almost serve as his proxy. Bertie relied on her loving glances and comforting touch to defuse his temper when fatigued and frustrated.

Their fortnight on the North Island included two respites—one day of deep-sea fishing, and a week later two days fishing for trout. Nevertheless, the subsequent four days in Wellington proved too much for the duchess. The entire New Zealand program, she told her sister May Elphinstone, "was simply ghastly, & I stuck it for 16 days, & then suddenly cracked." Early in the morning of March 9, 1927, *Renown* crossed the sixty-three-mile Cook Strait from Wellington at the bottom of the North Island to Picton at the top of the South Island. Their procession of cars took nearly all day—including five hours on dusty mountain roads through hairpin turns and steep declivities—to reach the coastal town of Nelson.

By the evening, Elizabeth was running a fever of 102 with a bad case of tonsillitis. The doctors insisted on bed rest and prohibited her from touring the South Island, which had an even more demanding schedule. Prince Albert momentarily considered canceling altogether but decided to press on alone. Compounding his anxiety, he was deflated by the prospect of losing Elizabeth's vital support and encouragement. "In his innate shyness and modesty, he believed that it was the Duchess whom the crowds were really cheering and that it was she whom they really wanted to see," wrote John Wheeler-Bennett.

By automobile and train the duke traversed the South Island from north to south, through Christchurch to Dunedin. Children, soldiers, and even hard-bitten coal miners greeted him heartily. The "Industrial Prince" was in his element. In an area supposed to be "Red," noted *The Times*, "he met nothing but patriotic demonstrations wherever he went." On one railroad platform he gave an impromptu speech. The "surging and wildly enthusiastic crowd" cheered him unceasingly for five minutes.

Elizabeth, meanwhile, returned to Wellington, where she could recuperate in more comfortable accommodations at Government House. Bertie kept in touch by telephone, and they exchanged affectionate letters. In mid-March she wrote to "My darling sweet" in Dunedin. She had received many kindnesses, but "all I wanted really was a nice comforting kiss from <u>you</u>."

She confessed to feeling "such a failure." But she emphasized that she and "everybody else" agreed that his perseverance was "marvellous." "Darling when you are feeling very depressed and tired," she wrote, "remember what wonderful work you are doing. They all loved you in N. Island and quite rightly." She prayed he would "get through the nightmare program" and looked forward to "the moment when I shall see you again." She sent him "hundreds of kisses & several hugs."

He replied to "my own little darling," that her letter had "spurred me on to greater efforts. Millions and millions of thanks for it you darling; it is just what I wanted & nothing could have given me greater help and encouragement." His main concern, though, was that she "have a real rest and get the throat strong again."

Back on *Renown,* she waited in rough weather for Bertie to arrive on the afternoon of March 22. The sea was so stormy he had to be transported by a harbor tug. When a gangplank proved inadequate, his only recourse was to jump from one vessel to the other. "It looked unpleasant," Elizabeth wrote, "but he did not seem to mind much." What mattered most was his father's judgment on the New Zealand tour. "I am delighted you are getting such excellent reception everywhere," George V wrote. "I congratulate you on the success of your visit."

THEY ARRIVED AT THE SPECTACULAR Sydney Harbour late in the morning on March 26 under sunny skies. The city's welcome was astounding, with a turnout of over a million people. Elizabeth wisely rested in the afternoon while Bertie did his rounds. That night, thirty thousand people clamored outside the town hall. Chains of Chinese lanterns and profusions of roses and laurels decorated the reception room inside, where three thousand invited guests "crushed and jostled" as the royal couple threaded through their midst.

And so it went for the rest of their forty-seven days of engagements in Australia. Their major stops after Sydney were Brisbane, Hobart, Melbourne, Adelaide, Canberra, and Perth. They had ten days set aside for travel and rest, mostly the former. They found brief downtime at a cattle station, a sheep station where Bertie went riding before breakfast, and a forty-three-thousand-acre ranch where the duke took part in a kangaroo hunt.

The emotional peak of their time in Australia was on April 25, Anzac Day in Melbourne, honoring the Australian and New Zealand Army Corps who had fought in the First World War. Surrounded by another massive crowd, the Yorks stood at a replica of the Whitehall Cenotaph, where the duke laid a wreath and took the salute as twenty-five thousand veterans marched past. They were preceded by the wrenching sight of seven hundred blind, disabled, and invalid soldiers in a procession of cars and trucks, some carrying the men in their hospital beds. At the brief commemoration ceremony, the duke spoke of the "traditions of loyalty, fortitude, and devotion to duty which animated those gallant men."

Although he and Elizabeth often felt besieged, the duke thrived on the Aussies' informality. At the University of Melbourne, students raucously "ragged" him after he received an honorary doctorate. "Come on, Albert!" they cried, as they bundled him into a landau escorted by "staff" in outrageous costumes. The chemistry students called him "Dear Bertie" and urged him to "give our kind regards to the Old Man and the Missus." The dentistry students described themselves as "people of good extraction."

At the students' clubhouse, he laughed and laughed as they sang "For He's a Jolly Good Fellow." He climbed on a chair to say he now knew "what a very good fellow the young Australian is." The students then carried him in the chair to the university quadrangle where dignitaries had been waiting nearly an hour for him to appear.

As expected, Australia fell in love with the Duchess of York. "The Smile That Captured All Hearts," read one headline. She had little to say, but her sunny presence was sufficient. By then she understood the power of her gaze. In a letter to the Prince of Wales, she described "the language of the eye" that she deployed. A newspaper in Melbourne captured the intimacy of her smile that would be remarked upon many times in the following years: "The strange thing is that everyone who has seen it feels it is for him or her alone."

The Yorks' aides were aware of the strain felt by both Elizabeth and Bertie: the mental, emotional, and physical energy needed to be "on" for hours at a time. Patrick Hodgson told Queen Mary that the duke "tends to get a little 'heavy' and snaps especially when he is tired. But this doesn't occur in public and the Staff quite understand it. These moods don't last." The duchess, on the other hand, "never appears bored or tired in public and is always ready to do what is wanted." Actually, as Elizabeth wrote to her mother, "Though we are working very hard," she confessed she found "some of it very boring."

Yet neither she nor Bertie displayed a whiff of the sort of cynicism characteristic of the Prince of Wales, who coined the term "stunts" for official engagements. Elizabeth wrote movingly to the Queen about the expression of the people's loyalty that "gives one quite a lump in the throat." The Yorks may have felt fatigued by the mind-numbing sameness of making small talk with one local official after another. But they grasped more keenly than ever that meeting a member of the royal family was a fresh experience that would endure as a treasured memory.

Wherever Bertie and Elizabeth went, they also witnessed an outpouring of affection for the baby breezily nicknamed "Princess Betty." Back in Britain, the little princess spent two solid months with the King and Queen, and Lady Strathmore saw her once in London, at tea on April 1 before the court moved to Windsor Castle. For her first stay in the ancient fortress, little Elizabeth lived in a nursery suite in Victoria Tower near the Queen's apartment. In honor of her first birthday on April 21, *The Illustrated London News* ran a full-page picture of the Queen and her granddaughter headlined "Britain's Most Popular Baby."

The princess was reunited with her non-royal grandparents at St. Paul's Walden Bury on May 10. She remained with them—with the exception of a week at Buckingham Palace for the King's and Queen's birthdays—until late June. Elizabeth thanked the King for "having been so kind" to her daughter. "I have missed her all day & every day," she wrote.

The main mission in Australia, opening the Federal Parliament in Canberra, took place on the morning of May 9 with "just a nip in the air." The Yorks arrived in a carriage with the usual panoply. Bertie was in his full-dress naval uniform and cocked hat, Elizabeth wore one of her signature cloche hats, and *Renown*'s silver bugles played a fanfare. A crowd of twenty thousand had assembled outside Parliament House. The duke was originally supposed to give only one speech to inaugurate the parliament in the Senate Chamber. But he also wanted to make remarks after unlocking the doors with a golden key.

From the top of the red-carpeted steps, he spoke for less than three minutes, his speech transmitted through loudspeakers and by radio across Australia. Looking out over the new capital city—in fact a small town of six thousand, with a few government buildings, bungalows for civil servants, dusty roads, and fields of grazing cattle and sheep—the Duke of York spoke of the dominion's future. "One feels the stirrings of a new birth, of quickened national activity, of a fuller consciousness of your destiny as one of the great self-governing units of the British Empire," he said.

In the crowded and overheated Senate Chamber, he and Elizabeth stood next to each other in front of two large leather chairs, surrounded by dignitaries. His formal inaugural address was judged "perfectly admirable in delivery." Afterward he told his father that the small room "was not a very easy one in which to speak." But he didn't feel nervous after having successfully spoken outside. His new confidence, he said, "comes from being able to speak properly at last."

The duke and duchess had two more weeks of official engagements that included a voyage on *Renown* to Western Australia, where jubilant crowds greeted them in Fremantle and Perth. On May 23, as *Renown*'s band played "Auld Lang Syne," the Yorks stood on their private deck and waved goodbye.

They arrived at Portsmouth on June 27, reasonably well rested, despite obligatory visits to Mauritius, Port Said, Malta, and Gibraltar. The Prince of Wales, Prince Henry, and Prince George boarded *Renown,* and David greeted Elizabeth with an affectionate kiss. The King typically had sent strict instructions about what Bertie and his staff should wear. Also typically, he wrote, "We will not embrace at the station before so many people. When you kiss Mama, take yr. hat off." On the platform at Victoria station, "Mama" ignored her husband's injunction and gave Elizabeth a hug. Elizabeth in turn enveloped her own mother with a warm embrace.

Defying a heavy rain, the duke and duchess rode to Buckingham Palace in an open carriage rather than let down the crowd lining the route. Sheltered under an umbrella, Elizabeth smiled continually as they proceeded up the Mall. The Yorks reunited with their fourteen-month-old daughter—cradled in the arms of her nurse—in the Grand Hall of the Palace. The little princess had only known her parents as the "Father" and "Mother" photographs framed in her nursery. "There's Mother!" Queen Mary exclaimed when Elizabeth appeared and cried, "Oh! You darling."

As attendants draped the balcony with crimson and gold cloth, the crowd began to cheer. Moments later, the King and Queen emerged, followed by the Strathmores and the Yorks. "Elizabeth held her baby in spite of the rain, which fell in torrents," George V noted admiringly in his diary. Princess Elizabeth "waved her hand vigorously" at the throng. Her face "radiant with smiles," the duchess walked twice with her baby toward the front of the balcony, to a crescendo of cheers.

Undaunted by the downpour, another crowd gathered in front of 145 Piccadilly as the happy trio arrived at their new home. They scarcely had time to look around when the double doors opened on a small balcony, and an oriental rug was thrown over the parapet. Out came the young family, the duchess still holding Princess Elizabeth in her arms. Bertie and Elizabeth waved to the crowd, thanking them for their welcome.

It had been a seminal experience for them both: thirty thousand miles by sea, and several thousand by land. The duke still felt anxious about public speaking, but he had proved himself at last. "Bertie has been wonderful, and is far less shy & more sure of himself," Elizabeth told Queen Mary. "I expect this Tour will mean a great deal to him." Bertie in turn told his father that Elizabeth had "done wonders. . . . I could never have done the tour without her help." Their mutual devotion had deepened, and they both realized how they depended on each other. They would carry out further consequential foreign tours together, but their antipodean journey would never be equaled in its scope and duration.

"Bertie and Elizabeth's firstborn cast a particular spell on the irascible George V."

An artist's rendering of King George V watching his favorite granddaughter, two-year-old Lilibet, on the grounds of Craigweil House, where the King was convalescing from a severe illness.

EIGHTEEN

Family Crises

THE YORKS' TOUR WAS SALUTED IN STYLE AT LONDON'S FIFTEENTH-CENTURY Guildhall in mid-July 1927. Trumpets heralded their arrival in an open carriage surrounded by enthusiastic crowds. After a luncheon attended by government officials and members of the royal family, Prime Minister Baldwin proposed a toast, emphasizing "the work, the anxiety, and the strain" imposed by the mission undertaken by the royal couple.

"From early morning until mid-day and from mid-day until late in the evening," they were "constantly seeing people of all kinds and in all circumstances." All who met them expected to be treated as though "the Duke and Duchess had come 10,000 miles to speak to them alone." Baldwin praised the Yorks for maintaining their equanimity, cheerfulness, and good temper throughout the long tour. And he praised the duke for being "prepared at any time to subordinate personal comfort to your duty . . . which is endearing you to the people of this country."

Bertie had resumed his regular sessions with Lionel Logue and was well prepared to reply. He spoke at unusual length—a half hour—touching on the high points of the journey and sharing his reactions. He was impressed by the unstinting loyalty to the throne and empire, along with "affection for the Mother Country." And he described the progress in both New Zealand and Australia that had taken place within three generations. "I return a thorough optimist," he said. "The same qualities that carried us successfully through the war will . . . enable us to surmount all difficulties."

Logue thought Bertie spoke "pleasantly, smoothly and with great charm." The duke redoubled his determination to improve his performance, which was still marked by pauses and periodic stumbles. Over the next two years, Bertie "never missed an appointment with me," Logue recalled. "He realized that the will to be cured was not enough but that it called for grit, hard work and self-sacrifice, all of which he gave ungrudgingly." Logue noted the support given by Elizabeth whenever Bertie made a speech. Once at a luncheon when the duke was struggling over his words, those nearby saw Elizabeth "reach out and squeeze his finger as if to encourage him to continue."

BERTIE REMAINED DAZZLED BY HIS older brother, but they had little time together before the Prince of Wales and Prince George set out in late July for a two-month tour of Canada with Prime Minister Baldwin and his wife, Lucy, along with Tommy Lascelles. Their main purpose was to preside over the inauguration of the international Peace Bridge built by Canada and the United States across the Niagara River. George was still a serving officer in the Royal Navy, a career he disliked, so the journey was a welcome respite from his duties.

In those years, as Bertie and Elizabeth grew more involved in their family life, the Prince of Wales gravitated toward the bachelor brother whose "unusual charm of manner" he found appealing. Despite their nearly nine-year age gap, David and George had much in common. They both adored café society, frequenting London nightspots.

At age twenty-four, Prince George was taller and more handsome than the Prince of Wales. He was easily the most cultivated of the brothers, with his impressive collection of antiques and a sophisticated interest in the arts that included talent as a pianist. But he was so far down the line of succession that he posed no threat to David and felt less pressure from their overbearing father.

As he had done with Bertie before Elizabeth entered the picture, the Prince of Wales encouraged his youngest brother's misbehavior. Writing from their first-class suites on the Canadian Pacific liner *Empress of Australia,* Edward and Georgie sent a joint letter on August 4 to Elizabeth on her twenty-seventh birthday. They boasted of their drinking escapades and pursuit of women, including, in David's words, "some choice pieces from the Middle West."

By the time they reached Ottawa, Tommy Lascelles felt so disillusioned with the Prince of Wales that he wrote his wife, Joan, to say he was on the verge of resigning as assistant private secretary. The British prime minister also witnessed for the first time Edward's careless behavior. One evening the Baldwins were invited to dinner with the royal brothers at Government House. They arrived promptly, only to see the two princes in shorts and sports shirts, heading out for a game of squash. The dinner party was forced to wait until they had finished playing and changed into dinner clothes.

Lascelles was in such despair that he asked for a confidential meeting with Baldwin. "I told him directly that, in my considered opinion the Heir Apparent, in his unbridled pursuit of wine and women, and whatever self whim occupied him at the moment, was rapidly going to the devil," Tommy recalled more than a decade later. Further, Lascelles said, "Unless he mended his ways," the Prince of Wales "would soon become no fit wearer of the British crown."

Baldwin surprised Lascelles by readily agreeing with everything he said. "You know," Tommy replied, "sometimes when I sit in York House waiting to get the result of some point-to-point in which he is riding, I can't help thinking that the best thing that could happen to him, and to the country, would be for him to break his neck."

"God forgive me," said Baldwin. "I have often thought the same."

In the following weeks, Edward performed well at the podium but misbehaved in private as Lascelles considered whether and how he should resign. Joan urged him to stay, arguing that he was "practically the only good influence" on the Prince of Wales. Lascelles decided to remain out of loyalty to the institution of the monarchy while harboring deep misgivings about its heir. As Tommy wrote to Joan, "the cold fact" remained that "it would be a real disaster if by any ill chance he were called to accede to the throne now." Nor did Lascelles see "any prospect of his fitting himself any better, as time goes on, for what is, ultimately, his job in life." Still, Lascelles viewed his calling as "making a good or at any rate a safe, King."

THE YORK FAMILY CIRCULATED THROUGH St. Paul's Walden Bury, Windsor Castle, Balmoral, Glamis, and Sandringham, but 145 Piccadilly—"the palace with a number and without a name"—formed the core of their life. Its front faced the busy Piccadilly thoroughfare, and net curtains on the ground-floor windows ensured privacy. The door had two bells, for "Visitors" and "House."

Only someone as grand as Mabell Airlie could describe the Yorks' new home as "cosy." It was a sizable establishment requiring a substantial staff that mostly lived in. The steward ran the household, which included at various times a butler, an underbutler, a housekeeper, two footmen, a cook, two kitchen maids, the duke's valet, the duchess's dresser, three personal maids, a nurse, an undernurse, a nursery maid, an odd-job man, an orderly, a telephonist, and a chauffeur. Mr. Ainslie, the tall and immaculate steward, would follow the family to Buckingham Palace. He was famously phlegmatic, and he took Bertie's temper in stride.

The central hall of what the royal family called "One-Four-Five" enjoyed natural light filtering from a large round glass dome set into the roof above the top staircase landing—also the final stop on the electric lift. Large oil paintings in gilded frames lined the walls, along with elephant tusk trophies from the Yorks' African safari.

The most welcoming place in the house was the spacious morning room on the ground floor, just off the central hall. Chintz covered the sofas and armchairs, a fine Persian carpet cloaked the floor, flowers always filled the vases, and the bookcase offered a generous selection of volumes. Elizabeth had her writing table in this room, as well as the requisite gramophone and radio.

Next door was Bertie's small, wood-paneled study equipped with several comfortable chairs. Prominent on his writing table was the miniature of Elizabeth painted by Mabel Hankey in 1923, encircled by a frame of sapphires topped by a jeweled crown. The dining room with a table for thirty faced Piccadilly, and Brussels tapestries hung along the wide staircase.

On the second floor were the more formal drawing room, Elizabeth's spacious bedroom, which overlooked Hyde Park, a boudoir that would later serve as a schoolroom, and the duke's bedroom. The floor above had a ballroom, a library, and more bedrooms. On the top floor the circular landing opened onto the nursery suite for Princess Elizabeth. There were day and night nurseries, a bathroom, a small kitchen, and rooms for nannies and nurses.

The Yorks entertained a lot, with small dinner parties for their friends. Their pet parrot from Australia set the tone by repeating, "Hullo Jimmie, have a drink." Sometimes after an evening at the theater, Bertie and Elizabeth would prepare supper for themselves. When they were on their own, Elizabeth played the piano or sat quietly with a book.

Her literary taste was eclectic and at times even subversive. In addition to her well-known fondness for humorist—and consummate stylist—P. G. Wodehouse, she enjoyed popular books such as Thornton Wilder's acclaimed first novel, *The Cabala*; Aldous Huxley's *Point Counter Point,* a sophisticated roman à clef with such recognizable figures as D. H. Lawrence among the characters; and *The President's Daughter,* a scandalous memoir by the mistress of the late U.S. president Warren G. Harding. Bertie wasn't an avid reader, but he enjoyed the *Times* crossword puzzle, something Elizabeth could never start but sometimes finished.

The duke worked in his study most mornings with his staff. He often invited business executives and trade union representatives to the house for meetings—intended, as always, to further his effort to improve industrial relations. When Commonwealth leaders came to London for conferences, Bertie met with them as well. At night he and Elizabeth formally entertained diplomats and politicians.

Elizabeth's parenting style mirrored her mother's informality, maintaining a fluidity between the nursery and the rest of the house—a sharp contrast to the rigidity of the duke's upbringing. Bertie and Elizabeth were openly demonstrative with their daughter and avoided the usual upper-class presentation of children at teatime. In the morning room, Elizabeth liked to pretend for Lilibet that the sofa was the clattering night train to Scotland. Bertie loosened up under his wife's influence. He played in the garden with his daughter and splashed her at bath time.

Bertie and Elizabeth's firstborn cast a particular spell on the irascible George V. Both he and Queen Mary singled out "Little Lilibet" as their favorite grandchild. They often insisted that Bertie and Elizabeth leave their daughter behind at Sandringham or Balmoral for weeks at a time, which enabled the Yorks to visit friends at their country estates. "She has been with us for over a month & I shall miss her dreadfully," wrote George V in his diary when they relinquished the child at the end of January 1928. Queen Mary told Bertie that "I don't think you & Elizabeth realize what a great joy your child is to us."

Now that they had become accustomed to the limelight, both the duke and duchess were learning to be canny about their images. Starting with their tour of Australia and New Zealand, they authorized a series of books about their lives. These accounts endured for decades as essential sources for future chroniclers.

Prince Albert took the first step, hiring fifty-one-year-old Taylor Darbyshire, born in England but raised and educated in Australia, to write the official record of their big tour. The Duke of York wrote the foreword for the book, which was published in September 1927.

He was so pleased with the result that he enlisted Darbyshire to write an authorized biography that appeared in the autumn of 1929. The title was a mouthful: *The Duke of York: An Intimate and Authoritative Life-Story of the Second Son of Their Majesties The King and Queen by One Who Has Had Special Facilities, and Published with the Approval of His Royal Highness*. While the book contained many fresh details about the duke's life to that time, the headlines highlighted revelations about Lionel Logue's work that led to Bertie's "curing himself of a speech defect."

Elizabeth recognized the merits of sanctioned books when she cooperated with Lady Cynthia Asquith for her own 228-page biography. Cynthia was a daughter of Hugo Charteris, the eleventh Earl of Wemyss, a Scottish title as storied as Strathmore. In 1910, she married Herbert "Beb" Asquith, the second son of Prime Minister Herbert Henry Asquith.

By the time a publisher proposed in 1927 that she write the life of the Duchess of York, she had authored numerous books for children and adults. Elizabeth didn't hesitate when Cynthia approached her. On their first meeting, Asquith "immediately fell under the spell of her charm, gentle radiance, delicate dignity, and that heaven-sent gift for setting others at their ease." Not only did the duchess grant her interviews, she also asked her friends and family members to share letters and speak to her. Crucially, the aristocratic writer allowed the duchess to approve "every word" in the manuscript before publication.

H.R.H. The Duchess of York: An Intimate and Authentic Life-Story, Including Many Details Hitherto Unpublished, Told with the Personal Approval of Her Royal Highness made a splash in the autumn of 1928. The book contained personal vignettes as well as astute observations such as "whatever she undertakes is carried off with a gaiety and cordiality which cloaks the strength of her personality," and "though she can express opinions very trenchantly and has a great love of argument, her manner is always gentle and disarming."

No less effusive was the story the duchess entrusted to her longtime confidante, Beryl Poignand. Elizabeth and her mother were fiercely loyal to Beryl and supported her financially by hiring her for various jobs with the family. Not long after the Asquith biography was published, Beryl began working on a magazine article that turned into a slender book about Princess Elizabeth. She wrote under the pseudonym "Anne Ring," who was "Formerly Attached to H.R.H. The Duchess of York's Household." Elizabeth assisted her wholeheartedly, supplying photographs and vetting the drafts.

"I have not altered anything except suggested a word or two," Elizabeth wrote after reading the "charming" manuscript. She agreed that Beryl should "vary Nurse with Nanny," as it is "much more friendly." When Beryl embroidered the narrative with "a forlorn Highland pony" named "Daisy" that received "love, caresses and carrots" from the toddler princess, the duchess didn't object. "It is a very harmless little invention," she told Beryl.

When *The Story of Princess Elizabeth* was published in 1930, it bore the imprimatur "Told with the Sanction of Her Parents." *The New York Times* previewed the U.S. publication in August 1931 with an article quoting "Anne Ring" on the little girl "who may some day be Queen of England" as "a sweet, unspoiled and perfectly lovable child."

IN SEPTEMBER 1928, THE PRINCE of Wales had been home for nearly a year after returning from Canada with Prince George. David was possessed, as he had been many times previously, with a "mania" to travel. At age thirty-four, he set off for an African safari, this time with Prince Henry as his companion. Once again, David was a malign influence.

Twenty-eight-year-old Henry had been honored the previous March when his father made him the Duke of Gloucester. He was at once the tallest and dullest of the King's sons. He squeaked through Eton, and his brief stint at Cambridge left no impression. But he found his niche at the Royal Military College at Sandhurst and became a dedicated army officer in his regiment, the Tenth Royal Hussars.

Edward squired Henry around Nairobi's Muthaiga Club, where the princes quickly got into trouble. By then the aristocratic English expatriates in Kenya, known as the "White Mischief" set, had a wild reputation. They entertained Edward and Henry with parties, polo, and thoroughbred racing. At a Muthaiga Club ball, Henry fell for Beryl Markham, a lissome blond horse trainer recently married to Mansfield Markham, a wealthy British coal magnate. She was also an aviatrix who would later become famous as the first woman to fly solo from east to west across the Atlantic.

In the autumn of 1928, she began an affair with Prince Henry. By some accounts she also shared her bed with Prince Edward. In early October, Henry set out on his own safari, accompanied by Beryl, who was about to turn twenty-six. David didn't expect to see his brother again until early December in South Africa, where they planned to spend Christmas.

Accompanied by Tommy Lascelles, the Prince of Wales and his party traveled west to Uganda for an elephant hunt, back to Nairobi, and south to Tanganyika (modern-day Tanzania). There they shot rhino, buffalo, and lions before their planned trip down to Cape Town by steamer, automobile, and train.

On November 26, 1928, a coded telegram from London arrived in Dodoma, Tanganyika, where it was conveyed to the Prince of Wales's safari camp. The message was the first in a series alerting Edward that his father was seriously ill. The safari party moved to Dodoma the next day to await further news. "The last and most urgent" telegram came from Prime Minister Baldwin, "begging" the Prince of Wales "to come home at once." After deciphering the message, Tommy read it aloud to Edward. "I don't believe a word of it," said the prince. "It's just some election dodge of old Baldwin's. It doesn't mean a thing."

Lascelles later wrote that Prince Edward's "incredibly callous behaviour" was "the last straw on my camel's back." For the first time in his eight years as assistant private secretary, Tommy Lascelles lost his temper. "Sir," he said. "The King of England is dying, and if that means nothing to you, it means a great deal to us." The Prince of Wales left without a word and "spent the remainder of the evening in

the successful seduction of a Mrs. Barnes, wife of the local commissioner," wrote Tommy. "He told me so himself next morning."

The King's health crisis had begun on the eleventh of November
when he caught a chill during the Armistice Day ceremony at the
Cenotaph. After shooting in raw weather at Sandringham, he took to
his bed ten days later at Buckingham Palace. His doctors diagnosed
acute septicemia and an infection in his right lung.

Over the following days, the Queen recorded her fluctuating anxiety over the King's condition. With David and Henry in Africa, and
George on a trip to the United States, she had only Bertie, Elizabeth,
and Princess Mary to rely on. At the first sign of George V's sickness,
Bertie returned to London from Naseby Hall, the Yorks' rented weekend home in Northamptonshire, where he had been hunting.

Prompted at least in part by Tommy's fury, the Prince of Wales
made a "sensational dash" home. He arrived in Folkestone, where
Stanley Baldwin accompanied him by train to Victoria station. Waiting
on the platform that evening was Bertie, who warned his brother that
he would find their father "greatly changed." He also expressed concern about their mother, who "has never once revealed her feelings to
any of us." Bertie said that Queen Mary was "far too reserved; she
keeps too much locked up inside of her. I fear a breakdown if anything
awful happens."

"At 10:30 David arrived to our great relief," Queen Mary wrote in
her diary on December 11. "I took him to G's room, he recognized
him & spoke to him quite clearly. G seemed more himself." But the
following day, the King lost consciousness. His lead doctor, Lord
Dawson of Penn, extracted some infected fluid from his lung. In the
evening, a surgeon removed one of the King's ribs and drained the
abscess causing the infection. George V's illness receded, and he
began a long and slow recovery. But he would never fully regain his
health.

Prince Henry made his own dash over land and sea from Africa,
and Prince George traveled from New York. They both arrived at
Buckingham Palace in time to join the family for a subdued holiday

"He was an intelligent child, with more force of character than anyone suspected."

Prince Albert (left) with his sister, Princess Mary, and brother Prince Edward in 1900.

"An elfin creature swift of movement, quick of intelligence, alive with humour."

Elizabeth Bowes Lyon with her younger brother, David Bowes Lyon.

"The humble soldiers were awestruck by 'the essence of politeness, a smile and a word for everyone.'"

Lady Elizabeth Bowes Lyon and her mother, Lady Strathmore, with wounded soldiers at Glamis Castle during the First World War.

*"David was the shining star,
and Bertie the fragile laggard."*

The Princess of Wales, later Queen Mary, with the Prince of Wales (left)
and Prince Albert in 1905.

"Bertie enthusiastically played tennis on the castle's new hard court."

Lady Elizabeth Bowes Lyon with Prince Albert on his first visit to Glamis in September 1920.

"Elizabeth is very kind to me. The more I see of her the more I like her."

A shooting party at Glamis Castle in September 1921, with Elizabeth Bowes Lyon and Prince Albert at the center and James Stuart on the far left.

> *"They bowed over and over to the immense roars at Hyde Park Corner."*

The newly married Duke and Duchess of York after their wedding, April 26, 1923.

> *"Bertie hoped that the 'home ties' would bring his brother closer to his family."*

A shooting party on the moors at Glamis with the Prince of Wales.

"'Of course poor baby cried,' noted Queen Mary."

The christening of Princess Elizabeth in Buckingham Palace.

"Bertie was overwhelmed by the noise and proximity of the crowd."

Prince Albert and Louis Greig defeated in straight sets at Wimbledon.

"Elizabeth held her baby in spite of the rain, which fell in torrents."

The Duke and Duchess of York with fourteen-month-old Princess Elizabeth on the Buckingham Palace balcony.

"A sweet, unspoiled and perfectly lovable child."

Three-year-old Princess Elizabeth on a royal engagement with her mother.

"Women in Marina's family 'make good wives.'"

THE BRIDAL GROUP AT BUCKINGHAM PALACE

Bassano

A group taken at Buckingham Palace, and the key to which, left to right, is: H.R.H. Princess Katherine of Greece, Lady Iris Mountbatten, H.R.H. the Prince of Wales, H.R.H. Princess Eugenie of Greece, H.R.H. the Duchess of Kent, H.R.H. the Duke of Kent, the Grand Duchess Kyra of Russia, H.R.H. the Duke of York, H.R.H. the Princess Irene of Greece, H.R.H. the Princess Juliana of the Netherlands: seated—Lady Mary Cambridge and the Princess Elizabeth

The wedding of the Duke and Duchess of Kent.

"George V told Bertie, 'You'll see, your brother will never become King.'"

George V with three of his sons—left to right, the Duke of Kent, Duke of Windsor, and Duke of York—five months before the death of the King.

"Four people whose lives form one spiritual whole."

The royal family on the grounds of Windsor Castle.

"Someone chalked up on the walls of Aberdeen, 'Down with the American harlot.'"

King Edward VIII and Wallis Simpson at Balmoral.

THE NEW REIGN DAWNS
The King, in Admiral's uniform, leaving No. 145 Piccadilly, to attend the Accession Council at St. James's Palace, December 12, 1936.

"He read his declaration 'in a low, clear voice, but with many hesitations.'"

King George VI leaving for his Accession Council.

"The torrential rain 'lessened the strain very much.'"

THE ILLUSTRATED LONDON NEWS

The World Copyright of all the Editorial Matter, both Illustrations and Letterpress, is Strictly Reserved in Great Britain, the British Dominions and Colonies, Europe, and the United States of America.

SATURDAY, JULY 2, 1938.

THE QUEEN'S MOTHER LEAVES HER HISTORIC HOME FOR THE LAST TIME: A FARM WAGON BEARING THE COFFIN OF LADY STRATHMORE, AND FOLLOWED ON FOOT BY THE KING, STARTING FROM GLAMIS CASTLE.

The Countess of Strathmore, mother of the Queen, was laid to rest on June 27 in the private burial ground beside the church at Glamis, Forfar, about a mile from Glamis Castle, where her life was mainly spent. After a simple service in the Castle chapel, attended by their Majesties and members of the family, the coffin was placed on a farm wagon drawn by two horses and borne in procession to the grave. Rain was falling heavily. The King walked behind the coffin, with the Queen's brothers, Lord Glamis and Mr. David Bowes-Lyon. The Queen followed in a car with her father, the Earl of Strathmore. Among the wreaths were those from their Majesties, Queen Mary, and the King and Queen of Norway, with a white cross of carnations from Princess Elizabeth and Princess Margaret. The Bishop of St. Andrews officiated at the family service in the chapel, and read the committal sentences at the grave.

PHOTOGRAPH BY SPORT AND GENERAL. (SEE ALSO ILLUSTRATIONS ON PAGES 4 AND 5.)

Lady Strathmore's funeral cortege at Glamis Castle.

"Watching on a newsreel in Berlin, Adolf Hitler called Britain's Queen 'the most dangerous woman in Europe.'"

Queen Elizabeth unexpectedly placing a poppy on the Australian war memorial in France.

"George VI praised the 'magnificent efforts of the Prime Minister in the name of peace.'"

Neville Chamberlain and his wife with the King and Queen on the Buckingham Palace balcony after signing the Munich Agreement.

"It was a milestone that took her to a new level in her preparation to be monarch."

Princess Elizabeth on her thirteenth birthday with her father and sister.

"One cried out, 'Ay, man, if Hitler could just see this!'"

The King and Queen in May 1939 with war veterans in Ottawa.

"'Good luck to you!' the president shouted. 'All the luck in the world!'"

Franklin and Eleanor Roosevelt waving goodbye to the King and Queen.

gathering. On Christmas Eve, the King was "clearer," Queen Mary observed. "We had a little talk. . . . All our children came to tea & sweet Lilibet."

The Queen arranged all the presents in the Throne Room around a small Christmas tree. "We missed dear George dreadfully," Queen Mary wrote, "but felt thankful he is improving at last." On Christmas Day, the family attended a Communion service in the Palace chapel. Queen Mary gave a small dinner party attended by her four sons, Mary, and Elizabeth.

To help speed the King's recovery, his doctors recommended that he move to Bognor on the English Channel "for the sea air." He stayed at Craigweil, a sprawling house protected by trees and high walls on one side, with an expansive sea view on the other. In addition to the constant monitoring by doctors, the King had a stream of visitors at his seaside villa. The "most favoured" was Lilibet.

"She is looking forward wildly to digging in the sand and talks knowingly of pails & spades!" Bertie wrote his mother the day before his daughter's trip to the seacoast on March 13—nearly a month shy of her third birthday. "I do hope that Lilibet will be good. She is very sensible really & understanding but like a piece of quicksilver nowadays!" The visit came at a convenient time. On the fourteenth, the Yorks traveled to Norway for the wedding of Bertie's first cousin Prince Olav to Princess Martha, a niece of the King of Sweden.

Lilibet's presence at Bognor delighted the King and instantly raised his spirits. The gardener created a sandpit on the lawn, and Queen Mary joined the King on a nearby bench to watch Lilibet play. At the end of their granddaughter's second day at Craigweil, Queen Mary wrote, "I played with Lilibet in the garden making sand pies!"

The princess stayed with her grandparents for nearly two weeks. Queen Mary took her back to London by train on March 26, the day after her parents returned from Norway, and drove with her to 145 Piccadilly. Lilibet's third birthday, usually celebrated with fanfare at Windsor Castle, was a more low-key occasion with her parents at Naseby Hall. In the United States, *Time* magazine gave her a rare gift:

a story recounting her brief life and a cover image by Marcus Adams with the headline "P'incess Lilybet."

When Bertie and Elizabeth visited the King at Craigweil in mid-April 1929, they had a memorable conversation that she recounted at least twice many years later. In a chat with biographer Kenneth Rose when she was seventy-nine, she said, "When the King was convalescing at Bognor, he said to us one day that he thought David would never take over from him. We were astonished, and hardly understood what he meant." Fifteen years on, she added some detail while reminiscing with Sir Eric Anderson. She recalled that George V told Bertie, "You'll see, your brother will never become King." George V "must have seen something we didn't, because I remember we thought, 'how ridiculous,' because then everybody thought he was going to be a wonderful King. . . . I remember we both looked at each other and thought 'nonsense.'"

But George V knew more than Bertie and Elizabeth, as did his advisers and Prime Minister Baldwin. Accelerating disillusion had marked Tommy's eight years of serving the Prince of Wales: from idolizing the man who "might have been a sculptor's model" to viewing Edward as a man "both vulgar and selfish." By early 1929, Lascelles could no longer serve someone who had "no comprehension of the ordinary axioms of rational, or ethical, behaviour," and for whom "fundamental ideas of duty, dignity and self sacrifice had no meaning."

On February 4, 1929, in a face-to-face meeting at St. James's Palace that lasted nearly an hour, Tommy Lascelles informed the Prince of Wales he was resigning. He told the King's heir "exactly what I thought of him and his whole scheme of life, and foretelling, with an accuracy that might have surprised me at the time, that he would lose the throne of England." The prince "took Tommy's scolding well," and thanked him for his candor.

"I suppose the fact of the matter is that I'm quite the wrong sort of person to be Prince of Wales," he said. Lascelles thought his words were "so pathetically true that it almost melted me." The next morning the Prince of Wales accepted the resignation and gave his former counselor an automobile as "proof that we parted friends." Lascelles immediately informed Prime Minister Baldwin of his conversation with the prince. "Whether what I said will have any permanent effect, I cannot of course say," Tommy wrote.

After a two-year break in the Dorset countryside with Joan and their children—a son named John and a daughter called Lavinia—Lascelles again became a private secretary, this time for the Earl of Bessborough, the governor-general of Canada. Tommy liked the job well enough, and he had plenty of opportunity to pursue his passion for fishing. It was a four-year interregnum that opened a useful window into North America. He kept his friendships within the royal household, but he had little awareness of the dramas swirling around the royal family.

WHILE THE KING WAS RECUPERATING in the late spring of 1929, he confronted unforeseen crises with both Prince Henry and Prince George. Shortly after Henry's return to England from Africa, Beryl Markham followed. She was six months pregnant, and the besotted prince installed her in a suite at the Grosvenor Hotel near Buckingham Palace. After she gave birth to a son in February, the baby was sent to live with relatives elsewhere in England. Henry moved in with Beryl at the hotel, and the gossips moved into overdrive. Although the boy had been conceived before Beryl met Prince Henry, he was erroneously tagged as the father rather than her husband, Mansfield.

The King and Queen were alarmed by their formerly staid son's outrageous behavior. They reacted by shipping him out to Japan at the end of March to attend the coronation of Hirohito as Emperor of Japan. Back in England in early July, Henry resumed his affair with Beryl.

Mansfield Markham was planning to file for divorce, and his older brother, Sir Charles Markham, hinted that Prince Henry could be named as corespondent unless he consented to "take care of Beryl." By the end of 1929, lawyers for the royal family quietly arranged a settlement providing a trust fund that would pay Beryl £500 (some £32,000 at current values) a year until her death, which came in 1985. The King kept a close watch on Henry, and the following autumn sent him overseas again, this time as his representative at Haile Selassie's coronation as Emperor of Abyssinia. By then, the romance had sputtered out.

The problems posed by Prince George that year were more severe. On leaving the navy in March 1929, the twenty-six-year-old moved into York House with the Prince of Wales. "Georgie," as his mother (but not his father) referred to him, was known for his louche behavior, but his parents could not have anticipated how wild he would become in 1929. Rumors flew that he was having affairs with women and men, among them the playwright Noël Coward, who boasted about it. But George's life darkened considerably when he took up with a wealthy American socialite named Kiki Preston. Known as "the girl with the silver syringe," Kiki introduced George to cocaine and morphine, and he became addicted to the drugs.

Toward the end of July, George V's diary entries reflected heightened alarm about his youngest son. The King was still in bad shape physically. He had left Bognor for Windsor Castle in mid-May, and shortly afterward had become feverish again. A fresh abscess had formed and broken through his old wound, which his doctors decided to leave open.

In the midst of his pain and weakness, George V had to navigate a new Labour government after the Conservative Party lost its majority in the general election on May 30—the first time women were allowed to vote. Once again, Baldwin was out, and Ramsay MacDonald was in. Both the old and new governments trooped out to Windsor Castle for the transfer of power. Wearing a yellow silk Chinese dressing gown, the King received the outgoing and incoming prime ministers in his bedroom at the castle.

He made a triumphal entry into London on July 1, buoyed by enormous crowds that he greeted from the Buckingham Palace balcony. Less than a week later, he and his family attended a service at

Westminster Abbey to give thanks for his recovery. He had planned to leave the next day for Sandringham, where he intended to remain for the summer. But his physicians forbade the journey after a portable X-ray machine revealed a large and ominous cavity beneath his open wound. He had more surgery in mid-July when his doctors removed another rib and cleaned out the abscess. He would not be well enough to move to Sandringham until the end of August.

Prince George was in a bad way, too. On the seventeenth of July, two days after his operation, the King saw his youngest son, little knowing how long he would wait to see him again. For the next seven months, George received unspecified treatment to rid him of his addiction. The point man for the prince's regimen was the person who originally abetted his reckless behavior: the Prince of Wales.

The King put considerable pressure on his eldest son to take his youngest son in hand. On July 26, 1929, he wrote in his diary, "Saw David twice about G." Over the following months, George V had further detailed conversations about Prince George, not only with Prince Edward but also with Sir Stanley Hewett, the royal family's deputy surgeon apothecary, and with at least one outside expert who said the young man was "not at all an easy case."

David took George to the country to escape London's temptations and undergo the hard work of drug rehabilitation. The Prince of Wales simultaneously ensured that Kiki Preston left England and told his brother she had moved overseas permanently. Queen Mary saw her "Georgie" just once, in the middle of August, accompanied by David.

Freda Dudley Ward, still very much in the picture for the Prince of Wales, helped by recommending nurses to care for George. David dutifully remained by his brother's side, particularly during what he described to Freda as "a tricky and critical stage" of "the cure." To ease his own stress, Prince Edward occupied himself with embroidery as he had done during the First World War. "It would make you laugh and maybe cry a little too," he told Freda.

By December, the treatment was showing success, and the Prince of Wales prepared to set sail in early January for nearly four months in

Africa—the resumption of the safari that his father's illness had interrupted. George still needed supervision, so the King enlisted forty-year-old Ulick Alexander, a seasoned courtier who had been overseeing the prince's finances since 1928.

On the last day of 1929, Alexander traveled to Sandringham, where he discussed plans for George with his parents and David. "It really is a terrible and terrifying thing to happen to anyone, and far worse to one's brother," David wrote to his father while at sea on January 16. The King expressed his gratitude in reply: "Looking after him all those months must have been a great strain on you, and I think it was wonderful all you did for him."

Prince George finally returned to Buckingham Palace for a luncheon with his parents on February 22, 1930. "I had not seen him since July," King George V wrote in his diary. His recovery held, and Prince George again appeared regularly at court, even attending church at Windsor Castle with his mother and father.

The thirty-five-year-old Prince of Wales had shown commendable determination and compassion in caring for Prince George. The entire unsavory episode went unmentioned in Edward's memoir as well as in the official biographies of his mother and father. And the rapprochement between the Prince of Wales and King George V proved short-lived.

*"She has got large blue eyes and a will of iron.
As long as she can disguise her will, & use her eyes,
then all will be well."*

Princess Elizabeth at age four with her mother, the Duchess of York, who holds
Princess Margaret Rose after her birth at Glamis Castle on August 21, 1930.

NINETEEN

Interlude

As a new decade began, Elizabeth and Bertie learned that they were expecting their second child in August. The ensuing six years were a quiet interlude of nesting with their family while keeping a lower public profile. The Duke and Duchess of York did their duty, but there were no more ambitious voyages overseas, nor any big challenges to alter their course.

Balancing the Yorks' delight over Elizabeth's pregnancy was their immense sadness over the death of her forty-three-year-old brother Jock from pneumonia on February 7, 1930. Sixty-seven-year-old Cecilia Strathmore was devastated over losing her fourth child. "It seems very hard that at her age she should have to go through such a thing," Elizabeth told Beryl. "Your poor Mother," Queen Mary wrote to Elizabeth, "my heart aches for her."

Elizabeth canceled the few engagements on her calendar and fretted about letting the world know she was pregnant. "My instinct is to hide away in a corner," she told Queen Mary in mid-April. The Queen reassured Elizabeth that she was "clever . . . to have kept it dark for so long a time," but advised her to make a brief public announcement. The duchess let her condition be known that spring.

Bertie was conscientious about keeping up with his various charities even if he was less active publicly. He continued to struggle with his stammer, which led his private secretary Patrick Hodgson to ask Lionel Logue in May 1930 if he could persuade the duke "to try to talk to people more when he goes to functions." Hodgson explained that when strangers were introduced to Bertie, his typical response was "shaking hands but remaining absolutely mute," which "makes a bad impression." Hodgson recognized that Bertie's reaction was partly due to his inherent shyness, but equally he avoided greeting people "and then finding he can't get his words out." It's unclear precisely what Logue tried, but Bertie resisted meeting with his therapist for another two years.

Elizabeth decided—and Bertie readily concurred—to have their baby at Glamis. With an estimated due date ranging from the sixth to the twelfth of August, she and Lilibet took the overnight train north in mid-July. Bertie followed shortly afterward.

The duke contented himself at Glamis by shooting with Claude Strathmore and his brother-in-law David. But he confessed to his mother in early August, "I find I get very nervous & anxious about everything. I know it is unnecessary & silly but I can't help it." Elizabeth found diversion in reviewing Beryl Poignand's manuscript about Princess Elizabeth. "I do hope you have a success with your little story & make a little money, which is very important nowadays," she wrote. "Don't forget that E is only four years old (Ma speaking!)."

Mostly the duchess was vexed by the weeks of waiting and discomfort. Her two obstetricians, Sir Henry Simson and Frank Neon Reynolds, had moved into the castle to be ready as soon as labor began. Simson "is hovering anxiously about," she told Queen Mary. "The more he hovers, the slower it all seems!"

The doctors took all their meals with the Strathmores and played bridge in the evenings. Frank Reynolds described Cecilia Strathmore as "a dear old thing with white hair who absolutely fitted into the picture, even to her Elizabethan collar standing up round the back of her neck." He was struck by Prince Albert's shy manner. "It makes one wonder if one is being backward and gauche, but it seems it is the same with everybody," he noted.

Mindful of the long-standing tradition based on the fear that royal babies might be switched, Bertie arranged for accommodations at Airlie Castle, eight miles from Glamis, for two government overseers, the Labour Party home secretary, John Robert Clynes, and his secretary, Harry Boyd. The duke had a special telephone line installed between the two castles, along with a motorcycle and dispatch rider situated at Glamis in case the wire broke down.

After six hours of labor on Thursday, August 21, 1930, the Duchess of York gave birth at 9:22 P.M. to a six-pound, three-ounce girl. Clynes had arrived at Glamis at nine o'clock. Claude Strathmore—a Tory to his core—was reported to have said, "Give him a glass of wine in the housekeepers' room." Simson fetched Clynes and Boyd at 10:15 and guided them through "the narrow winding stone corridors" into the sitting room next to the duchess's bedroom. There Clynes found the Duke of York, the Strathmores, and Elizabeth's sister Rose standing around the cot. He peered in to see "a fine chubby-faced little girl" lying wide awake. "A very nice baby, and everything went smoothly," Frank Reynolds wrote to his wife.

The next morning, the York family's nanny, Clara "Alah" Knight, took Lilibet into the nursery for her first glimpse of the baby. Ever obedient, she heeded her nurse's instruction not to disturb her sleeping sister, and "she stole softly out of the room." That night, thousands of people gathered in the village of Glamis and followed a kilted band of bagpipers to the top of nearby Hunter's Hill where a thirty-foot-high bonfire had been erected. At half-past nine, three little girls lit "the mighty beacon" of bracken and fir wood. Cheering revelers joined hands and danced around the bonfire as the bagpipes played "Highland Lassie" and "The Duke of York's Welcome," which had been composed for the occasion. In her room at Glamis Castle, Elizabeth watched the fire glow, which could be seen in six counties.

According to courtier Clive Wigram, Queen Mary was initially disappointed not to have a boy. George V, however, "said he was glad it was a girl; one could play with girls longer than with boys, and the parents were young and had plenty of time to have a son." Queen Mary typically followed her husband's line of thinking in her congratulatory note to Bertie.

When the King and Queen arrived at Balmoral on August 23, they summoned Bertie to join them the next day. He obediently but grudgingly complied. "How I hated going away yesterday & leaving you my angel & that lovely precious new born baby of ours," Bertie wrote Elizabeth on the twenty-fifth from Royal Deeside. He was thankful that she was "going on so well & strong. I don't mind at all that it's a girl. I would have liked a boy & you would too." But he was pleased that "at last Lilibet has a playmate in the nursery."

The King and Queen traveled to Glamis with Bertie on August 30 and immediately went to see Elizabeth and the baby. "E looking very well & the baby a darling," the Queen noted in her diary. After a family luncheon, the Strathmores "showed us round their most interesting & historic castle," wrote the King, a first-time visitor. "Lilibet seemed delighted to see us," wrote Mary.

On September 6, Elizabeth told the Queen, "Bertie and I have decided now to call our little daughter 'Margaret Rose,' instead of M. Ann as Papa does not like Ann. I hope that you will like it." Margaret had been a family name among the Strathmores for some five hundred years. As *The Scotsman* proclaimed in a headline on September 23, "Scottish Name for Daughter of Scotland." The middle name was a tribute to the duchess's sister, one of the baby's first visitors.

Elizabeth remained bedridden for two weeks after Margaret's birth. "I am getting on well, and am having massage which is helping my flabby muscles back wonderfully," she told the Queen. "I expect that next week I shall start getting up . . . that I always think is a bad moment, as one feels so weak out of bed."

The family of four returned to London in early October. According to the wishes of the King and Queen, Archbishop of Canterbury Cosmo Lang officiated at Margaret Rose's christening in the Palace. The godparents balanced Windsor and Strathmore loyalties: Great-Aunt Toria, Uncle David, and Princess Ingrid of Sweden (a cousin of the King) on one side, Aunt Rose Leveson-Gower and Uncle David Bowes Lyon on the other. Princess Margaret Rose was dressed in the same vintage christening robe Lilibet had worn. "She has got large blue eyes and a will of iron," Elizabeth wrote. "As long as she can disguise her will, & use her eyes, then all will be well."

IN THE EARLY THIRTIES, THE world outside the cosseted life of the Duke and Duchess of York was shifting in alarming ways. The crash of the New York stock market in October 1929 triggered a global economic decline characterized by business failures and high unemployment, as leaders struggled to contain the damage. British newspapers featured photographs of civil unrest in the United States: Salvation Army depots handing out clothing and food in New York to prevent rioting, and demonstrations by unemployed men as the government considered a welfare system to ease the distress. Eight million Americans were out of work—an unemployment rate of nearly 16 percent compared to 3 percent in 1929 before the crash.

Bank collapses and business failures rocked Europe, where inflation ravaged the value of currencies. Germany, with a population of 63 million, had 4.5 million unemployed. Germans blamed their distress on the reparations mandated by the Treaty of Versailles after the First World War that drained the government's treasury. Austrian-born Adolf Hitler gathered popular support by promising German renewal and fiercely opposing Communism. His Nazi party triumphed in the German general election in September 1930, increasing its seats in the Reichstag from 20 to 107. It was the first step toward absolute power for the forty-one-year-old fanatic.

By 1931, the crisis engulfed Britain, where unemployment had more than doubled in one year to over 2.5 million—one-fifth of the country's workforce. That summer Labour's minority government couldn't fulfill its commitment to balancing its budget without major cutbacks in expenditures—including already minimal aid to the poor and unemployed—along with public sector wage reductions and significant tax increases. With his cabinet divided and incapable of taking action, Ramsay MacDonald declared they should all resign.

On August 22, George V traveled from Balmoral to London for a series of meetings with the jittery leaders of the three political parties. At the insistence of the King—a rare overt assertion of royal power in politics—MacDonald agreed to break the deadlock and form a national government with the Conservatives and Liberals. MacDonald continued as prime minister, and his cabinet included Stanley Baldwin as lord president of the council.

The coalition increased the income tax from 22.5 percent to 25 percent, and cut unemployment pay and public sector wages by 10 percent. From the garden at 10 Downing Street, MacDonald made a speech for British Movietone News imploring his countrymen to "bear equitable sacrifices." The two other party leaders made similar appeals, all of which were featured in movie theaters.

To show solidarity with the national effort, the King reduced his government-funded "Civil List" allowance by £50,000 a year (some £3.5 million—$4.7 million—today) for the duration of the national emergency. Prince Edward donated to the national exchequer an equal amount from the Duchy of Cornwall, his substantial investment portfolio as the Duke of Cornwall—the most important of his titles next to the Prince of Wales. The Duke of York sold his six horses and resigned from the Pytchley, his favorite hunt.

Writing from 145 Piccadilly to the Queen at Balmoral in mid-September 1931, Elizabeth described their finances as "down to bedrock, it seems. . . . We are getting rid of a footman & a kitchenmaid, and if we reduce any further, it will mean shutting up this home." Such a measure would be "rather useless," she admitted, given the requirements of royal duties in London.

That same month, the King offered Bertie and Elizabeth a country house in Windsor Great Park called Royal Lodge. It was a quirky place, located just three miles from Windsor Castle and originally built in the early nineteenth century for King George IV, who retreated there toward the end of his reign when he became unpopular. As a grace-and-favor lodging owned by the Crown, Royal Lodge had been occupied rent-free by George V's racing manager, Major Fred Fethers-tonhaugh. Known to the royal family as "Fether," the major had died unexpectedly of cardiac arrest at the end of July.

When Queen Mary wrote to the Duke of York in mid-August to alert him to the forthcoming offer from his father, she emphasized that "Mrs. 'Fether' cannot afford to keep it on." The Queen did not think the King was "frightfully keen" that they accept the house, and he only offered it from a sense of fairness to give them first refusal. "Personally I think you will be making a mistake" in taking on the house. It was "too small" and the garden "expensive to keep up." She gave this advice "for what it is worth," but added, "I believe you will agree with me, both of you."

The Queen underestimated the Yorks' desire for a nearby country home. Bertie and Elizabeth visited the house several weeks later. Despite an awkward layout and state of "dilapidation," the Yorks grasped the potential of Royal Lodge. Backpedaling from the "bedrock" finances that threatened 145 Piccadilly, Elizabeth shrewdly made her case for Royal Lodge to the Queen in a letter on September 21.

"I think we shall be able to manage it alright," she wrote. Con-cerned about the cost of curtains and carpets, she offered to "fill it up with linoleum" instead. She was relieved, however, that the Crown would pay for a gardener. She emphasized that "the children will be able to spend some happy and peaceful weeks there, & keep up riding etc, which is rather important." (For her fourth birthday, the King had given Lilibet a Shetland pony named Peggy.) Writing gratefully to his father, Bertie said, "I think it will suit us admirably."

The fact was, despite Britain's overall economic despair and the economies that the royal family had publicly made, they still had many millions from lucrative private investments to quietly finance their way of life. Once the Royal Lodge matter was settled, Queen Mary shifted into her project manager mindset. In a letter to Bertie the next day, she suggested they use one of the sitting rooms as his dressing room, and install a new bathroom "in the cloak rm just opposite yr room." For carpets and curtains, she advised that they secure "the same advantageous terms we get thro' the Office of Works" as they had done for the Big House at Sandringham, "only do not mention this as we arrange this privately."

The Yorks found £5,000 (the equivalent of some £360,000 at current values) to cover the renovations, which took a year to complete. Bertie did much of the designing himself. By January 1933, with the children installed at Sandringham for the month, Bertie and Elizabeth were "arranging pictures, & curtains & furniture" and "busy here with lights & chintzes and all the extras that are wanted nowadays." They had bought "quite a lot" from J. Rochelle Thomas, a noted antiques dealer in St. James's. "I hope & trust that nothing else will be wanted or we shall be completely bankrupt!" she told Queen Mary.

As it happened, the Yorks needed still more alterations. In early 1934 they added rooms for their servants: a necessity, Elizabeth explained to the Queen, "or they will all become too miserable & leave." She reassured her mother-in-law that "we are really very economical & have cut down our expenditure as much as we can and we have no expensive habits." Two years later came an additional pair of bedrooms and two drawing rooms on the upper floor. "There really was not enough room" for guests, Elizabeth explained to Queen Mary. The new rooms were small, but they made it possible "to have four or five people in comfort."

It is unclear how precisely the Yorks managed these expenditures, although special royal discounts doubtless helped. Queen Mary arranged for the Duke of Westminster—one of the wealthiest aristocrats in Britain—to lend the Yorks "a shop for 3 months" to help with some of the work. Still, early in 1935, Sir Basil Brooke, Bertie's comptroller who monitored his finances, confided to Chips Channon that "The Duke of Y has a difficult time" living on his annual government stipend of £25,000 (£1.6 million today) "with all those demands on him." All her life, Elizabeth was known for obliviousness to the cost of supporting her expensive tastes.

When Bertie and Elizabeth finished, they had created a "considerable mansion" of two stories. They restored the "magnificent proportions" of George IV's original saloon, with wings on either side, and "the whole exterior pink-washed in a colour of warm rose." Marion "Crawfie" Crawford, the governess to Elizabeth and Margaret who arrived in the spring of 1933, described Royal Lodge as "the most up-to-date of the royal establishments." The overall effect was "plain and simple."

Unusually, the duke and duchess had their bedrooms on the ground floor. Her double bed was covered in blue silk "with lemon pleatings," the carpet her favorite "misty blue." All her furniture was painted white, and the cupboards were illuminated by electric lights on opening. Bertie's room reminded Crawfie of a ship's cabin. It had a "blue-green draped bed, very hard-looking," with a dressing table and bookcase, with everything laid out neatly "as if for parade inspection."

Bertie and Elizabeth both loved gardening, and the fifteen acres surrounding Royal Lodge provided their first opportunity to plant and cultivate according to their respective talents. They redid the borders and added pools as well as terraces next to the house. The Duke of York cleared the "wilderness" at the bottom of the lawn and created a series of vistas punctuated by long "rides" similar to the wide grassy paths at St. Paul's Walden Bury. Elizabeth emphasized scent as well as color in her mixed herbaceous borders. Hedges of lavender and rosemary were planted near the house to carry fragrance through the open windows.

Even before they occupied Royal Lodge, the Yorks began lobbying for a third house—also rent-free—Birkhall on the Balmoral estate, which was seven miles from the castle. When George V was convalescing in 1929, he had remained at Sandringham rather than taking his customary holiday at Balmoral. At the Queen's suggestion, Bertie and Elizabeth had settled that autumn into Birkhall.

It was a small "pure Queen Anne" house built in 1715 that Queen Victoria had purchased in the mid-nineteenth century. Courtiers had mainly lived there, most recently Sir Frederick "Fritz" Ponsonby, a senior adviser for nearly forty years—serving Queen Victoria, King Edward VII, and King George V. Ponsonby was one of the few people who could argue with the King. George V felt intense loyalty to him.

The Queen was taken aback by Bertie's request in May 1932. "With all yr expenses with Royal Lodge this year how can you afford to take a place in Scotland besides," she replied with evident vexation. She said that the King would ask if Fritz was "agreeable to giving up Birkhall." The Queen expressed puzzlement that her son and daughter-in-law wished to stay elsewhere in Royal Deeside. "Surely life at Balmoral is not strenuous & you are practically free to do what you like," she wrote. "Besides which we like having you with us, as alas the other brothers come to us so little," and Mary "has her duties in Yorkshire."

Ponsonby evidently knew his place. Five days later, the Queen wrote Bertie to say that "Papa has arranged everything with Fritz about Birkhall." She set one condition for the King's consent: "that we shld like yr children to come to us to stay for one week while you are at Birkhall, otherwise we shall see so little of them if they do not stay in the Castle with us." The Yorks readily agreed.

Two months later, Bertie and Elizabeth moved into Birkhall, perched above the murmuring River Muick, a tributary of the Dee. They spent hours in the flower and vegetable gardens below the house. With stags' heads mounted everywhere, the carpets and curtains in Balmoral or Royal Stewart tartan, and the wallpaper adorned with Queen Victoria's gold cipher, Birkhall resembled the Castle but was infinitely cozier. "They are very happy & comfortable there," the King wrote in his diary after he and Queen Mary visited for the first time on August 24, 1932.

In mid-October, shortly before their return to London, Elizabeth wrote to D'Arcy Osborne about their two-month stay. The wild natural beauty was "most helpful and calming," as was the freedom from the formalities of the castle. "The birches are golden & silver, the river is an angry black & blue, every other tree is scarlet & yellow," Elizabeth told Osborne. "I feel very satisfied every time that I look out of my window."

"As George V's disillusion with the Prince of Wales grew, it was becoming increasingly clear that the future of the monarchy lay with his favorite grandchild."

King George V and Queen Mary take eight-year-old Princess Elizabeth to Westminster Abbey in July 1934 for a special service inaugurating a pilgrimage to aid the unemployed.

TWENTY

A Certain Person

ON THE EDGE OF BERTIE AND ELIZABETH'S CONTENTED EXISTENCE, they could feel disturbing vibrations from the frenetic parallel life of the Prince of Wales. Paradoxically, David devoted himself more conscientiously to Britain's welfare even as his personal entanglements became more troubling. His aura of modernity captivated the public, who had no idea about the dramas of his love life, which remained shielded by the protective British press. Not only did his private behavior contrast sharply with that of the obliging and thoroughly domesticated Yorks, his two other brothers fell into line in the mid-1930s and found suitable women to marry. All this came against a backdrop of King George V's declining health.

The hidden agenda behind the Prince of Wales's trip to Africa in January 1930 was a safari rendezvous with his newest lover, twenty-five-year-old Thelma, Viscountess Furness. The American-born daughter of a diplomat, Thelma had been married briefly at age seventeen and since 1926 had been the wife of a wealthy shipping magnate twenty years her senior, a viscount named Marmaduke Furness.

Although Prince Edward still called Freda Dudley Ward every

morning and visited her in the afternoon, he frequented nightclubs with Lady Furness. When Thelma and Marmaduke traveled to Kenya in February 1930, the viscount went his own way while she joined the Prince of Wales for a safari.

Back in England, Prince Edward installed Thelma as his hostess during weekends at Fort Belvedere, his country home on the outer reaches of Windsor Great Park. George V owned "the Fort"—as it became known—as a property of the Crown Estate, and in 1929 the prince became enchanted by the miniature Gothic Revival castle. Six miles from Windsor and three miles beyond Royal Lodge, the turreted Fort was distant enough to ensure the prince's comings and goings would be reasonably private. It was also near Sunningdale, one of Edward's favorite golf clubs. He badgered George V into giving it to him, and the Prince of Wales set about lavishly modernizing the Fort as his "own creation."

In close consultation with Freda—who had a flair for tasteful décor—the Prince of Wales splurged £21,000 (more than £1.5 million in today's money), drawn from his Duchy of Cornwall funds, for central heating, en suite bathrooms, a swimming pool, a tennis court, a gymnasium, a steam room, renovated stables, and a private landing strip. The furniture was Chippendale, the paintings by Canaletto. David took special interest in the garden, which was created by Norah Bourke Lindsay, an aristocratic designer catering to elite clients.

Freda and Thelma were well aware of each other, and neither woman had any illusions about a long-term future with Prince Edward. As divorcées, they were both precluded from marrying him under church and civil law. Thelma was a Catholic as well, and Catholics were prohibited by centuries-old law from being either monarch or consort. Freda and Thelma appeared simply to enjoy the royal ride as long as it lasted.

Thelma was less influential than Freda, who kept the prince's irresponsibility somewhat in check and could assuage his insecurities. Thelma may have appeared more often publicly on the prince's arm, but Freda remained confident that she held the dominant position.

After all, while Edward was canoodling with Thelma in Africa, he was writing love letters to "my darling Angel" Freda in London.

Thelma Furness was a key player in the life of Prince Edward for one reason. She had been befriended by a fellow American, Mrs. Wallis Warfield Simpson, who migrated from Baltimore, Maryland, to England when she was thirty-two. In a modest ceremony at the Chelsea Register Office in 1928, Wallis married Ernest Aldrich Simpson, a prosperous thirty-one-year-old Anglo-American shipbroker described by Chips Channon as "a good looking barber's block of a boy."

Wallis Warfield had been a poor relation in a prominent Maryland family. At the age of twenty, she had married Earl W. Spencer, an alcoholic aviator in the U.S. Navy, and eleven years later they divorced. Ernest Simpson, whom she first got to know in New York, offered the prospect of financial stability as well as social networks in Manhattan and London. Wallis met Thelma through connections at the American Embassy in London, and they became fast friends.

With her broad shoulders, flat chest, and large hands, Wallis had an almost mannish appearance. She pulled her dark hair into a tight chignon, and she had a bold nose and strong chin. She did make the most of her one advantage: "beautiful dark sapphire blue eyes, full of sparkle and nice mischief," as described by her biographer Anne Sebba. She also wore stylish clothes to full effect on her svelte figure.

Personality was Wallis's long suit. She was known for arch repartee and forthright irreverence. When Thelma's husband was away, she asked Wallis and Ernest Simpson to join her for a foxhunting weekend with the Prince of Wales at her country estate, Burrough Court, at Melton Mowbray in Leicestershire.

As a married couple, the Simpsons would be "chaperones" of a sort for Thelma and her royal lover. At their first encounter on January 10, 1931, Wallis cheekily challenged Edward's conversational shortcomings: "I had hoped for something more original from the Prince of Wales." Prince Edward was thirty-six at the time, and Wallis was thirty-four. He was intrigued, and Wallis felt drawn to his vivacity as well as his hint of melancholy.

Over the following year, Edward and Wallis saw each other from time to time, including her presentation at court that June, when she caught his eye with "the grace of her carriage and natural dignity of her movements." In early 1932, Wallis invited Edward to dinner at the Simpsons' flat at Bryanston Court in London's respectable but then-unfashionable Marylebone neighborhood. Although the prince judged it "small but charming," the three-bedroom apartment had spacious and elegantly decorated rooms.

Wallis served such delicious food that the Prince of Wales asked for one of her recipes. He stayed until four A.M., captivated by the "gay, lively and informed company" she had gathered. He found her to be "complex" and "elusive" as well as "the most independent woman I had met." The Prince of Wales began inviting Ernest and Wallis to the Fort as regular weekend guests.

The royal household had yet to hear about the prince's new companion, but the King decided in March 1932 to raise the issue of marriage with his eldest son as he approached his thirty-eighth birthday. At a meeting in Buckingham Palace detailed in a memorandum by Sir Clive Wigram—George V's private secretary since the death of Lord Stamfordham a year earlier—the King emphasized David's responsibilities as the heir to the throne.

While people "worshipped" the Prince of Wales, George V wondered, "Would this last when the Public began to realize at last the more or less double life that the prince was leading?" David disagreed, saying people were "more tolerant," but the King insisted that the public expected members of the royal family "to have a decent home life."

George V specifically criticized the affair with Thelma and said David was beyond the age when young men "sowed their wild oats." There had never been an unmarried king, which George V considered an "invidious" position. David countered that he had no interest in marrying a foreign princess. When the King said a "suitable well-born English girl" would be acceptable, the prince—conveniently forgetting the example of Elizabeth Bowes Lyon—said he didn't realize this was an option.

The Prince of Wales told his father that the only woman he wished to marry was Freda Dudley Ward, who by then had been divorced for nearly two years. "The King said he did not think that would do." At that point, the conversation ended. "It had been a highly charged encounter," wrote Wigram, and David "had smoked countless cigarettes and frowned most of the time, but on the whole it had been 'amicable.'"

Bertie and Elizabeth first crossed paths with Wallis Simpson in January 1933 when Thelma invited them to a skating party on Virginia Water Lake, near the Fort. Elizabeth and Thelma laughed together as they clung to kitchen chairs so they could "navigate around the pond safely if not gracefully." Thelma fondly remembered "the lovely face of the Duchess, her superb colouring heightened by the cold, her eyes wrinkled with the sense of fun that was never far below the surface." Rather less exuberantly, Wallis wrote to her aunt, Bessie Merryman, "We have been skating out on the water with the D and Duch of York. Isn't it a scream?"

An early hint of the Yorks' view of Wallis came in a letter Elizabeth wrote to Queen Mary the following August. Her language was elliptical, but she was unmistakably discussing Wallis. "Papa one day mentioned to me that he had heard that a certain person had been at the Fort when Bertie & I had been there & he said that he had a very good mind to speak to David about it," she wrote. Elizabeth said they didn't have an opportunity to continue their conversation, but she urged the Queen to prevent the King from bracing his oldest son.

"I am sure David would <u>never</u> forgive us for being drawn into anything like that," she continued. "Relations are already a little difficult when naughty ladies are brought in. . . . I would like to remain quite outside the whole affair." Queen Mary replied several weeks later, "Of course Papa never said a word to D. about Belvedere so all is well for I agree with you that it wld never do to start a quarrel, but I confess I hope it will not occur again for you ought not to meet D's lady in his own house, that is too much of a <u>bad</u> thing!!!"

The relationship between Prince Edward and Mrs. Simpson

deepened in the early months of 1934 when Thelma traveled to New York to spend time with her twin sister, Gloria (the mother of socialite Gloria Vanderbilt and grandmother to media star Anderson Cooper). Before her January departure, Thelma had lunch with Wallis at the Ritz in London and asked her friend to "look after" Edward.

Wallis socialized with him nonstop and fielded as many as three telephone calls a day. On her return to England that March, Thelma noticed a change in the atmosphere at the Fort as she observed Wallis's possessiveness with the prince. "Darling, is it Wallis?" Thelma asked David when they had a private moment. He told her not to be silly. Thelma left the Fort the next morning, little realizing their five-year affair was over.

Two months later, Edward brutally ended his sixteen-year romance with Freda. By then her role had turned into more of a mother figure than a lover, but she still counted on his companionship—and his loyalty. When she didn't hear from him for several weeks, she rang up York House, only to be told by the operator, "I have orders not to put you through." The Prince of Wales never spoke to her again.

WHEN FREDA WAS STILL HIS confidante several years earlier, the Prince of Wales told her that he was tired of royal "stunting," which he called "artificial nonsense." Nevertheless, he seemed to tackle his job with renewed vigor in the early 1930s. The secret weapon that fueled his popularity was his frequent use of an airplane: the ultimate cutting-edge symbol. He loved the thrill of flying, and an airplane allowed him to do more official engagements in less time. His public activities also aligned with the most pressing issues of the day, unemployment and poverty.

Through his much-praised tours of impoverished areas across Britain, the Prince of Wales defined himself as a man concerned with the welfare of those hit hard by the Depression. This was crucial image-making for the royal family, especially after "hunger marchers" of unemployed men and women converged on Hyde Park to protest against benefits cutbacks in the autumn of 1932.

It was difficult in those years for the Yorks to compete with the Prince of Wales, who grabbed most of the headlines. They certainly saw ample evidence of Britain's economic upheavals when they visited their charities. Writing to Queen Mary in October 1932, Elizabeth noted "the sad & lean faces of the men in the villages we passed through near Glasgow. I am afraid there is a great deal of misery." The duchess exchanged long letters on pressing issues of the day with D'Arcy Osborne, who was serving as an "Envoy Extraordinary" at the British Embassy in Washington.

By then Osborne had become an informal tutor to Elizabeth on domestic and foreign policy. "I am feeling very thwarted at this moment," she wrote at the end of 1932. She confessed that there was "so much to be done in this country, things that I could easily do, but a combination of Press & Precedent make it impossible." It would be "almost dangerous," she wrote, "to flout convention."

The inexhaustible appeal of Princesses Elizabeth and Margaret—"the two most popular children in the world," in the words of *The Illustrated London News*—also detracted at times from interest in their parents. The November 1932 issue of *Vanity Fair* even named four-year-old Lilibet to its Hall of Fame, declaring that "she seems destined to inherit the crown and become in her own right Queen of England and Empress of India." There were pictures in the newspapers of the princesses at big events such as Trooping the Colour and the Braemar Gathering, along with more personal glimpses of Lilibet on her pony in Windsor Great Park and walking Dookie, the first in her long line of Welsh Corgis, who arrived in the summer of 1933. (He was formally named Rozavel Golden Eagle, but the staff nicknamed him after the Duke of York.)

As George V's disillusion with the Prince of Wales grew, it was becoming increasingly clear that the future of the monarchy lay with his favorite grandchild. In the summer of 1934, Lilibet accompanied the King and Queen to a service at Westminster Abbey to launch a pilgrimage to aid the unemployed, and the following year her parents brought her to the Abbey to watch the Archbishop of Canterbury distribute the Royal Maundy—the annual ritual before Easter when the monarch recognizes a group of elderly subjects for their service to churches and local communities.

Privately she was being groomed as well. At age four, Lilibet was included in Queen Mary's party for the wives of Indian princes. At seven, she attended a Buckingham Palace luncheon hosted by the King for Harry Oppenheimer, who showed her a large diamond that had been discovered in South Africa. And when Queen Wilhelmina of the Netherlands came to lunch at Balmoral, the only child to attend was nine-year-old Princess Elizabeth.

DESPITE THE ATTENTION ON DAVID and the Yorks, the King had his other sons to consider as well. Since his successful drug rehabilitation with the help of the Prince of Wales in 1929, Prince George had been following a conventional path. When he turned thirty-one in 1934, his parents were eager to see him well married. They had one European royal specifically in mind: twenty-eight-year-old Princess Marina of Greece and Denmark. She was the granddaughter of King George I of the Hellenes, Queen Alexandra's brother, who had been assassinated in 1913. Marina's father, Prince Nicholas of Greece and Denmark, was one of the late king's eight children, who were often entertained by the British royal family following their exile from Greece in the 1920s after a military coup and formation of a republic.

Princess Marina and her two sisters, Princess Olga—the wife of Prince Paul of Serbia—and Princess Elizabeth, had grown up in Paris with little money and high position. They had been raised by an English governess in a cultivated and multilingual environment. Prince Nicholas was a modestly successful artist, and his wife, the former Grand Duchess Elena of Russia, did charitable work for Russian orphans and refugees. Marina was beautiful enough to model for the top French couturiers.

Queen Mary had been carefully observing the fetching Greek princess—one of her goddaughters—during her family's periodic visits at Buckingham Palace. She told Mabell Airlie that women in Marina's family "make good wives. They have the art of marriage." Chips Channon expressed the hope in early May 1934 that Marina would "make a suitable marriage with the House of W."

Little did Channon know that the very next day, Prince Paul and Princess Olga would bring Marina to a Buckingham Palace luncheon with George V and Queen Mary. During Cowes Week aboard the *Victoria and Albert* three months later, both the King and the Duchess of York talked to George about the Greek princess. While he and Marina were second cousins, they didn't really know each other. "I was glad that I had the opportunity of having long talks to George," Elizabeth wrote to Queen Mary in early August. "I hope that something will come of the Marina idea. He <u>must</u> get to know her well."

A scant nine days later, at Paul and Olga's villa beside Lake Bohinjsko in Yugoslavia, Prince George proposed to Princess Marina, and she accepted. By all accounts, they had found much in common—especially a love of music and the arts, as well as shooting and other country pursuits. "This girl is sophisticated as well as charming," Queen Mary told Mabell Airlie. "Theirs will be a happy marriage." George V rewarded Prince George in October by entitling him Duke of Kent, Earl of St. Andrews, and Baron Downpatrick.

Two nights before George and Marina's wedding on November 29, 1934, the King and Queen hosted a late-evening reception at Buckingham Palace for eight hundred guests. The Prince of Wales brazenly brought the Simpsons to the party. As Ernest stood alone, Wallis—bejeweled with gifts from David and a diamond tiara she borrowed from Cartier—was escorted by the prince to meet his parents as they walked through the state rooms. Queen Mary remembered their perfunctory greeting as the only time she exchanged words with Wallis. George V reacted with fury, reportedly shouting afterward, "That woman in my own house!"

The wedding ceremony at Westminster Abbey replicated the nuptials of Princess Mary and Prince Albert. Eight-year-old Lilibet was the youngest of the eight bridesmaids. She and her ten-year-old cousin

Lady Mary Cambridge proudly held high the bridal train of the newly married Duchess of Kent during the procession from the altar.

Big crowds hailed the bride and groom outside the Abbey, and afterward George and Marina had a Greek Orthodox marriage service in the Buckingham Palace Chapel, followed by what the King described as a "great ovation" when they appeared on the Palace balcony. George V hosted a traditional wedding breakfast for 150 family and close friends in the Supper Room. Among the guests was thirteen-year-old Prince Philip of Greece: Lilibet's cousin who shared ancestry with Queen Victoria and Prince Albert.

PRINCE HENRY WAS FAR AWAY on the day of his younger brother's nuptials, midway through a seven-month tour of Australia and New Zealand. The Duke of Gloucester acquitted himself well representing the monarch, and on his return in late March, George V and Queen Mary gave him a full-dress welcome and carriage drive from Victoria station.

As with Prince George, the King and Queen steered thirty-five-year-old Henry toward a desirable match with a woman well known to the family. She was Lady Alice Montagu Douglas Scott, a daughter of the seventh Duke of Buccleuch, the wealthiest landowner in Scotland. The duke and George V had been friends since they served together in the Royal Navy, and Henry had spent time with Alice and her seven siblings at her family's six enormous houses in England and Scotland.

Alice was thirty-four, which prompted Chips Channon to dismiss her as a "hopeless old maid." She was far better than that. Pretty and lively in the company of those she knew well (although reserved in public), she was a talented watercolor artist and a surprisingly independent woman who had postponed marriage to travel the world. Later describing herself as "a kind of pre-beatnik," she sold her paintings at London galleries to finance her adventures.

She had just returned in May 1935 from Africa, and she had been the maharajah of Jaipur's guest at a tiger shoot in India. She played polo, rode regularly with the Buccleuch Hunt in the Borders, and enjoyed stalking. Her sporting passions meshed with those of Prince Henry, but she found him "terribly shy." When he asked for her hand in August 1935, he "muttered it as an aside during one of our walks." Still, Prince Henry was a known quantity, and they were fond of each other. She accepted his proposal because "it was time I did something more useful with my life."

She fit in perfectly with the royal family, although she took the King aback on her first day at Balmoral when she asked if she could go stalking with the men. Women weren't even allowed to follow the guns on George V's grouse moors, so she and her mother contented themselves with Queen Mary's excursions. The King forgave Alice's presumption and described her in his diary as "charming and nice looking." After several days together, the Queen wrote, "We like her immensely."

The death of the Duke of Buccleuch from cancer in late October thwarted plans for a big Westminster Abbey wedding. Instead, Henry and Alice were married quietly by the Archbishop of Canterbury in the Buckingham Palace Chapel on November 6, 1935. After the two families did the requisite turn on the Palace balcony, they had a traditional wedding breakfast. Out in the forecourt for the going-away ritual, the cameras caught Lilibet beaming as she and the other wedding guests pelted Henry and Alice's carriage with rose petals. That night, George V wrote in his diary: "All the children are married but David."

"Queen Mary described 'wonderful crowds of sorrowing people mourning their dear King.'"

King George V's funeral cortege on January 28, 1936, when 124 Royal Navy sailors pulled his coffin on a gun carriage through the streets of London for two hours.

TWENTY-ONE

The Sunset of Death

THE DISTRESS OF THE ROYAL FAMILY OVER THE PRINCE OF WALES heightened in 1935. The year marked George V's quarter century on the throne—his Silver Jubilee—and was meant to be celebratory from beginning to end. But the King's persistent respiratory illness now required periodic oxygen administered by Sister Catherine "Blackie" Black, his nurse since his life-threatening septicemia in 1928–29. He had fallen ill at Sandringham after George and Marina's wedding, and in late February 1935, his doctors recommended he spend a month at the Duke of Devonshire's Compton Place estate at Eastbourne in East Sussex on England's south coast.

On Sunday, March 3, five days after the arrival of the King and Queen, David came for a brief visit. He had been flaunting his affair with Wallis for months. They had recently flown to the Continent for a ski holiday in Austria at Kitzbühel. The pair then traveled to Vienna for evenings of waltzing, and to Budapest, where they listened to gypsy music. The prince returned to London only days before he saw his parents at Eastbourne.

In the preceding weeks, George V had met twice with David's

comptroller, Lionel Halsey, and once with the prince's private secretary, Godfrey Thomas. In each instance the long-suffering aides had
spoken in detail about the Prince of Wales. What passed between
David and his parents at Compton Place is unknown. But Queen
Mary was "fully informed and desperately worried" about the situation
with Wallis, according to James Pope-Hennessy.

A month later, Clive Wigram met with Prince Edward to remind
him of his father's precarious health and warn him that his relationship with Mrs. Simpson was inappropriate. The middle class, he said,
"would not tolerate a sovereign keeping company with another man's
wife."

None of the appeals mattered to David. Writing after a luncheon
party in early April, Chips Channon proclaimed Wallis the prince's
"*maîtresse-en-titre.*" He noted that she had acquired "the air of a per-
sonage and walks into the room as if she almost expected to be curtsied to. . . . She has complete power over the PoW."

The King's health appeared restored when the royal family inaugu-
rated the jubilee on Monday, May 6, 1935, with a magnificent procession of royal carriages, massed bands, and row upon row of troops
down the Mall to St. Paul's Cathedral for a midday Service of Thanksgiving. The Duke and Duchess of York led the way in the landau they
shared with Lilibet and Margaret. He wore his admiral's uniform and
cocked hat, and she wore a long white gown with a fur stole draped
around her shoulders. The princesses, dressed in pink coats and
cloche hats, smiled at the tumultuous crowds. On arriving at St. Paul's,
Lilibet lingered on the steps "to take stock of the scene."

The King in his field marshal's uniform and the Queen in "white
and silvery splendour" led the final and most elaborate procession.
They rode in a large carriage drawn by six gray horses that arrived last
at the cathedral with a sovereign's escort of Life Guards.

Archbishop of Canterbury Cosmo Lang's address to 4,406 of the
great and the good praised George V's "quiet dignity" and "unaffected
friendliness" toward his subjects. Lang said the King had become "the
Father of his people, and to loyalty has been added the warmth of love.

This is the secret of the real personal emotion which today fills the heart of his Realm and Empire." As the family arrayed itself across the Buckingham Palace balcony afterward in brilliant sunshine, Lilibet and Margaret had pride of place between the King and Queen. The little girls "waved again and again to the dense crowds cheering below."

The King and Queen kept up a punishing pace in subsequent weeks, with carriage processions through all the boroughs of London, banquets, a concert of British music at the Royal Albert Hall, receptions with dignitaries, and repeat performances on the balcony. The Yorks represented the King at celebrations in Edinburgh, and the Prince of Wales did the same in Cardiff. Twice George V and Queen Mary singled out Lilibet by treating her to private automobile drives through the back streets of the East End and north London to see the jubilee decorations.

The most glamorous event was the state ball at Buckingham Palace on May 14, which David turned into a family crisis. Four days beforehand, he had a "long talk" over tea at Buckingham Palace with his father and veteran courtier Lord Claud Hamilton, who had served David as well as the King since 1919. Yet again George V pressed his eldest son on the need to get married.

David replied that marriage held no appeal for him, and he disingenuously claimed he had ended his relationship with Thelma Furness because of the family's objections to her. At that point, the King confronted his eldest son about keeping Wallis as his mistress. David insisted that she was not his lover and begged his father to ask the Simpsons to the jubilee ball. It is unclear whether George V took him at his word, but he relented and invited Wallis and Ernest to the Palace.

A crush of twenty-five hundred guests filled the state rooms at ten P.M. on the night of the ball. "It was a fine sight, but no room to dance," wrote the King. Somehow David and Wallis found space for an audacious foxtrot in front of the royal family. "I thought I felt the King's eyes rest searchingly on me," Wallis later wrote. "Something in his look made me feel that all this graciousness and pageantry were but the glittering tip of an iceberg that extended down into unseen depths I could never plumb, depths filled with an icy menace for such as me."

When Bertie and Elizabeth heard that David had lied to the King about his affair with Mrs. Simpson, they were incensed. Staff working for the Prince of Wales may have lacked confirmed sightings of him in bed with Wallis but knew they were living together. Everyone in the prince's circle had seen Wallis, in the words of their friend Lady Diana Cooper, "dripped in new jewels and clothes." What's more, the King had been told that David was giving Wallis an income of £6,000 a year—nearly a half million dollars at today's values.

After dining with his parents in Buckingham Palace at the end of July, the Prince of Wales did not see them again until October. Relations were strained to the breaking point, especially after the King reprimanded David for a speech to military veterans in which he praised Nazi Germany.

By 1935, Adolf Hitler had consolidated his absolute power. He had been named chancellor early in 1933 when the Nazis became the dominant political party. A fire in the Reichstag soon afterward emboldened Hitler to arrest the elected Communists and declare himself dictator.

That year the Prince of Wales had first made his pro-Hitler views known publicly, saying Britain had no right to meddle in Germany's internal affairs. He not only aligned with Hitler's fervent anti-communism but also admired the Nazi policies on unemployment and housing. By contrast, Bertie and his father deeply mistrusted Hitler and found his views and policies repellant. Since the First World War, Elizabeth had harbored a visceral dislike of the "Hun."

A growing number of prominent figures led by Winston Churchill, Duff Cooper, and Anthony Eden raised the alarm over Hitler's rapid rearmament as well as Nazi persecution of Jews and dissidents. Yet much of the British establishment appeared to be sleepwalking as Germany gained strength. In the summer of 1935, pro-Nazi society hostess Emerald Cunard introduced the Prince of Wales to Joachim von Ribbentrop, Hitler's close confidant who would become Germany's ambassador to Britain in the summer of 1936. Wallis also got to know Ribbentrop, who was instructed by Hitler to flirt with her in order to gain favor with the prince. The führer's personal envoy socialized with them both, prompting "much gossip about the Prince of Wales's Nazi leanings," as Chips Channon noted.

In June 1935, Ramsay MacDonald resigned as premier due to failing health. George V asked Stanley Baldwin to return as prime minister and form a reconstructed cabinet. A general election in November gave Baldwin's overwhelmingly Conservative national government a healthy majority of 242 seats. "Splendid," wrote the King in his diary.

AT BALMORAL THAT AUTUMN, BERTIE went out stalking with his father on the hills a few times—far less than was the King's custom. George V's health was obviously deteriorating. Blackie and a second nurse alternated shifts to administer oxygen and care for him. He had what turned out to be his final glimpse of Royal Deeside on September 27. Bertie brought Lilibet and Margaret to tea, and afterward the King and Queen took the train to London. The Yorks followed in early October.

George V conscientiously kept up with his government documents and audiences with various officials. But he was too sick to lead the Armistice Day ceremony at the Cenotaph on November 11, so the Duke of York took his place. The Queen and the Duchess of York watched from their customary vantage point at the Home Office.

The King suffered a "sad loss" when his close friend and long-serving courtier, Fritz Ponsonby, died unexpectedly at age sixty-eight in late October. Days later, Clive Wigram contacted Tommy Lascelles, who had recently ended his five-year stint as private secretary to the Earl of Bessborough, the governor-general of Canada.

Wigram entreated him to fill the vacancy and return to royal service as assistant private secretary to the King. Lascelles initially resisted, figuring correctly that if George V died, he would end up working again for Edward, whom he couldn't abide. But Wigram deliberately misled

Tommy, telling him the King was "in splendid health" and would certainly have "several more years" on the throne.

The enticements worked, and Tommy assembled his courtier's wardrobe, including levee dress coat and white knee breeches. He met the King at Buckingham Palace on Thursday, November 21, and prepared to report for work in January at a salary of £1,500 a year (around £110,000 today).

As December approached, George V was beset by worry about Toria, his favorite sister who devotedly called him on the phone every day. After not having seen her since July, the King and Queen Mary visited her in late November to find her ill and bedridden. Early in the morning of December 3, 1935, Toria died at age sixty-seven. George V was so devastated that he canceled the State Opening of Parliament: "perhaps the first and last time in his life his tremendous sense of public duty faltered," wrote John Wheeler-Bennett. The chancellor of the exchequer stood in to read the King's speech.

The entire royal family gathered for Toria's funeral on December 7 at St. George's Chapel in Windsor. Lord Dawson of Penn, the chief royal physician, observed that the shock of his sister's death had "a further depressive influence" on George V's "failing vitality." The King was also denied the cheerful company of Elizabeth when she was stricken in mid-December with influenza that turned into debilitating pneumonia. Bertie had no choice but to stay with her at Royal Lodge for the Christmas holidays, while Lilibet and Margaret went on the train with the King and Queen to Sandringham.

The Queen did her best to enliven the holiday for Lilibet and Margaret, who visited the King in the mornings and at teatime. The Gloucesters came from York, where Prince Henry was stationed with his regiment. George and Marina arrived on the afternoon of Christmas Eve with their infant son, born in October. To Queen Mary's annoyance, David didn't appear until more than an hour after the exchange of gifts began in the ballroom at the Big House.

Elizabeth told the Queen she was "miserable" to miss Christmas with her children and the royal family. As she remained confined to her bed, Bertie was "ploughing through a turkey all by himself poor darling." Together, they imagined all the festive scenes at the Big House. "It was rather nice being able to guess what you were doing fairly accurately," she wrote.

The shooting parties continued without the King, and houseguests came and went. Tensions between George V and his eldest son erupted three days after Christmas when Sandringham neighbors John and Dorothy Maffey witnessed the King shouting that David must "get rid of that woman." The Prince of Wales left for London the next day, and a week later George V had back-to-back discussions with Lionel Halsey about the prince.

Soon afterward, Blanche Gordon-Lennox—a long-standing member of the royal inner circle—was talking to the King during one of his brief walks outdoors. As she recounted their conversation to Mabell Airlie, "King George had said passionately, 'I pray to god that my eldest son will never marry and have children, and that nothing will come between Bertie and Lilibet and the throne.'"

ON JANUARY 7, 1936, NURSE "Blackie" wrote to Lord Dawson about the King's "sleepiness" and "breathlessness." Unable to walk more than a few steps at a time, he took to riding Jock, his white pony, with Queen Mary or Lilibet. Frederick John Corbitt, who served the royal family for twenty years managing household logistics, caught a poignant scene when "out of the mist" came King George V on Jock: "Walking by the head of the pony, as if leading it along, was the little figure of Princess Elizabeth. She was taking her grandfather back to the house along the pathway that runs through the golf course."

On the afternoon of Wednesday, January 15, the King "felt rotten" and went to bed early. "Didn't feel very grand," he duly noted the next morning. When he stayed in his room all day, Queen Mary wrote, "Most worrying."

Her first instinct was to summon Bertie to Sandringham the next day. David was hosting a shoot at the Fort "in the highest spirits," noted Duff Cooper, one of his guests. The prince "hadn't heard a word of his father's illness." Although Elizabeth was still bedridden, the Duke of York left Royal Lodge for Norfolk.

On the train to Wolferton, he encountered Tommy Lascelles, en route to his first stint of duty as a member of the royal household. The duke "burst into my carriage and said, 'What's all this about the King not being well?'" Lascelles recalled. "That was the first intimation I had that anything was amiss." Tommy was pleasantly surprised by the "very amiable" duke. "I thought him much changed for the better since I last saw him eight years ago," he wrote to his wife, Joan.

By the time Tommy and Bertie arrived late in the afternoon on Thursday the sixteenth, two doctors and two nurses were closely monitoring George V's rapid decline. "Only half of each lung functions properly in the best of times," noted Lascelles. "The machine might gradually run to a standstill at any time."

The next day the King was so weak he could manage just two lines of shaky handwriting in his diary. The doctors issued their first carefully worded medical bulletin that night noting that the King's "bronchial catarrh" was "not severe" but warning that "cardiac weakness" was causing "some disquiet." In fact, George V's kidneys were barely functioning and he was semiconscious.

On Saturday, January 18, Dawson sent for Sir Maurice Cassidy, a cardiac specialist, who confirmed that the King's heart was failing. Alah Knight took Lilibet and Margaret home to Royal Lodge, and all the houseguests left as well. Elizabeth wrote to Queen Mary that she was praying for "you and Papa . . . I cannot bear to think of your anxiety." She felt "cut off & far away" and offered to come to Sandringham "if I can be of any use."

David and Bertie were driven to London on Sunday so the Prince of Wales could alert Stanley Baldwin that the King would survive only a few more days. A series of medical bulletins in the press and on the radio underlined the gravity of the situation as the Archbishop of

Canterbury arrived at the Big House for a bedside vigil. He blessed the King as he was sleeping.

Back in London, Baldwin asked Duff Cooper to meet at 10 Downing Street on Monday the twentieth. The prime minister described to Cooper his conversation with the Prince of Wales the previous day. Not only was Baldwin alarmed by the news of the King's terminal illness, he was also "very much disturbed" about the prince's relationship with Mrs. Simpson, wrote Cooper. "'The country won't stand it,'" said the prime minister. "'If she were what I call a respectable whore,' he said, he wouldn't mind, by which he meant somebody whom the Prince occasionally saw in secret but didn't spend his whole time with."

That morning at Sandringham, a Privy Council of senior government officials, Cosmo Lang, Clive Wigram, and Lord Dawson, appointed Counsellors of State including the Queen, the Prince of Wales, and the Duke of York to conduct business on the King's behalf while he was incapacitated. As the King sat propped up in a chair with pillows, the Privy Counsellors watched him sign two crosses on the document. With Dawson's encouragement, he struggled to say "approved." "He was unable to sign his name, which distressed him," Queen Mary wrote. But as the men withdrew, George V "nodded and smiled to them just as he always had at the close of an interview."

David and Bertie flew back to Sandringham on Monday afternoon. Reporters and photographers camped outside the estate, clamoring for news. The family took walks, had dinner together, and visited the King. At around nine P.M., Dawson consulted with Wigram in the household dining room about how to handle George V's imminent demise. Dawson wrote a simple message on a menu card: "The King's life is moving peacefully towards its close." He and the other two doctors signed it, and after gaining the approval of the Queen and the Prince of Wales, it was read on the BBC at 9:25 P.M.

In her diary, Queen Mary described her husband "becoming weaker in the evening" when the family "realized the end was approaching." They went to his room "at intervals & at 5 to 12 my darling

husband passed peacefully away. My children were angelic." At the
top of her diary entry, she wrote, "Am brokenhearted," and on an extra
page came her valedictory: "The sunset of his death tinged the whole
world's sky."

Her placid account omitted the truth about King George V's death
at age seventy-one that would not be revealed until 1986 with the
opening of Lord Dawson's private diary. It was, in the words of medical
examiner J. H. Rolland Ramsay, a "convenience killing." Dawson wrote
that he recognized the King's "last stage might endure for many hours,
unknown to the patient but little comporting with the dignity and the
serenity which he so richly merited and which demanded a brief final
scene." As a consequence, he decided "to preserve the King's dignity
and ease the strain on his family by cutting short the King's life."

Dawson recorded that Queen Mary and the Prince of Wales had
told him they did not wish George V's life to be prolonged if he was
certain to die. It was unlikely that the deeply religious Queen Mary
would have overtly approved euthanasia, but what the doctor said
about the measures he planned was unclear. Dawson believed such
actions were within a physician's discretion, as he said in a speech to
the House of Lords ten months later when he called euthanasia "a
mission of mercy."

Around eleven P.M., Dawson called Cosmo Lang to the uncon-
scious King's bedroom for final prayers and a benediction. According
to the doctor's notes, after the archbishop left, he administered a fatal
injection of three-quarters of a gram of morphine and one gram of
cocaine into the King's "distended jugular vein." To ensure that the
death announcement would appear "in the morning papers rather
than the less appropriate evening journals," Dawson asked his wife to
call the editor of The Times and advise him to withhold publication
until he had the final word.

As the Queen, the Prince of Wales, the Duke of York, Princess
Mary, and the Duke and Duchess of Kent sat at the King's bedside
with the doctors, his "life passed so quietly that it was difficult to de-
termine the actual moment," Dawson wrote. The bulletin at 11:55 P.M.

on January 20—just shy of *The Times'* deadline and less than an hour after the injection—said "death came peacefully." The cause of death was described as cardiorespiratory failure.

The Queen's observation notwithstanding, one of her children was hardly "angelic." According to a memorandum written that night by Clive Wigram, as George V lay dying, the Prince of Wales "became hysterical, cried loudly and kept on embracing the Queen." Helen Hardinge described David's outburst as "frantic and unreasonable. . . . While he demanded attention for his own feelings, he seemed completely unaware of those of others."

Had the King been sentient in his final moments, he might have recalled what he had latterly told Stanley Baldwin about his heir: "After I am dead the boy will ruin himself within twelve months."

"Pictures of the King and his paramour on holiday appeared everywhere but in Britain."

King Edward VIII with Wallis Simpson and her American friend Katherine Rogers during the cruise of the *Nahlin* in August 1936.

TWENTY-TWO

Tears of Destiny

KING EDWARD VIII WAS PROCLAIMED MONARCH AT 4:00 P.M. ON TUESDAY, January 21, 1936, the day following his father's death. With Bertie looking on, David stood before the Accession Council of British grandees in St. James's Palace after their official proclamation. He made his accession declaration, took his oath, and gave his first speech as king. He was said to be "debonair, self-possessed, full of youthful charm and buoyancy," wrote John Wheeler-Bennett.

The next morning, heralds read out the proclamation during a colorful ceremony at Friary Court in St. James's Palace and three other locations in the city. Rather unnervingly, Edward was spotted at a palace window watching the proceedings with Wallis, his married mistress, at his side. A dismayed Duff Cooper wrote that such behavior "causes so much criticism. . . . Already people are beginning to talk about her and to criticize him."

The brothers were back at Sandringham on Wednesday afternoon, joined by Elizabeth after her five bedridden weeks. Queen Mary wrote in her diary that she "did business with David who was most helpful and kind." To put it mildly, the Queen's description glossed over an extremely uncomfortable meeting that evening with the new king, his siblings, and private secretary Clive Wigram.

After George V's will had been read by a solicitor, Edward VIII was "much perturbed that his father had left him no money and kept on saying, 'Where do I come in?'" Wigram recorded. To each of his other children, George V left some £750,000 in cash (around £54 million at today's values). He bequeathed David a life interest in the private estates at Sandringham and Balmoral—as his own father had done for him.

The private secretary and the lawyer tried to explain that as Prince of Wales for twenty-five years, Edward had been expected to have a "nice surplus" from the revenues of the Duchy of Cornwall portfolio of properties and other investments that had provided private income to male heirs to the throne since 1337. As a result, David's father saw "no necessity to provide for him." The lawyer added that for the same reason, Edward VII had left no direct financial bequest to George V. Wigram wrote, "We failed to comfort the new king. He kept on saying that 'my brothers and sister have got large sums but I have been left out.'"

David "was not reasonable," noted Wigram, who tried to reassure him that he would be "very well off" as king. It was only later that Wigram and other courtiers discovered that Edward VIII "had tucked away over a million in sterling" (some £75 million—more than $100 million—at current values) from the Duchy of Cornwall. Nevertheless, "His Majesty continued to be obsessed about money," wrote Wigram.

After the reading of the will, Tommy Lascelles encountered Edward VIII "striding" along a corridor "with a face blacker than any thunderstorm. He went straight to his room," and for a long time was "glued to the telephone" in conversation with Wallis. "Money, and the things that money buys, were the principal desiderata in Mrs. Simpson's philosophy, if not his," Lascelles later wrote.

Equally insensitive was one of Edward's first acts as king: turning back the clocks by a half hour and abolishing his father's sacrosanct

"Sandringham Time" that he had used to extend the daylight for shooting. Yet he showed appropriate solidarity with his family on Thursday the twenty-third when they all accompanied the late king's coffin by train from Sandringham to London and in a cortege from King's Cross station to Westminster Hall for five days of lying in state.

Marring the solemnity was an unfortunate incident as the procession neared its destination. The coffin on the gun carriage was draped with George V's royal standard and carried the Imperial State Crown. Perhaps because the crown's frame was in disrepair, the Maltese Cross on its top—consisting of a huge sapphire and two hundred diamonds— suddenly clattered into the gutter. A quick-thinking sergeant-major in the bearer party of Grenadier Guards picked up the cross and slipped it into his pocket so it could be reaffixed in the hall once the coffin was placed on a catafalque. "A most terrible omen," wrote Harold Nicolson, George V's future biographer, who was then a member of Parliament. The sight of the historic crown falling apart seemed to signal trouble ahead for Edward VIII's reign.

Nearly a million mourners filed past George V's bier. The most touching moment occurred at midnight on Monday the twenty-seventh, when his four sons, all in uniforms of the army and navy, stood for twenty minutes with bowed heads at the four corners of the catafalque covered in purple cloth.

Under a cold drizzle the next morning, Edward, Albert, Henry, and George followed the gun carriage drawn by Royal Navy sailors in a cortege for two hours through what Queen Mary described as "wonderful crowds of sorrowing people mourning their dear King." They slowly proceeded through London to Paddington station amid muffled drums, the skirl of bagpipes, and the tolling of bells. After debarking from the train at Windsor, the sons followed their father on his final journey up the hill to St. George's Chapel for the funeral service and burial in the ancestral vault. Queen Mary, her daughter Mary, and the wives of Princes Albert, Henry, and George made the trip by automobile and train.

Queen Mary's children took turns consoling her over lunches and dinners at Buckingham Palace in the following weeks. But in the company of her lifelong friend Mabell Airlie, the sixty-eight-year-old Queen's composure cracked, and she revealed her "passionate grief." While reading condolence letters, "her tears would break out afresh" and "sometimes she would be unable to speak for a few minutes," Mabell recalled.

To "shut out her loneliness and anxiety," Queen Mary occupied herself with sorting through her masses of possessions and planning her move in the autumn out of Buckingham Palace to Marlborough House, which she was busily redecorating. While she remained in her palace apartment, Edward VIII set aside a suite of rooms for his official business but continued to live at York House in St. James's Palace and, increasingly, Fort Belvedere in Windsor.

In February, Queen Mary confided her anxiety about David to Mabell Airlie, as stories about his flagrantly keeping company with Wallis filtered back to the Palace. She told Mabell she had hesitated to broach the subject primarily because "he is the most obstinate of all my sons. To oppose him over doing anything is only to make him more determined to do it. At present he is utterly infatuated, but my great hope is that violent infatuations usually wear off."

The press and the people praised Edward VIII for his charm, informality, modernism, and the perception that he could relate to the man in the street. The British public still had not heard of Mrs. Simpson and expressed considerable sympathy for the forty-one-year-old King's lack of a wife and family. But the cognoscenti viewed David's mistress as the problem rather than the solution; the idea of his marrying Wallis after a divorce seemed remote to some, unthinkable to most others. J. H. Thomas, the longtime general secretary of the National Union of Railwaymen and a confirmed Labourite, had been a close friend of George V. As early as February 1936, Thomas told Harold Nicolson that "this little obstinate man with 'is Mrs. Simpson . . . won't do. . . . I know the people of this country. I *know* them. They 'ate 'aving no family life at Court."

While David continued to spend extravagantly on Wallis, he

became fixated on making economies at Sandringham and Balmoral—cherished royal havens he disliked. He deputized Bertie to spend two weeks in Norfolk surveying the Sandringham estate and submitting recommendations for cost cutting. The duke obediently prepared a report that was, in the words of John Wheeler-Bennett, "a remarkable example of clarity and common sense." He conceded that some changes were advisable and sought to preserve rather than destroy.

Bertie carried out royal engagements, but Elizabeth couldn't shake the respiratory infection that had plagued her since mid-December. As George V had done the previous year, she decamped to the seaside in Eastbourne on March 4 for restorative salt air and sunshine. Bertie came and went as his work allowed, and the princesses, now nine and four, played on the beach. "I am religiously going out morning & afternoon so I expect that soon I shall be very well," Elizabeth told Beryl Poignand. The family stayed for a month.

Throughout the full court mourning period extending to July 20, King Edward VIII fulfilled an array of public duties. His popularity seemed secure, yet his private behavior unnerved palace officials as well as savvy close observers such as the twenty-seventh Earl of Crawford, an eminent and well-connected Tory whose brother Ronald Lindsay was the British ambassador to the United States. In early February, Crawford wrote to his good friend John Buchan, the celebrated Scottish novelist (*The Thirty-Nine Steps,* among others) who had been appointed governor-general of Canada and ennobled as the first Baron Tweedsmuir in November 1935.

Crawford confided to Tweedsmuir that Edward VIII was "surprised to find how great is the gulf" between life as "His Royal Highness" the Prince of Wales and "His Majesty" the King. These differences, Crawford pointed out, included the need to submit his speeches to the government for approval. The routines of kingship—audiences with officials as well as signing government documents in his daily dispatch boxes—were already proving "irksome. . . . He finds himself a little non-plussed that his freedom should be so much curtailed."

Shortly after taking the throne, the King told one friend that "he could not bear to feel that he would be cooped up in Buckingham Palace all the time within the iron bars." Through David's own cavalier disregard for his father's duties, George V's unwillingness to share much with his heir, and the new king's inattentive attitude, Edward VIII was shockingly unprepared for his role.

Crawford reported to Tweedsmuir in early May that the King "breaks precedents without rhyme or reason," and that his indecision "offends everybody. . . . It is all very discouraging, this lack of intuition about people who have served the Throne for so long." The King persisted with his heedless behavior, especially while at Fort Belvedere with Wallis. Tommy Lascelles later revealed to Harold Nicolson that "nobody would ever know what the Private Secretaries had had to endure" during Edward VIII's 326-day reign. "The King refused to have regular hours and would escape from Thursday to Tuesday to Belvedere where none of them were allowed to go."

Not only did Edward VIII fail to read and sign many government documents, he also carelessly left them lying about. Some papers were returned to Downing Street and Whitehall marked with rings left by cocktail glasses. Lascelles recalled that even when the King did attend to his papers, "he shut himself up at Buckingham Palace with Mrs. Simpson." "The lady is still there," the footmen would say. By the time Tommy got the King's attention, David would be "too bored to listen."

Helen Hardinge, whose husband, Alec, would be promoted from assistant private secretary to private secretary in July 1936, recorded her dismay at the monarch's worrying ways that spring: his "strange hours" that kept his advisers up late, the "confusion" created because he was so "impractical," and his all-round "irresponsibility." Fearing possible leaks, the Foreign Office began withholding documents from the King.

Edward VIII was superficially attentive to his mother. He regularly had luncheon with her, sometimes bringing luminaries such as King Farouk of Egypt and the Aga Khan. For the Queen's

sixty-ninth birthday on May 26, Edward VIII hosted a family luncheon, where she was "much spoilt" by everybody. But her happiness proved short-lived.

On the following night, the King presided over a dinner at York
House, and the "Court Circular" in *The Times* the next day published
the guest list. In addition to Prime Minister Baldwin and his wife, it
noted the presence of Mr. and Mrs. Simpson—the first time they were
mentioned in the official chronicle of royal and upper-class doings.
Queen Mary showed the notice to Mabell Airlie. "He gives Mrs. Simpson the most beautiful jewels," she said. After a long pause, the Queen
added, "I am so afraid that he may ask me to receive her." Mabell noticed
that "bright spots of crimson were burning on her cheek bones."

Only weeks later, Edward VIII, who was prevented by court
mourning from attending Royal Ascot, offended his family again by
arranging a royal carriage to transport Mrs. Simpson to the races. After
Wallis and her husband Ernest separated that summer, the King paid
for a house on Cumberland Terrace in Regent's Park as her new London residence, and Wallis filed for divorce.

The King put her name in the "Court Circular" a second time after
a York House dinner for twenty-two that he hosted on July 9, which
was also attended by Bertie and Elizabeth, Winston and Clementine
Churchill, and Alec and Helen Hardinge. "The unfortunate Court
Circulars," former Labour prime minister Ramsay MacDonald said to
Harold Nicolson, have "a bad effect on the country. The people do not
mind fornication, but they loathe adultery."

The York House dinner was one of the few times Elizabeth and
Bertie socialized with Edward VIII outside official events such as
Trooping the Colour to celebrate David's forty-second birthday on
June 23. He had been conspicuously keeping Bertie and his wife at
arm's length, and they painfully felt his chill. Their only encounter as
a foursome had occurred in April when David and Wallis came to
Royal Lodge for tea. The King had been eager to show Bertie his new
American station wagon and proudly drove over with Wallis from the
Fort.

The King and Elizabeth conversed with relative ease, but Bertie had trouble talking to Wallis. Afterward they all strolled in the garden, comparing the plantings at the Fort and Royal Lodge. While Wallis recalled that Elizabeth's "justly famous charm was highly evident," she got the "impression that while the Duke of York was sold on the American station wagon the Duchess was not sold on David's other American interest."

THE BEGINNING OF THE END for King Edward VIII was his holiday cruise with Wallis along the Dalmatian Coast from mid-August to early September 1936. They sailed on the *Nahlin*, a friend's luxurious yacht equipped with a swimming pool and gymnasium.

"What a pity David went abroad when there is so much for him to do here & at Balmoral," Queen Mary wrote to Bertie from Sandringham on August 13. She was especially concerned about what the King planned for the Balmoral estate. "You will I know be able to advise him to do the right thing up there & be liberal up to a point without overdoing it."

By then Edward VIII was aboard the *Nahlin* entertaining guests including Duff and Diana Cooper, Tommy Lascelles, and Wallis's wealthy American friends Herman and Katherine Rogers. It was during this cruise that Lady Diana Cooper watched the King trying to free Wallis's dress from under a chair. "She stared at him as one might at a freak," and said, "'Well, that's the *maust* [*sic*] extraordinary performance I ever saw in my life,'" recalled Lady Diana, who was taken aback by Wallis's "coldness" toward the King.

Pictures of the King and his paramour on holiday appeared everywhere but in Britain. Only *Cavalcade,* an English *Time* magazine–style weekly with a small circulation, broke the British press silence and covered the trip honestly. Publications like *The Illustrated London News* deliberately withheld photographs of the couple.

"One must not forget that, as he said pathetically the other night, he is acutely depressed by what he calls his 'little black coat & striped trousers' & is, no doubt, a very different creature inside B.P. from what he is when he is happy & comparatively free, as now," Tommy Lascelles wrote to his wife, Joan. "There may be many faults of temperament & character & . . . certain cells in his brain have never grown up," he added. Still, he thought it was "ridiculous to make him out either a loony or a reckless libertine."

Yet much of the British establishment turned on Edward for a particularly reckless act during his visit to Balmoral in September. Bertie accompanied his older brother from the railroad station to the castle when the King arrived on September 19, dressed in a Balmoral tartan kilt. The next morning David attended the service at Crathie Church along with the Yorks and other members of the royal family.

Bertie and Elizabeth had already been in their Birkhall home for a month. Four days before Edward VIII's arrival at Royal Deeside, Elizabeth wrote to her mother-in-law that Bertie "loves this place & is a little worried about its future. . . . I do hope that David will take a liking to the whole property. . . . It means a lot to Scotland as a whole." Contrary to their hopes, however, David made staff cutbacks and other stringent changes at Balmoral without even consulting his younger brother. "David only told me what he had done after it was over, which I might say made me rather sad," Bertie wrote to his mother.

As David was stalking his first stags on the hills above the castle on the nineteenth, Elizabeth wrote to Queen Mary that she was "secretly rather dreading next week, but I haven't heard if a certain person is coming or not." The King had been scheduled to open a new hospital in Aberdeen on the twenty-third, but he asked the Yorks to do the honors. His excuse was that he was still observing official mourning—a blatant lie, since he had been carrying out similar engagements both before and since the end of full court mourning on July 20.

The Yorks went through their paces at Aberdeen, little knowing that simultaneously David was arriving at the train station to greet Wallis, along with Herman and Katherine Rogers. He bundled them into his car, slipped behind the wheel in his driving goggles, and motored the sixty miles to the castle himself. The next day the Aberdeen *Evening Express* ran side-by-side photographs of the King on a "surprise visit in car to meet guests" and of the Yorks at the hospital opening. The people of Scotland never forgave Edward VIII. "It is quite true that someone chalked up on the walls of Aberdeen . . . 'Down with the American harlot,'" Lady Londonderry told Lord Tweedsmuir.

Wallis Simpson was conspicuous among the Balmoral guests announced in the "Court Circular"—all prominent titled aristocrats as well as David's brother and sister-in-law George and Marina. The sixth Earl of Rosebery gave a full account of the house party to his friend Lady Londonderry, who passed along the details to Tweedsmuir in Canada. The King and Wallis occupied rooms next to each other on the ground floor, and the Roseberys were assigned George V's and Queen Mary's rooms upstairs.

"The whole of the gold plate was taken up to Balmoral for the week—a thing that had never been done before in all the weeks the late King was there," Lady Londonderry wrote. "In fact, more stuff went up that one week than in any previous time—all in order for Mrs. S to dine off the gold plate belonging to the British Sovereign, surrounded by Dukes and Duchesses!!" Edward VIII was as capricious in his private conduct as he was in his public duties: "all kept waiting until any hour of the morning, before they knew what the King wished them to do."

Three days after the notorious Aberdeen incident—by then known throughout the British upper-class—David invited Bertie and Elizabeth to dinner. On their arrival, Wallis committed a provocative faux pas. As host of the dinner, the King was expected to greet his guests. Instead, Wallis moved forward to extend her hand to the Yorks. Already simmering about Aberdeen, Elizabeth breezed past her brother-in-law's mistress and said, "I came to dine with the King." Her discourtesy enraged David.

To Bertie, Edward VIII's stay at Balmoral was "a nightmare. . . . He felt shut off from his brother, neglected, ignored, unwanted," wrote Wheeler-Bennett. Beyond the King's unilateral decisions about the estate, the Duke of York despaired over "the hopelessly complicated personal element. He felt that he had lost a friend and was rapidly losing a brother."

In a letter to Queen Mary, Elizabeth lamented that "David does not seem to possess the faculty of making others feel <u>wanted</u>. It is very sad, and I feel that the whole difficulty is a certain person. I do not feel that I can make advances to her & ask her to our house. . . . This fact is bound to make relations a little difficult. . . . The whole situation is complicated & horrible, and I feel so unhappy."

But after the Yorks returned to London in mid-October, Elizabeth wrote to "Darling David," thanking him "for lending us Birkhall" for "six weeks of complete peace." She described him as "ANGELIC and kind," adding, "you are always so sweet & thoughtful for us." Without Birkhall, she wrote, "I honestly don't believe that I could cope with all the problems of modern life."

On October 27, the royal family's problems worsened when a circuit court judge in Ipswich on the Suffolk coast—a provincial location deliberately chosen in an ill-conceived effort at secrecy—granted Wallis her decree nisi—conditional approval for a divorce that would become final in six months. "King's Moll Renoed" went one headline in the American press, referring to the Nevada city known for its easy divorces. Suddenly the notion that Edward VIII could contemplate marrying a woman twice divorced "with two husbands living" became "a devastating revelation" of the new king's "intentions," in the Earl of Crawford's words. While previously Crawford and his friends had been "inclined to laugh, now we are frightened of a first class constitutional crisis" that could set the King against the British government.

The silence of the British press gave the King a false feeling of security and inflated his sense of invincible popularity. Yet Prime Minister Baldwin and others in the government and the Palace had evidence that "beneath the surface of a Loyal Press" in Britain, there was within the ruling class "a growing volume of criticism of the King's domestic affairs," in the words of Alec Hardinge, the King's private secretary.

Baldwin had actually made one attempt to persuade the King to stop the divorce action. On Tuesday, October 20, he had met with Edward VIII at the Fort to discuss Mrs. Simpson for the first time. During extensive talks together three days earlier, Baldwin and Hardinge had calculated that a decree nisi was imminent, and that an absolute decree at the end of April 1937 could enable the King to marry Wallis before his coronation scheduled for May 12.

What's more, the overseas press—especially in the United States—had been "dragging the name of the King of England in the mud," in the view of Hardinge. These reports were being widely read in Canada. Baldwin feared that rampant criticism of the King there would seriously undermine the monarchy by spreading to the other four dominions—Australia, New Zealand, South Africa, and the Irish Free State—that recognized the British monarch as head of state. The prime minister needed to confront the King as soon as possible.

In the Fort Belvedere meeting on the twentieth, which lasted about an hour, Prime Minister Baldwin recounted that his "post bag" was "beginning to show widespread resentment about Mrs. Simpson." The prime minister even brought along a representative sampling of the correspondence. "I spoke plainly and he listened," Baldwin told Tweedsmuir several days later. "The ice is broken but whether I made a real impression I don't know. I used Canada with him and the inevitable result of the impact of the American press."

Worryingly, the King had insisted to Baldwin that he, as monarch, had no right to interfere in the Simpsons' private affairs, and the divorce case must proceed. Despite frequent requests from Baldwin, the two men would not meet again for nearly a month. Still, Baldwin's words made an impression. The King promptly contacted Walter Monckton, a barrister who had served as attorney general to the Prince of Wales and legal adviser to the Duchy of Cornwall since 1932.

After lunch at the Fort, the King told Monckton about his conversation with the prime minister. "I am beginning to wonder whether I really am the kind of King they want," Edward VIII said. "Am I not a bit too independent? . . . My make-up is very different from that of my father. I believe they would prefer someone more like him. Well, there is my brother Bertie."

The evening after Baldwin's meeting with the King, Alec Hardinge gave a report to Queen Mary. "How unsatisfactory it all is, so underhanded and unpleasant," the Queen wrote to Bertie on October 22. "How will it end, you may imagine how worried I feel." Bertie subsequently had his own briefing from Hardinge. For the first time, Bertie understood that his brother might abdicate to marry Wallis. Bertie "recoiled from it with consternation and incredulity," wrote Wheeler-Bennett, "but in his heart he began to realize the inevitability of his destiny."

The family went through the motions as Queen Mary moved into Marlborough House in October, and Prince Henry and his wife, Alice, prepared to live in York House after the King's departure for Buckingham Palace. But Bertie complained to his mother that David was "very difficult to see & when one does he wants to talk about other matters; never knowing what will happen tomorrow, & then the unexpected comes."

The two brothers finally met on November 6, mainly to settle arrangements for Christmas, which Queen Mary would host at Sandringham. The King had initially said he had no wish to spend the traditional holiday in Norfolk, but Bertie persuaded him to come for two days, which the Queen thought would "certainly look better."

Strictly speaking, Edward VIII could marry Wallis, who would become his queen. The Royal Marriages Act of 1772 required the monarch to approve all marriages in the royal family, presumably including his own. But Church of England law would not recognize the marriage of the sovereign—the church's supreme governor—to a divorcée. If the King's ministers advised against the marriage, he would be violating the constitution.

Alec Hardinge decided to force the issue by laying out the increasingly dangerous situation on paper to avoid any misunderstanding. In a letter to Edward VIII on November 13, 1936, his private secretary said "the silence of the British Press" would likely break in "a matter of days," and the criticism of the King in Britain would be "calamitous." If the monarch persisted in marrying Wallis, the government could resign, triggering a dissolution of Parliament and general election "in which Your Majesty's personal affairs would be the chief issue." Even those who sympathized with Edward VIII "would deeply resent the damage which would inevitably be done to the Crown," Hardinge wrote. To defuse this "dangerous situation," Hardinge urged the King to send Wallis abroad *"without further delay."*

The King not only ignored Hardinge's advice, he furiously broke with his private secretary. Three days later, he summoned Prime Minister Baldwin to the Palace and told him that he would definitely marry Wallis as soon as she was fully divorced, and that she would be his queen. He wished to remain king, but if the government opposed him, he would abdicate.

That evening he arrived at Marlborough House in white-tie and tailcoat for dinner with his mother, his sister, and Prince Henry's wife, Alice. By David's account, at the end of the meal Alice said she was tired and asked to be excused. After her curtsey, "she almost fled from the room." Alice had a different recollection: "He was in a great state of agitation and asked his mother if I could leave the room." Queen Mary "was discernibly angered by this request, but with many apologies she asked me to go, which of course I did."

In Queen Mary's boudoir, the King informed his mother and sister of his marriage plans. "They comprehended that even the alternative of abdication did not deter me," he later wrote. He understood that his mother could not accept that a sovereign—to her a sacred entity—would actually give up the throne. "The word duty fell between us," he recalled.

Still, he begged his mother and sister to receive Wallis so they could "understand what she means to me and why I cannot give her up." But "they could not bring themselves to unbend." Queen Mary later told Clive Wigram, her late husband's private secretary, that she thought she had been "extremely outspoken" to her son, and that "I tried to express my displeasure, but I suppose he never listened to what I said."

The next day, the Queen wrote David to express "true sympathy" for his difficult position and her hope that he was "making a wise decision" for his future—her wish that he would part company with Wallis. As he had the night before, he misinterpreted her words and sent her an almost giddy reply several days later. "I feel so happy and relieved to have at last been able to tell you my wonderful secret," he wrote. "Now that Wallis will be free to marry me in April it only remains for me to decide the best action I take for our future happiness and for the good of all concerned. . . . God bless you darling Mama for all your sweetness to and understanding of your always very loving and devoted David."

On Tuesday, November 17, Queen Mary wrote to Elizabeth, "I am more worried than I can say at what is going on. I long to have a talk with you & Bertie. . . . What a mess to have got into & for such an unworthy person too!!!" Meanwhile, David was busy unburdening himself to his three brothers, starting with Bertie that afternoon. The Duke of York "was so taken aback by my news that in his shy way he could not bring himself to express his innermost feelings at the time," the King later wrote. "His genuine concern for me was mixed with the dread of having to assume the responsibilities of kingship."

Back at 145 Piccadilly, Bertie shared the news with his wife. "Bertie has just told me of what has happened, and I feel quite overcome with horror and emotion," Elizabeth immediately wrote to her mother-in-law. "One feels so helpless against such obstinacy." She asked to meet the following morning and signed off, "God help us all to be calm & wise."

EDWARD VIII'S DECLARATIONS TO THE prime minister and his own family essentially sealed the outcome, although many permutations played out over the following three and a half weeks. On Wednesday, November 18, the King left London for a highly publicized two-day tour through sixty miles of the "distressed" mining areas in South Wales. Everywhere he went, enthusiastic crowds packed the streets, and the press noted his "deep compassion for the unemployed and a desire to ameliorate their conditions."

The dramatic centerpiece of the tour was on the first day during an unscheduled stop at the Dowlais Steel Works, which had once employed nine thousand men and had been closed for several years. As workmen formerly employed at Dowlais sang Welsh hymns, the King bowed and said, "These works brought all these people here. Something should be done to get them at work again." His words, repeated in the press as "Something must be done," became a touchstone for the King and fueled his delusion that he would remain popular whatever he did in his personal life.

Despite the favorable publicity, the King's performance in South Wales prompted criticism. Now that he was king, his comments appeared to be overtly political and violated the public neutrality expected of a sovereign. What's more, Victor Cazalet, a well-regarded Conservative member of Parliament, noted that "it was known among a good many people that he had spent at least 100,000 pds on jewelry" for Wallis (over $100 million in today's values). "Sympathising . . . in South Wales, telling them something must be done . . . at the same time he was sacking literally dozens of people from his estates . . . and lavishing jewels on his mistress."

On November 23, Bertie and Elizabeth both sent letters to the King—evidently unbeknownst to each other. The duke apologized for his speechless reaction on hearing his older brother's news. "I do hope you did not think that I was unsympathetic about it," Bertie wrote. "Since then I have been thinking a great deal about it, as I do so long for you to be happy with the one person you adore. I, of all people, should understand your own personal feelings at this time, which I do indeed." He said he grasped the King's "great difficulties" and expressed confidence that "whatever you decide to do will be in the best interests of this Country & Empire."

Elizabeth made a more forceful case in her own confidential letter. "For God's sake don't tell [Bertie] that I have written," she pleaded. "Please read this," she wrote. "Please be kind to Bertie when you see

him, because he loves you, and minds terribly all that happens to you."
She emphasized how "loyal & true" he was to David. "You have no idea
how hard it has been for him lately. I know that he is fonder of you
than anybody else. . . . I am terrified for him—so DO help him." She
reassured the King that they both wanted him to be happy "more than
anything else, but it's awfully difficult for Bertie to say what he thinks,
you know how shy he is—so do help him."

Bertie told veteran courtier Godfrey Thomas that if he became
king—the "worst" outcome, in his view—he would work hard to "clear
up the inevitable mess, if the whole fabric does not crumble under the
shock and strain of it all." Both Bertie and Elizabeth found it to be "a
great strain having to talk & behave as if nothing was wrong during
these difficult days," she wrote to Queen Mary.

In late November, Edward VIII seized on the idea of a "morganatic" marriage: Wallis would become his wife but would take a lesser
title such as duchess, and any children they might have would be
ineligible to succeed him as sovereign. But under English law and
tradition, the King's wife is automatically the Queen Consort. Only a
special Act of Parliament would permit a morganatic union, and an
identical bill would need to be passed by each of the five dominion
parliaments in Canada, Australia, New Zealand, South Africa, and the
Irish Free State.

Baldwin sounded out Clement Attlee, leader of the Labour Party,
and Sir Archibald Sinclair, leader of the Liberal Party. Neither of them
would form a new government if the King defied the prime minister's
advice against a marriage to Mrs. Simpson and forced Baldwin and his
cabinet to resign. Nor would either party chief condone a morganatic
union.

"It is not only the law of our country but it is also, I believe, a
sound, healthy and essential element in the monarchical principle
itself, that the lady whom the King marries must become Queen and
share with him, before the whole people, the glorious burden of sover-
eignty," said Sinclair. He strongly believed that a morganatic marriage
bill passing through the parliaments of the dominions could involve

the throne "in prolonged controversy" which could damage "its prestige and dignity."

Prime Minister Baldwin also queried prominent Tory politician
Winston Churchill, a friend of Edward VIII who professed to support
the government. At the King's urging, Churchill pushed the morganatic
option. He also unwisely pressed Baldwin to give the King time to con-
sult his subjects and allow Parliament to examine the issue before making a formal statement. Churchill's position had more to do with a
romantic loyalty to the sovereign as a revered institutional figure than
personal fealty to a flawed man. But his passionate defense of Edward
VIII put Churchill crosswise with the future King George VI, a rift that
wouldn't heal until they were thrown together during World War II.

On November 28, Stanley Baldwin sent telegrams to the dominion prime ministers asking them to consider three scenarios for the
King: He would marry Wallis and she would become his queen; he
would wed her morganatically with the approval of their parliaments;
or he would voluntarily abdicate so he could marry her as a private citizen. All the dominion leaders considered a morganatic marriage
unworkable, and they strongly opposed twice-divorced Wallis as
queen. The only outcome was abdication.

Australian prime minister Joseph Lyons pointedly said that
whether the King married Mrs. Simpson or not, he had lowered the
prestige of the monarchy so far that he would have to step down in any
event. Elizabeth wrote emphatically to her sister May, "If Mrs. Simpson is not fit to be Queen, she is not fit to be the King's morganatic
wife. The crown must be above all controversy."

Speaking to the House of Commons on Friday, December 4, Baldwin said that if the King were to marry Mrs. Simpson, she would
"automatically have the same status as Queen Alexandra or Queen
Mary." Harold Nicolson felt "a shudder of horror" pass through the
chamber. When the prime minister declared that the government had
no intention of introducing ad hoc legislation to permit a morganatic
marriage, the House burst into loud cheers.

By then the King's affair with Mrs. Simpson was front-page news in Britain as well as the rest of the world. The improbable trigger for the British press's abandonment of its silence was a speech by the Right Reverend Walter Blunt, the Anglican Bishop of Bradford, at a diocesan conference on December 1. Referring to the upcoming coronation, Blunt noted the necessity of the King's "prayer and self-dedication." He added that he hoped Edward VIII was "aware of his need. Some of us wish that he gave more positive signs of such awareness."

Whatever Blunt intended, the press made the connection to Wallis Simpson. Two days later, newspaper placards on the streets of London blared "The King's Marriage." Some surveys showed initial popular support among ordinary Britons for Edward and Wallis, but soon politicians recognized that even the workingmen who had previously cheered the King now opposed his marrying Wallis.

Throughout these weeks of machinations—including almost daily meetings of the cabinet and periodic encounters between Baldwin and the King—Bertie tried to see his older brother, to no avail. He was shocked by the headlines and upset that "the whole matter had been published." Suddenly, all the photographs of the King and his mistress—on the *Nahlin,* in Salzburg, at Lake Como and Kitzbühel and Ascot—flooded the newspapers, along with profiles of "the cause of the constitutional crisis: Mrs. Ernest A. Simpson."

Hate mail quickly followed, and someone broke windows in Wallis's Regent's Park home. She was already suffering from "nervous exhaustion" at Fort Belvedere, where the King raged against the "damn politicians" who made her ill. As the news spread across Britain, she fled to France to stay with her American friends Herman and Katherine Rogers at their villa near Cannes.

Bertie had two brief meetings in London with his older brother on December 3, the first including the prominent barrister Walter Monckton. Since the King cut contact with Hardinge and the other private secretaries in mid-November, Monckton had been serving as David's principal adviser and point of contact with the government. Before midnight, Monckton would travel with the King to the Fort and live there until the abdication. He maneuvered through the crisis so skillfully that he earned the trust of Bertie, Queen Mary, and government ministers as well as Edward VIII.

Bertie began his own anguished chronicle of the abdication that day. In their conversation at the Palace, he was taken aback that his older brother "was in a great state of excitement," saying "he would leave the country as King after making a broadcast to his subjects & leave it to them to decide what should be done." This audacious idea was summarily rejected by the cabinet at a special session.

Bertie's second encounter with David occurred later in the evening, after the King had again met with Baldwin. In the presence of Bertie and his sister Mary, David made the "dreadful announcement" to his mother that "he could not live alone as King & must marry" Wallis. "I feel so terribly sad for you darling Mama," Bertie wrote afterward. "I am feeling very overwrought as to what may befall me, but with your help I know I shall be able to carry on."

Bertie tried repeatedly to reach the King throughout the weekend by phone. He was rebuffed each time. But he quietly stayed in the loop thanks to Stanley Baldwin. "Three or four times" in the days before the abdication, he traveled incognito to 10 Downing Street in an unrecognizable car and entered by the garden unobserved.

On Saturday, December 5, the Palace announced that "all the King's official engagements are canceled for the present." Even Chips Channon, one of Edward VIII's most ardent defenders, said he was behaving "like a petulant lunatic." Stanley Baldwin told Channon that during one of their meetings, Edward VIII "lost all control and threw books and anything he could lay his hands on *at* the PM." "The last days at Fort Belvedere were a nightmare," wrote Lord Crawford. The King "stayed in mostly solitude resisting every argument based on good sense and propriety. As time went on he became more & more impossible."

Among those who did see Edward VIII at the Fort was Winston Churchill, who came for dinner on Friday the fourth and Saturday the fifth. David had been spending hours on the phone with Wallis in

Cannes, and his behavior was at times panicky and erratic. "He had two marked and prolonged blackouts, in which he completely lost the thread of his conversation," Churchill recalled.

Monckton described life inside the Fort as "disorganized, a series of interruptions, with snatches of sleep." But Monckton denied rumors that the King was frequently inebriated. "Among all the great men who saw us both constantly throughout those days I never heard of one who thought either of us had been drinking!" Monckton recalled.

In the middle of these dramatic events, Elizabeth came down with influenza on Sunday, December 6, after walking to the Royal Lodge church with her husband and daughters in a storm of sleet and snow. Her illness would keep her confined to her bedroom at 145 Piccadilly for nearly two weeks. For a woman robust enough to live past one hundred, Elizabeth's susceptibility to serious respiratory ailments starting in her teens was noteworthy. Even more striking was her tendency to take to her bed at especially stressful moments: the end of their tour of the North Island of New Zealand with Bertie, during the final illness of George V, and now at the peak of the abdication crisis.

"The strain is terrific," she wrote to May Elphinstone that Sunday. "Every day lasts a week." It's unlikely her ailments were psychosomatic, but they were partly caused by exhaustion. In a letter to Beryl Poignand, Elizabeth's mother blamed "over fatigue" and the "terrible . . . constant strain."

As Edward VIII's reign disintegrated, Bertie had to manage his tense conferences without the crucial emotional support of his wife. Writing from 145 Piccadilly, Elizabeth told Queen Mary she was distressed "that at this most vital and unhappy moment in the history of our country, I cannot leave the house."

On Monday, December 7, David finally took Bertie's call in the early evening and asked him to come to Fort Belvedere after dinner. "No, I will come & see you at once," Bertie replied. He found the King "pacing up & down the room, & he told me his decision that he would go." After dinner at Royal Lodge, Bertie went back to the Fort. "I felt having once got there I was not going to leave."

He vowed to help his brother "in his hour of need." Finally, later that night, he returned to London to be with his ailing wife. In the meantime, Prince George spent hours with his older brother at the Fort "trying by every means in his power to persuade the King to stay." But there was no deterring the mulish King Edward VIII.

Edward's advisers, Palace courtiers, and Prime Minister Baldwin began working together to ensure that the King could make a dignified exit. One of the oddities of this denouement was a statement released by Wallis from Cannes on Tuesday, December 8, saying she was prepared "to withdraw forthwith from a situation that has been rendered both unhappy and untenable." In some quarters of the press this was interpreted as the "end of the crisis." In fact, it was a meaningless diversion requested by the King to help improve Wallis's "position . . . in the eyes of the public." David had approved the statement in advance. "We at the Fort knew . . . that his intention was quite unchanged," wrote Walter Monckton.

That night the King hosted a surreal stag dinner for eight in the paneled dining room at the Fort. The guests included two brothers—Bertie and George—as well as the prime minister, Monckton, and three other advisers. Baldwin had earlier made one vain last effort to dissuade the King. Knowing the decision was "final & irrevocable," Bertie and the others were "very sad."

Yet with a sense of awe tinged with envy, Bertie marveled that David was "the life & soul of the party." Monckton called the dinner the King's "tour de force." Wearing a white kilt, Edward VIII took his seat at the head of the table "with a good fresh colour while the rest of us were pale as sheets." He was "rippling over with bright conversation." At one point, Bertie turned to Monckton and said, "Look at him. We simply cannot let him go."

The next day Bertie and David met with the King's advisers to tackle practical details of the transition. The Duke of York faced the hard reality of his situation late in the evening of Wednesday, December 9, when he and Monckton went to Marlborough House to review the Instrument of Abdication with Queen Mary. For the first time she wrote about the crisis in her diary, expressing dismay that her eldest son was giving up "the Throne of this Empire because he wishes to marry Mrs. Simpson!!! The whole affair has lasted since Nov. 16th and has been very painful. It is a terrible blow to us all & particularly poor Bertie."

"I broke down and sobbed like a child," Bertie wrote in his own chronicle. Thirteen years later, in a conversation with Harold Nicolson at Marlborough House in the very same sitting room, the memory of her second son's torment remained indelible for the Queen. "The whole abdication crisis made him miserable," she recalled. "He sobbed on my shoulder for a whole hour—there upon that sofa."

Shortly before ten A.M. on December 10, 1936, Edward VIII sat at a desk in his octagonal drawing room at Fort Belvedere and signed seven copies of his Instrument of Abdication and eight copies of his message to the parliaments of the empire. His three brothers stood nearby and then signed each document as his witnesses. Bertie called it a "dreadful moment." From her bed in London, Elizabeth wrote to Queen Mary that she had "great faith in Bertie—he sees very straight."

Monckton gave the documents to Stanley Baldwin, who addressed the packed House of Commons in midafternoon. After the Speaker of the House read the King's message of abdication in a shaky voice, the prime minister spent a half hour describing the final two months of Edward VIII's reign of less than a year. "There is no moment when he overstates emotion or indulges in oratory," wrote Harold Nicolson. The members of Parliament sat in silence, and afterward Nicolson encountered Baldwin in the corridor. "The man is mad. MAD," the prime minister said. "He could see nothing but that woman. He did not realize that any other considerations avail. He lacks religion. . . . The Duke of York has always been bothered about it. I love the man. But he must go."

Bertie spent most of the day in an agitated state with David, repairing to Royal Lodge for rest when "the tension was getting unbearable at the Fort." After dinner with Clive Wigram at Royal Lodge, he returned to London, where "remarkable scenes of enthusiasm" greeted him. The tremendous crowd engulfed his car, and after he entered the house, the throng sang, "God Save the King" and "For He's a Jolly Good Fellow," followed by chants of "We want the King." Bertie was, by his own admission, "overwhelmed."

The House of Commons expeditiously passed the abdication bill before lunch on Friday, December 11, 1936. With the announcement of the abdication at 1:52 P.M., forty-year-old Prince Albert Frederick Arthur George became king. Chips Channon, who relied on his Belgrave Square neighbor Prince George ("Wildly indiscreet. I call him the BBC") for inside information on the royal family, had already written six days earlier, "He will call himself George VI instead of Albert I, which people think too Germanic." But George VI (as he will now be known in these pages, along with "the King" and "Bertie") also sought to honor his father's memory and underline the traditions that had been interrupted by Edward VIII.

At the moment of his succession, George VI was in London planning his Accession Council and proclamation on Saturday the twelfth. The new Queen Elizabeth was still sick in bed at 145 Piccadilly. Walter Monckton visited George VI to discuss David's new title. Monckton pointed out that "His Royal Highness" remained, and would in fact require an Act of Parliament to remove. While Edward was renouncing for both himself and any children the right to the throne, he kept "the royal birth he shared with his brothers." Monckton noted that George VI "saw the point and was ready to create his brother the Duke of Windsor as the first act of his new reign."

Lilibet and Margaret, who had been shielded from the agonies and uncertainties of the constitutional crisis by their parents and governess, grasped the significance of the day's events. The ten-year-old heiress presumptive glanced at an envelope on their hall table addressed to Her Majesty the Queen. "That's *Mummy* now, isn't it?" she said. Six-year-old Margaret complained, "I had only just learned to spell York, and now I'm not to use it any more."

Bertie went to Fort Belvedere at seven P.M. for a final one-on-one conversation with David as he packed for a trip to Austria that night.

"You are not going to find this a difficult job at all," David told Bertie. "You know all the ropes, and you have almost overcome that slight hesitation in your speech that used to make public speaking so hard for you."

"By the way, David, have you given any thought to what you are going to be called now?" Bertie asked. David had not, but it was clear that Bertie had considered the question and decided on a title equivalent to those of his younger brothers. "I shall create you a duke," he said. "How about the family name of Windsor?"

"Duke of Windsor," replied David, nodding his agreement.

The former and new kings had dinner at Royal Lodge with their mother, brothers, sister, Prince Henry's wife, Alice, and Queen Mary's brother Alge, the Earl of Athlone, and his wife, Princess Alice. In addition to the ailing Queen Elizabeth, the heavily pregnant Marina, Prince George's wife, was also absent. (She would give birth to a daughter, Princess Alexandra, on Christmas Day.) The meal "passed pleasantly enough under the circumstances," wrote David. Uncle Alge recalled that what "might have been quite a gloomy occasion" turned out to be quite cheerful.

Walter Monckton collected David for the drive to Windsor Castle, where he gave his farewell radio address at ten P.M. He had written it with Monckton and Winston Churchill, who "vastly improved the form . . . though he did not alter the substance," Monckton recalled. The most memorable passage—that he could not "discharge my duties as King . . . without the help and support of the woman I love"—was included at David's insistence, and against the advice of others.

His family listened together at Royal Lodge. Queen Mary judged the speech "good & dignified." At ten-thirty, David returned for what his mother called "the dreadful goodbye. . . . The whole thing was too pathetic for words." Princess Mary "sobbed hysterically," prompting the former king to say "For God's sake, don't go on like that, Mary! You are making it more difficult for us all."

The Queen and her daughter left first, as the former king bowed to his mother. The brothers lingered for another hour of conversation—

talking "of all subjects except the one we were thinking," noted Monckton. Before midnight, they had a farewell drink and walked with David
to the door. He bowed over his younger brother's hand, kissed it, and
said, "Thank you, Sir, for all your kindness to me," and "God bless you,
sir. I hope you will be happier than your predecessor." Seeing Bertie's
distressed expression, David put a hand on his shoulder and added, "It
is all right old man but one must step off on the right foot from the
first."

In the car bound for Portsmouth and a voyage across the Channel,
the former king opened a letter written that day by Elizabeth. She
apologized that her illness prevented her from coming to Royal Lodge,
"as I wanted so much to see you before you go, and say 'God bless you'
from my heart. We are all overcome with misery, and can only pray
that you will find happiness in your new life." She said she often
thought of the old days and how he helped them in the first years of
their marriage. "I shall always mention you in my prayers, & bless you,
Elizabeth."

She may well have been sincere in the moment, but her affectionate tone toward the new Duke of Windsor would not be repeated in
the years to come.

The coronation in Westminster Abbey of King George VI and Queen Elizabeth, seated in their Chairs of Estate in front of the royal box, where Queen Mary, Princess Elizabeth, and Princess Margaret look on, May 12, 1937.

PART FOUR

A Royal Beginning

"The new sense of confidence pervades us all."

"We will, God helping us, faithfully discharge our trust."

King George VI and Queen Elizabeth with Queen Mary, Princess Elizabeth, and Princess Margaret on the Buckingham Palace balcony on May 12, 1937, following the coronation in Westminster Abbey.

TWENTY-THREE

Upright Bearing and Grave Dignity

In the front hall at 145 Piccadilly on the morning of Saturday, December 12, 1936, Lilibet and Margaret hugged their father before he set off for St. James's Palace. Dressed in the uniform of Admiral of the Fleet, he emerged from the house bareheaded to enter a royal Daimler. The crowds cheered "Long Live the King" and "God Save the King."

His Accession Council convened at eleven A.M. in the crimson and gilded Throne Room, with its imposing portraits and battlefield paintings, and its massive golden canopy above the solitary throne. He seemed diffident, and his face looked pale and drawn as he read his 122-word declaration "in a low, clear voice, but with many hesitations." He spoke of the unparalleled circumstances of his accession and said, "With My wife as helpmeet by My side, I take up the heavy task which lies before Me." His first act, as promised, was to declare his older brother His Royal Highness the Duke of Windsor. He then greeted, one by one, the representatives of the overseas dominions and India who stood near the door of the Picture Gallery.

On returning home, King George VI watched his two daughters

drop elegant curtsies. "He stood for a moment touched and taken aback," Marion Crawford recalled. "Then he stooped and kissed them both warmly." Bertie and Elizabeth would soon discard the stilted custom of children curtseying to their sovereign and consort parents, although the princesses would continue the practice with Queen Mary.

At three P.M. came the proclamation from Friary Court at St. James's Palace. Floodlights illuminated the scarlet-draped balcony above the forecourt in the failing winter daylight, and a light mist softened the scene. As a reassuring counterpoint to the surreptitious glimpse of Edward VIII and Mrs. Simpson eleven months earlier, George VI, his daughters, Queen Mary, and the Duke and Duchess of Gloucester watched the colorful medieval ceremony from a window of Marlborough House. The kings, heralds, and pursuivants of arms stood in a row along the main balcony, resembling "the gay figures on playing-cards come to life," while silver trumpets sounded the fanfares. After reading the proclamation from a great parchment, the Garter principal king of arms called out "God Save the King!" The guardsmen in their greatcoats presented arms, and a military band played the national anthem followed by cheers for King George VI.

The new queen was still bedridden on Sunday morning with what the newspapers described as "a mild attack of influenza." The King, the princesses, Queen Mary, and other family members attended a service in the chapel at Marlborough House. George VI stepped into the sunshine afterward and walked across the courtyard before returning home with Lilibet and Margaret. The princesses smiled at the cheering crowd outside 145 Piccadilly, and the King tipped his hat.

Monday, December 14, marked George VI's forty-first birthday. He specifically requested that there be no official observance. But he carried out his own touching tribute, not to himself, but to his wife, by conferring the Order of the Garter on Queen Elizabeth. On learning that his father had given Queen Mary the Garter on his birthday, he thought "the coincidence was so charming" that he followed suit. He was also signaling to the public the partnership that would define his reign, a symbol of "gratitude and affection to one who had shared with him so bravely the burdens of the past, and was to bear with him so nobly the trials of the future."

It has often been noted that George VI confessed to Lord Louis Mountbatten that he felt "quite unprepared" for his new role. His cousin reassured him that his experience in the Royal Navy had sufficiently trained him, as it had George V. But this vignette underestimates the new king's accumulated experience, especially with industrial workers, and the knowledge he had acquired through his sharp powers of observation. He had been with George V more than any of his brothers, and he had absorbed much by example.

Still, his nervous temperament nearly undid the King at the outset. Although his official biographer avoided the word "breakdown," he alluded to George VI's emotional turmoil during the first weeks of his reign when he remained out of public view. "At first he had been emotionally disturbed," wrote John Wheeler-Bennett, "then a merciful numbness had supervened, to be followed . . . by a gradual reawakening to the realities of life, which demanded all his courage."

In this task, he relied heavily on Elizabeth. She, too, initially felt rattled in the aftermath of David's departure, which she likened to "a heavy blow on the head" that left her feeling temporarily dazed. Yet, as she wrote to several of her friends, including Archbishop of Canterbury Cosmo Lang, "the curious thing is that we are not afraid."

Queen Mary provided support with a written message she released on December 12. She mentioned the "distress which fills a Mother's heart" on learning her son had "deemed it to be his duty to lay down his charge." She asked that the people of the United Kingdom and the empire give the new king "the same full measure of generous loyalty which you gave to my beloved husband" and to the new queen "the same unfailing affection and trust you have given to me for six and twenty years."

Cosmo Lang wrote Queen Mary's message, and on Sunday the thirteenth he said his own piece in a BBC broadcast. The general population had no knowledge of the former king's decadence, but the

Archbishop of Canterbury offered the first hint of the misbehavior that had turned the royal family and the establishment against him. Lang lamented that Edward VIII's "craving for private happiness" had led him to "abandon a trust so great. . . . Even more strange and sad is that he should have sought his happiness in a manner inconsistent with Christian principles of marriage, and within a social circle whose standard and ways of life are alien to all the best instincts and traditions of his people."

The archbishop's candid rebuke stirred protests from members of the public that he was unnecessarily vindictive. The Duke of Windsor himself "complained bitterly" about it to a friend. But Lang had the quiet backing of Elizabeth and George VI as well as his mother. As the new queen explained to her friend Victor Cazalet, Queen Mary "felt he said exactly what he should and was grateful to him. All the family feels the same. I think the nation vaguely *felt* it, but *he* put the true issue clearly and as no one else had the right to do. . . . I think it well that for once someone should speak out in plain and direct words, what after all was the truth."

On Tuesday, December 22, the King and Queen, the princesses, and Queen Mary took the train to Sandringham for Christmas. Queen Elizabeth was dressed in black, and she "smilingly acknowledged the cheers" from a crowd of several hundred people while walking along the red-carpeted platform at King's Cross station. Tenants from the Sandringham estate stood in the rain at Wolferton station to greet the royal family. The King and Queen were reported to be "emotionally and physically exhausted."

Queen Mary, who had stoically borne incalculable strain during the crisis, succumbed to a respiratory infection and retired to her bedroom on Christmas Eve. "At dinner I nearly choked with my awful cough," she wrote in her diary. She didn't come downstairs again until New Year's Eve. Elizabeth later told Victor Cazalet that the abdication "very nearly killed poor Queen Mary. There is indeed such a thing as a broken heart and hers very nearly collapsed."

The royal family managed to celebrate the holiday in familiar fashion. Following church on Christmas Day they had a luncheon of Sandringham beef, Norfolk turkey, and plum pudding. In the ballroom afterward, the King touched a switch to illuminate the large Christmas tree. He carried out his father's custom in the afternoon by presenting each of the estate workers with a joint of beef as Lilibet and Margaret looked on. Three days later, the King led a shooting party in the fields surrounding Appleton, Queen Maud's house. Elizabeth and the princesses joined the shooting luncheon in a tent, and the King enjoyed the day so much he didn't return to the Big House until dusk.

Only two weeks into his reign, George VI declined to give a Christmas Day radio address—an occasion that would have imposed enormous stress. He simply wasn't up to it. His anxieties about his stammer had been inadvertently worsened by his friend Cosmo Lang.

In his remarks on the BBC, the archbishop had generously praised the new king's character and qualities of leadership. Then he had added, "When his people listen to him they will note an occasional and momentary hesitation in his speech. But he has brought it into full control, and to those who hear it need cause no sort of embarrassment, for it causes none to him who speaks."

The archbishop's effort at reassurance was as unnecessary as it was misleading. George VI had by no means mastered his stutter. It would be a lifelong struggle requiring relentless practice and concentrated effort to keep the wayward consonants in check. Lionel Logue was irritated by the archbishop's remarks and worried that they would dent Bertie's already shaky confidence. Logue was right to be concerned. Several years later, George VI said he had been "so stunned" by Lang's words that it had taken "a long time" to get over them.

During his six-week stay in Norfolk, George VI came to grips with two shocking discoveries that would forever alter his relationship with his older brother. In the months before his abdication, Edward VIII had secretly arranged to sell two significant tracts of land on the Sandringham estate—the Anmer and Flitcham farms—to a prominent farming family in Lincolnshire. George VI urgently instructed his land agent, William Fellowes—the chief administrator at Sandringham—to stop the sale. "It was a complicated business, because the contract had been signed," said a man whose father was privy to the arrangements. Fellowes was able to unwind the sale, and George VI was deeply angered by his brother's duplicity.

Even more upsetting was Bertie's realization in those weeks that David had deceived him by concealing his private Duchy of Cornwall fortune of more than £1 million in accumulated revenue that he had hoarded. Under the system of Civil List annuities distributed by the government, Edward VIII as an unmarried monarch had been receiving £370,000 a year—nearly $38 million at today's values—which ceased on his abdication. After receiving £25,000 annually (some $2.5 million today) as Duke of York, Bertie got a significant pay raise upon taking the throne: £410,000 a year ($42 million today)—the amount designated for a married king. It covered the family's expenses, including the costs of the royal household—the private secretaries and other officials and staff who ran the day-to-day operation.

In the midst of their intense financial discussions on December 10—what Bertie described as "a terrible lawyer interview"—David had pleaded his own special form of poverty. He said his assets amounted to only £90,000 (around $9 million at today's values)—a fraction of his real wealth. He insisted he needed an annual payment of £25,000 tax free for his life as a private citizen. Bertie had signed off under duress, without proper investigation, and had left hanging David's life tenancy of Sandringham and Balmoral.

"I understood from you when I signed the paper at the Fort that you were going to be very badly off," Bertie wrote to David early in 1937. "The fact remains that I was completely misled." George VI felt that under those circumstances, the Duke of Windsor was no longer entitled to an annual pension. What's more, the British government refused to pay him out of the Treasury's funds. Baldwin and his ministers had no interest in debating the former king's finances with the Labour Party in Parliament.

To secure the amount he wanted, David essentially held the Sandringham and Balmoral properties hostage. At one point he even threatened to return to Britain and assert his ownership of both estates. Contentious negotiations dragged on for more than a year as Walter Monckton worked out a new settlement that was completed in 1938. George VI ended up paying David the £25,000 a year from his own pocket, and he bought out his brother's interest in the two estates for nearly £300,000—almost $30 million at current values.

One of the King's persistent worries was that David and Wallis would return to Britain and undermine his reign by stirring up discontent and seeking publicity. His family felt the same way. Even Prince George, David's favorite brother, confided to Chips Channon that he had told Bertie, "Don't ever let David come back. He will only cause you trouble." As Elizabeth explained years later, "You can't have two Kings."

On George VI's behalf, the government secured the Duke of Windsor's concession that he would not travel to Britain without the King's express permission—on penalty of having his pension payments suspended. The duke complied, but under vehement protest, calling the arrangement "unfair and intolerable . . . tantamount to my accepting payment for remaining in exile." To David, this violated his assumption—based on informal assurances from Bertie before the abdication—that his brother would allow him to come back to Britain after several years and resume his life at Fort Belvedere.

YET THERE WAS NO ESCAPING the Duke of Windsor and Mrs. Simpson, even in the remote reaches of Sandringham. From his redoubt in Austria where he waited for Wallis's divorce to become final at the end of April, David began regularly telephoning his brother at inconvenient times. He offered unsolicited advice—often contrary to government policy—but more frequently he harangued his brother about money and his insistence that Wallis be named "Her Royal Highness" after their marriage. The duke took advantage of these telephone calls, knowing that his fast-paced glibness could stymie his brother and make him stutter. After these long-distance conversations, the

King often erupted in anger, his nerves jangling. At Elizabeth's urging, Walter Monckton eventually persuaded the duke to stop the calls.

At the very height of tension in January 1937, Elizabeth's friend Osbert Sitwell offered the royal family comfort in ridicule. He composed a fifty-six-line poem that made the rounds of all the great houses. Titled "Rat Week," it skewered the Duke of Windsor's social set that had abandoned him after the abdication. They were the "rats"—including leading hostess Sibyl Colefax in her "iron cage of curls"—who had left the "sinking ship" and now scarcely admitted even knowing him.

Lord Crawford first heard "Rat Week" at Chequers, the prime minister's country house, where Stanley Baldwin had been reading it aloud to entertain his guests. "The spirit I might almost say the animation with which SB declaimed the verses, indicated I thought some measure of his feelings, of his sense of indignation towards the crowd who let down the poor King so heartlessly," Crawford wrote to Tweedsmuir, adding, "Do not let us be too charitable, for HM himself never showed the smallest hesitation or reluctance to outstrip the worst of his bad companions."

Sitwell worried that his caustic doggerel might not go down well with the King and Queen. But it proved as popular at Sandringham as at Chequers. "I must tell you first of all, that we all thought your satire absolutely brilliant," Elizabeth wrote to the author. "It really is perfect—it hits hard (and never too hard for me) and is wickedly amusing."

THE ROYAL FAMILY SAID GOODBYE to 145 Piccadilly and moved into Buckingham Palace on February 15. While the rooms formerly occupied by George V and Queen Mary on the first floor were being prepared for the new king and queen, they stayed in the pink-and-gold-brocaded Belgian Suite on the ground floor—what Crawfie described as "camping in a museum." Bertie had lived in the Palace for thirteen years before his marriage, and Elizabeth was familiar with some of its 775 rooms. Yet it was another matter to inhabit the vast building—really more an office complex than a home—as a family. Lilibet wondered if a tunnel might be dug so they could sleep in their old house. Soon enough, she and her sister were "delighted with the wide passages to play in," Queen Mary noted a week after their arrival.

As was her habit, Queen Mary immersed herself in the Buckingham Palace redecoration, spending hours going over the rooms with her daughter-in-law. But Elizabeth proceeded prudently in the shadow of the continuing economic depression. She replaced carpets and silk curtains—one set of which was donated by Queen Mary's friend Mrs. Charles Rothschild—and filled the rooms with flowers brought from Windsor to brighten the atmosphere.

Over tea in the Queen's temporary sitting room, Mabell Airlie noticed "the little feminine touches which I had always associated with her." "It looks like home already," she said. George VI added with a smile, "Elizabeth could make a home anywhere." At the end of April, the King and Queen moved into their apartments: "nice and comfortable," Queen Mary wrote.

Their first public engagement as king and queen on February 13, 1937, took them into the heart of the East End, one of London's impoverished districts. There they visited the People's Palace, a community center for social and recreational activities that had been recently constructed to replace a similar building that had burned down in 1931. Their drive from Buckingham Palace to the People's Palace was highly symbolic. In the words of *The Times,* they were able to "show in action the link that binds the two palaces together."

Above all, the King and Queen wanted to make clear—after Edward VIII's showy demonstrations of solidarity with the poor of South Wales before his abdication—their record of concern for the working class and the dispossessed. *The Times* got the message, noting that the King's long association with the Industrial Welfare Society had brought him into "peculiarly close touch with the circumstances of industrial life," a cause to which "he gave not merely support but leadership."

Thick crowds of East Enders cheered and waved to the monarch and consort along streets decorated with flags and bunting. Inside the building, George VI and Elizabeth walked among five hundred representatives of youth organizations and questioned them about their activities. As they left, they received a rousing send-off.

In subsequent months, George VI and Elizabeth did the usual appearances, and they made a good impression everywhere, raising the stature of the monarchy. At a Buckingham Palace dinner in March, Harold Nicolson watched the Queen approvingly. "Nothing could exceed the charm or dignity which she displays," Nicolson wrote. "I cannot help feeling what a mess poor Mrs. Simpson would have made of such an occasion."

Courtiers and grandees equally admired the young king. Tommy Lascelles reported to his wife, Joan, that "I really like him awfully. He talks to me & I to him with naturalness that was never there with the other man." The influential Earl of Crawford told Lord Tweedsmuir, "We have had 3 months of our new Sovereign—a contrast almost unbelievable with the last regime. The new sense of confidence pervades us all."

Still, rumors persisted that George VI was not up to the job—especially after the Palace announced in February that the royal couple would not travel to India later in the year to celebrate the accession as they had hoped. The given reasons were the cost, an uncertain political situation on the subcontinent, and the need for the King to be in Britain during the first year of his reign. The strain such a trip would impose was also a crucial factor, which fed a perception that George VI was somehow frail and unwell, on top of concern that his stammer would prevent him from communicating with his people.

The main mission of forty-one-year-old Bertie and thirty-six-year-old Elizabeth in their first year as king and queen was to rebuild the foundations of the monarchy badly battered by Edward VIII. The apex of that reconstruction would be the coronation on Wednesday,

May 12, 1937. George VI had to show that he was capable of leading Britain and the empire as well as inspiring his subjects. That meant performing at a high level not only during the lengthy coronation ceremony but also in the evening during a radio broadcast from Buckingham Palace to the empire. For the first time, the "elaborate ritual of personal and national dedication" in Westminster Abbey would also be transmitted to hundreds of millions of listeners around the world, which raised the stakes even more for Bertie.

After having been out of touch with Lionel Logue, he invited his speech therapist to Windsor Castle in mid-April. In the weeks before the coronation, Logue worked steadily with the King at a desk in Buckingham Palace that allowed him to broadcast standing up—which George VI believed would help him breathe more easily and speak with less effort. They also had to deal with the microphone fright that had persisted long after his two halting appearances at Wembley in 1925.

The King and his teacher, assisted by BBC sound engineer Robert Wood, built on the drills Logue had practiced with Bertie a decade earlier—sessions that would be touchingly depicted many years later in the film *The King's Speech*. They couldn't alter his speaking part in the coronation service—five brief responses to the Archbishop of Canterbury that needed to be flawlessly delivered. But they cut troublesome words from the speech text and substituted easier ones. Wood helped with "tone formation and lip formation," showing how to "let the microphone do the work." When they recorded the King and played it back, the results frustrated him. "He is indeed a gallant fighter," Logue wrote, "and if a word doesn't go right, he looks at me so pathetically and then gets on with the job."

Elizabeth's presence in the room for many of these meetings bolstered the King. She invariably steadied him when he became agitated. "He is a good fellow and only wants careful handling," Logue noted. "He always speaks well in front of the Queen."

THE BLARE OF LOUDSPEAKERS BEING tested near Buckingham Palace jolted Bertie and Elizabeth out of bed at three A.M. on Coronation Day. Soon afterward, the sound of bands practicing prevented their return to sleep. The King was unable to eat breakfast and "had a sinking feeling inside." But having prayed with the Archbishop of Canterbury three days earlier, they were both ready to embrace the most profound religious aspects of the thousand-year-old ceremony. "There were tears in their eyes when we rose from our knees," Cosmo Lang recalled.

They would be the thirty-eighth sovereign and twenty-sixth consort to be crowned in Westminster Abbey, "the temple and shrine of English history." The coronation procession began at eight-thirty A.M. with more than fifty cars carrying foreign dignitaries. For the next two hours, as the King and Queen readied themselves at Buckingham Palace, came wave upon wave of carriages, bands, cavalrymen, and foot soldiers. It was a pleasantly noisy cavalcade, with drums and brass, jingling harnesses, and clattering hooves. Five million spectators packed the sidewalks, parks, and grandstands, filling the air with cheers and waving handkerchiefs and flags.

After the empire procession featuring delegations from the dominions, Princesses Mary, Lilibet, and Margaret appeared in a glass coach, the eleven-year-old heiress presumptive grinning through the window. They were followed by more carriages carrying members of the royal family, the last of whom was Queen Mary, with her sister-in-law Queen Maud of Norway.

Coronations had not typically included dowager queens. Alexandra had happily stayed away from the formal investiture of George V. But Queen Mary felt it her duty to support her son, and she had thrown herself into preparations for the big day. She chipped in on the design of Queen Elizabeth's platinum crown, which incorporated the famous 108-carat Koh-i-Noor diamond from Queen Mary's own coronation crown. She attended rehearsals, and she visited foreign royals when they arrived in London.

The long wait at the Palace was "nerve-wracking," Bertie wrote that night, but their moment finally came when they left the forecourt at ten-thirty A.M. They traveled to the Abbey in the massive (twenty-four feet long and twelve feet high) Gold State Coach dating from 1762 and first used by King George III. It is a stunning piece of royal equipage, decorated with carved and gilded symbols—palm trees, tritons, and scepters, topped by the Imperial State Crown—its sides embellished with richly painted allegorical panels. It had to be pulled by eight Windsor Greys driven by four postilions in short red jackets and jockey caps.

The King wore white knee breeches and stockings, a red satin surcoat, a red velvet robe, an ermine cape, and a red velvet cap of maintenance rimmed by ermine—a medieval-era signifier of the King's authority in the absence of a crown. The Queen was costumed in a white satin dress embroidered in gold thread with symbols of the British Isles and Empire. Her purple ermine-lined cloak was affixed to her shoulders by white satin bows and gold tassels.

The coach gleamed in the sunshine that had emerged only fifteen minutes before their departure. Behind its shimmering windows, the royal couple bowed to the masses of onlookers. "The size and magnificence of Their Majesties' procession were astounding," wrote *The Times.* In addition to their sovereign's escort of mounted Life Guards in scarlet uniforms, shiny breastplates, and plumed helmets, they were accompanied by admirals and field marshals, regular troops, mounted and massed bands, Yeomen of the Guard, the King's barge-master, and twelve scarlet-coated watermen.

The first members of the royal family to enter the Abbey were Lilibet and Margaret flanking their Aunt Mary: "small figures advancing with pretty wonder" in long white silk and lace dresses and miniature purple velvet robes lined with ermine. The princesses carried their plain gold coronets.

They passed through the nave and choir and into the "coronation theatre" in the crossing of the Abbey between the choir and the sacrarium. In the middle were two platforms with thrones for the King and Queen—his atop five steps, hers two steps lower. Both chairs faced the sacrarium's "golden radiance of the high altar" at the eastern end of the mammoth church. It was, of course, where Bertie and Elizabeth had consecrated their marriage fourteen years earlier.

Eight thousand people crowded into the Abbey. Seated in the south transept were the dukes, marquesses, earls, viscounts, and barons in red velvet and ermine-trimmed robes. Opposite the peers in the north transept sat the peeresses—"a vitrine of bosoms and jewels and bobbing tiaras"—robed just like the peers. In stands above were politicians, clergy, and the judiciary. Thousands more guests filled tiers of seats that gave the immense nave "the containment of a chapel."

On the south side of the sacrarium, up a curving staircase, was the royal box. Within the sacrarium stood three more thrones. Positioned in front of the royal box were the two Chairs of Estate with a faldstool before each. In the center, the fourteenth-century oaken King Edward's Chair faced the altar: a conspicuously plain counterpoint to the kaleidoscope of surrounding color.

Seventy-year-old Queen Mary cut a regal figure in her gown of gold cloth hand-embroidered with sparkling flowers, rows of diamonds garlanding her neck, a diamond circlet on her silver hair. "Grannie looked too beautiful," wrote Lilibet in her account of the coronation meticulously recorded on six lined pages "From Lilibet by <u>Herself</u>." This was Queen Mary's third coronation, and she was a thorough professional. As she passed through the choir filled with dignitaries, everyone bowed, and she slowly bowed right and left. The princesses followed their grandmother up the steps to the royal box, where Lilibet sat between her and Margaret.

All rose with a fanfare of trumpets for the procession of the bareheaded Queen, moving at a measured pace alongside two bishops in their colorful copes. Six maids of honor wearing identical white gowns and diamond tiaras carried her outspread train, and diamonds sparkled at her throat. From high above in the triforium, forty King's Scholars from nearby Westminster School chanted, "*Vivat Regina Elizabetha! Vivat! Vivat! Vivat!*" After the Queen and her maids of honor had bowed to the altar, she smiled at the "two eager little faces" in the royal box. As she settled into her Chair of Estate, she kept her eyes forward.

The King made an equally spectacular entrance, a slender figure with his own pair of bishops. Nine pages held his ermine-bordered train. *"Vivat, Vivat Rex Georgius!"* shouted the schoolboys on high. George VI looked strikingly young, almost boyish. He calmly took his place near his own Chair of Estate.

The service lasted two and a half hours, with many intricately choreographed components. The King first doffed his cap of maintenance and stood in the sacrarium before the entire congregation for his "Recognition" as "the Undoubted King of this Realm." The cry from the triforium went up: "Long Live King George." He turned to show himself to each quadrant and bowed in turn. "Long Live King George!" the people exclaimed amid trumpets and beating drums.

Back in his Chair of Estate and wearing his cap of maintenance, George VI held the book containing his solemn oath. "Sir, is Your Majesty willing to take the Oath?" asked the Archbishop of Canterbury. "I am willing," George VI replied without missing a beat.

In response to the archbishop's questions about whether he would govern by all laws and customs, judge in the spirit of law, justice, and mercy, and uphold the Church of England, he read the affirmative replies. He signed the oath, twice dipping his pen in the ink. Afterward he could be seen wiping his hands. Only later did he ruefully admit, "the ink got all over my fingers," but he was glad nobody appeared to notice. He rose and walked to the altar with bared head and knelt on a solitary faldstool, where he laid his right hand on an open Bible and said, "The things which I have here before promised, I will perform, and keep. So help me God."

George VI's words, *The Times* declared, "though quiet, were so careful and deliberate that they were clearly heard on the loudspeakers through which the service was broadcast." In a letter to Lionel Logue five days later, George VI recalled his intense anxiety and shared his relief that all went well: "Not a moment's hesitation or mistake!" He thanked Logue for his "expert supervision & unfailing patience."

His speaking part ended, he moved into the most sacred element of the service, which began with removing his crimson velvet robe, red satin under-robe, and ermine cape. Clothed simply in a white shirt and breeches—"a curiously slight and modest figure"—George VI sat in King Edward's Chair, his back to the congregation. He was, however, visible to his wife, daughters, and mother to his right.

Four Knights of the Garter in deep blue velvet cloaks grasped four silver poles and raised a golden canopy above his head. From an ampulla in the shape of a little golden eagle, the archbishop poured holy oil into a twelfth-century silver gilt spoon. The prelate daubed the substance on his finger and anointed George VI on the palms of both hands, his chest, and the top of his head. Cameras filming the ceremony for newsreels caught Queen Mary wiping tears from her eyes at this moment—a scene that would be edited out of the film shown in cinemas.

Now consecrated, in the words of the archbishop, as "King over the Peoples, whom the Lord your God hath given you to rule and govern," George VI was ready to be arrayed in the emblems of his high office, starting with layers of splendid garments. As he stood in front of King Edward's Chair, the Dean of Westminster helped him slip on the Colobium Sindonis, a sleeveless white tunic. It nearly went inside out, "had not my Groom of the Robes come to the rescue," Bertie wrote. Next came the glorious supertunica of golden cloth, along with a girdle of the same material tied around his waist.

Seated again in the Coronation Chair, he received his royal regalia, including golden spurs, the Sword of State, and the gold jewel-encrusted orb, in an elaborate series of maneuvers. On the fourth finger of George VI's right hand, the archbishop placed the King's ring—"a great sapphire, slashed with a cross of rubies"—representing the sovereign's defense of the faith. His final garment was the heavily embroidered gold Imperial Mantle. The total weight of the coronation robes was thirty-six pounds.

In his hands he held two scepters—one the symbol of his earthly power topped by a jeweled cross, the other with an ivory dove signifying divine guidance—as he waited for what he called "the supreme moment." At the altar, the archbishop consecrated St. Edward's Crown, the official crown of England: five pounds of gold and 444 semi-precious stones. He turned and walked toward King Edward's Chair with the dean, who carried the crown on a velvet cushion.

George VI sat still as the archbishop lifted the crown with both hands and lowered it onto the monarch's head. "God Save the King!" the schoolboys shouted again, this time joined by the congregation and accompanied by silver trumpets. In unison, the peers put on their gold and velvet coronets. At the crowning moment, "the arches and beams at the top were covered with a sort of haze of wonder," Lilibet precociously wrote, little knowing that in sixteen years she would be the focus of the same ritual.

The religious investiture was complete, but the homage remained. Surrounded by bishops, archbishops, and secular officials, George VI walked to his gilded throne on the platform in the center of the theater. There, the dignitaries put their hands under his arms and, in a gesture demonstrating the power of Church and State, they lifted him onto the throne.

The archbishop dropped to his knees and expressed fealty to his "Sovereign Lord," walked up the five steps, and kissed George VI's left cheek. More bishops repeated this gesture, followed by similar tributes from Bertie's brothers, Prince Henry and Prince George, along with senior representatives of each rank of the peerage. They vowed to be the King's "liege man of life and limb" and touched the crown after kissing the sovereign's cheek.

Throughout these hours of ceremony, Queen Elizabeth sat mute in her Chair of Estate. As the trumpets, drumrolls, and shouts for the King faded, she advanced to a faldstool in front of the altar for her much briefer anointing and crowning. She would not be crowned by the will of the people like her husband, but rather by the command of the King. Nor would she swear an oath.

As Queen Elizabeth knelt, four duchesses held the golden canopy above her. The Archbishop of Canterbury carried out the same procedure with the ampulla and spoon, but he anointed her just once, on the crown of her head. After blessing the Queen's ruby ring, he placed it as he had done for her husband—on the fourth finger of her right hand. From the altar, the archbishop brought her crown and set it upon her head.

The peeresses instantaneously raised their arms "like swans from a crimson lake" and put on their coronets. Lilibet marveled at the hovering coronets, and how "the arms disappeared as if by magic." The archbishop then gave Queen Elizabeth her smaller versions of the scepter and the ivory rod that she held upright.

The Queen turned and bowed to her husband. She took her place on the platform, where she and the King sat side by side "crowned, sceptred, and enthroned." For Holy Communion, they removed their crowns, put aside their scepters, and knelt on faldstools before the altar. Seated again in their thrones with their crowns and scepters, they heard the benediction concluding the ceremony.

While the choirs sang, the King and Queen retired to St. Edward's Chapel behind the altar. There they rested briefly, and the King exchanged his coronation crown for the Imperial State Crown that he would use at occasions such as the State Opening of Parliament. Weighing in at nearly two and a half pounds, it contained a staggering array of three thousand gems, including the Black Prince's Ruby, the Stuart Sapphire, and the 317-carat Cullinan II diamond.

When they reemerged in the sacrarium, they both wore purple velvet and ermine robes. The King—"with upright bearing and grave dignity"—carried his scepter and his orb, and the Queen still held her scepter and ivory rod. The two princesses, now wearing their little coronets, peered over the edge of the royal box as their mother followed their father in the procession through the choir and nave to the Abbey's Great West Door.

The royal family spent around a half hour in their specially built rooms in a temporary annex at the front of the Abbey, where they were offered sandwiches, stuffed rolls, orangeade, and lemonade. The return procession through the streets of London was the longest on record: more than six miles in the rain, which began as the King and Queen climbed into the lumbering state coach.

Outside Buckingham Palace, the crowds called repeatedly for the monarch and consort, who obliged by appearing on the balcony in their crowns and robes with Queen Mary, Lilibet, and Margaret. Lilibet imitated the way her Grannie twirled her right hand to acknowledge the cheers from what she correctly reckoned were "millions" of people beyond the Palace railings. A lip-reader picked up Queen Mary's words to her Bertie: "It's not for me they are cheering but for you, my son."

At eight P.M., King George VI faced the final trial of the day, his ten-minute radio address. Logue was nearby, and the King stood (not sat, as reported in the press) alone in a small room opposite his study, overlooking the quiet quadrangle in the middle of the Palace. An old desk had been retrieved from the basement and raised on blocks of wood, with two gilt microphones mounted on top.

"It is with a very full heart that I speak to you tonight," King George VI began. His voice was "deeply charged with the emotion which he felt," *The Times* observed, "but as he proceeded the King spoke calmly and with confidence." He stumbled just once, on the word "distress," which created "dramatic effect," noted Cecil Beaton. George VI thanked his people for their "love and loyalty," and he promised to maintain the "honour and integrity" of the Crown, "a grave and constant responsibility." Above all, he pledged to devote himself to "the Ministry of Kingship . . . with the Queen at my side. . . . We will, God helping us, faithfully discharge our trust." After many hours of practice, Logue considered Bertie's speech "a triumph."

At nine o'clock, George VI and Elizabeth appeared again on the balcony, now floodlit. He had changed into evening dress with his blue ribbon of the Garter. She was wrapped in a white fur-trimmed cloak and wore a diamond tiara. It still rained lightly, but they remained in the blaze of illumination for several minutes, as he waved and she bowed. When they left, the crowd sang the national anthem. Yet the people demanded more. After continuous loud cheering, the royal couple came out again three more times, retiring for the night at eleven-thirty P.M.

"Bertie and E looked so well," Queen Mary wrote, "& did it all too beautifully. . . . We were all much moved." She told her son that she felt "Papa's spirit was near us in blessing you. . . . I could not help feeling that poor foolish David has relinquished for nothing!!! But it is better so & better for our beloved Country."

Elizabeth later said she had a "great sense of offering oneself," and that "I was not conscious of there being anybody else there at the Communion." Bertie told Cosmo Lang, "I felt I was being helped all the time by Someone Else as you said I would," and he revealed to Ramsay MacDonald that for long stretches of the ceremony he was "unaware what was happening." One close observer also noticed the King's jaw muscles twitching, indicating his extreme tension.

The Earl of Crawford, who sat among his fellow scarlet-robed peers, detected "a great sense of security, and a feeling of apprehension removed." The King and Queen had maintained "a quiet but very resolute dignity, which has already given them status, and as time goes on will enhance their prestige. The King's appreciation of the solemnity of his calling as Sovereign, of his duties to the exalted post, are very keenly developed, and manifest also to us all."

Leo Amery, a member of Parliament, could not help considering the alternative history. "Neither Edward, let alone Edward and Mrs. Simpson, could have figured in that solemn dedication which seemed so natural and fitting from those two simple and good young people," he wrote several weeks later.

It was, in fact, unimaginable that King Edward VIII—a man cynical in his conduct and superficial in his grasp of the spiritual core of the British monarch's role—could have convincingly carried out the timeless rituals of the coronation. It was laughable to imagine that twice-divorced Wallis Simpson was capable of understanding the requirements for a queen consort, not to mention the nature and needs of the British people.

However costly the toll on their respective psyches, George VI and Elizabeth were the right couple at the right time. They were poised by temperament and a sense of duty to save the monarchy—not only from Edward VIII's damage but also from challenges to Britain's very existence.

"The Nazi leaders bowed to the duchess, and the ladies curtsied."

Adolf Hitler greeting the Duke and Duchess of Windsor during their tour of Germany in October 1937.

TWENTY-FOUR

His Brother's Shadow

THROUGHOUT EDWARD VIII'S BRIEF AND CALAMITOUS REIGN, EUROPE'S two menacing dictators, Adolf Hitler in Germany and Benito Mussolini in Italy, were expanding their power. Mussolini had taken the first step in late 1935 when he defied international agreements and invaded Abyssinia (present-day Ethiopia), adding it to Italy's African colonies. Hitler carefully observed the failure by Britain and France to impose meaningful sanctions or otherwise curtail Mussolini's territorial ambitions. In the spring of 1936, an emboldened German army marched unimpeded into the Rhineland—the industrial region along the Rhine River. It was a strategic stretch of territory that had been demilitarized after the First World War as a buffer zone to prevent Germany from attacking neighboring countries.

Less than two months into his reign, Edward VIII had accepted Germany's aggression despite Hitler's clear violation of the Treaty of Versailles. Leopold von Hoesch, the German ambassador to Britain at the time, had even written to his superiors two months before the Rhineland occupation that he had become convinced "during frequent, often quite lengthy, talks" with Edward VIII "that his sympathies" for Nazi Germany were "deep-rooted." The British government under Stanley Baldwin felt no such affinity for Hitler but had little appetite for opposing him. Germany was rebuilding its military at an unprecedented pace while Britain was only slowly rearming.

King George VI was not yet attuned to these international developments. After the abdication trauma, Bertie and Elizabeth were more intent on establishing themselves and stabilizing their rattled country. Like his father, George VI embodied family values, although he was more visibly devoted to his wife than his father had been. George V had dominated Queen Mary, whose reverence for him defined her subordinate position.

The dynamic between Bertie and Elizabeth reflected her status as a confidante and her essential role in helping him cope with a disability his father never suffered. To the jaundiced eye of Chips Channon (who ran hot and cold on the King and Queen and could be relied on for caustic digs), "all his mature life he has been entirely under the dominion of his wife" who "has him *completely* under her thumb." Still, Channon conceded that Elizabeth had "enormously improved" Bertie.

While George V intimidated his children, George VI doted on Lilibet and Margaret. Bertie had none of his father's bluffness, nor his natural volubility. George VI had inherited his mother's reserve and had been observing and listening since childhood. But among people he knew, he was seldom tongue-tied, as he could be with strangers in a public setting. British ambassador to the United States Ronald Lindsay found that except for the "occasional and momentary check" the King could talk "well and vigorously."

Elizabeth balanced Bertie's diffidence with her open-hearted enjoyment. She set the more relaxed and less formal tone of their entertaining. Out went knee breeches, in came trousers for dinner parties. When the King and Queen gave a ball at Buckingham Palace, "there was very little ceremony," observed Duff Cooper. For the supper procession, men were "simply told to take a lady. There was a crooner with the popular Ambrose's band, and guests could smoke everywhere."

Six months into his reign, Bertie set himself apart from his father in his relations with the courtiers. Tommy Lascelles told Harold Nicolson that George V had regarded his decades-long private secretary, Lord Stamfordham, as his "intimate" confidant and friend. He had shared all his thoughts and impressions with Stamfordham, who wrote detailed memoranda describing the King's conversations with officials.

Unlike his father, who often held forth in his audiences with his prime ministers, George VI said little. He annoyed his private secretaries by declining to share with them what had passed in his private audiences. Lascelles blamed George VI's secretiveness on Elizabeth, who felt that his private secretaries "were inclined to be bossy." The King tackled all the documents in his dispatch boxes and was determined to analyze problems and make his own judgments. As her husband's number one listener, Elizabeth understood his thinking better than Alec Hardinge and Tommy Lascelles ever did.

DURING THE WEEKS AFTER THE coronation, the new king and queen felt the love of the British people at every turn—not without some cost to their own well-being. Lionel Logue expressed concern to Alec Hardinge in midsummer that the King was being "overloaded." In an audience with George VI on July 20, the speech therapist noted that he "seemed very drained." The King confided that his "weak stomach" was affecting his speech. Noted Logue in his diary, "Give him too much work and make him too tired," and it affects "his weakest part— his speech."

Nevertheless, the King and Queen swept through all the events and rituals: the Guildhall luncheon, the Thanksgiving service at St. Paul's Cathedral, Trooping the Colour, a historical pageant and torchlight parade at Windsor Castle, the procession of the Knights of the Garter and service at St. George's Chapel, military and naval reviews, and tours of Scotland, Northern Ireland, England, and Wales.

Lilibet and Margaret were reliable crowd pleasers when they appeared with their mother and father. At the first garden party given by

George VI and Queen Elizabeth on the grounds of Buckingham Palace, the princesses strolled among the guests with their parents, pausing to speak to specially honored individuals. The Queen instructed her daughters to walk slowly and always be polite. "People liked to see them at these affairs," wrote their governess Marion Crawford, "but I don't think the children much enjoyed them."

The girls accompanied their parents on the Edinburgh leg of the Scottish tour at Holyroodhouse, arriving in an open landau. Onlookers massed on the nearby slopes, forming "an immense natural 'grand stand.'" When the King, Queen, and their daughters emerged from the Palace gates, "a tremendous burst of cheering echoed round the hills." In the Thistle Chapel at St. Giles' Cathedral, Lilibet and Margaret watched their father install their mother as the first lady of the Order of the Thistle. The honor bestowed by the British monarch dates from the seventeenth century and is Scotland's counterpart to the Order of the Garter.

All this should have been a source of great satisfaction, but for the persistent problem of Edward, the former king "over the water." The flashpoint for a deepening rift was George VI's decision to officially deny Wallis the title of "Her Royal Highness." Bertie, his mother, and his wife had made up their minds on the matter early in the year. On February 4, Queen Mary had told the King that it was "unfortunate" the Duke of Windsor "does not understand our point of view with regard to the H.R.H. and that this rankles still, but there is no doubt you must stick to this decision, as it wld make great difficulties for us to acknowledge her as being in the same category with Alice & Marina."

Their stance, while understandable, contradicted law and precedent. Bertie knew from his conversation with Walter Monckton the night before his Accession Council that Edward's royal birth meant he retained "His Royal Highness" for his lifetime; his title could be removed involuntarily only by an Act of Parliament. The new king used those three crucial words in naming his brother Duke of Windsor at St. James's Palace. Prince Edward's wife was, in fact, entitled to the same status as her husband.

But the royal family couldn't condone that outcome, on the grounds that Wallis was not a "fit and proper person . . . after what she has done to the country," George VI told Stanley Baldwin. To circumvent the law, the King's advisers and government officials created the fiction that the abdication itself invalidated David's royal status for himself, his spouse, and his future children. As king, George VI could bestow the HRH through his position as "Fount of Honour"—his power to grant and remove titles. This enabled him to "restore" his brother's HRH that had never actually been removed.

With the approval of Baldwin's cabinet, King George VI issued letters patent on May 27. He announced that Edward was "entitled to hold and enjoy for himself only" the title Royal Highness, and that "his wife and descendants if any shall not hold said title style or attribute." Tommy Lascelles, in one of the most blinkered understatements of his courtier career, wrote to his wife, Joan, three days later, "The question of Mrs S's 'style & title' has at last been satisfactorily settled & answered. They took it quite calmly in the end & saw, I think, that it was to her own interest to be definitely in the non-royal category, rather than to be mortified for the rest of her life by people refusing to give her royal courtesies to which she was technically entitled—as they undoubtedly would refuse."

The Duke and Duchess of Windsor were actually livid and implacably remained so. David never gave up his campaign to persuade Bertie to reverse Wallis's HRH exclusion. Each refusal from the King deepened the acrimony. George VI made the debatable decision on his own, with the crucial reinforcement of his wife and mother, both of whom emphatically declined to "receive" Wallis.

Sharpening the Windsors' ire was the King's order—again backed by Baldwin's cabinet—that nobody in the family could attend his brother's wedding. The ostensible reason was that the Church of England wouldn't sanction such a ceremony. In reality, distaste for Wallis was at the heart of Bertie, Elizabeth, and Queen Mary's entrenched opposition.

"None of us can go to the wedding," the King's mother wrote to him in mid-April. "It wld look as if we approved of it which of course we do not." She said she got "endless letters . . . imploring us not to go out for the wedding as it wld do great harm especially after the terrible shaking the Monarchy received last Dec." Bertie blocked his brother Prince George—the one member of the family still close to David—from participating.

The Duke and Duchess of Windsor chose to be married at a friend's home in France, the Château de Candé, with seven guests in attendance, presided over by a publicity-seeking English clergyman. The date was June 3, 1937—the birthday of King George V. This choice further incensed the royal family. "It must be too ghastly for you," Elizabeth wrote Queen Mary on May 21. "I feel so outraged for you . . . I can hardly speak." Queen Mary replied the same day that David had "hurt me very deeply, as you can imagine of course she did it, but how can he be so weak. I suppose it is out of revenge that none of the family is going to the wedding." She declared that every aspect of the marriage was "sickening," including "her 40-odd gowns for the trousseau!!!"

BERTIE, ELIZABETH, AND THEIR DAUGHTERS arrived at Balmoral on August 4, 1937—Elizabeth's thirty-seventh birthday. It was their first stay in Royal Deeside since Bertie became king. After taking the night train to Aberdeen, they were driven for sixty miles along roads decorated with bunting, arches, and flags to a spot near the castle gates, where they transferred to a nineteenth-century open landau and were greeted by tenants and servants.

They had ten weeks in the Highlands that summer, interrupted only by the traditional visit to Glamis. Elizabeth gave the Balmoral interiors a brightening makeover. She had the woodwork pickled, and replaced a lot of the tartan curtains and upholstery. The King and Queen filled the bedrooms with old friends, including James and Rachel Stuart, as well as Elizabeth's brothers. After being banished by Edward VIII, Cosmo Lang contentedly resumed his place in the court circle. He was impressed by the "homely family regime" set by the Queen, who "seems to reproduce the country house atmosphere of Glamis."

Among the new visitors was Osbert Sitwell, who likened the Ghillies Ball to "Elizabethan times, quite devoid, the whole thing, of class feeling." The designer Rex Whistler—another unconventional addition to the guest roster—watched with delight as "the King and Queen jigged with great abandon. . . . The pipes squealed, people hooted and laughed." For Princess Margaret's seventh birthday on August 21, Tommy Lascelles was conscripted for a hide-and-seek game in the garden after tea. In a letter to his wife, he described the King and Queen as "very domestic & friendly. The meals are short & no strain at all."

George VI conscientiously tended to his official duties throughout his holiday. He set aside time each day to read and sign the documents in his red dispatch boxes, and he entertained officials and politicians, chief among them Neville Chamberlain, who had become prime minister on May 28 upon the voluntary retirement of Stanley Baldwin.

As chancellor of the exchequer, Chamberlain had been involved in the fractious financial negotiations with the Duke of Windsor, which were still months away from resolution. Chamberlain had taken a hard line against the duke, so he was a receptive listener for George VI's litany of complaints about his brother during their first audience on May 30.

At age sixty-eight, Chamberlain was only a year younger than his predecessor. The new prime minister's biographer described him as "masterful, confident, ruled by an instinct for order . . . his mind, once made up, hard to change." Although his demeanor could be severe and distant, Chamberlain went out of his way to establish a warm relationship with the forty-one-year-old king and his thirty-seven-year-old consort.

During his four days at Balmoral at the end of August, Neville Chamberlain had the customary audiences with George VI and joined the royal family for shooting, fishing, and al fresco lunches. After three days together, the King wrote to his mother at Sandringham, where she was spending much of the summer, that Chamberlain "is getting over his natural shyness, which makes me the same."

Yet the pall of the Duke of Windsor persisted. "The world is in a very troubled state & there is plenty to worry about & D seems to loom ever larger on the horizon," Bertie wrote to his mother on October 4. Despite their manifest popularity, the King and Queen seemed haunted by David's charismatic force field.

"The solitude and its reflections began to make them timorous," wrote the Earl of Crawford after his brother Sir Ronald Lindsay visited Balmoral in early October. "Previously it was the burden and responsibility of Court ceremonial which appeared to weigh them down—but in the freedom of Scotland it transpired that they felt a rival was always hovering in the background and planning an open appeal to publicity, to popularity." In Crawford's opinion, "their modesty" made them "misjudge their position."

The King and Queen had good reason to feel apprehensive about the Windsors' plans and intentions. In late September, the royal family was blindsided by the duke's announcement—"a bombshell & a bad one, too," said George VI—that he would shortly be visiting Germany. His purpose would be to show solidarity with laborers and study their living and working conditions, and he would later travel to the United States on a similar mission.

He was, of course, posturing, as the duke had neither the official position nor the means to carry out social welfare policies. Indeed, in his radio broadcast following his abdication, he had clearly said "I now quit altogether public affairs." Yet there he was, proposing "private stunts for publicity purposes," in the words of Alec Hardinge.

In his meetings with Lindsay, the King—backed up by Tommy Lascelles—spoke heatedly about the duke for "behaving abominably" and "trying to stage a comeback"—a highly unlikely event that reflected the King's insecurity. Bertie was especially concerned that his brother would try to create his own following in America. The Queen lamented that David had changed and was no longer kind to his family. "She was backing up everything the men said," Lindsay wrote, "but protesting against anything that seemed vindictive."

Lindsay memorably concluded that George VI did not feel "safe" on the throne and was "like the medieval monarch who has a hated rival claimant living in exile." Queen Mary complained to Elizabeth that David "only thinks of his and her point of view" and "not a bit of this Country & all of us—of course we know she is at the back of it."

There was nothing George VI could do about the duke's imminent trip to Germany, and the United States plans eventually fell apart. But the King and his government could curb any effort by David to visit Britain, which in late December they finally codified by tying his £25,000 yearly stipend to his enforced absence. Meanwhile, during their twelve days in Germany that October, the Windsors flouted protocol and shamelessly sought attention. Even worse, they revealed their Nazi sympathies amid growing evidence of Hitler's authoritarianism, plans for further territorial expansion, and persecution of German Jews.

They followed an ambitious itinerary with visits to eight cities. They inspected factories, garden settlements, sports and leisure facilities, and Nazi headquarters in several locales, including Nuremberg. "Heil Edward!" and "Windsor! Windsor!" the crowds shouted. "Heil Hitler!" he replied, several times returning the stiff-armed Nazi salute. The Nazi leaders bowed to the duchess, and the ladies curtsied. To them, she was "Her Royal Highness."

The couple met the Nazi high command, with whom the duke cheerfully conversed in German. Their friend Joachim von Ribbentrop, the German ambassador to Britain, wined and dined them. They took tea with Minister of Propaganda Joseph Goebbels (who noted afterward that had Edward remained on the throne, "an alliance would have been possible. . . . What a shame"), visited the country house of Hermann Göring, creator of the Gestapo secret police, and had dinner with Deputy Führer Rudolf Hess at his home in Munich. The capstone at the end of their tour on October 22 was tea with the führer himself at his mountain retreat near Berchtesgaden.

The German tour was widely criticized. The Windsors' evident partiality for Hitler specifically and Nazism generally partly accounted for the cancellation of the visit to the United States. Most concerned of all was George VI, who read press accounts of his brother's tour with growing alarm.

THE ROYAL FAMILY HAD RETURNED to London the day after David and Wallis arrived in Berlin. George VI and Elizabeth faced a full schedule of engagements, among them a tour of Yorkshire—the first by a reigning monarch—Armistice Day at the Cenotaph, and a state visit by King Leopold of the Belgians.

Lilibet and Margaret had a busy agenda as well, with their schooling once again assuming top priority after a long Scottish idyll. The education of the heiress presumptive had taken on greater significance after her father became king. Marion Crawford continued as the princesses' main governess, with tutors brought in for supplementary instruction in French, German, music, and dancing.

The King relocated the schoolroom at Buckingham Palace from a gloomy space on the top floor to a light-filled room overlooking the gardens. Crawfie walked a delicate line between her eagerness, as she once wrote, to have "knowledge poured in as fast as I can pour it in" and her sensitivity to Queen Elizabeth's wish that her daughters not be too burdened by academic routine. Helping the governess to find a proper course was Queen Mary, who became a sub-rosa ally in bolstering the girls' curriculum.

Crawfie provided written progress reports and lesson plans to Queen Mary, and sometimes expressed frustration when Elizabeth pulled her daughters away for the "odd distractions like dentists, tailors and hair-dressers" that impinged on morning lessons. One letter in early November 1937, sent by way of Queen Mary's lady-in-waiting Lady Cynthia Colville, illustrated Crawfie's intellectual discipline and educational philosophy.

The governess confessed to impatience when "sometimes . . .

things are not made easy for me," adding, "I have been more or less commanded to keep the afternoons as free of 'serious' work as possible." She managed to subvert this edict by teaching the girls as they walked or played in the Palace garden. Queen Mary had objected that two and a half hours a week of history instruction seemed inadequate. Crawfie said that was all she was permitted until Christmas, when she planned to drop arithmetic to create more time.

"Princess Elizabeth should be absolutely 'soaked' in History and all the wide and wonderful avenues that such a subject opens up," she wrote. Crawfie emphasized the importance of dates as well as the geography of the empire, noting that Lilibet possessed "a good visual memory." She played educational games with the princesses, and they even devised "History chants."

The omission of Bible study "looks quite shameful," Crawfie admitted. The reason, she explained, was the Queen's determination to teach the Bible to her daughters each morning "through story from herself" as she had been taught by her mother. Poetry, on the other hand, was a linchpin of the girls' instruction. They averaged three or four long poems each month. Both princesses learned quickly and retained what they had learned. Crawfie also sought to humanize literature. Before teaching Chaucer's *Canterbury Tales,* she would review over tea the author's life and the "history and characteristics of his period."

The range of literature the girls covered over the years was impressive: works by Coleridge, Dickens (at the time of the November 1937 letter, Lilibet was reading *A Tale of Two Cities*), Keats, Austen, Trollope, and Robert Louis Stevenson, as well as popular fiction by Arthur Conan Doyle, John Buchan, and Queen Elizabeth's favorite, P. G. Wodehouse.

This was the vital foundation for the little princess who would be George VI and Elizabeth's living legacy for an unparalleled—and unforeseen—reign spanning more than seven decades. The curriculum was at once conventional and unconventional, and it gave Lilibet the tools to think for herself, to comprehend the scope of her responsibilities leading Britain and the Commonwealth, and to better understand human nature. There may have been vexing interruptions, but both her parents recognized the need to foster Lilibet's curiosity as well as her knowledge of the world around her.

To that end, in the autumn of 1937, Queen Mary also began taking the girls on weekly educational outings. After the State Opening of Parliament, they went to the Tower of London, where the governor took them everywhere. They spent more than an hour at the Natural History Museum. Lilibet had a special tour of the Bank of England, where she held currency valued at £1 million. At the British Museum, Lilibet and Margaret peered at the Rosetta Stone as they were conducted around by the director. Museumgoers were mostly unaware of the presence of the girls, who were "so absorbed they remained considerably longer than intended." On other days they toured the Royal Mint and saw the dollhouses, costumes, and watches at the Victoria and Albert Museum.

GEORGE VI'S MAIN PREOCCUPATION DURING the autumn of 1937 in London was his first speech at the State Opening of Parliament in late October. Not only would he be required to sit—which he believed impeded his breathing rhythms and impaired his ability to speak smoothly—he would also be wearing the two-and-a-half-pound Imperial State Crown as he read out the government's legislative program for the coming year. He was plagued by what Lionel Logue called his "inferiority complex about his father," who had always spoken fluidly and sonorously.

Logue and the King practiced diligently, replacing tricky words with simpler ones. On the eve of the ceremony, Logue found the King at his desk wearing the crown. They did two run-throughs before George VI put the crown aside for another practice. Logue was cheered that the King spoke and looked well. "His voice was beautiful tonight," he wrote. He was not alone in his view. Harold Nicolson once called the King's voice "truly fine rich and very English," but sadly hampered by "throwing emphasis on the wrong words."

The next day, the King and Queen led a procession of six carriages from the Palace to the Houses of Parliament in Westminster: "a very pretty sight in the sunshine," wrote Queen Mary. Elizabeth wore a white gown and diamond tiara, and George VI was dressed in a field marshal's uniform. In the robing room, the King put on his crown and crimson imperial robe with an ermine cape, and the Queen donned a similar but shorter robe and cape. For the first time the princesses attended the ceremony. They sat in the Lord Great Chamberlain's box outside the robing room to be "the first to make obeisance."

As the King and Queen entered the House of Lords hand in hand, the dimly lit chamber suddenly flooded with bright light. The King sat on his throne, with the Queen's throne situated on the same dais but slightly lower. Chips Channon noticed the Queen "toying with her jewels"; she confessed later to Queen Mary that her first-time experience in that setting made her "very very nervous." She kept her eyes fixed on her husband as the King read the speech "in slow, modulated monotonous tones."

The *Sunday Express* noted the absence of a discernible stammer: "Indeed the words took on a dignity and actual beauty from the tempo that he had wisely imposed on himself." The King's confidence appeared to grow as he progressed, and he even glanced a few times around the chamber. When he finished, the Queen "could not keep from her eyes the pride of a woman in her husband."

Nearly two months to the day later, George VI faced another ordeal with his first Christmas radio broadcast, which he delivered from Sandringham House. His father had originated the practice in 1932. His intention had been to forge a direct and personal bond between the monarch and the people of the British Empire. George V's maiden speech, written by Rudyard Kipling, emphasized his life of dedicated service. "I speak now from my home and from my heart to you all," he had said, striking a resonant emotional chord.

George VI resisted picking up his father's tradition. In the immediate aftermath of his accession, he had avoided the speech in 1936. A year later he felt pressure to put his own stamp on what some—

although not Bertie—considered an important ritual for the monarch. He was leery of the inevitable comparisons with his father, and he feared the dreaded microphone. He finally yielded in late November, insisting that the broadcast wouldn't be an annual event.

Logue worked with him steadily, and on Christmas morning he traveled to Sandringham, where the royal family gave him a coveted place at lunch between the Queen and Princess Marina. The King had already been rehearsing with the BBC's Robert Wood, who set up the broadcasting room where Bertie could walk around as he spoke. (Logue remembered the King's laughter whenever he saw the posed photos of him sitting at a table before a microphone like his father.)

The Queen both observed her husband's practice sessions and was an important contributor to the substance of the message. "The King always wrote his own speech for the Christmas Day broadcast, with the help of Queen Elizabeth," recalled Robert Wood. "They worked together as a team. If they didn't like the sound of a passage during rehearsal they would go away together and work on it . . . until they had exactly what they wanted, and what they meant—and what the King could say without difficulty."

Logue and the King did one last run-through, and at 2:55 P.M. on December 25, 1937, Bertie lit a cigarette and began to pace. After tossing the butt into the fireplace, he waited for the red light and started to speak, as his family listened on a radio in the nursery upstairs. He stumbled on one word and spoke more quickly than in the rehearsals before he began "pulling himself up." Logue fretted that the King went "just a shade too long on two words through trying to get too much of an emphasis," but he congratulated him with a reassuring handshake. In return, George VI flashed "that lovely schoolboy grin of his."

Now he could relax. He had not only put his nerve-racking speech behind him but also listened to a playback in Wood's room filled with audio equipment. Logue recalled the King "leaning against the wall and the Queen, her face animated and flushed," standing in the door-way. Seventy-year-old Queen Mary asked Wood, "Was all this done when my late husband broadcasted?" Wood replied affirmatively. "And I knew nothing about it," she replied.

Of equal importance to his successful radio address was the knowledge that after a year of negotiations, George VI now had the power, backed by his government, to keep his embittered and trouble-making brother away from Britain for the foreseeable future. He had also decisively put his sister-in-law in her place by denying her the HRH. As a result, the King and his elder brother were no longer on speaking terms.

The family invited Lionel Logue for an informal tea followed by gift giving in the ballroom. The previous year Queen Mary's staff had overseen the holiday, but this year Queen Elizabeth orchestrated everything. Fabergé ornaments decorated the ceiling-high Christmas tree, and the adults played "Ring a Ring o' Roses" with Lilibet, Margaret, and their cousins. Bertie gaily wore the paper crown from his Christmas cracker. "Look at him now," Elizabeth said to Logue. "I do not think I have ever known him so light-hearted and happy."

"To the French the Royal Visit seemed to safeguard against the dreaded war."

King George VI and Queen Elizabeth with French president Albert Lebrun during a garden party at the Château de Bagatelle in the Bois de Boulogne on July 20, 1938, during their state visit to France.

TWENTY-FIVE

Simplicity and Dignity

IN THE TWO YEARS OF HIS REIGN BEFORE THE ONSET OF WORLD WAR II in September 1939, King George VI learned the scope of his role. Queen Elizabeth, in turn, tested her unique potential as his consort. Adhering to constitutional requirements, he was constrained from exercising real power by the need for his political neutrality and his role as a unifying national force. When he tried to intervene in foreign policy, his government ministers gently rebuffed him. Once he overstepped his constitutional position in a symbolic moment during the Munich crisis that Elizabeth later admitted was a mistake. Yet the King did make a difference in one substantive way, by forging a personal alliance with Franklin D. Roosevelt on the eve of war that would prove vital in the early years of the conflict.

But the major impact of George VI and Elizabeth in 1938 and 1939 was their service as impeccable representatives of the monarchy, upholding the values and principles of a free society. They embodied the resolve and spirit of Britain on behalf of France, their chief ally on the Continent, and for their Canadian dominion. They also projected a fresh image of the royal family to the people and the government of the United States, strengthening the special relationship in new ways.

Their enemies were paying attention as well, notably at the end of their triumphant state visit to France in the summer of 1938, after the King had dedicated a monument to eleven thousand Australian servicemen who died on the World War I battlefield at Villers-Bretonneux. George VI had laid his wreath of crimson poppies at the foot of the new war memorial, when something unexpected and deeply moving occurred. As the King stood with his head bowed, the Queen briefly whispered a word to him. She then stepped forward on her own. In her hand she held a Flanders poppy that a young French schoolboy had given her—its color a vibrant counterpoint to her white dress. Spontaneously and reverently, she walked to the memorial, stooped, and placed the poppy atop the King's wreath. Watching the impressively dramatic gesture on a newsreel in Berlin, Adolf Hitler famously called Britain's Queen "the most dangerous woman in Europe."

AFTER THEIR SIX-WEEK WINTER BREAK at Sandringham, the royal family returned to Buckingham Palace in early February 1938 in "splendid health and spirits."

Their principal focus was the visit to France set for the end of June. Germany's aggressive designs on neighboring countries in February and March heightened the diplomatic urgency behind the planned public display of Anglo-French friendship.

Hitler first targeted Austria, the land of his birth, which he had been plotting to take over since mid-1936. He bullied the Austrian chancellor and fomented unrest among what he portrayed as persecuted Austrian Nazis. Insisting that German troops were necessary to restore order, Hitler invaded Austria unopposed in the middle of March 1938. His "Anschluss" incorporated the führer's "dear homeland" as a province of the German Reich. Neither England nor France was prepared to resist Germany on Austria's behalf, and Hitler maintained that outsiders had no business in what he described as "a German family affair."

Germany's next objective in its expansionist campaign was Czechoslovakia, where Hitler planned to annex the German-majority district of Sudetenland. He paved the way as he had done in Austria, by inciting the Sudeten Germans to press for a union with Germany. France had pledged to defend Czechoslovakia against outside aggression, but Britain remained uncommitted.

Prime Minister Chamberlain's response to these threatening maneuvers was a policy of appeasement rooted in his determination to prevent the horror of another war. He also believed he could apply personal diplomacy to rein in the dictators of Germany and Italy. The overarching question was how far the Chamberlain government would go in sacrificing the freedom of democracies in central and eastern Europe. Austria had been eliminated, and despite Hitler's lies to the contrary, Czechoslovakia would surely fall without the intervention of France and Britain.

The King and Queen, as well as a substantial portion of the Conservative Party and the British public, supported appeasement and recoiled from a repetition of the First World War's carnage. Winston Churchill, however, adamantly opposed placating dictatorial regimes and warned frequently of the Nazi menace. Churchill's chief ally was Anthony Eden, who resigned as foreign secretary in late February 1938 out of his "strong political convictions" that Chamberlain's policy was too lenient with dictators. In his place, the prime minister appointed Edward, Viscount Halifax, who had sterling pro-appeasement credentials. George VI was also more comfortable with Halifax, a tall patrician with a withered left arm, an amiable manner, and worldly experience as a former viceroy of India.

In the face of the European pressures and crosscurrents, preparations for the state visit to France proceeded apace. "The French are leaving nothing undone," reported Alec Hardinge. But just five days before the planned departure of the King and Queen on June 28, seventy-five-year-old Cecilia Strathmore died at two A.M. in her London home.

Bertie and Elizabeth, as well as Elizabeth's father and her sister Rosie, were by the bedside at the end. The next day, the King and Queen agreed to an offer from French president Albert Lebrun to postpone their visit by three weeks. They left Lilibet and Margaret at the Palace, and late Saturday night they made the mournful journey to Glamis on the royal train with Cecilia's coffin of unpolished oak in the last of ten coaches. Thousands of people paid their respects at Euston station, and a large crowd greeted the family at Glamis station the next morning.

Estate workers carried the coffin, draped with gold and blue brocade, to a farm cart drawn by two horses. Atop the coffin was Elizabeth's wreath of lilies of the valley and pink carnations. Three cars carrying Elizabeth and her family followed the cart on the half-mile route to Glamis. At midday on Monday, June 27, family and close friends assembled in the castle's private chapel for Lady Strathmore's funeral service that Elizabeth described to her mother-in-law as "exquisite in its simplicity and beauty."

The humble horse-drawn farm wagon transported Lady Strathmore's flower-bedecked coffin for the mile-long drive to the family's private burial ground. Despite a heavy rain, the King, in overcoat and top hat, walked behind the cart with Elizabeth's brothers and brothers-in-law. Elizabeth and her eighty-three-year-old father rode in the first car of a small cortege, with hundreds of mourners following. At the gravesite lined with rhododendron boughs, Bertie urged Elizabeth to remain in the car while he, "bare-headed in the rain," helped to carry flowers to the grave, and estate workers brought the coffin to Cecilia's final resting place.

The King carefully set down a small cross of white carnations from Lilibet and Margaret. The Queen, dressed in black with a heavy veil, emerged from the car with her father for the committal service led by the Bishop of St. Andrews. By then, the noise of the wind and rain beating against the nearby oak trees was so loud that the priest's voice could barely be heard.

After the choir sang the Nunc Dimittis, Lord Strathmore stepped to the grave and stood with his head bowed. He handed his wreath of liliums, irises, and carnations—all grown at Glamis—to his son Michael, who knelt and placed it on the coffin next to Elizabeth's wreath. With that, Bertie, Elizabeth, and the rest of the family each paused briefly by the grave before returning to Glamis.

The next day, George VI and Elizabeth retreated to Birkhall for the remainder of the week to console each other in the place they both adored. Elizabeth found solace by climbing the nearby hills. "They are so nice & big & everlasting & such a lovely colour," she wrote to Arthur Penn, who organized a memorial service in London. To her friend she reflected on her mother's character: "modest to a fault," she told Arthur, "<u>very</u> proud & sensitive." Elizabeth said she had always relied on Cecilia's unerring judgment, and her "uncanny instinct about human beings (whether they were nice or nasty)."

She wrote revealingly to Queen Mary from Birkhall. The torrential rain, she said, "lessened the strain very much. The elements taking a part made the whole mournful affair less agonizing." Elizabeth observed that her mother "gave things their due importance, and the things that did not matter were relegated to the background. That is so rare in women, & a great gift. You have it <u>very</u> strongly, darling Mama."

Elizabeth's generous words were a testament to the closeness of her relationship with her mother-in-law compared to the early days when she resented Queen Mary's well-intentioned interference. The two women had tightly bonded during the abdication crisis. Now Queen Mary was Elizabeth's mother figure, and the affection was genuine.

THE KING AND QUEEN WERE back in London on Saturday morning, July 2. They had decided against court mourning to avoid disturbing the social events at the height of the London season, although Elizabeth wanted to observe "family mourning" and stay away from public engagements, such as her intended visit to the opera at Glyndebourne.

She nevertheless had a busy two weeks of unanticipated preparations before their voyage across the English Channel to France. She had to scuttle the entire colorful wardrobe prepared by her new dress designer, Norman Hartnell. The King had inspired the couturier's creations by asking that his wife's dresses resemble the romantic crinolines in Franz Xaver Winterhalter's portraits of Empress Eugénie of France and Elisabeth of Austria. In the same spirit, Hartnell and his seamstresses had to quickly create an all-white mourning wardrobe—as acceptable in court circles as black.

Elizabeth occupied herself with fittings and other arrangements while Bertie carried out solo duties, including debutante courts at the Palace on July 5 and 6. On Saturday the ninth at Royal Lodge, George VI suddenly succumbed to what his doctors called "gastric influenza." He was running a fever and immediately went to bed, where he remained for six days. When Queen Mary offered to visit early in the week, Elizabeth suggested she wait "in <u>case</u> of infection. It is very catching, I believe, & he would like to be <u>out</u> of his room before seeing anybody." Every measure had to be taken to ensure the King and Queen could travel to France as planned.

The King canceled all his engagements, and Elizabeth felt duty bound to substitute at one of them, the presentation party at the Palace on July 12. She "decided to set aside her own wishes in order not to disappoint the guests," wrote *The Times*. At ten P.M., she arrived at the state room in a gown of black velvet trimmed with lace and seed pearls, a diamond tiara, diamond necklace, and diamond bracelet. It could not have been easy for her, scarcely three weeks after losing her mother, to smile graciously before twelve hundred guests and receive the curtseying debutantes. Her performance showed her inner strength as well as what her childhood friend David Cecil called her "astonishing self-control."

Having made a full recovery, the King was able to join the Queen at the Buckingham Palace garden party for ten thousand guests on the eve of their journey. Bertie and Elizabeth put on their happiest expressions, accompanied by Lilibet and Margaret, wearing matching silver-gray crepe de chine dresses. The princesses "have learned to face the gaze of hundreds of eyes without seeming to notice they are the centre of interest," commented *The Manchester Guardian*.

OVER FOUR DAYS IN FRANCE, George VI and Elizabeth followed the routines they had carried out repeatedly for fifteen years. In the City of Light, surrounded by Gallic extravaganza, they moved from one elaborately decorated venue to another in a spectacular progress. The French had spent eight million francs (the equivalent of some $230,000, which would be nearly $4 million at today's values) to create opulent apartments for the royal couple at the Quai d'Orsay, the headquarters of the French Foreign Ministry, with artwork brought from the Louvre, Versailles, Fontainebleau, and Chantilly.

The royal couple attended a gala performance at the opera and were feted at one banquet after another. At the state dinner in the Élysée Palace hosted by President Lebrun and his wife, Marguerite, the Queen dazzled in her crown sparkling with the Koh-i-Noor diamond. The King "spoke well and clearly in French with practically no hesitation," reported diplomat Oliver Harvey.

George VI and Elizabeth traveled on the Seine in a white "royal barge" to the Hôtel de Ville, where the King again spoke in French. "Our entente has lost nothing of its strength or of its vitality," he said—a theme he sounded, along with a commitment to peace, in all his remarks. In the Bois de Boulogne they were entertained at a "Bagatelle garden party" by ballet dancers on rafts moored in a lake. The Queen's white wardrobe—especially her floor-length full-skirted gowns of satin, organdy, tulle, and crepe—bowled over the French, who set the highest bar for fashion excellence.

The pièce de résistance came on the final day in Versailles. At the château where the treaty ending the First World War was signed, the

King reviewed fifty thousand troops—a display of France's "modern military might" that would prove illusory two years later against a German onslaught. The midday formal luncheon in the Hall of Mirrors extravagantly re-created the seventeenth-century milieu of the court of Louis XIV, the Sun King.

George VI and Elizabeth and 280 guests were served by 125 footmen in white powdered wigs and coats of royal blue. They watched a performance by the Comédie-Française, also in period costume— "one of the most elaborate pageants ever devised for royalty in modern times." Lady Diana Cooper marveled at the "thirteen glasses apiece for thirteen precious wines, all bottled on the birthdays of the presidents and kings."

That night, after a banquet at the Quai d'Orsay, the British King and Queen appeared on a floodlit balcony, smiling and waving to tens of thousands of Parisians mobbing the streets below. Lady Diana Cooper stood among the throng and later observed, "To the French the Royal Visit seemed to safeguard against the dreaded war. That at least is what they told me but I could see nothing to allay fears."

George VI and Elizabeth received an ecstatic welcome when they returned to London. The crowds were so thick on the route from Victoria station to the Palace that they engulfed the royal car several times. Out on the balcony for five minutes of sustained cheering, the Queen blew kisses, and the couple stood still for the singing of "God Save the King." The trip was "a great personal triumph for the King and Queen," wrote *The Illustrated London News*. They had emphatically reinforced Britain's strong ties with France in a manner that "should make the dictators think," Oliver Harvey wrote. He ascribed Bertie and Elizabeth's impact to "their simplicity and dignity."

THE ROYAL FAMILY SETTLED INTO Balmoral in early August for ten weeks. Their only planned public engagement was in late September, when the King and Queen were scheduled to launch the new ocean liner *Queen Elizabeth*. It turned out that they had just three carefree weeks in the Highlands until the arrival of Neville Chamberlain on August 31 for the annual four-day prime minister's visit.

In their private audiences, George VI and Chamberlain discussed the grim news from the Continent: German troops were massing at the Czech border, and an invasion to secure Sudetenland and "return" its three million German citizens (nearly a quarter of the Czech population) to the "Motherland" seemed imminent. At the heart of the emerging crisis was France's pledge to support its Czech ally and whether Britain would be obliged to do the same, sparking another European war.

Capitulating to Hitler's demands would mean tearing apart the democratic Czechoslovakian Republic and consigning a swath of its territory to authoritarian Nazi rule. The führer gave a venomous speech at Nuremberg on September 12, insulting the Czech prime minister and provoking Sudeten Germans to revolt. Queen Mary wrote to Bertie that she had listened to the speech on the radio and was "horrified at his voice & shouting & what he said, so theatrical & awful." But she added, reflecting the King's own view, "God grant we may not have war . . . the Czechs are not worth fighting for."

George VI headed for London in mid-September, eager to be close at hand for a major foreign policy emergency. When the King arrived at Buckingham Palace on the fifteenth, Chamberlain had already departed on the first airplane flight of his life, a mission to meet Hitler at Berchtesgaden.

Over the following fourteen days, Chamberlain made two further flights to Germany in his effort to preserve peace. Hitler outmaneuvered him each time. During their initial encounter, Chamberlain gave in to Hitler's demand that the Sudeten Germans could leave if a majority of them supported the change in a referendum. At the second meeting, Hitler reneged on his earlier terms and insisted that German troops occupy Sudetenland before a plebiscite.

It was clear that Germany planned to deploy its military might, and Chamberlain could only agree to Hitler's postponement of his move across the border until October 1. Jittery about its alliance with

Czechoslovakia, France joined Britain to urge the Czechs to surrender Sudetenland or risk a European conflagration. Chamberlain stressed this point in a memorable speech on September 27, when he declared that Britain should not go to war "because of a quarrel in a faraway country between people of whom we know nothing."

Chamberlain's third meeting, a conference convened by Hitler in Munich, resulted in an agreement signed by Britain, France, Germany, and Italy on September 30, 1938. It ratified the dismemberment of Czechoslovakia, and Chamberlain took Hitler's word that he had no further territorial ambitions in Czechoslovakia or elsewhere. The führer mollified the prime minister with an Anglo-German agreement confirming friendship and "the desire of our two peoples never to go to war again." With that, the German army rolled into Czechoslovakia on October 1 and seized the Sudetenland.

George VI remained in London throughout the crisis, alternating between bouts of anxiety and efforts to use his influence to help avoid conflict. Three times he offered to send personal messages to Hitler, and each time Chamberlain deflected him. Bertie shared his distress with Tommy Lascelles, at one point confiding, "Everything is in a maze." In meetings with and letters to the prime minister, the King praised his courage and exhorted him to pursue appeasement.

Bertie had the wholehearted support of his wife. In a preview of how closely he would keep Elizabeth's counsel during World War II, he sent papers to Scotland for her to read. "You will see I have marked the different papers with notes, as it is easier," he wrote to "my own darling Angel" on September 19. "The Cabinet Minutes of Saturday are very interesting & gives [sic] the P.M.'s impressions of Hitler." He cautioned her to avoid traveling to London "as it might make people feel nervous. We will keep you well informed as to the daily progress of the situation." He admitted, "My brain is getting addled & I have told Alec to send you a précis as well. They won't tally probably!"

On September 21, Elizabeth finally took the train to London to support her husband. Three days later she told her sister May that

Bertie "has had such a terribly anxious and worrying time, & still has now."

The Queen found a city immersed in frenetic preparations for the war that seemed likely. Basements were converted into air raid shelters, and Londoners registered to receive gas masks in case Germany waged chemical warfare. The government mobilized the Royal Navy and called up the Auxiliary Air Force. Antiaircraft guns appeared in Horse Guards Parade and on Westminster Bridge. In Hyde Park and Kensington Gardens, workers dug "slit trenches" to serve as shelters from bombs. Hospitals were cleared for potential casualties, and schoolchildren were evacuated to the countryside.

Elizabeth performed her greatest service on September 27—the peak of international tension—when she traveled to Glasgow to deliver her husband's speech before she launched the *Queen Elizabeth* liner meant to travel between Britain and the United States. The new ship was the largest afloat, and "the greatest engineering feat of the century." At the King's request, the speech had been written by Lord Tweedsmuir in consultation with Alec Hardinge.

The gravity of the hour required Elizabeth to begin her remarks with a special message from the King. Speaking not only to the quarter million spectators at the launch but also millions of BBC listeners across the nation, her voice "rang out clearly" as her daughters watched from the dais.

The Queen said that the King "bids the people of this country to be of good cheer, in spite of the dark clouds hanging over them, and indeed, over the whole world. He knows well that, as ever before in critical times, they will keep cool heads and brave hearts; he knows, too, that they will place entire confidence in their leaders, who, under God's providence, are striving their utmost to find a just and peaceful solution of the grave problems which confront them."

Elizabeth paid tribute to the "fabric of friendship and understanding between the people of Britain and the people of the United States." It was "altogether fitting," she said, that "the noblest vessel ever built in Britain . . . should be dedicated to this service." Back in London,

George VI "listened to every word," he told her sister May. "I was <u>so</u> proud of Elizabeth taking on that ordeal of broadcasting the speech at a moment's notice. . . . I knew how well she would do it."

Three days later, the Queen was back in London when Neville Chamberlain returned in triumph from Munich, clasping the Anglo-German friendship agreement. Amid a wildly cheering throng at the airport, he read the joint declaration aloud and described it as "a prelude to a larger settlement in which all Europe may find peace." Later that day, he called the Munich achievement nothing less than "peace with honour" and "peace for our time."

AT THE KING'S INVITATION, THE prime minister drove straight to Buckingham Palace where his wife waited with George VI and Elizabeth in the monarch's private apartments. The crowds outside chanted, "We want Neville," and soon the royal couple appeared on the illuminated balcony with the Chamberlains. They stood together for four minutes—the men in morning dress, the women in unadorned coats—until George VI motioned his prime minister to move forward. With evident pride, Neville Chamberlain acknowledged the enthusiastic ovation.

George VI issued a message praising the "magnificent efforts of the Prime Minister in the name of peace" and expressing his "fervent hope" that "a new era of friendship and prosperity will be dawning among the peoples of the world." To his mother, he described the "great day. . . . I am so relieved that the crisis is over."

Before the royal couple left for Balmoral on the evening of Sunday, October 2, Elizabeth told her mother-in-law how relieved she was to return to Royal Deeside. "I am sure that it will do Bertie good," she wrote. "He has been marvellously calm all these ghastly days & so courageous. It has helped him, I feel, to have complete trust in Mr. Chamberlain."

The balcony appearance was at odds with the monarch's proper role. George VI appeared to be endorsing a political position when he was expected to be above politics. Many politicians and other figures took exception to the Munich Agreement for its inherent weakness, its betrayal of the Czechs, and its mistaken assumption that Hitler could be trusted. Parliament approved it, but there was strong debate, not only with the Labour opposition but within the Conservative Party as well. Thirty Tories abstained, although none voted against the government. Duff Cooper resigned his cabinet position as First Lord of the Admiralty in protest.

Queen Mary expressed the royal family's general opinion when she wrote to Elizabeth, "You & Bertie must be as angry as I am at the criticism there is now about the P.M.'s meeting at Munich. It really is a shame after all his hard work." She wished "people wld only back him up."

Many years later, in a rare interview with historian D. R. Thorpe, Elizabeth admitted that "the balcony appearance was a constitutional error," according to William Shawcross. Still, she believed it was a "venial" mistake "because the British people were so relieved by Chamberlain's agreement." And she insisted, along with many other Chamberlain supporters, that the agreement gave Britain "one year to re-arm and build a few aeroplanes." This was actually an illusion. Although Britain would accelerate its rearmament in the following year, Germany did so at an even faster pace. In September 1939, Britain's military posture was relatively weaker than it had been at the time of Munich.

*"Many of them felt that her bow was
really for them personally."*

THE ILLUSTRATED LONDON NEWS

SATURDAY, JUNE 17, 1939.

THE FIRST KING AND QUEEN OF ENGLAND TO VISIT AMERICA : THEIR MAJESTIES DRIVING TO THE WHITE
HOUSE WITH PRESIDENT AND MRS. ROOSEVELT ON THEIR ARRIVAL IN WASHINGTON.

King George VI with President Franklin D. Roosevelt and Queen Elizabeth with
first lady Eleanor Roosevelt on their arrival in Washington, D.C., on June 8, 1939.

TWENTY-SIX

Transatlantic Triumph

WHEN THE KING OPENED PARLIAMENT FOR THE SECOND TIME IN November 1938, the reason for the Queen's effusive remarks in Glasgow about Anglo-American friendship became clear. He announced that in addition to taking their first trip to Canada in May 1939, he and Elizabeth had accepted President Franklin D. Roosevelt's invitation to visit the United States. It would be a "practical expression of the good feeling that prevails between our countries," he said.

Roosevelt had set a cozy tone in September 1938 by initiating a direct correspondence with "My Dear King George," the first such exchange between a British monarch and an American president. The purpose of a trip to America was undeniably political; Eleanor Roosevelt wrote that her husband wanted it because he believed "that we all might soon be engaged in a life and death struggle, in which Great Britain would be our first line of defense," and "he hoped that the visit would create a bond of friendship between the people of the two countries."

But FDR had a personal motivation as well. The crucial element for him was a stay at the Roosevelt estate on the Hudson River in Hyde Park, New York. "As I said to [George VI], the American people admire the essential democracy of the King and Queen," the president wrote to Canada's governor-general, Lord Tweedsmuir, that November. "It would help if the formal 'functions' could be supplemented by a peaceful and simple visit to a peaceful and simple American country home."

The need for British preparedness for war came into disturbing focus in March 1939 when Hitler dramatically broke the terms of the Munich Agreement. On Wednesday the fifteenth, his troops invaded Czechoslovakia and seized the territory that remained. That evening in Prague, he announced that "Czechoslovakia has ceased to exist." Appeasement was in tatters.

A shaken Chamberlain broadcast a speech from Birmingham calling Hitler an untrustworthy liar and voicing Britain's new policy for Germany: "The liberty that we have enjoyed for hundreds of years . . . we would never surrender." He promised to resist any further aggression by Germany. George VI sent him a letter commiserating over the prime minister's "deep distress," adding, "I am sure that your labours have been anything but wasted."

Only days later, Hitler began making menacing noises about Polish territory that he insisted belonged to the Reich. On March 31, Chamberlain drew his line in the sand, announcing in the House of Commons that Britain and France had given guarantees to Poland that they would declare war if Germany attacked. In the following weeks the British government extended that protection to Greece, Romania, Denmark, the Netherlands, and Switzerland. Soon afterward came Britain's first compulsory military service in peacetime. Germany countered by signing an alliance with Italy, which had already invaded neighboring Albania.

It was no small matter that when the Polish foreign minister, Colonel Józef Beck, went to Windsor in early April for lunch with the King and Queen, Lilibet sat at the table with more than a dozen adults, as the string band of the Scots Guards played in the background. Beck was in England to negotiate the terms of a British-Polish pact following Chamberlain's pledge of support. Exactly three weeks later, Lilibet turned thirteen, a milestone that took her to a new level in her preparation to be monarch.

Elizabeth told her friend Jasper Ridley that she wanted her older daughter to take instruction in constitutional history from Sir Henry Marten, then the vice provost of Eton College. Crawfie carried this out, accompanying the young princess twice a week to the ancient school down the hill from Windsor Castle. Marten was as eccentric as he was erudite. "Piles of books stood like stalagmites on the floor," Crawfie recalled.

Under Marten's tutelage, Lilibet's curriculum included H.A.L. Fisher's *History of Europe* as well as United States history. He stirred her interest in politics, which George VI amplified in his own discussions with her. "Try and learn as much as you can from [Marten], & mark how he brings the human element into all his history," the Queen wrote to her daughter. "Of course history is made by ordinary humans, & one must not forget that."

KING GEORGE VI AND QUEEN Elizabeth set sail on May 5 aboard the liner *Empress of Australia* for their planned twelve-day voyage to North America. On their seventh day at sea, a thick fog enveloped the ship. The next morning, the gray curtain lifted briefly to reveal all around them icebergs "as big as Glamis," the Queen told Lilibet. For three days the ship sat motionless in the mercifully calm water, moving gingerly at intervals as the horns blasted every two minutes in what Elizabeth likened to "the twang of a piece of wire." She told Queen Mary that "one kept imagining that a great iceberg was bearing down on the ship, & starting up at night with a beating heart."

They tried to make the best of what Tommy Lascelles described as a "sensation of being suspended somewhere right outside the world, with no dimensions. Space was limited to the grey wall outside & time was nonexistent. We might have been there three days or three

months." The Queen somewhat improbably occupied herself by reading Hitler's anti-communist, expansionist, anti-Semitic, and authoritarian tract *Mein Kampf,* which she considered "very soap-box, but
very interesting." Six months later, she would give a copy to Foreign
Secretary Halifax, saying, "I do not advise you to read it through, or
you might go mad. . . . Even a skip through gives one an idea of his
mentality, ignorance and obvious sincerity."

The alarming interruption ended on Sunday, May 14, when the
fog dispersed and the *Empress* skirted around a wall of ice on three
sides. In the bright sunshine, they had to push through a quarter mile
of thick ice before they reached open water and steamed toward the
St. Lawrence River. They arrived in Quebec on Wednesday morning,
two days late.

George VI had enjoyed an unintended benefit of the three-day
pause. It was "the only really idle & irresponsible spell he has had
since he acceded" as there was "nothing for him to do," Tommy told
his wife. The King hardly even mentioned Hitler's name and expressed
relief to have had "his first real rest."

Lascelles and the Canadian officials reorganized the schedule so
no engagements were dropped, but the early days of the tour were
more condensed than anticipated. The Canadians came out in force
for the first visit to their country by a British sovereign and consort.
French-speaking Quebecois began referring to "*our* King and Queen"
after George VI gave a bilingual speech—somewhat nervously at first,
then in a strong voice.

In Toronto, Elizabeth dropped to her knees and embraced the
four-year-old Dionne quintuplets—a global phenomenon at the
time—who smothered her with kisses. She was many decades ahead
of Diana, the Princess of Wales, whose hugging on her official tours
was applauded for breaking royal norms and establishing unprecedented intimacy with ordinary people.

During three jammed days in Ottawa, the King and Queen stayed
with Lord Tweedsmuir and his wife, the former Susan Grosvenor, a
relative of the Dukes of Westminster and Wellington. At a garden

party for five thousand, George VI and Elizabeth mingled with the "genteel of Ottawa" who "cheered the whole time like children at a school feast." After Elizabeth laid the foundation for a new Supreme Court building, she and the King insisted on spending some ten minutes with the building's masonry workers.

The most dramatic moment of the tour occurred after George VI had unveiled Ottawa's National War Memorial in the presence of ten thousand veterans. The Queen told Tweedsmuir that she "must go down" among the troops. The governor-general considered the risk worthwhile, so "sure enough the King and Queen and Susie and I disappeared in that vast mob!—simply swallowed up. The police could not get near us." The elderly veterans "made a perfect bodyguard," and their reaction to the young royals was "extraordinarily touching." Many of them were weeping, and one cried out, "Ay, man, if Hitler could just see this!"

The American reporters were "simply staggered" and said no American president would have braved a crowd that way. To Tweedsmuir, George VI was nothing less than "a people's king." He couldn't understand how the King and Queen could "face these gigantic crowds with equanimity," he told his sister. "As a matter of fact, the Queen's eyes pretty often filled with tears."

The royal couple even made themselves accessible to the press corps. In Ottawa they sipped sherry with some eighty journalists, walking among them and shaking hands. While no questions were allowed, it was an opportunity to recognize their work and pay a compliment to their profession. Elizabeth thought the reporters were "really very nice . . . so shy and polite!" The Americans in particular were easy to talk to. They "were surprised & delighted to find that we were ordinary & fairly polite people with a big job of work," Elizabeth told Queen Mary.

Each night in Ottawa, George VI kept Tweedsmuir up talking into the small hours. The governor-general had long felt a "sincere affection" for George VI. Now more than ever Tweedsmuir realized "what a wonderful mixture he is of shrewdness, kindliness and humour." In addition to admiring the King's character, Tweedsmuir had formed "a very deep respect . . . for his brains."

He remarked on more than one occasion that both the King and his consort had "simply a genius for unrehearsed effects. They are so simple and straightforward themselves that everyone feels at ease with them. The Queen is an extraordinarily clever woman in her quiet way."

Canadian prime minister Mackenzie King came to the same conclusion. He had been a strong advocate of appeasement, and Elizabeth found that their views coincided. They both believed Hitler would avoid going to war—her reading of *Mein Kampf* notwithstanding—and they agreed that Britain should continue to take the lead for the cause of peace. "I was quite impressed with the earnestness with which she spoke," the prime minister wrote in his diary. She said to him, "It is very nice to be able to say what you think."

The King and Queen covered nearly ten thousand miles in twenty-nine days—through cities and small towns, from the Atlantic to the Pacific and back. Accompanied by Mackenzie King, they traveled mainly on the governor-general's train, which had been redone with new furnishings and a fresh coat of pale blue and silver paint on the exterior. The task of filling the train's library shelves fell to Lady Tweedsmuir, who understood the inclinations of an aristocratic queen. Elizabeth told her the library was a "great joy." Her favorites were a short volume on Canadian history and a collection of ghost stories that she read twice.

As they passed the mountains and prairies and far-flung towns, Elizabeth shared her impressions with Lilibet. She described taking a hike at Banff, where "the pine trees smelt delicious in the hot sun." She also sprinkled her letters with motherly reminders and words of advice. "I am sure that you are being wonderfully kind & thoughtful for other people," she wrote, adding that Lilibet needed to control herself when Margaret teased her: "You can do it, & I know you will." To the thirteen-year-old heiress presumptive, she emphasized that the final two weeks in Canada would be "very hard work, but it is worth while, for one feels how important it is that the people here should see their King & not have him only as a symbol," and "to give the people an opportunity to show how British they are."

———

Franklin D. Roosevelt watched with rising anticipation as the King and Queen made their royal progress across Canada. George VI delivered four effective speeches, capped by his Empire Day broadcast to the people of the Commonwealth and the United States from Winnipeg on May 24. Tweedsmuir had written the remarks, and Logue had practiced with the monarch back in England. Logue had also coached Tommy Lascelles on how to prepare the King for a broadcast, including his all-important need to stand up.

Lascelles was alone in the broadcasting room with George VI on Empire Day, which "was rather nerve-wracking," but he thought the speech was done "admirably." Logue agreed, wiring Lascelles: "tremendous success." The voice was "beautiful" and "resonant." George VI struck a compelling chord by advocating "freedom, justice and peace in equal measure for all, secure against attack from without and from within."

Roosevelt told Tweedsmuir that the King and Queen had already made a "splendid impression" among Americans. The president joked that the "only contretemps" in Washington "has been caused by social climbers and the newspaper girls who failed to get their 'pasteboards' [stiff paper invitations]" to the British ambassador's garden party. FDR mostly looked forward to "the thirty hours of comparative quiet" at Hyde Park.

Although George VI and Elizabeth were in the United States for only four days, their visit had an outsize impact. They arrived in the nation's capital by train late in the morning of June 8, 1939, and withstood what Elizabeth described to Lilibet as "two burning, boiling, sweltering humid furnace-like days." Not only was it the first time a reigning British sovereign had visited America, it was also the first opportunity for most Americans to see an actual King and Queen. "In the course of a long life I have seen many important events in Washington, but never have I seen a crowd such as lined the whole route between the Union Station and the White House," wrote fifty-four-year-old Eleanor Roosevelt in her diary.

George VI wore his Admiral of the Fleet uniform. Elizabeth fit the part in a mauve ensemble and small straw hat trimmed along the crown with mauve ostrich feathers. *Time* magazine encapsulated her queenly perfection: "eyes a snapping blue, chin tilted confidently . . . fingers raised in greeting as girlish as it was regal." *The Times* took special note of the Queen as she wiped away tears while listening to "The Star-Spangled Banner," a gesture that "set her in the people's hearts." The King drew ovations, but "the tide of sound lifted even higher as the Queen came into sight."

More than seven hundred thousand people lined the two miles of downtown streets to hail the royal visitors. The president in his topper and the King in his cocked hat led the procession in an open limousine. The first lady and the Queen, sheltering from the sun with her long-handled parasol held high above her head, followed in their own convertible. A cushion equipped with springs gave Elizabeth extra buoyancy as she continuously bowed to the left and right. Eleanor Roosevelt admired the Queen's uncanny ability to connect with individuals in vast crowds, creating the illusion that "many of them felt that her bow was really for them personally."

The royal couple kept up a punishing pace throughout their first day—sightseeing that included visiting the Lincoln Memorial, meeting prominent Washingtonians at Ambassador Lindsay's garden party, and attending a family luncheon, diplomatic reception, and State Dinner at the White House. On their second day, they smiled their way through ten engagements in eleven hours, taking them from the Capitol (where they individually greeted 426 senators and representatives) to Mount Vernon (where the King put the ghost of King George III to rest by laying a wreath on George Washington's tomb).

They even attended Eleanor Roosevelt's morning press conference with seventy female reporters. "Oh!" said the Queen as she walked into the room. "There are quite a lot of them, aren't there?" The first lady told them about Elizabeth's "keen sense" of the problems of laborers and her understanding of "the conditions which push people to desperation." Privately, she described the Queen with a touch of asperity: "gracious, informed, saying the right thing & kind but a little self-consciously regal."

Despite temperatures in the mid-nineties, the King and Queen didn't wilt in public, although Elizabeth's skin reddened from sunburn. She later said she had "never seen a hotter place than the White House." At one point she was so exhausted she lay on the floor of her bedroom—formerly Abraham Lincoln's study—to cool off.

While the president and first lady were predictably enchanted with the royal couple's cordial and easygoing manner, they were equally struck by how well informed and inquisitive they were. Both the King and Queen had studied a thirty-four-page briefing book prepared by the Foreign Office that provided overviews of foreign and domestic issues as well as biographies of top officials. When Eleanor Roosevelt took them to visit a Civilian Conservation Corps camp for unemployed young men—a project they had asked to see—they quizzed each camper with detailed questions.

At tea on the White House lawn with sixteen heads of government agencies, the first lady could scarcely make her introductions before the King launched his queries about the New Deal policies each of them was carrying out. The Queen carefully remained in the background, smiling and watching the King attentively as he was speaking. He, in turn, would catch her eye "with a swifter, shyer glance."

George VI and Elizabeth hosted a final dinner for the Roosevelts at the British Embassy on Friday, June 9. Shortly before midnight, they boarded their train for the journey northward. Still dressed in their formal clothes—the King in white-tie and the Queen in a diamond tiara and a Hartnell "Victorian picture frock" of sumptuously embroidered deep rose tulle—they waved goodbye to Washington from the platform of the rear coach.

At seven A.M. on Saturday, they left the train in New Jersey and traveled on the destroyer *Warrington* past the Statue of Liberty to Lower Manhattan. Escorted by Mayor Fiorello La Guardia and Governor Herbert Lehman, they drove in a convertible through the city's streets past three and a half million overjoyed New Yorkers massed thickly on the sidewalks. Almost from the start, the royal couple was behind schedule and never caught up.

Their main event was a tour of the World's Fair—optimistically designed to celebrate an expansive "world of tomorrow." The British Pavilion was "very good & very interesting historically," Elizabeth told Queen Mary. But as a veteran of many such exhibitions, she added, "one big Fair looks much like another." Their last brief stop was Columbia University to see the founding charter that had been granted by King George II in 1754.

George VI and Elizabeth were utterly wrung out when they set off on their seventy-mile drive to Hyde Park. His temper had flared at the World's Fair halfway through his introduction to hundreds of people when he turned on his heel and walked away. One newspaperwoman saw him clenching his teeth from the strain, and others observed that both of them were waving like automatons. By the last hour of their New York City rounds, "the King's cheek muscles ceased to work," and he was unable to smile. He and the Queen arrived an hour and a half late at Springwood, the Roosevelt family's Georgian-style home overlooking the Hudson River. When FDR offered George VI a martini, he gladly drank it.

As the president had anticipated, the setting of his country residence offered the perfect opportunity to seal his friendship with the British sovereign and his wife. The Roosevelts were pure American aristocracy. Their Hyde Park estate for more than a hundred years was a smaller version of Sandringham. Springwood was even known as "the Big House." Like the King at York Cottage, Franklin Roosevelt had been born at Springwood. Both men thrived in the countryside, knew every inch of their old growth woodlands, and enjoyed gardening. At Hyde Park, FDR "was Squire, not President," wrote John Wheeler-Bennett. "With his quick intuition he sensed that all this would appeal unfailingly to King George."

FDR reinforced his bond with the King at dinner by proposing a toast to seventy-two-year-old Queen Mary as he gazed across the table at his eighty-five-year-old mother, Sara Delano Roosevelt, a similarly formidable matriarch. Sara had "the greatest affection & admiration" for the Queen Mother, and her son spoke "in the most touching terms," Elizabeth wrote to her mother-in-law. "It was so nice & friendly, & of course I found tears coming into my eyes!"

In the library afterward, George VI and Roosevelt had the second of three extended discussions about the looming threat of war with Germany. They had begun in FDR's White House study following the state banquet at the end of George VI's long first day in Washington. As the president told the press the next morning, they had spoken "as would any two men at a time of grave world tension."

Their first conversation had lasted until one in the morning. "He is so easy to get to know," George VI later wrote, "& never makes one feel shy. As good a listener as a talker." One key factor in their instantaneous rapport was that each of them had overcome a challenging disability. In the case of the president, it was a crippling case of poliomyelitis that had infected him at age thirty-nine, leaving him paralyzed from the waist down. Showing the same determination the King had applied to his severe stutter, Roosevelt had pursued political office and been elected president twice.

Now the fifty-seven-year-old American leader and the forty-three-year-old monarch could have what the King described as a "frank & friendly" exchange. Although FDR outpaced George VI in experience and knowledge, his magnetic charm lessened any anxieties the King may have had. Tweedsmuir once said that Roosevelt's "vitality oxygenates all his surroundings, and his kindliness diffuses a pleasant warmth about him wherever he goes. . . . His thought is not only spacious, but close-textured."

Canadian prime minister Mackenzie King participated in Saturday night's conversation, although George VI needed no particular assistance. He had read his briefs and was well prepared. Shadowing the discussion was the Neutrality Act passed by Congress in 1935. Roosevelt had been trying to amend the act—if not outright repeal it—to enable America to supply armaments to Britain, but isolationist senators were firmly opposed.

FDR told George VI that he still hoped "something could be done to make it less difficult for the USA to help." The president also pointed out the importance of setting up a western Atlantic patrol, with bases from Canada into British colonies in the Caribbean, to protect America and defend those regions against enemy forces at sea.

When the hour approached one-thirty A.M., FDR recognized the King's fatigue and said, "Young man, it's time for you to go to bed." But as was his habit, George VI insisted on staying up with Mackenzie King to share his impressions. "Why don't my Ministers talk to me as the President did to-night?" he asked. "I feel exactly as though a father were giving me his most careful and wise advice." The president appreciated that the King "was completely natural and put all the 'royalness' aside when in private."

The King excluded the Canadian prime minister from his conversation with Roosevelt the following afternoon when they delved into more detail on what George VI called the "firm & trusted" Anglo-American alliance. FDR not only showed the King a map of his proposed naval patrols and bases but also gave it to him. The president made promises he probably knew he couldn't keep if Britain went to war with Germany: "If he saw a U boat he would sink her at once & wait for the consequences" and "If London was bombed U.S.A. would come in." It would be seventeen more months—long after the Luftwaffe had terrorized London with the Blitz—before the United States entered the war following the Japanese bombing of Pearl Harbor.

George VI wrote a detailed memorandum of their talks as well as a document he titled "F.D.R.'s ideas in case of War." Back in London he would convey "the essence" of these discussions to "the proper quarters." The actual documents he would keep to himself and carry with him in his red dispatch box wherever he went during the Second World War. He would, however, share Roosevelt's map with officials at the Admiralty and explain "what Roosevelt had in mind." The ocean patrol plan led to the essential "destroyers for bases" and "Lend-Lease" deals that would eventually offer Britain lifesaving assistance from the United States.

ON SUNDAY, THE KING AND Queen attended the service at St. James, the Roosevelts' Episcopalian parish church. Fifty years later, Elizabeth remembered with amusement, "We saw a large notice outside saying 'Church of the President,' and under it some wag had written, 'Formerly God's.'" FDR gave the royal couple a tour of his estate in his car specially equipped with hand controls for accelerating and braking. The president careened around at high speed, pointing out the sights and flourishing his cigarette holder. "He was conversing more than watching the road," Elizabeth recalled. "There were several times I thought we could go right off the road and tumble down the hills. It was frightening, but quite exhilarating." The Queen pronounced Roosevelt "such a delightful man and _very_ good company."

The centerpiece of the day was the picnic at Top Cottage, the president's hideaway three miles from the Big House. Under trees on the veranda overlooking the Hudson River, they ate a lunch featuring quintessentially American hot dogs—a first for the King and Queen—served on silver dishes. In a letter to Queen Mary, Elizabeth observed that the president invited "all his own farm servants, gardeners etc at tables to right & left"—a conspicuously egalitarian touch. To Lilibet she described "all our food on one plate—a little salmon, some turkey, some ham, lettuce, beans & HOT DOGS!" George VI chomped down on his American-style sausage "with gusto," said Roosevelt historian Arthur Schlesinger, Jr., while the baffled Queen daintily resorted to a knife and fork.

After lunch, they all drove to Val-Kill Cottage, "Mrs. R's own little house," noted Elizabeth to her mother-in-law. The King and the president swam in the pool while Elizabeth sat alone in the shade. "It was deliciously peaceful," she wrote to Lilibet, "and the first really quiet moment we have had for WEEKS."

They ate a simple dinner of fish chowder before the royal couple caught their train at Hyde Park station for the return trip to Canada, where they were winding up their tour in the Maritime Provinces.

Onlookers packed the riverbank in the gloaming and sang "Auld Lang Syne" as the Roosevelts bid goodbye. "Good luck to you!" the president shouted. "All the luck in the world!" The first lady thought the King and Queen, "standing on the rear platform on the train as it pulled slowly away, were deeply moved. I know I was."

George VI and Elizabeth reunited with the Tweedsmuirs aboard the royal train en route to Halifax, Nova Scotia, where they made their farewell speeches to the Canadian people. The governor-general had long talks separately with the King and the Queen during their rail journey together. "It is unbelievable the way he has matured in the last two years," Tweedsmuir told a friend.

In a letter to Roosevelt, Tweedsmuir underlined the couple's enthusiasm for their visits to Washington and Hyde Park. "The King especially was very full of his talks with you. You have given him many things to think about, and he really thinks." Mackenzie King seconded these impressions in his own letter to FDR, saying the King "found it easier to carry on a conversation with you than with almost anyone else."

To Stanley Baldwin, Tweedsmuir observed, "The King has a remarkable flair for political questions, and his judgment, especially after his talks with the president, seemed to me very shrewd." In his letter to Neville Chamberlain, the governor-general promised that the King would reveal particulars of his discussions with FDR: "He is profoundly interested both in the President's personality and in the problems he is facing."

The evening send-off from Halifax on Thursday, June 15, was intensely emotional. "I nearly cried at the end of my last speech in Canada," George VI later admitted, "and everyone around me was crying." Accompanied by three Canadian destroyers, the royal couple's homebound ocean liner, the *Empress of Britain,* steamed out of the spectacular harbor under clear skies. Tweedsmuir watched "the tiny figures of Their Majesties on the bridge, and the grey, menacing cruisers following."

He reported to his sister that "we have all fallen deeply in love" with George VI and Elizabeth. "She has a kind of gentle, steady radiance . . . and he is simply one of the best people in the world. I never thought that I should feel the romantic affection for my sovereign that I feel for him." More to the point, he told Lord Crawford, "What a piece of luck that the Abdication happened. We have got precisely the monarchs who are needed at this moment in the Empire and the world."

"There may be dark days ahead, and war can no longer be confined to the battlefield."

King George VI's radio address to citizens of Britain and the Commonwealth on September 3, 1939, at the start of World War II.

TWENTY-SEVEN

～～

We Shall Prevail

THE REUNION OF THE KING AND QUEEN WITH THEIR DAUGHTERS ON the *Empress of Britain* off the Isle of Wight was as raucous as it was joyful. After being apart from their parents for seven weeks, Lilibet and Margaret could barely contain themselves as they raced up the wooden steps of the companionway from a barge. "Hullo!" shouted eight-year-old Margaret at the top of her voice. "Hullo, Mummy!" Lilibet cried out.

On reaching the deck, they rushed to their parents and "kissed them and hugged them again and again," wrote Crawfie. "The King could hardly take his eyes off Lilibet." They all had lunch in the ship's dining room, festooned with streamers and balloons, which the princesses and the King tossed through the portholes to people in pleasure boats below.

Queen Mary and the King's immediate family accompanied them on the train to Waterloo station, where George VI shook hands with his ministers, and Elizabeth was surrounded by curtseying and kissing royals. Lilibet and Margaret, dressed alike in pink coats and hats, chatted with everyone on the platform, including Neville Chamberlain, with whom Lilibet was seen having a "long talk."

The princesses rode with their parents at the head of the carriage procession to Buckingham Palace. Elizabeth was beaming, and Bertie had a "quiet, happy smile lighting up his face as he raised his hand again and again" in response to the crowds. The cheering "was like a continuous wave of sound, rising in a succession of crescendos," reported *The Times*.

The House of Lords and House of Commons suspended their sittings and paid an unprecedented homage, gathering together on the pavements of Parliament Square. The sun broke through heavy clouds just before the royal carriage appeared. As the King saluted his government, the Queen smiled and bowed. "We lost all our dignity and yelled and yelled," wrote Harold Nicolson. "We returned to the House with lumps in our throats."

Fifty thousand people surged around the Palace gates. "The roar could be heard in the Strand above the noise of London's traffic," reported the *Daily Mirror* under the headline "To Our Love and Gratitude You Enter Once Again Your Home in the Empire's Heart." Responding to the clamor of the crowd, the King and Queen appeared on the balcony with the princesses. Shortly before nine P.M., George VI and Elizabeth made an encore to another "hurricane of cheers." It was "the greatest of all homecomings," announced the *Daily Mirror*.

Lionel Logue came to the Palace late the next morning, Friday, June 23. In a few hours, George VI had to deliver his report on the trip at the Guildhall after a luncheon with seven hundred dignitaries. He was understandably "a little nervous," Logue noted, but he relaxed after they ran through the speech, which had been written by Tweedsmuir at the King's request.

Under the imposing stone arches and stained-glass windows of the Guildhall Library, George VI listened to the Lord Mayor of London express his "deep gratitude to the King and Queen for their historic journey." Their determination "to undertake such a heavy responsibility in these confused and difficult times," he added, "had profoundly stirred the feelings of the nation."

The King delivered a twofold message. "Even in this age of machines and mass-production," he said, "the strength of human feeling is still the most potent of all forces affecting world affairs." Equally, Britain had "made a helpful contribution to the gradual weaving of that fabric of humanity." Institutions of liberty and justice that evolved in Britain, "century after century . . . British in origin, British in their slow and almost casual growth," had benefited countries around the world.

His audience rewarded his remarks fourteen times with cheers, the loudest and most prolonged near the end of his speech when he singled out the Queen for assisting him in "promoting peace and good will among mankind." The *Daily Express* called the speech "admirable and shapely" and noted that "one is not now conscious of any impediment." Tommy Lascelles reported to Mackenzie King that he had "never heard the King . . . speak so effectively or so movingly. One or two passages obviously stirred him so deeply that I feared he might break down."

Logue listened on the radio and told Tommy that "everyone was pleased, *particularly the King.*" George VI proudly told his old mentor Louis Greig that the experience "was a change from the old days when speaking I felt was 'hell.'" Yet he was more unguarded in a letter to Tweedsmuir. He expressed gratitude for "all the help you gave me with my speeches, which I am sure struck the right note. I was able to carry it on in my Guildhall Speech, which was a great ordeal."

The tour marked an inflection point for King George VI. The King and Queen each remarked that the trip had "made us." "I have been struck with the King's increased confidence and more assured mastery of himself in public," Neville Chamberlain told Tweedsmuir. The prime minister's wife had noticed the change in newsreels from Canada. "She was more struck with the bearing of the King than of the Queen, and you know how much that is saying."

George VI himself reported to the Canadian governor-general that "everybody here says that our tour has done untold good to the people of Canada, & I can tell you that our tour has done me untold good in every way." Seeing the United States "was an enlightening experience, full of surprises. . . . I am so glad to have met and talked with a man such as the President." The King had returned to Britain "with a renewed vigor to all the problems which beset this Old World of ours."

Tweedsmuir took from these comments that the King now saw himself not as "a mere symbol or link . . . but a very real person who, alone in the world, can do certain things of the utmost importance." In the view of his biographer John Wheeler-Bennett, George VI was emboldened "to trust his own judgment and to size up men for himself." The royal couple's more accessible approach had clearly resonated. "There must be no more high-hat business," the King said, "the sort of thing that my father and those of his day regarded as essential as the correct attitude."

Elizabeth was likewise newly empowered, but in a different way, with a sharper awareness of the influence of her image as well as her personality. In contrast to her husband, who didn't like to consciously perform, Elizabeth understood her skills as an actress. Tweedsmuir knew that Elizabeth had a "perfect genius for the right kind of publicity."

To that end, in late July 1939, she summoned Cecil Beaton to Buckingham Palace to photograph her for a series of portraits intended to uplift British spirits. Choosing him was "a daring innovation," he wrote. "My work was still considered revolutionary and unconventional." Elizabeth wanted a change from the stilted portraits of the coronation, and it was the first time the renowned society photographer had captured the Queen. She ended up spending far longer in front of his lens than anticipated. They began in the midafternoon and ended at seven P.M.

They first met in her drawing room to discuss the dresses she would wear. Beaton was transfixed by the "blue haze" that "emanated from the French silk walls embroidered of silver" and the "pointillist bower of flowers—hydrangea, sweet peas, carnations." She offered her suggestions "wistfully . . . with a smile and raised eyebrows" and an "infectious" charm. He found himself wrinkling his forehead "in imitation of her look of inquiry."

As she changed from one Hartnell creation to another—tiers of spangled tulle, crimson crinoline embroidered in gold and silver, golden fabric encrusted with pearls and diamonds—they moved from one opulent setting to the next: the Music Room, the Bow Room, the Yellow and Blue Drawing Rooms. In the late afternoon, at Beaton's suggestion, they shifted to the Palace garden, where she wore a champagne-colored lace dress and hat, and carried one of her signature parasols.

Beaton clicked his camera "with monkey-like frenzy," which amused Elizabeth. When she fretted that three rows of large pearls seemed excessive and the photographer reassured her that it was fine, she removed one strand anyway, saying, "I think three rows *are* too much!" She wore two different diamond tiaras and a necklace of diamonds "almost as big as walnuts"—a coronation gift from the King.

She reminded Beaton of a "porcelain doll, with a flawless little face like luminous china in front of a fire . . . altogether a face that reveals what the owner is—someone with the best instincts, strict in her likes, gay, sympathetic, witty, shrewd, wistful . . . a great lady & childish, an angel with genius" who "makes every man feel she needs his protection though she can well get along on her own merits."

As Beaton "sweated with the effort," the Queen kept smiling with fresh enthusiasm. "It is so hard to know when *not* to smile," she confessed. Out on the terrace, the sun began to drop, and the sky turned rosy. It was as if, she said, "Piccadilly were on fire every night," an evocative foreshadowing of London scenes during the Blitz little over a year later.

The resulting photographs were a propaganda coup for the King and Queen. Elizabeth worked closely with Beaton on the selections. Simultaneously businesslike and gossipy, she summed up people "in a brilliant & penetrating way," observed Beaton. She let slip that "she refuses to have anything to do with 'Chips' Channon." (As a partisan of the Duke of Windsor, the diarist had been aware of his diminished status even before the abdication, when he admitted to being "out of the royal racket" for "having backed the wrong horse.")

An exquisite Beaton image of the Queen in profile graced the cover of *The Queen's Book of the Red Cross,* published that November with a handwritten message from Elizabeth praising the "noble work" of the global humanitarian organization. A compendium of prose, poetry, and artwork from fifty of Britain's "distinguished authors and artists," including Daphne du Maurier, Rex Whistler, and T. S. Eliot, the book raised money for what the Queen called "the great work of mercy on the battlefield."

In the following weeks, more portraits from the sessions with Beaton appeared in newspapers and magazines around the world, displaying a romantic and serene consort. The picture on the cover of *The Tatler* society magazine was an effulgent vision of the bareheaded Queen seated in her flowing tulle gown on a sofa in the Blue Drawing Room. "H.M. the Queen—God Bless Her!" ran the headline. The setting, explained *The Tatler,* made an "appropriate background for Her Majesty's distinguished beauty," but reminded readers that "nowadays, the Queen is more often seen in the workmanlike surroundings" of a Palace room where she was leading "a party of ladies and palace employees in preparing comforts" for the British armed forces.

THE SUMMER OF 1939 WAS forever known as the last season of peace. The most consequential event for the royal family occurred far from Buckingham Palace on July 22, when George VI, Elizabeth, Lilibet, and Margaret arrived at the King's alma mater, the Royal Naval College at Dartmouth, for a two-day visit. The King's cousin Dickie Mountbatten accompanied the royal foursome for George VI's first visit since 1919, when he was a lieutenant in the Royal Navy. They disembarked from the royal yacht *Victoria and Albert* in a downpour, which didn't dampen the reaction of Lilibet when she was introduced to Cadet Captain Prince Philip of Greece. In a coup de foudre similar to her father's first sighting of Elizabeth nearly two decades earlier, thirteen-year-old Lilibet fell in love with the strikingly handsome eighteen-year-old.

They were third cousins and great-great-grandchildren of Queen Victoria and Prince Albert. Philip's mother and father, Prince Andrew of Greece and Princess Alice of Battenberg, along with many members of his extended family, had been entertained over the years by the British royal family. Lilibet and the young prince had met glancingly at the wedding of Prince George and Princess Marina five years earlier, and Philip had attended the 1937 coronation.

At Dartmouth, Lilibet "never took her eyes off him the whole time," Crawfie recounted. He was polite to her "but did not pay her any special attention." Remembering the day many years later, Philip said to Lilibet, "You were so shy. I couldn't get a word out of you." In her own reminiscences more than seven decades after their marriage, Queen Elizabeth II spoke of Philip's "mischievous, enquiring twinkle" that captivated her "when I first set eyes on him."

Lilibet and Philip had tea with her parents and other cadets, although Lilibet "was not allowed to stay up," according to Crawfie, to attend dinner on the yacht that evening when her cousin was among the guests. Crawfie noticed that at tea the next day, Lilibet plied Philip with food. The princess sat "pink-faced, enjoying it all very much."

When the *Victoria and Albert* steamed away early that evening, a "huge flotilla" of cadets in their blue boats escorted the yacht into the bay and "cheered lusty farewells." Prompted by the King's concern that the harbor conditions were unsafe, the ship's captain signaled the cadets to turn around. The one exception was Philip, "rowing away as hard as he could," according to Crawfie. Lilibet watched him through binoculars, and her exasperated father said, "The young fool. He must go back, otherwise we will have to heave ho and send him back." Philip heeded the order shouted through a megaphone and duly turned around.

Ten days later, the King and his family arrived at Balmoral, where he and the Queen began preparing for the two hundred boys scheduled to attend what had been renamed "the King's Camp." It was the eighteenth season, and George VI had moved the gathering to the grounds of his boyhood home at Abergeldie—located three miles from the castle—so he could spend more time with the campers. He halved the usual number to provide a more intimate experience, but the camp was still equally divided between public schoolboys and factory workers. Within hours of his Royal Deeside arrival, George VI was inspecting the big tents for sleeping, dining, and entertainment, and the Queen was busy consulting on the catering arrangements.

When the campers appeared on Saturday, August 5, George VI greeted them. The next day, he and the Queen gave them tea at the castle and showed them around the grounds. The royal family visited the camp on Monday morning in the bright sunshine after a weekend of rain, entering the site through tall fir trees and a narrow lane formed by the cheering boys.

The King personally planned the week meticulously, with games scheduled on only one day. Otherwise, the boys went with him for long daily hikes across the moors, mountains, and deer forests. George VI explained to them that the treks would build their endurance and foster comradeship. Walking over the heather in twos and threes, "we got to know each other properly," wrote a boy from Bryanston School. "Class distinction vanished in our common appreciation of nature."

To set a casual tone that Monday, the King wore an open-neck sports shirt with his Balmoral tartan kilt and tweed jacket, and the Queen was dressed in a simple linen frock. He took home movies and operated a newsreel camera for a "talkie" featuring the boys singing "For He's a Jolly Good Fellow." The royal couple and the princesses grinned throughout the hand signals and silences of the traditional camp song, "Under the Spreading Chestnut Tree." While Elizabeth, Lilibet, and Margaret watched, the King took part with the boys in their games. The Queen reported to Queen Mary that it was "wonderful how happily they mix with each other."

After lunch, George VI led the boys on their first five-mile hike together, through Balmoral Forest on a long climb to Birkhall. He "pointed out activity going on all round them which their inexperienced eyes had failed to see. Herds of deer . . . the sparrow hawk hovering in the sky," recalled the camp chief, Captain J. G. Paterson. The boys from "the more crowded parts of the Kingdom" shared their experiences of industrial life with the monarch.

"We talked to the King as if he was an assistant schoolmaster," said the Bryanston student. "His Majesty is a very good walker," recalled a factory boy. "He talks and jokes with us . . . and sits down and has lunch with us." Tommy Lascelles marveled that "without any fore-warning," he couldn't tell "which came from Eton & which from a pitman's cottage. How intelligent the young are nowadays & how thirsty for information about world-affairs."

The final night, Friday, August 11, Elizabeth and the girls were at Glamis for the weekend, which enabled the King to celebrate with his campers on his own. They met at the castle grounds, where he led them up the steep Craigowan hill. At the summit, he lit a huge pile of wood for a bonfire as the boys sang "God Save the King," and six bag-pipers played Highland airs. At the end, the King and his two hundred campers held hands and sang "Auld Lang Syne." When they left Bal-moral in buses, they saw King George VI, standing in the road, illumi-nated by headlights, waving goodbye.

Three weeks later, Britain would be at war with Germany, and many of the seventeen-to-nineteen-year-old campers would be in uni-form. The Abergeldie King's Camp was his last. It would be an indel-ible memory for the participants as well as a lasting legacy for the seven thousand boys who in the years since 1921 had been touched by George VI's unusually egalitarian spirit.

THE FIRST WAR ALARM SOUNDED suddenly, on August 22, with the stunning announcement that Germany and the Soviet Union had signed a nonaggression pact negotiated in secret. Their undisclosed aim was to divide Poland between them after launching attacks from the east and west. Even without that specific knowledge, Chamber-lain and his government knew that Hitler's threats of aggression against Poland would mean fulfilling the British commitment to safeguard the country. Britain reaffirmed that guarantee in a message to Hitler, and sealed it on the twenty-fifth by signing a formal treaty with the Polish government. By then two million German troops had massed on Poland's border.

The King had arrived in London the previous day, determined to do what he could to promote a peaceful resolution. Once again, he proposed a personal appeal to Hitler, and once more Chamberlain politely rejected the idea. The British government continued to try dissuading Germany from its planned invasion, and other leaders from around the world, including Franklin D. Roosevelt and Pope Pius XII, issued pleas for peace. As Hardinge explained to Tweedsmuir, "No one any longer has any illusions about the Nazi regime, and everyone is quite convinced that the only thing to do is to remain absolutely firm." Britain would only negotiate if "it is not at the point of a pistol."

On August 25, George VI wrote to Elizabeth at Balmoral enclosing a letter from Chamberlain to Hitler and the führer's answer, possibly offering the basis for some kind of settlement. "All hope is not gone anyhow for the moment," he wrote. He sent the documents in a locked box "which I know your key will fit."

Elizabeth followed her husband to Buckingham Palace on the twenty-ninth. She found him "very calm and cheerful despite the great anxiety that he is going through." In the midst of this high tension, the Duke of Windsor resurfaced in a burst of breathtaking presumptuousness, not to mention grandiosity, and sent a telegram to Hitler. Edward told Walter Monckton that "as a citizen of the world," he asked "not to plunge the world in war." According to the duke, Hitler replied by saying "he never wanted a war with England, and if it took place it would not be his fault."

The prospect of a conflict with Germany meant that Edward would need to be in Britain if only for his safety. A year earlier, George VI had confided to a senior diplomat that "one of the minor calamities" of war would be the return of the Duke of Windsor. In the last days of August, Monckton was already "speaking constantly to the Duke from 10 Downing Street, making elaborate arrangements" for the former king's return. He offered George VI's airplane and personal pilot to retrieve him from Antibes. After Edward refused to come "unless he was promised accommodation at Windsor or one of the royal castles," Monckton regretfully had to cancel the arrangements.

Still, the duke and duchess would certainly return to England on terms yet to be defined. "What <u>are</u> we going to do about Mrs. S?" Elizabeth wrote to Queen Mary on August 31. "Personally I do not wish to receive her at all, tho' it must depend on circumstances. . . . I am afraid that if they do return, they will wriggle their way into things. . . . It is a very difficult position & a great nuisance, with many pitfalls."

The Wehrmacht surged across the Polish border on September 1. Britain and France countered with an ultimatum stating that unless Hitler withdrew his troops by 11:00 A.M. on Sunday, September 3, they would declare war. On Saturday, George and Elizabeth accepted the inevitable. "We went to bed with sad hearts," she wrote. She later told Lionel Logue that the King scarcely slept because "he was so worried."

She awakened on Sunday morning at 5:30—the dawn of a radiant London day—saying to herself, "We only have a few hours of Peace left." From that instant until 11:00 A.M., "every moment was an agony," she wrote in a diary of the day's events. She clocked her last cup of tea and last bath "in peace" and thought of Britain's people: "their courage, their sense of humour, their sense of right and wrong." She believed that they would "come through the wicked things that war lets loose." At 10:30, she joined Bertie in his sitting room at Buckingham Palace.

The King began a diary that would continue throughout the war and for nearly two years afterward. When the eleven o'clock deadline came and went, "I had a certain feeling of relief," he wrote. Fifteen minutes later, Bertie and Elizabeth listened on the radio to Neville Chamberlain's announcement that Britain was at war. "He spoke so quietly, so sincerely, & was evidently deeply moved & unhappy," Elizabeth wrote. "I could not help tears running down my face." But she and her husband agreed that "if there was to be any freedom left in our world . . . we must face the cruel Nazi creed & rid ourselves of this continual nightmare of force." The King reassured himself that "the country is calm, firm & united behind its leaders."

Within minutes, they heard the "ghastly, horrible wailing of the air raid siren." They descended "with beating hearts" to a shelter in the Palace basement that had been prepared for them. "We felt stunned & horrified," Elizabeth wrote, "waiting for the bombs to fall." George VI noted that he and his wife were "very well trained in Air Raid Precautions" and took their gas masks along. When they returned to their rooms, "We prayed with all our hearts that Peace would come about," Elizabeth wrote. "Real peace not a Nazi peace."

George VI faced one of the biggest challenges of his reign that night: a radio broadcast at six P.M. to the empire. Logue arrived at the Palace with less than an hour to spare. As they reviewed the text, Logue marked pauses and substituted more easily pronounced words such as "ourselves" for "government."

"In this grave hour," King George VI began, "perhaps the most fateful in our history," he asked his listeners to vanquish the "selfish pursuit of power" that sought to keep people "in the bondage of fear." He held out the challenge to preserve "all that we ourselves hold dear." He called upon his people at home and abroad to "stand calm and firm and united in this time of trial." He warned that "there may be dark days ahead," as "war can no longer be confined to the battlefield." But he emphasized the rightness of their cause and urged "one and all" to "keep resolutely faithful to it" and prepare to make the necessary sacrifices. "With God's help, we shall prevail."

It was a stirring and beautiful speech that lasted just under six minutes. The King delivered it slowly, with sturdy solemnity. The prearranged pauses imposed control, and he stumbled only slightly toward the end, at the word "prevail." "That was good, Bertie," said the Queen, who was waiting for him outside the broadcasting room. Queen Mary told him that he "came through very well," adding, "of course I wept, yr voice is so like dear Papa's."

FRANCE DECLARED WAR WITHIN HOURS of Britain, and in the days afterward so did Australia, New Zealand, Canada, and South Africa, followed by the other Commonwealth countries. The Republic of Ireland, however, stubbornly maintained its neutrality. The subsequent eight months were known as the "Phoney War" because the anticipated bombings of Britain didn't happen, and Hitler held off further invasions. Still, the country remained on nerve-jangling high alert. Blackout paper covered all windows, trenches and air raid shelters scarred the parkland, and more than a million children were evacuated to the countryside. Gasoline rationing began at once. Food rationing followed several weeks later.

As a temporary measure, the King and Queen decided to keep the princesses in Scotland. They moved from the castle to the more sheltered Birkhall, under the care of the Queen's sister Rosie, who promised to "try my very best to smooth their lives," and the ever-faithful Alah Knight. Crawfie, who had been away on holiday, and Madame "Monty" Montaudon-Smith, the French tutor, joined them there, and their lessons resumed. When Henry Marten mailed Lilibet history assignments, she wrote essays that Crawfie sent to him at Eton.

George VI and Elizabeth keenly missed their daughters and telephoned them every day at six P.M. "Stick to the usual programme as far as you can Crawfie," said the Queen. It was a mercifully contented existence for the princesses, who had their cousins, Margaret Elphinstone and Jock's daughter Diana Bowes Lyon, for companionship. They rode on ponies and had picnics, and they signed on with the local Girl Guides troop, where they got to know evacuees from "the Gorbals," one of Glasgow's worst slums.

Some of them were housed around Balmoral and Abergeldie, and staff members taught their mothers practical household skills. At weekly sewing parties, the princesses "handed round teacups and cake, and talked away happily" to the ladies. But Lilibet was taken aback that her adored countryside unsettled the evacuees. "The children were terrified of the silence, scared to go into the woods, and frightened if they saw a deer," Crawfie recalled.

The London skies filled with gray barrage balloons—inflatable devices designed to disrupt low-flying dive bombers. Elizabeth described them as "swimming over our heads like pretty fishes when high & very like elephants & sheep when low!"

At Buckingham Palace, crystal chandeliers in the state rooms were taken down, packed, and sent to the country for storage, along with chinaware, furniture, and precious objects. The famous "gold plate" was removed from the basement strong room and similarly dispatched. The priceless art collection was tagged, catalogued, and buried in distant caves. Sandbags surrounded the Palace, where the guards now wore khaki uniforms and steel helmets instead of the traditional bearskins.

Windsor Castle was similarly fortified, its most valuable contents removed and hidden away. Antiaircraft guns were installed on the grounds and in barrels next to the Thames. Air raid shelters were fitted out in former basement dungeons. Glass-fronted cabinets were emptied and turned to face the walls, while dust sheets were draped over the remaining furniture. Workers lowered the chandeliers close to the floor to minimize breakage from bomb blasts. High-wattage lightbulbs were replaced with low-power substitutes. It took weeks to fully cover the castle's many windows with blackout paper and paint, along with wire mesh.

Two chambers were dug at the castle to hide the Crown Jewels. Unmarked cars from Garrard jewelers transported them from London to Windsor. There the King and Owen Morshead, the royal librarian, used pliers "to wrench the major gems off their settings." Wrapped in cotton wool, some jewels ended up in leather hatboxes, while others were tucked into cookie tins.

The King and Queen planned to live at Buckingham Palace "until the raids get bad, then probably to Windsor or further west," he told Queen Mary. But he decided that his mother was unsafe at Marlborough House or at Sandringham, a potential bombing target with its proximity to the seacoast. The day after the declaration of war, she moved to Gloucestershire to stay with her niece Mary, the Duchess of Beaufort, on the Badminton estate, where she would live for six years. Set on more than fifty thousand acres, Badminton approached Sandringham in scale, with eighteenth-century Palladian elegance. Badminton House had some twenty bedrooms and bathrooms as well as multiple drawing rooms and a massive library.

Even Queen Mary had to admit her cavalcade of automobiles filled with fifty-five servants and some seventy personal pieces of luggage was "quite a fleet." She and her entourage immediately displaced the Beauforts, who had to make do with two bedrooms and a sitting room. The tenth duke, known as "Master," was off with his cavalry regiment, the Blues, returning periodically for short visits. "I run Badminton with my own staff," Queen Mary explained. "Master & Mary are my guests." Once ensconced, she knitted, did crossword puzzles, and delved into the Beaufort family archives to label and organize every paper she could find.

With her usual industriousness, Queen Mary set to work stripping ivy from walls, a lifelong activity rooted in her horror of anything that obscured stonework and brickwork.

She even extended her tidying mania to "wooding"—her "unprofitable crusade against nature." On many days she would head to the "verge," the strip of woodland around the nine-mile perimeter of the Badminton parkland, to clear brush, brambles, branches, and tree limbs. In this task she enlisted the help of assorted servants, guardsmen in her security detail, and local children, as well as young evacuees from Birmingham and even houseguests. When they took breaks, she handed out cigarettes and contentedly smoked as she chatted.

Throughout the Phoney War, the septuagenarian matriarch visited London nearly every week and frequently had lunch at the Palace with Bertie and Elizabeth. In Gloucestershire, she visited troops, hospitals, schools, and factories. She promoted and participated in a "salvage scheme" to collect scrap iron, bottles, and other rubbish for the war effort. Not only did she strictly enforce rations at Badminton, "she used every piece of soap until it could be used no more," recalled Osbert Sitwell.

She also "discovered democracy," in the words of her longtime courtier Claud Hamilton, by making a habit of picking up hitchhikers in uniform. "Their surprise and gratitude brought pleasure to the Queen, who in turn enjoyed the military gossip and varied descriptions of Army life," according to her lady-in-waiting Cynthia Colville.

An imperious presence in her long gowns and multiple strands of pearls, she supplanted Mary Beaufort and presided at meals. After dinner, she would perch on a high armless chair placed in the middle of the drawing room, leafing through picture books. "Her personality and temperament permeated everything she did, said, or wore," wrote Sitwell. When the Duchess of Beaufort was later asked where Queen Mary resided in the house, she remarked, "She lived in all of it."

As THE KING AND QUEEN concentrated on matters of war—including the Soviet Union's invasion of Poland in mid-month—Edward and Wallis made their way from the south of France to England, arriving on Tuesday, September 1. They stayed with their friends Fruity and Lady Alexandra "Baba" Metcalfe. Two days later David went to Buckingham Palace for his first encounter with Bertie since he'd left England on December 11, 1936. Walter Monckton brokered the meeting "by excluding women as I explained to Alec Hardinge that it would save trouble if it were a stag party."

The brothers spent an hour together with "no recriminations on either side," noted the King, who thought his brother "looked very well & had lost the deep lines under his eyes." Edward displayed his familiar but unnerving swagger as he tried to "lay down the law" throughout their conversation. "He seemed to be thinking only of himself & had quite forgotten what he had done to his country in 1936," wrote George VI. For his part, the duke considered his brother to be "agreeably weak."

The Duke of Windsor had expressed a wish to serve his country in wartime, and they explored two options: a civilian job in Wales or a military position in Paris. Edward preferred the former, which would enable him to reestablish himself in Britain—an outcome neither Elizabeth nor George VI could condone. "I touched on the question of his reception" in Wales and "also that of his wife if she went with him. He had not thought about the job from that point of view," the King recorded. In the end, Edward agreed to take the military appointment in Paris.

The King told Neville Chamberlain that "the sooner he went to France the better for all concerned. He is not wanted here." He informed war minister Leslie Hore-Belisha that he "did not want D attached to any unit of the British Army." Unlike previous monarchs, he said that his predecessor "is not only alive, but very much so!"

General Sir Edmund Ironside, the chief of the imperial general staff, "put it very strongly" to the King "that in the British Military Mission in France," the duke "would get access to the secret plans of the French," and he "would pass them on to his wife." Ironside "did not trust her." George VI instructed Ironside that the chief of the Mission in Paris "must not tell [Edward] or show him anything really secret."

The mutual mistrust and harsh feelings between the duke and his family were now deeply ingrained. Such endearments as Bertie's "My dear old David" and Elizabeth's "My darling David" were unthinkable. The Windsors already knew that neither Queen Mary nor the Queen wished to see Wallis. Elizabeth had even taken the "precaution" of sending the duchess a message in France "saying that I was very sorry I could not receive her." As she explained to her old friend Prince Paul of Yugoslavia, "I thought it more honest to make things quite clear."

In their meeting at the Palace, David inquired about Princes Henry and George, but "he did not ask about his mother or any female member of the family." Over lunch with Bertie the next day, Queen Mary said she had "no intention" of seeing David "if she could avoid it." The King "was able to reassure her on this point." Elizabeth felt relieved that Wallis "kept away, & nobody saw her" and hoped that the duke "<u>at last</u> realizes that there is no niche for him here." She strongly believed that the British had not forgiven "what he did to this country, and they <u>HATE</u> her! . . . What a curse black sheep are in a family!" The Windsors had originally planned to stay for a month in England, but after the King made clear that length of time "would be difficult," they cut their visit to two weeks.

THAT AUTUMN AND WINTER THE King visited all units of the British Expeditionary Force before they left for the Continent, as well as Air Force headquarters and the Royal Navy fleet. In one Palace audience after another, he absorbed a great volume of classified information. "It is all an amazing puzzle," he wrote after three weeks of war.

He regarded Chamberlain as "a man of great vigour & stamina at the age of 71." Winston Churchill, brought into the cabinet by Chamberlain as First Lord of the Admiralty, was "very pleased to be back in harness again," George VI recorded after their first audience. He dutifully showed him the notes of his discussion with Roosevelt at Hyde Park, including the proposal for American naval bases on British colonies in the Caribbean. But the King felt uneasy, not least because of Churchill's support for Edward VIII during the abdication. By their third audience a month later, he noted that "Winston is difficult to talk to, but in time I shall get the right technique I hope."

One visitor who rubbed George VI the wrong way was Joseph P. Kennedy, the U.S. ambassador to the Court of St. James's since March 1, 1938. Joe and Rose Kennedy and their nine photogenic children had landed in Britain with a tremendous splash of publicity. Despite his Irish Catholic heritage, with its intrinsic suspicion of England, the wealthy businessman known for his pugnacious personality and gleaming smile had found himself enchanted by the British royal family. His wife, Rose, had basked even more in their proximity to the King and Queen, who turned on their high beams of charm.

During the Kennedys' first weekend at Windsor that April, scarcely a month after the ambassador had presented his credentials to the

King, the Queen impressed Joe with her intelligence—in his words she had "a fine head." Elizabeth seated Lilibet on the ambassador's right at one luncheon. Asked her favorite subject, the soon-to-be-twelve princess replied, "geography." She added, with an ingenuousness certain to please the envoy, that she had "just finished studying the Atlantic Coast of the U.S.A."

As a fervid supporter of appeasement, Joe Kennedy held views that initially lined up with those of the royal family and the establishment. When the British government's policy shifted after Hitler's occupation of Czechoslovakia, Kennedy's pro-appeasement stance hardened, and FDR increasingly marginalized him. The first hint of the chill came when the State Department wouldn't allow Kennedy to travel with the royal couple to the United States.

Six days after war was declared, the ambassador went to the Palace for a meeting with the King and Queen. What disturbed George VI during their conversation was Kennedy's belief that the war would be a "financial and material disaster" for Britain, and that Hitler should be allowed to occupy eastern Europe, which was "of little use" to Britain "from a monetary standpoint." Equally alarming was the ambassador's inability to comprehend the moral principles at stake: that a war with Germany was a matter of honor, despite its heavy toll on Britain and its allies. George VI worried that this downbeat view would influence the Roosevelt administration.

The King followed up with a stern letter to Kennedy expressing his irritation. He stressed that there were only "three really free peoples in the World"—the United States, France, and the British Empire. Two of these "great democracies" were now "fighting against all that we three countries hate & detest, Hitler & the Nazi regime and all that it stands for." He pointed out that England was part of Europe and defended its role as "the upholder of the rights of smaller nations." Contrary to Kennedy's assertions, he said his country's prestige in the world remained high.

Kennedy's reply acknowledged Britain's position in Europe and

expressed his esteem for the monarch. He softened his previous truc-
ulence to say the Roosevelt administration wished "to help England
and France economically but not to send American troops to Europe."

The King recognized that Kennedy's pessimistic and coldly calculated views ran counter to his own. The American ambassador would
continue to adamantly insist, in public and in private, that Germany's
superior military power would surely defeat Britain, and that American forces should never be deployed. George VI and Elizabeth saw Joe
Kennedy just once more socially, at a Buckingham Palace luncheon
after a scaled-back State Opening of Parliament in late November
1939.

Gone were the opulent robes and the carriage procession. The
peers in the House of Lords chamber wore morning suits or military
dress. The King and Queen arrived by car, he in his Admiral of the
Fleet uniform, she in black velvet and pearls for a ceremony of "stern
simplicity." A senior peer, Lord Chatfield, also in his admiral's uniform, bore the Imperial State Crown on a purple-covered salver. The
"deep significance" of the proceedings, said *The Times,* "was symbolized in the crown which remained visible but unworn while the King
put on his naval cap." The crown had been retrieved from its hiding
place at Windsor and would not be seen again until V-J Day in August
1945.

During lunch afterward at the Palace, Joe Kennedy thought the
King "didn't look very well, thin and drawn, and stuttered more than I
had ever seen him." The Queen was "sweet as usual," although Kennedy tried her patience by declining to eat the main course of roast
hare. "Madam, I don't like it," the famously blunt ambassador told her.
"What an honest man!" she said with a laugh and offered him pheasant instead. "I staggered through," he wrote.

The King would meet Joe Kennedy at a half dozen audiences between their luncheon and the ambassador's final visit in October 1940
before flying home to submit his resignation. Kennedy had by then
been sidelined for many months by Roosevelt, against whom he had
turned overtly antagonistic. Kennedy alienated many Britons whom he

had initially impressed. Harold Nicolson dismissed him as a "cowardly and conceited man." Halifax regarded him with "contempt."

Besides objecting to Kennedy's defeatism, George VI judged him "always the shrewd hard business man" who thought "in terms of dollars as against the terms of human feelings." He concluded that the ambassador was "a very disappointed & rather embittered man, to run down his own chief." George VI and Joseph P. Kennedy never met again.

THE QUEEN SOMETIMES ACCOMPANIED THE King during the Phoney War, but she was often on her own, carrying out visits to regiments, hospitals, schools, factories, and volunteer organizations to encourage their work and raise their morale. She tapped into the empathy she had shown as a teenager at the Glamis hospital during the First World War along with skills honed in her royal role. "I feel that it is so important that the people can feel free and able to tell me anything they like," she wrote to Prince Paul.

Lord Tweedsmuir, among others, began encouraging her to use the radio to "speak words of comfort and encouragement" to women at home and abroad. On November 11, 1939—Armistice Day, when there was no ceremony at the Cenotaph for the first time in two decades—she broadcast to the women of the empire.

Archbishop of Canterbury Cosmo Lang gave her some religious notes, but the "skeleton" of the remarks reflected her considered thinking and genuine feelings. Others who contributed included future prime minister Harold Macmillan, then working for the Ministry of Information.

The Queen sat alone before the microphone in the small room where her husband had broadcast his speech on the first day of the war. As Bertie listened on a radio nearby, Elizabeth spoke for seven minutes. She singled out the women of Poland, who deserved "deep and abiding sympathy" for having sustained "the first cruel and shattering blows" of the war, as well as the "gallant womanhood of France" called upon "to

share with us again the hardships and sorrows of war." She thanked
"from my heart" the women of "our great Empire" for taking on tasks
"whether at home or in distant lands, over every field of national service." Equally, she understood "the humbler part" played by so many
women, "the thousand and one worries and irritations in carrying on
war-time life in ordinary homes which are often so hard to bear."

She made common cause with her listeners by acknowledging that
"many of you have had to see your family life broken up," with husbands leaving to fight, and children being evacuated for their safety.
"The King and I know what it means to be parted from our children,"
she said. "We can sympathize with those of you who have bravely consented to this separation for the sake of your little ones." She also
thanked the women of the home front who had opened their doors to
evacuees. After she had finished, "God Save the King," "La Marseil-
laise," and the national anthem of Poland were played.

"It went off very well," Bertie wrote in his diary. The Queen was a
natural broadcaster, her clear voice soft, youthful, and soothing. Her
accent was unmistakably upper-class, but her delivery came across as
appealingly conversational. Sir John Reith, former director-general of
the BBC, called it "one of the best broadcasts that have ever gone out
to the world." Listeners as far away as Adelaide, Australia, tuned in
and sent messages of thanks.

Three weeks later, the King traveled to France for a weeklong tour
of the British Expeditionary Force—numbering more than 150,000
men. The conditions were cold and the itinerary exhausting, packed
with reviews and briefings. The King "very much enjoyed it, strenuous
though it was," wrote Alec Hardinge. "It gave pleasure and encouragement to the troops whose greatest enemy so far has been boredom."

George VI spent three days at the main headquarters and visited
the Maginot Line on the Saar front—the supposedly impregnable de-
fenses built by France in the 1930s to protect from a German invasion. Through binoculars, he saw the German positions some ten
miles away. "Lovely undulating country, with woods on the hills," he
wrote. He marveled at Hackenberg, the biggest fort, with accommoda-

tions for over one thousand men, where he inspected the underground electric railway and elevators to the gun turrets.

He found the French generals "very impressive"—a premature judgment, as it turned out. But he succumbed to the strain after a visit with forces commanded by General Sir Alan Brooke. On the drive back to headquarters, the King fell asleep in the car, which became "a bit awkward as the villages were full of troops and civilians cheering and saluting," Brooke recalled.

The biggest event that month for the King and Queen was Lilibet and Margaret's arrival in London on December 20. Elizabeth had spent one week with them at Birkhall in October, but George VI hadn't seen them for four months. They soon went to Sandringham for their last holiday break at the Big House. After skipping the Christmas broadcast the previous year, the King reluctantly agreed to resume his father's traditional address "if all goes well."

The speech was meant to gently shake Britons out of the passivity created by the absence of battlefield action. The King held up as a worthy example the troops he had met during his recent visit to the BEF. "They are waiting," he said, "and waiting is a trial of nerve and discipline."

But it was his peroration that caught the public imagination. It came from an obscure poem titled "God Knows" by Minnie Louise Haskins, a lecturer at the London School of Economics. The Queen had found it inspirational and brought it to the attention of the King. He was similarly moved, and immediately incorporated it into the speech.

In closing, he offered the poem's "message of encouragement" by saying, "And I said to the man who stood at the gate of the year, 'Give me a light that I may tread safely into the unknown.' And he replied, 'Go out into the darkness, and put your hand into the Hand of God. That shall be to you better than light, and safer than a known way.'"

The Haskins poem made the live nine-and-a-half-minute broadcast the King's most famous. But his delivery was more halting than usual. At the beginning he audibly gulped three times before saying "above." He

periodically stumbled before gathering himself to repeat a word he had
initially mangled. His palpable effort made his words more affecting as he
doggedly pressed on. "This is always an ordeal for me," he wrote in his
diary. "I don't begin to enjoy Christmas until after it is over."

THE KING AND QUEEN RETURNED to Buckingham Palace in mid-
January. They settled the girls at Royal Lodge, which offered seclusion
and safety as well as access to music, art, and dancing teachers from
London. "At their age, their education is too important to be neglected,"
wrote the King. George VI and Elizabeth continued to live and work at
Buckingham Palace and join the princesses on weekends in Windsor.

Toward the end of January 1940, the royal couple began hosting
Monday-night dinners for members of the government. "They go with
quite a swing," wrote George VI. On these evenings, as in other meetings with senior officials, the Queen kept abreast of wartime issues.
The King increasingly relied on her counsel, knowing that she understood the value of total discretion.

During this unnervingly static time, the King found the greatest
cheer in his regular visits with the armed forces. In March he endured
a "blizzard of snow and a strong gale" in Dover, where he inspected
vessels in the Dover Patrol that kept the sea clear for British troops
being ferried to and from France. After walking through the tunnels of
the fort inside the Dover cliffs, he watched nearly one thousand BEF
soldiers debarking from ships for short home leaves. They were in
such a hurry that most failed to recognize the man in a greatcoat on
the quayside. He stepped out to tear a pass from the voucher book of
one sergeant, who looked astonished when he realized that the King
was standing in as a ticket collector.

In audiences at the Palace, the King leaned the most on Chamberlain, who reassured him about the quickening pace of rearmament.
But in a burst of frustration, he wrote to the prime minister urging him
to get "new blood" into his government—evidence of George VI's
growing assertiveness. He found Churchill surprisingly good company,

telling "amusing" stories about the War Cabinet. Halifax was "his usual calm self" even when delivering disappointing news.

The King was vexed by Roosevelt's failure to deliver on promises made at Hyde Park. He felt "very angry," he wrote in his diary in mid-March, "that the U.S. Administration & the U.S.A. are going to do nothing until after the Presidential election" in November.

Everything changed for Britain on Tuesday, April 9, with the news that Germany had invaded Norway and overtaken Denmark. It was an unanticipated lightning operation—a "Blitzkrieg"—comprising swiftly moving columns of tanks and sustained bombing from the air. The British and French governments sent troops to Norway, only to withdraw when they were overwhelmed in early May. Days later, Parliament rounded on Chamberlain and delivered a vote of no confidence.

On Friday, May 10—also without warning—Germany invaded Holland, Belgium, and Luxembourg and aggressively attacked France. As the prime minister scrambled to stay in office by forming a multi-party national government, Clement Attlee, leader of the Labour Party, refused to participate as long as Chamberlain was the leader. The King's first choice for his replacement was Viscount Halifax, who declined on the grounds that he couldn't effectively govern while serving in the House of Lords. He told the King he would be "a shadow or a ghost in the Commons, where all the real work took place." At that point, George VI knew the "only person" who could take the job was Winston Churchill, "who had the confidence of the country." Churchill came to Buckingham Palace and pledged to form a government. "He was full of fire & determination," noted the King.

Both George VI and Elizabeth greatly regretted losing Chamberlain. The Queen wrote him a sorrowful letter expressing how much they had valued his "support and comfort" during "these last desperate and unhappy years." She added that when Lilibet heard his resignation speech on the radio she said, "I <u>cried</u>, mummy."

On an April 1940 visit to a munitions factory in the Midlands, King George VI examines a tracer shell while Queen Elizabeth talks to a factory inspector.

PART FIVE

The War Years

*"The challenge is not to fight to survive,
but to fight to win."*

*"We have now had a personal experience
of German barbarity."*

King George VI, Queen Elizabeth, and Prime Minister Winston Churchill
inspecting the bomb damage at Buckingham Palace on September 10, 1940.

TWENTY-EIGHT

Sharing the Suffering

THUS BEGAN THE MOST TUMULTUOUS AND HARROWING PERIOD IN THE lives of the King and Queen and their daughters. In mid-May 1940, on instructions from the Queen, Crawfie bundled Lilibet and Margaret out of Royal Lodge and into well-fortified Windsor Castle. Three days later a company of Grenadier Guards soldiers arrived to provide additional protection for the girls.

Events on the Continent advanced with blistering speed in May and June. First Holland fell, followed ten days later by Belgium. At the same time, the French army was collapsing after German troops breached the Maginot Line that had impressed the King less than six months earlier. On May 21, George VI wrote in his diary, "The French command is apparently hopeless." The German army had roared out of the densely forested Ardennes region, which the French generals had considered "an impossible place for an army to deploy from," wrote the King. "However, the Germans have done it." (Churchill had predicted the Ardennes' vulnerability back in August 1939.)

The Germans' powerful, multipronged attack put the British Expeditionary Force into a vise. Hemmed in on three sides, the British troops had to fight their way to the French coast at Dunkirk. There, as Prime Minister Churchill told the King, he planned to evacuate the entire army across the English Channel, leaving behind all their equipment—"guns, tanks, ammunition & all stores." The potential consequences were "appalling," wrote George VI, "as the loss of life will probably be immense." The initial estimate was that only about fifty thousand men could be saved in such an evacuation from France.

Against this background, George VI prepared for a major radio speech on May 24, Empire Day. He practiced for hours at the Palace with Lionel Logue. On the appointed evening, the King took time shortly before the broadcast "to practise the emphasis on two or three of the more difficult passages."

"On Empire Day last year I spoke to you," he began his broadcast, recalling his speech from Canada when the world was at peace, and when he had believed that "the grievous onslaught of war" could be avoided.

Logue listened as the King spoke for twelve minutes, managing "hitherto impossible" words without effort. "The decisive struggle is now upon us," George VI said. "It is no mere territorial conquest that our enemies are seeking. It is the overthrow, complete and final, of this Empire and of everything for which it stands, and after that the conquest of the world."

When he ended by saying "with God's help we shall not fail," Logue clasped the King's hands to commend his success. The Queen entered the room, kissed her husband, and told him he had been "grand." He knew as much. "I was very pleased with the way I delivered it," he wrote that night. "It was easily my best effort. How I hate broadcasting!!"

In the early evening two days later, an extraordinary armada of some seven hundred civilian craft of all sorts and sizes—from fishing boats to small pleasure yachts—set off across the Channel to join Royal Navy vessels for a remarkable evacuation from France that the King called "an epic for history." Churchill and his military leaders—operating from the tunnels under Dover Castle that George VI had inspected the previous March—displayed imagination and determination in organizing the navy, air force, and army to carry out the rescue they called Operation Dynamo. They were also providentially assisted when Hitler inexplicably stopped his tanks outside Dunkirk for twenty-four hours. The evacuation took nine days and brought home 338,226 soldiers, including some 140,000 French, Belgian, and Dutch. George VI was on tenterhooks throughout the operation, keeping a daily tally of the number brought to safety.

On the last day, June 4, Churchill gave one of the most stirring speeches of his career, remembered mainly for its peroration: "We shall go on to the end, we shall fight in France, we shall fight on the seas and oceans, we shall fight with growing confidence and growing strength in the air. We shall defend our Island, whatever the cost may be. We shall fight on the beaches, we shall fight on the landing grounds, we shall fight in the fields and in the streets, we shall fight in the hills. We shall never surrender." The words chimed with George VI, who paraphrased in his diary the prime minister's vow to "go on fighting to the end, even after this country has been laid waste, we shall fight from the New World to redeem the Old."

In a matter of weeks, the King had forged an enduring partnership with Churchill, about whom he had initially felt doubt. "I cannot yet think of Winston as P.M.," he had written the day after Churchill took office. He was, of course, well known to George VI, who had worked for him at the Admiralty in 1916 when Churchill had first admitted him to a clandestine War Room. They had met in audiences and socialized over the years: The Churchills had attended the wedding of Bertie and Elizabeth and had been entertained at Windsor Castle and Balmoral by George V and Queen Mary. On several occasions, the future king had stalked stags with the future prime minister on the hills at Balmoral.

Elizabeth had forever felt indebted to Churchill for suggesting to her over dinner at Maggie Greville's in 1924 that she and Bertie travel to East Africa.

Winston Churchill was now sixty-five—twenty-one years older than the King. The new prime minister was, in the words of his biographer Andrew Roberts, "superbly prepared" for his wartime challenges "in experience, psychology, and foresight." He also possessed "a calmness under pressure and a sense of humour that allowed him to crack jokes however bad the situation had got." These traits in particular helped build his alliance with the King and leaven their gloomiest moods. The prime minister entrusted the King with his government's deepest secrets, including the Enigma messages detailing German communications from the code breakers at Bletchley Park. (President Roosevelt wouldn't learn of this highly sensitive intelligence until the United States entered the war late in 1941.) Above all, George VI and Churchill shared a passionate resolve to preserve democracy against the authoritarian Nazi juggernaut.

ITALY DECLARED WAR ON GREAT Britain and France on June 10, 1940, and days later France formally surrendered to Germany. On the seventeenth, the new leader of the French government, Marshal Philippe Pétain—"a defeatist . . . Aged 84" in the words of George VI—signed an armistice. Britain was now on its own in Europe. "Personally, I feel happier now that we have no allies to be polite to & to pamper," the King wrote to his mother.

Britain's solitary position prompted Churchill to deliver another memorable speech the next day. At stake in the coming Battle of Britain, he said, was "the survival of Christian civilization. . . . The whole fury and might of the enemy must very soon be turned on us. . . . If we fail, then the whole world, including the United States . . . will sink into the abyss of a new Dark Age." Britons must prevail, he said, so that "if the British Empire and its Commonwealth last for a thousand years, men will still say, 'This was their finest hour.'"

It became the King's duty to deal with imperiled monarchs on the Continent. The first distress call came from fifty-nine-year-old Queen Wilhelmina of the Netherlands at five A.M. on May 13, 1940, begging in vain for air support to help defend her country. As German soldiers made a determined effort to capture her, a British destroyer swept her off to England.

The King met her at Liverpool station and brought her to Buckingham Palace, where she was reunited with her daughter, Princess Juliana, and son-in-law, Prince Bernhard (affectionately called "Bernilo" by the British royal family), and their two little girls. The redoubtable Queen Wilhelmina—a widow since the death of her husband, Prince Henry, in 1934—arrived wearing a tin hat supplied by the ship's commander. She was feeling "very upset & had brought no clothes with her," observed the King.

When the Dutch army surrendered two days later, Wilhelmina rallied her government-in-exile on the terrace at the Palace. George VI was conferring with an official when he spotted them through a window and remarked, "One very seldom happens to see a reigning Sovereign talking to her Ministers in one's own country." That evening Wilhelmina delivered a bracing radio address calling for resistance against the Nazis—the first of many such broadcasts that established her as Holland's symbol of freedom and independence.

Queen Mary, who had entertained Wilhelmina and Juliana for tea at Balmoral five years earlier with Elizabeth and Lilibet, listened on her radio. When the Dutch national anthem played afterward, Queen Mary respectfully stood to attention. She traveled to London the next morning for luncheon at the Palace and found Wilhelmina "very calm & courageous & very interesting as to her unpleasant experiences."

George VI considered Queen Wilhelmina to be "a remarkable woman & wonderfully courageous after all that she has gone through." Since the Dutch queen was quite stout, no appropriate clothing could be found in the Palace. Elizabeth asked her dressmakers to produce some outfits. Wilhelmina chose a "sensible black hat with a brim" and opted for practical suits.

The King settled her in a friend's house on Eaton Square, while Elizabeth thoughtfully suggested the private chapel at Buckingham Palace for the christening of her nine-month-old granddaughter, Princess Irene. Juliana and the children soon moved to Canada for the rest of the war, while her husband, Bernhard, stayed in Britain with his mother-in-law and later successfully commanded Dutch resistance forces.

George VI's anxiety over the fate of the Norwegian royal family was considerably more intense, not least because they were such close kin. King Haakon VII ("Uncle Charles" to the British royals) had been widowed in August 1938 when his wife, Queen Maud, was stricken with heart failure at age sixty-eight—the last of George V's siblings to die. Their thirty-six-year-old son, Crown Prince Olav, had been a good friend since childhood, and George VI had been the best man at his first cousin's wedding.

Haakon and Olav evaded the Nazis through Norway's forests and mountains for nearly two months until they were rescued by a British warship. Olav's wife, Crown Princess Märtha, and their three young children, escaped to neutral Sweden. Even there, staying with her family was dangerous for Princess Märtha. Franklin D. Roosevelt—who had met Olav and Märtha in Washington shortly before the outbreak of war—intervened by offering her safe passage to the United States on an American ship. After an initial stay in the White House, Märtha and the children spent their war years at a spacious home in suburban Bethesda, Maryland. She avidly promoted the Norwegian cause with the American public and government, especially with Roosevelt, who was famously smitten with her.

On June 10, the King welcomed Haakon and Olav to Buckingham Palace, which was beginning to resemble an exclusive refugee encampment. He gave them rooms on the ground floor and lent Uncle Charles clothes from his own wardrobe. Cousin Olav was dispatched to the royal tailor for uniforms and suits.

Like Wilhelmina and Bernhard, Haakon and Olav established their Norwegian exile government in London, with an office in Kensington. George VI and Elizabeth enjoyed their company, but she told Queen Mary she was worried that the Norwegians were burdening the "depleted" Palace staff. "Uncle Charles and Olav seem to have completely settled down here!" Elizabeth wrote. "It is rather a bore <u>never</u> to be alone."

WITH THE FALL OF FRANCE on June 22, the Duke and Duchess of Windsor faced capture unless they left the country. Once more, David became a recurring problem for George VI and Elizabeth. After briefly disappearing from sight, he and Wallis surfaced in Spain. Although formally neutral, the fascist government led by Generalissimo Francisco Franco sympathized with Germany. In a meeting with Churchill on the evening of June 25, the King and Queen expressed their strong opposition to the duke's permanent return to Britain. "We must guard against his becoming a champion of the disgruntled," they said. "We told him we could not meet 'her.'"

Less than a week later, they were taken aback by two importunate telegrams from the Duke of Windsor in Madrid demanding that "he could only return to this country on the condition that his status & financial position were first regulated." In essence, he wanted an official job in Britain, extra compensation from the government to make up for losing his French tax-free status, and an ironclad assurance that Wallis would be received by the King and Queen at Buckingham Palace and elsewhere in Britain. Walter Monckton told Harold Nicolson that the idea of paying income tax to England "filled [Edward] with appalling gloom." The King and Queen were astonished that Edward could be obsessed by pettiness at such a dangerous time for Britain. "He is going to be very difficult I can see," wrote George VI.

Under pressure from the British government, the Windsors relocated to Lisbon. Portugal was neutral but also infested with German spies. Churchill and other top officials were aware of intrigues by Hitler's minions—chiefly Joachim von Ribbentrop, by then serving as foreign minister—to return the Windsors to Spain, under coercion if necessary, where Nazi operatives could more easily exploit their Nazi sympathies.

A series of German telegrams asserted that the duke was a "firm supporter of a peaceful compromise with Germany," that he believed "with certainty" that a bombing campaign would "make England ready for peace," and that he "spoke strongly against Churchill and against this war." Ribbentrop planned to "accommodate any desire" of

Edward's upon a successful German invasion of Britain, including "the assumption of the English throne" with Wallis as his queen.

George VI faced two unpalatable alternatives: that the Windsors return to Britain, where they might form a "movement for peace"—essentially a fifth-column Nazi front—or that they stay in Europe and become German pawns. Churchill laid bare his concerns in a draft memorandum to the prime ministers of the dominions. The duke's "activities" on the Continent "in recent months have been causing HM and myself grave uneasiness as his inclinations are well-known to be pro-Nazi, and he may become a centre of intrigue. We regard it as a real danger that he should move freely on the Continent." The message that was actually sent was less stark, but the concerns were equally grave about potentially treasonous activities by the duke and duchess.

Churchill decisively broke the impasse on July 3 in an audience with George VI. "I did not see what job he could have here in this country, & that 'she' would not be safe here," the King recorded in his diary. "W. suggested his going to the Bahamas as Governor during the war." George VI initially balked at the unconventional idea and asked the prime minister to seek guidance from Lord Lloyd, the colonial secretary. When Churchill offered Edward the position without further consultation, the King grumbled that it was "most annoying as the matter has not been thought out." Churchill convinced him that the posting was a necessary measure during wartime and that "D. must leave Lisbon" as soon as possible. The duke promptly accepted the job.

George VI conceded that "this arrangement may be the best one in the end." He told Churchill, "I am sure D could do no good here, as 'she' would be a nuisance." The King reassured his mother that David "must have a job during the War." While he disliked the appointment, he told her that the former king's "return here would be an embarrassment to everybody."

Elizabeth acquiesced as well, but she couldn't resist sharing her displeasure with Lord Lloyd about the unsuitability of the duchess as an envoy's wife with "three husbands alive." Instead of "looking up" at a representative in a British colony, "the Duchess of Windsor is looked upon as the lowest of the low," she wrote. Alec Hardinge told her the posting was "the lesser of two evils," adding that "she will do harm wherever she is, but there is less scope for it in a place like the Bahamas than elsewhere."

The King kept worrying about Edward's potential treachery, especially after he read a report on July 7 from Sir Alexander Cadogan, a foreign office undersecretary. According to Cadogan, a credible source had learned that the Germans expected the Windsors to help with propaganda against Britain before forming an opposition government in England. Churchill assured George VI in mid-July that he would write to both of the Windsors "telling them that they must be careful what they say in the Bahamas," and as representatives of the government they "must conform" to its policies. "Before as a free lance he could say what he liked," noted the King, "& his ideas were not always ours."

The duke and duchess vacillated for weeks about their departure from Lisbon, issuing demands for their travel arrangements that infuriated the King. In an audience with Lord Lloyd on July 18, he complained about the "preposterous propositions" Edward was making. "I said to [Lloyd] D has got to obey orders now. From telegrams I have read D has forgotten that we are at war & that the authorities here are busy with great problems." It took yet another visit from Walter Monckton to persuade the Windsors to leave on August 1 as they had promised.

Nevertheless, there were strong indications that Edward kept on intriguing with German emissaries. The day after their departure, Baron Oswald von Hoyningen-Huene, the German minister in Lisbon, reported to Ribbentrop that the duke had promised to "remain in continuing communication" with his Portuguese host, who was, in fact, a German agent. Edward "had agreed with him on a code word" to signal his return to Europe, which would be "possible at any time."

A week later, Monckton reported to George VI that "D. had different ideas about the war to what we had, & that he would be quite ready to make peace," George VI recorded. "D's attitude was a selfish one, as all he had to live for now was his private & comfortable life."

THE FIRST INKLING OF THE Battle of Britain came at the end of June, with scattered German air attacks on ships and south coast ports. At the outset, these attacks inflicted little damage. But the bombings intensified over the summer when the Germans tried to destroy the Royal Air Force and hit factories, airfields, and other defense facilities to clear the way for Operation Sea Lion, Hitler's planned invasion of Britain. The RAF had spent weeks bombing German positions in the fight to save France, Norway, Belgium, and Holland. Now they turned their attention to the Luftwaffe's bombers and escort fighter planes flying to their homeland.

The pummeling by German forces accelerated on July 10 with widespread raids on convoys in the English Channel as well as attacks on port cities. During the day, dogfights between British and German fighters over southern England transfixed those down below. At his home in Kent, Harold Nicolson witnessed the soundless waves of German bombers, "twenty little silver fish in arrow formations," as well as "the rattle of machine gun fire as we see two Spitfires attacking a Heinkel."

George VI and Elizabeth took a train to Hull in East Yorkshire on August 1, and for the first time they "talked with people whose houses had been bombed." The King began keeping track of RAF and enemy losses with an "Air Activity" log in his diary.

Then, on Tuesday, August 13, he wrote, "This looks like the beginning of the German Air Blitzkrieg." It was indeed a deadly new phase of ferocious aerial bombardments, with nearly fifteen hundred daylight assaults. Hermann Göring, the commander of the Luftwaffe, called it "Eagle Day." He told Hitler it would take less than a week to crush the RAF.

Churchill silenced that claim in an extraordinary speech on the night of August 20, taunting the führer with Britain's bravery and strength. He pledged retaliation against Germany's military installations and factories that "will continue upon an ever-increasing scale until the end of the war." And he praised the "British airmen who, undaunted by odds, unwearied in their constant challenge and mortal danger, are turning the tide of the World War by their prowess and by their devotion. Never in the field of human conflict was so much owed by so many to so few."

Toward the end of August, the Luftwaffe bombers fanned out over Leicester, Birmingham, Liverpool, and other cities as the toll of death and destruction began to climb. On Saturday, August 24, George VI and his family hurried to the air raid shelter under Windsor Castle after midnight and stayed for two hours as "the enemy dropped bombs round about . . . without doing any damage." The shelter had been specially constructed for maximum protection underneath the Brunswick Tower near the East Terrace. Elizabeth hated having to "descend into the bowels of the earth" to seek safety.

The next day, Germany hit London's outer perimeter and suburbs, and Britain launched its first bombing raid on Berlin. Between August 24 and September 6, Germany targeted Britain with more than one thousand raids a day. As the RAF's Spitfire pilots did their best to fight off the Luftwaffe, British bombers counterpunched with sorties against military and industrial targets in Germany.

On Saturday, September 7, Germany made what Churchill biographer Andrew Roberts described as a "major strategic blunder," shifting from daylight raids aimed at airfields and other military structures to the launch of a fifty-seven-day assault on London, soon to be known as the Blitz. It was a savage campaign, carried out mostly at night, to terrorize the citizenry and destroy vital infrastructure.

As the King and his family spent the weekend at Windsor Castle, they were well aware of the fierce onslaught throughout Saturday and Sunday against the Thames docks and east London by two hundred airplanes each night. The indiscriminate bombing inflicted severe damage on dwellings and warehouses and ignited raging fires. An estimated four hundred Londoners perished, and some fourteen hundred were seriously injured. The King and Queen and Lilibet and Margaret stayed most of Sunday night in the castle's roomy but gloomy shelter.

On reaching London the next morning, George VI learned that an unexploded bomb had landed next to Buckingham Palace below his own study and the Queen's sitting room and dressing room on the north side of the building. The home secretary strongly advised that it would be "wiser for us to remain at Windsor with the bombing of London going on at night."

George VI and Elizabeth did not spend another night at the Palace until fourteen months later, in November 1941, although they continued to work there during the days. (Haakon and Olav finally left the Palace as well, moving to a house in the country.)

At Windsor, the royal family slept mainly in the ground-floor rooms of the Victoria Tower, which had been fortified with concrete and sandbags surrounded by scaffolding. They retreated to the deep underground shelter only when the bombings became "really intense."

That first Monday in September 1940 marked the start of a dramatically dangerous week for the King and Queen. Their actions on those days also set the pattern for their leadership during the most critical year of the war and put to the test their nerves, perseverance, and courage. Britain itself had become a battlefield, its citizens as integral to the country's defense as its frontline military.

Men and women operated antiaircraft guns and served as air raid wardens and in ambulance crews. More than a million men who couldn't serve in the armed forces joined the Local Defence Volunteers, which became the Home Guard. Women signed up for their own branches of the army, navy, and air force. The danger from the air meant that everyone—monarch as well as commoner—was on an equal footing. Nothing symbolized that new dynamic more than the attack on the home of the sovereign.

On the morning of Monday, September 9, the King spent three hours with Captain Euan Wallace, commissioner for the London Region, touring bomb-damaged neighborhoods in the East End and south of the Thames. They saw burnt-out docks and visited several shelters. In one of them, fifty people had died, including three children whose grieving mother the King comforted. As he watched people removing their belongings from a damaged apartment house, a woman cried out, "Are we downhearted?" "No!" came the hearty reply from her neighbors.

Captain Wallace was struck by the King's interest in talking to "all and sundry." He "insisted on carrying out the program in full," Wallace wrote. "It is almost impossible to believe that he is the same man who took the oath before the Privy Council less than four years ago." Back at the Palace, the King spent time working in his study. While he was having lunch, a delayed-action bomb detonated in Green Park. "We felt the concussion all right," he wrote.

The bomb embedded next to Buckingham Palace exploded at 1:25 A.M. on Tuesday, September 10, while the King and Queen were at Windsor Castle. Its force catapulted a block of Portland stone weighing nearly two tons twenty feet into the air. The high-explosive charge severely damaged the swimming pool built by the King for his daughters two years earlier in the northwest corner of the Palace. The blast shattered all the windows in the north front. The wire netting on the broken windows of the King's and Queen's rooms prevented major interior damage, although the floors were covered with glass and other debris. George VI felt distinctly unnerved that "I had been sitting in my room the day before without knowing that it was a time bomb." It was the first of nine direct hits on the Palace and its grounds between that day and late June 1944.

The Queen accompanied the King into London later that day to inspect the damage and collect belongings to take back to Windsor. They also hosted the first of what would become weekly luncheons with Winston Churchill that replaced the formal audiences typical of the King and his first minister. To ensure confidentiality, no servants were allowed. It was self-service from a side table, which also fostered a more relaxed mood. They helped themselves to grilled fish or chicken, and poured whisky and bourbon from small decanters. There were plenty of cigarettes for the King and two or three cigars for Churchill.

George VI called his prime minister "Winston"—a familiarity he didn't extend to the three other men who held that high office during his reign. (In his diary he referred to "Chamberlain" and "Baldwin" and, later, "Attlee.") Churchill savored what he called the King's "gracious intimacy." George VI appreciated that Churchill "does tell me what is in his mind."

Even more unusual was the Queen's regular attendance at the luncheons—an acknowledgment of the prime minister's trust. Churchill told the King how much he valued "our weekly luncheons in poor old bomb-battered Buckingham Palace" as well as knowing "that in Yr. Majesty and the Queen there flames the spirit that will never be daunted by peril, nor wearied by unrelenting toil." George VI's diary is silent on the Queen's role in these wide-ranging discussions—"many things both of a serious & of a frivolous nature" in the King's words—nor did Churchill reveal what, if anything, she contributed.

Many years later, Elizabeth said that the King "told me everything," wrote William Shawcross. "There was only us there. So obviously he had to tell one things. But one was so dreadfully discreet. . . . You knew something and you couldn't say a word about it, when you heard people talking absolute nonsense." It is unclear if Elizabeth was privy to the secret Enigma intelligence from the government's code breakers or, later in the war, the development of the atomic bomb. Given the degree to which the King confided in her, she may well have known.

After their initial lunch, the King and Queen took Churchill outside to show him the damage. Tommy Lascelles arranged for forty journalists and photographers to be present as well. "It will make a fine story for the American press," Lascelles told Harold Nicolson. The trio stood in front of the swimming pool's ruined pavilion and the twisted remnant of the diving board. The King was in his naval uniform and the Queen wore a pastel dress, coat, and hat with smartly turned-up brim. Churchill sported his trademark homburg and bow tie. The photos were so compelling that the King and Queen selected one for their Christmas card that year.

The next day George VI returned to the East End, and the Queen joined him for the first time to tour the blighted poor neighborhoods of Camberwell, Lewisham, and Lambeth. "The usual collapsed houses & homeless people who had lost all their belongings," George VI recalled. "But here again their fortitude in adversity is amazing." As the royal couple passed one heavily damaged block of workers' flats, a small crowd cheered them and sang, "There'll always be an England."

They made an unscheduled stop that underlined the risk of such outings. When the air raid alarm sounded, a police car sped them to a basement room in the Lewisham Police Station. As the King and Queen entered the dimly lit shelter, the uniformed policemen, court officials, and other staff looked at them with disbelief, and then burst into cheers. The royal couple sat down, George VI lit a cigarette, and they waited to have some tea.

Before tea could be prepared, the "all clear" sounded, but the King insisted on staying. Canteen workers served them biscuits along with tea in thick china cups, and the Queen said it was delicious. Such spontaneous moments would be a regular feature of their wartime tours, linking them to the people in unforeseen ways. As the Queen later recalled, "I think we must have taken refuge in every single police station in London. We were always given a cup of very, very strong tea."

That Friday—the thirteenth as the fates would have it—they arrived at the Palace in a downpour. After Tuesday's explosion blew out the windows in their rooms, they had moved their quarters into a suite overlooking the quadrangle—the central courtyard in the Palace. At midday a "Red Warning" for an air raid in progress sounded, signaling that they should hurry to the shelter. The King was in his new sitting room, and he asked Elizabeth to first remove a lash from his eye.

At that moment, George VI wrote, they "heard an aircraft making a zooming noise above us, saw two bombs falling past . . . then heard 2 resounding crashes as the bombs fell in the quadrangle about 30 yds away." Elizabeth recalled in a letter to Queen Mary "the noise of aircraft diving at great speed, and then the scream of a bomb" was followed by the explosion and "a great column of smoke & earth thrown up into the air." The King and Queen both remembered that they "looked foolishly at each other," in Elizabeth's words, and seconds later dashed to the safety of an interior red-carpeted corridor. Another explosion followed, and they stood still with a pair of Palace pages. "We all wondered why we weren't dead," the King wrote.

They miraculously escaped injury, not to mention death. Except for family and a few members of the household, they didn't tell anyone what a close call it had been. They even kept Churchill in the dark until he was writing his memoirs after the war. As Churchill wrote then, "Had the windows been closed instead of open, the whole of the glass would have splintered into the faces of the King and Queen, causing terrible injuries."

But everyone knew that the Palace had been bombed. Harold Nicolson was at his office in the Ministry of Information when he encountered Walter Monckton. "They have just dive bombed Buckingham palace and hit it three times," Monckton whispered. "The King's safe." The most Nicolson could glean was that "the King and Queen were in their own rooms and not in the shelter and were 'much shaken.'"

The Times ran eyewitness accounts of the airplane diving out of a cloudbank, the pilot flying low over the Palace, releasing the whistling bombs, and quickly disappearing back into the cloudbank. The two bombs in the quadrangle made huge craters, and a ruptured water main created a ten-foot-high fountain. Most of the windows on the south side of the inner quadrangle were shattered, and bomb fragments scarred the walls. The worst damage was to the private chapel in the south wing of the Palace, which was destroyed by a direct hit, its alabaster altar shattered and organ broken beyond repair.

George VI and Elizabeth took a quick look at the wreckage, in the words of one member of the household, "calmly making their way about it, like people crossing a river on stepping-stones!" They then went down to the shelters, a series of fortified basement rooms, to check on all the servants.

The shelter for George VI and Elizabeth—originally a housemaid's room—had an incongruous décor. Oriental rugs were strewn about on the linoleum floor. Against one wall stood a large old-fashioned house-maid's sink, and a table formerly piled with sheets and towels had been arranged for the Queen with an oval mirror, ivory brushes, and a comb. Tufted upholstered sofas were juxtaposed with a Victorian table, a Regency settee, and antique gilt chairs. Old Master Dutch landscape paintings decorated the walls. The Queen later said she "had developed an unreasonable dislike for these little scenes of cows and bridges over canals."

When the "all clear" sounded, the King and Queen picked them-selves up and went out as planned for a tour of damage in East and West Ham, two neighborhoods in east London. One official who accompanied them said that knowledge of the bombing endured by the King and Queen "made their reception even more enthusiastic." "Their Majesties appeared to be quite unshaken by their experience," observed *The Times*.

The appearances were deceptive. Elizabeth told Queen Mary that as they walked down an empty street past evacuated houses, it felt like "a dead city." Through the broken windows "one saw all the poor little possessions, photographs, beds, just as they were left." They visited a bombed school that had collapsed on five hundred people, with two hundred still buried in the ruins. "It does affect me seeing this terrible and senseless destruction," she wrote. "I think that really I mind it much more than being bombed myself. The people are marvellous and full of fight."

George VI described the Palace bombing as "a ghastly experience, & I don't want it to be repeated. It certainly teaches one to 'take cover' on all future occasions, but one must be careful not to become 'dugout minded.'" That night he slept well and hoped "for no ill effects" from being targeted. But over the weekend two "dud" bombs hit the Palace in their absence. One landed near a bathtub in the Belgian Suite on the ground floor where Haakon and Olav had recently stayed. Demoli-tion experts blew it up at the far end of the garden.

George VI dutifully traveled to the Palace the first three days of the following week, which proved a more disorienting experience than he anticipated. "I should not put it down in writing," he wrote, "but I did feel the reaction after the bombing. . . . I quite disliked sitting in my room in B.P. on Monday & Tuesday. I found myself unable to read, always in a hurry, & glancing out of the window." He soon felt better, with no lasting post-traumatic effects. Indeed, the King and Queen continued to conduct their tours during air raids, with fighter planes battling overhead.

On Thursday, September 19, George VI and Elizabeth went to Chelsea, Fulham, and Marylebone on the western side of London. *The Times* noted that they moved freely among the people "with whom they are sharing—and with the same cool tenacity—the peril from the air. . . . Men, women, and children brushed shoulders with Their Majesties as they made their way among scenes of destruction." In Fulham, George VI and Elizabeth walked with difficulty, hemmed in by the pressure of a crowd in a narrow alley. "Let us give three cheers for our King," shouted a workman. The response was "thunderous."

Hitler may have been hell-bent on killing the monarch and consort, but he failed to anticipate the galvanizing effect of the Buckingham Palace bombings. Churchill told the House of Commons that the attacks "unite the King and Queen to their people by new and sacred bonds of common danger."

In a public message to the prime minister, George VI said, "Like so many other people we have now had a personal experience of German barbarity, which only strengthens the resolution of all of us to fight through to final victory." He told his mother privately that in comforting the bereaved and homeless in bombed areas, "we have both found a new bond with them as Buckingham Palace has been bombed as well as their homes, & nobody is immune from it."

Elizabeth went even further: "I'm glad we've been bombed. It makes me feel I can look the East End in the Face." There had been concern in the government about bitterness and resentment among East Enders. Harold Nicolson had even heard that "the King and Queen were booed" on their tour two days before the Palace bombing. Their new solidarity and repeated displays of compassion quelled discontent. Again and again, they returned to the poorest neighbor-hoods. The Queen also scoured the attics and storerooms of royal resi-dences for spare beds and clothing. She dispatched sixty suites of royal furniture for residences to shelter the homeless.

THE FIRST PRIORITY OF THE King and Queen was protecting their daughters and ensuring that even in wartime they would enjoy a rela-tively normal life. During the summer of 1940, there had been some discussion about possibly sending Lilibet and Margaret overseas. In mid-June, the King asked Churchill if the princesses would be "a lia-bility in case of invasion. He said, 'No.'" The Queen famously declared when asked if her daughters should be evacuated, "The children could not go without me. I could not possibly leave the King, and the King would never go." She emphasized to Harold Nicolson the importance of "personal patriotism," saying, "That is what keeps us going. I should die if I had to leave."

But George VI and Elizabeth took measures for their own safety and the security of their daughters. The King's "Brontosaurus," his special armored Humber, ferried him around London. Another car was fitted out with small armchairs for the princesses, who took a trial trip around Windsor's Home Park with Crawfie and one of their corgis.

The King set up shooting ranges at Windsor and in the Bucking-ham Palace garden so they could practice with rifles, pistols, and even a Tommy gun. The King "always felt that one day one will be called upon to use a Tommy gun or revolver in self defence, or, being able bodied, one will have to be ready to help others in the defence of one's own immediate surroundings." As early as July, the Queen told Harold Nicolson that she took lessons in firing a revolver because, "We are not going to be caught like the others." Wherever he went, the King always had a rifle and revolver in the car with him.

The government also organized a top-secret group of one hundred officers and men from the Coldstream Guards. Known as the "Coats

Mission," it was headed by Major James Coats, a friend of the King and Queen. The "mobile column" was positioned at all times near the family. With a fleet of bulletproof "saloon cars," they stood ready to defend the monarch and his family from invading parachute troops, or to escort them to one of several designated safe houses in the remote countryside. The officers had an easy relationship with the family, meeting them for drinks, playing golf with the King, and joining shooting parties at Sandringham.

The girls kept up their schoolwork, and Henry Marten now walked up the hill to the castle for Lilibet's lessons in history and the English constitution. Marion Crawford reported to Queen Mary that the provost saw "great stuff" in Lilibet. At meals the princesses practiced their language skills by speaking only in French. They had art and music classes as well as dancing lessons with courtiers' children. The girls played duets at the piano for the household and performed minuets and waltzes at dance concerts. They especially loved their Thursday Madrigal Society meetings—the beginning of a lifetime singing together. After the death of Margaret in 2002, her older sister would never sing a madrigal again.

Lilibet and Margaret had an active Girl Guides troop. They made jam tartlets and drop scones in the castle kitchen for their cook's badge and hiked to a campsite where they roasted sausages on sticks over an open fire. It was an eclectic group, including both cockney refugee girls from the East End and an aristocratic neighbor from across the Great Park, Alathea Fitzalan Howard. She was nearly three years older than Lilibet and a shrewd observer of the princess's adolescent progress.

Alathea came to the castle for weekends and slept on the bunk beds in the bomb shelter. She worshipped Queen Elizabeth, who always made her feel at ease. "She is so sweet and kind, and without being beautiful she has such an irresistible charm one could not help loving her," she wrote in her diary. She saw the royal family as "four people who mean everything to each other, whose lives form one spiritual whole, independent of the aid of all outsiders, or even relations."

Alathea was one among many friends and family members who

stayed at the castle. Another was Princess Victoria, Marchioness of Milford-Haven, the maternal grandmother of Prince Philip of Greece and Denmark, as well as George V's first cousin. In a "very hurried moment when the bombs were so bad," the seventy-six-year-old princess fled her apartment at Kensington Palace to Windsor, where the Queen took special care of her. "How she does talk!" Elizabeth reported to Queen Mary. "It's fantastic. I have never experienced anything like that before—some of it most interesting but too much of it!"

Princess Victoria was an extraordinary woman with a modern outlook and a quick brain, one of many granddaughters of Queen Victoria. She had also closely overseen the education of Lilibet's future husband, who described her approach as "the right combination of the rational and the emotional." At their mother's request, Lilibet and Margaret regularly walked the elderly marchioness down Castle Hill and back.

Lilibet had become an accomplished hostess by age fourteen. She presided over lunches with the Grenadier Guards officers stationed at the castle, as well as with boys visiting from Eton. One Sunday in November 1940, the latter included the future eighth Earl Spencer, father of Diana, the Princess of Wales. Lilibet also began regularly receiving RAF officers in the Red Drawing Room.

Alathea noticed that Lilibet found "making conversation very difficult. . . . She had to stand by herself for over an hour talking to each one in turn. She insisted on bringing the dogs in because she said they were the greatest save to the conversation when it dropped!" It was a tactic she would deploy frequently when she became queen.

Lilibet's most prominent contribution to the early war years was her first radio broadcast in October 1940, exactly a month after her parents were bombed at Buckingham Palace. She rehearsed assiduously, concentrating on her breathing and phrasing, and her parents listened approvingly as she practiced the speech in front of them. According to Crawfie, "Lilibet herself put in several phrases that were quite her own."

At 5:15 on Monday, October 13, the red light came on in a room near her Windsor Castle apartment, while the King and Queen stood in an adjacent room. Lilibet sat with Margaret behind a microphone set upon a table, with the pages of her remarks spread out in front of her. George VI admired his daughter's equanimity. "She was not at all nervous & did not mind doing it a bit," he told Queen Mary.

In a piping voice similar to her mother's, Princess Elizabeth spoke for three minutes during the BBC's *Children's Hour* program. Her primary audience was children who had been evacuated to Canada and the United States. "I feel so much for you," she said, having also been parted "from those we love most of all." She reassured her listeners that the children of Britain "are full of cheerfulness and courage," trying "to bear our own share of the danger and sadness of war." She sent "our love and best wishes to you and to your kind hosts."

She emphasized that "it will be for us, the children of today, to make the world of tomorrow a better and happier place." Surprising her listeners with a well-kept secret, she finished by saying, "My sister is by my side, and we are going to say good night to you. Come on Margaret." With that, ten-year-old Margaret said "Good night" in a clear voice, and Lilibet followed by saying, "Good night and good luck to you all."

It was a magical moment that moved many listeners to tears. In Canada, "thousands of children were delighted by her voice." One report from the United States said the broadcast "was one of the most effective ever received from London." In an editorial, *The Times* called it "most admirably executed." As heiress presumptive, Princess Elizabeth had demonstrated the "unaffected dignity and courage which her royal parents have so unflinchingly displayed in sharing the sufferings of their people."

THE KING NOTED IN HIS end-of-year reflections that the second half of 1940 "certainly showed the world what we can stand." The RAF had demonstrated its superiority over the Luftwaffe, and by October 31, the fifty-seven-night assault of the Blitz had effectively concluded.

The cost was horrific: More than one million homes were destroyed or damaged, and some twenty thousand Londoners had died. By then Hitler had already postponed his planned invasion to the following spring, even as German propaganda kept threatening its imminence.

Punishing bombings nevertheless continued all over Britain at a regular pace through June of 1941. In April and May there was a new "hot blitz." Harold Nicolson witnessed "a gale of fire as red as an Egyptian dawn." The night "shrieks and jabbers like an African jungle," he wrote. More than twenty-three hundred people perished on two successive nights in mid-April.

Aside from entire neighborhoods blown to bits, the civilian targets included numerous schools and hospitals. Even the King and Queen's old house at 145 Piccadilly was bombed. The list of "architectural and historic glories" leveled or extensively damaged was staggering. "It really makes one wild with rage to see all the insane destruction of beautiful & so often dearly loved buildings," Elizabeth wrote to Queen Mary.

Among the iconic targets were the Tate Gallery, the Tower of London, St. Clements Dane on the Strand and numerous other seventeenth-century churches designed by Sir Christopher Wren, and the fifteenth-century Guildhall ("vandalism, pure and simple," wrote George VI). The vividly symbolic survivor of a firestorm in the City of London on December 29, 1940, was St. Paul's Cathedral. The Luftwaffe dropped more than ten thousand incendiary bombs that night. On Churchill's order to save St. Paul's at all costs, firefighters and other heroic volunteers battled the blaze with sandbags and water pumps—their victory enshrined in a photograph of the gleaming dome framed by black smoke.

Also hit were Westminster Abbey and the House of Commons, which was reduced to "a mass of tangled girders & masonry," in the King's words. He and the Queen were deeply upset by the sight of the Abbey, where debris and charred rafters littered the sacrarium in front of the high altar. "It is just four years ago that we were crowned in the Abbey," he noted ruefully. "We had a photograph taken on the spot."

It is difficult to single out any one tragedy among thousands, but the dramatic bombing of the Midlands city of Coventry in mid-November 1940 stood out for its ferocity and scale. It was an eleven-hour assault by more than five hundred aircraft that demolished the city. George VI, who by then had seen more than his share of mayhem inflicted by the Nazis, arrived there two days later and was "horrified" by the sight. "I walked amidst the devastation," he wrote. "The cathedral, hotels, shops, everything was flat & had been gutted by fire. The people in the streets wondered where they were, nothing could be recognized."

He spent five hours in the smoldering ruins, talking to as many victims as he could. Herbert Morrison, the home secretary, toured along with the King. In his report on the visit, Morrison said "he had done much to restore morale." George VI was gratified to hear his visit had been appreciated and had helped, as he said, "to alleviate their sadness. . . . I feel that this kind of visit does do good at such a moment."

Buckingham Palace was attacked five more times between September 17, 1940, and April 10, 1941. Nearly all the windows were broken and covered with flimsy cardboard. Wind rushed through the cracks, and the interior was constantly cold, with dust everywhere, making it "terribly difficult to keep the house clean," Elizabeth reported to Queen Mary. The King felt it was "so depressing sitting in a room with no outside light coming in." He also found "the journey to London & back every day is tiring & very boring, & I cannot read in a car." Yet George VI and Elizabeth withstood the discomfort and came to the Palace most weeks for appointments and their regular tours of the city's bombed neighborhoods.

It was vital for the King and Queen to circulate widely throughout Britain, regardless of the risks. It was also the King's personal preference. "I would much rather go & see things than to have long interviews with people in London," he wrote in the summer of 1940. "The latter have to be got through. . . . Some are interesting & others are deadly." In addition to comforting the afflicted, they gathered insights about conditions on the ground to share with Churchill and other government leaders.

Together and separately, George VI and Elizabeth had been taking the royal train since the beginning of the King's reign. Such were its creature comforts that one newspaper called it a "Palace on Wheels." The King's coach had a day compartment in the Jacobean style plus a bedroom and smoking room. The Queen's day compartment had a Georgian décor, with a bedroom upholstered in blue silk brocade next to a smaller room for her dresser. The rest of the train consisted of a dining car and coaches for members of the household, as well as a special office for the King to conduct his business with all the latest communications equipment.

In wartime, the royal train—code-named "Rugged" or "the Grove Special"—became the mobile nerve center where the King and Queen worked, ate, and slept when they traveled outside London. To ensure their comfort and safety, the London Midland and Scottish Railway company renovated the carriages by installing air-conditioning as well as modern bathrooms, with bathtubs and washbasins providing hot and cold running water. (Previously, hot water had to be carried from the engines.) Steel plates armored the train, including the roof, and the windows were fitted with steel shutters. The food supplied by the railway companies was basic. The only specific requirements for the royal couple were a few items from the farm and dairy at Windsor Castle: small round cream cheeses, pats of butter, and fresh eggs.

George VI and Elizabeth were equally mindful of how they looked while on tours. Starting with the first day of the war, the King always wore a military uniform from one of the three services he commanded. The Queen, however, found uniforms unbecoming. "Some clothes do not like me," she said.

In close collaboration with her dress designer Norman Hartnell, she chose "gentle colours . . . dusty pink, dusty blue and dusty lilac." "She wished to convey the most comforting, encouraging and sympathetic note possible," wrote Hartnell. Elizabeth usually wore a single strand of pearls and avoided flashy jewelry. She always sought to set a good example for those she met: "If the poor people came to see me they would put on their best clothes."

The royal family took pains to show the people their participation in the war effort. Periodically photographs of "us four" would appear in newspapers and magazines—the princesses tending their wartime gardens, or snapshots of them all enjoying each other's company, with their corgis and Lilibet's pet chameleon playing cameo parts. George VI and Elizabeth even opened their doors for a film called *Royal Road* that offered anodyne glimpses of their home life.

An example of Elizabeth's media savvy occurred during a visit to a communal feeding center in the autumn of 1940. At one point, a "very dirty child" reached out and grabbed the Queen's pearls. A nearby photographer rushed to get a picture, but the moment passed. Lord Woolton, the minister of food, who was escorting the royal couple, whispered in the Queen's ear: "Your Majesty, you've broken a press man's heart." Without missing a beat, she shifted her position so the child was able to play with her pearls again. The photographer got his shot. It was the only image of the visit that appeared in the press.

In their many rounds, carried out so often under the shadow of German warplanes overhead, both the King and Queen appeared fearless. The Queen showed her sangfroid when an intruder emerged from behind the curtains of her bedroom at Windsor Castle and grabbed her by the ankles. After her initial shock, she recognized that he was mentally ill and quietly said, "Tell me about it." He then revealed that his family had been killed in the Blitz, and he was an army deserter. As he spoke, she slowly moved to a call button and pushed it to summon assistance. "Poor man, I felt so sorry for him," she recalled. "I realized quickly that he did not mean any harm."

But the repeated exposure to scenes of death and destruction, along with the strains of maintaining their own morale as well as that of the people, inevitably took an emotional toll. In public, the King and Queen showed concern without losing control, although Lord Woolton once saw Elizabeth tearful and dumbstruck when a group of newly homeless people in south London cried out "God bless you."

She told Queen Mary that such scenes exhausted her, and confessed to her sister May that she had come to "loathe" visiting bomb sites, although the heroism and spirit gave her a boost. "I am still just as frightened of bombs & guns going off as I was at the beginning," Elizabeth told her niece Elizabeth Elphinstone. "I turn bright red and my heart hammers, in fact I'm a beastly coward but I do believe that a lot of people are, so I don't mind!"

The King's nervous nature made him particularly vulnerable to wartime traumas. Tommy Lascelles coined the term "Nashvilles" and described them as "sudden outbursts . . . accompanied by gnashing of his teeth and raising his clenched fists to heaven." He told his wife he didn't think the King was "always conscious of his actions in those outbursts. . . . They are extremely tiresome to live with, but one can only ignore them & look on them as a physical failing."

Many years later, Lascelles said he thought the King's temper was "partly epileptic. You could see it coming when his foot began to tap and the veins in his neck to pulsate." Edward Ford, who also served as one of George VI's private secretaries, subscribed to the same theory. He said that fellow courtier Owen Morshead "never knew how to handle the King. He treated him as if he were soothing a fractious child" rather than Tommy's more effective tactic of letting the moments pass without comment.

The Queen's gentle touch worked best, although Margaret knew how to defuse her father with humor. Once at a dinner with guests, George VI got so angry he threw his knife and fork over his shoulder. Margaret then "threw her fork and spoon over <u>her</u> shoulder," Lascelles recalled. "The King said, 'Margaret, you are impossible,' and laughed."

George VI and Elizabeth worried about the impact of the war on their daughters. In the autumn of 1940, there was a lot of air activity over the castle, and a number of bombs dropped in Windsor Great Park. One of the war's mysteries was why the Germans didn't directly hit one of the most conspicuous targets in Britain. The persistent rumor was that the Luftwaffe avoided Windsor Castle because Hitler wanted to live there when Germany invaded Britain.

But on October 22, they dropped three high-explosive bombs within 150 yards of the castle, landing near the cricket field and tennis courts.

"We heard the 'swish' as they were falling," the King wrote. The following night, eight bombs exploded in the vicinity of the castle, half of them near Royal Lodge. "It was the first time that the children had actually heard the whistle and scream of bombs," Elizabeth wrote to May Elphinstone.

The princesses were enviably resilient. Down into the shelter they trudged through frigid corridors, carrying their little suitcases packed with books, personal treasures, and clothing. They practiced wearing their gas masks, comically designed to look like Mickey Mouse. They passed the time with the Queen doing jigsaw puzzles and playing the card game Racing Demon. They all watched movies for diversion, laughing uproariously at Charlie Chaplin.

On Saturday, December 21, 1940, Lilibet and Margaret appeared in a Nativity play staged in St. George's Hall, where a temporary platform had been built at one end of the gigantic Gothic room decorated with shields of Knights of the Garter. The princesses shared the stage with pupils from the Royal School in Windsor Great Park, some of them east London evacuees. Costumes were fashioned for the children from lengths of brocade and other materials scavenged from castle cupboards.

Lilibet played one of the three kings in a golden crown and a velvet tunic of pink and gold. As the Christ child, Margaret sang "Gentle Jesus Meek and Mild." She did it "remarkably well & was not shy," noted the King. Crawfie recorded that George VI and Elizabeth "were absolutely amazed at the entire performance." The King confessed to his diary, "I wept through most of it."

Winston Churchill wrote that year's Christmas speech, and the King called him "a past master in this art." Lionel Logue traveled by bus to the castle, arriving as "a frozen mass." After warming himself with a fireside glass of sherry, he helped the King prepare for the midafternoon broadcast. Logue was touched that the Queen gave him a gold cigarette case and that the family included him in their luncheon featuring boar's head and prunes.

George VI stood alone with the microphone, while the Queen and princesses listened together through a loudspeaker elsewhere in the castle. *The Times* described his voice as "firm and deliberate," but it was punctuated by the now-familiar gulps and pauses. In the ten-minute address, George VI struck a note of "hope and sober confidence in victory." He lamented that "many family circles are broken" by "the sadness of separation." Yet he urged his listeners to keep in mind that "if war brings its separations, it brings new unity also, the unity which comes from common perils and common sufferings willingly shared."

" 'I am sure you will agree,' the King wrote to Roosevelt, that Churchill is 'a very remarkable man.'"

British prime minister Winston Churchill with American president Franklin D. Roosevelt aboard the HMS *Prince of Wales* off Newfoundland on August 10, 1941.

TWENTY-NINE

⟨⟨✦⟩⟩

American Friends

TWO DAYS AFTER CHRISTMAS, THE ROYAL FAMILY TRAVELED TO THE Sandringham estate for "a little rest & change." It was the first time the princesses had left the Windsor Castle environs in more than a year. With the exception of three days the King and Queen spent in London and Windsor in mid-January 1941, the family was based in Norfolk for an entire month.

They stayed in Appleton House, Queen Maud's residence until her death. Built of brick and surrounded by woodlands and formal gardens, it was modest compared to Sandringham's Big House, which had been shuttered for the duration of the war. Appleton had twenty rooms, with eight sitting rooms on the ground and first floors.

The King had supervised the construction of a concrete air raid shelter connected to the house, which he considered "well camouflaged by trees." But at his specific request, it was not further protected the way the Big House had been "surrounded completely by waves of barbed wire," looking "so forlorn," in the Queen's words.

Elizabeth had furnished Appleton with pieces from the Big House, including a piano and radio for the main drawing room. "It is warm &

comfortable," wrote the King. They were served by a reduced staff: two ladies' maids, Ainslie the King's steward, the King's valet, two footmen, a chef, and two kitchen helpers.

In the coldest winter on record, Lilibet and Margaret had snowball fights and played ice hockey on the frozen lake with the Coats Mission soldiers. "The children are looking quite different already," Elizabeth reported to her mother-in-law after two weeks of their "quiet stay at dear little Appleton."

Despite the frigid temperatures, icy winds, and thick snow cover, shooting partridges and wild pheasants invigorated the King. "The fresh air & exercise has done me no end of good," he wrote. Still, he couldn't help feeling it was "all wrong being away from London & from my work," especially during the intense bombing raids concentrated on the City of London at the turn of the year.

He and the Queen ventured out for a day trip by train in early January to inspect bombing damage at Sheffield in Yorkshire. The city had been hit three weeks earlier with special ferocity. "The damage to the centre of the city is pitiful to see," the King wrote. "We talked to many people rendered homeless." Lord Harlech, a local civil defense commissioner who accompanied the royal couple that day, told Harold Nicolson, "The effect of these visits is tremendous. The people feel flattered in their martyrdom."

Recalling the day's events, Harlech said, "When the car stops, the Queen nips out into the snow and goes straight into the middle of the crowd and starts talking to them. For a moment or two they just gaze and gape in astonishment. But then they all start talking at once. 'Hi! Your Majesty! Look here!'"

Harlech reckoned that the Queen's "quality of making everybody feel that they and they alone are being spoken to" resulted from her having "very large eyes which she opens very wide and turns straight upon one." She also had the power to enchant with her "clear, soft voice," in the view of diarist James Lees-Milne. "Her voice is her secret weapon. It could disarm the most hostile adversary."

Lilibet and Margaret had been carefully shielded from the horrors of bomb sites, but in late January 1941 their parents introduced them to Britain's wartime fighting spirit with a visit to the Coastal Command station of the RAF at Bircham Newton in Norfolk. Lilibet held the pilot's control column, peered at the instrument panel of a Hudson aircraft, and declared, "It is very much smaller than I thought it would be." Margaret sat in the bombardier's seat, focusing the bomb sights through the glass-bottomed nose of the aircraft toward an imaginary enemy.

The princesses "asked innumerable questions of the pilots as to what they had been doing & most of them were so modest about their activities," wrote the King. By then George VI could detect a pronounced difference between fighters and bomber pilots. "The former are much more awake & highly strung," he astutely observed, "while the latter are plodders. Both types are very efficient."

For the first time, the two princesses watched their father carry out an investiture, decorating twenty RAF officers and noncommissioned officers for valor. The King conducted these ceremonies diligently throughout the war—first monthly, then weekly. Before the Blitz, he often held them in the quadrangle of Buckingham Palace. Even during Red Warnings he kept pinning on medals. When necessary, he herded the recipients into the Palace shelter. At times, the investitures ran well over an hour and involved as many as three hundred recipients, leaving him exhausted. "I find that they take a lot of energy out of me," he wrote. "I have to do all the talking & I have found men much easier to talk to than the officers. The latter are very nervous."

The highest military award for heroism in combat was the Victoria Cross. Since the first weeks of the Blitz, the King had also recognized comparable "bravery & outstanding deeds" by civilians, as well as military personnel outside the field of battle. He called these awards the George Cross, with a stature equal to the Victoria Cross. In addition, he conceived of the George Medal for "wider distribution."

He had dramatically announced this "new mark of honour" in a radio speech from the Buckingham Palace shelter during an air raid on

September 23, 1940. "The spirit of the Londoner stands resolute and undismayed," he said. In the four months since, George VI had commended some two dozen men for extraordinary gallantry and "undaunted devotion to duty," most of them for bomb disposal, defusing mines, and tunneling through unsafe wreckage to carry out rescues.

DURING THEIR EXTENDED WINTER STAY at Sandringham, the King and Queen could reflect on the previous traumatic six months. They grieved together over the death of Neville Chamberlain on November 10. He had been suffering from cancer when he resigned in May, and George VI and Elizabeth had been able to visit his bedside just weeks before he died. In his review of the year, the King lamented that the former prime minister's "untimely death" had "robbed me of an adviser & friend." That December, Britain had also unexpectedly lost Lord Lothian, the country's popular and highly valued ambassador to the United States, when he died of food poisoning. Shortly before Christmas, Lord Halifax was appointed as his successor, and Churchill's protégé Anthony Eden returned as foreign secretary.

The King, Queen, and Churchill agreed on the need to strengthen Britain's relationship with the United States. George VI had long since quelled his disappointment that America had not—contrary to FDR's overly optimistic talk at Hyde Park—come to Britain's aid the moment London was bombed. The King recognized that isolationist sentiment in America was too strong, and Roosevelt didn't have the votes to overturn the neutrality laws dating from the late 1930s. But George VI was an active participant in the decisions around the American president's steadily escalating policies to help Britain "by all means short of war."

The King and Roosevelt had been secretly corresponding since April 1940. The tone of these letters was friendly, even affectionate, but the two men dealt with substantive issues as well. In June 1940, the United States had begun sending crucial arms shipments across the Atlantic to replace those lost at Dunkirk. Soon afterward, Churchill requested fifty reconditioned American destroyers. George VI reiterated that appeal in his own letter to FDR, in which he spoke of the "magnificent" spirit in Britain.

After some adroit maneuvering between the two governments, delivery of these ships was linked to ninety-nine-year leases in British West Indian territories for American air and sea bases to build up the defense of the United States. This agreement fulfilled the proposal FDR had made to George VI at Hyde Park for a Western Atlantic patrol. "I often think of those talks we had at Hyde Park, when you gave me your ideas of bases & patrols in the Atlantic," the King wrote Roosevelt. "I am very glad to know now, that those ideas have become real facts."

The King and Queen had watched the American presidential election campaign "with deep interest." Roosevelt's decisive reelection in November 1940 had prompted the King to write privately that he and the Queen were "delighted & thankful." He expressed relief that FDR's "wise & helpful policy" would "continue without interruption," and he emphasized that "we are keeping our end up here very well . . . our people are full of courage & determination to win through."

George VI and Elizabeth still wanted America's direct engagement by its declaring war against Germany, but they were cheered by Roosevelt's reply in late November that he was "doing everything possible" to accelerate shipment of "literally everything we can spare" that would help Britain's war effort. He added that with their courageous behavior, the King and Queen had "deepened the respect and affectionate regard in which you are held in this country by the great majority of Americans."

Roosevelt reinforced his pledges early in 1941 by dispatching his closest adviser, Harry Hopkins, to London for meetings with the British government and the King and Queen. Bertie and Elizabeth had returned to Windsor from Sandringham at the end of January and resumed their regular trips to Buckingham Palace. Hopkins, whom George VI and Elizabeth had met during their stay in Washington, told the King that FDR "meant every word" in his recent statements of support for Britain, and that the president had public opinion behind him. Crucially, Hopkins brought encouraging news about the Lend-Lease bill making its way through Congress.

A month before his death, Lord Lothian had begun working on Roosevelt's plan to ship much-needed arms and supplies to Britain without compelling payment from the cash-strapped nation. These armaments and essential goods would, in effect, be "leased" to Britain, with the accounts settled at a distant date. Churchill called this long-term loan scheme a "glorious conception." Roosevelt would sign it into law on March 11.

Over a congenial Palace luncheon on January 30, Hopkins had a candid and wide-ranging conversation with the King and Queen, finishing it in the shelter "as there was a good deal of air activity overhead with guns firing," the King noted. Hopkins had been touring the country with Churchill, who had earlier reported to George VI that the American envoy was "much impressed by all he has seen."

The King thought Hopkins looked "rather tired after his numerous visits & countless interviews." Hopkins's gaunt appearance belied his inner strength—he had survived cancer surgery two years earlier—and workaholic determination. He spoke slowly, often with a dead cigarette between his lips, but projected thorough confidence in his opinions and assurances.

Hopkins was impressed that George VI had "intimate knowledge" of all the high-ranking officers in Britain's armed services. "He reads very carefully all the important dispatches," Hopkins wrote in his diary. He said the King "did not have a very high opinion" of his ministers. He "felt there was no one even remotely as competent as Churchill in managing the affairs of Britain." George VI also dismissed Irish president Eamon de Valera as "a fanatic who, while not necessarily pro-German, is so bitterly anti-British that his actions amount to the same thing."

The Queen didn't hesitate to share her strong opinions either. She told Hopkins "she felt Hitler and the German people were a pretty cruel lot and realized they would have no mercy on them." Hopkins observed that "she seemed to have a wide acquaintance with British politics and affairs and showed great interest in all I had to tell her about our trip throughout the country."

The Queen "quite casually" told Hopkins "she had written to Mrs. Roosevelt three times and had no answers to any of her letters but that she was going to persist and send a fourth." Hopkins urged them both to continue writing to the president and first lady—to keep Britain and America "closely related." The King observed that Eleanor Roosevelt "seemed to be busy at press conferences and lectures, which he said he was never able to understand," adding with a smile that he didn't "presume to criticize any of the ways of my country."

George VI was pleased that Hopkins had already cabled Roosevelt "to send us more long distance bombers & flying boats." He noted that Hopkins was "greatly struck" by Churchill's "personality & power to get things done & wants him to meet Roosevelt."

The Queen was relieved that Hopkins was "very helpful and all out for our cause. A very nice American." Hopkins in turn admired Elizabeth's conviction that "victory in the long run was sure, but that the one thing that counted was the morale and determination of the great mass of the British people."

Roosevelt subsequently appointed Hopkins as the administrator of the Lend-Lease program, which would total nearly $85 million and would not be paid off by Britain until 2006. Both the King and Queen would count on Hopkins as a reliable conduit of information from the president. "If ever two people realized that Britain is fighting for its life, it is those two," Hopkins concluded.

In those early months of 1941, Roosevelt and George VI conspicuously broke protocol to send a strong message to the American and British people that the United States may have been nominally neutral, but it was inexorably shifting toward intervention. When Lord Halifax, the new British ambassador, debarked at Annapolis, Maryland, from the battleship *King George V* on January 24, the president was there to greet him personally. According to Harold Nicolson, "the newspapers were full of the arrival." George VI told FDR it was "a gesture which I and my countrymen deeply appreciated."

Scarcely a week later, Joe Kennedy's replacement as U.S. ambassador to the Court of St. James's arrived at Windsor station. In an unprecedented signal of goodwill by a British sovereign, King George VI met fifty-one-year-old John Gilbert "Gil" Winant himself "to return the compliment" extended by FDR to Halifax. During a long talk at the castle, the King was drawn to the darkly handsome envoy who was "very shy & not a good talker." He was gratified to learn that Winant "knows England well" and "is very keen that we should have all we want from U.S.A." Winant found George VI to be "completely informed on the day-to-day progress of the armed forces and on any other subject that concerned his people."

In addition to German onslaughts by air, Britain was suffering through the Battle of the Atlantic, with sustained attacks by German submarines against convoys of merchant ships carrying supplies from North America. Britain was also fighting Italy in the Middle East, where its army had scored initial victories in Egypt and Libya. Once Germany's Erwin Rommel entered the battle in February 1941, his Afrika Korps defeated the much smaller British force. The only enclave Britain held was the besieged Libyan port of Tobruk, which would be the target of repeated German raids.

At times the King felt overwhelmed by the growing complexities of the war. "I have a lot to read in the way of papers & as there is so much going on everywhere my brain is full of conflicting facts at the end of the day, which I cannot properly sort out," he wrote in early April. "Luckily other people find it the same."

His most daunting mission was as Churchill's go-between with eastern European monarchs under pressure from Hitler to abandon neutrality. These efforts failed as they all knuckled under, and Hitler assumed control of Romania, Bulgaria, Hungary, and Yugoslavia. "If only those idiotic balkan countries could have got together, instead of allowing themselves to be gobbled up one by one," Elizabeth wrote to Queen Mary.

Among these reversals, the most painful personally for the King and Queen was the tragic tale of their close friend and extended family member Prince Paul of Yugoslavia. When King Alexander I of Yugoslavia was assassinated by a terrorist in 1934, his first cousin, Prince Paul, was called upon to govern as regent until Alexander's son Peter, then eleven years old, came of age. Oxford-educated Paul—an art connoisseur and bon vivant far more comfortable in the salons of Mayfair than in Belgrade's corridors of power—was ill-suited for the regency. The manner of his capitulation to the Nazis badly damaged his reputation.

After meeting with Hitler, he signed an alliance with Britain's Axis enemies on March 25, 1941. Two days later, a military coup expelled him from Yugoslavia, as German troops swept through the country to stage an invasion of neighboring Greece, which Italy had attacked the previous October. Paul ended up exiled to Africa and branded a traitor by Churchill and the British foreign policy establishment.

Peter, then seventeen years old, reigned as Yugoslavia's monarch for only a few weeks until the German army fully occupied the country. The Nazi air attack on Belgrade in early April was especially vicious, killing some seventeen thousand people. King Peter II fled to Britain, where he led a feeble government-in-exile, studied at Cambridge University, and periodically consulted with his godfather, George VI.

King Peter II later told George VI that Paul "was definitely in the wrong" by signing the Axis pact, and that he "actually saw Hitler twice quite a short time before." What's more, when Hitler was sending "sealed wagons" across Yugoslavia, Paul knew they contained German troops for the invasion of Greece—contrary to his denying that he was aware of their purpose. "Poor Paul has a lot to answer for, I am afraid," wrote George VI.

Churchill's War Cabinet refused Paul's request to come to England and placed him under house arrest in Kenya with his wife and children. "Nobody wants him," George VI noted in his diary that May. Many years later Paul would be exonerated of war crimes and judged a victim of circumstance who actually opposed Nazism. But during the war and afterward, the ardent Anglophile was unfairly accused of being pro-German. He minded deeply and suffered from depression. The King even heard that he was "on the verge of a nervous breakdown."

Elizabeth felt particularly sorry for her longtime friend. "He has made such a mess of his job in the eyes of the world," she wrote Queen Mary. "One knows that he is very timorous & sensitive & subtle minded." But she admitted that he must have grasped the consequences of aligning with Germany. She guessed he was in over his head. "I am sure that he was afraid & perhaps weak," she told Lord Halifax.

Along with the setbacks in the Middle East, Britain's attempts to assist Greece collapsed that spring as well. The outmanned British and Commonwealth forces (four divisions against Germany's fifteen divisions) withdrew to Crete, where they were overwhelmed by the German army and air force and had to be evacuated—a "grave defeat," wrote Harold Nicolson.

Among those airlifted from Greece were King George II and his government ministers, first to Palestine, and on to London. George VI wrote to the deposed Greek king sympathizing with his "bitter blow" that "left unbroken the spirit of Your gallant people." He welcomed George II to be "at our side" in the continuing struggle to reclaim his homeland. By the beginning of June 1941, Germany completely dominated the Balkans.

On Saturday, June 14, 1941, at Windsor Castle, George VI noted with puzzlement that "we have been left alone from bombing lately." A week later, on June 22, the King had his answer when he tuned in to the nine A.M. BBC News. Just before dawn, Germany had launched Operation Barbarossa, a surprise invasion of the Soviet Union, with 161 divisions and three million men. The King marveled that there had been "no ultimatum . . . no declaration of war . . . no demand for concession."

Hitler was greedy for oil and other natural resources, so he turned on his ally of convenience and tore up the nonaggression pact they had signed in August 1939. Dedicated anti-communist Churchill flipped with astonishing speed in a speech on June 23 promising full support of the Soviet Union. The following day he told the King he was replacing General Archibald Wavell, the commander in chief in the Middle East, with General Claude Auchinleck. "When Winston has made up his mind about somebody or something, nothing will change his opinion," George VI observed. "He looks to one goal & one goal only, winning this war. No half measures."

In a diary entry on June 25, the King shrewdly observed that "this war with Russia may be a great mistake on Hitler's part." The führer and his generals believed that the Wehrmacht could roll over the Red Army as easily as it had done in western and eastern Europe. But the campaign turned into a protracted struggle and diverted German resources to the east, lessening the pressure on Britain, where the bombardment ended, not to resume for many months.

With the cessation of bombing, the King and Queen were no longer called upon to routinely inspect ruins and console victims. Their emphasis shifted to tours of factories and shipyards, and inspections of military bases and civil defense installations, hospitals, schools, shelters for the homeless, and social service organizations. During one visit to an ordnance factory, the Queen described the women workers as "bright-eyed and obviously happy at their job." On the same tour, she visited a French convalescent home where she spoke French to nearly all of the sixty patients, "charming them all with her smile and her command of their language."

Elizabeth took special interest in women's civilian and military war efforts, such as the Auxiliary Territorial Service, the women's branch of the British Army. In July 1941, she spent a day reviewing ATS units with Princess Mary, who held its most senior rank as chief controller. Elizabeth thoughtfully reported to her mother-in-law that "it was so nice going round with her, she is so keen & I think has done a great deal to put the service on its feet by her really deep interest & good advice. They all love her."

Women formed the vanguard of American public opinion favoring more involvement in the Allied fight against the Axis powers. With that in mind, government and royal advisers urged the Queen to give a radio broadcast to the United States, directed yet again to women, as she had in her 1939 Armistice Day speech. The text had several contributors, including Churchill. "I fear it is not very polished—a good deal of my own," she told the prime minister, who added some rhetorical flourishes.

Sitting before the microphone at Windsor Castle on Sunday, August 10, 1941, the Queen described British women "working in factory and field, turning the lathe and gathering the harvest. . . . Their courage is magnificent, their endurance amazing. I have seen them in many different activities." In the armed services they were "driving heavy lorries, cooking, cyphering, typing, and every one of them working cheerfully and bravely under all conditions." Others were "air raid wardens or ambulance drivers" who had "quietly and calmly" faced "the terrors of the night bombings." She singled out the heroism of nurses who "in the black horror of a bombed hospital" had never faltered, even those wounded themselves. She paid tribute, as before, to the gallantry of housewives tackling the difficulties of wartime deprivation.

Above all, she thanked "American generosity" that had "touched beyond measure the hearts of all of us living and fighting in these islands. . . . In the hour of our greatest need you came forward with clothes for the homeless, food for the hungry, comfort for those who were sorely afflicted. . . . Unless you have seen, as I have seen, just how your gifts have been put to use you cannot know, perhaps, the solace which you have brought" to those who are "suffering and toiling in the cause of freedom."

Americans warmly received her words of "quiet eloquence and sincerity." Roosevelt cabled his congratulations in a letter to the King, asking him to tell the Queen that "her radio address yesterday was really perfect in every way and that it will do a great amount of good."

The president's location—unknown to the world at the time—was the USS *Augusta*, an American cruiser anchored in Placentia Bay off Newfoundland, where he and Churchill had been conducting secret talks. The president and the prime minister, who had traveled across the Atlantic on the battleship *Prince of Wales,* had met for the first time on Saturday, August 9.

On boarding *Augusta,* Churchill had given FDR a letter from the King. In it, George VI expressed his pleasure that the two leaders were meeting at last. "I am sure you will agree," he wrote, that Churchill is "a very remarkable man." Among the prime minister's many advantages was being half American. His beautiful socialite mother, Jennie Jerome, the daughter of a wealthy financier, was born in Brooklyn and grew up in Manhattan as well as Paris.

The four-day conference was the American president's most overt violation of neutrality to date. The *Miami Herald* called the meeting "an admission by the President that we are engaged in an undeclared war on the Axis partners in crime." The previous May, Roosevelt had declared an "unlimited state of national emergency" and empowered U.S. naval patrols to defend convoys of merchant ships steaming to Britain.

The main outcome of the Placentia Bay conference—the first of nine meetings between the prime minister and president that would total 113 days—was the Atlantic Charter. The document set forth "common principles" designed to ensure "a better world" after the defeat of the Axis powers. It would become the foundation of the eventual United Nations Declaration.

Over luncheon at the Palace on August 19, the day after his return, Churchill reassured the King that although Roosevelt "at the moment . . . would not declare war," he "would wage war with us, against Germany." Three months later, on November 14, the U.S. Congress would finally amend the Neutrality Act to permit U.S. merchant ships to enter war zones. This pleased the King, but he couldn't help observing, "America is not nearly ready for war."

THE PRIVATE LIFE OF THE royal family lightened during the second full year of World War II. In early April 1941, Lilibet revealed to her friend Alathea Fitzalan Howard that she had been corresponding with a nineteen-year-old naval officer. "He's called Prince Philip of Greece," the princess confided. "Can you keep a secret?" Philip, she said, was her "boy." She had been in love with him for nearly two years.

Around the same time, Philip's cousin Princess Alexandra of Greece watched him writing a letter and asked the name of the recipient. "Lilibet," he said. "Princess Elizabeth, in England."

"But she's only a baby," said Alexandra. After a beat she realized "he's angling for invitations."

Philip was by then six feet tall, with vivid blue eyes, flaxen hair, and a cheeky, confident personality. At age fifteen, Lilibet wasn't exactly a "baby." She already had a curvy figure (a friend of Alathea's thought she had an "enormous chest"), a wide smile, and lovely blue eyes. Behind her "outward calm and matter-of-factness," Alathea saw "something lovable and sincere" as well as "a dignified grace peculiar to herself."

At Windsor the royal family could roam freely again without casting their eyes overhead. The girls punted on the lake next to Frogmore and swam in the pool at Royal Lodge. Toward the end of July, the King and Queen hosted Lilibet's first dance. Among the two hundred guests in the Red Drawing Room were aristocratic officers in the Brigade of Guards stationed at Windsor and from the Royal Military College at Sandhurst. The Queen and her daughters wore white tulle dresses designed by Norman Hartnell, and the princesses put flowers in their hair. Everyone danced the Palais Glide as well as an assortment of reels. The party was meant to end at midnight, but it lasted until three in the morning.

The family took the train to Balmoral on August 20 for a stay of two uninterrupted weeks for the King and Queen, plus three more for Lilibet and Margaret. It was "a real change, as I need it in every way. Both mentally & physically," wrote the King. They hadn't been in the Scottish Highlands for two years.

The King shot grouse each day, which he said did him "a great deal of good." Almost immediately, the princesses looked "ten times better, with pink cheeks and good appetites!" Elizabeth told Queen Mary. She felt the experience helped her conserve energy "for whatever may lie ahead."

Canadian prime minister Mackenzie King came for a weekend of conversation, primarily with George VI. The Queen took him to a cot-tage on the moors where they met the shooting party for a picnic lunch. They helped themselves to a simple meal of cold grouse, salad, sandwiches, bread and butter, and cake that they ate on a plain table decorated with lettuce leaves by the princesses.

Relaxing by the fireside later that afternoon in his room upstairs at the castle, George VI discussed the state of the war with the prime minister. The King was gratified that his Canadian guest "feels as I do that America should declare war on Germany. Until she does the American public will never realise what the war means to us or to her in the long run." Mackenzie King was impressed by the informal atmo-sphere at Balmoral. He found Lilibet to be "very natural" in her man-ner. Margaret, on the other hand, "tried to amuse the others," at one point by crossing her eyes, which drew rebukes first from the Queen, then the King.

Back at Windsor, the King and Queen hosted Prince Philip of Greece and Denmark on October 18 for his first weekend in the castle where his mother was born and where his grandmother was a refugee resident. Now holding the rank of acting sub-lieutenant in the Royal Navy, the Greek prince was taking courses at Portsmouth following a stint of duty in the Mediterranean. He had been "mentioned in dis-patches" (cited for gallant conduct) during the Battle of Cape Mata-pan the previous March.

His job on the battleship *Valiant* had been to operate searchlights during the Royal Navy's daring night raid on Italian ships threatening an Allied convoy. As a result of Philip's "alertness and appreciation of the situation," his ship had sunk two Italian cruisers within five min-utes. In his commendation, Admiral Andrew Cunningham singled out Philip's "successful and continuous illumination of the enemy" that "greatly contributed to the devastating results."

The King was impressed by the young officer's description of the Mediterranean battle. Afterward, Lilibet told Alathea that she had been with her "beau" and urged her friend to meet him on his next visit. "She said he's very funny, which doesn't sound my type actually,"

Alathea wrote. A month later, Lilibet said she was "very excited over Philip coming for the weekend."

Life at dusty and drafty Buckingham Palace edged closer to normal. The King and Queen resumed dinner parties for government ministers, and in late November they began spending nights at the Palace again. "We felt we had to break the idea that we could not stay there for reasons of security," George VI wrote.

They were winding up a weekend at Windsor Castle on Sunday night, December 7, 1941, when "a bomb shell arrived in the 9 o'clock news . . . saying that the Japanese had bombed Pearl Harbour in Honolulu, the U.S. Fleet base, without warning," wrote the King. The Queen heard the bulletin on a radio in her room and hurried to her husband to share the news.

Since entering the Tripartite Pact with Germany and Italy in the summer of 1940, Japan's principal incursions had been in China and Southeast Asia. Churchill did not believe that Japan would risk American intervention in the Pacific. During one luncheon in August, Churchill told the King that "Japan would remain quiet." Two months later, FDR himself reassured George VI that American officials were working with Japanese moderates to check the more aggressive elements in the government.

These foot-dragging maneuvers turned out to be a smokescreen, as the King put it, "so that the Japanese Fleet & Army could take up their strategic positions for a lightning attack on American islands in the Pacific without warning." The well-planned attack sank or seriously damaged seven of the eight battleships at Pearl Harbor. Japanese forces followed with assaults on Malaya, the Philippines, Borneo, Thailand, Hong Kong, and the Dutch East Indies.

Britain joined America on Monday, December 8, in declaring war on Japan, and Hitler declared war on the United States three days later. "We are proud indeed to be fighting at your side against the common enemy," the King wrote to Roosevelt. "We share your inflexible determination." The Queen was less sanguine, telling Queen Mary that the United States was "not well armed & their pilots have no experience. . . . I do feel rather sorry for them . . . 'tho they have persistently closed their eyes to such evident danger, for they are a very young and untried nation."

The princesses lifted spirits with a pantomime performance held in the Waterloo Chamber at the castle on Friday, December 19. The Christmas pantomime was a boisterous tradition in Britain stretching back two centuries: "warm-hearted stage revels blending the homely fun, the heroic sentiment, and the spectacular splendour of tradition" interspersed with "bits and pieces" from contemporary music hall comedy.

For the first Windsor Castle "panto," the princesses chose *Cinderella*. It was written and directed by Hubert Tannar, a local schoolmaster whose pupils filled out the cast. Eleven-year-old Margaret, wearing a white wig and crinoline dress, took the lead role, and Lilibet played Prince Charming. "All very good," wrote the King of the production, which was duly announced in the "Court Circular."

The only "uneasy moment," recalled BBC sound engineer Robert Wood, came at the end of the show when Mr. Tannar, "rather overcome with the success of the venture and the audience's applause, kept on bowing and bowing and looked as though he would never leave the stage." Wood grabbed a sound-effects recording of the thundering Flying Scotsman train, "wheels, whistles and all," and slammed it on the turntable. Tannar "shot off the stage like a startled deer, and the show collapsed in laughter."

In his Christmas radio address from Windsor, George VI made a special plea to "the boys and girls of today" to prepare themselves to "be ready for whatever part you may be called to play" in building a better world. "Make yourselves ready—in your home and school—to give and offer your very best." After the broadcast, there was a family party around the Christmas tree that Lilibet and Margaret had decorated. The job of distributing the gifts was taken up by the King, who enlivened the proceedings by wearing a Santa Claus costume.

THE THIRD YEAR OF WORLD War II pivoted from a cascade of losses in the first half of 1942 to steady gains that culminated in the defeat of German forces in North Africa early in 1943. There were many moments of despair, but once the United States entered the war, the powerful combined Allied forces had a decisive advantage. Churchill saw as much in January 1942 when he told the King "in private" that he was "confident now of ultimate victory . . . U.K. and U.S.A. were now 'married' after many months of 'walking out.'"

It took optimism, assurance, and strategic vision for Churchill to make such a prediction of ultimate victory. Hong Kong and Manila had fallen at the turn of the year. When Britain's island base of Singapore surrendered in February 1942, more than eighty thousand Commonwealth troops were captured. By the end of May, Japanese armies had conquered the East Indies, Burma, and the Philippines, where they took thirty-five thousand American troops prisoner on the Bataan peninsula. Rommel claimed Tobruk in June—a victory that put him in striking distance of Alexandria, Egypt. "Bertie & I have been very tired & troubled of late," Elizabeth wrote to her mother-in-law in February, but she retained faith in "the good sense & wonderful fighting spirit of this wonderful people of ours."

The King and Queen concentrated their hopes on the island of Malta, a British colony sixty miles south of Sicily. It was a critical location in the Mediterranean for the Royal Navy and RAF to disrupt Axis shipping routes to Rommel's army. By the spring of 1942, Malta had undergone sustained night-and-day attack by the Luftwaffe for nearly a year. The Maltese not only withstood the bombardment but also faced possible starvation. On the fifteenth of April, George VI awarded the "Island Fortress of Malta" the George Cross for "heroism and devotion that will long be famous in history."

By then Britain was itself about to endure another wave of aerial bombing. These new attacks were reprisals for British raids on what Germany said were civilian targets (although the King wrote in his diary that "aircraft works" had been heavily damaged). These "Baedeker" raids—so named because German officials said they would bomb every English building given three stars in the Baedeker guidebook—lasted for six weeks, killing or injuring nearly four thousand people. The cities in the German bomb sights—Exeter, Bath, Canterbury, Norwich, and York—were renowned for their ancient cathedrals. "There are no war industries in Exeter," George VI pointedly wrote.

The King and Queen visited scenes of destruction that angered them both. In Bath they saw extensive damage from a hilltop: "A great many historical buildings have been destroyed, including the Assembly Rooms in the centre of town," noted the King. They clambered around the rubble and spoke to homeless people who "behaved splendidly, & felt quite all right." Several days later they were in Exeter, where they visited the famous cathedral, one of the oldest in Britain. "Devon people are very tough," wrote the King.

George VI followed the events of the war with unceasing attention, logging every development in his diary, quizzing his visitors (now including senior American military advisers), reading their reports, and hearing their plans. They felt free to unburden themselves in his sympathetic presence, and he bucked them up when they despaired. Air Chief Marshal Sir Hugh Dowding, the architect of the radar system that helped the RAF win the Battle of Britain, had "nearly wept" in the early days of the Blitz over the devastation caused by night bombing in London.

After a bumpy start when the King had referred to Anthony Eden as a "know-it-all," he developed a good relationship with the foreign secretary. At the end of April 1942, he observed that Eden "is very good at telling me things, & I feel I can ask him about people frankly." He similarly trusted Kingsley Wood, the chancellor of the exchequer, who made his budget briefings "much more intelligible for me & I can ask questions." As for Churchill, the King told his mother that he had "studied the way in which his brain works. He tells me, more than people imagine, of his future plans & ideas & only airs them when the time is ripe to his colleagues & Chiefs of Staff."

LILIBET WAS CONFIRMED IN THE Church of England at a service in
Windsor Castle's private chapel at the end of March 1942, with Queen
Mary and Princess Mary attending as two of her godparents. Lilibet,
her mother, and her father—all devout Christians—took her confirmation seriously, with Cosmo Lang as her instructor. The Queen
thought the service, conducted by Lang shortly before his retirement
as Archbishop of Canterbury, was "so straightforward and so inspiring." He ended his address by saying, "I can do all things through
Christ who strengthened me," and he blessed Lilibet by placing both
hands on her head.

Mabell Airlie, who hadn't seen the princess since the war began,
watched her with fresh eyes: "a grave little face under the small white
net veil. . . . The carriage of her head was unequalled, and there was
about her that indescribable something which Queen Victoria had.
Although she was perfectly simple, modest and unselfconscious, she
gave the impression of great personality."

Several days later, the family went to Royal Lodge for a week. It
was the first time they had stayed there since the bombing began in
1940. "There we can be alone & we leave the staff in the Castle," the
King wrote. "I can do my papers by box & by telephone. We spent a lot
of time outdoors in the Park."

In the chapel near Royal Lodge, Lilibet took her first Communion on
Easter Sunday. Elizabeth, the King, and Lilibet walked over early in the
morning and returned to Royal Lodge for breakfast & Easter eggs. "It was
so nice to be together & quiet after three years of war & turmoil & perpetual anxiety, for even a few moments of true peace," Elizabeth wrote.

They marked a further milestone for Lilibet on her sixteenth birthday. The King had appointed her colonel of the Grenadier Guards, a
number of whom she knew from teas and luncheons at the castle. On
the morning of April 21, 1942, she conducted her first inspection of a
Grenadier troop on parade in the quadrangle. Afterward, Lilibet and
her parents had lunch with the officers and watched a performance in
the Waterloo Chamber by Tommy Handley, a popular radio comedian,
and his BBC troupe.

Seated in the front row was Grenadier Captain Hugh FitzRoy, the Earl of Euston and heir to the Duke of Grafton. The Queen invited Hugh, as well as Lilibet's friend Alathea, to a "quiet birthday tea" with chocolate cake. Alathea, who had a crush on Hugh, noted that the King and Queen were "so pointedly nice to him that one wonders if there's anything behind it." They did, in fact, consider him a highly eligible candidate to marry Lilibet.

The following month Hugh turned up again at a dance in the Green Drawing Room. "Everyone's talking of the way in which the Royal Family single him out," Alathea wrote. "He's staying the night . . . and he sat by the princess at supper." But Princess Elizabeth had no romantic interest in him. Scarcely six weeks later, Alathea took note when Lilibet "scribbled on a piece of paper . . . that Philip was coming for the weekend."

The royal family celebrated yet again on the Fourth of July, with the birth of Prince Michael of Kent, the second son and third child of the King's brother George and his wife, Marina. Queen Mary had always felt protective of her son "Georgie," and she welcomed the way his marriage and fatherhood had settled him. Elizabeth had a strong affinity with George, the Duke of Kent, as well. She considered him "like a brother," someone to whom she could talk about "many family affairs." She appreciated his "quick & sensitive mind & a very good & useful sense" as well as "a great many jokes."

In wartime, Prince George had found professional satisfaction when the King appointed him an air commodore in the Royal Air Force. His principal duty was to conduct inspections of RAF facilities at home and overseas. The previous year he had reviewed pilot training programs in Canada and visited the Roosevelts at Hyde Park. The president had written to the King that he felt "a great affection" for his younger brother. In honor of the newborn prince's birthdate, FDR agreed to be a godfather.

On Tuesday, August 25, the King and Queen and their daughters had been at Balmoral Castle for two weeks. The weather was "filthy," with "low mist, rain & an East wind," which didn't dissuade the King from shooting grouse on the moors with his brother Prince Henry. That afternoon, one hundred miles north at a naval base, thirty-nine-year-old Prince George boarded a Sunderland flying boat in similarly bad conditions. He took off for Iceland, where he was due to inspect an RAF base. Shortly afterward, flying too low in the "haar," the thick coastal fog, the airplane smashed into the top of a hill, killing the duke and fourteen other passengers. It was a ghastly case of pilot error.

During dinner that evening, George VI was summoned from the table for a phone call. It was Archibald Sinclair, the secretary of state for air, who told him of George's death. In a state of shock, the King took a pencil and wrote on a note card headed with the red insignia of Balmoral Castle: "Darling, What shall we do about ending dinner? I am afraid George has been killed flying to Iceland. He left Invergordon at 1:30 pm and hit a mountain near Wick. What a day to start on. B." He handed the note to the Queen and sat silently until she beckoned Alice Gloucester to join her in leading the ladies from the table into the drawing room. They assumed Queen Mary had died and were stunned when the King walked in to share the devastating news.

George VI was shattered, as was his mother. On the evening of the twenty-fifth, her lady-in-waiting Cynthia Colville had been reading aloud to Queen Mary when a phone call came through from one of the King's private secretaries, Sir Eric Mieville, at Balmoral. "What is it? Is it the King?" Queen Mary said as Lady Cynthia rejoined her in the sitting room. "No, Ma'am," replied the lady-in-waiting. "I'm afraid it is the Duke of Kent."

"My most precious son Georgie," Queen Mary wrote in her diary. "I could not believe it."

Mabell Airlie felt that Queen Mary "never really recovered from the shock of the Duke of Kent's death. Of all her sons he had the most in common with her." She managed to hide her sorrow, "but it still remained." The next morning, she was driven to Coppins, the Kents' home in Buckinghamshire, to console his widow, thirty-five-year-old Marina, who was heartbroken. "We were a comfort to each other in our own grief," Queen Mary wrote.

The King and Queen arrived in London on Thursday the twenty-seventh and set in motion plans for the duke's funeral in St. George's Chapel at Windsor on Saturday morning with military honors: The coffin was borne by eight noncommissioned RAF airmen, with blue-jackets, marines, and other regiments lining the aisle into the nave. It was an appropriately subdued wartime service attended by fewer than one hundred mourners.

Elizabeth felt a "terrible loss," and George VI expressed deep sorrow in his diary. "I have attended very many family funerals in the Chapel, but none of which have moved me the same way," he wrote. "Everybody there I knew well but I did not dare to look at any of them for fear of breaking down. His death & the form it took shocked everybody. . . . The war had brought him out in many ways. Always charming to people in every walk of life."

Back at Balmoral in early September, George VI steeled himself for a melancholy task: a visit to the site of his brother's death. He thanked those who led search parties and talked to the man who had found Prince George's body. The King noted that "the remains of the aircraft had been removed, but the ground for 200 yards long & 100 yards wide had been scored & scorched" by the trail of the plane and the fireball that engulfed it. "The impact must have been terrific," wrote the King. "I felt I had to do this pilgrimage."

He resumed his work in London the next day, while Elizabeth and the princesses stayed in Scotland, where the Queen had developed a bad respiratory infection. The King arranged for Princess Olga to be flown from Africa to stay with her sister Marina at Coppins. Churchill approved the trip as an act of compassion, but he wouldn't permit Prince Paul to accompany his wife. George VI visited Marina and Olga several times in September. "Marina is still stunned from shock," he noted, "but she is very calm and collected."

Queen Mary had been touched by a telegram from the Duke of Windsor sending "all my loving thoughts" and wishing he could be with her to give "comfort and help." She replied with a long grief-stricken letter offering her eldest son consolation, "knowing how devoted you were to him." She even sent a "kind message to your wife who will help you to bear your sorrow." She told Bertie that she hoped her reference to Wallis "was not compromising," adding, "I hope you will approve." David replied thoughtfully to his mother, but again he asked her to receive Wallis.

In a letter to Bertie, David wrote of sharing with him "this irreparable loss." He reminded his brother that he "took [George] under my wing and guided him safely through the most difficult period of his life, which might have otherwise turned out disastrously." He praised their mother's courage and exemplary fortitude. He complimented the King and Queen for doing "a fine job" in "difficult times." But perhaps inevitably, he undermined his compassionate sentiments by adding that it was "a source of great pain to me now to think that on account of your 'attitude' towards me, which has been adopted by the whole family, [George] and I did not see each other last year when he was so near me in America."

The King sent a copy of this letter to his mother. In a reply to Bertie, she expressed hope that the "ice has at last been broken," although she wondered "why he accused you 'of your attitude towards him' when the boot fits on the other leg, I fail to see, & after all it was D. who wrote us such very rude letters." Elizabeth expressed her own irritation several days later, writing to Queen Mary that "it is a good thing to communicate, but what a typical 'attitude!' We are always in the wrong."

The Duke of Windsor predictably pushed for more in a letter several weeks later to Churchill, requesting that the "H.R.H." title be "restored" to his wife (who never actually had been granted it). The King sent his mother the pertinent passage, saying, "I feel that this is impossible, especially in these days, when their names are never mentioned here. . . . Has he done it because of the letters we have interchanged lately & is this what he calls my 'attitude' towards him?"

Bertie emphasized Wallis's status as a "doubly divorced woman." He acknowledged that "she may have done quite well in the Bahamas," but reiterated "that is not sufficient to reverse a decision taken

*"One or two passages obviously stirred him so
deeply that I feared he might break down."*

At the Guildhall in London, the King reporting on the trip to North America with
the Queen.

"It is so hard to know when not to smile."

The Queen as photographed by Cecil Beaton in July 1939.

*"We talked to the King as if he was
an assistant schoolmaster."*

The royal family with the boys at the King's Camp at Balmoral on the eve of war.

*"She understood 'the thousand and one worries
and irritations in carrying on in war-time life
in ordinary homes.'"*

Queen Elizabeth broadcasting from Buckingham Palace to the
women of the empire.

*"It gave pleasure and encouragement to the troops
whose greatest enemy so far has been boredom."*

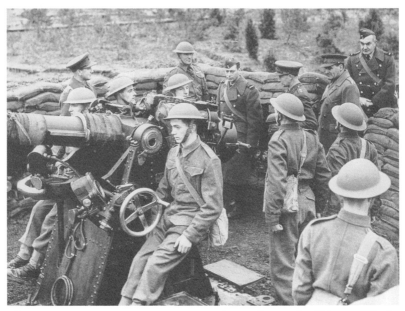

The King inspecting troops on a visit to France during the "Phoney War."

"Buckingham Palace was beginning to resemble an exclusive refugee encampment."

The leaders of the exiled European governments with the King and Queen.

*"Elizabeth considered herself 'very much
a part of the team with the King.'"*

The King and Queen with Winston Churchill during
the Blitz.

*"Originally a housemaid's room, it had
an incongruous décor."*

The Buckingham Palace bomb shelter for the King and Queen.

"The attacks 'unite the King and Queen to their people by new and sacred bonds of common danger.'"

The King and Queen in a bomb-damaged area of London in October 1940.

"She was not at all nervous & did not mind doing it a bit."

Fourteen-year-old Princess Elizabeth makes her first radio broadcast with her sister at her side.

"I should die if I had to leave."

The Queen emerges from the royal armored car, named "Brontosaurus."

"Winant found George VI to be 'completely informed on the day-to-day progress of the armed forces.'"

The King greets John Gilbert Winant, the new American ambassador.

"The King was most in his element when inspecting the masses of British troops."

George VI greeting soldiers during his trip to North Africa.

*"I have never known Lilibet
more animated."*

Princesses Elizabeth and Margaret
performing the *Aladdin* pantomime.

*"A new character has slipped demurely
upon the stage of public life."*

Princess Elizabeth celebrating her eighteenth birthday with her family
at Windsor Castle.

"He is entirely bound up in himself & leads his own life."

George VI with Field Marshal Montgomery in October 1944 on a tour of the Normandy invasion armies in Holland.

"Truman 'understood European difficulties from a new standpoint.'"

George VI meets President Truman before the end of the Second World War.

"We did not want to disappoint the people."

On V-J Day in 1945, the King and Queen travel in an open carriage despite the rain.

"There we can be alone & we leave the staff in the Castle."

George VI with his daughters at Royal Lodge near Windsor Castle.

*"It is a far more moving
thing to give away your
daughter than be
married yourself."*

Princess Elizabeth arrives at Westminster
Abbey with the King for her wedding to the
Duke of Edinburgh.

*"He gave thanks for their
'supremely happy married life.'"*

The King and Queen during a service at St. Paul's Cathedral on their silver
wedding anniversary.

*"Princess Margaret thought her father
was 'in the best of health.'"*

The King and Queen celebrate Prince Charles's third birthday with his sister Princess
Anne six weeks after George VI's lung surgery.

"The Queen 'could <u>not</u> help one huge tear forcing its way out of my eye.'"

Princess Elizabeth and the Duke of Edinburgh departing for a five-month tour of Africa, Australia, and New Zealand.

"Yr. Majesty's devotion & love made it possible for him to reach the pinnacle."

Queen Elizabeth, now the Queen Mother, at the funeral of King George VI.

with much thought only six years ago. Elizabeth agrees with this too." It was not time "to wake up the past. This worry coming on the top of all one's other work is too bad."

Queen Mary replied on the same day to express her disappointment that "D. should bother you with this tiresome question once again." She urged him to write to his brother saying that he must abide by his original decision. Wallis "is not the kind of person to hold the title of H.R.H.," she wrote. "Thank goodness for some time they have been 'out of the picture' & we do not wish this revived." The King went along with his mother's advice and put the matter to rest.

"Every bastion and every view point lined with people who cheered as we entered."

King George VI arriving in Malta's Grand Harbour aboard HMS *Aurora* on June 20, 1943.

THIRTY

The Tide Turns

ALONE WITH THE GIRLS AT BALMORAL IN THE AUTUMN OF 1942, ELIZABETH missed her "Bertie darling." She couldn't shake a severe respiratory infection, and the princesses were ailing as well. The Queen had been treated by the royal homeopathic doctor, John Weir, who administered what George VI called "his remedies." But she was sensible enough to take M&B (named for its manufacturer, May & Baker), the first widely available antibiotic, a sulfa medication that had been in use for five years. She was skeptical of the drug at first, but eventually touted its efficacy, telling Queen Mary that it "eats up the bad germs like lightning."

In mid-October the family was back at Windsor as the King and Queen prepared for the arrival of Eleanor Roosevelt on a fact-finding mission to see British women's wartime work and visit American forces. "I want you and the Queen to tell Eleanor everything in regard to problems of our troops in England which she might not get from the Government or military authorities," FDR wrote to the King.

There was little George VI and Elizabeth could do to clean up "dirty and dark and draughty" Buckingham Palace for the first lady's two-night stay starting on Friday, October 23. They decided to put her in Elizabeth's bedroom, where sheets of mica, the clearest material available, were fitted into small wood frames replacing the large shattered windows. The Queen's sitting room remained "windowless," so they provided her with the King's sitting room heated by a coal fire.

The first lady met Lilibet and Margaret at tea and sized up the heiress presumptive as "quite serious . . . with a great deal of character and personality. She asked me a number of questions about life in the United States, and they were serious questions." She noted how much the King and Queen had matured since 1939 when she had viewed them as "a young and charming couple who would have to undergo some very difficult experiences."

Not only had they survived those challenges, "they were anxious to tell me about them." She wrote that she had "gained the greatest respect" for them both and could see that they were "doing an extraordinarily outstanding job for their people in the most trying times." She admired "their character and their devotion to duty."

The wartime austerity in the Palace shocked the first lady. Black lines were painted five inches from the bottom of every bathtub to restrict water use, rooms were scarcely warmed by little electric heaters, and the food was comparable to that served in a commoner's cottage. The menu for their first dinner together included fish croquettes, cold ham and chicken, a salad, brussels sprouts, dessert, and fruit— incongruously served on gold and silver plates.

Unlike George V, who banned alcohol from all royal residences during the First World War, George VI kept the drinks flowing to help morale. His cocktail of choice was a small whisky before dinner and a second with his meal. The Queen favored "a small gin and orange" before lunch and a dry martini before dinner. During meals she typically drank claret or champagne.

Winston and Clementine Churchill joined the dinner for the first lady. The prime minister was "like a cat on hot bricks," awaiting news of the massive assault launched that evening by General Bernard Montgomery on Rommel's forces at El Alamein in western Egypt.

Unable to contain himself, he left the table to call 10 Downing Street. When he returned, he was singing "Roll Out the Barrel" (a wartime hit also known as the "Beer Barrel Polka") to the astonishment of the footmen he walked past.

On Saturday, the King and Queen hosted a Buckingham Palace luncheon for the first lady with eight heads of women's organizations. "I was the only man," wrote the King, who took time to talk to the women he had not previously met. Afterward, the royal couple escorted their visitor on an extensive tour of London.

They spent a half hour at the city's great symbol of survival, St. Paul's Cathedral. The first lady saw the hole where a bomb had penetrated the dome, as well as the damage near the high altar. They visited the equally iconic Guildhall, which looked "comparatively normal" from the outside with a temporary new roof. But the historic library where George VI had spoken of the triumphant North American trip three years earlier was still "an appalling mess." In the blitzed East End, they were cheered by large crowds.

For the first lady's second Buckingham Palace dinner, the King and Queen invited Labour Party stalwart Ernest Bevin, the minister of labour and national service since 1940, and Lord Woolton, the minister of food. "They both gave Mrs. R a good idea of what we have been doing," the King wrote in his diary. A former farmworker and trade union leader, Bevin was stout and blunt-spoken. George VI had initially regarded him as "very egotistical" but equally recognized that he was "a strong man & a capable one."

Bevin "got on like a house on fire with Mrs. Roosevelt," wrote Tommy Lascelles. After dinner, the King urged Bevin to pinch one of his favorite brandy goblets to test its strength. When the goblet "exploded like a shell," wrote Lascelles, "the King merely said, 'Now you'll want some more brandy.' To which Ernie replied, 'Thank you, Sir, I think I will.' Two great gentlemen."

Eleanor Roosevelt left George VI and Elizabeth on Sunday morning for a countrywide tour that lasted two weeks. Elizabeth described her as a "charming guest . . . so interested in all our war efforts, & so understanding and sympathetic of our ideals and difficulties." Before she flew back to the United States, the first lady said goodbye to the King and Queen over tea at Windsor Castle. "She is much impressed with all she has seen & heard," wrote George VI. But she irritated the monarch and his wife by bringing along her friend Beatrice Gould, editor of the *Ladies' Home Journal* in New York City. In addition to "flagrantly gate-crashing," Beatrice presented the Queen with a "long and elaborate questionnaire" about an array of issues affecting women around the world.

Lascelles knew that Eleanor Roosevelt was the author of "My Day," a regular newspaper column in which she had thoroughly recounted her activities and ideas during her visit to Britain. She was "a personality in her own right . . . free to speak her mind forcibly, and to advance controversial opinions."

But Lascelles, along with the royal couple, firmly believed that neither the Queen Consort nor other members of the royal family should "publicize themselves in the Press à la Mrs. Roosevelt"—and certainly not according to terms dictated by journalists. He turned down Beatrice Gould on the spot, and yet again when she offered a "wholly imaginary conversation" with the Queen that she wanted permission to publish in her magazine: a "palpable *fake*," sniffed Tommy.

Eleanor Roosevelt reported her impressions at a White House press conference. She marveled that the British remained cheerful after three years of blackouts. She came away with "enormous pride in the ability of human nature to rise above things that usually bother us most—the little things." The Queen told Tommy Lascelles that the first lady had drawn "quite a good & sober picture of this incredibly gallant country" while somewhat understating the "sacrifices and hardships." Elizabeth knew that Eleanor was "anxious not to appear too pro-British. Very wise of her."

"I BRING YOU VICTORY," ANNOUNCED Winston Churchill when he arrived at Buckingham Palace for his weekly luncheon with the King and Queen on November 3, 1942. "We thought, 'Is he going mad?'" Elizabeth recalled. Inside his red dispatch box, he carried two telegrams from Rommel to Hitler that had been decrypted by the code breakers at Bletchley Park. In these messages, known by their top-secret "Ultra" classification, the German general had given "a very depressing account" of the battle in Egypt. He "did not see how he could hold out." Everything else the King and his first minister discussed that day was "trivial as compared to this," wrote George VI.

The next afternoon, the King was working with Logue on his speech for the State Opening of Parliament—still held each year without frills—when the telephone rang. "Yes! Yes! Well read it out, read it out," he said. It was a telegram from General Harold Alexander, the commander in chief in the Middle East, to report Montgomery's defeat of Rommel's army in Egypt "after 12 days of heavy & violent fighting" at El Alamein.

"The enemy is in full retreat," said George VI with a smile. "Well," he added, "that's grand." "A Victory at last," he wrote in his diary. "How good it is for the nerves." The King instantly sent his congratulations to Churchill. After the prime minister's "many arduous hours of work" and "many miles you have travelled . . . you have every right to rejoice. . . . At last the Army has come into its own."

Four days later, a British and American combined force of more than one hundred thousand troops landed in North Africa. Code-named "Torch," the operation gained a strong foothold in Morocco and Algeria, taking control from the French Vichy regime. "It is some 4 months ago since I first heard of the idea of this expedition on such a vast scale," wrote the King. The government ordered church bells to peal throughout Britain, the first time they were rung since June 1940.

The two successful assaults shifted the momentum of the conflict in the Allies' favor, not least because Torch was the first major operation carried out on their own initiative. The Germans were stunned by its scale, which also gave a psychological boost to the British and Americans. Torch had been conceived by Churchill as the linchpin of his Mediterranean strategy that would lead to victories in Europe.

One crucial consequence was that "relief of Malta" was "now in sight," wrote the King, as convoys carrying food and supplies reached the beleaguered island. Concurrent with the victories in North Africa, Russia was making substantial gains against the Germans, as was the United States against Japan in the Pacific.

At the end of the month, the King and Queen hosted their first Thanksgiving Day party for two hundred officers of the U.S. Army, Air Corps, and Navy, along with twenty-five American nurses and Britain's top military brass. Lilibet and Margaret were on hand with their friend Alathea Fitzalan Howard, and Winston Churchill brought his twenty-year-old daughter Mary, who was serving in the ATS on an antiaircraft battery in Hyde Park. This was the first time she had been officially presented to the King and Queen.

George VI, Elizabeth, and the princesses stood in the Grand Hall of the Palace for nearly three hours and spoke to most of their guests. A buffet table stretched the length of the corridor next to the Bow Room, footmen served tea and cocktails, and a string band of the Grenadier Guards played in a corner. Admiral Harold Stark, commander of U.S. Forces in Europe, noted that Princess Elizabeth was "a very nice-looking girl, bright and pleasant to talk to just like her mother." Margaret Rose was "tiny for her 12 years, but also bright as can be."

Their friend Alathea understood that while Lilibet was "good at trying to find the right words for strangers," it was "a great strain for her. Not so for Princess Margaret Rose, who burbles away naturally and easily." Admiral Stark was struck by the informality of the reception, with the royal family freely circulating among the guests. "Everybody felt at home," he recalled. The Americans had "very good manners & waited for their turn," the King noted. "They all seem happy here."

At last George VI could offer optimistic words in his Christmas broadcast from "the study of a country house," as Windsor Castle was always referred to in the press for security reasons. With Churchill as his speechwriting collaborator, he dramatically described "the First and Eighth Armies, our Fleets, and Air Forces . . . advancing towards each other, heartened and greatly fortified by the timely and massive expeditionary armies of the United States. Tremendous blows have been struck by the armies of the Soviet Union. . . . In the Pacific we watch with thrilled attention the counterstrokes of our Australian and American comrades." He cautioned that hard tasks lay ahead, but "today we stand together, no longer alone, no longer ill-armed, but just as resolute as in the darkest hours to do our duty whatever comes."

The Luftwaffe sporadically bombed Britain in the early months of 1943, once again prompting the King and Queen to inspect and console. Elizabeth railed against the "unspeakable Huns" after she visited seriously injured children in a hospital. They both traveled to areas of Newcastle that had been targeted and visited facilities turning out munitions. One factory producing explosives employed sixteen thousand workers, mostly women. George VI and Elizabeth were "impressed by the spirit of work people & their smiling faces . . . all doing a real job . . . and they know it."

At the urging of the government, Elizabeth broadcast another tribute to the women of the British Empire on April 11: her ninth broadcast as Queen and her fifth during the war. As she considered the postwar world, she felt conflicted about the sort of guidance she should give. "One would like to congratulate women on the way they are tackling men's jobs," she told Alec Hardinge. "Yet they must be ready to stay down (& by) after the war." As much as she valued her role as the King's partner in substantive as well as symbolic matters, Queen Elizabeth was no feminist.

She gave her "very rough draft" to Churchill for suggestions, asking him to "be ruthless with the extra bad bits, & cut them out firmly!" He added only ten lines, telling her it was most important that her remarks reflect her "own words and feelings." She said she put in his contribution "just as you wrote it," hoping his words would "comfort many an aching heart." Other contributors were the Bishop of Lichfield, who had become a spiritual mentor to the Queen, as well as Tommy Lascelles. "You understand what I feel about things," she told Lascelles.

As she prepared to speak, she galvanized herself by thinking of "the grey & narrow streets of places like South Shields or Sunderland"— two coastal towns near Newcastle that were devastated by the Luftwaffe. "If one can help those gallant people, everything is worthwhile." To "my fellow countrywomen all over the world," she said she wanted to share something "deep in my heart." They had "earned the gratitude and admiration of all mankind," and it was "high time that someone told you so."

She said that their contributions in their "different spheres" were "just as much 'war-work' as that which is done by the bravest soldier, sailor or airman who actually meets the enemy in battle. And have you not met that enemy, too? You have endured his bombs, you have helped to put out the fires . . . you have tended those he has maimed, brought strength to those he has bereaved."

In the view of *The Times,* ordinary people saw in the Queen "a friend whom they know to be one with them not in heart only but also in experience and in toil. . . . Very little of her ceaseless activity gets into the newspapers. It is impossible to put into print the qualities of head and heart which give a vitalizing power to her public life. The Queen's job, like the King's, demands unrelaxing energy and sincerity if it is not to be tainted with the poison of routine."

MATCHING THE HOPEFUL MOOD THAT spring was incomparably beautiful weather in battered old England. The royal family spent more time at Appleton House, where they celebrated Lilibet's seventeenth birthday by bicycling around the Sandringham estate. The King and Queen marked their twentieth wedding anniversary with a cocktail party for local friends and army officers.

In Windsor, the family now often stayed at Royal Lodge, which was livable again after work to repair bomb damage had been completed. There they had tea on the lawn under a canopy, and the girls played the game of Consequences with the officers from the Windsor barracks. One weekend, George VI and Elizabeth watched the races at Ascot. Although his horse failed to win, the King was pleased that the public had full use of what had previously been the exclusive Royal Enclosure. And for the first time, they took Lilibet and Margaret to see a play in London's West End, *Arsenic and Old Lace*. The audience cheered them, and they went behind the scenes to speak with members of the cast.

At the end of March, the King and Queen gave a dance for Lilibet and Margaret in the Green Drawing Room at the castle for 150 guests. The Queen looked chic in a black net dress and black gloves. Lilibet was in white lace and wore lipstick. They had supper and champagne, and "did so enjoy it," remarked the King. "We kept it going until 3:30 A.M. In these days the young get so little enjoyment."

Tommy Lascelles was amused the next day as he climbed the hill from the Windsor railway station to see "the whole royal family basking in the sun under the terrace wall." They were "obviously sleepy and complained of sore feet, but seemed to have enjoyed their party."

By midyear the Allies had achieved two major victories: The German army capitulated at Stalingrad following an arduous siege, and on May 13, 1943, the Axis forces surrendered at Cape Bon in Tunisia, giving the British and American armies complete control of North Africa. "It is an overwhelming victory," wrote the King. He and Churchill, who was in Washington with Roosevelt for talks on war plans, exchanged congratulatory messages that were released to the press.

The Times ran an editorial singling out George VI for particular praise. While prime ministers come and go, "the King remains, always at the centre of public affairs, always participating vigilantly in the work of government from a standpoint detached from any consideration but the welfare of his people as a whole," said *The Times*. "He is the continuous element in the constitution, one of the main safeguards of the democratic character."

Churchill's telegram revealed "the help that one of the strongest of Prime Ministers has received from his Sovereign," continued *The Times*, a "powerful reminder that King George VI is doing a work as indispensable for English governance as any of his predecessors, just as he has set his peoples from the first day of the war an unfailing public example of courage, confidence, and devoted energy."

With all he had done over more than three years, George VI felt a need to do more. For some months, he had been spending his spare time in the castle basement, side by side with male household servants. One of them had taught the King "how to prepare & assemble the striker mechanism for the breech block of a 6 pounder anti-tank gun," he wrote in his diary. He had set up the workshop to produce these important precision parts so he and his employees could turn the lathes together to "help in the war effort. I want to do my bit during weekends."

Most of all, the King yearned to see his troops out in the field. His last visit had been to the British Expeditionary Force in December 1939, and now he wanted to commend them personally in North Africa. In early June, Alec Hardinge began planning a two-week itinerary with British and American military leaders. "Secrecy is all important as no one must know I am going there," the King wrote.

He disliked flying and faced the long air journey with considerable apprehension. On June 9, two days before he was scheduled to leave, George VI wrote a memorandum of instructions to the Queen. In the event of his death, he stipulated that she should "take the entire charge of & go through all my personal papers." Only she could read his diaries before she committed them to the care of the Royal Archives. "I do not wish anyone else to read them," he wrote. She would know "if there is anything in them which should be used in reference to these days of war."

The next day he packed, weighed his luggage, and authorized a Council of State—including the Queen, Princess Mary, and Prince Henry—to act on his behalf while he was overseas. The morning of his departure he met with his solicitor and "discussed matters with him owing to war risks. I think it better on these occasions to leave nothing to chance."

He traveled incognito as "General Lyon" and gave his wife "an anxious few hours" when a heavy fog over Gibraltar scuttled a planned refueling stop. The Queen "imagined every sort of horror and walked up and down my room staring at the telephone!" she told Queen Mary. Accompanied by Alec Hardinge and several other aides, the King landed in Algiers on June 12. At age forty-seven, he followed a backbreaking schedule over the next fourteen days, traveling sixty-seven hundred miles, shuttling among North African cities and encampments, and carrying out forty-five engagements, including seven in one day. He inspected tens of thousands of Commonwealth and American troops and conferred with his own senior military officers, as well as General Dwight D. Eisenhower and the other top American commanders.

The King had been keeping an eye on the tough yet genial supreme commander of American forces—known by his nickname "Ike"—since his early days in Britain. The previous July they had spent nearly an hour together at Buckingham Palace. The King knew that Ike got on well with his British counterparts. Ike, in turn, found George VI to be "most personable and very much 'in the know'" regarding current and planned Allied operations.

George VI also enjoyed telling the general about an incident at Windsor Castle nearly two months before their first meeting. Long-time courtier Clive Wigram had been asked to show two senior American officers around the gardens at the castle. Wigram alerted the King, who agreed to avoid any awkwardness with the visitors by remaining indoors.

But on the appointed Sunday afternoon, the King and Queen and their two daughters decided to spend some time in the sunshine on a small terrace in the garden. As they were having their tea, they heard the unmistakable Wigram voice identifying various flowers, and they spotted his two guests—"one very tall and the other simply tall": five-foot-ten Eisenhower and his deputy General Mark Clark, who was six foot five. Bertie, Elizabeth, Lilibet, and Margaret quickly ducked behind a hedge, squeezed through a low opening in the terrace wall, and crawled undetected into the castle.

In the intervening months, through conversations with Churchill and other officials, the King had followed Eisenhower's plans and strategic thinking. Now in North Africa, George VI and the general had dinner on successive nights. Ike was "fond of the King," according to Harry C. Butcher, his naval aide, and thought he was "democratic" and not "aloof from military matters."

After their first dinner together, the King "soberly and with dignity," in Butcher's words, privately invested "our Kansas farm boy" with a GCB, the Grand Cross of the Most Honourable Order of the Bath. Several days later, George VI knighted General Montgomery for his brilliant victory at El Alamein.

The King was most in his element when inspecting the masses of British troops and seeing "the smiles on their faces" showing "they were pleased with what they have done." On one such drive in an open car, he got so sunburned a doctor had to treat him with "grease & a lotion." On another tour he stopped by the roadside to award the Victoria Cross to a Gurkha officer. Whenever he could, he slipped away to swim in the sea.

The high point of his trip was a stealth visit to Malta. After awarding the indomitable islanders the George Cross the previous year, he was determined to honor them in person. It was a dangerous proposition, given Malta's proximity to fascist-controlled Sicily only sixty miles away. But the secret mission held, and after a rocky voyage across the Mediterranean, he arrived in the Grand Harbour at Valletta on HMS *Aurora* at 8:15 A.M. on Sunday, June 20, 1943.

Standing atop a special platform, he saluted from the bridge of the ship, a slender vision in a white naval uniform. "A lovely sunny morning," he wrote. "A wonderful sight. Every bastion and every view point lined with people who cheered as we entered." Landing an hour later as church bells rang across the island "brought a lump into my throat," he told his mother, "knowing what they had suffered from 6 months constant bombing."

Over the next twelve hours, he toured Malta by car. He saw the devastation from the bombing, and he was shown the George Cross on display in the Palace in Valletta. As he drove through the flag-bedecked villages, the crowds cheered and threw so many flowers that bright colors streaked his white uniform. He left the island as he had arrived: "by sea and by night." When the island's lieutenant governor told him he had made the people of Malta "very happy," George VI replied, "But I have been the happiest man in Malta today."

Elizabeth did her duty as a Counsellor of State, putting her initials on about a half dozen papers each day. She hosted the weekly luncheon with Churchill, who kept her informed about the King's activities. One morning she carried out her first investiture ceremony for several hundred recipients. Among the honors was a Victoria Cross she pinned on one of the "dambuster" RAF pilots who had destroyed German hydroelectric facilities. For an evening's diversion, Tommy Lascelles took the Queen and Lilibet to a concert of Bach and Handel at the Royal Albert Hall. Lascelles, a keen connoisseur of music, observed that Lilibet "obviously enjoyed the concert. . . . I think she may be really fond of music."

But the Queen felt an undercurrent of worry about her husband's strenuous schedule. "Please don't get overtired," she wrote. She told Queen Mary "he looks very thin in photographs." She had good reason for concern. Always on the move, the King didn't sleep well, and midway through his tour he came down with "internal trouble known as 'Gyppy Tummy'"—a euphemism for dysentery. He felt weak from insufficient food, and he had to spend most of one day in bed. By the end of the trip, he had lost nearly a stone—fourteen pounds—in weight.

His night flight home was smooth and landed in England an hour early at six A.M. on Friday, June 25. In the car to Buckingham Palace, Churchill thanked him for having done so much good on his journey. "I found Elizabeth in bed waiting anxiously for me," George VI wrote. "It was lovely seeing her again. She had had very little sleep, & it was then only 7.0 A.M."

THOROUGHLY EXHAUSTED FROM HIS TRAVELS, George VI recuperated for more than a week at Royal Lodge. It turned out he needed a different sort of fortitude to deal with a high-level crisis that had been brewing in the royal household in his absence. The problem was his private secretary, Alec Hardinge. Although they had been friends for many years, and his wife, Helen, had grown up with Elizabeth, Alec had fallen out of favor with the King, and Elizabeth had turned on him as well. A genuine and complicating factor was Hardinge's own bouts of poor health; at the beginning of the year, the King had noted in his diary that Alec "has not been well & has been away." But the nub of the crisis was a power struggle with Tommy Lascelles.

While the King and Hardinge were in North Africa, Lascelles had the Queen's complete attention, and he unloaded his feelings about the private secretary. His objections centered on what he considered Alec's "great secrecy" over the King's North Africa tour and his overall "reluctance to delegate." In his diary, Lascelles cataloged his grievances against Hardinge, among them his "flat refusal to admit he is ever anything but 100 per cent right" and a lack of civility toward "the great majority of his fellow men." Tommy also believed that Hardinge and the King "were so temperamentally incompatible that they were rapidly driving each other crazy."

The upshot was a meeting requested by Lascelles on Tuesday, July 6, to tell Hardinge "he could no longer work with him" because of his "policy of splendid isolation." Lascelles's threatened resignation compelled Hardinge to force the issue by submitting his own resignation letter that evening to the King—an offer the private secretary believed would be refused outright.

This development "came as a great shock" to the King. After dinner he met with Lascelles, who "explained the whole position . . . & told me the cause of it," notably that he and other courtiers had been kept "in the dark by Alec." To Tommy's surprise, the King "at once" decided to accept Hardinge's resignation—"remarkable proof," Lascelles wrote, of his "diagnosis of the intolerable relationship between him and Alec."

The King confirmed his unhappiness with Hardinge in his diary, noting that he "had always found him difficult to talk to & to discuss matters with. I knew & felt he was doing me no good. . . . I knew that I should not get this opportunity again." Hardinge took the news badly in a meeting with the King the next day and asked "point blank if I really wanted him to resign. I told him I did. . . . I am sure he expected me to say, do go on 3 months sick leave."

Lascelles insisted that he had not coveted the private secretary job, nor had he attempted to influence the King. He professed to have been the "unwilling target" of a "Hardinge must go" barrage "from almost everybody from the King and Queen downwards, and outside it." He claimed to have "turned a rigidly deaf ear" to such complaints until he could see a clear deterioration in the relationship between monarch and private secretary.

The murky X factor in the drama was the role of the Queen behind the scenes, just as it had been two decades earlier with Louis Greig. Whatever doubts Elizabeth had about Hardinge were likely reinforced by her conversations with Lascelles while the King and his private secretary were away.

In a letter written after the King's return, she thanked Lascelles for his "kindness & support & understanding." It had been "a deep relief to be able to speak quite freely to such a sympathetic & discreet person. If I was a trifle _in_discreet—well who better qualified to listen than yourself? It is so important to be able to discuss rather delicate matters in a broadminded & I hope balanced way, and there are very few people in the world alas! to whom one can occasionally speak freely."

At least two people close to the situation believed Elizabeth had helped push Alec overboard. Oliver Harvey, private secretary to Anthony Eden—a strong supporter of Hardinge—regarded the resignation as "a serious thing." Hardinge "had a mind of his own and didn't hesitate to state it." Harvey traced "friction" back to Hardinge's anti-appeasement views during the Munich crisis when the King and Queen supported Chamberlain. Harvey said that the Queen "was determined to get him out." He rightly assessed the Queen's character as "a strong one out of a rather reactionary stable."

Helen Hardinge also detected the hidden hand of the Queen. She told Elizabeth that well-informed sources said the Queen had been trying to ease Alec out for a long time. The two women met, and Helen wrote in her diary that the Queen was "very angry at me for believing they could have ill wished Alec."

The announcement of Tommy Lascelles's appointment came in the "Court Circular" on July 17, 1943. Cynthia Colville wrote that it was "simply grand when the right person & the right place come together." Mabell Airlie praised his varied experience, along with his "extended knowledge of family reactions and family characters" that would make his advice valuable. Tommy admitted to sitting "rather wearily" in his new chair, "only too conscious of the heavy burden of responsibility and business I have shouldered. Still, I have reached the top of my profession at the age of fifty-six," he wrote in his diary. "I suppose that is something."

"The dreadful shadow of war has passed
far from our hearths and homes."

King George VI, Queen Elizabeth, Princess Elizabeth, and Princess Margaret
with Prime Minister Winston Churchill on the Buckingham Palace balcony on
May 8, 1945, Victory in Europe Day.

THIRTY-ONE

Overlord

THE PACE AND NATURE OF THE WARTIME DUTIES OF GEORGE VI AND Elizabeth shifted from the middle of 1943 onward. They traveled less and spent more working hours at Buckingham Palace, where they hosted lunches and receptions for visiting officials. George VI immersed himself even more deeply in military strategy now that Britain and the United States were on the offensive.

The first significant thrust came with Operation Husky, an ambitious Anglo-American attack on Sicily launched on July 9 with 160,000 troops. Little over two weeks later, they had conquered the island and landed on the Italian mainland to begin their march northward. Mussolini was deposed at the end of the month. In early September, the Italian army surrendered unconditionally and joined the Allied armies fighting the Germans.

By then the King had turned increasing attention to plans for Operation Overlord, an Allied invasion across the English Channel into France scheduled for late spring 1944. During an August 1943 conference in Quebec, Roosevelt had persuaded Churchill to join him in giving the massive offensive a green light. Over the course of the

next nine months, George VI would have some forty briefings on Overlord with political and military leaders. No detail was too small for the
King, as he threw himself into reviewing the preparations from as
many angles as possible. "The more one goes into it, the more alarming it becomes in its vastness," he wrote.

IN ADDITION TO HER TRADITIONAL tours of defense facilities, hospitals,
and women's organizations, the Queen was active in Britain's cultural
sphere. Since the late 1930s she had taken a keen interest in expanding the royal collection with contemporary British artists, although
their work was by no means avant-garde or abstract. The painters
whose work she bought included Paul Nash, Graham Sutherland,
Duncan Grant, Augustus John, and Walter Sickert. Not only did they
give her pleasure, but she also saw her patronage of the arts as a facet
of patriotic duty.

She commissioned artist John Piper to paint a series of watercolors memorializing Windsor Castle. Kenneth Clark, the surveyor of
the King's pictures since 1934, and Jasper Ridley, another of the
Queen's art advisers, suggested Piper for the project at a time when
the Windsor environs were threatened by Luftwaffe bombers. Clark
described Piper's style as "romantic" without being "artificially old-
fashioned." From 1941 to 1944, Piper turned out twenty-six haunting
watercolors dominated by inky clouds and monochromatic vistas—
some of which he painted from the castle rooftops.

The Queen appreciated the artistry of these brooding images and
told Kenneth Clark she thought them "really exquisite. . . . The King
likes them enormously, too, and altogether I am <u>delighted</u>." Nevertheless, she tried to nudge Piper toward more colorful depictions. At her
urging, Arthur Penn asked Clark if he could persuade Piper to paint a
Gothic arbor in the Frogmore gardens while it was "covered with wisteria in full bloom." The fiercely independent artist ignored her plea
and painted Frogmore's gray summerhouse against a black sky, with
scarcely a hint of color. King George VI was amused by his wife's effort

to tame Piper. As he reviewed the series of paintings one day at Windsor, he took a long look, turned to Piper, and said, "You seem to have very bad luck with your weather, Mr Piper."

BOTH THE KING AND QUEEN took particular interest in *Aladdin,* the 1943 Christmas pantomime at Windsor Castle. As in previous years, it was a charity performance to raise money for the Royal Household Wool Fund, which provided yarn for knitted comforters sent to soldiers fighting on the front lines. The King watched the rehearsals and chipped in with suggestions. Standing in the back of the room, he would shout, "I can't hear a word any of them say!"

The presence of Prince Philip, home on leave from the Royal Navy, added excitement to the Saturday matinee performance when he sat with the King and Queen in the front row. As usual, Lilibet played the male lead; her Aladdin wore a green and gold brocade tunic and leg-revealing shorts. Margaret was Princess Roxana in an elaborate red and gold floor-length silk gown and paste tiara. "It was admirably done," wrote Tommy Lascelles. "The principals and chorus alike would not have disgraced Drury Lane."

"I have never known Lilibet more animated," Crawfie observed. "There was a sparkle about her none of us had ever seen before." Alathea noticed as well. Philip "seems so suited to P.E. and I kept wondering today whether he <u>is</u> her future husband. I think it is the most desirable event that could possibly happen." Prince Philip stayed for the weekend, and he was invited back for Christmas.

They sang carols at St. George's Chapel, and the King wore his Inverness tartan tuxedo to Christmas dinner. After dinner came the customary game of Charades. "They rolled back the carpet in the crimson drawing-room, turned on the gramophone and frisked and capered away till near 1 A.M.," wrote Tommy Lascelles. Lilibet reported to Crawfie that "we had a very gay time, with a film, dinner parties and dancing to the gramophone."

Philip thoroughly enjoyed himself, although he cautiously wrote to the Queen that he hoped his "behaviour did not get out of hand." At the risk of seeming presumptuous, he said that Windsor Castle was now one of his favorite places. "That may give you some small idea of how much I appreciated the four days you were kind enough to let me spend with you."

Before the turn of the year, the royal family traveled to Sandringham, where they remained at Appleton House for the month of January. One of the King's guests for two days of shooting was Sir Alan Brooke, chief of the imperial general staff. The King and the general talked of Operation Overlord. All the senior officers for the operation were now in place, with Eisenhower as the supreme Allied commander.

George VI interrupted his holiday for three days in London to see Churchill and meet with Ike. The general reported that 875,000 American servicemen had arrived in Britain, with a total of 1.5 million expected by April. "From now on I shall be very busy in London & elsewhere going round seeing the preparations for 'Overlord,'" wrote the King as he ended his winter break in Norfolk.

By late spring he had managed to visit all the Allied troops taking part in Overlord. His review of the British fleet at Scapa Flow in Scotland's Orkney Islands extended over three days and included the destroyer *Whelp,* where he saw Prince Philip. For the first time, the King and Queen brought Lilibet along for a half dozen military inspections, including an overnight journey on the Royal Train to South Wales, where they were hailed by cheering crowds. On Salisbury Plain they watched demonstrations of gliders and parachutists: "a wonderful sight," said the King.

In the months leading to Lilibet's eighteenth birthday in April, Parliament amended the Regency Act of 1937 to enable her to be a Counsellor of State rather than wait until she turned twenty-one. At the same time, elements of the press and some politicians pushed to change her title to Princess of Wales. The King strongly opposed that effort and insisted to Churchill that it was a "family matter." As he explained to his mother, "How could I create Lilibet the Princess of

Wales when it is the recognized title of the wife of the Prince of Wales?" The prime minister and his War Cabinet agreed, and the Palace issued a statement on February 12 saying the King would not make "any change in the style and title of the Princess Elizabeth" when she turned eighteen.

One important voice on the King's side in the debate was the editor of *The Times,* Robert Barrington-Ward. At a Buckingham Palace reception several days later, he was introduced to Lilibet, who told him straightaway that she read *The Times* every day and "liked it very much." She added, "very modestly, 'I was interested in the article which you had about me the other day.' . . . We then agreed that the decision about her title was right," recalled Barrington-Ward.

The Times followed up with a thoughtful tribute to Princess Elizabeth, noting that she was "beginning to move more freely among her future subjects. Without any 'building up' . . . a new character has slipped demurely upon the stage of public life. She has few lines to speak at present, but in a later act she will have many. . . . The audience will watch with a lively curiosity the gradual revelation of her character. . . . She has a real feeling for history and a marked sense of the richness of the tradition into which she has been born."

Along with the military reviews with her parents, Lilibet did a solo engagement with Sea Scouts and Sea Rangers, whose uniform she wore for an eighteenth-birthday portrait. In London she had lunch with her aunt Marina at Claridge's: her first visit to a hotel, which "fascinated her." Alathea Fitzalan Howard felt sad, because "her life is becoming so less and less her own." No longer could her friends call her Lilibet; now she was "Ma'am" except with her family.

April 21 was a "lovely hot day" for Lilibet's celebration. The Grenadiers did a special Changing of the Guard in the castle quadrangle in their colonel's honor. The regiment's lieutenant colonel handed her a smaller version of the King's Colour featuring in each corner her monogram in gold thread. On the lapel of her hyacinth-blue coat she wore her diamond brooch of the Grenadiers' badge and cipher that the regiment had given her two years earlier. A family luncheon followed the ceremony, with extravagant gifts for the princess: a diamond and sapphire bracelet from her father, a diamond and ruby "pin-on" watch, a bracelet and necklace from Queen Mary, a small diamond tiara from her mother, and a dressing case from King Haakon of Norway.

ON THE MORNING OF MAY 15, under a mantle of secrecy, George VI and Churchill attended a briefing at St. Paul's School in London, General Montgomery's alma mater that was serving as the headquarters of his Twenty-first Army Group. Members of the War Cabinet and top military brass were on hand. The King had previously met them all in audiences at Buckingham Palace and at a series of dinners at 10 Downing Street over the previous three months—once in the very small air raid shelter during a spate of Luftwaffe raids over London in the late winter.

Now the King and the prime minister were seated in armchairs, while everyone else perched on the schoolboy benches in the pine-paneled room. From Eisenhower on down, each military commander described his part of the operation using maps to outline the plan of attack and the expected opposition. As the last military man concluded his remarks, the King stepped up to the platform without any advance notice. To the "astonishment" of Tommy Lascelles, he "delivered an admirable impromptu speech, in which he said exactly the right things and said them very well."

George VI described how he had followed the planning since the inception of Overlord. "This is the biggest Combined Operation ever thought out in the world," he said. "But it is so much more than this. It is a Combined Operation of two countries, the United States & the British Empire. As I look around this audience of British & Americans I can see that you have equally taken a part in its preparation. I wish you all success & with God's help you will succeed." Afterward, Ike thanked George VI and joked that his ground troops needed to "capture some villas for the hot shots, particularly one to accommodate the King."

The King and Queen had formed a close bond with Eisenhower. Ten days before the scheduled June 5 crossing, now called "D-Day," the supreme commander had lunch with them at the Palace. As they did with Churchill, they ate "cafeteria style," serving themselves from a side table. Ike reassured them that the troops were "in fine shape for the coming battle." Ike later told Harry Butcher he had a "grand time" with the royal couple. "Even if they weren't King and Queen you would enjoy being with them." He said Elizabeth was "particularly personable and radiates hospitality." She was "more talkative than the King," and he was tickled that she recalled "details of their crawling on their hands and knees" during the Windsor Castle garden incident the previous year.

With only days to go before the invasion, both George VI and Churchill decided they should witness the historic landing on the beaches of Normandy at close range from one of the "bombarding ships." At their weekly luncheon on May 30, the King told the prime minister the idea had been "in my mind for some time." Churchill suggested they go together. "I told Elizabeth about the idea & she was wonderful as always & encouraged me to do it," the King wrote in his diary. Tommy Lascelles was horrified by the proposal. He "shook the King" by asking "whether he was prepared to face the possibility of having to advise Princess Elizabeth on the choice of her first Prime Minister in the event of her father and Winston being sent to the bottom of the English Channel."

The next morning Lascelles easily persuaded George VI that it was "not right" for either of the men to "go on this expedition." The King immediately sent Churchill a letter to that effect, but the prime minister was determined to go. They met again on Thursday, June 1, for a briefing by Admiral Sir Bertram Ramsay, the naval commander in chief of the Allied Naval Expeditionary Force. Churchill asked Ramsay if he and the King could cross the Channel as observers.

"As I thought he would," wrote the King, the admiral "gave a very definite 'no' to the question." When Churchill insisted on going anyway, George VI strongly criticized the idea of his prime minister on a "joy-ride" in the middle of a battle and said he would be taking "unnecessary risks." Ramsay, a veteran of the First World War who had overseen the Dunkirk evacuation and naval operations during Torch and Husky, was visibly "shaken" by the prime minister's obstinacy. Churchill's "seemingly selfish way of looking at the matter" rattled the King as well.

On Friday, June 2, the King wrote an even longer letter to Churchill, outlining all the reasons he should stand down, and ending with a personal plea: "I have been very worried & anxious over the whole of this business & it is my duty to warn the P.M. on such occasions. No one else can & should anything dreadful happen I should be asked if I had tried to deter him." George VI was so desperate to stop him he considered driving to Portsmouth and physically standing in his way. Churchill finally phoned Tommy Lascelles and said that "in deference to the King's wishes, he would abandon his plan of going to sea."

While the Germans remained in the dark about the destination of the expeditionary force, everyone in England privy to the plans was on tenterhooks. The apprehensiveness intensified on the morning of Sunday, June 4, when Eisenhower scrutinized the rainy and windy weather forecast for the next day and postponed Overlord for twenty-four hours.

At Windsor the King diverted himself by riding on horseback for the first time in four years, with Lilibet and Margaret. But he brooded about the men waiting on board the ships in quarters that were "very cramped." Lilibet told Alathea "how terrible a strain it was for the King" and that the Queen "spent almost the whole of Monday night at the window looking at the planes, unable to sleep."

George VI and Elizabeth were in London on Tuesday, June 6, when they heard the invasion was under way. They had lunch with Churchill at the Palace, and the King went off with his prime minister for updates at the Supreme Headquarters Allied Expeditionary Force (SHAEF) command center in Bushey Park on the perimeter of London. By nightfall some 165,000 troops had been transported by more than 5,000 ships. In the first twenty-four hours, there had been 9,000 casualties, including 3,000 killed.

Elizabeth had urged her husband to deliver the invasion message to the public rather than leave it to Churchill. Queen Mary backed her up, saying, "Bertie's message will be far more popular. Do persuade him to do it." George VI worked with Lionel Logue for three hours before his D-Day radio broadcast at nine P.M. The Bishop of Lichfield had helped the King write it, and only a few words needed to be changed.

The King reminded his listeners that four years earlier, Britain's back had been against the wall, and the nation had survived the most severe tests. "Once more a supreme test has to be faced," he said. "This time the challenge is not to fight to survive, but to fight to win the final victory for the good cause." He asked for a "revival of the spirit," and for "young and old" to join in a "vigil of prayer as the great crusade sets forth." Writing to his mother, the King said, "It was a great opportunity to call everybody to prayer. I have wanted to do it for a long time."

The King and Queen spent the week monitoring what he described as the "very fierce" battle. "These are very anxious days," he wrote. They had Winston and Clementine for tea, and in Churchill's map room they viewed models of the "Mulberry" harbors, the artificial ports with floating piers that were being built on the Normandy beaches.

George VI, Tommy Lascelles, and top British and American military officers made a daylong visit to the armies in Normandy on the sixteenth of June. They crossed the choppy Channel in gusty weather and boarded a "Duck" amphibious landing craft that "waddled" up the beach. At General Montgomery's headquarters in a small château, their lunch in the garden included Camembert cheeses, which they had not tasted in four years.

The front lines were six miles away, and Monty "would not hear of the King going nearer," as the intervening territory was filled with snipers. The King did an investiture for a small group of officers and men, "elaborately staged by Monty," who gave a full briefing on progress and planned attacks. "It was most encouraging to know that it was possible for me to land on the beaches only 10 days after D Day," the King wrote.

When he returned to Windsor Castle that evening, Elizabeth told him about the V-1 "Vengeance" bomb that Germany had unleashed on Britain. Nicknamed the "buzz-bomb" and "doodlebug," it was a pilotless airplane packed with nearly a ton of high explosives that arrived with a terrific buzzing noise. When the engine cut out at a designated moment, the noise ceased, and about fifteen seconds later the aircraft dropped to the ground with a massive explosion. "It looks as if the 'secret weapon' phase has started," commented George VI. He called its arrival "a new trial for our people" that would likely mean "a change in our daily routine."

Launching from sites along the French coast, thousands of V-1s landed day and night in London and in areas of Kent along their route. The most personal attack for the royal family came on Sunday, June 18, when the Guards' Chapel at Wellington Barracks near Buckingham Palace took a direct hit during the morning service, just as the choir had begun the sung Eucharist. The King and Queen knew the chapel well and had often worshipped there. One hundred twenty-one soldiers and civilians were killed, and 141 more were seriously injured.

Although the chapel itself was destroyed, the gilded apse survived. Within it, the six altar candles—in silver candlesticks George VI had given to the chapel in 1938—miraculously still burned. "It was a great shock to us, as we know so many people who use it," wrote the King.

Two days later, another doodlebug blasted open seventy-five yards of the Buckingham Palace wall along Constitution Hill. "We felt the concussion of the blast in the shelter where we were," wrote the King. Afterward, George VI and Elizabeth went into the garden to pick up bomb fragments, and they were dismayed to see extensive damage to the little Admiralty summerhouse that Lilibet had used for her Girl Guides troop. The King shifted all investitures, audiences, and lunches with the prime minister to the Palace shelter. Windsor Castle didn't get hit, but a V-1 crashed onto the Long Walk with an explosion that burst some windows at Royal Lodge.

The King, Queen, and Churchill worried about the impact of these terror weapons on "our normal life & the effects on people's nerves and energy," in the prime minister's words. The Queen believed that the new barrage was "much worse than the Blitz of 1940. . . . Perhaps because after 5 years of war people have been through so much that this extra burden lies heavier," she told Queen Mary. "There is something very inhuman and beastly about death dealing missiles being launched in such an indiscriminate manner."

The King and Queen stepped up their tours of military facilities, especially antiaircraft batteries near the Channel coast, and British and American air stations carrying out sorties against the V-1 launching sites in France. Elizabeth took particular note of the efforts of the women operating heavy guns aimed at the doodlebugs: "constantly on the alert night & day."

A second and equally sinister unmanned German bomb first fell in early September 1944. The V-2 was a new ballistic missile fired into the stratosphere, after which it would fall to earth at such ferocious speed—about 2,500 mph on impact—it could make a crater thirty feet deep. Unlike the doodlebug, the arrival of the V-2 wasn't preceded by loud warning noises. "You can't take shelter," explained the Queen. "It's just luck or perhaps the Almighty keeping an eye." From June 1944 to March 1945, when the last of the launch sites was destroyed, the two murderous weapons killed some 9,000 people, injured 25,000, and destroyed more than 100,000 homes.

George VI and Elizabeth did their best to carry on with their lives even as the rockets fell. But mindful of the risks, at the end of June the Queen sent a letter to Lilibet giving instructions about dividing up her jewelry "in case I get 'done in.'" She counted on her older daughter to "do the right thing & remember to keep your temper & your word & be loving."

That July, the King made plans to see his troops in Italy who had been "put in the shade" by all the action following D-Day. Despite her "intense anxiety," Elizabeth understood that her husband felt "so much not being more in the fighting line." Rome had been liberated on June 4, two days before D-Day. The Germans had continued to fight tenaciously, and Allied progress had been slow.

By the middle of the summer, the Allies had secured enough Italian territory that it was reasonably safe for George VI to visit for "a strenuous eleven days." As he did when he visited North Africa, the King felt a need to put in writing to his "darling Angel" some "matters which might want clearing up." He told Elizabeth that she should continue living in the Palace, Windsor Castle, Sandringham, and Balmoral "for the present until such time as Lilibet is on her own." He said he hoped that Royal Lodge, Appleton, and Birkhall "will always be your house on the private estates. The former is our home; the house we built & made for ourselves in Windsor Park."

On Saturday night, July 22, 1944, Elizabeth and Lilibet went with the King to the Northolt aerodrome to say goodbye. "It was nearly dark when we drove onto the airfield," the Queen wrote to Queen Mary. She and her daughter climbed into the same York airplane that the King had taken to North Africa. "It looked as big as Noah's ark, and a deal more comfortable," Tommy Lascelles observed.

After they had inspected the accommodations, including "a nice little kitchen to prepare the food," the Queen got an unexpected jolt when she entered the cockpit and tried out the pilot's seat. "The first thing I saw through the glass was a flying bomb caught in the searchlights," she wrote. It seemed to be headed directly for them, and she averted her eyes, more in anger than fear. "Luckily it buzzed over and was going strong when I looked again!"

The King arrived in Naples on Sunday afternoon. With General Harold Alexander as his guide, George VI traveled eight thousand miles by air and one thousand by road. He reviewed British, American, French, Polish, and even Brazilian troops. He and "Alex" awakened at six-thirty each morning and took swims in nearby lakes. He had tea in the Villa d'Este at Tivoli and sat in the ruins of Hadrian's Villa built in A.D. 130. Yet he yearned for Elizabeth. "I have only been away a week & I feel it is 10 years," he wrote from Lake Bolsena. "I hope you are not too lonely angel."

Most important of all was the time he spent one-on-one with General Alexander, with whom he had many frank talks: "I got to know him very well & he told me a great deal on the military side about his generals." Alexander lent him his caravan, and the King had lighting installed and added a small tent. He brought his own rubber bathtub, which he left behind for the general's use.

In Arezzo, a town that only nine days earlier had been occupied by the Germans, the King admired the "panorama of mountains to the north," one of which looked like "several Lochnagars placed together." As he sat in his bath, he took in "the view in all its glory on a most lovely clear evening at the same time as I was listening to our guns firing 6 miles off & the Grenadier Guards band was playing 'The White Horse Inn.' What could have been nicer."

On his return from Italy at seven A.M. on August 3, the King went straight to Windsor to be with the Queen and his daughters before meeting Churchill at the Palace for lunch and giving a full report on his impressions. He was "very well and cheerful, having evidently enjoyed himself," noted Tommy Lascelles.

The Queen was "longing to get the children away for a change because life is rather un-normal," she wrote to Queen Mary from Windsor on August 4, her forty-fourth birthday. It was a day of "warnings and explosions," which "does give a feeling of uncertainty!" She was proud of Lilibet and Margaret for being "so good & composed" despite the strain of constant "listening & occasionally a leap behind the door."

A week later they were all on the train to Balmoral. George VI felt guilty about staying away from the action in London while battles played out on the Continent. But he reassured himself that much could be done on the telephone.

"The most important thing is that one (I) cannot go for ever without a rest," he wrote. "This is the only place where one (I) can have a real change, though strenuous exercise is the order of the day. I feel my visit to Italy demands a rest." What he didn't reckon was that his grouse moors had been thoroughly trampled by troops training for Overlord. Not that he especially minded, since "that training has enabled them to fight as they have & are fighting in Normandy."

A few days in the Highlands yet again brought out Lilibet and Margaret's "very bright eyes and pink cheeks." Lilibet went out deer stalking and caught her first salmon, an eight-pounder, in the river near Birkhall. Elizabeth was savoring the "peace and beauty" after a "violent two months." Yet like her husband, she was "almost conscience stricken" thinking about everyone in London "carrying on so splendidly amongst all the ruin and death."

GEORGE VI CLOSELY TRACKED ALLIED progress toward victory over Germany. The war in the Pacific concerned him less, at least in part because it was more in the purview of the United States. He had always had a "Germany first" policy. The King and Queen rejoiced over the liberation of Paris on August 25, 1944, followed by Brussels on September 3. In late September they traveled to London, where the King invested Queen Wilhelmina of the Netherlands with the Order of the Garter to show his "admiration for the way she has upheld the traditions of her country from a distance during its occupation by the enemy for four years." George VI stayed behind at the Palace while Elizabeth returned to Balmoral, where she and the princesses remained until late October.

While they were on holiday, the King flew to Allied territory in Holland and Belgium for a weeklong visit with the Normandy invasion armies. As Montgomery's guest, he stayed in two caravans, with a bath tent attached. His bedroom was equipped with electric lights, a comfortable bed, and a writing table. He and the general had lunch in the mess tent, where the King met Monty's dogs, Hitler and Rommel, along with his pet rabbits.

Over the next week, George VI had briefings from all the top commanders, among them Montgomery, Eisenhower, Omar Bradley, and George Patton. He inspected troops and grilled pilots about their missions. Monty occupied most of his time and proved a source of bemused fascination.

"I found out that he had no hobbies, had never hunted or shot, or played any game in his life," wrote the King. "He is entirely bound up in himself & leads his own life with his small personal staff who are all very young. Besides telling me all about the Battle of Normandy, he gave me an account of it to read written by himself as the battle progressed, which reads like a novel." On leaving for England in mid-October, George VI wrote, "I have got to know how the Army works & lives."

He was reunited in London with Elizabeth, Lilibet, and Margaret, just back from Balmoral. "I had not seen them for 3 weeks & it seemed several years," he wrote. Less than a month later, on Monday, November 6, word reached Elizabeth from Glamis that her father was gravely ill. Claude Strathmore had been suffering from influenza for a month and had taken a sudden downward turn. He died in his sleep that night at age eighty-nine, with his daughter May at his bedside.

Despite the constraints of the war, Elizabeth had traveled to Glamis a half dozen times to be with her father, most recently on his birthday the previous March. She described him to her mother-in-law as "active & virile," even in his eighties: "One could not wish him to live as an invalid." *The Times* observed that despite his youngest daughter's "great position," Claude Strathmore "never altered his unostentatious and almost simple mode of life." Elizabeth told Winston Churchill that she was "very grateful to have had him so long," and she was comforted to know that Glamis "was a centre of good will & unity for the people around."

Lord Strathmore's funeral echoed the austere rites for Cecilia in 1938: a small service for family and a handful of friends in the Glamis private chapel, followed by a procession to the burial ground. Three foresters and three gamekeepers bore the coffin, draped with a Union Jack, to a farm wagon drawn by two horses. The cart followed four pipers of the Black Watch regiment, playing the lament "The Flowers o' the Forest." Walking behind were the King and Michael Bowes Lyon, as well as May's husband, Sidney. Elizabeth rode in a car with May and Rosie, and their brother Patrick, now the fifteenth Earl of Strathmore.

For Patrick, permanently shell-shocked from the First World War, this was the second tragedy in three years. His eldest son, John, the

Master of Glamis, a lieutenant in the Scots Guards, had been killed in action in September 1941 while serving in Egypt. Elizabeth clung to the hope that Patrick would settle at Glamis. "He seems to really love the place," she wrote to her brother David, who was posted at the British Embassy in Washington and unable to attend the funeral. "Perhaps he will become more ordinary & easy when he is 'himself' at Glamis."

THE FAMILY HAD ANOTHER QUIET Christmas at Windsor. From his deployment in the Indian Ocean, Prince Philip sent Lilibet a photograph of himself, and she "danced round the room with it for joy!" She had last seen him the previous July when he visited her at Windsor Castle. As he often did on weekend evenings, the King had shown a film in his private cinema: Noël Coward's *This Happy Breed*. Alathea Fitzalan Howard sat behind Philip and noted that the prince "laughed v. loudly," while the King kept a running commentary on his visit to Normandy after D-Day. "I guessed that P.E. was v. happy and I wished her success in my heart." Philip had sent an effusive note to the Queen, thanking her for sharing with him "the simple enjoyment of family pleasures." He touchingly admitted to being "incapable of showing you the gratitude I feel."

Princess Elizabeth took on fresh responsibilities in 1945. She was, by her mother's account, working hard with Henry Marten and had "learnt quite a lot of European and constitutional history." In the final year of the war, she visited miners in South Wales, gave her first public speeches in London, and launched HMS *Vanguard*, "the greatest battleship yet built in the British Isles."

The launching was the first time she appeared on her own in what *The Times* called a "ceremony of national significance." She acknowledged her enthusiastic welcome "with smiles and a little movement of her right hand, very like that of her mother. . . . She asked questions about anything that claimed her interest, and many things did." After she pressed the button to release the great ship into the water, she "watched with rapt eyes," a "brave and winsome figure."

Lilibet's most unusual new challenge that spring was a three-week course at the No. 1 Mechanical Training Centre run by the ATS. "I think it will be a good thing for her to have a little experience from the inside into how a women's Service is run," Elizabeth told her mother-in-law. "She will learn something about the inside of a car as well, which is always useful."

The princess proudly wore her battledress with trousers and soft peaked cap when she registered as Second Subaltern Elizabeth Alexandra Mary Windsor. Every day an ATS officer drove her to Camberley in Surrey, where she crawled under cars and learned how to change tires along with the mechanics of ignition systems, brakes, and spark plugs. Since Windsor wasn't far from the training center, she could spend her nights at the castle. But otherwise she had to salute senior officers and was treated equally with the other young women in her training course.

Before long she was driving three-ton trucks and spending her days in "new and utterly unaccustomed surroundings, quite on her own as it were."

"I've never worked so hard in my life," the princess told a friend. "Everything I learnt was brand new to me." As she was wrapping up her course on April 9, the King and Queen came to watch her demonstrate her new skills under the hood of a car, her face proudly smudged with grease.

Three days later the King and Queen heard that Franklin D. Roosevelt had died of a cerebral hemorrhage at age sixty-three. Churchill had reported to the King in February after meeting on postwar plans with Roosevelt and Soviet leader Joseph Stalin at Yalta that FDR "has become very feeble," so his death wasn't surprising. "He was a very great man, & his loss will be felt the World over," George VI wrote in his diary. He ordered a week of court mourning, and he and the Queen attended a memorial service the following week at St. Paul's Cathedral. The King knew little of Roosevelt's successor, Vice President Harry S. Truman, but he was intent on meeting him as soon as possible.

Over subsequent weeks, the German army collapsed rapidly. The King recorded the most shocking news on Thursday, April 19, 1945, after the U.S. Army liberated the concentration camps at Belsen and Buchenwald. "Internment Camp Horrors" and "Camp of Death and Misery" read the headlines in *The Times,* accompanied by gut-wrenching photographs of the atrocities.

There had been awareness in Britain of Jewish "persecution and in fact the extermination"—as Harold Nicolson described it—since late 1942 when a parliamentary committee took evidence of horrors on a "gigantic scale." On December 17 of that year, Foreign Secretary Anthony Eden had read out a statement in the House of Commons about "barbarous and inhuman treatment" of Jews, prompting all the members of Parliament and journalists in the chamber to stand for two minutes of silence. But there was no follow-up by the British or American government to intervene with measures such as bombing railway lines used to transport imprisoned Jews to the camps.

The King made no mention in his diaries at the time, but while not specifically referring to the persecution of Jews, he did express outrage in his diary on April 19, 1945: "Tens of thousands of people of all nationalities have been allowed to die of starvation after bestial mal-treatment. They have found bodies littered about the camps & the ovens where they were cremated. Coal shortage prevented the Ger-mans from carrying out their work & we found bodies already stacked in the ovens." While he had yet to hear of the gas chambers at Ausch-witz and other extermination camps in occupied Poland, he said unequivocally that "the German people are all guilty in allowing these things to happen. They have no sense of shame that it is wrong."

"Events are moving very fast now," the King wrote the weekend of April 28, after U.S. armies entered Munich. Mussolini had been mur-dered by Communist "Italian Patriots" in northern Italy on the twenty-eighth, and Hitler was reported to have died at his command post in the Reich Chancellery—by suicide, it turned out—on the thirtieth. On May 2, one million men in the German army surrendered to Har-old Alexander, promoted by the King to field marshal. "A great victory," wrote the King. The same day, the Russians took over Berlin. Total German surrender came early in the morning of May 7. Hostilities officially ended on Tuesday, May 8, 1945, Victory in Europe Day.

Preparations for V-E Day had been under way for months. Floodlights and loudspeakers were positioned throughout London and in front of Buckingham Palace. Churchill came to the Palace for his customary lunch, this time in a mood of elation. "No more fear of being bombed at home & no more living in air raid shelters," wrote the King, who wisely added, "There is still Japan to be defeated & the restoration of our country to be dealt with."

But on that day, the first of two national holidays, all of Britain let loose. Nearly a million people clogged the streets across London. They sang "Roll Out the Barrel" and wore paper hats. They scaled lampposts and scrambled atop double-decker buses. But they fell silent when Churchill spoke at three P.M. from 10 Downing Street, his words broadcast on the radio and through loudspeakers in vans at Parliament Square. The "evil doers," he said, were "now prostrate before us."

Soon afterward, the King and Queen and princesses stepped onto the Buckingham Palace balcony to a roar of acclamation from the massive crowd—the first of eight appearances by the monarch and consort that afternoon and evening. The second time, about an hour later, Churchill joined them to acknowledge the jubilation of the British people. The most poignant feature of the scene was the partly boarded window behind them, a reminder of what the Palace—and the royal family—had endured.

"Speaking from our Empire's oldest capital city, war-battered but never for one moment daunted or dismayed," George VI began his victory speech that evening at nine P.M. from the broadcasting room in the Palace. He had been practicing at intervals with Logue since Saturday, and he felt confident in front of the microphone. He vowed to turn with "utmost resolve" to defeating the Japanese, "but at this hour when the dreadful shadow of war has passed far from our hearths and homes in these islands, we may at last make one pause for thanksgiving."

Harold Nicolson listened with a group of friends at the Travellers Club. "The words are excellent, and he does not stammer too badly," Nicolson wrote. "But it is agony to listen to him—like a typewriter which sticks every third word." Logue knew the King was exhausted, "and it showed; he stumbled over his words, but it didn't seem to matter."

The King let Lilibet and Margaret slip into the crowds with a group of friends to join the fun. Lilibet wore her ATS uniform with her cap pulled low, and the girls were accompanied by friends and guards officers. They all linked arms and plowed through the throng, danced the Lambeth Walk and the Hokey-Cokey, and did a conga line through the Ritz hotel. Lilibet and Margaret even stood near the Palace railings to see their parents dramatically illuminated on the balcony, their mother in a white ermine wrap and a glittering diamond tiara. When they returned to the Palace by the private garden entrance, they eagerly ate sandwiches made by the Queen. The next night they were out again. "Embankment. Piccadilly. Pall Mall, walked simply miles," Lilibet wrote in her diary. "Saw parents on balcony at 12:30 am—ate, partied, bed 3 am!"

When the King released Lilibet and Margaret from the Palace, he made a comment in his diary that was subsequently much quoted: "Poor darlings they have never had any fun yet." But what was so remarkable was the amount of enjoyment Princesses Elizabeth and Margaret *had* found in the war years, even in the most harrowing moments. They had danced into the small hours in the drawing rooms at Windsor Castle and Buckingham Palace a half dozen times and had watched more than forty movies—including *Casablanca* and *Gone with the Wind*—as well as theatrical performances. The Grenadier guardsmen at Windsor had organized countless other entertainments— teas, treasure hunts, and games of Charades, Sardines, Clumps, and Consequences. The girls had taken pride in their own pantomime performances and had savored weeks of freedom at Balmoral and Sandringham. And, of course, Prince Philip had courted Lilibet at Windsor whenever he was free on leave.

On May 9 and 10, the King and Queen took long carriage drives through neighborhoods in east and south London that had been hit so mercilessly by the bombings. The people responded in kind, with a "great ovation." There was a thanksgiving service at St. Paul's Cathedral commemorating the end of the war in Europe, and on May 17, both Houses of Parliament paid tribute to the King and Queen in the Great Hall of Westminster.

The hall was jammed, and after short addresses from the Lord Chancellor and House Speaker, the King spoke for fifteen minutes on "what this country & Empire have done." His remarks had "a dignity and eloquence surpassing anything that I have yet heard from him," wrote Tommy Lascelles. "He had one bad stammer, on the word 'imperishable,' but otherwise it was all good; and a wholly spontaneous touch gave the speech a really dramatic and moving quality when, in alluding to the Duke of Kent's death, his voice faltered and broke." The crowd remained briefly silent before Churchill, "with his sense of occasion," waved his top hat, leapt to the dais, and called for three cheers. As Harold Nicolson recalled the moment: "All our pent up energies responded with three yells such as I should have thought impossible to emanate from so many elderly throats."

King George VI with Princess Elizabeth in 1946.

PART SIX

An Indelible Legacy

"Boundless hopes are centred in yr daughter's gleaming personality & reign."

*"Privately he called his new prime minister
'Clem the Clam.'"*

King George VI with his new prime minister, Clement Attlee, at Buckingham
Palace on July 28, 1945, after the Labour Party defeated Winston Churchill
and the Conservative Party.

THIRTY-TWO

Changing of the Guard

SINCE THE BEGINNING OF THE WAR, KING GEORGE VI HAD TURNED repeatedly to questions about Britain's postwar outlook, and he assiduously read papers on reconstruction from various departments in the government. In early 1940 he and Roosevelt had discussed setting up an international mission to provide relief for food and clothing. Anticipating the Common Market in July 1940, Ernest Bevin had brought up his concept for a "Customs Union" comprising Britain, France, Holland, and Belgium. Two years later, South African prime minister Jan Smuts raised a similar proposal for a "northern bloc" including Britain, Holland, Norway, Belgium, Denmark, and Sweden.

To Bevin and other Labour ministers in the War Cabinet, George VI stressed that labor union leaders should coordinate with leaders of industry in peacetime. The King's objective, rooted in his boys' camps and his long-standing work with the Industrial Welfare Society, was to encourage dialogue between economic and social classes. The home secretary, Labour's Herbert Morrison, agreed with George VI in late 1940 that the two parties "must stick together afterwards so as to rebuild & replan it together."

The King was adamant that "we must get rid of all those bureau-cratic regulations as soon as possible. In war time people know and realise that rules and regulations have to be made & obeyed, but in peace time they want them to cease at once, which is impossible." As a consequence, he emphasized that changing from wartime to peace-time conditions needed to be "done gradually, so as to obviate unem-ployment on a large scale."

With these ideas in mind, the King believed he would be working with Winston Churchill to help rebuild Britain's postwar society. The British public had other ideas. Within weeks of V-E Day, Labour min-isters led by Clement Attlee resigned from the national government. They told the King they were sorry to leave but felt it was time to break away. "Parliament is ten years old, and no one under the age of 30 has ever voted," they said. "The House of Commons needs rejuvenating." Churchill formed an interim government, and a general election was called for July 5. "Thus has ended the Coalition Government which during the War has done admirable work," wrote the King. "Country before Party has been its watchword. But now what?"

The King and Queen expected Churchill would coast to an easy victory. On July 25, the day before the announcement of election results, the prime minister predicted to the King that the Conserva-tives would be elected with a majority ranging between 30 and 80. In fact, Labour won with an enormous majority of 146 seats.

Everyone was stunned by the result. It wasn't so much an overt repudiation of seventy-year-old Winston Churchill as it was an urgent call for change felt by a war-weary populace. Churchill explained his defeat to Tommy Lascelles as "the people's reaction from their suffer-ings of the past five years . . . all the horrors and discomforts of war, and, automatically they have vented it on the government that has been in power throughout the period of their discontent."

It didn't much matter that the Tories had already embraced the wartime coalition's plans for a national health service and educational reforms. Labour advocated more sweeping programs that had popular appeal. Its agenda was overtly socialist, calling for nationalization of crucial parts of the economy, including the central bank, railroads, gas, electricity, and the production of coal, iron, and steel. Only then, Attlee had written, could Britain redress "gross inequalities of wealth and opportunity."

The King reacted to the result "with great calm and reasonableness," according to Lascelles, although he wearily wrote in his diary, "The change of Govt. will of course give me a great deal more work & even less leisure." The King noted sympathetically that the retiring Tory ministers assured him that they "would help the new Govt. unless they tried to do some dreadful piece of legislation against the Country's interests."

At seven P.M. on July 26, Churchill came to the Palace to submit his resignation. "It was a very sad meeting," George VI recalled. "I told him I thought the people were very ungrateful after the way they had been led in the War." He offered Churchill his highest honor, the Order of the Garter, "in recognition of his services during the War." Churchill declined on the grounds that it would be wrong to accept "after the rebuff that the electorate have given him as a leader." He hoped he could receive it at a later date (which he did in April 1953 from the King's elder daughter). Churchill told George VI he worried that the socialists "could remain in power for years" and promised to carry on the Tory cause as leader of the opposition.

A half hour later, when Clement Attlee arrived—"obviously in a state of some bewilderment," noted Lascelles—the King "found he was very surprised his Party had won." At age forty-nine, George VI took on the unexpected role of elder statesman to his sixty-two-year-old prime minister when Attlee admitted he hadn't given much thought to his key appointments.

Attlee had met with the King dozens of times during the war as Churchill's deputy prime minister. In their first wartime meeting late in 1939, the King had found him "shy & reserved and difficult to talk to." As recently as February 1945, he had written that Attlee "as usual was very reticent." Privately he called his new prime minister "Clem the Clam."

When asked his choice for foreign secretary, Attlee mentioned Hugh Dalton, an economist who had held several Labour Party positions during the war. George VI disliked the "anarchist son" of his father's stern tutor, Canon Dalton. After one wartime audience with Hugh Dalton, George VI was notably uncharitable about his departure from the Ministry of Economic Warfare. "I did not tell him," he wrote, that the ministry had reacted "with delight" that he was leaving. "He has a schoolmaster manner." George VI also took a dim view of Dalton's apparent sympathy toward the Soviet Union and its territorial ambitions.

In his first conversation with Attlee as prime minister, the King pointedly disagreed with the Dalton suggestion. Foreign affairs was "the most important subject at the moment," George VI told Attlee. "I hoped he would make Mr. Bevin take it. He said he would." Tommy Lascelles put the matter more emphatically, writing that "HM begged him to substitute Bevin." Attlee later denied that George VI had "insisted" he appoint Ernest Bevin rather than Hugh Dalton. But George VI didn't back away from the robust stand he took on Bevin's behalf, even if it seemed to exceed the monarch's constitutional duty to "be consulted."

George VI's conviction that Bevin was the right man for the job turned out to be correct. He admired Bevin's muscular approach toward the Soviet Union, and he found him easy to deal with. He wrote to his brother Prince Henry that Bevin told him "everything that is going on." After a "long talk," the King was "much struck" by Bevin's knowledge of foreign affairs.

DURING THE FINAL STRETCH OF the Pacific war that summer, hundreds of American B-29 Superfortresses dropped more than six thousand tons of firebombs and high explosives each day on Japanese industrial towns. As the endgame played out, the King met Harry Truman aboard HMS *Renown* off the battered port city of Plymouth in Devon on August 2, 1945. The American president was en route to Washington from the Potsdam Conference in Berlin with Attlee and Stalin. Their purpose had been to work out the terms of an unconditional Japanese surrender and the governance of postwar Germany. Soviet domination of Eastern Europe following its battlefield victories was already a fait accompli that would later harden into the Cold War.

The King and President Truman spent twenty minutes together before having lunch on shipboard, where they established an immediate rapport. George VI was pleased that at Potsdam, Truman "had learnt a great deal & understood European difficulties from a new standpoint." Truman was "impressed with the King as a good man." The King was taken with Secretary of State James Byrnes, calling him "a great talker." Byrnes, in turn, was pleasantly surprised by George VI's "informality and wide knowledge."

They all discussed at length the "T.A. bomb"—the atomic "tube alloy" weapon developed by the Manhattan Project in the United States. Churchill had been secretly briefing the King on its progress, and the monarch had been exceedingly circumspect. It was only on the twenty-fifth of July that he wrote in his diary, "The Prime Minister told me the Tube Alloy experiment in U.S.A. had been a success & that one of these bombs would be dropped on Japan in the near future. Its effect would probably bring the Japanese War to an end very soon."

When Byrnes freely talked about the weapon's properties and potential in front of the stewards serving the meal, the King was "horrified," according to Tommy Lascelles. It was "so secret a matter in this country that only about six people have ever heard of it." The secretary of state's indiscretion prompted the King to say, "I think, Mr. Byrnes, that we should discuss this interesting subject over our coffee."

Four days later, the United States dropped the first atomic bomb on the Japanese city of Hiroshima—killing more than 100,000 people—followed by a second three days later on the port city of Nagasaki. Some 40,000 people died in that second attack. In a speech to the House of Commons, Churchill said that the alternative would have been an invasion of Japan, which could have cost "a million American, and a quarter of a million British, lives." On August 15, the

Japanese government accepted the terms of surrender, ending the Pacific war.

In London, "Victory Over Japan Day" coincided with the first peacetime State Opening of Parliament. The splendid pageantry was only partly restored, but it was sufficient to give the massive crowds on the streets an unanticipated victory parade. The monarch and consort traveled to the House of Lords in an ornate state landau pulled by four gray horses, ridden by wigged and jockey-capped postilions, with two footmen standing at the back and scarlet-coated outriders trotting alongside. The escort of Household Cavalry wore khaki, and the route was lined by the Brigade of Guards.

Despite intermittent showers, the royal couple insisted on an open carriage. "We did not want to disappoint the people," said the King. Neither George VI nor Elizabeth wore ceremonial robes; he was in a naval uniform and cap, and the Queen wore a dress and feather-trimmed halo hat of pale blue with fox furs draped on her shoulders. Hand in hand they walked into the chamber at the Palace of Westminster and sat in the thrones on the dais. Preceding them was the Imperial State Crown carried on a cushion by the Admiral of the Fleet.

Speaking for sixteen minutes, the King announced the surrender of Japan and outlined the ambitious "public ownership" of "our industries and services" to ensure their "maximum contribution to the national well-being." Foremost among these measures were bills to nationalize the Bank of England and the coal-mining industry. The King and Queen returned to the Palace as they arrived, in the open landau, this time in a downpour. The King wore a raincoat, and the Queen held a black umbrella with one hand "while with the other she acknowledged the cheering, no less fervent than before."

In the House of Commons, Clement Attlee praised the King and Queen for their example of "courage and devotion throughout the war," which had strengthened the "bond of affection and understanding between the Throne and people." The prime minister and his cabinet gathered on the Palace terrace to congratulate the King and Queen on the final victory and pose for photographs. A half hour after the

Labour ministers left, Winston Churchill arrived on his own and had a private conversation with George VI.

That day and evening the King and Queen stood on the balcony a half dozen times, the first appearance in the late afternoon with the two princesses. At nine P.M., the King delivered his "Victory Talk to His Peoples," alone in his Buckingham Palace study, without Logue's assistance. "Our sense of deliverance is overpowering," he said in a firm and resonant voice, "and with it all, we have a right to feel that we have done our duty." He asked his listeners to remember those who had laid down their lives and the "sufferings of those who fell into the hands of the enemy."

"The war is over," he said. "You know, I think that those four words have for the Queen and myself the same significance, simple yet immense, that they have for you. Our hearts are full to overflowing, as are your own." He ended by thanking, "from the bottom of my heart," his "Peoples, for all they have done, not only for themselves but for mankind."

In addition to its transmission on BBC radio, the King's speech was relayed through loudspeakers in front of the Palace. Tommy Lascelles listened in the forecourt "with a vast crowd . . . in 'pin-drop silence,' stretching out behind us half-way down the Mall." Tommy thought that George VI "surpassed himself. . . . He has never yet spoken so fluently or forcefully." When the monarch finished, there was a "great burst of cheering."

"We want the King," chanted the crowd. "For He's a Jolly Good Fellow," they sang. The rain had cleared, and a half-moon shone in the starlit sky. After floodlights illuminated the Palace façade, the royal family appeared for a fourth time, the Queen in diamond tiara, the King in his navy uniform, Lilibet in a flowered silk gown, and Margaret in blue. Behind them, nearly all the windows on the Palace front were still covered with boards. Nobody else shared the balcony, and the King missed his former prime minister. "I wish he could have been given a proper reception by the people," he wrote in his diary.

Late in the evening, Lilibet and Margaret sneaked into the

crowds again, this time escorted by two plainclothes police officers. They stood for a while in front of the Palace and watched the King and Queen on the balcony, the final appearance just before midnight. Some revelers recognized Lilibet and Margaret and began cheering them, but the police "informed the crowds that the princesses wished to be treated as private individuals," and they were allowed to go on their way. They "walked miles," Lilibet recalled. "Ran through Ritz . . . drank in Dorchester, saw parents twice, miles away, so many people."

OVER TIME, GEORGE VI AND Attlee grew more comfortable with each other. The King respected his fourth prime minister for having fought in the First World War, and for volunteering as a social worker as a young man in the impoverished East End. He wasn't shy about urging Attlee to slow down his nationalization program and cautioning that it threatened to "stifle all private enterprise"—arguably a legitimate exercise of his prerogative "to warn."

Like so many others who passed through the King's audience room, Attlee came to appreciate George VI's steadfast character and fundamental humanity. "He was a very hard worker," Attlee wrote. "Few people realize how much time and care he gave to public affairs, and visitors from overseas were often astonished at his clear familiarity with all kinds of questions. With this close study went a good judgement and a sure instinct for what was really vital. . . . He was essentially broad-minded and was ready to accept changes that seemed necessary."

Elizabeth shared her husband's dismay at the election results, which she thought "very depressing. . . . One must try now to build up another good sound government. But the material is not too inspiring." Like the King, she admired Attlee for his modest manner and evident integrity. Years later she said that Attlee "wouldn't strike one as a star," and she thought "at first he was quite cagey, you know, difficult to get on with, but then he soon melted. But I think he was very practical. Seemed to get a grip of things."

Nevertheless, even more than the King, Elizabeth had grave doubts about the radical social and economic policies and extreme austerity measures being imposed on Attlee's watch. The government rationed bread for the first time in British history and tightened wartime strictures on many necessities, along with import controls on oil and tobacco. Britain's huge debt to the United States had to be renegotiated, and the government significantly hiked taxes to finance the new welfare state.

Winston Churchill remained preeminent in the affections of the King and Queen, and they continued to socialize with him and seek his counsel. After Winston and Clementine came to the Palace for dinner late in 1945, the King wrote in his diary, "How refreshing to have a friend to talk to for a change." When the King needed to give a speech to United Nations delegates at a banquet early in 1946, he even ran the government version past Churchill. Nearly a year after Churchill's defeat, George VI told Mackenzie King that he missed his former prime minister "very much."

BOTH CHURCHILL AND ATTLEE INEVITABLY got involved when the Duke of Windsor popped up again in the autumn of 1945 with another set of demands. He had resigned his position as governor of the Bahamas at the beginning of the year and returned to France with Wallis when the European war ended. Now he was seeking a postwar job and a place to settle. As always, he wanted his mother and the Queen to meet with Wallis, and for the King to grant her the HRH title. Unexpectedly, he also asked to be named Britain's ambassador to Argentina.

Tommy Lascelles had already weighed in on the duke's postwar prospects in a "personal and secret" letter to Churchill in May 1944. Given the duke's history of poor judgment and "undesirable" associates, Lascelles had concluded that he would not be "safe" in any official role. It was also untenable for the duke to live in Britain. "There is no room for two kings in England," wrote Lascelles. The physical proximity of the Duke and Duchess of Windsor "would be a constant agony" to George VI, "which might have really serious consequences." The only viable option, in Tommy's view, was for the duke to live in the United States—perhaps "a nice place in Virginia"—and use his wealth in a positive way as a private citizen.

Churchill kept pressing George VI to reconcile with his brother and persuade his mother and wife to receive Wallis. He also unwisely suggested that the government give the duke a foreign posting. The King countered that his family's relations with David were a "purely private matter," and he reminded Churchill that the duke, "on more than one occasion," had been "extremely rude to, and about, the Queen, Queen Mary, and other royal ladies." Any meeting between his wife and mother and Wallis "would imply that the Abdication had been all a mistake."

The King confirmed this stance with Queen Mary in early November 1944, writing in his diary, "The same conditions prevail now as they did in 1936." In an extraordinary move, the two queens then signed a brief statement of their ironclad opposition to "receiving" the duchess. Lascelles sent a stern message to Churchill warning that "constant harping on this problem might have a really serious effect on the present King's health."

The situation with the Duke of Windsor grew even more complicated in August 1945 when a series of top-secret telegrams between Ribbentrop and the German ambassador to Spain in 1940 were discovered among archives at Marburg in Germany. This "Marburg file" added damning details of treasonous collusion with the Nazis by the duke and duchess that British intelligence had first detected before the Windsors were sent to the Bahamas. The most serious revelation was the duke's willingness to return as king should the Germans conquer Britain.

After reading the cables, Tommy Lascelles recognized a "substratum of truth" that would be "highly damaging" to the duke and duchess. Churchill, Bevin, and Halifax came to the same conclusion. The day after V-J Day, Lascelles shared the telegrams with the King, who discussed them at length with Bevin.

Against this troubling backdrop, the Duke of Windsor arrived at Marlborough House on Friday, October 5, 1945, for a weeklong visit. It was the first time he and his mother had seen each other in nine years. She had written Bertie the previous week to say she was "dreading" the visit. "Though I shall be so glad to see him again . . . his odd behaviour in 1936 has made a great barrier between us, which will be next to impossible to break down, when ideas are so far apart."

Before the King met with his brother, he and Attlee agreed that the Duke of Windsor should never be offered the ambassadorship in Argentina or anywhere else. Among the reasons were the contents of the Marburg file, held under lock and key in the United States and Britain. In the evening David dined with his mother and brother and asked again if Queen Mary would receive Wallis. "After some moments in a strong silence," recalled the King, "she replied that she could never do so, as nothing had happened to alter the circumstances which had led to his Abdication." George VI noted hopefully that the duke "could see this was final."

Yet David requested still another meeting the next day with Bertie at the Palace. For ninety minutes, they "discussed the whole matter, very thoroughly & quietly," wrote the King. He repeated to his older brother how "profoundly shocked" everyone had been by the abdication, and emphasized their belief that David "had not thought out the consequences of his behavior." The duke said he was "happily married" to Wallis, and "he knew he had done the right thing, as he felt he could never have done the King's job properly without her."

The King also delivered the disappointing news that "a job under the Crown was very difficult, as he had already been King. His war job in the Bahamas was really to get him out of Europe after France fell." Later, over dinner with Lascelles, George VI said he had convinced his brother that Wallis would never be received, nor would she be given the HRH title.

It fell to Tommy Lascelles, backed up by Attlee, Churchill, and Bevin, to summarize for David "a real truthful statement of the whole position," as the King put it. This the veteran courtier did the following

Tuesday in a meeting at Marlborough House. Lascelles noted that the duke's voice had become "shriller" and "more pronouncedly American than that of many Americans." At age fifty-one, he was "almost painfully thin," and his face "much lined."

They spoke for an hour and a half, seated in armchairs flanking the drawing room fireplace. To Lascelles's relief, the duke's manner was "courteous . . . even when I spoke most frankly." Lascelles explained that if Wallis were formally received, "it would have a very damaging if not dangerous effect on public opinion."

Regarding an official job, Lascelles likened the British Empire to a clock with delicate machinery. The "inclusion of an extra wheel—the wheel of an ex-king," couldn't be done "without damaging the works." When the duke countered that his "wheel" had fit fine in the Bahamas, Tommy admitted he had done "remarkably well" as governor. But that appointment had been an "emergency solution" in wartime, an "experiment that had worked once but it couldn't be safely repeated."

"What am I going to do?" asked the duke, if he and Wallis did settle in the United States. Lascelles suggested they could make their house a high-level meeting place promoting Anglo-American projects. The duke warmed to this notion, and Tommy was relieved that the visit had proceeded "without a breach of the peace," although he felt "as one did on hearing the all clear after a prolonged air-raid."

The duke still wasn't finished. In a telephone call with Bertie before returning to France, he "characteristically" asked for "some sort of diplomatic immunity" from the embassy in Washington to shield himself from American taxes. Over the next several months, officials in Washington and London batted around this idea, unhelpfully abetted by Churchill, that the duke could be attached to the embassy with an unofficial "silken thread." Finally, early in 1946, Attlee and Bevin unequivocally shot down any quasi-diplomatic status for the duke.

Faced with the prospect of paying high income taxes as private citizens in America, the Duke and Duchess of Windsor opted to remain in France, which allowed them to live tax free. Neither of them spoke the language very well, nor did they much admire French culture and society. Surrounded by American and British visitors, they created their own sybaritic realm, where the duchess indulged her "chief hobby," running a household to her highest standards of perfection.

George VI did his best to maintain tranquil relations with his difficult older brother. In the autumn of 1946, they had a long talk over tea at the Palace. Although "she" was also in London, "he never mentioned his wife. Nothing acrimonious was brought up." But the Windsors' bitterness ran deep. Privately, the duke called his mother and Elizabeth "ice-veined bitches."

Several years later the Queen reported to Lilibet that on a visit to London, David "had one of his violent yelling conversations" with the King, "stamping up & down the room & very unfairly saying that because Papa wouldn't (and couldn't) do a certain thing that Papa must hate him. So unfair, because Papa is so scrupulously fair & thoughtful & honest about all that has happened. It's so much easier to yell & pull down & criticize, than to restrain, & build, & think right—isn't it?" During her husband's lifetime, Elizabeth could not bring herself to see David, and she would meet Wallis only three times after Bertie's death, all at family gatherings. The barrier described by Queen Mary was simply too high.

THE ROYAL FAMILY SPENT THE month of September 1945 at Balmoral—less time than usual. The Queen managed to squeeze in an extra week with the princesses in the Highlands while her husband dealt with David's London visit. But George VI and Elizabeth seemed careworn, especially the King, who complained of feeling "burnt out." He wrote to his brother Henry that he had been "suffering from an awful reaction from the strain of war."

A *Time* magazine report described how he had aged: "his sandy-coloured hair" was "well streaked with grey," his face "prominently lined. . . . He continually worked the muscles of his jawbone, a reflex common among nervous people." At the end of October, Winston Churchill turned up at the Palace looking like "a new man" after a prolonged stay in Italy. The King complained to Tommy Lascelles that he never had such time for recuperation: The boxes, official papers, and audiences continued even while he was on holiday.

George VI and Elizabeth returned to Sandringham's Big House at Christmas for the first time since 1939. When Mabell Airlie joined Queen Mary for lady-in-waiting duties after a six-year absence, she was struck by a new informality. The entrance hall now featured a green baize table covered with jigsaw puzzles that the princesses and their friends "congregated round" at all hours of the day and night. "The radio, worked by Princess Elizabeth, blared incessantly." Mabell found the atmosphere more friendly than in the days of George V. "We still assembled in the drawing-room in the traditional way, but no orders or medals were worn," she recalled. "One sensed far more the setting of ordinary family life."

At dinner on Mabell's first evening, she could see that the King looked "tired and strained, and he ate practically nothing. I knew that he was forcing himself to talk and entertain me. When I told him how much I had liked his Christmas broadcast, and how well written I thought the script had been, he looked across at the Queen. 'She helps me,' he said proudly." He had been working on his boxes before dinner, and he would resume reading government documents afterward. "Looking at him and realizing how hard he was driving himself," Mabell wrote, "I felt a cold fear of the probability of another short reign."

The wise old lady-in-waiting, soon to turn eighty, also saw Lilibet anew. "She seemed to me one of the most unselfish girls I had ever met," Mabell reflected, "always the first to give way in any of the small issues that arise in every home." The two sisters seemed utterly unalike: "the elder with her quiet simplicity, the younger with her puckish expression and irrepressible high spirits—often liberated in mimicry."

George VI was devoted to both of his daughters. Mabell felt he spoiled fifteen-year-old Margaret and "continued to treat her as an *enfant terrible*." But Lilibet "was his constant companion in shooting, walking, riding—in fact everything. His affection for her was touching." Mabell wondered "whether he was secretly dreading the prospect of an early marriage for her."

"With the secret and unofficial betrothal in the air, it was the last opportunity for 'us four' to spend extended time together."

King George VI, Queen Elizabeth, Princess Elizabeth, and Princess Margaret in Cape Town, South Africa, during their 1947 tour.

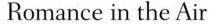

THIRTY-THREE

Romance in the Air

THE NEW YEAR BEGAN WITH A BLACK MG SPORTS CAR ZOOMING INTO the Palace forecourt. At the wheel was Prince Philip of Greece and Denmark, "hatless," and "always in a hurry to see Lilibet." He had served in the Far East for more than a year, and since his return in mid-January 1946 he had been training naval cadets at a base near Bath. When he was in London, he would stay either with his maternal grandmother, Princess Victoria Milford-Haven, who was back in her apartment at Kensington Palace, or on a camp bed at 16 Chester Street, the home of his uncle Louis Mountbatten—"Uncle Dickie"— his mother's brother. Philip liked to joke that he had "no fixed abode."

Now that he was a familiar presence at Buckingham Palace— stopping by for dinner in Lilibet's new suite of rooms overlooking the Mall—the King and Queen faced the reality that their daughter and the officer in the Royal Navy were very much in love. They had spent enough time with Philip during his wartime visits to Windsor Castle to have assessed his character and temperament. In purely dynastic terms, he was completely royal: descended from Queen Victoria on his mother's side and the Greek royal family—which was actually Danish and German, lacking even a drop of Greek blood—through his father. Except for his Royal Navy salary, Philip was also penniless.

His parents had separated in the early 1930s; his mother, Princess Alice of Battenberg, had been institutionalized following a mental breakdown; and his father, Prince Andrew of Greece and Denmark (a first cousin of King George V through Queen Alexandra), had lived an idle life with his mistress in Monte Carlo. Princess Alice, who had been deaf since childhood, had ultimately found a calling as a nun in a Greek religious order.

When King George II of Greece (Prince Andrew's nephew) fled his country with the rest of his family during the German invasion in 1941, Alice remained in Athens, at times verging on starvation. She risked her life by heroically shielding a Jewish family from the Gestapo in her home, saving them from the death camps. Prince Andrew died of a heart attack at age sixty-two in December 1944. Like Princess Alice, he was a pauper, leaving his son a suitcase filled with worn clothes, an ivory shaving brush, and a gold signet ring that Philip would wear for the rest of his life.

With neither a mother nor a father to guide him, Prince Philip relied on Dickie Mountbatten and his grandmother, both of whom ensured he received a good education in England. From the age of nine, he attended two British boarding schools, Cheam in England and Gordonstoun in Scotland, followed by the Royal Naval College at Dartmouth, where he had first spent time with Lilibet in 1939. Once that spark had been struck, Dickie Mountbatten worked every angle he could to ensure that the King and Queen saw Philip in the most positive light.

Throughout the war, George VI had closely followed the fate of his Greek royal relatives, particularly King George II, who headed a government-in-exile first in London, then in Cairo. George VI periodically met the exiled king at Buckingham Palace and invited him to stay at Sandringham and Windsor. The King felt a personal commitment to help George II "get back to his country," which eventually happened in 1946 after a plebiscite returned him to the throne.

At some point after Prince Philip's Christmas visit to Windsor in 1943, George II learned of his cousin's romantic interest in the heiress presumptive and mentioned it to George VI and Elizabeth, who told Queen Mary. The King's mother already had a high opinion of Philip, whom she had met when he visited Marina (also his cousin) and the Duke of Kent on holidays from Gordonstoun before the war. "He's very handsome," she told Mabell Airlie. "He seems intelligent, too. I should say he has plenty of common sense." Queen Mary had followed his "brilliantly successful" career in the navy and had even knitted him several scarves and sweaters while he was deployed overseas.

In the spring of 1944, George VI and his mother had a flurry of correspondence about Philip and Lilibet. Queen Mary wrote to say she thought he was a suitable prospect for marriage. The King agreed with his mother about the prince's intelligence, adding that he "has a good sense of humour and thinks about things in the right way." But he and the Queen felt that at age eighteen, Lilibet was too young to make a decision and needed to meet more young men of her own age. Queen Mary concurred, but added, "P. sounds extremely nice." She liked the idea of an old-fashioned dynastic alliance that was also a love match. Having suffered her own share of slights and cruel judgments as a poor relation before marrying the heir to the British throne, Queen Mary had a special affinity for Philip's circumstance.

There the matter rested until his return to England early in 1946. At Sandringham, Queen Mary spoke to Mabell Airlie about the situation for the first time. "They have been in love for the last eighteen months, in fact longer I think," she said. The King and Queen still felt that at nineteen Lilibet was too young to get engaged. "They want her to see more of the world before committing herself." Yet Queen Mary knew that Lilibet "would always know her own mind. There's something very steadfast and determined in her—like her father. She won't give her heart lightly, but when she does it will be for always."

None of the aristocratic guards officers the King and Queen invited to Windsor, Sandringham, and Balmoral had turned their daughter's head. Lilibet kept a photograph of Philip on her mantelpiece, and when Crawfie cautioned it might lead to gossip, she simply replaced it with one of the prince with the beard he had grown while on duty in the Far East. "I defy anyone to recognize who that is," said Lilibet.

That June, Philip wrote to thank the Queen for a weekend at Windsor, apologizing for the "monumental cheek" of having invited himself. "However contrite I feel there is always a small voice that keeps saying, 'nothing ventured, nothing gained'—well I did venture and I gained a wonderful time." Elizabeth, whose own correspondence sparkled with sly wit and colorful observations, recognized the same qualities in Philip. "You certainly can write a letter!" she once told him. "Which alas is a rare thing nowadays, & so delightful & important."

The King and Queen bowed to the inevitable, and in early September 1946 they invited Philip to Balmoral for a two-week stay. The King made no note of Philip's presence in his diary. All he wrote was, "We have had several young people to stay. Some had never seen a grouse or a stag." Philip may well have been among the "some." Growing up, he had shot pheasants at his uncle Dickie's country estate, but his exposure to field sports was limited.

On an unspecified day and at an undisclosed place—most likely on a walk through the heather on the Royal Deeside hills, Philip proposed, and Lilibet accepted. Together, they announced their betrothal to her parents. The King gave the engagement a conditional blessing. He and his family were scheduled to make a tour of South Africa for three months the following year, and he asked that Philip and Lilibet postpone a final decision until their return in May—after she had turned twenty-one.

Tory diehard Queen Elizabeth was said to have mistrusted Philip's liberal opinions, prompting him once to apologize for "a rather heated discussion." He reassured her that he was not "violently argumentative and an exponent of socialism." He also showed her a more sensitive side during his first Highlands visit by confiding that he "had always played a lone hand," compelled to stand up for himself without parental support. In his effusive letter of thanks to the Queen for her hospitality, he wrote that he had "fallen in love completely and unre-servedly." At last, he said, his life "had a purpose."

To help smooth the path to marriage, Dickie Mountbatten worked with Philip on his application for British citizenship, which meant renouncing his Greek royal title (Prince Philip of Greece and Den-mark) and his sixth place in the line of succession to the Greek throne. His service in the Royal Navy gave him the right to be naturalized, with the approval of George VI and the prime minister. Dickie met with Attlee in November 1946 for the go-ahead, which included the King's offer of the title "H.R.H. Prince Philip." But Philip declined to be named a British prince. He preferred to be a simple subject, and took as his surname Mountbatten, the anglicized version of his moth-er's Battenberg—an expression of humility that pleased George VI.

Within the list of some eight hundred newly adopted British citi-zens published in *The London Gazette* on March 18, 1947, was Philip Mountbatten, "Serving Officer in His Majesty's Forces." An ironic twist was that the citizenship process was actually unnecessary. Under a 1705 British law, Philip was, through his mother, a direct descen-dant of King George I and therefore automatically British.

By GOING TO SOUTH AFRICA in 1947, George VI and Elizabeth intended to strengthen the connection between the monarch and his African dominion, to thank its people for fighting with Britain during the Sec-ond World War (more than two hundred thousand had joined the Allied armies, and over eleven thousand had died), and to promote reconciliation amid persistent interracial tensions and the stark divi-sions between the two "distinct white races"—the Dutch Afrikaners and the British. They also wanted to show solidarity with the prime minister, Field Marshal Jan Smuts, who was facing reelection. They revered him as a shrewd internationalist who at age seventy-six had become a sort of "philosopher-king." George VI considered him a "real friend of England's" and a source of optimism during some of the war's darkest days.

The royal couple equally viewed the tour as an important rite of passage for their daughters, especially for Lilibet as heiress presumptive. With the secret and unofficial betrothal in the air, it was the last opportunity for "us four" to spend extended time together.

At the same time, the King and Queen felt guilty about leaving Britain at an especially difficult moment. Austerity had bitten more deeply than ever, and the country was experiencing record-breaking cold weather. The King ended his diary on Thursday, January 30, 1947, two days before their departure on Saturday, February 1. In his penultimate entry, he described an hour-long conversation with Winston Churchill at Buckingham Palace in which they "discussed everything."

The King made clear to his former prime minister his exceedingly dim view of the Labour government: "I told him I was doing my best to warn them that they were going too fast in their legislation & were offending every class of people who were ready to help them if they were asked to, but were swept aside by regulations etc."

As the royal family left Portsmouth, the "dawn lightened the sky," and they steamed south for three weeks aboard the battleship HMS *Vanguard* that Lilibet had dedicated two years earlier. At first, they were hit by such strong gales that the royal standard was torn to ribbons and had to be replaced. The waves broke over the quarterdeck, and the royal family kept to their cabins. When they reached calm waters and a warm climate, the Queen said, "It's like being stroked."

All along their route, the King received grim telegrams from Clement Attlee about conditions in Britain. Everyone was suffering under freezing temperatures and blizzards, followed by floods. An extreme coal shortage forced the government to ration gas and electricity. The King worked himself into such a swivet of remorse that he offered to fly back to Britain to share the travails with his people. Attlee prudently told the King he thought "it would only make people feel that things were getting worse." The prime minister "was not anxious for him to come back." But the King kept fretting, nonetheless.

The King and Queen understood the tensions and complexities of South African life. They knew the trip would be diplomatically tricky and perhaps even uncomfortable. Among the King's many obligations was opening the parliament with a speech aimed at both political factions and including several sentences in Afrikaans. To that end, he and the Queen were tutored in the language, and she wrote down phonics to help guide their conversations.

In 1910, the Union of South Africa had been created as a self-governing British dominion with the British monarch as its head of state. The South African provinces consisted of former British colonies and the two former Boer (Dutch) republics, the Transvaal and the Orange Free State, that had been defeated by British forces during the Boer Wars at the turn of the twentieth century.

The white minority governed at every level, while black and mixed-race people—the country's overwhelmingly majority population—were segregated and discriminated against politically, economically, and socially. Under long-standing policies, only whites could vote in South Africa. The country had two capitals—Cape Town for the parliament and Pretoria for the administrative government—two national flags, and two national anthems, "God Save the King" and a Dutch song that omitted the name of the monarch.

Jan Smuts's principal opponent, Daniel Malan, and his National Party were avowedly pro-white and sought to tighten segregation further with their newly named policy of apartheid. Smuts was less doctrinaire on race relations and had implemented some minor concessions on wages and social mobility for blacks. Facing a general election in 1948, Smuts hoped a visit by the King and his family would help the prospects of his United Party. As a longtime friend of the British royal family and adviser to the British government, the Afrikaner-born but pro-English Smuts was an avowed monarchist. Malan and his Afrikaner allies wanted South Africa to become a republic, eliminate the British monarch as head of state, and leave the British Commonwealth.

IT WAS 105 DEGREES WHEN the royal party landed in Cape Town on Monday, February 17, 1947. Smuts greeted the King and Queen of South Africa as their official host. The crowds were unexpectedly large and enthusiastic throughout the day. That evening the royal foursome attended a state banquet for five hundred people in suffocating heat.

"In 30 years of public dinners, I can't recall one that caused me greater misery," Lascelles wrote. But the King spoke well and pleased all the guests. To Tommy's surprise, "the royals had enjoyed it & thought it great fun—especially the young ones." He noted that Lilibet was "delightfully enthusiastic & interested."

They were all overwhelmed by the "staggering amounts" of food, the tables "piled high with grapes & peaches & pears & beautiful flowers," Elizabeth wrote to Queen Mary. But the "serious racial problems" were evident to the Queen as well. The routes of their motorcades reflected the divisions: whites on one side of the street, blacks and mixed-race "coloureds" on the other.

The King opened the parliament on February 21, their fifth day in Cape Town, with a simplified version of the ceremony in Westminster. All parties in both Houses attended "in full force," wrote *The Times*. George VI was in a white uniform, and Elizabeth wore a white gown with a short train. Her massive tiara had been made for Queen Mary with diamonds she had been given during a royal tour in 1901.

Unexpectedly, George VI had "repeated spasms of stage fright" before the ceremony. The problem was not the short speech, which he delivered faultlessly, but rather the prospect of having to declare the session open in Afrikaans as well as English. He ultimately "got out his few sentences of Afrikaans to his own satisfaction and that of all who heard him." But the episode gave Tommy Lascelles "much trouble."

That afternoon they boarded the "White Train" of fourteen coaches that extended a third of a mile. For long stretches of their ambitious tour over the next ten weeks, the luxurious train—with its white-and-gold-painted exterior and paneled and air-conditioned interior—served as their home. They spent thirty-five nights on board and traveled nearly seven thousand miles by rail alone, with another four thousand miles flying and driving.

The train stopped frequently so the royal family could greet crowds assembled at small stations and road crossings, much as George VI and Elizabeth had done in Canada. When these encounters occurred late in the evening, the Queen and the girls would wear jewelry over their nightgowns to simulate evening dresses. On their periodic stays at government residences and hotels, they found relief in horseback rides at dawn, tennis matches, swimming, and picnics.

The tour was a kaleidoscopic experience of cities (Durban, Pretoria, Johannesburg), spectacular countryside (the Drakensberg mountains towering above Natal National Park), historic battlefields, and the thrilling sight of steenboks, wildebeest, giraffes, zebra, hippos, and more in the Kruger game reserve. The royal family wore white overalls and helmets to descend seventy-eight hundred feet into the shaft of a mine. They cut feathers at an ostrich farm, attended elegant garden parties, and watched tens of thousands of ululating and dancing natives. A group of Bantu schoolchildren sang in exquisite harmony, with "the basses coming in like an organ, wild and sad." At one indigenous gathering, the chiefs all wore European clothes, "lest the King should think we are naked savages." Elsewhere, on the slopes of steep green hills, Zulu warriors did their tribal dances with sticks and shields, clad only in leopard skins.

The King and Queen felt most apprehensive about their reception in the heavily Afrikaner Orange Free State. But as Elizabeth wrote to her niece Elizabeth Elphinstone, "even the old Boer farmers who have been brought up Republicans & to look upon England as an enemy have come to greet us, so simply & kindly." Afrikaner politician Colin Steyn told Tommy Lascelles that he was "astounded" by the fervor of his fellow countrymen for the British royal family.

On Easter Sunday, they visited Jan Smuts's modest farmhouse outside Pretoria to have tea with the prime minister's wife, Ouma, and twenty-four family members. But their real purpose was a clandestine visit with Prince Paul of Yugoslavia and Princess Olga and their three children, who had been living as disgraced exiles in Johannesburg. Despite objections from both Attlee and Churchill, George VI and Elizabeth had long since forgiven Paul's doomed alliance with the Axis powers during the war, and were determined to see their friends. Knowing of Paul's chronic depression, Smuts had arranged the secret meeting.

After tea, the royal family met with Paul and Olga in Smuts's study for over an hour. "Olga very pretty & Paul hardly changed at all," Bertie reported to his mother. "They were very pleased to see us again but their life is dull as they cannot go about much." Princess Marina wrote to Elizabeth of her "deep happiness" over the reunion. She thanked her sister-in-law for describing the meeting with "details I longed to know & you write so sweetly of my beloved Olga . . . such a noble person." The visit was the first step in the eventual rehabilitation of the beleaguered couple.

During their ten-day visit to Southern and Northern Rhodesia, the family spent three nights in the Victoria Falls Hotel and were awed by the massive waterfall discovered by Scottish explorer David Livingstone in the mid-nineteenth century. On their last day, the family turned its attention to the speech Lilibet was scheduled to broadcast on her twenty-first birthday.

The remarks had been drafted by Dermot Morrah, a *Times* journalist who moonlighted as a royal speechwriter as well as the official chronicler of the South Africa tour. Tommy Lascelles "lavished much care" on the speech, but the most important contributors were the King, Queen, and Lilibet. They correctly recognized its importance, and they spent two hours huddled in deck chairs on the lawn behind the hotel, fine-tuning the words. Under the direction of the BBC's Frank Gillard, Princess Elizabeth rehearsed and made a recording to serve as a backup in case the radio transmission failed on the appointed day.

Early in the evening of April 21, 1947, Lilibet sat before a microphone at Government House in Cape Town and delivered her profoundly moving coming-of-age address in a live radio broadcast to an estimated two hundred million people around the world. In a confident yet palpably emotional voice, she spoke of her bond with the people of the Commonwealth, and of feeling "at home" in South Africa despite being six thousand miles from "the country where I was born." She asked young people to "take some of the burden off the shoulders of our elders, who have fought and worked and suffered to protect our childhood." She called for her listeners to go forward with "a high courage and a quiet heart" to make the Commonwealth "more free, more prosperous, more happy . . . and an influence for good in the world."

But the message that would resonate across the decades was her "solemn act of dedication" at the end. "It is very simple," she said. "I declare before you all that my whole life, whether it be long or short, shall be devoted to your service and the service of our great imperial family to which we all belong." Queen Mary listened at Marlborough House in London and thought the broadcast "perfect," she wrote to Elizabeth. "There were the most charming articles in the papers, really moving, & of course I wept." So did Lilibet's mother and father, as well as Winston Churchill, never dreaming that in just five years, he would be her first prime minister.

Three days later, the royal party embarked on *Vanguard* for their voyage to England. The pace of their eleven-thousand-mile tour—from the Cape of Good Hope to the River Zambesi and back again—had been exhausting for everyone, even the Queen, who had carried off an impeccable performance at every step. The writer Enid Bagnold had watched with fascination the "delicate control" of Elizabeth's facial muscles, the way she could "cast a small look" to "create a rain of pleasure." Yet instead of being buoyed by the energy of the people, the Queen had often felt depleted. She told her sister May she had been so tired that she felt "quite sucked dry sometimes."

It was worse for the King, whose nerves periodically frazzled under the pressure of the heat and confined quarters, compounded by his unceasing worry over conditions in Britain. Lascelles noted that these "internal storms" were "comparatively infrequent," but they were

nevertheless disquieting. Once during a long drive in the royal Daimler, the King kept up an "incessant tirade" from the back seat, unnerving the chauffeur. As the Queen tried to gently tamp down the
outburst, the King's equerry, Commander Peter Townsend, shouted,
"For heaven's sake shut up or there's going to be an accident!" Before
midnight that evening, the King summoned Townsend to his room and
said, "simply and with complete sincerity, 'I am sorry about today. I
was very tired.'"

The tour was by all accounts a triumph for the British royal family.
In the view of Tommy Lascelles, they had achieved their main objective, "to convince the South African people that the British monarchy
is an investment worth keeping, and that the present royal family in
particular can mean a good deal to them." George VI told Smuts that
the tour had "given me a new outlook on life after those terrible war
years in Britain. . . . I shall now be able to return to my work in London
with renewed energy."

Elizabeth came away with equally vivid impressions, not only of
South Africa's many points of beauty, but also of the troubling under-
currents she had sensed. In a shipboard letter to her sister May, she
wrote that "it is such a complex country, with the white races quarrel-
ling & hating each other, and the black races growing enormously in
numbers & at that dangerous moment of leaving savagery & being
educated & yet not out of the jungle by a thousand years. But there are
signs that the white people are beginning to come together & with
intermarriage & a little toleration, one hopes that much will be
achieved."

Unfortunately for Jan Smuts, the royal tour likely hurt rather than
helped his chances in the 1948 election. Nationalist sentiment was
too strong. Smuts's party was decisively defeated by Malan's forces,
whose bid to protect the white race led to the intolerable policies of
apartheid that would last for nearly fifty years.

The most promising outcome of the tour was "the remarkable development of Princess Elizabeth," wrote Tommy Lascelles. Faced with
new responsibilities, she had emerged from her instinctive reticence

to show "a perfectly natural power of enjoying herself without any trace of shyness." She not only displayed "an astonishing solicitude for other people's comfort," she had become "extremely businesslike." When necessary, Lascelles wrote, she even "tells her father off to rights." But the most important impact on the young princess, unknown at the time, was her formative exposure to cultural and racial divisions she had never previously witnessed. What she saw and heard at age twenty-one would create a bedrock for her understanding of South Africa as queen, and her ability to maintain the integrity of the Commonwealth during testing times.

"Colour came back for a little while into the life of a people starved of visual inspiration."

Princess Elizabeth and the Duke of Edinburgh after their marriage at Westminster Abbey on November 20, 1947.

THIRTY-FOUR

❧

Sunlight and Clouds

AFTER THREE WEEKS AT SEA, THE ROYAL FAMILY ARRIVED AT PORTSMOUTH on May 12, 1947—by happy coincidence the tenth anniversary of the coronation. *The Times* said George VI's tour "crowned a decade of unremitting public service by carrying through with flawless success a mission which he alone was qualified to undertake." The newspaper took note of the "peculiar divisions and difficulties" of South Africa but said "it was not the function of the royal visit to provide political remedies."

The return trip aboard *Vanguard* had been smooth, marred only by the King's "slight chill" that kept him bedridden for three days. Given the quantities of food they had eaten in South Africa, he should have been "getting fatter," he told his mother. Instead, he had dropped seventeen pounds in four months, an alarming loss from his already slender frame. It's impossible to know, but his gaunt appearance may have been an indication that he was already afflicted with the coronary artery disease and lung cancer that would eventually kill him.

"We are all glad to have Their Majesties home again," Clement Attlee said in the House of Commons. So too were the Londoners who gave their carriage procession a rousing welcome and cheered them on the Palace balcony. Three days later the King and Queen and princesses, along with Queen Mary and the Duke and Duchess of Gloucester, were out in the landaus again, en route to a luncheon at the Guildhall, "still showing the scars of its wartime adventures."

In his remarks, George VI described the sweep of their travels and touched on South Africa's "unique" task: "nothing less than adjusting, almost from day to day, the progress of a white population of well over two million, whose future must always lie in South Africa, with that of a far greater number of other peoples, very different in race and background—coloured, Indian, and above all African." It was, at best, an attempt to paper over South Africa's deep racial divisions that would draw growing condemnation within and beyond the Commonwealth in the decades ahead.

His twenty-minute speech—written by Tommy Lascelles, with crucial additions from Jan Smuts—was unusually long. The King was said to be suffering from laryngitis, and *The Times* noted that delivering it must have been "a miserable ordeal." His voice grew hoarser as he went along, and his pauses weren't prompted by his stammer but, rather more worryingly, by a persistent cough. Nevertheless, *The Times* concluded that "the tones were forceful and resolute, and it was one of his most effective utterances."

FOR PHILIP MOUNTBATTEN, WAITING IN the wings, those days offered a preview of the life he had marked out for himself. Lilibet had written to him "constantly" from her travels. According to Crawfie, she had kept his photograph on her dressing table or bureau at all times. During the four months they were apart, their commitment to each other had grown even stronger. Writing to the Queen a month after the royal family's return, Philip said that while the delay had been appropriate, it was time to take the next step to a life with her daughter.

"This is one line to tell you <u>very secretly</u> [with additional underlining in wavy red pencil] that Lilibet has made up her mind to get engaged to Philip Mountbatten," Elizabeth wrote to May Elphinstone on Monday, July 7, 1947. "I think that she is <u>really</u> fond of him, & I pray that she will be very happy." The Queen emphasized his "interest in many things & ideas." One surprising interest was artistic. Using his mother's diamonds that his father had placed in a bank vault nearly twenty years earlier, Philip designed Lilibet's platinum engagement ring made by the London jeweler Philip Antrobus, Ltd.

Two days later, the King and Queen announced the engagement "with the greatest pleasure." "It is so <u>lovely</u> to know you so well," the Queen wrote to Philip, "and I know that we can trust our darling Lilibet to your love and care." But she couldn't resist offering guidance on how he and the princess could provide "example & leadership." Recognizing Philip's tendency to be outspoken, she cautioned that their role would not be easy: "It often means remaining silent when one is <u>bursting</u> to reply, & sometimes a word of advice to restrain instead of to act! But I have great confidence in your good judgement."

Philip and Lilibet made their first public appearance together at a Buckingham Palace garden party on July 10, 1947. Mabell Airlie—who had been so instrumental in the engagement of Bertie and Elizabeth twenty-four years earlier—was on hand with Queen Mary and watched the princess "flushed and radiant with happiness. . . . Prince Philip shook hands rather shyly. I noticed that his uniform was shabby—it had the usual after-the-war look—and I liked him for not having got a new one for the occasion. . . . Observing him I thought that he had far more character than most people would imagine."

The five thousand guests on the lawn paused their strolling and lined up to get a good view of the bridal pair, indifferent to a light drizzle. "Everybody is straining," Harold Nicolson noted, "irreverently and shamelessly straining." In the evening, huge crowds congregated in front of the Palace railings, calling out for an appearance. At nine o'clock, they got their wish when Philip and Lilibet emerged on the balcony to greet the throng with smiles and waves. The King and Queen and Margaret joined them, and "the whole party stood smiling down at the cheering people."

Philip fell in quickly with the royal family's routines. The following week he traveled to Scotland for nine days with the princesses and their parents. It was a master class in royal touring that ran the gamut of duties he would be expected to carry out. They stayed in Holyroodhouse, where Philip and Lilibet joined the King and Queen at a presentation party for eight hundred guests. The next day Philip watched intently as his future wife received the Freedom of the City of Edinburgh, an honorary citizenship award. The couple attended two balls, and he accompanied her to the Hamilton Park races as well as the opening of a center for young leaders.

With the King and Queen, they traveled 150 miles by car through the Scottish borders, stopping at seven towns and shaking over one thousand hands. Lilibet strode confidently and greeted people with her mother's ease. Philip appeared tentative but alert, learning to walk two steps behind Lilibet, left hand behind his back—a familiar gesture in the years ahead. He wore a well-tailored double-breasted suit similar to the King's, a sign that he had already come up in the world. In Glasgow they visited homes for the elderly, and the King kidded the Queen, saying, "I have put our names down for one of these."

Philip was in his element during the final two days of the busy program, when they spent a night on HMS *Duke of York* between two days inspecting the Home Fleet. From the royal barge they boarded five ships on the first day, and on the second they led a procession of torpedo boats for fifteen miles between two lines of one hundred ships. Back in London, they were on show again at the last Buckingham Palace garden party of the season, mingling with more than one thousand guests.

In August, Philip stayed with his future in-laws at Balmoral for ten days. "He is so nice & helpful," the King wrote to his mother. They were busy with wedding arrangements, torn between something quiet and spare in keeping with the hard times, or what Churchill called "a flash of colour on the hard road we have to travel." The former prime minister's view prevailed over the killjoys.

———

DESPITE THE PROSPECTS OF A glittering wedding, George VI couldn't shake gloomy feelings while he was in Royal Deeside. "Whenever I come here for a little peace & rest there seems to be more worry & unrest for me than when I am in London," he wrote to Queen Mary in August. Scarcely a month later he shared his feelings of depression again with his mother: "I do wish one could see a glimmer of a bright spot anywhere in world affairs. Never in the whole history of mankind have things looked gloomier than they do now, & one feels so powerless to do anything to help."

It was a genuinely concerning time for George VI. In March 1946, with President Truman sitting nearby, Winston Churchill had delivered a historic speech at Westminster College in Fulton, Missouri. His focus was the challenge posed by the Soviet Union's "indefinite expansion of their power and doctrine": "From Stettin in the Baltic to Trieste in the Adriatic, an iron curtain has descended across the Continent. Behind that line lie all the capitals of the ancient states of Central and Eastern Europe." The "iron curtain" metaphor defined the new Cold War, and Churchill warned that Russia planned to consolidate its power further through "communist fifth columns" elsewhere in Europe.

George VI applauded the speech, especially Churchill's call for an even closer "special relationship" between Great Britain and the United States. The King considered it the "statesmanlike" analysis that "the whole world has been waiting for." Accepting the King's congratulations in person a month later over dinner at Windsor Castle, Churchill told him his remarks had taken two months to prepare.

Equally troubling to the King was the fate of India, Britain's "jewel in the crown" of colonies. He had been obsessed with Indian affairs for years. Throughout the Second World War, the King had quizzed every English official connected with India who visited him at Buckingham Palace.

He believed firmly that Britain had benefited India enormously over the years, and that "many Indians still want to owe allegiance to me as King-Emperor." He mistrusted independence leaders Jawaharlal Nehru and Mahatma Gandhi—the latter a "humbug," in the opinion of Lord Linlithgow, viceroy of India during the early war years. Gandhi "wants us out of India completely. . . . This we shall never do," the King wrote in 1942. A year later, after another meeting with Linlithgow, he said, "We cannot leave Indians to govern themselves"—a view Churchill shared.

The arrival of the Labour government meant that such opinions mattered little. The agitation for independence was too strong, and Britain's depleted treasury could no longer finance the government's control of India from afar. Attlee's choice for the twenty-ninth and last British viceroy was the King's cousin Louis Mountbatten, who took charge in March 1947. It was no small irony that he was the great-grandson of Queen Victoria, the first empress of India, but his modern outlook made him ideal for the task. In the words of his daughter Patricia, he "was considered pink—very progressive."

Nevertheless, Dickie Mountbatten went to the King to express his misgivings about the post. "You've got to do it," George VI said. Dickie replied, "It will be awful if I make a muck of it. I will be letting the family down." According to Dickie's daughter Lady Pamela Hicks, the King insisted, "If you make a success, it will redound to the family. You must do it."

With his customary determination, Dickie plunged into the task of transferring power into Indian hands, attempting to satisfy the antagonistic factions. His deadline for British withdrawal was June 1, 1948. When it became clear that Nehru and his opposite Muslim number, Mohammed Ali Jinnah, could not agree on the hoped-for unitary government, a partition creating two countries, one Hindu, the other Muslim, became inevitable.

As boundaries were drawn up, Parliament's Indian Independence Bill became law on July 18, with two months allotted for the transfer of power. The split proceeded in hasty and acrimonious confusion when millions of people relocated in the border areas. As many as a half million people died in brutal fighting.

After two centuries of British domination and seventy years of direct rule under the British Crown, the Indian Empire ended on August 15, 1947, with the creation of India and Pakistan as self-governing dominions. Britain's King now had a new signature duly noted by Queen Mary on the back of an envelope containing a letter from her son on August 18: "The first time Bertie wrote me a letter with the *I* for Imperator of India left out, very sad."

Other former colonies also began breaking away, first Ceylon (later to be Sri Lanka), followed closely by Burma. But as the old British Empire crumbled, one source of reassurance for the King was the creation of a new commonwealth consisting of former British colonies in a voluntary alliance. It was nurtured by India's new prime minister Nehru, whom the King ended up liking "very much" when they met in London in 1948.

With a fortuitous sleight of hand, Nehru managed to drop George VI as India's king but to welcome the British monarch as head of the Commonwealth—"the symbol of the free association of its independent member nations." This guiding principle would be enshrined in the London Declaration of April 27, 1949, agreed upon by the governments of the United Kingdom, Canada, Australia, New Zealand, South Africa, India, Pakistan, and Ceylon—a group that would expand to fifty-four nations over the following decades.

Absent from the ranks of the Commonwealth was Ireland, the source of great acrimony and strife with England over the years. The Government of Ireland Act in 1920 had carved out the six counties of Protestant Northern Ireland as part of the United Kingdom, with the island's twenty-six primarily Catholic southern counties called the Irish Free State—also known as Eire. The King had been distressed when Eire remained neutral during World War II and denied Britain the use of its ports to combat German submarines. "The Southern Irish were patriots to Ireland but to nobody else," he wrote in 1940. The ultimate insult came at the end of the war when Irish leader Eamon de Valera offered the German minister in Dublin his condolences on Hitler's death.

Yet the King and Queen had a sentimental reaction when Eire

became the Republic of Ireland in 1948, severing all connection to the Crown. At a Buckingham Palace reception, they took aside John Dulanty, Ireland's high commissioner in London. George VI had believed relations with Ireland were improving; he and the Queen even thought about spending a summer holiday there. "Why leave the family?" they asked Dulanty. According to Harold Nicolson, the King told Dulanty, "Now it was all impossible. Was it any personal fault in himself?" Dulanty "assured him that 'even the angel Gabriel' could not have prevented it. 'Well, whatever we are,' said the Queen, 'we are not the angel Gabriel.'"

THE WEDDING ON THURSDAY, NOVEMBER 20, 1947, of Princess Elizabeth and the newly ennobled HRH the Duke of Edinburgh, Baron Greenwich, and Earl of Merioneth fulfilled expectations and lifted spirits in the royal family and around the world. The celebrating began three nights earlier with a Palace dinner dance for friends, family, and visiting royalty. For each table of eight, five footmen in scarlet livery served dinner on gold plate.

Philip started the dancing with a Hokey-Cokey, and Lilibet led the conga line out of the Music Room, through the Picture Gallery and Blue Drawing Room. "I mustn't miss this, Bertie," whispered the Queen, who grabbed the King's tailcoat as they joined the line. At around four A.M., Eileen Parker, the wife of Philip's equerry, Michael Parker, noticed the King "having a quiet smoke in a corner" and watched him "give a slight nod of the head" for the last dance. Just like the old days, the King and Queen did a slow waltz. After everyone stood to attention for "God Save the King," the royal family said good night.

The next evening, the King and Queen hosted a grand ball at Buckingham Palace for more than one thousand guests. Once again, the King was in white-tie and tails. The Queen wore one of her signature crinoline gowns of white satin heavily embroidered in gold, with a diamond tiara and necklace. Princess Elizabeth, dressed in a gown of tulle embellished with gold paillettes, honored one of the guests, Field Marshal Smuts, by wearing the necklace of twenty-one diamonds that he had given to her on her birthday.

Smuts was in high spirits, talking to a group of queens—from Britain, Greece, and Yugoslavia. As eighty-year-old Queen Mary approached them, Smuts exclaimed, "Ah, here, is the Queen of Queens. The rest are just little potatoes!" Elizabeth registered the flippancy, and the next year when Smuts came to lunch at the Palace, the Queen said to the butler, "No potatoes for Field Marshal Smuts. He doesn't like them."

Duff and Diana Cooper arrived an hour late at ten-thirty and found all the guests drinking champagne and standing around the enormous buffet table laid out with a feast including caviar and chocolate gateau. "Presently all the royalties arrived in a herd," Duff recalled. He noted that the Queen had grown "very large, but she looked queenly and was very well dressed." Princess Elizabeth was "everything that a princess in a fairy tale ought to look like on the eve of her wedding." Philip escorted Winston Churchill, who glanced around the enormous red ballroom and exclaimed, "Isn't this a marvellous occasion?" The dancing lasted until after midnight, and the King led the conga line snaking through the state rooms and corridors.

For their daughter's wedding day, the King and Queen made certain that the two regiments of the Household Cavalry escorting the bridal procession wore their full-dress uniforms—one regiment in blue tunics, the other in scarlet, both with plumed helmets and breastplates shining—the first occasion for ceremonial dress since 1939. Princess Elizabeth's wedding gown was an exquisite Hartnell creation—ivory silk satin encrusted with pearls and crystals—and she wore a diamond tiara borrowed from Queen Mary. On his naval uniform, Philip pinned the insignia of the Order of the Garter that the King had given him the day before. As heiress presumptive, Lilibet had received her Garter a week earlier. "I know Philip understands his new responsibilities in his marriage to Lilibet," the King wrote to his mother. Lilibet's title became Her Royal Highness the Princess Elizabeth, Duchess of Edinburgh.

The King, looking regal in his Admiral of the Fleet uniform, rode to Westminster Abbey with his daughter in the Irish State Coach. They were preceded by the Glass Coach carrying the Queen—in apricot silk brocade with a matching upturned hat—and Princess Margaret. It was a cold and cloudy day, with brief glints of sunshine for the masses of well-wishers who filled the parks and lined the streets—fifty deep in some places. As Lilibet and her father passed the Cenotaph, still banked with flowers from Remembrance Day, the King gave a salute and the princess bowed her head.

The hour-long ceremony at eleven-thirty A.M. in Westminster Abbey evoked the service twenty-four years earlier on George VI and Elizabeth's wedding day. In its essence, said the Archbishop of York, Cyril Garbett, it was "exactly the same as it would be for any cottager who might be married this afternoon in some small country church in a remote village on the dales." One significant difference was "the miracle of wireless" that allowed an estimated two hundred million listeners to hear Elizabeth and Philip say "I will."

Shortly after their return to the Palace, the newlyweds stepped onto the crimson-and-gold-draped balcony. The King, the Queen, Queen Mary, and Princess Margaret joined them and then withdrew, allowing the bride and groom to absorb the enthusiasm of the cheering, handkerchief-waving, and smiling throng. "Colour came back for a little while into the life of a people starved of visual inspiration," observed *The Times*.

Underlying the entire day's pageantry was the recognition that the princess and Philip were the "leaders to whom the coming generation will look for inspiration," wrote *The Times*. She was not only the King's daughter but also the future queen regnant. In a still incalculable sense, the royal dynamic shifted in a new direction on that momentous day.

The wedding breakfast for 150 in the white and gold supper room was relatively modest at three courses compared to the Duke and Duchess of Kent's ten-course feast after their wedding in 1934. Philip and Lilibet sat with the King and Queen, Queen Mary, and Princess

Alice of Battenberg at a table in the center, with the other guests at small round tables. The main centerpiece of white flowers contained heather along with myrtle from a bush that had grown from a sprig of Queen Victoria's wedding bouquet. The King and his son-in-law gave the briefest of toasts. "To the bride," said George VI as he raised a glass of champagne. Bagpipers from Balmoral played, and the bridal couple cut the four-tier wedding cake with a sword that had belonged to Philip's maternal grandfather, Admiral of the Fleet Louis Mountbatten, the Marquess of Milford Haven.

One of the King's nieces, Alexandra of Yugoslavia, could see that he was "looking quite miserable." In an effort to cheer him, she said that Philip—who had been so deprived of family life—has "got you and Aunt Elizabeth, as well as Lilibet. He *belongs* now." Replied George VI with a smile, "He *does belong*. You're so right! Come and have a drink."

The family reappeared on the balcony in midafternoon, surrounded by their wedding attendants and more family members. Shortly afterward, an open landau pulled into the quadrangle to take Philip and Lilibet to Waterloo station for their honeymoon getaways, first to the Mountbatten estate at Broadlands, then for a more extended stay at Birkhall. Family and friends pelted them with rose petals as they dashed to the carriage. The King held the hand of the Queen, who picked up her silk skirts, and together they ran with everybody else to the Palace railings as the carriage clattered away. "My mouth, my eyes, everything was jammed with rose petals," Lilibet wrote to her mother. "I felt as if I might cry if there was any more delay."

Duty called the King and Queen yet again that evening as a new throng outside the Palace summoned them with a "deep-throated roar." They came to the floodlit balcony four times, once with Margaret, as the crowds grew larger and more insistent. Their last appearance was at eleven P.M. They stayed for around two minutes "amid tumultuous applause and cheers." When they retired into the Palace, the floodlights were switched off.

However many times they had stood on the balcony over the years, those performances that night cannot have been easy. The King and Queen were both overcome with emotion. George VI later told the Archbishop of Canterbury that he had been on the verge of tears when they signed the registry after the service. "It is a far more moving thing to give away your daughter than be married yourself," he wrote. In a letter to Lilibet he described his pride walking her through the Abbey, "but when I handed your hand to the Archbishop I felt that I had lost something very precious. . . . I can, I know, always count on you, & now Philip, to help us in our work." Still, he said, her leaving had created a "great blank" in the lives of her parents.

The Queen wrote to Lilibet that "Papa & I are happy in your happiness, for it has always been our dearest wish that your marriage should be one of the heart, as well as the head." She hoped that Lilibet and Philip should "love each other through good days and bad or depressing days." To Philip, she expressed her joy that he would "cherish and look after" Lilibet "because however independent minded women are nowadays, they still need a man to lean on!" She understood he might feel burdened by the demands of public life but advised that he could find balance in the knowledge that he would be "giving so much towards the happiness and stability of the country."

She also slid in some guidance from the royal playbook. Philip now had "a great chance for individual leadership as well as 'married couple' leadership." As a family, she explained, "we do try to work as a team, but each going their own way." She expressed confidence that he could "make very valuable contributions towards the common pool." She was equally certain that he could "help Papa very much. He will talk to you on subjects that you will be able to support him on, and I do look forward to that, for he has many & great burdens to bear."

Philip took this role seriously, as did George VI, who arranged for Winston Churchill to give him a private tutorial in the constitution over lunch. The courtiers who had initially looked askance at the Duke of Edinburgh came to appreciate his attributes. Tommy Lascelles told Harold Nicolson that the family had at first viewed Philip as "rough, ill-mannered, uneducated and would probably prove unfaithful."

While the "last point has still to be proved," Philip "has tipped out as far the best Prince Consort there has ever been anywhere. In fact he is so good and speaks so well that jealousies will before long be aroused and people will say he does too much."

One day while Nicolson was visiting Lascelles at the Palace, the private secretary asked Philip to join them in reviewing a speech he had to give at the Guildhall. "The young man came in like a school boy," Nicolson noted. "We made him go through it. He did it so seriously and so well." After Philip had left, Tommy remarked, "What a bit of luck, such a nice young man—such a sense of duty—not a fool in any way—so much in love poor boy."

Five months after the royal wedding, George VI and Elizabeth celebrated their silver wedding anniversary on April 26, 1948, with a service of thanksgiving at St. Paul's Cathedral. The sun shone brightly, and the crowds hailed them during their two-mile procession of landaus from the Palace. Margaret accompanied her parents, and the Edinburghs followed. The King wore a naval uniform, and the Queen was dressed in a long silver-gray crepe gown and a flamboyant boa of blue-tinted ostrich feathers. Twenty-five years on, they had withstood travails they could never have anticipated, and they were more devoted and interdependent than ever.

A congregation of four thousand attended the midday service, which was broadcast on the radio. George VI and Elizabeth sat on gilt and velvet chairs under the great dome, and as the service began, they knelt in prayer. A tall red canopy behind the high altar "concealed the wounds, not yet fully healed, that the cathedral suffered in the war." The bells pealed, trumpet fanfares sounded, and the organ boomed. The choir sang Hubert Parry's "I Was Glad" and in a reprise of the coronation, Handel's "Zadok the Priest."

At the Palace they hosted a three-course luncheon for seventy in the state dining room and cut their single-tier silver wedding cake topped by a silver bowl filled with gardenias and white roses. There was an afternoon appearance on the balcony and several more under floodlights in the evening. In between, the King and Queen rode in an open car for nearly twenty-two miles, mainly in east and south London, where they had a rapturous reception. Flags and bunting decorated nearly every house. The East Enders in particular "remembered how the King and Queen had come among them when the bombs had been dropping the night before, and the cold, damp winter air was fouled with the dust and smoke of explosives."

They returned to the Palace with only minutes to spare before delivering back-to-back radio broadcasts. The King said it had been a "memorable and a very happy day," and he gave thanks for their "supremely happy married life." He referred to periods of "difficulty, of anxiety, and often of sorrow" they had shared. It would have been "almost too heavy" a burden "but for the strength and comfort which I have always found in my home."

The Queen's message was similarly brief, at once personal and universal. She expressed her gratitude for the opportunity to serve their "beloved country" and for "the blessings of our home and children." Married lives, she said, are "in a sense, communities in miniature . . . in some way the highest form of human fellowship." She expressed hope that those who lived in "uncongenial surroundings" would rely on "patience, tolerance, and love" to "help them to keep their faith undimmed and their courage undaunted when things seem difficult." Writing to his mother afterward, George VI said, "We were both dumbfounded over our reception. . . . It does spur us on to further efforts."

NOBODY COULD POSSIBLY HAVE REALIZED that the spring of 1948 marked the beginning of the King's physical decline that would hobble the rest of his reign. The pain began slowly, in his legs, and his feet periodically felt cold and numb. He began keeping track of the sensations as early as January. In the summer he was walking in the hills above Holyroodhouse in Edinburgh with Peter Townsend, his equerry.

Usually the King walked with a "remarkably long, steady stride," Townsend recalled. "That evening he labored and kept muttering, 'What's the matter with my blasted legs? They won't work properly.'" By the autumn, his feet were chronically numb, and he had trouble sleeping.

The first doctor he consulted that October was Sir Morton Smart, the royal "manipulative surgeon," essentially a physical therapist who had treated George V for a painful shoulder. Smart initially focused on relieving the symptoms without addressing the source. The King continued to work as usual, participating in the State Opening of Parliament and entertaining the queen of Denmark. On October 26, the Queen wrote to Tommy Lascelles, asking for his help in making "a real break for the King to have treatment for his leg. I am not at all happy about it, and rather think that a fortnight or three weeks set aside now, might avert much trouble later."

Smart prescribed much-needed bed rest and placed the King's legs in clamps for eight hours a day to ostensibly improve the flow of blood—a remedy that conjured unpleasant memories of Bertie's boyhood agonies from wearing splints on his legs. But Smart was sufficiently alarmed by the King's problems that he brought in more medical specialists, including cardiologist Sir Maurice Cassidy and Professor James Learmonth, a vascular surgeon.

In his appointment with Learmonth on November 12, the King received a sobering diagnosis: arteriosclerosis, a hardening of the arteries that resulted in less blood flow to his legs and feet. Also known as Buerger's disease, its incidence was aggravated, if not caused, by smoking. George VI's lifelong two-pack-a-day habit—by some estimates as many as fifty cigarettes a day—had been a concern to both his wife and his elder daughter, neither of them a smoker. Both Edward VII and George V had died relatively young of tobacco-related respiratory illnesses. On his wedding day, at Lilibet's urging, Philip had emptied his ashtray for the last time.

While George VI refused to give up his nicotine habit, he did follow the doctors' orders when they warned that his impeded circulation could cause gangrene and possibly result in the amputation of his right leg. He continued to work on his boxes and tend to other business of the monarchy, but he was confined to his bedroom for two months with the clamps on his legs. His circumstances irritated him, but the squalls of temper subsided.

He rose from his bed on November 14, 1948, to celebrate the birth of his first grandchild, Prince Charles, who arrived at 9:14 P.M. in Buckingham Palace. After the King and Queen had seen the baby in his little white cot, they celebrated over champagne in the Equerry's Room with Queen Mary and members of the royal household. Elizabeth was "beaming with happiness," and the King was "simply delighted by the success of everything," wrote the Queen's private secretary, Major Thomas Harvey. "I think everything seemed a bit unreal to him, even the little red baby upstairs. But a Prince had been born" and "his daughter was all right."

The King and Queen had to accept some bad news only two days later, when the medical team said their planned trip to Australia and New Zealand with Princess Margaret in the spring of 1949 had to be canceled. In a carefully worded statement a week later, the doctors cited the "obstruction" to circulation in the King's legs that had "only recently become acute." The King needed "complete rest," they said, adding that "the strain of the last twelve years has appreciably affected his resistance to physical fatigue." As a consequence, "it would be hazardous for His Majesty to embark on a long journey."

Nor was he allowed to travel anywhere nearby. After examining George VI on December 12, the doctors ordered that he be confined to his bed for another three weeks "to do this treatment in the same atmosphere." If he moved, he could risk a setback. As a consequence, the family celebrated Christmas at Buckingham Palace. Elizabeth promised her mother-in-law she would "try and make it as cheerful as possible." Her husband's "courage & perseverance" had "brought him through." The threat of amputation receded, as he did as he was told, but he complained to his mother that he was "tired & bored with bed."

By the end of 1948, Elizabeth was optimistic that the King would be able to "take up his life again." He was able to do all his work, but he remained bedridden because, she said, "rest is essential to bring the circulation back to his legs." She agreed with the doctors that "overwork & strain & mental worry" had contributed to his condition, although she avoided naming the primary culprit, his smoking habit.

The doctors allowed the King to travel to Sandringham early in 1949. He shot rabbits in the mornings, and in the afternoons he rested and used the leg clamps for four hours. One of their guests, the Queen's friend Giles St. Aubyn, an eccentric housemaster at Eton, said that since the King had turned into "a recognized invalid," he had become "as sweet and patient as could be." He was not given to reading for pleasure, but he did enjoy Eisenhower's memoirs, a reflection of his personal fondness for the general. He read Ike's book from "cover to cover" and considered it a "wonderfully true picture of the great events it records."

After a follow-up examination that March, his doctors concluded that the King's only chance of resuming a normal life would be a surgical procedure called a right lumbar sympathectomy. The exasperated King exploded in anger. "So our treatment has been a waste of time!" he barked. It hadn't actually. He had needed the convalescence to prepare for surgery.

On Saturday, March 12, 1949, Professor Learmonth performed the operation in a surgical suite created in the Buhl Room at Buckingham Palace—a guest room on the first floor overlooking the Mall, only steps away from the famous balcony. His task was to cut the nerves at the base of the King's spine that had been contracting the arteries in his right leg. Eliminating them was meant to allow more blood to reach his feet. But the procedure was only a palliative. The hardening of the arteries would continue, and the disease risked a clot, or thrombosis, which could fatally stop the blood flow to the King's heart.

In the short run, though, George VI felt better and carried out a limited number of engagements. For Trooping the Colour that year, the King led the parade, but he rode alone in a landau, with Lilibet on horseback behind him. As colonel in chief of the Welsh Guards, he wore the regiment's full-dress red tunic and the heavy bearskin. She, too, was in uniform—a dark blue jacket and peaked cap with regimental badge.

The princess confidently rode sidesaddle while her father looked uneasy until he mounted a small dais in Horse Guards Parade to watch the trooping by the Welsh Guards. The juxtaposition of father and daughter felt poignant, and it illustrated the candid advice Learmonth gave to George VI: His situation was "both psychological and physical, and the change in the tempo of the King's life must be permanent."

At Balmoral, George VI ingeniously adapted his grouse shooting for his disability. First a Land Rover would transport him from the castle, then on the hill he would hitch himself into a harness attached to a pony that pulled him. "I've only got to *move* my legs without having to exert myself at all," he explained. Should the pony bolt, he could press a mechanism to release him from the trace.

Philip and Lilibet stayed at Birkhall with their toddler son, and they invited friends to small house parties for shooting and stalking. The princess joined the men to stalk but didn't participate in the grouse drives. Instead, she followed tradition and accompanied the other women to organize picnic lunches with the guns, typically cold meat, salad, and plum pudding. Eileen Parker was pleasantly startled at the end of her first such meal when the King said, "Let's take the plates down to the stream and clean them up a bit. It saves the fat settling." After rinsing the plates together in a nearby burn, they methodically stacked them in the hampers.

George VI reported to his mother that the weather was "lovely & warm," and that he had not tired himself with too much walking. "I feel ever so well in this good fresh air & am trying to worry less about matters political." But he did worry about government policies, especially those that threatened ancestral estates with new taxes. "It is so disastrous the way all the old families are going," he wrote. "It does the countryside no good."

As newlyweds, Lilibet and Philip had to live in her Buckingham Palace suite while they spent eighteen months doing a top-to-bottom renovation of Clarence House, down the Mall next to St. James's Palace. A gift from the King, the early nineteenth-century house had been damaged by wartime bombing and had fallen into disrepair. Philip and Lilibet immersed themselves in the plans and construction, finding the work a welcome distraction from the King's illness and the ever-growing demands on their time to carry out official engagements.

The young couple had Windlesham Moor in Surrey near the Sunningdale golf course for their weekends, but living under the same roof with his in-laws proved less than ideal for Philip. He also disliked his desk job at the Admiralty, which he reached by walking down the Mall every day, ignoring the double takes he invariably encountered from passersby.

After finally moving in midsummer 1949, Philip and Lilibet had only a few months in Clarence House before he resumed active service as the second-in-command on the destroyer *Chequers* based in Malta. The Queen thanked him for having "plunged into the life of the country here during your two years ashore." She told him "how tremendously it was appreciated," and she hoped he would return to Britain and apply his "good mind & brain," as there was "so much to be done."

Over the next two years, Lilibet made frequent monthslong visits to Malta, where she could live as an ordinary officer's wife far from the Palace. She returned to London in the late spring of 1950 and delivered their second child, Princess Anne, in Clarence House on August 15. She and Philip were "very delighted to have achieved the 'double,'" she wrote to Tom Harvey. From the beginning, Anne was "completely unlike Charles." Philip came home for the birth, but weeks later took command of his own ship, HMS *Magpie,* in Malta.

As Queen Mary and King George V had cared for Lilibet and Margaret when Bertie and Elizabeth traveled the world, Charles and Anne spent extended periods with their grandparents from late 1949 until mid-1951. The Queen gave Lilibet reports on the progress of "those heavenly little creatures"—from teething to baby Anne's cooing and "short vulgar laughs" to Charles's fascination with snowflakes.

She was tickled when toddler Charles "bumped his leg & patting that sturdy limb he said, 'Mind my nylons,' which was of course exactly what he heard daily! I don't suppose that he had the vaguest idea what it meant!" Elizabeth told Philip that Charles was "a strong manly little boy, & extremely brave too!"

But she equally recognized Charles's sensitivity and urged Lilibet to be vigilant about protecting him: "You will have to see that he doesn't get frightened by silly people." The time the Queen spent with Charles laid the groundwork for a lifelong devotion that provided him with crucial nurturing when his mother was preoccupied by her work.

For the King, the presence of Charles and Anne was a welcome distraction from troubling world developments. "They cheer us up more than I can say," the Queen told her daughter. The invasion of South Korea by the North Korean military in June 1950 worried him, especially when American forces entered the battle to protect the South, and the British Army joined with other United Nations ground troops in support. George VI was upset when U.S. General Douglas MacArthur advanced his forces into the North and was pushed back by Chinese troops.

"I do hope the Americans won't precipitate a war by their wanting to make China an aggressor," the King wrote his mother in January 1951. "They are in a very hysterical state I am afraid & they refuse to listen to us & our more moderate counsels. Now that they are at war & have suffered their first defeat they don't like it & won't take it. In other wars they have come in after the defeats to help win the war & say that they have done it alone. But we must hope they will see reason in our idea of moderation." The Queen agreed, telling Lilibet that the Americans should be persuaded "to think before they act."

Not only did the King despair about relations with America, he also worried about the uneasiness in Britain before and after the general election in February 1950. Since 1945, Labour had passed nearly 350 laws, launched the National Health Service, pushed through education reforms, and built more than a million new houses, in addition to nationalizing large swathes of British business. But the continued rationing, high taxes, and sacrifices of austerity had alienated many voters. The Tories gained eighty-five seats, and Labour's commanding majority shriveled to a mere five seats, which left the government unable to pursue the rest of its socialist agenda.

Always more outspokenly Tory than her husband, Elizabeth wrote to Lilibet in Malta that "here prices are <u>roaring</u> up. . . . State ownership does not work. I can't think why the Government doesn't do what worked well in the war—a high authority over individual industries—you could have state interference at a high level, & yet keep competition, without which all industry seems to wilt and almost die."

IN THE MIDDLE OF THE King's illness came an episode concerning Marion Crawford that was unnecessarily acrimonious and ultimately sad. On her retirement as governess early in 1949, she received a grace-and-favor house, Nottingham Cottage, near Kensington Palace, along with a generous pension. But when Crawfie proposed to write a memoir about her fifteen years with the royal family, the Queen objected, identifying the clamlike discretion that she expected: Those in "positions of confidence with us must be utterly oyster."

Yet, since the 1920s the Queen and the King had permitted carefully selected individuals to write about the royal family: Lady Cynthia Asquith, Beryl Poignand (under the pseudonym Anne Ring), Taylor Darbyshire, and most recently, Dermot Morrah, who published a book on Princess Elizabeth in 1949. That year Elizabeth asked Philip to review a magazine article about him by "Old Miss Poignand." The Queen said it seemed "innocuous," but asked him to reply "O.K. or not on your life or whatever you feel."

There had also been two sanctioned books about George V. In 1941, John Gore, one of Tommy Lascelles's oldest friends, had published a slender volume subtitled *A Personal Memoir.* Seven years later, Lascelles had again overseen a more comprehensive biography of the late king by Harold Nicolson, Tommy's intimate friend since Oxford days. Each author was considered to be "a safe pair of hands," mindful of areas to be avoided. Their books were informative, expertly written, polished, thorough, and professional.

Crawfie's approach was more chatty and less formal, along the lines of the women who had collaborated with Elizabeth. But unlike the others, Crawfie would not submit to royal control. Nor did she help her cause by working with *Ladies' Home Journal* editor Beatrice Gould, who had offended royal propriety during Eleanor Roosevelt's wartime visit. The Queen told Crawfie, "You must resist the allure of American money and persistent editors." Crawfie succumbed to the allure and insisted on doing the memoir on her own terms, and under her own name, unlike Beryl Poignand.

The Queen was appalled by what she considered Crawfie's betrayal—essentially, writing without royal approval. She disliked the familiarity and personal details in the manuscript, and the implication that the Queen was lax about her daughters' education. In the end, the Palace persuaded Crawfie to change thirteen offensive passages. The eventual book, titled *The Little Princesses*, became a bestselling classic of the genre, to modern eyes affectionate and anodyne. The royal family hated it, and cut off all contact with the woman they once considered their "true & trustworthy friend."

"Alone at the center of the elaborate military drill, she 'acquitted herself extremely well,' and showed 'perfect poise and composure.'"

Twenty-five-year-old Princess Elizabeth substitutes for her bedridden father to lead the Trooping the Colour ceremony in Horse Guards Parade in London for the first time on June 7, 1951.

THIRTY-FIVE

~≪✕≫~

Farewell, with Love

OSBERT SITWELL WROTE ABOUT THE "CURIOUS AIR OF MYSTERY THAT always surrounds any illness, however slight, in a member of the royal family." Kings and queens "must not appear to be in any sense fallible." The possibility of illness could produce "a sense of shock," as well as a reminder of "the transitoriness of their human splendour." So it was with George VI from 1949 onward, when his condition was more precarious than the public realized, and those around him found it easier to deceive themselves than to directly confront the implications of his diminishing stamina.

The King's deterioration wasn't precipitous at first, but small and alarming signals were evident to those paying attention. After the King carried out an investiture in March 1950, the author Patrick Leigh Fermor told Harold Nicolson that while George VI was charming, he was "heavily made up with sun tan and rouge."

By the spring of 1951, there was no disguising the King's infirmity. Fearing the danger of a thrombosis, he had significantly curtailed public engagements on his doctors' orders. In May, he and the Queen opened the Festival of Britain—a tribute to the centenary of Prince

Albert's Great Exhibition of 1851 and an attempt to showcase Britain's postwar comeback. Several weeks later on May 24, when the King attended a special ceremony at Westminster Abbey installing his brother Prince Henry as a Grand Master of the Order of the Bath, he was running a fever. "It was remarked by many present on that occasion how ill he looked," wrote John Wheeler-Bennett.

George VI took to his bed that night, the beginning of his final decline. He had already been suffering from what the Queen described to Lilibet as "flu" that had "got him very down." Now his cough had worsened. An X-ray revealed a spot of "catarrhal inflammation" on his left lung. The doctors diagnosed the "shadow" as "pneumonitis," a precursor to pneumonia, and prescribed a course of penicillin injections. "I feel now that I have got the chance of a rest & had much better take it & get really well," he wrote to his mother in early June. He canceled all his engagements for the following six weeks.

Over the summer, the King was unable to "chuck out the bug," as he put it, despite extended periods of recuperation at Royal Lodge and Sandringham. When it became clear he couldn't fulfill any public duties, Lilibet and Philip left Malta and returned to Clarence House, and she began carrying out engagements on her father's behalf.

At Trooping the Colour, the princess led the parade mounted on a police horse called Winston while the King stayed at home in bed. She wore the scarlet and gold tunic of the Grenadier Guards, a dark blue skirt, and a black tricorne hat with a tall white plume. Princess Elizabeth, alone at the center of the elaborate military drill, "acquitted herself extremely well," and showed "perfect poise and composure," said *The Times*. The Queen and Prince Charles, standing on a chair and waving excitedly, watched from a window overlooking Horse Guards Parade.

With the approval of Clement Attlee, Princess Elizabeth began reading cabinet papers to familiarize herself with public issues. The Queen and Princess Margaret took the King's place on a visit to Northern Ireland, and the Queen hosted an official visit by King Haakon that June. At his state banquet, Princess Elizabeth read her absent father's speech. Nor was the King "strong enough to cope" with the Buckingham Palace garden parties. Queen Elizabeth and Queen Mary did the honors together.

George VI and Elizabeth traveled to Balmoral in early August, hoping the restorative powers of Royal Deeside would work their magic again. The King had several days of successful shooting with Philip and assorted houseguests. Even as the weather turned cold and rainy, George VI went out on the hill, moving slowly, coughing, and frequently pausing to lean on his crummock. The unsurprising result was a chill and sore throat.

Princess Margaret celebrated her twenty-first birthday at Balmoral on August 21, 1951, with a group of aristocratic young men and women. After dinner, the celebrating turned raucous when they went outdoors and lit torches, which the men carried in "flaming and dancing" relays to the top of the hill. There they ignited a bonfire that "shot up a glorious tongue of flame and lit up everything for miles," Margaret recalled. "We were all in tears by this time, and the pipers were playing." The Queen then "had one of her most brilliant ideas, and we all danced an eight-some reel on the gravel in & out of the puddles in our Diors! It was splendid and exhausting."

Feeling fretful up in his room, George VI called for his equerry Peter Townsend. The King looked a "lonely forlorn figure," Townsend recalled. "In the eyes was that glaring, distressed look which he always had when it seemed that the tribulations of the world had overcome him. Above the rhythm of the music and the dancing coming up from below, he almost shouted at me: 'Won't those bloody people ever go to bed?'"

Ten days later, at Elizabeth's insistence, the King summoned Dr. George Cordiner, a radiologist, and Dr. Geoffrey Marshall, a chest specialist, to Balmoral. After the first series of X-rays in late May and early June, Dr. Cordiner had suspected lung cancer, but his colleagues had rejected his diagnosis. Now Cordiner and Marshall persuaded the King to come to London for further examinations.

The day before the King boarded the night train on Friday,

September 7, with Tommy Lascelles, he attended the Braemar Gathering with Elizabeth. Among the family party were the Duke of Edinburgh and his mother, Princess Alice of Battenberg, who had been
staying at Birkhall. It was the first public appearance by George VI in
more than three months, and he looked exceptionally frail.

On Saturday morning, the King spent an hour and a half in Cordiner's consulting rooms on Upper Wimpole Street, where he underwent more precise tomography X-rays. He couldn't get away from
London fast enough. By three P.M., he was on a flight from London
Airport. In the early evening he was back at Balmoral, where he immediately headed for his "sand table-model" of the moors and woodlands
for a recap of the day's shooting in his absence. The next day it was
business as usual at Crathie Church, where he and the Queen, accompanied by Margaret, Lilibet, Philip, and Princess Alice, attended the
morning service.

The images taken by Cordiner confirmed that the "shadow" in the
left lung was in fact a tumor. Among the additional specialists called
in was Clement Price Thomas, a chest surgeon specializing in cancer
treatment. The medical team unanimously recommended that the
King return to London as soon as possible for an exploratory bronchoscopy and biopsy of the left lung.

"Royal shooting ceased on September 14th," wrote Aubrey Buxton, one of the King's sporting companions. The next day the King flew
back to London in rough weather. He had said goodbye to Balmoral,
as it turned out, for the final time. Elizabeth, Lilibet, and Philip would
follow three days later.

The test results confirmed what the medical men suspected.
George VI had a malignant tumor—a diagnosis they withheld from
him as well as his family. In fairness, it was common practice at the
time for doctors to be secretive about cancer, which carried a stigma.
As with his cardiovascular illness, the culprit was decades of heavy
cigarette smoking.

The official medical bulletin on Tuesday, September 18, now
signed by nine doctors, was couched in euphemism. It cited "struc-

tural changes" in the left lung and said the King had been advised to "stay in London for further treatment." When Winston Churchill asked his personal physician, Lord Moran, to cut through the ambiguity, he indicated it was cancer. Why had the doctors used the phrase "structural changes"? Churchill asked. "Because they were anxious to avoid talking about cancer," Charles Moran replied.

On September 21, another opaque medical bulletin disclosed that George VI needed his left lung removed due to the previously mentioned "structural changes." *The Times* offered a tortuous interpretation, blaming "scarring and narrowing of the bronchial tubes" that caused "inflammatory matter" to accumulate "in the depths of the lung." If left unattended, said *The Times,* "further structural damage may continue to occur."

The only remedy was to deal with the "bronchial obstruction" through "modern surgery" and take out the infected lung entirely. "Poor fellow, he does not know what it means," Churchill told Moran. *Time* magazine, which likely never crossed the King's desk, described the procedure as "drastic surgery" and said the "obstruction" was "probably cancerous, but the King's doctors still would not say."

"If it's going to help to get me well again I don't mind but the very idea of the surgeon's knife again is hell," the King told a friend. Writing to his mother, Elizabeth also expressed guarded optimism. "He is so wonderfully brave about it all," she said, "and it does seem hard that he should have to go through so much. But if only this operation is successful, it may help him to regain a certain amount of health."

Clement Price Thomas performed the surgery on Sunday, September 23, with four other doctors in attendance. Once again, the physicians worked in the bespoke operating theater in the Buhl Room. Tommy Lascelles sent the Queen a note reporting that "Winston said to me just now, 'I did a thing this morning that I haven't done for many years—I went down on my knees by my bedside & prayed.'"

The operation began at ten A.M. and lasted some three hours— a "long hell" of "endless waiting" for the Queen. The physicians saw evidence of malignancy in the right lung and concluded that the King was unlikely to live more than two years—a grim prognosis they kept to themselves.

In midafternoon, Elizabeth reported to Queen Mary that the operation had succeeded. It would be touch-and-go for several days as Bertie's body recovered from "reaction & shock," but he had steady blood pressure and his heart was sound. "It does seem hard that he should have to go through so much, someone as good as darling Bertie who always thinks of others," Elizabeth wrote. One hitch was the surgeon's need to cut several nerves in his larynx, which could have permanently reduced his voice to a whisper. That didn't happen, but his voice did lose some resonance. As the King later told Queen Mary, "Thank goodness there were no complications."

On October 5, Elizabeth wrote to her sister May that Bertie was "making steady progress." He was still in considerable pain, but he could "move about a little in bed . . . propped up with pillows." She reported that the doctors "are amazed at the way things have gone (so far)."

At Tommy Lascelles's suggestion, the Queen, the princesses, Prince Henry, and Princess Mary were appointed as a Council of State to deal with day-to-day matters. Lascelles also reported to Elizabeth that the Duke of Windsor was in London. He had called for an update on his brother and asked if the Queen would meet with him. She immediately replied to Tommy, "You can imagine that I do not want to see the Duke of Windsor—the part author of the King's troubles."

Elizabeth had good reason for her pique. David had come to London in September not to see his brother, but to speak at an event to promote the recent publication of his memoir, *A King's Story.* George VI and Elizabeth had been aware since mid-1949 of a book in progress with an American ghostwriter. They saw it as yet another instance of betrayal and poor judgment, and they were distressed that David was exploiting the royal family for financial gain and dredging up traumatic memories of the abdication. Excerpts had already been published twice by *Life* magazine in America.

Within days of the King's surgery, *The Times Literary Supplement* ran a front-page article on the memoir, although the duke did decline to attend the dinner in his honor, in light of "continued anxiety" over his brother's condition. After a meeting with Lascelles at the Palace, the duke returned to Paris on the Dover-Dunkirk train ferry. He came back to England several weeks later and tried again to see the Queen. She rebuffed him once more, even after Queen Mary had asked her "to bury that hatchet at last."

WITH GEORGE VI OUT OF danger, Philip and Lilibet left on October 7 for a trip to Canada and the United States. As a precaution, Princess Elizabeth's private secretary, Martin Charteris, brought along the essential papers in the event of the King's death, and Princess Elizabeth packed mourning clothes in her suitcases. Their itinerary recalled the triumphant 1939 tour: a ten-thousand-mile journey by rail crisscrossing Canada in thirty-five days, followed by two days with President Truman and the first lady in Washington.

The princess charmed Americans with her "smiling confidence" and "her calmness and ease of manner when faced with big crowds." Truman proclaimed that the Edinburghs' visit had "tightened the bonds" between the United States and Britain.

In mid-October, the Queen wrote her daughter that "Papa" was getting stronger and "beginning to take an interest in things again." She couldn't resist adding some motherly advice, reminding the princess to "put a bit of <u>inflection</u> into your speeches. . . . They have been excellent so far, so clear too & good <u>pauses</u>—Philip came over splendidly."

Britain voted in a general election that month, and on October 25, 1951, the Conservatives prevailed with a majority of seventeen—less than decisive but "enough to keep the new Government in office for quite a long time," said *The Times*. The King listened to the election results on the radio in his room, while Elizabeth and Margaret stayed up late in the Queen's Palace apartment to get the final tallies. Five weeks shy of his seventy-seventh birthday, Winston Churchill became George VI's prime minister for the second time.

Clement Attlee drove to the Palace late in the afternoon of October 26 to tender his resignation after serving for six and a half years. Despite their political differences, the King respected Attlee and expressed his admiration by conferring on him, as he had on Churchill in 1946, the Order of Merit. The prestigious honor founded in 1902 by King Edward VII recognized distinction in the military, arts, and sciences and was limited to twenty-four members.

Churchill arrived at 5:45 P.M., and the King welcomed his long-time friend with pleasure, as did the Queen. But given the King's continued fragility, they would have far fewer dealings than during Churchill's first premiership.

Everyone around the King shared the illusion that he would eventually be restored to good health, and that the surgery had made all the difference. When he got out of bed for the first time, he raised his arms repeatedly above his shoulder as if he had a shotgun in his hands, showing a "twinkle of merriment" at the prospect of resuming his favorite sport. He managed to review the entire manuscript of Nicolson's official biography of his father and made only minimal comments. When Tommy Lascelles—the overseer of the project at every step—told Nicolson that in mid-January the King had completed the last part, the biographer wrote "FINISHED" in his diary.

Applying the same determination he had summoned to tame his stutter, George VI regained his mobility. He proudly recounted to his mother that he was ready "to get up & do more to get stronger. Always an ordeal to begin with as one does not know how much one can do on one's own." He walked the grounds at Windsor on November 30, when he and the Queen stayed at Royal Lodge for the first time. "As we drove through the gates, we felt at once the calm of this place," he wrote to a friend.

He told Lionel Logue that his "remarkable recovery" had been helped immeasurably by the "right breathing" techniques he had learned from his speech coach. He said he had "no trouble in walking upstairs & there is no extra exertion. Though with one lung, the right one, the left side ribs still work as well as before." His voice was "quite another matter," he confessed. Both the surgical and bronchoscopy procedures had damaged his vocal cords. "The voice is getting stronger all the time but is husky."

Still, he was unable to carry out once-routine public duties because of "undue fatigue." On October 29, the Queen attended the twenty-second Royal Variety Performance with Princess Margaret and the Duchess of Gloucester. A landline was set up between the Victoria Palace theater and the King's room at Buckingham Palace so he could listen to the performance and feel included. A week later, he was absent from the opening of the new Parliament, where the Lord Chancellor stood in to read the King's speech. In its twenty-first medical bulletin since the monarch's surgery, the Palace emphasized that he was "up the greater part of the day," although "the need for care" remained.

His most laborious task was preparing his Christmas broadcast that was written, as always, in collaboration with Elizabeth. The Palace announced that his voice was "liable to be a little uncertain," and he lacked the stamina for a live broadcast. With the Queen's encouragement, he worked with BBC sound engineer Robert Wood to record his remarks in mid-December.

They proceeded slowly, with the King speaking a few words before pausing to rest. "It took a very long time, at least two hours, before the few hundred words were finally complete," recalled Wood. "It was very very distressing for him and the Queen, and for me, because I admired him so much and wished I could do more to help."

THE FAMILY HAD A HAPPY Christmas holiday at Sandringham, with the biggest gathering there since before the Second World War. They drove through fog and rain to the West Newton church on the Sandringham estate for the annual carol service, and there were shooting parties on many days. Princess Margaret thought her father was "in the best of health—having triumphantly recovered from an appalling operation." Spared the anxiety of the microphone in midafternoon on

Christmas Day, the King was relaxed and upbeat. The voice in his six-minute-long address was "both familiar and yet worryingly different," in the view of Lionel Logue. "He sounded uncomfortably husky and hoarse, as if he were suffering from a particularly heavy cold." Logue noticed that at times the King's voice "dropped to almost a whisper."

"Not only by the grace of God and through the faithful skill of my doctors, surgeons, and nurses have I come through my illness," George VI told his listeners. He acknowledged the "support and sympathy" of his friends and the people of the Commonwealth. He also shared his "great disappointment" that he and the Queen had to give up for the second time their tour of Australia, New Zealand, and Ceylon, but he was glad to announce that Princess Elizabeth and the Duke of Edinburgh would do the tour on his behalf.

When the family went to church on Christmas Day, several thousand people turned up to see them and listen to the service on loudspeakers. The King was vigorous enough to walk back to Sandringham House with the Queen and Margaret across the snow-covered park.

He resumed shooting with a light gun, joining the party on Boxing Day. The following morning, he was out with a family group including the Duke of Edinburgh and the Duke of Gloucester. One of his companions in the field was his neighbor, Maurice Roche, Lord Fermoy, the maternal grandfather of the future Diana, Princess of Wales. "I shot with the King the other day," Fermoy wrote to a friend in late January. "I thought he was very well, but he looked tired. He smokes a lot, too. I'm surprised the doctors allow that with only one lung."

George VI and Elizabeth traveled to London for the King's follow-up examination by his doctors at Buckingham Palace on January 29, 1952. Although they released no public bulletin, his specialists told the King they were "well satisfied." His activity that day buttressed their sanguine assessment. He carried out a half dozen investitures and had an audience late in the day with Winston Churchill.

The next evening the King and Queen took Philip, Lilibet, and Margaret, along with equerry Peter Townsend, to see the hit musical *South Pacific* at the Theatre Royal, Drury Lane. It was to be their last night together before the Edinburghs departed the next morning for Kenya, their first stop on the way to Australia, New Zealand, and Ceylon.

They all assembled on the tarmac at London Airport on the morning of January 31. The skies were gray, and a brisk cold wind blew. A large party including the King and Queen, Princess Margaret, Winston Churchill, and several high commissioners boarded the British Overseas Airways plane to inspect the royal quarters while the family exchanged private farewells.

As the airplane taxied down the runway, the princess and the duke waved from a forward window to the King and Queen and their entourage. George VI had effortlessly climbed up and down the boarding stairs and walked with a firm stride, but he looked haggard as he stood bareheaded, his hand raised in a goodbye salute to his daughter. Yet Churchill told Lord Moran that the King was "gay and even jaunty, and drank a glass of champagne." The Queen blew Lilibet a kiss and later told her she "could not help one huge tear forcing its way out of my eye, & as we waited to wave goodbye, as you taxied off, it trembled on my eyelashes."

George VI and Elizabeth took Prince Charles and Princess Anne with them on the train to Sandringham the next day, ready to settle in for a long winter visit. The King and Queen were planning a recuperative trip to South Africa in March, a measure of their optimism, not to mention their ignorance of his true condition. "I do hope that a good soaking from the sun will do him good," the Queen wrote to Lilibet.

The King did appear to be recovering, and his mood was upbeat. He wrote a heartfelt letter on February 3 to Sir John Weir, his homeopathic physician and friend of three decades. He thanked Weir for carefully prescribing his "various remedies, never hurrying, always allowing the medicine to take effect before changing to something else." Weir was regarded as a quack by the other royal doctors, but the King was a "firm believer" in his curative powers. The nurses, he wrote, "were quite dumbfounded at times at the effect of the white powder in that small piece of paper!" He closed by saying that with Weir's "generous help I shall get back my health to normal."

Two days later, under blue skies and bright sunshine, George VI went out with tenants, friends, local farmers, estate workers, policemen, and staff for an informal day shooting hares, rabbits, and pigeons. In deference to medical advice, the King moved from stand to stand in his Land Rover while the others walked. He also wore a custom-designed heated waistcoat to ward off chills.

Maurice Fermoy joined the King in the woods and fields that morning. "It was one of the loveliest winter days I have ever known in Norfolk," he recalled. "It was perfect for shooting. . . . The King was in great form." Fermoy observed that George VI's major surgery "had not meant the loss of any of his skill." When they sat together at the shooting luncheon, the King "didn't complain of being tired or ill."

On the last drive of the day, George VI got nine hares, three of them with his final three shots. As Aubrey Buxton described it, the third hare was running at "full speed," and the King "killed it cleanly against the hedge. It was his last shot." There was also an uncanny symmetry in that moment. Forty-four years earlier, at age twelve, Bertie had shot his first three rabbits at Sandringham.

While the King was enjoying his country pursuits, the Queen and Princess Margaret spent much of the day with Edward Seago, one of Elizabeth's favorite artists. He gave them lunch at his riverside home and took them out in his boat along the expansive waterways of the Barton Broad. They looked at his new paintings and made a selection to show to the King. Lady-in-waiting Delia Peel, the sister of Elizabeth's childhood friend Lavinia Spencer, invited them for tea at her house, and they returned to Sandringham in the late afternoon.

They laid out the Seago paintings for the King, who was "enchanted with them all," Elizabeth later told the artist. "We spent a very happy time looking at them together." They had a convivial dinner, Princess Margaret played the piano, and they all listened to the radio for news of Lilibet and Philip's visit to Africa. "With his customary precision," wrote Wheeler-Bennett, George VI "planned the next day's sport."

The evening ended at ten-thirty, when the King asked a servant to bring some hot cocoa to his ground-floor bedroom. He was contentedly reading a hunting magazine and "said good night cheerfully." The watchman in the garden saw the King come to the window at midnight and fiddle with the latch.

The next morning at seven-thirty, on February 6, 1952, his valet, James Macdonald, brought the King his customary cup of tea and noticed him lying motionless in his bed. At age fifty-six, he had died in the night of a coronary thrombosis—the blood clot menace that had shadowed him for three years.

"I flew to his room & thought that he was in a deep sleep," Elizabeth wrote to Queen Mary. "He looked so peaceful—and then I realized what had happened." Princess Elizabeth was now the monarch, and it was paramount that she be notified. On the night of her father's death, she and Philip had been at the Treetops Hotel in Kenya's Aberdare National Park, enjoying a unique vantage point above the wildlife. When she became queen, she may have been asleep, or having breakfast, or, as Harold Nicolson imagined it, "in a perch in a tree in Africa, watching the rhinoceros come down to the pool to drink."

The courtiers used "Hyde Park Corner" as their code word to signal the King's death, which they immediately sent to Nairobi. But the telegraph operator didn't have access to the codebook, so the message never got through. Lilibet's private secretary, Martin Charteris, heard the news from a journalist who caught a bulletin from the Reuters wire service in London. Once the courtiers confirmed the report, Prince Philip told his wife, now Queen Elizabeth II.

Just as instantly, fifty-one-year-old Elizabeth became Queen Elizabeth the Queen Mother, her daughter became the Queen, and Queen Mary became the Queen Dowager. Despite the years of illness, the sudden death of George VI came as a shock. The night before "he was in wonderful form and looking so well," Elizabeth told Queen Mary. The two royal widows consoled each other with tender letters. "He was my whole life," wrote Elizabeth. "One can only be deeply thankful for the utterly happy years we had together." She emphasized how devoted Bertie had been to his mother. "I do feel for you so darling Mama. . . . Bertie so young still, & so precious."

Queen Mary described the "great affection between our darling Bertie and us <u>all</u>. . . . You have been such a wonderful wife to him in 'weal and woe' & such a prop when things were a little difficult and he was upset." She worried about twenty-five-year-old Lilibet taking the throne "when she is so young." But she knew her "steadfast character" would carry her through, and she would be greatly helped by "dear Philip." Once in a letter to Philip, Elizabeth had perceptively described her daughter's "ardent & controlled nature," qualities that would prove vital in the near and long term.

At age eighty-four, Queen Mary couldn't manage the trip to Sandringham from Marlborough House "at this most tragic moment." She noted to Elizabeth "how curious it is that I should lose <u>3</u> sons in such a sudden way, first my poor Johnnie at 17, then precious Georgie & now most precious Bertie." She didn't mention her fourth loss, David, to estrangement. She signed her letter as "Ever your v. devoted sad old Mama."

ON FEBRUARY 7, 1952, THE new queen and her consort touched down at London Airport in the late afternoon. They were greeted by Winston Churchill and members of the Accession Council who the previous day had signed the Proclamation of Queen Elizabeth II. Dressed in black, she smiled to acknowledge the deep bows from the men lined up on the tarmac.

The prime minister's secretary, Jane Portal, had accompanied him to the airport so he could dictate the remarks he would be broadcasting that evening. She knelt behind the wheels of a nearby airplane and watched "this beautiful young woman come out on the steps, walking down, so young, so slim, so beautiful. She shook hands with all of her cabinet." In the car on the return trip to 10 Downing Street, Churchill "remained completely silent the whole way back, and weeping."

When the Queen and duke arrived at Clarence House around five P.M., Queen Mary was waiting to receive them. "Her old Grannie and subject must be the first to kiss Her hand," she later said. She wrote in her diary that "they looked well on the whole, & having much enjoyed their week in Africa poor dears."

That night on the radio, in a "moment of serenity and sorrow," Churchill spoke of the King's sterling qualities and achievements. Drawing on his deep well of knowledge—"No Minister saw so much of the King during the war as I did"—he said that for the fifteen years that George VI reigned, "never at any moment in all the perplexities at home and abroad, in public or in private, did he fail in his duties."

Churchill praised the "love match" of George VI and Elizabeth, who married "with no idea of regal pomp or splendour." The Queen Mother had "sustained King George through all his toils and problems and brought up with their charm and beauty the two daughters who mourn their father today."

On Friday the eighth, the Queen made her Accession Declaration to her first Privy Council at St. James's Palace, followed by the public proclamation of the new sovereign "with befitting pomp and colour." The Queen and Philip then drove to Sandringham in snow and sleet, arriving at around four-thirty, to console the Queen Mother and Margaret. The body of George VI was placed in a coffin made of oak from the Sandringham estate, as his father had been.

In the evening, the coffin was transported on a wheeled bier from Sandringham House to the Church of St. Mary Magdalene several hundred yards away. Following the coffin were the Queen, the Queen Mother, the Duke of Edinburgh, and Princess Margaret, accompanied by the skirls of a kilted pipe major. Inside the church, estate workers placed the coffin on a trestle before the altar and covered it with the King's standard and Elizabeth's wreath. On the chancel floor at the head of the coffin lay another wreath with a card: "Darling Papa, from your loving and devoted daughter and son-in-law. Lilibet. Philip." The rector, the Reverend H. D. Anderson, conducted a short service for the family.

Guarded by four estate foresters and gamekeepers in their tweed suits with plus fours, the coffin remained in the church through the weekend as Sandringham tenants and employees filed past and paid their respects. The grieving family returned to the church on Sunday for another short service. As they walked slowly across the park to Sandringham House, the four estate workers took up their vigil again, but the church remained closed.

Monday, February 11, was a day of solemn drama as a cortege with the coffin left Sandringham. Soldiers of the King's Troop of the Royal Horse Artillery pulled the gun carriage for two miles to Wolferton station. The royal train carried the mourners and the King's remains to King's Cross station in London. There the coffin was draped with George VI's royal standard, and the Imperial State Crown and Elizabeth the Queen Mother's wreath on top. The Dukes of Edinburgh and Gloucester followed the gun carriage on foot for the three-mile journey to Westminster Hall, where the coffin would lie in state for three days and four nights.

"Poured in sheets all day, alas," wrote Queen Mary in her diary. She, the Queen Mother, the Queen, and Princess Margaret waited in the majestic hall for the coffin to arrive. The three queens made a striking tableau in black, with their heavy veils. Queen Mary looked the most distinctive in her black point cap and long veil typical of a German widow. Eight Grenadier guardsmen linked arms and bore the coffin on their shoulders to the purple-draped catafalque in the center of the hall. Four sentries from the King's Body Guard of the Yeomen of the Guard positioned themselves to stand watch day and night.

The royal family, along with members of both Houses of Parliament, foreign royals, and numerous dignitaries, participated in a short and simple service conducted by the Archbishop of York. "We had a few prayers & the Hymn 'Abide with Me,'" wrote Queen Mary. "It was all very touching and thank God we did not break down." In the following days, 305,806 people filed past the bier, many of them waiting as long as five hours in the biting cold.

On Friday, February 15, a bearer party of Grenadiers carried the coffin—covered now with the King's standard, the Imperial State Crown, the gold orb, scepter, and insignia of the Order of the Garter, along with the Queen Mother's white wreath—from Westminster Hall to the gun carriage. Big Ben tolled fifty-six times, and a shoulder-to-shoulder phalanx of 150 Royal Navy bluejackets tightened ropes to begin pulling. The gun carriage "rode like a ship, while bells tolled and solemn music filled the air and the black muffled drums rolled and rumbled" as the mile-long procession passed through the streets of London to Paddington station in a gauzy mist.

Riding in the Irish State Coach directly behind the coffin were the Queen, the Queen Mother, Princess Margaret, and Princess Mary. They were followed at a slow pace by the four royal dukes: Edinburgh, Gloucester, Windsor, and Kent, the sixteen-year-old son of the late Prince George. More gilded coaches carrying dignitaries filled out the cortege. The crowds were huge and silent, some standing thirty deep, many in tears.

As the procession made its way up the Mall, Queen Mary could be seen standing in a window at Marlborough House. By her side was the ever-faithful Mabell Airlie. "Here *he* is," Queen Mary "whispered in a broken voice." To Mabell, she was "past weeping, wrapped in the ineffable solitude of grief." In their carriage on the Mall, the Queen, the Queen Mother, and Princess Margaret saw the stoic Queen Dowager watching them, and they leaned toward the window for a lingering look.

And then, riding up Piccadilly, the cortege passed what was left of the home where the Duke and Duchess of York had lived happily with Lilibet and Margaret. After sustaining a direct hit during the war, 145 Piccadilly was now partly demolished. On this day its remaining single story was draped in black and purple, with a Union Jack flying at half-mast.

At Windsor, a shorter procession climbed the hill to the castle from the train station. There was only one carriage for the Queen, the Queen Mother, Princess Margaret, and Princess Mary. They rode again behind the gun carriage, followed by the four royal dukes and other mourners on foot. The cortege crossed the castle quadrangle, went past the Round Tower and down to St. George's Chapel for the funeral. The guard of honor included Grenadiers as well as cadets from Eton, and massed bagpipers played the familiar funeral lament "Flowers o' the Forest."

Among the mourners, General Eisenhower sat with Winston Churchill. When the congregation had settled, the two-minute silence requested by the new Queen was observed throughout Britain and beyond. Grenadiers carried the coffin up the steps and through the Great West Door for the King's last procession through the nave and choir, and onto the catafalque before the altar.

Elizabeth II walked beside her mother, with Princess Margaret and Princess Mary behind. "Very slight and very young the Queen looked in that solemn hour and in her solemn place," wrote *The Times*. The Archbishop of Canterbury conducted the Order for the Burial of the Dead from the Book of Common Prayer—"noble, lovely, and consoling." The liturgy referred to the late king as "our brother."

At the end of the service, the King's standard, crown, and regalia were replaced with heaps of flowers. "Ashes to ashes, dust to dust," said the archbishop. As the coffin descended into the royal vault, his elder daughter, now the Queen, stepped forward to sprinkle it with earth from a gilded bowl. The Queen Mother, the Queen, and Princess Margaret each made one final slow curtsey, and the royal dukes bowed their farewell. They all left by the unobtrusive North Door and turned their attention to their new and much-altered lives.

In his broadcast the night after George VI died, Winston Churchill observed that during his last months, "the King walked with death, as if death were a companion, an acquaintance, whom he recognized and did not fear." It was a haunting image that entered the lore of the late monarch. In the House of Commons, Clement Attlee, speaking of George VI less dramatically but no less movingly, said, "It was his fate to reign in times of great tension. He could never look round and see clear sky."

That much was true of his relationship with the wider world. But at home, within the family he cherished, he could look round, day by day, and feel warmth and encouragement from the steady radiance of his "own darling Angel Elizabeth." As Churchill wrote in a consoling letter, "Yr. Majesty's devotion & love made it possible for him to reach the pinnacle on [which] He stood at his death. . . . But then there is the future. Boundless hopes are centred in yr daughter's gleaming personality & reign."

Queen Elizabeth II would apply herself with dignity and diligence for more than seven decades—an astonishing record of stability and continuity made possible by the careful nurturing of George VI and Elizabeth. Together, they had indeed saved the British monarchy.

ACKNOWLEDGMENTS

I am deeply grateful to Her Majesty the Queen for affording me the privilege of working in the Royal Archives at Windsor Castle. She granted me extensive access to the papers of King George VI and Queen Elizabeth and permitted me to quote from this historic material. Reading diaries and correspondence dating to the early years of the last century allowed me to immerse myself thoroughly in the lives and times of a sovereign and consort who had a profound impact on Britain and the world.

My gratitude extends to the archivists at Windsor for their many courtesies and expert assistance. Oliver Urquhart Irvine, the librarian and assistant keeper of the Queen's Archives at the time, initially facilitated my research. He was ably assisted by archives manager Bill Stockting and senior archivist Julie Crocker, who worked closely with me throughout the three months I spent in the research room atop the Round Tower. Julie later checked my source notes in record time, and with impressive accuracy. I would also like to thank archivists Allison Derrett, Laura Hobbs, and Kathryn Johnson, as well as research room and enquiries assistants Lynne Beech and Colin Parrish. I much appreciated the efficiency, thoughtfulness, and patience with which they fielded my lengthy document requests.

Sir Edward Young, private secretary to the Queen, also gave considerate attention to my project, for which I am most appreciative.

With the kind permission of Simon Bowes Lyon, the nineteenth Earl of Strathmore and Kinghorne, I had the pleasure of spending time in the archive at Glamis Castle in Scotland, where archivist Ingrid Thomson opened the family papers to me. I would also like to thank Linda Cumming and Lynne Topping, who prepared documents and answered my questions. On my final day, I had a complete tour of the castle, which made even more vivid all that I had been reading— the letters as well as the game books and photo albums. Ingrid Thomson was helpful yet again when I asked to reproduce photographs I had seen.

Andrew and Sue Jardine-Paterson kindly invited me to stay in their home at Auchterarder while I was doing my Glamis research. They were hosting friends for a neighbor's wedding, and the next morning their description of dancing "The Dashing White Sergeant" and other Scottish reels unexpectedly brought to life passages in Lady Elizabeth Bowes Lyon's correspondence.

Sir Simon Bowes Lyon, the son of Queen Elizabeth's younger brother, David, welcomed me to St. Paul's Walden Bury, the family's home in Hertfordshire. He and his wife, Lady Bowes Lyon, gave me a delicious lunch accompanied by delightful reminiscences and followed by a tour of the house and grounds.

The Harold Nicolson Papers at Balliol College, University of Oxford, were enormously useful to me. Harold Nicolson's diaries not only offered his astute appraisals of everyone who was anyone in the early to mid-twentieth century—from the King and Queen on down—they also provided a sweeping perspective on events in Britain and around the world. His granddaughter Juliet Nicolson graciously permitted me to have unlimited access to these unpublished chronicles of historic importance. Anna Sander, archivist and curator of manuscripts at Balliol, expedited my research, and I was well looked after during my stay by librarians Stewart and Naomi Tiley. My thanks to Norah Perkins at Curtis Brown, who handles the

Harold Nicolson Literary Estate, for granting me permission to quote from the diaries.

Anna Sander also guided me through the Monckton Papers, which provided a detailed and highly informed view of the abdication, particularly the actions of King Edward VIII and his subsequent behavior in the first year of World War II.

I am grateful to Allen Packwood, the director of the Churchill Archives Centre at the University of Cambridge, and his deputy Andrew Riley for their help with the papers of Sir Alan Lascelles. At the Getty Research Institute in Los Angeles, I found an eye-opening cache of letters between Lascelles, who served three sovereigns as a private secretary, and Queen Mary's authorized biographer, James Pope-Hennessy. My thanks to Aimee Lind, reference specialist at the Getty, for expediting my search of the John Pope-Hennessy Papers.

In the special collections at the Bodleian Libraries, University of Oxford, I was able to read the diary of David Euan Wallace and the papers of Frederick James Marquis, first Earl of Woolton, which offered dramatic observations of the King and Queen in wartime. My thanks to Susan Thomas, head of archives and modern manuscripts at the Bodleian, as well as library assistants Victoria Joynes and Gillian Humphreys.

The John Buchan (Lord Tweedsmuir) Papers at the Queen's University Archives in Kingston, Ontario, Canada, yielded a trove of previously unexplored correspondence illuminating the brief reign of Edward VIII and his abdication. These letters also provided fresh insights into the early years of George VI's reign, particularly his landmark trip with Queen Elizabeth to North America in the summer of 1939. Michael Borsk was my intrepid research assistant for this collection.

At the Eton College Library, I was pleased to see the Cazalet family papers, with the permission of Sir Edward Cazalet, and the Diana Cooper correspondence, thanks to her son, Viscount Norwich. Librarian Lucy Gwynn thoughtfully assisted me.

I am grateful to Emily Astor, who searched the archives of her grandmother Lady Nancy Astor at the University of Reading and gave me unpublished correspondence with the Duke and Duchess of York. Sarah Jane Dumbrille of Ontario, Canada, a discerning collector of royal memorabilia, generously shared with me some important letters from Beryl Poignand, a governess and companion to Lady Elizabeth Bowes Lyon. I am indebted to my friend David Harvey for permitting me to quote from the papers of his father, Major Thomas Harvey, the private secretary to Queen Elizabeth from 1946 to 1951. Mark Barrington-Ward gave me permission to quote from the diary of his father, Robert Barrington-Ward, a former editor of *The Times* of London. Thanks to my friend Philip Astor, I was given access to a revealing unpublished interview with Sir Alan Lascelles by Oliver Woods, a longtime journalist at *The Times,* from the archives at McMaster University in Hamilton, Ontario, Canada.

Jacqueline Williams, who has been helping me with research in England at various times over nearly three decades, stepped up yet again by compiling chronologies of the lives of George VI and Queen Elizabeth that she culled from an array of published sources. Jackie also uncovered some significant correspondence in the Lady Airlie Papers at the British Library.

Writing a biography is by its nature a solitary effort, yet the wisdom and knowledge of many people are essential. For this book, I relied on several experienced allies whose guidance helped make my research possible. Samantha Cohen, a former assistant private secretary to Queen Elizabeth II, understood from the outset my vision for the book and encouraged me to pursue it. William Shawcross, who published the two indispensable works about Queen Elizabeth— a magisterial official biography and a comprehensive collection of her letters—put his shoulder behind my project from its inception, for which I am most grateful. Historian Jane Ridley, the acclaimed biographer of Edward VII and George V, gave me crucial advice about the Royal Archives and was a most congenial companion in the Round Tower research room as well as in the tearoom, where we ate lunch at lightning speed. Jane also joined me on tours of Frogmore House at Windsor and White Lodge in Richmond Park. At the latter, we were guided by Anna Meadmore, manager of special collections for the Royal Ballet School at White Lodge.

While I had read descriptions of York Cottage on the Sandringham estate, it was not until I was shown around the premises by Simon Hickling, the deputy land agent, that I fully understood the atmosphere and significance of this unusual house where King George V and Queen Mary lived for thirty-three years and King George VI was born. My thanks to Simon for his time and his expertise.

I was fortunate to interview friends and relatives of George VI and Elizabeth who gave me illuminating insights: the Earl and Countess of Airlie, John Bowes Lyon, the Right Reverend Dr. John Cairns, Dame Frances Campbell-Preston, Lady Charteris, Lady Mary Clayton, Annabel Cope, Jane FitzGerald, Geordie Greig, Lady Pamela Hicks, Jamie Lowther-Pinkerton, Countess Mountbatten of Burma, Sir Michael and Lady Angela Oswald, Mary Charteris Pearson, Lady Penn, Margaret Rhodes, Sir Adam Ridley, Kenneth Rose, Lady Elizabeth Shakerley, Rosie and William Stancer, Viscount Stuart of Findhorn, Lady Williams, and Ashe Windham.

Many others with knowledge of the royal family generously assisted me with suggestions and information: Charles Anson, David Astor, Anne Baker, Michael Bishop, Tim Bouverie, Sarah Bradford and Viscount Bangor, Johnny Cunningham-Reid, Robert Cunningham-Reid, Nicky and Jasmine Dunne, Philip Eade, David Friend, Nicky Haslam, Bill Husselby, David Ker, Edward Luce, Lord Luce, the Earl of Moray, Howard Morgan, Christopher and Brina Penn, Justine Picardie, the Earl of Rosslyn, and Colonel Simon Vandeleur.

I also relied on good friends for support, encouragement, and hospitality. Chief among those who opened their homes to me during my overseas travels were Bernie and Joan Carl, whose generosity over the years has been immeasurable. During my research trips to Oxford, Margaret MacMillan graciously invited me to stay at her lovely flat.

Victor and Isabel Cazalet entertained me at their cozy retreat in Norfolk near Sandringham and shared wonderful family reminiscences about George VI and Elizabeth.

For kindnesses of all sorts, I am indebted to Sarah Baxter, Darcie Baylis, Paul Benney, Chris and Wendy Born, Nina Campbell, Graydon Carter, Lyman and Diana Delano, Michael Estorick and Jane Gordon-Cumming, Douglas and Sue Gordon, Rupert and Robin Hambro, Patrick and Annie Holcroft, Perry Pidgeon Hooks, Pico Iyer, Brenda and Howard Johnson, Jamie Kabler, Manfred Kuhnert and Peter Iacono, Hopie Lapsley, Wayne Lawson, Ellen and Pettus LeCompte, Jeff and Elizabeth Louis, Valentine Low and Eliza Thompson, Sir David and Lady Manning, Judy Martin, David and Liz McCreery, Terry and Trisha Mulchahey, Caroline Nation, Peggy Noonan, Richard Nye and Francesca Stanfill, Maureen Orth, Ben Pentreath, John and Suzy Redpath, Viscount Ridley and Lady Ridley, Jimmy and Cindy Rowbotham, David and Natasha Royds, Joth Shakerley, Robert Shaughnessy, Olga Shawcross, Jeremy and Susanna Soames, Brendan Sullivan, Evan and Oscie Thomas, Carole and Anthony Turner-Record, Philip Volkers, Louise Wellemeyer, Jacqueline Winspear, and Terry and Bente Wise.

I am incredibly blessed to have Kate Medina as my editor nonpareil. She showed remarkable patience and understanding as I spent longer than anticipated writing the book during the COVID pandemic. When I turned in the manuscript, she responded with her usual perceptive comments, invaluable guidance, and much-appreciated enthusiasm. I benefited greatly from Kate's two stellar assistants, first Noa Shapiro, followed by Louisa McCullough, who adroitly handled text as well as photographs as we proceeded to publication. My thanks as well to managing editor Rebecca Berlant.

Production editor Steve Messina yet again expertly oversaw the copyediting, which was meticulously carried out by Michelle Daniel. Others on the production team were designer Susan Turner and production manager Richard Elman.

Under the imaginative supervision of art director Robbin Schiff, designer Belina Huey created a jacket cover that combines grandeur and tenderness, perfectly evoking an observation from one of Princess Elizabeth's friends: "four people who mean everything to each other, whose lives form one spiritual whole."

From the moment I start a book, I am aware of the importance of photographs as a visual complement to the text. Finding the best possible images for the interior pages as well as the photo section is a treasure hunt that I have now happily shared with Carol Poticny, an admirably resourceful photo researcher, for four biographies. No matter how obscure the source, Carol can track down the perfect shot.

Gina Centrello, president and publisher of Random House, and Tom Perry, senior vice president and deputy publisher, brought their skillful leadership to ensuring that *George VI and Elizabeth* was launched and marketed in the best possible way. I remain endlessly thankful for their continuing support. Maria Braeckel, vice president and director of publicity, and her team—Rachel Rokicki, Karen Fink, Katie Horn, Ayelet Durantt, and Michelle Jasmine—came up with inventive promotion strategies. My gratitude as well to Denise Cronin, Rachel Kind, Leigh Marchant, Andrea DeWerd, Joelle Dieu, Toby Ernst, and Carolyn Foley for their sure-footed work on foreign and subsidiary rights.

For the fourth time, my friend Max Hirshfeld focused his matchless talent on taking my author photograph. Because of the pandemic, he was unable to bring along his wife, Nina, to serve as his eagle-eyed stylist, but his assistant, Michael Jones, helped as usual with the setup, and Lori Pressman made sure I looked my best for an outdoor shoot on a frigid January day.

I wrote this book during a testing period for everyone, and I benefited greatly from the unstinting love of my family. My daughter, Lisa, and her husband, Dominic, gave me respites in the Kentish countryside at the height of the pandemic, for which I will be everlastingly grateful. Their three children, Henry, Lexi, and Zara, were a constant source of joy during my research trips to England. My older son, Kirk, his wife, Sally, their children, Sophie and Beau, and my younger son, David, sustained me with their affection and constant encouragement.

Not long after I finished *George VI and Elizabeth,* my beloved husband, Stephen, and I celebrated forty years of marriage. From day one he has been my inspiration, and he was endlessly tolerant when I immersed myself for hours, not to mention days, in organizing and writing a story that inspired him as much as it did me. He applied his consummate editing skills to two drafts, helping me to compress and trim and hone my prose. He was also moved to tears several times by Bertie and Elizabeth, which touched me deeply. Stephen has seen me through eight biographies, an expression of love and devotion matched only by mine for him.

Amanda Urban is the best literary agent in the business, and an exceptional advocate. But for me she is so much more. We have been friends since we were students together at Wheaton College in Massachusetts more than five decades ago. She is as confident as she is supportive, and I always count on her to give me an honest reaction to my writing. For this book, it was only a matter of days before she shared her excitement—well before she had finished reading. She followed up with a reliably incisive assessment, and then thrilled me by writing, "I really hated saying goodbye to them!" In honor of all the work she has done on my behalf and for consistently believing in me, I am dedicating this book to her.

Sally Bedell Smith

Washington, D.C.
June 2022

SOURCES

ABBREVIATIONS

Asquith I   Lady Cynthia Asquith, *H.R.H. The Duchess of York: An Intimate and Authentic Life-Story, Including Many Details Hitherto Unpublished, Told with the Personal Approval of Her Royal Highness* (Philadelphia: J. B. Lippincott, 1928).

Asquith II   Lady Cynthia Asquith, *Her Majesty the Queen: An Entirely New and Complete Biography Written with the Approval of Her Majesty* (New York: E.P. Dutton, 1937).

Channon I   Sir Henry Channon, *Chips: The Diaries of Sir Henry Channon,* ed. Robert Rhodes James (London: Weidenfeld and Nicolson, 1967).

Channon II   Sir Henry Channon, *The Diaries 1918–38,* ed. Simon Heffer (London: Hutchinson, 2021).

Donaldson I   Frances Donaldson, *Edward VIII: A Biography of the Duke of Windsor* (Philadelphia: J. B. Lippincott, 1975).

Donaldson II   Frances Donaldson, *King George VI and Queen Elizabeth* (Philadelphia: J. B. Lippincott, 1977).

Harvey I   Oliver Harvey, *The Diplomatic Diaries of Oliver Harvey, 1937–1945,* ed. John Harvey (London: Collins, 1970).

Harvey II   Oliver Harvey, *The War Diaries of Oliver Harvey, 1941–1945,* ed. John Harvey (London: Collins, 1978).

Lascelles I	Sir Alan Lascelles, *End of an Era: Letters and Journals of Sir Alan Lascelles, 1887–1920,* ed. Duff Hart-Davis (London: Hamish Hamilton, 1986).
Lascelles II	Sir Alan Lascelles, *In Royal Service: The Letters and Journals of Sir Alan Lascelles 1920–1936,* ed. Duff Hart-Davis (London: Hamish Hamilton, 1989).
Lascelles III	Sir Alan Lascelles, *King's Counsellor: Abdication and War: The Diaries of Sir Alan Lascelles,* ed. Duff Hart-Davis (London: Weidenfeld and Nicolson, 2006).
Nicolson I	Harold Nicolson, *Diaries and Letters,* vol. I, *1930–1939,* ed. Nigel Nicolson (New York: Atheneum, 1966).
Nicolson II	Harold Nicolson, *Diaries and Letters,* vol. II, *The War Years 1939–1945,* ed. Nigel Nicolson (New York: Atheneum, 1967).
Nicolson III	Harold Nicolson, *Diaries and Letters,* vol. III, *The Later Years 1945–1962,* ed. Nigel Nicolson (New York: Atheneum, 1968).
Pope-Hennessy I	James Pope-Hennessy, *Queen Mary, 1867–1953* (New York: Knopf, 1960).
Pope-Hennessy II	James Pope-Hennessy, *The Quest for Queen Mary,* ed. Hugo Vickers (London: Zuleika, 2018).
Rhodes James I	Robert Rhodes James, *Victor Cazalet: A Portrait* (London: Hamish Hamilton, 1976).
Rhodes James II	Robert Rhodes James, *A Spirit Undaunted: The Political Role of George VI* (New York: Little, Brown, 1998).
Rose I	Kenneth Rose, *Who's In, Who's Out: The Journals of Kenneth Rose, Volume One, 1944–1979,* ed. D. R. Thorpe (London: Weidenfeld and Nicolson, 2018).
Rose II	Kenneth Rose, *Who Loses, Who Wins: The Journals of Kenneth Rose, Volume Two, 1979–2014,* ed. D. R. Thorpe (London: Weidenfeld and Nicolson, 2019).
Shawcross, *QEQM*	William Shawcross, *Queen Elizabeth, the Queen Mother: The Official Biography* (London: Macmillan, 2009).
Shawcross, *QEQM Letters*	*Counting One's Blessings: The Selected Letters of Queen Elizabeth the Queen Mother,* ed. William Shawcross (London: Macmillan, 2012).

Windsor I	Edward, Duke of Windsor, *A King's Story: The Memoirs of the Duke of Windsor* (New York: Putnam, 1951).
Windsor II	Edward, Duke of Windsor, *Letters from a Prince: Edward, Prince of Wales to Mrs. Freda Dudley Ward, March 1918–January 1921,* ed. Rupert Godfrey (London: Warner, 1999).
Ziegler I	Philip Ziegler, *Diana Cooper* (London: Hamish Hamilton, 1981).
Ziegler II	Philip Ziegler, *King Edward VIII* (New York: Knopf, 1991).
Balliol	Balliol College Archives and Manuscripts, University of Oxford
CAC	Churchill Archives Centre, University of Cambridge
CH	Glamis Archives, Clarence House Collection
John Buchan Fonds	Records from John Buchan, first Baron Tweedsmuir, former governor-general of Canada, Queen's University Archives, Kingston, Ontario, Canada
LASL	Papers of Sir Alan Lascelles, Churchill Archives Centre, University of Cambridge
RA	Royal Archives

PROLOGUE

xvi   **he had no idea:** William Shawcross email, January 7, 2011.

xix   **"Tommy Tadpole":** Lascelles I, p. xi.

xx   **"sharpest blue-pencil":** Victoria Schofield, *Witness to History: The Life of John Wheeler-Bennett* (New Haven, Conn.: Yale University Press, 2012), p. 209.

xx   **two of the royal biographers:** "first Harold, then Julian," Sir Alan Lascelles to James Pope-Hennessy, n.d. [2 May 1959]; "lots and lots of love; cold, pure love," Sir Alan Lascelles to James Pope-Hennessy, 5 March 1960; "how splendid to be so excitable at the age of 70!," Harold Nicolson to James Pope-Hennessy, 10 April 1958, John Pope-Hennessy Papers 1617–1995, bulk 1930–1995, the Getty Research Institute, Los Angeles, accession no. 990023.

xxi   **"Now darling, you must look":** Shawcross, *QEQM Letters,* p. 17; Queen Elizabeth, conversations with Eric Anderson, 1994–95, RA QEQM/ADD/MISC.

xxii   **"Get it out!":** Geordie Greig, *The King Maker: The Man Who Saved George VI* (New York: Open Road, 2014), p. 28.

xxiii   **"Such a sweet little couple":** Diana Cooper, *The Light of Common Day* (Boston: Houghton Mifflin, 1959), p. 73.

xxiii **"tinkety-tonk"**: Queen Elizabeth to Elizabeth Elphinstone, 7 February 1941, RA QEQM/OUT/ELPHINSTONE; Shawcross, *QEQM Letters,* pp. 304–5.

xxiii **"what ho"**: Lady Elizabeth Bowes Lyon to David Bowes Lyon, 18 July 1913, Glamis Archives.

xxiii **"to the accompaniment"**: Lady Elizabeth Bowes Lyon to Jock Bowes Lyon, 6 March 1921, RA QEQM/OUT/SHAKERLEY; Shawcross, *QEQM Letters,* p. 90.

xxiv **"where nobody quarreled"**: Rose II, p. 39.

xxiv **"Papa & I were so lucky"**: Queen Elizabeth to Princess Elizabeth, 21 December 1949, RA QE II/PRIV/RF; Shawcross, *QEQM Letters,* p. 422.

xxv **"marshmallow made on a welding"**: Piers Brendon, *The Royal House of Windsor,* Channel 4, 2017.

xxv **"bolshie"**: Edward, Prince of Wales, to Mrs. Freda Dudley Ward, 26 March 1920, Windsor II, p. 323.

xxv **"kind of man who needs"**: Ibid., 14 January 1920, p. 304.

xxv **Once when he was on all fours**: Ziegler I, p. 178.

xxvi **"You've got to get rid"**: Bill Husselby email, 23 April 2019, quoting Penelope Maffey Aitken; Queen Mary, diary, 28 December 1935, RA QM/PRIV/QMD/1935.

xxvi **"I don't know"**: Hector Bolitho, *Their Majesties* (London: Max Parrish, 1952), p. 51. This was Princess Helena Victoria, nicknamed "Thora" in the family. She was the daughter of Queen Victoria and Prince Albert's third daughter, Princess Helena.

xxvi **"the right to be consulted"**: Walter Bagehot, *The English Constitution* (New York: Cosimo Classics, 2007), p. 75.

xxvii **"personal feelings are nothing"**: King George VI, diary, 24 June 1941, RA GVI/PRIV/DIARY/WAR/1939–1947 (vols. I, II, III, IV, V, VI, VII, VIII, IX, X, XI, index).

xxvii **"partly to blame"**: King George VI, diary, 24 May 1940, RA GVI/PRIV/DIARY.

xxvii **"to keep the spirit"**: King George VI, diary, 5 September 1940, RA GVI/PRIV/DIARY.

xxvii **"looks a small quiet man"**: King George VI, diary, 22 May 1942, RA GVI/PRIV/DIARY.

xxvii **"unprecedented"**: Shawcross, *QEQM,* pp. 514–15.

xxviii **"immense catacomb"**: Lascelles III, p. 63.

xxviii **"very much a part"**: Shawcross, *QEQM,* p. 515.

xxviii **"one of my main jobs"**: King George VI, diary, 17 November 1940, RA GVI/PRIV/DIARY.

xxviii **"war expediency"**: King George VI, diary, 3 July 1940, RA GVI/PRIV/DIARY.

xxviii **remove him from Europe**: King George VI, diary, 6 October 1945, RA GVI/PRIV/DIARY.

xxix "practical little man": Queen Elizabeth, conversations with Eric Anderson, 1994–95, Shawcross, *QEQM*, p. 602.

xxix "shriveled & small": King George VI, diary, 15 May 1940, RA GVI/ PRIV/DIARY.

xxix "I find I have to tell him": King George VI, diary, 3 August 1945, RA GVI/PRIV/DIARY.

xxx "cheerful and undaunted": *The New York Times,* 8 February 1952.

PART ONE: LOSS AND LOVE

ONE: Twelve Days

4 "heavy cold": Lady Elizabeth Bowes Lyon, diary, 3 January 1923, RA QEQM/PRIV/DIARY/3.

4 a popular revue: Stephen Banfield, "English West-End Revue," in *The Oxford Handbook of the British Musical,* ed. Robert Gordon and Olaf Jubin (New York: Oxford University Press, 2016), pp. 158–60.

4 "great fun": Lady Elizabeth Bowes Lyon, diary, 3 January 1923, RA QEQM/PRIV/DIARY/3.

4 There he asked for her hand: Lady Elizabeth Bowes Lyon, diary, 3 January 1923, RA QEQM/PRIV/DIARY/3.

4 "had a long talk": Duke of York to Queen Mary, 12 January 1922 [archivist note: wrongly dated; must be 1923], RA QM/PRIV/ CC11/21.

5 "serious proposal": Queen Elizabeth, conversations with Eric Anderson, 1994–95, Shawcross, *QEQM,* p. 149.

5 "She was so uncertain": Author interview with Lady Elizabeth Anson, 19 March 2019.

6 "must not go": Lady Elizabeth Bowes Lyon to Duke of York, Xmas Day 1922, RA GVI/PRIV/RF/26/47.

6 "My dearest Cecilia": Lady Airlie to Lady Strathmore, 23 December 1922, British Library, Add. MS 82763, ff. 37–38.

7 "Perhaps you know": Lady Elizabeth Bowes Lyon to Duke of York, Xmas Day 1922, RA GVI/PRIV/RF/26/4.

7 invited to stay: Lady Elizabeth Bowes Lyon to Beryl Poignand, 2 January 1923, Glamis Archives (CH).

8 "It is the limit": Duke of York to Lady Elizabeth Bowes Lyon, 29 December 1922, RA QEQM/PRIV/RF.

8 "much wiser if you did": Lady Elizabeth Bowes Lyon to Duke of York, 30 December 1922, RA GVI/PRIV/RF/26/48.

8 "inspiration": Duke of York to Lady Airlie, 30 January 1923, British Library, Airlie Papers, Add. MS 82571, ff. 3–4.

8 "final effort": The Countess of Airlie, *Thatched with Gold: The Memoirs of Mabell, Countess of Airlie* (London: Hutchinson, 1962), p. 131.

9 "the cornerstone": Ibid., p. 93.

9   "grown to love": Ibid., p. 168.
9   "talked it all over": Lady Elizabeth Bowes Lyon to Duke of York,
      4 January 1923, RA GVI/PRIV/RF/26/49.
9   "for yr <u>kind help</u>": Queen Mary to Lady Airlie, 9 January 1923, British
      Library, Airlie Papers, Add. MS 82748.
9   "so angelic": Lady Elizabeth Bowes Lyon to Duke of York, 4 January
      1923, RA GVI/PRIV/RF/26/49.
10   peregrinations: Lady Elizabeth Bowes Lyon, diary, 4 January 1923, RA
      QEQM/PRIV/DIARY/3.
10   "desperately fond": Channon II, p. 54.
10   "very amusing": Lady Elizabeth Bowes Lyon, diary, 4 January 1923,
      RA QEQM/PRIV/DIARY/3.
10   "conceal her thoughts": Shawcross, *QEQM Letters,* p. 104.
10   *"I am most perplexed"*: Lady Elizabeth Bowes Lyon, diary, 4 January
      1923, RA QEQM/PRIV/DIARY/3.
10   *"thinking too much"*: Lady Elizabeth Bowes Lyon, diary, 5 January
      1923, RA QEQM/PRIV/DIARY/3.
11   "well-known Scottish peer": Sarah Bradford, *The Reluctant King: The
      Life and Reign of George VI, 1895–1952* (New York: St. Martin's Press,
      1989), p. 104.
11   "Not mentioning my name": Lady Elizabeth Bowes Lyon, diary,
      5 January 1923, RA QEQM/PRIV/DIARY/3.
11   "We all bowed and bobbed": Channon II, pp. 53–54.
11   "One rainy afternoon": Channon I, p. 397.
12   "very amusing": Lady Elizabeth Bowes Lyon to Lady Strathmore,
      20 March 1918, Glamis Archives, 270/1/4.
12   "old gargoyles": Lady Elizabeth Bowes Lyon to Beryl Poignand,
      18 May 1921, Glamis Archives (CH).
12   "great send-off": *The Times,* 19 May 1921.
12   "was away all day": Lady Elizabeth Bowes Lyon to Beryl Poignand,
      18 May 1921, Glamis Archives (CH).
12   "Wilton was great fun": Lady Elizabeth Bowes Lyon to Duke of York,
      7 November 1922, P.S., RA GVI/PRIV/RF/26/36.
13   "nice old friends": Lady Elizabeth Bowes Lyon, diary, 5 January 1923,
      RA QEQM/PRIV/DIARY/3.
13   "watched her unseen": Channon II, p. 54.
13   "no extravagance": Asquith II, pp. 22–23.
13   Elizabeth read, knitted: Lady Elizabeth Bowes Lyon, diary, 6 January
      and 7 January 1923, RA QEQM/PRIV/DIARY/3.
13   "about my rumoured": Lady Elizabeth Bowes Lyon, diary, 8 January
      1923, RA QEQM/PRIV/DIARY/3.
13   "It's too extraordinary": Lady Elizabeth Bowes Lyon to Duke of York,
      n.d. [8 January 1923], RA GVI/PRIV/RF/26/50.
14   She and Lady Strathmore: Lady Elizabeth Bowes Lyon, diary,
      9 January 1923, RA QEQM/PRIV/DIARY/3.

14 **Elizabeth's dance card:** Lady Elizabeth Bowes Lyon, diary, 10 January 1923, RA QEQM/PRIV/DIARY/3.

14 *"feeling very ill"*: Lady Elizabeth Bowes Lyon, diary, 11 January 1923, RA QEQM/PRIV/DIARY/3.

14 **a prospect that filled him:** Duke of York to Lady Elizabeth Bowes Lyon, 26 January 1923, RA QEQM/PRIV/RF.

15 *"I am very worried"*: Lady Elizabeth Bowes Lyon, diary, 11 January 1923, RA QEQM/PRIV/DIARY/3.

15 **"very tired":** Ibid.

15 **"dashed off":** Lady Elizabeth Bowes Lyon, diary, 12 January 1923, RA QEQM/PRIV/DIARY/3.

15 **"pretty Strathmore girl":** Penelope Mortimer, *Queen Elizabeth: A Life of the Queen Mother* (New York: St. Martin's Press, 1986), p. 55.

15 **"my darling Mama":** Duke of York to Queen Mary, 12 January 1923, RA QM/CC11/21.

16 **"quite steadfastly":** Lady Strathmore to Lady Christian Martin, 17 January 1923, Joicey-Cecil Papers, Shawcross, *QEQM Letters,* p. 107.

16 **"I never really had":** Duke of York to Queen Mary, 12 January 1923, RA QM/CC11/21.

16 **something unexpected:** Lady Elizabeth Bowes Lyon, diary, 12 January 1923, RA QEQM/PRIV/DIARY/3.

17 **"Prince Bertie sawed hard!":** Lady Elizabeth Bowes Lyon, diary, 13 January 1923, RA QEQM/PRIV/DIARY/3.

17 **"not to be disturbed":** Rev. John Stirton, diary, 31 August 1923, RA AEC/GG/026.

17 **"for hours":** Lady Elizabeth Bowes Lyon, diary, 13 January 1923, RA QEQM/PRIV/DIARY/3.

17 **"Woke at 9 . . . to London at 5":** Lady Elizabeth Bowes Lyon, diary, 14 January 1923, RA QEQM/PRIV/DIARY/3.

17 **"the haunt of fairies":** Asquith II, p. 202.

17 **"came down to St. P.W.":** Lady Strathmore to May Elphinstone, 16 January 1923, RA QEQM/OUT/ELPHINSTONE.

18 **"I am so happy":** Lady Elizabeth Bowes Lyon to Beryl Poignand, 21 January 1923, Glamis Archives (CH).

18 **"The excitement was great":** Helen Hardinge, *Loyal to Three Kings* (London: Kimber, 1967), p. 39.

18 **"Bertie has just appeared":** Queen Mary to Lady Elizabeth Bowes Lyon, 15 January 1923, RA QEQM/PRIV/RF.

18 **"I am very very happy":** Duke of York to Queen Mary, 16 January 1923, RA QM/PRIV/CC11/22.

TWO: An Honorable Boy

21 **"darling Georgie":** John W. Wheeler-Bennett, *King George VI: His Life and Reign* (London: Macmillan, 1958), p. 8.

22   flocked to a marquee: Pope-Hennessy I, p. 292.

22   "regret": Wheeler-Bennett, *King George VI*, p. 7.

22   As a token: Ibid.

23   it could sleep forty: Kenneth Rose, *King George V* (New York: Knopf, 1984), p. 98.

23   "no proper space": Ibid., p. 269.

24   worked on her canvases: Ibid., p. 118.

24   "most kind-hearted": Harold Nicolson, diary, 27 April 1949, Balliol.

24   "bathing them in turn": Wheeler-Bennett, *George VI,* p. 16.

24   "remained a distant figure": Ibid.

24   "never stand up": Pope-Hennessy II, p. 234.

24   "foully rude": Ibid., p. 284.

25   "cozy room overflowing": Windsor I, p. 26.

25   "as a means of killing time": Ibid., p. 27.

25   embroider in petit point: Marion Crawford, *The Little Princesses: The Story of the Queen's Childhood by Her Nanny* (1950; New York: St. Martin's Press, 2003), p. 36.

26   "masculine discipline": Wheeler-Bennett, *George VI,* p. 22.

26   "Handsome, stalwart": Ibid.

26   poor teacher: Windsor I, p. 59.

26   a crippling affliction: Wheeler-Bennett, *George VI,* p. 27.

26   Bertie's nightmare: Windsor I, pp. 42–43.

27   This inhumane treatment: Wheeler-Bennett, *George VI,* p. 29.

27   "tragedies of the stammerer": Ibid., p. 27.

28   "I found that far from being": Airlie, *Thatched with Gold,* pp. 113–14.

28   "It has come too late": Jane Ridley, *Bertie: A Life of Edward VII* (London: Chatto and Windus, 2012), p. 347.

29   "fidgeted and whispered": Wheeler-Bennett, *George VI,* p. 30.

29   emphasis on Highland reels: Windsor I, p. 31.

29   "scatter-brain": Wheeler-Bennett, *George VI,* p. 34.

THREE: Stuck in Sick Bay

31   "Sardine": Greig, *King Maker,* p. 21.

31   "never say I'm beaten": Wheeler-Bennett, *George VI,* p. 41.

32   On his eighteenth birthday: Ibid., p. 70.

33   On the King's crowning: Ibid., p. 51.

33   his attitude generally softened: Ibid., p. 58.

33   "on which I took a great step": Ibid., p. 57.

34   lugging heavy bags of coal: Greig, *King Maker,* p. 38.

34   "no manners at all": Wheeler-Bennett, *George VI,* p. 64.

34   "he listened, he encouraged": Greig, *King Maker,* p. 43.

35   he showed greater maturity: Wheeler-Bennett, *George VI,* p. 72.

36   "a pygmy among giants": Windsor I, p. 111.

36   "Please God it may soon": Wheeler-Bennett, *George VI,* p. 76.

36 "gastric attacks": Ibid., p. 77.

36 "violent pain in the stomach": Ibid.

37 "not doing his bit": Ibid., p. 80.

37 "Nothing to do as usual": Ibid., p. 82.

37 "is sick every time": Imperial War Museum, Hamilton Papers, MS 75/41/1, 20 June 1915, Bradford, *Reluctant King*, p. 61.

37 "the weakening of the muscular": Wheeler-Bennett, *George VI*, p. 85.

37 "careful dieting": Bradford, *Reluctant King*, p. 62.

37 "change of scene": Wheeler-Bennett, *George VI*, pp. 85–86.

38 "never quite the same": Harold Nicolson, *King George the Fifth: His Life and Reign* (London: Constable, 1952), p. 268.

38 "emotional excitement": Wheeler-Bennett, *George VI*, pp. 88–89.

38 "lost seriously in weight": *The Manchester Guardian*, 14 December 1915.

38 "light duty": Wheeler-Bennett, *George VI*, p. 89.

39 severe shell shock: Michael Bowes Lyon to Lady Elizabeth Bowes Lyon, 18 October 1916: "poor Pat is an awful wreck," Glamis Archives, 270/7/15.

39 head wound: Shawcross, *QEQM*, p. 64.

39 His right leg was blown: Ibid., p. 71.

40 "It really is all so ghastly": Lady Lavinia Spencer to Lady Elizabeth Bowes Lyon, 5 October 1915, Glamis Archives, 270/4/28.

40 "Mary" . . . "George R": Glamis Archives, Box 270.

40 When Elizabeth failed: Shawcross, *QEQM*, p. 75.

40 Lavinia wrote to invite: Lady Elizabeth Bowes Lyon to Lady Strathmore, 28 March 1916, Glamis Archives (CH).

40 "rather frightening": Lady Elizabeth Bowes Lyon to Lady Strathmore, 4 April 1916, Glamis Archives (CH).

40 "he's rather nice": Ibid.

40 "staying and staying": Beryl Poignand to her mother, n.d. [4 April 1916], Poignand Papers, Shawcross, *QEQM*, p. 75.

FOUR: The Rent You Pay for Life

44 he would first carefully part: Crawford, *Little Princesses*, p. 53.

44 Unlike most of them: Grania Forbes, *My Darling Buffy: The Early Life of the Queen Mother* (London: Richard Cohen Books, 1997), p. 9.

45 "left wounds which never healed": *The Times*, 24 June 1938.

45 "an elfin creature": Asquith I, p. 88.

45 "the personality which I see": Elizabeth Longford, *The Queen Mother: A Biography* (London: Granada, 1981), p. 16.

45 "You feel very safe": Queen Elizabeth, conversations with Eric Anderson, 1994–95, Shawcross, *QEQM Letters*, p. 4.

46 "can there ever have been": Asquith II, p. 34; author interview with Caroline, Lady Bowes Lyon, 2 March 2019.

46   "holiday place": Asquith I, p. 34.

46   She excitedly showed: Forbes, *My Darling Buffy*, p. 29.

46   riding astride a donkey: Asquith I, p. 91.

47   "She was a great force": Author interview with Lady Mary Clayton,
        12 March 2009.

47   "Work is the rent": Shawcross, *QEQM Letters*, p. 4.

47   "Life is for living": Forbes, *My Darling Buffy*, p. 9.

47   "insisted he be included": Shawcross, *QEQM*, p. 24.

48   "follow the birds": Hugo Vickers, *Elizabeth the Queen Mother* (Lon-
        don: Arrow Books, 2005), p. 3.

48   "He lived more of his own life": Queen Elizabeth, conversations with
        Eric Anderson, 1994–95, Shawcross, *QEQM Letters*, p. 15.

48   "She never muffed it": Forbes, *My Darling Buffy*, p. 28.

48   "magnificent cypresses": Shawcross, *QEQM*, p. 28.

49   "a tumour at the base": Vickers, *Elizabeth the Queen Mother*, p. 13.

49   "My darling preacious": Lady Elizabeth Bowes Lyon to Lady Strath-
        more, 19 September 1912, Glamis Archives (CH).

49   "It is a curious thing": Queen Elizabeth to Arthur Penn, 30 June
        1938, Penn Papers, Shawcross, *QEQM Letters*, p. 256.

49   "Lovie I was so sorry": Lady Elizabeth Bowes Lyon to Lady Strath-
        more, 17 October 1912, Glamis Archives, 270/11.

50   "play is the highest": early-education.org.uk/friedrich-froebel.

50   "not a believer": Beryl Poignand to her mother, 22 November [1914],
        Poignand Papers, Shawcross, *QEQM*, p. 56.

50   "my dearest Medusa": Lady Elizabeth Bowes Lyon to Beryl Poignand,
        1 October 1918, Glamis Archives (CH).

50   "dearest Pig": Lady Elizabeth Bowes Lyon to Beryl Poignand, 9 March
        1920, Glamis Archives (CH).

50   "My dear silly ass": Lady Elizabeth Bowes Lyon to Beryl Poignand,
        26 December 1915, Glamis Archives (CH).

50   "Zut! I mean Phut": Lady Elizabeth Bowes Lyon to Beryl Poignand,
        1 May 1916, Glamis Archives (CH).

51   "The streets were full": Queen Elizabeth, conversations with Eric
        Anderson, 1994–95, Shawcross, *QEQM Letters*, p. 22.

51   "the essence of politeness": Asquith I, p. 122.

51   "appeared to sail through": *The Times*, 24 June 1938.

52   "She always rose early": Forbes, *My Darling Buffy*, p. 77.

52   "awful blow": Beryl Poignand to her mother, 1 October 1915, Sarah
        Jane Dumbrille Collection.

52   "has all her meals": Beryl Poignand to her mother, 3 October 1915,
        Sarah Jane Dumbrille Collection.

53   "All I can say": Lady Elizabeth Bowes Lyon to Beryl Poignand,
        26 April 1916, Glamis Archives (CH).

53   congregation comprised: *The Times*, 25 May 1916.

FIVE: Coolness and Courage

56   "the young prince": *The Times,* 18 September 1916.
56   "I am pleased with my son": Wheeler-Bennett, *George VI,* p. 97.
56   "It was certainly a great": Ibid., p. 96.
56   "When I was on top": Ibid., p. 97.
57   "deeply depressed": Ibid., p. 102.
57   "squalls of temper": Ibid., p. 104.
57   successful operation: *The Times,* 30 November 1917.
57   "small house": Greig, *King Maker,* p. 115.
57   "maternal tyranny": Nicolson, diary, 9 September 1948, Balliol.
57   "most simple": Greig, *King Maker,* p. 115.
58   "damned funny": Ibid.
58   "treated her like": Greig, *King Maker,* p. 116.
58   "most frightfully": Ibid.
58   "unrestrained": Ibid.
58   "a curious sensation": Prince Albert to Queen Mary, 5 March 1918,
       RA QM/PRIV/CC10/271.
58   made no friends: Greig, *King Maker,* p. 131.
59   Greig had introduced: Ibid., pp. 132–33.
59   "amused": Windsor II, 26 October 1918, p. 125.
59   "didn't sleep at": Ibid.

SIX: Do's and Don'ts

61   "Gud [sic] how I loathe": Windsor II, 27 November 1918, p. 136.
61   "It's rotten having to": Windsor II, 28 November 1918, p. 136.
62   "wear the wings": A. Cunningham Reid, *Planes and Personalities: A
       Pot-Pourri* (London: Philip Allan, 1920), p. 44.
62   "stand the strain": Ibid., p. 46.
62   "practical flying": Ibid.
62   "sheer determination": Ibid.
62   "painful to see": Alexandra Churchill, *In the Eye of the Storm: George
       V and the Great War* (Warwick, UK: Helion, 2018), p. 190.
63   "lovely day": Queen Mary, diary, 18 January 1919, RA QM/PRIV/
       QMD/1919.
63   "very peaceful": Ibid.
63   "I feel rather stunned": Queen Mary to Prince Albert, 18 January
       1919, RA GVI/PRIV/RF/11/305, Churchill, A, p. 331.
63   "It must have been": Prince Albert to Queen Mary, n.d. [January
       1919], RA GV/PRIV/CC1/4, Churchill, A, p. 331.
63   "chilling insensitivity": Ziegler II, p. 70.
64   "the greatest relief": Windsor II, 20 January 1919, p. 158.
64   "had become more": Ibid.

64 "cold-hearted": Prince Edward to Queen Mary, 27 January 1919, Ziegler II, p. 70.

64 "crammed with": Queen Mary to Prince Albert, 21 January 1919, RA GV/PRIV/RF/11/306, Churchill, A, p. 333.

64 "It must have been": Prince Albert to Queen Mary, n.d., RA GV/PRIV/CC11/5.

64 an idealistic: Bolitho, *Their Majesties,* p. 28.

65 "I'll do it": Wheeler-Bennett, *George VI,* p. 164.

65 "good will between": *The Times,* 22 May 1919.

66 "the Foreman": Wheeler-Bennett, *George VI,* p. 168.

66 "I never met one": Ibid., p. 166.

66 chance meeting: Robert Wainwright, *Sheila: The Australian Ingenue Who Bewitched British Society* (Sydney: Allen and Unwin, 2014) [February 16, 1918], pp. 57–58.

66 "Her entire appearance": Ibid., p. 89.

67 "I don't expect to see": Windsor II, 14 May 1919, p. 179.

67 "The 4 Do's": Windsor II, 28 June 1920, p. 420.

67 "What marvellous fun": Windsor II, 23 May 1919, p. 180.

68 "He is going to make": Wainwright, *Sheila,* p. 92.

68 "Christ! How I loathe": Windsor II, 21 May 1920, p. 373.

68 "If he really loved": Windsor II, 24 May 1920, p. 379.

68 "fine old title": Wheeler-Bennett, *George VI,* p. 140.

68 "I can tell you": Duke of York to King George V, 6 June 1920, RA GV/PRIV/AA61/27.

68 "I know that you have": Wheeler-Bennett, *George VI,* 7 June 1920, p. 140.

68 "I am very proud": Ibid.

69 "what fun they all had": Wainwright, *Sheila,* p. 95.

69 on June 1, 1920: *The Times,* 2 June 1920.

69 "he was not an easy": James Stuart, Viscount Stuart of Findhorn, *Within the Fringe: An Autobiography* (London: Bodley Head, 1967), p. 48.

SEVEN: Radiant Vitality

71 "went straight to": Queen Elizabeth, conversations with Eric Anderson, 1994–95, Shawcross, *QEQM,* p. 96.

71 "very old for her age": Lady Strathmore to Beryl Poignand, 9 October 1914, Glamis Archives, Box 270.

71 "gay and giddy": Victor Cochrane-Baillie to Lady Elizabeth Bowes Lyon, 18 September 1918, Glamis Archives, Box 270.

72 "perpetually rough": Asquith I, p. 86.

72 "clear, rather high": Ibid., p. 184.

72 "Mad Hatters": Forbes, *My Darling Buffy,* p. 93.

72 "cocktail-drinking": Airlie, *Thatched with Gold,* p. 166.

72   "radiant vitality": Ibid.
73   "great sweetness": Longford, *Queen Mother,* p. 16.
73   "mildly flirtatious": Channon II, p. 629.
73   "People were rather": Queen Elizabeth, conversations with Eric
      Anderson,1994–95, Shawcross, *QEQM,* p. 116.
73   "soulful correspondence": Lady Elizabeth Bowes Lyon to Beryl
      Poignand, Tuesday [9 May 1922], Glamis Archives (CH).
74   "It was all over": Queen Mary, diary, 6 July 1920, RA QM/PRIV/
      QMD/1920.
74   "a pretty match": *The Times,* 9 July 1920.
74   "the education of": *The Times,* 29 June 1920.
75   "Lady Elizabeth managed": Forbes, *My Darling Buffy,* p. 148.
75   "I was on duty": Stuart, *Within the Fringe,* p. 57.
75   "It really was most": Lady Elizabeth Bowes Lyon to Beryl Poignand,
      13 July 1920, Glamis Archives (CH).
75   "nice": Ibid.
75   "fallen in love": Airlie, *Thatched with Gold,* p. 166.
75   "It was a more": Stuart, *Within the Fringe,* p. 57.

EIGHT: Improved in Every Way

77   Scarcely nine days: Shawcross, *QEQM,* p. 118.
77   "famous electric launch": Helen Cecil to Captain Hardinge, n.d.
      [18 September 1920], Hardinge Papers, Centre for Kentish Studies,
      Maidstone, U 2117-C2/33, Shawcross, *QEQM,* p. 118.
78   "quite worth it": Ibid.
78   The list of thirty-six: Queen Mary, diary, 23 July 1920, RA QM/PRIV/
      QMD/1920.
78   "invited to meet": *The Times,* 24 July 1920.
78   Elizabeth had a full: Forfar County Ball, 8 September 1920, Lady
      Elizabeth Bowes Lyon dance card, Glamis Archives, 270/7/2.
78   "completely exhausted": Lady Elizabeth Bowes Lyon to Beryl Poi-
      gnand, n.d. [14 September 1920], Glamis Archives (CH).
79   "Prince Albert is coming": Ibid.
79   "There is a <u>fearful</u>": Helen Cecil to Captain Hardinge, n.d. [18 Sep-
      tember 1920], Hardinge Papers, Centre for Kentish Studies, U 2117-
      C2/33, Shawcross, *QEQM,* p. 120.
79   "You won't let James": Captain Hardinge to Helen Cecil, 11, 13 Sep-
      tember 1920, Hardinge Papers, Centre for Kentish Studies, U 2117-
      C1/19, 21, Shawcross, *QEQM,* p. 120.
79   "sliding races": Helen Cecil to Captain Hardinge, n.d. [18 September
      1920] and 20 September 1920, Hardinge Papers, Centre for Kentish
      Studies, U 2117-C2/35, 36, Shawcross, *QEQM,* p. 120.
80   "did it with more gusto": Ibid.
80   "rather alarming": Ibid.

80   "signals of distress": Helen Cecil to Captain Hardinge, n.d. [19 September 1920], Hardinge Papers, Centre for Kentish Studies, U 2117-C2/34, Shawcross, *QEQM*, p. 120.

80   "I wonder he isn't": Helen Cecil to Captain Hardinge, n.d. [19 September 1920] and 20 September 1920, Hardinge Papers, Centre for Kentish Studies, U 2117-C2/34, 36, Shawcross, *QEQM*, p. 121.

80   "for the very abrupt": Duke of York to Lady Strathmore, 21 September 1920, Glamis Archives.

80   "no other house": James Stuart to Lady Strathmore, 21 September 1920, Glamis Archives.

80   "leaving him in peace": Helen Cecil to Lady Elizabeth Bowes Lyon, 21 September 1920, Glamis Archives.

80   "babies": Lady Elizabeth Bowes Lyon to Beryl Poignand, n.d. [23 September 1920], Glamis Archives (CH).

80   "most awfully nice": Ibid.

80   "much improved": Ibid.

80   "worked wonders": Margaret Rhodes, *The Final Curtsey* (London: Umbria Press, 2011), p. 145, quoting a letter from Lady Elizabeth Bowes Lyon to Margaret's mother, May Elphinstone.

80   "royalty staying": Ibid.

81   "Of course we didn't": Lady Doris Gordon-Lennox to Lady Elizabeth Bowes Lyon, n.d. [14 October 1920], Glamis Archives.

81   "I have got to start": Lady Elizabeth Bowes Lyon to Beryl Poignand, n.d. [est. late October 1920], Glamis Archives (CH).

81   "Our <u>Bert</u>": Lady Elizabeth Bowes Lyon to Beryl Poignand, n.d. [November 1920], Glamis Archives (CH).

81   "Don't say one word": Lady Elizabeth Bowes Lyon to Beryl Poignand, n.d. [November or December 1920], Glamis Archives (CH).

82   "terrifies me": Lady Elizabeth Bowes Lyon to Duke of York, Monday, n.d. [13 December 1920], RA GVI/PRIV/RF/26/01.

82   "I couldn't leave": Lady Elizabeth Bowes Lyon to Duke of York, 23 December 1920, RA GVI/PRIV/RF/26/02.

82   "always talking": Airlie, *Thatched with Gold*, p. 167.

82   "I'm sure you would": Lady Elizabeth Bowes Lyon to Beryl Poignand, Friday, n.d. [31 December 1920], Glamis Archives (CH).

82   "frankly doubtful": Airlie, *Thatched with Gold*, p. 167.

82   "enormous": Lady Elizabeth Bowes Lyon to Duke of York, n.d. [6 January 1921], RA GVI/PRIV/RF/26/03.

83   "very ill": Lady Elizabeth Bowes Lyon to Duke of York, 10 January 1921, RA GVI/PRIV/RF/26/04.

83   Armstrong Siddeley: Queen Mary, diary, 16 January 1921, RA QM/PRIV/QMD/1921.

83   "ill expressed": Lady Elizabeth Bowes Lyon to Duke of York, n.d. [24 February 1921], RA GVI/PRIV/RF/26/05.

83   a charity matinee: *The Times*, 1 March 1921.

83   **"romance was on"**: Author interview with Dominic, the third Viscount Stuart of Findhorn, 30 July 2019.

84   **"Prince Bertie"**: Lady Elizabeth Bowes Lyon to Duke of York, 28 February 1921, RA GVI/PRIV/RF/26/07.

84   **"I have written"**: Lady Strathmore to Lady Airlie, 5 March 1921, British Library, Airlie Papers, Add. MSS 82762, ff. 48–49.

84   **"much relieved"**: Lady Elizabeth Bowes Lyon to Duke of York, n.d. [7 March 1921], RA GVI/PRIV/RF/26/08.

84   **"Dearest Mabell"**: Queen Mary to Lady Airlie, 9 March 1921, British Library, Add. MS 82748, f. 39.

85   **typical day**: Queen Mary, diary, 14 March 1921, RA QM/PRIV/QMD/1921; "Court Circular," *The Times,* 15 March 1921.

85   **"very flourishing"**: Lady Elizabeth Bowes Lyon to Duke of York, 25 March 1921, RA GVI/PRIV/26/09.

85   **"the spirit of"**: *The Times,* 2 March 1921.

85   **"human factor"**: *The Times,* 3 March 1921.

85   **"excellent speeches"**: Lady Elizabeth Bowes Lyon to Duke of York, n.d. [7 March 1921], RA GVI/PRIV/RF/26/08.

85   **"longing to get over"**: Duke of York to Queen Mary, 30 April 1920, RA QM/PRIV/CC11/15.

86   **"gift of vision"**: Bolitho, *Their Majesties,* p. 32.

86   **"although in private"**: Ibid., p. 31.

86   **The crowd included:** *The Times,* 8 July 1921.

86   **To tunes played:** *The Times,* 12 July 1921.

86   **They also played:** Lady Elizabeth Bowes Lyon to Duke of York, n.d. [18 July 1921], RA GVI/PRIV/RF/26/12.

87   **He had conceived:** Wheeler-Bennett, *George VI,* p. 175.

87   **"play the game"**: *The Times,* 4 November 1921.

87   **"welfare spirit"**: Ibid.

87   **"Your Boys Camp:** Lady Elizabeth Bowes Lyon to Duke of York, 6 August 1921, RA GVI/PRIV/RF/26/13.

NINE: More Than an Ordinary Friend

89   **"expeditions"**: Queen Mary to Lady Airlie, 24 July 1921, Lady Airlie Papers, British Library, Add. MS 82748, ff. 40–41.

89   **eight attendants:** Airlie, *Thatched with Gold,* p. 155.

89   **"From the way"**: Rev. John Stirton, diary, 28 August 1921, RA AEC/GG/026.

89   **"Lady Elizabeth filled"**: Airlie, *Thatched with Gold,* p. 167.

90   **"shot so badly"**: Duke of York to Lady Elizabeth Bowes Lyon, 2 October 1921, Glamis Archives, 270/5/3.

90   **"good talk"**: Duke of York to Queen Mary, 29 September 1921, RA QM/PRIV/CC11/19.

90   **"Elizabeth is very kind"**: Ibid.

90   Their last engagement: *The Times,* 18 July 1921.

90   Mabell Airlie reported: Lady Airlie to Queen Mary, 2 October 1921, RA QM/PRIV/C47/ 684, Shawcross *QEQM,* p. 132.

90   Elizabeth described: Lady Elizabeth Bowes Lyon to Beryl Poignand, 11 October 1921, Glamis Archives (CH).

91   "tremendous spirits": Duke of York to Lady Elizabeth Bowes Lyon, 2 October 1921, Glamis Archives, 270/5/3.

91   "touched": Lady Elizabeth Bowes Lyon to Duke of York, 4 October 1921, RA GVI/PRIV/RF/26/15.

91   "good progress": Lady Elizabeth Bowes Lyon to Duke of York, 11 October 1921, RA GVI/PRIV/RF/26/16.

91   "I have been leading": Duke of York to Lady Elizabeth Bowes Lyon, 12 October 1921, Glamis Archives, 270/5/4.

91   "felt so deeply": Queen Mary to Lady Elizabeth Bowes Lyon, 19 October 1921, RA QEQM/PRIV/RF.

92   James needed to go: Stuart, *Within the Fringe,* p. 57.

92   "ruined my life": Vickers, *Elizabeth the Queen Mother,* p. 47.

92   "still too weak": Lady Elizabeth Bowes Lyon to Beryl Poignand, 28 November 1921, Glamis Archives (CH).

92   "no evidence": Shawcross, *QEQM,* p. 134.

92   "The point is": Author interview with Dominic Stuart, 30 July 2019.

93   "insisted on taking": Lady Elizabeth Bowes Lyon to Beryl Poignand, 28 November 1921, Glamis Archives (CH).

93   James officially: *The Times,* 5 December 1921.

93   he set sail: Stuart, *Within the Fringe,* p. 58.

93   "He used to go": Queen Elizabeth, conversations with Eric Anderson, 1994–95, Shawcross, *QEQM Letters,* p. 84.

93   "her mother had": Princess Margaret to Queen Elizabeth II, 8 March 1954, RA QEII/PRIV/RF, Shawcross, *QEQM,* p. 134.

94   "solid and endearing": Lascelles III, p. 622.

94   "She wrinkles": Lascelles II, p. 8.

94   Through an inheritance: Ibid., p. x.

94   "poor girl": Ziegler II, p. 149.

94   "rather dull": Lady Elizabeth Bowes Lyon to Beryl Poignand, 28 November 1921, Glamis Archives (CH).

94   "What colours": Lady Elizabeth Bowes Lyon to Duke of York, n.d. [23 November 1921], RA GVI/PRIV/RF/26/20, Shawcross, *QEQM,* p. 134.

95   "I should have": Lady Elizabeth Bowes Lyon to Duke of York, 16 December 1921, RA GVI/PRIV/RF/26/21.

95   "with a chill": Lady Elizabeth Bowes Lyon to Duke of York, n.d. [December 1921], RA GVI/PRIV/RF/26/22.

95   Elizabeth received: Princess Mary to Lady Elizabeth Bowes Lyon, 5 January 1922, RA QEQM/PRIV/RF, Shawcross, *QEQM,* p. 135.

95   "Princess Mary's": *The Times,* 16 January 1922.

95   **"longing to hear"**: Queen Mary to Duke of York, 22 January 1922, RA GVI/PRIV/RF/11/315.

95   **"I was rather depressed"**: Duke of York to Queen Mary, 25 January 1922, RA QM/PRIV/CC/11/24.

96   **"I am beginning"**: Lady Elizabeth Bowes Lyon to Duke of York, 23 February 1922, RA GVI/PRIV/RF/26/25.

96   **The sun shone**: Queen Mary, diary, 28 February 1922, RA QM/PRIV/QMD/1922.

96   **"living ribbon"**: *The Times,* 28 February 1922.

96   **"a man of her own"**: *The Times,* 27 February 1922.

96   **After the carriage**: *The Times,* 1 March 1922.

96   **depressed for days**: Queen Mary, diary, 29 February 1922, RA QM/PRIV/QMD/1922.

97   **"Dreadful saying"**: Queen Mary, diary, 28 February 1922, RA QM/PRIV/QMD/1922.

97   **"The whole nation"**: *The Times,* 28 February 1922.

97   **"I am so terribly"**: Lady Elizabeth Bowes Lyon to Duke of York, 8 March 1922, RA GVI/PRIV/RF/26/26, Shawcross, *QEQM,* p. 136.

97   **"somewhat depressed"**: Duke of York to Lady Elizabeth Bowes Lyon, 8 March 1922, RA QEQM/PRIV/RF/8 March 1922.

98   **"Please do try"**: Lady Elizabeth Bowes Lyon to Duke of York, n.d. [12 March 1922], RA GVI/PRIV/RF/26/27, Shawcross, *QEQM,* p. 137.

98   **"would be too sad for me"**: Duke of York to Lady Elizabeth Bowes Lyon, 16 March 1922, RA QEQM/PRIV/RF/16 March 1922.

98   **"was not very upset"**: Duke of York to Lady Elizabeth Bowes Lyon, 26 March 1922, RA QEQM/PRIV/RF.

98   **"most extraordinary"**: Hon. James Stuart to Lady Elizabeth Bowes Lyon, 24 March 1922, RA QEQM/PRIV/PAL, Shawcross, *QEQM,* pp. 138–39.

99   **"tragic" victim**: Channon II, p. 54.

99   **"Not that it's any"**: Hon. James Stuart to Lady Elizabeth Bowes Lyon, 24 March 1922, RA QEQM/PRIV/PAL, Shawcross, *QEQM,* pp. 138–39.

99   **"The fact that he"**: Author interview with Dominic Stuart, 30 July 2019.

99   **"So long as we"**: Duke of York to Lady Elizabeth Bowes Lyon, 26 March 1922, RA QEQM/PRIV/RF.

99   **"still so far"**: Queen Mary to Lady Strathmore, 6 May 1922, Glamis Archives.

100   **"most charming"**: Lady Elizabeth Bowes Lyon to Duke of York, 16 May 1922, RA GVI/PRIV/RF/26/29.

100   **"He says it's exactly"**: Lady Elizabeth Bowes Lyon to Beryl Poignand, Tuesday [9 May 1922], Glamis Archives (CH).

100   **"in her private"**: Forbes, *My Darling Buffy,* p. 160.

100   **"Yes, I did put"**: Lady Elizabeth Bowes Lyon to May Elphinstone, n.d. [12 May 1922], RA QEQM/OUT/ELPHINSTONE.

100   **He thought Davidson**: Greig, *King Maker*, p. 178.

101   **"crisis"**: Ibid., 179–80.

101   **"much brighter"**: Ibid.

101   **"new spring"**: Ibid., p. 181.

101   **"so that I can collect"**: Lady Elizabeth Bowes Lyon to Duke of York, Wednesday [26 July 1922], RA GVI/PRIV/26/30.

101   **Bertie replied**: Duke of York to Lady Elizabeth Bowes Lyon, 28 July 1922, Glamis Archives, 270/5/7.

101   **"I do hope you won't"**: Lady Elizabeth Bowes Lyon to Duke of York, 12 September 1922, RA GVI/PRIV/RF/26/31B.

101   **"I am very sorry"**: Rev. John Stirton, diary, 26 September 1922, RA AEC/GG/026.

102   **"the pipers playing"**: Channon I, p. 397.

102   **"horrid"**: Duke of York to Queen Mary, 30 September 1922, RA QM/PRIV/CC1/28.

102   **"ten million"**: Lady Elizabeth Bowes Lyon to Duke of York, 3 October 1922, RA GVI/PRIV/RF/26/34.

102   **"I play the records"**: Lady Elizabeth Bowes Lyon to Duke of York, 7 November 1922, RA GVI/PRIV/RF/26/36.

102   **"Wonderful day"**: Duke of York to Lady Elizabeth Bowes Lyon, 27 November 1922, RA QEQM/PRIV/RF.

103   **"not think really"**: Duke of York to Lady Elizabeth Bowes Lyon, 30 November 1922, RA QEQM/PRIV/RF.

103   **"I should love"**: Lady Elizabeth Bowes Lyon to Duke of York, 6 December 1922, RA GVI/PRIV/RF/16/42.

103   **"at once!"**: Lady Elizabeth Bowes Lyon to Duke of York, 7 December 1922, RA GVI/PRIV/RF/26/43.

103   **he celebrated with**: Queen Mary, diary, 14 December 1922, RA QM/PRIV/QMD/1922.

103   **"unmasking and highlighting"**: Stephen Leacock, *The Essential Stephen Leacock* (Limerick, Ireland: Pillar International, 2015), p. 7.

103   **"I cannot thank"**: Duke of York to Lady Elizabeth Bowes Lyon, 16 December 1922, RA QEQM/PRIV/RF.

104   **"was torn between"**: Longford, *Queen Mother*, p. 23.

PART TWO: HALCYON DAYS
TEN: Don't Forget Your Honey Lamb

109   **"In the public mind"**: *The Times,* 26 April 1923.

109   **"character sketch"**: *The Times,* 17 January 1923.

110   **"Great headlines"**: Lady Elizabeth Bowes Lyon, diary, 16 January 1923, RA QEQM/PRIV/DIARY/3.

110   "Awful . . . appalling": Lady Elizabeth Bowes Lyon, diary, 16 January 1923, RA QEQM/PRIV/DIARY/3.

110   "Scotch reporters": Lady Elizabeth Bowes Lyon, diary, 16 January 1923, RA QEQM/PRIV/DIARY/3.

110   "badly . . . fond": *The Star,* 17 January 1923.

110   a large Kashmir: *The Illustrated London News,* 27 January 1923.

110   "proposed in the garden": *The Star,* 17 January 1923.

110   "it was news to me": Ibid.

110   She had not: Lady Elizabeth Bowes Lyon, diary, 4 July 1923, RA QEQM/PRIV/DIARY 3.

110   "I had no idea": Captain William Leveson-Gower to Lady Elizabeth Bowes Lyon, 16 January 1923, RA QEQM/PRIV/BL.

110   "How tiresome": Queen Mary to Duke of York, 18 January 1923, RA GVI/PRIV/RF/11/318.

111   "grammy": Lady Elizabeth Bowes Lyon, diary, 10 February 1923, RA QEQM/PRIV/DIARY/3.

111   baked potatoes: Lady Elizabeth Bowes Lyon, diary, 24 March 1923, RA QEQM/PRIV/DIARY/3.

111   "my own little": Duke of York to Lady Elizabeth Bowes Lyon, 26 January 1923, RA QEQM/PRIV/RF/26 January 1923.

111   "just a month": Duke of York to Lady Elizabeth Bowes Lyon, 11 February 1923, RA QEQM/PRIV/RF/11 February 1923.

111   "I do love you": Lady Elizabeth Bowes Lyon to Duke of York, n.d. [25 January 1923], RA GVI/PRIV/RF/26/51.

112   "little P.A.": Lady Elizabeth Bowes Lyon to Duke of York, n.d., Thursday [29 March 1923], RA GVI/PRIV/RF/26/57.

112   "don't forget": Lady Elizabeth Bowes Lyon to Duke of York, n.d., Saturday [31 March 1923], RA GVI/PRIV/RF/26/58.

112   "Bertie do you": Ibid.

112   "I think they have": Lady Joan Verney to Lady Airlie, 24 January 1923, British Library, Airlie Papers, Add. MS 82763, ff. 50–51.

112   "a very warm": Queen Mary to Lady Elizabeth Bowes Lyon, 15 January 1923, RA QEQM/PRIV/RF.

112   "I know you will": King George V to Lady Elizabeth Bowes Lyon, 15 January 1923, RA QEQM/PRIV/RF.

112   "humble & obedient": Lady Elizabeth Bowes Lyon to Queen Mary, 17 January 1923, RA QM/PRIV/CC11/34.

112   to support Bertie: Lady Elizabeth Bowes Lyon to King George V, 17 January 1923, RA GV/PRIV/AA61/342.

112   "very happy": Lady Elizabeth Bowes Lyon to Queen Mary, 17 January 1923, RA QM/PRIV/CC11/34.

113   Her brother Mike: Michael Bowes Lyon to Lady Elizabeth Bowes Lyon, 20 January 1923, RA QEQM/PRIV/BL.

113   "railway trains": Pope-Hennessy II, p. 157.

113   "**They were all**": Lady Elizabeth Bowes Lyon to May Elphinstone, n.d.
       [20 January 1923], RA QEQM/OUT/ELPHINSTONE.
113   "**managed with**": Queen Elizabeth to Charles, Prince of Wales, n.d.
       [1960s], Clarence House Archives, 10086–600, Shawcross, *QEQM*,
       p. 155.
113   "**terrible squash**": Pope-Hennessy II, p. 89.
114   "**orders and decorations**": Ibid., p. 115.
114   "**terrifying**": Lady Elizabeth Bowes Lyon to May Elphinstone, n.d.
       [20 January 1923], RA QEQM/OUT/ELPHINSTONE.
114   "**We got on**": Queen Elizabeth, conversations with Eric Anderson,
       1994–95, Shawcross, *QEQM Letters,* pp. 126–27.
114   "**As he told**": Rose I, p. 576.
114   "**rather enjoyed**": Queen Elizabeth, conversations with Eric Anderson,
       1994–95, Shawcross, *QEQM Letters,* p. 126.
114   "**sat on hot water**": Lady Elizabeth Bowes Lyon, diary, 21 January
       1923, RA QEQM/PRIV/DIARY/3.
114   **a sunburst diamond:** Lady Elizabeth Bowes Lyon, diary, 21 January
       1923, RA QEQM/PRIV/DIARY/3.
114   "**some wonderful lace**": Lady Elizabeth Bowes Lyon, diary, 17 Febru-
       ary 1923, RA QEQM/PRIV/DIARY/3.
115   "**minor mausoleum**": Pope-Hennessy II, p. 90.
115   "**radiant faces**": Queen Mary to Lady Strathmore, 25 January 1923,
       Glamis Archives.
115   "**dear people**": Queen Mary to Duke of York, 24 January 1923, RA
       GVI/RF/11/319.
115   "**I can't tell you**": Lady Joan Verney to Lady Airlie, 24 January 1923,
       British Library, Airlie Papers, Add. MS 82763, ff. 50–51.
115   "**When all is said**": Lady Strathmore to Lady Salisbury, British Library,
       Add. MS 82763, ff. 48–49.
116   "**simply marvelous**": Lady Elizabeth Bowes Lyon, diary, 17 February
       1923, RA QEQM/PRIV/DIARY/3.
116   "**the only completely**": Asquith I, p. 13.
116   "**Old as the hills!**": Lady Elizabeth Bowes Lyon, diary, 4 February
       1923, RA QEQM/PRIV/DIARY/3.
116   "**mulligatawny soup**": John Matson, *Sandringham Days: The Domestic
       Life of the Royal Family in Norfolk 1862–1952* (Stroud, Gloucester-
       shire: History Press, 2011), p. 138.
117   **As a teenager:** Asquith I, p. 99.
117   "**to Zyrot**": Lady Elizabeth Bowes Lyon, diary, 2 March 1923, RA
       QEQM/PRIV/DIARY/3.
117   **Her selections were:** Lady Elizabeth Bowes Lyon, diary, 20 April and
       21 April 1923, RA QEQM/PRIV/DIARY/3.
117   "**very simple**": *The Times,* 23 April 1923.
117   he "**seems not to**": Rev. John Stirton, diary, 31 August 1923, RA AEC/
       GG/026.

118   "talked hard": Lady Elizabeth Bowes Lyon, diary, 17 January 1923 and 5 March 1923, RA QEQM/PRIV/DIARY/3.

118   "Mike, Mother & I": Lady Elizabeth Bowes Lyon, diary, 11 February 1923, RA QEQM/PRIV/DIARY/3.

118   "Have you written": Michael Bowes Lyon to Lady Elizabeth Bowes Lyon, 20 January 1923, RA QEQM/PRIV/BL.

118   "Cable of": Lady Elizabeth Bowes Lyon, diary, 1 February 1923, RA QEQM/PRIV/DIARY/3.

118   "James rang up": Lady Elizabeth Bowes Lyon, diary, 6 February 1923, RA QEQM/PRIV/DIARY/3.

118   Mike arrived: Lady Elizabeth Bowes Lyon, diary, 8 February 1923, RA QEQM/PRIV/DIARY/3.

118   "Mikie still dressing!": Lady Elizabeth Bowes Lyon, diary, 9 February 1923, RA QEQM/PRIV/DIARY/3.

119   Elizabeth talked to Mike: Lady Elizabeth Bowes Lyon, diary, 10 February 1923, RA QEQM/PRIV/DIARY/3.

119   "talked hard": Lady Elizabeth Bowes Lyon, diary, 11 February 1923, RA QEQM/PRIV/DIARY/3.

119   "it all happened": Author interview with Dominic Stuart, 30 July 2019.

120   "to the Berkeley": Lady Elizabeth Bowes Lyon, diary, 24 April 1923, RA QEQM/PRIV/DIARY/3.

120   a diamond and emerald: *The Times,* 17 April 1923.

120   "a prominent Quaker": *The Times,* 26 April 1923.

120   "Of course do ask": Duke of York to Lady Elizabeth Bowes Lyon, 14 March 1923, RA QEQM/PRIV/RF.

120   "I hope you don't mind": Prince of Wales to Duchess of York, 15 January 1923, RA QEQM/PRIV/RF.

121   Instead, they spent: Lady Elizabeth Bowes Lyon, diary, 25 March 1923, RA QEQM/PRIV/DIARY/3.

121   "I do hope": Lady Joan Verney to Lady Airlie, 18 January 1923, British Library, Airlie Papers, Add. MS 82763, ff. 41–43.

121   Built in 1730: *Country Life,* 21 April 1923; *The Illustrated London News,* 28 April 1923; author tour with Anna Meadmore, manager of special collections for the Royal Ballet School at White Lodge, 29 March 2019.

122   "I was simply": Lady Elizabeth Bowes Lyon to Queen Mary, 25 January 1923, RA QM/PRIV/CC11/36.

122   "I am a hopeless": Duke of York to Lady Elizabeth Bowes Lyon, 13 March 1923, RA QEQM/PRIV/RF.

122   "Don't worry": Lady Elizabeth Bowes Lyon to Duke of York, n.d. [13 March 1923], RA GVI/PRIV/RF/26/54.

123   "Bertie & I had to": Lady Elizabeth Bowes Lyon, diary, 5 March 1923, RA QEQM/PRIV/DIARY/3.

123   "Very pompous": Lady Elizabeth Bowes Lyon, diary, 23 March 1923, RA QEQM/PRIV/DIARY/3.

123   "throat burnt": Lady Elizabeth Bowes Lyon, diary, 6 February 1923,
      RA QEQM/PRIV/DIARY/3.

123   "I thought so much": Duke of York to Lady Elizabeth Bowes Lyon,
      13 March 1923, RA QEQM/PRIV/RF.

123   "the morning sun": Lady Elizabeth Bowes Lyon to Duke of York, n.d.
      [13 March 1923], RA GVI/PRIV/RF/26/58.

123   "blow the germs": Longford, *Queen Mother,* p. 141.

123   "How I loved": Duke of York to Lady Elizabeth Bowes Lyon, 14 March
      1923, RA QEQM/PRIV/RF.

124   "very sad": Lady Elizabeth Bowes Lyon, diary, 16 March 1923.

124   "very little": Lady Elizabeth Bowes Lyon, diary, 18 March 1923.

124   "rich with ornamentation": *The Times,* 19 March 1923.

124   "so grievously disabled": Ibid.

124   "gave them a rousing": Ibid.

124   "one of the most": *The Illustrated London News,* 24 March 1923.

125   "I shall always": Duke of York to Lady Elizabeth Bowes Lyon,
      29 March 1923, RA QEQM/PRIV/RF.

125   "Having never seen": Lady Elizabeth Bowes Lyon to Duke of York,
      Saturday, n.d. [31 March 1923], RA GVI/PRIV/RF/26/58.

125   "Another 2 days": Duke of York to Lady Elizabeth Bowes Lyon, 1 April
      1923, RA QEQM/PRIV/RF.

126   "much chaff": Lady Elizabeth Bowes Lyon, diary, 5 April 1923, RA
      QEQM/PRIV/DIARY/3.

126   "You are not late": Hardinge, *Loyal to Three Kings,* p. 40.

127   "ragged about": Lady Elizabeth Bowes Lyon, diary, 7 April 1923, RA
      QEQM/PRIV/DIARY/3.

127   The most eye-catching: *The Times,* 24 April 1923; *The Illustrated
      London News,* 28 April 1923.

127   "Feel very odd": Lady Elizabeth Bowes Lyon, diary, 21 April 1923, RA
      QEQM/PRIV/DIARY/3.

128   "donors of presents": *The Times,* 25 April 1923.

128   "looked so pretty": Queen Mary, diary, 23 April 1923, RA QM/PRIV/
      QMD/1923.

128   "huge glass cases": Christopher Warwick, *King George VI and Queen
      Elizabeth* (London: Sidgwick and Jackson, 1985), p. 4.

ELEVEN: A Gilded Carriage

131   On his wedding eve: King George V, diary, 25 April 1923, RA GV/
      PRIV/GVD/1923.

131   "felt terribly moved": Lady Elizabeth Bowes Lyon, diary, 25 April
      1923, RA QEQM/PRIV/DIARY/3.

131   She rose late: Lady Elizabeth Bowes Lyon, diary, 26 April 1923, RA
      QEQM/PRIV/DIARY/3.

131   "the simplest ever": *The Times,* 25 April 1923.

132   "frank smile": *The Times,* 27 April 1923.

132   numerous Americans: *The Times,* 23 April 1923.

133   "the many multitudes": *The Times,* 27 April 1923.

133   She leaned over: Ibid.

134   "the white and green": Ibid.

134   "gleaming Roman": Ibid.

135   "very good seats": *The Duff Cooper Diaries: 1915–1951,* ed. John
       Julius Norwich (London: Weidenfeld and Nicolson, 2005),
       p. 174.

135   Bertie seemed unsettled: *The Times,* 27 April 1923.

136   "in his best form": Herbert Henry Asquith, *Letters to a Friend,* vol. 2,
       pp. 52–53; Shawcross, *QEQM,* p. 174.

136   "with shining eyes": *The Times,* 27 April 1923.

136   "Did not feel very": Duchess of York, diary, 26 April 1923, RA
       QEQM/PRIV/DIARY/3.

136   "I was very nervous": Duke of York to Queen Mary, 27 April 1923, RA
       QM/PRIV/CC11/40.

136   "very kindly": *The Times,* 27 April 1923.

136   "the King's eyes": Ibid.

136   "so brief, so momentous": Ibid.

136   "When you are at the top": Author interview with Lady Elizabeth
       Anson, 24 November 2010.

137   "homely sentiment": *The Times,* 27 April 1923.

137   One gold pen: *The Times,* 20 April 1923.

137   "so dignified": Lady Strathmore to Beryl Poignand, 10 May 1923,
       Glamis Archives 270/3/11.

138   "Thank you": *The Times,* 27 April 1923.

138   It included *consommé:* Gabriel Tschumi, *Royal Chef: Recollections of
       Life in Royal Households from Queen Victoria to Queen Mary* (London:
       Kimber, 1954), pp. 153–54.

139   "Awful saying goodbye": Duchess of York, diary, 26 April 1923.

139   one of the postilions: *The Times,* 27 April 1923.

140   "very fine": King George V, diary, 26 April 1923, RA GV/PRIV/
       GVD/1923.

140   "beautiful": Queen Mary, diary, 26 April 1923, RA QM/PRIV/
       QMD/1923.

TWELVE: A Splendid Partner

143   "my dearest Papa": Duke of York to King George V, 27 April 1923, RA
       GV/PRIV/AA61/155.

143   "I am quite certain": King George V to Duke of York, 29 April 1923,
       RA GV/PRIV/AA61/156.

144   "I hope you will not": Duke of York to Queen Mary, 27 April 1923,
       RA QM/PRIV/CC11/40.

144   "with all my heart": Queen Mary to Duke of York, 28 April 1923, RA
      GVI/PRIV/RF/11/323.

144   "I felt so worried": Duchess of York to Lady Strathmore, n.d. [27 April
      1923], Glamis Archives.

144   "I won't say what": Lady Strathmore to Duchess of York, 27 April
      1923, RA QEQM/PRIV/BL.

145   "always take care": Duke of York to Lady Strathmore, 28 April 1923,
      Glamis Archives.

145   "at peace about": Lady Strathmore to Duke of York, 1 May 1923, RA
      GVI/PRIV/PAL/S/33.

145   "What shall I do": Mollie Cazalet to Queen Elizabeth, 8 August 1938,
      RA QEQM/PRIV/PAL, with enclosed note, Lady Strathmore to Mollie
      Cazalet, n.d.

145   "I cannot tell you": Lady Strathmore to Lady Christian Martin,
      17 January 1923 (Joicey-Cecil Papers), Shawcross, *QEQM Letters,*
      p. 107.

145   "I hope you will": Queen Mary to Duke of York, 28 April 1923, RA
      GVI/PRIV/RF/11/333.

145   The Queen even spent: Queen Mary, diary, 4 June 1923, RA QM/
      PRIV/QMD/1923.

145   "as nice as possible": Queen Mary to Duchess of York, 16 June 1923,
      RA GVI/RF/11.

145   royal sibling slang: Duchess of York, diary, 25 January 1923, RA
      QEQM/PRIV/DIARY/3.

145   "Everything was plain": Greig, *King Maker,* p. 185, citing Greig
      Papers.

146   "an ornately carved": Toni Ford, "Great British Houses: Polesden
      Lacey—Where the Queen Mother Spent Her Honeymoon," *Angloto-
      pia for Anglophiles,* 20 March 2015, anglotopia.net/british-history
      /great-british-houses-polesden-lacey-queen-mother-spent
      -honeymoon/.

146   "so shrewd": Queen Elizabeth to Osbert Sitwell, 27 September 1942,
      Sitwell Papers (Weston), Shawcross, *QEQM Letters,* p. 325.

146   "Mrs Greville has": Duke of York to King George V, 27 April 1923, RA
      GV/PRIV/AA61/155.

146   "woody glade": *The Illustrated London News,* 5 May 1923.

146   "delicious": Duchess of York to Beryl Poignand, 22 May 1923, Glamis
      Archives (CH).

147   "troublesome": Duchess of York, diary, 16, 17, 18 May 1923, RA
      QEQM/PRIV/DIARY/3.

147   The three-story: Author tour of Frogmore, 31 May 2019.

147   "a heavenly place": Duchess of York to Beryl Poignand, 22 May 1923,
      Glamis Archives (CH).

147   "the smartest": P. G. Wodehouse and Guy Bolton, *Bring on the Girls*
      (1953; London: Everyman's Library, 2014), p. 189.

147   **"danced hard"**: Duchess of York, diary, 22 May 1923, RA QEQM/ PRIV/DIARY/3.

147   **"The cure for it"**: Duke of York to Queen Mary, 25 May 1923, RA QM/PRIV/CC11/42.

147   **"How she got"**: Ibid.

148   **"arranged things"**: Duchess of York, diary, 12 June 1923, RA QEQM/ PRIV/DIARY/3.

148   **The duke's ground-floor:** *The Illustrated London News,* 4 August 1923.

148   **"I had better warn"**: Duke of York to Queen Mary, 21 June 1923, RA QM/PRIV/CC11/43.

148   **"went all over"**: King George V, diary, 28 June 1923, RA GV/PRIV/ GVD/1923.

148   **Elizabeth had her first:** *The Times,* 10–12 July 1923.

148   **She spotted:** Shawcross, *QEQM,* pp. 191–92.

149   **Dressed informally:** *The Times,* 9 August 1923.

149   **"not only the founder"**: John Cornwell account, n.d., RA GVI/PRIV/ CAMP.

149   **"restraints, etiquette"**: Unsigned account, n.d., RA GVI/PRIV/CAMP.

150   **"Whiters"**: Duchess of York, diary, 19 June 1923, RA QEQM/PRIV/ DIARY/3.

150   **"Felt depressed"**: Duchess of York, diary, 4 August 1923, RA QEQM/ PRIV/DIARY/3.

150   **"hope it will be"**: Ibid.

151   **"He had the ability"**: Author interview with Dominic Stuart, 30 July 2019.

151   **"She dispensed"**: Ibid.

THIRTEEN: Family Affairs

154   **"the truth was"**: Pope-Hennessy II, p. 224.

154   **"loathed it"**: Ibid., p. 181.

154   **"tranquility of spirit"**: Wheeler-Bennett, *George VI,* p. 240.

154   **"Elizabeth I hope"**: Duke of York to Lady Strathmore, 6 September 1923, Glamis Archives (CH).

154   **"It is so boring"**: Duchess of York to Lady Strathmore, n.d. [14 September 1924], Glamis Archives (CH).

154   **"even though I am"**: Duchess of York to Queen Mary, 19 September 1923, RA QM/PRIV/CC11/47.

155   **"When I first married"**: Pope-Hennessy II, p. 224.

155   **"colossal kilted"**: *The Times,* 7 September 1923.

155   **"not amusing"**: Queen Mary, diary, 6 September 1923, RA QM/PRIV/ QMD/1923.

155   **"as usual"**: King George V, diary, 6 September 1923, RA GV/PRIV/ GVD/1923.

156   **She sparkled**: Rev. John Stirton, diary, 11 September 1923, RA AEC/
       GG/026.
156   **"He would put"**: Rose I, p. 546.
156   **"Koom"**: *The Illustrated London News,* 27 October 1923.
157   **"up to the ropes"**: Greig, *King Maker,* p. 195.
158   **"often discussed"**: Ibid., p. 196.
158   **"miserable"**: Ibid., p. 200.
158   **"The success"**: Asquith II, p. 154.
158   **"I feel that now"**: Duke of York to Queen Mary, 9 October 1923, RA
       QM/PRIV/CC11/49.
158   **"Talked after lunch"**: Duchess of York, diary, 11 October 1923, RA
       QEQM/PRIV/DIARY/3.
158   **"I don't care"**: Greig, *King Maker,* p. 199.
158   **"Greig is going"**: Duchess of York to Lady Strathmore, n.d. [12 No-
       vember 1923], Glamis Archives (CH).
158   **"saving his life"**: Greig, *King Maker,* p. 202.
159   **"force to be reckoned"**: Ibid.
159   **"I have been trying"**: Louis Greig to Duchess of York, 15 November
       1923, RA QEQM/PRIV/HH.
159   **"I am not going to say"**: Greig, *King Maker,* p. 201.
159   **"We are off to Suburbia"**: Duchess of York to Beryl Poignand, 17 Oc-
       tober 1923, Sarah Jane Dumbrille Collection.
159   **turned on the taps**: Author interview with Jamie Lowther-Pinkerton,
       23 March 2021.
159   **"How we all lived"**: Duke of York to King George V, 26 October 1923,
       RA GV/PRIV/AA61/189.
159   **"drowned the singing"**: Ibid.
159   **"like a musical"**: Duchess of York to Lady Strathmore, 26 October
       1923, Glamis Archives (CH).
159   **"He was enchanted"**: Ibid.
159   **Photographs of the baptism**: *The Illustrated London News,* 27 Octo-
       ber 1923.
160   **"How dull"**: Duchess of York to Lady Strathmore, 12 November 1923,
       Glamis Archives (CH).
160   **"Everybody looking"**: Duchess of York, diary, 22 December 1923, RA
       QEQM/PRIV/DIARY/3.
160   **"treat"**: Duchess of York, diary, 24 December 1923, RA QEQM/PRIV/
       DIARY/3.
160   **At age seventy-nine**: Queen Mary, diary, 24 December 1923, RA QM/
       PRIV/QMD/1923.
161   **"pretty bracelet"**: Duchess of York, diary, 24 December 1923, RA
       QEQM/PRIV/DIARY/3.
161   **"arrived just before"**: Queen Mary, diary, 24 December 1923, RA
       QM/PRIV/QMD/1923.

161   "hated dawdling": Rose I, p. 567.
161   "crackers & much": Duchess of York, diary, 25 December 1923, RA QEQM/PRIV/DIARY/3.
161   "an incubus": Wheeler-Bennett, *George VI*, p. 189.
161   They also chafed: Ibid.
162   "HIDEOUS": Duchess of York to Lady Strathmore, 18 October 1923, Glamis Archives 270/1/6.
162   "I went to White": Queen Mary, diary, 12 January 1924, RA QM/PRIV/QMD/1924.
162   *"he'd had a talk"*: Duchess of York, diary, 13 January 1924, RA QEQM/PRIV/DIARY/4.
162   "Old House": Duchess of York, diary, 14 October 1923, RA QEQM/PRIV/DIARY/3.
162   "It is really tiny": Duchess of York to Lady Strathmore, 18 October 1923, Glamis Archives 270/1/6.
162   "the gloom of": *Duff Cooper Diaries*, p. 181.
163   "David ought to": King George V to Queen Alexandra, 24 August 1923, RA GV/PRIV/AA38/57.
163   "I am sure it will": Duke of York to Queen Mary, 4 October 1922, RA QM/PRIV/CC11/29.
163   "selfish, ill-tempered": Windsor II, p. 406.
163   "exceeded the most": Piers Legh to A. L. Lascelles, 23 February 1922, LASL, CAC.
164   "a chap younger": Windsor II, p. 466.
164   "He won me": Lascelles I, p. 334.
164   "the future of": Ibid., p. 333.
164   "People began to": Lascelles II, p. 10.
165   "county cricketers": Lascelles I, p. xviii.
165   "own tribe": Ibid., 65.
165   "lonely and": Sir Alan Lascelles to James Pope-Hennessy, n.d. [2 May 1959], John Pope-Hennessy Papers, 1617–1995, bulk 1930–1995, the Getty Research Institute, Los Angeles, accession no. 990023.
165   "empty pedestal": Ibid.
165   "never more than": Ibid.
165   "What is to most": Sir Alan Lascelles to James Pope-Hennessy, 22 June 1959, the Getty Research Institute.
165   The first: Sir Alan Lascelles to James Pope-Hennessy, 2 May 1959, the Getty Research Institute.
165   "If their marriage": *The New York Times*, 25 September 2004.
165   "god": Sir Alan Lascelles to James Pope-Hennessy, 2 May 1959, the Getty Research Institute.
165   "looked best in": Lascelles I, p. 307.
165   "natural and unaffected": Ibid., p. 322.
166   "being a secretary": Ibid., pp. 208–9.

FOURTEEN: Out of the Welter

169 "first-hand knowledge": Wheeler-Bennett, *George VI,* p. 196.

170 "I am extremely": Duchess of York to D'Arcy Osborne, 17 March 1924, RA QEQM/OUT/OSBORNE.

170 "fairies and owls": Ibid.

170 "I think the Labour": Duchess of York to D'Arcy Osborne, 22 March 1924, RA QEQM/OUT/OSBORNE.

170 "terrific excitement": Duchess of York, diary, 26 April 1924, RA QEQM/PRIV/DIARY/4.

170 "pyrotechnics": *The Times,* 11 April 1924.

171 "*They have offered*": Duchess of York, diary, 4 March 1924, RA QEQM/PRIV/DIARY/4.

171 "They danced": Channon II, p. 110.

171 "a very beautiful sight": Duchess of York, diary, 3 June 1924, RA QEQM/PRIV/DIARY/4.

172 "breakie in bed": Duchess of York, diary, 20 June 1924, RA QEQM/PRIV/DIARY/4.

172 "delectable & idle": Duchess of York to Osbert Sitwell, 27 September 1942, Sitwell Papers (Weston), Shawcross, *QEQM Letters,* p. 325.

172 Among the prominent: *The Times,* 28 June 1924.

172 "Winston was": Queen Elizabeth, conversations with Eric Anderson, 1994–95, Shawcross, *QEQM,* p. 218.

173 "Marvellous": Duchess of York, diary, 14 July 1924, RA QEQM/PRIV/DIARY/4.

173 "always been grateful": Queen Elizabeth, conversations with Eric Anderson, 1994–95, Shawcross, *QEQM,* p. 218.

173 "the most awful": Duchess of York, diary, 1 September 1924, RA QEQM/PRIV/DIARY/4.

173 "Mother nearly": Duchess of York, diary, 6 September 1924, RA QEQM/PRIV/DIARY/4.

173 "looked so pretty": Rev. John Stirton, diary, 17 September 1924, RA AEC/GG/026.

173 "I am feeling very": Duke of York to Duchess of York, 29 September 1924, RA QEQM/PRIV/RF.

173 "I miss you": Duchess of York to Duke of York, Wednesday [1 October 1924], RA GVI/PRIV/RF/26/63.

173 "Two lunches": Duke of York to Duchess of York, 2 October 1924, RA QEQM/PRIV/RF.

174 "The election news": Duchess of York, diary, 30 October 1924, RA QEQM/PRIV/DIARY/4.

174 "grinding his teeth": Greig, *King Maker,* p. 5.

174 "never to be without": King George V to Duke of York, 28 November 1924, RA GV/PRIV/AA61/228.

174 **"very sad having"**: Duke of York to Queen Mary, 30 November 1924, RA QM/PRIV/CC11/67.

174 **"I am feeling"**: Duchess of York to D'Arcy Osborne, 4 December 1924, RA QEQM/OUT/OSBORNE.

175 **"The place is growing"**: Duke of York to King George V, 24 December 1924, RA GV/PRIV/AA61/232.

175 **"absolutely wild"**: Ibid.

175 **sung in Swahili**: Duke of York, tour diary, 25 December 1924, RA GVI/PRIV/DIARY/African Safari 1924–1925.

176 **"charming . . . with an"**: Duchess of York to D'Arcy Osborne, 31 January 1925, RA QEQM/OUT/OSBORNE.

176 **six hundred native**: Duke of York, tour diary, 21 February 1925, RA GVI/PRIV/DIARY/African Safari 1924–1925.

176 **"exactly like"**: Duchess of York to Lady Strathmore, 29 December 1924, Glamis Archives (RA), Shawcross, *QEQM,* p. 225.

177 **in an open-top Rolls-Royce**: Duchess of York, diary, January 2, 1925, RA QEQM/PRIV/DIARY/5.

177 **"a proper safari"**: Duke of York to King George V, 31 January 1925, RA GV/PRIV/AA61/239.

177 **rocks the size of**: Duchess of York, diary, 21 January 1925, RA QEQM/PRIV/DIARY/5.

177 **killed her first**: Duke of York, tour diary, 26 January 1925, RA GVI/PRIV/DIARY/African Safari 1924–1925; Duchess of York, diary, 26 January 1925, RA QEQM/PRIV/DIARY/5.

177 **"Don't tell your"**: Duchess of York to Prince of Wales, 13 January 1925, RA EDW/PRIV/MAIN/B/76, Shawcross, *QEQM Letters,* p. 135.

177 **"a very good rifle"**: Duke of York to King George V, 31 January 1925, RA GV/PRIV/AA61/239.

177 **Shouting and singing**: Duke of York, tour diary, 14 February 1925, RA GVI/PRIV/DIARY/African Safari 1924–1925.

178 **"immense"**: Duchess of York, diary, 22 February 1925, RA QEQM/PRIV/DIARY/5.

178 **ninety pounds each**: Duke of York to King George V, n.d., Wheeler-Bennett, *George VI,* p. 205.

178 **"It is rather nice"**: Duchess of York, diary, 5 March 1925, RA QEQM/PRIV/DIARY/5.

178 **Rowland Ward**: Duchess of York, diary, 17 July 1925, RA QEQM/PRIV/DIARY/5.

178 **"a different being"**: Duchess of York to Prince of Wales, 13 January 1925, RA EDW/PRIV/MAIN/B/76, Shawcross, *QEQM Letters,* p. 135.

179 **"speaks very slowly"**: Captain Roy Salmon to his mother, 19 February 1925, private collection, Shawcross, *QEQM,* p. 231.

179 **It took additional**: Duke of York, tour diary, 11 January 1925, RA GVI/PRIV/DIARY/African Safari 1924–1925.

179   "made a terrible": Duke of York, tour diary, 27 February 1925, RA GVI/PRIV/DIARY/African Safari 1924–1925.

179   "a smell you don't": Duke of York, tour diary, 1 January 1925, RA GVI/PRIV/DIARY/African Safari 1924–1925.

179   "calmly began": Captain Roy Salmon to his mother, 25 March 1925, private collection, Shawcross, *QEQM*, p. 234.

179   "very small": Duchess of York to Prince of Wales, 13 January 1925, RA EDW/PRIV/MAIN/B/76, Shawcross, *QEQM Letters*, p. 135.

179   "khaki shirt": Captain Roy Salmon to his mother, 25 March 1925, private collection, Shawcross, *QEQM*, p. 232.

179   "I have become": Duchess of York to May Elphinstone, 6 March 1925, RA QEQM/OUT/ELPHINSTONE.

179   "very funny": Duchess of York to D'Arcy Osborne, 31 January 1925, RA QEQM/OUT/OSBORNE.

179   "a wonderful place": Duchess of York to May Elphinstone, 6 March 1925, RA QEQM/OUT/ELPHINSTONE.

179   "was simply wonderful": Duchess of York to Rose Leveson-Gower, n.d. [March 1925], Glamis Archives, RA, Shawcross, *QEQM Letters*, p. 137.

180   "very big men": Duke of York, tour diary, 25 March 1925, RA GVI/PRIV/DIARY/African Safari 1924–1925.

180   "changed into": Duchess of York, diary, 31 March 1925, RA QEQM/PRIV/DIARY/5.

180   "like a violoncello": Duchess of York to Lady Strathmore, 31 March 1925–1 April 1925, Glamis Archives, 270/II.

180   "I never knew": Duchess of York to D'Arcy Osborne, 31 January 1925, RA QEQM/OUT/OSBORNE.

180   "I love meandering": Duchess of York, diary, 12 March 1925, RA QEQM/PRIV/DIARY/5.

180   "our own little world": Duke of York to Queen Mary, 3 January 1925, RA QM/PRIV/CC11/70.

180   "We shall have": Duke of York to King George V, 31 January 1925, RA GV/PRIV/AA61/239.

180   tinned tongue: Duchess of York, diary, 24 January 1925, RA QEQM/PRIV/DIARY/5.

180   had to filter: Asquith I, p. 204.

180   bathed in dirty: Duke of York to Prince of Wales, 6 March 1925, RA EDW/PRIV/MAIN/A/2506.

180   poured with: Duchess of York to May Elphinstone, 6 March 1925, RA QEQM/OUT/ELPHINSTONE.

180   confidently finished: Duchess of York, diary, 2 April 1925, RA QEQM/PRIV/DIARY/5.

180   "a sort of Jaeger": Captain Roy Salmon to his mother, 25 March 1925, private collection, Shawcross, *QEQM*, p. 231.

180   "We are all so pally": Duchess of York to D'Arcy Osborne, 31 January 1925, RA QEQM/OUT/OSBORNE.

181 **She never used soap:** Captain Roy Salmon to his mother, 25 March 1925, private collection, Shawcross, *QEQM,* p. 236.

181 **" 'Watch so & so' ":** Ibid.

181 **"feeling too tattered":** Duchess of York to Sir Geoffrey Archer, April 1925, quoted in Sir Geoffrey Archer, *Personal and Historical Memoirs of an East African Administrator* (Edinburgh: Oliver and Boyd, 1963), p. 191; Vickers, *Elizabeth the Queen Mother,* p. 95.

181 **"We met a lot of":** Duchess of York, diary, 10 April 1925, RA QEQM/ PRIV/DIARY/5.

181 **"It is so difficult":** Duchess of York to May Elphinstone, 6 March 1925, RA QEQM/OUT/ELPHINSTONE.

181 **"best bit":** Queen Elizabeth, conversations with Eric Anderson, 1994–95, Shawcross, *QEQM,* p. 241.

FIFTEEN: My Heart Goes Pit-a-pat

183 **"I am enclosing":** Duke of York to King George V, 4 May 1925, RA GV/PRIV/AA61/254.

184 **"I do hope I shall":** Ibid.

184 **"His stammer was":** Wheeler-Bennett, *George VI,* p. 207.

184 **Bertie was so worked:** Duke of York to Prince of Wales, 27 May 1925, RA EDW/PRIV/MAIN/A/2516.

184 **"very downhearted":** Duchess of York, diary, 9 May 1925, RA QEQM/ PRIV/DIARY/5.

185 **"deep hush fell":** *The Illustrated London News,* 16 May 1925.

185 **"cloud of witnesses":** Wheeler-Bennett, *George VI,* p. 208.

185 **"nervous in the legs":** Duke of York to Prince of Wales, 27 May 1925, RA EDW/PRIV/MAIN/A/2516.

185 **"present its lessons":** *The Times,* 11 May 1925.

185 **"I declare this":** Ibid.

185 **"It was an ordeal":** Duke of York to Prince of Wales, 27 May 1925, RA EDW/PRIV/MAIN/A/2516.

185 **"It was marvelously":** Duchess of York, diary, 9 May 1925, RA QEQM/PRIV/DIARY/5.

185 **"easily the best":** Duke of York to Prince of Wales, 27 May 1925, RA EDW/PRIV/MAIN/A/256.

185 **"seemed pleased":** Ibid.

185 **"Bertie got through":** King George V to Prince George, 10 May 1925, Wheeler-Bennett, *George VI,* p. 208.

185 **"Horrible":** Duchess of York, diary, 19 April 1925, RA QEQM/PRIV/ DIARY/5.

186 **"Between ourselves":** Duke of York to Prince of Wales, 27 May 1925, RA EDW/PRIV/MAIN/A/2516.

186 **"the lives and devotion":** *The Times,* 25 June 1925.

186 **"I quickly saw":** Channon II, p. 151.

186　"relief and freedom": Duchess of York to Prince of Wales, 13 January 1925, RA EDW/PRIV/MAIN/B/76, Shawcross, *QEQM Letters,* pp. 134–35.

186　"stand up to them": Prince of Wales to Duchess of York, 27 February 1925, RA QEQM/PRIV/RF, Shawcross, *QEQM,* p. 228.

186　"stick up for yourself": Duchess of York to Duke of York, 10 September 1925, RA GVI/PRIV/RF/26/65.

186　"I loved what": Duke of York to Prince of Wales, 11 September 1925, RA QEQM/PRIV/RF.

187　"I still long for": Duke of York to Prince of Wales, 9 August 1925, RA EDW/PRIV/MAIN/A/2528.

187　"I am feeling": Duchess of York to Duke of York, 10 September 1925, RA GVI/PRIV/RF/26/65.

187　"that we may look": Queen Mary to Duke of York, 20 October 1925, RA GVI/PRIV/RF/11.

187　"It will be much": Duke of York to Queen Mary, 27 October 1925, RA QM/PRIV/CC11/81.

187　"they would have": Ibid.

187　"owing to a cold": *The Illustrated London News,* 21 October 1925.

188　"very well": *The Times,* 2 November 1925.

188　"Hearing him speak": Reginald Pound, *Harley Street* (London: Michael Joseph, 1967), p. 155.

188　"deepest & truest": Duchess of York to King George V, 24 November 1925, RA GVI/PRIV/AA56/105.

188　"my own little": Duke of York to Duchess of York, 8 December 1925, RA QEQM/PRIV/RF.

189　"awful & deadly": Ibid.

189　"We brought": Duchess of York to May Elphinstone, 19 December 1925, RA QEQM/OUT/ELPHINSTONE.

189　"My heart still": Duke of York to Duchess of York, 24 December 1925, RA QEQM/PRIV/RF.

189　"I am just sitting": Duchess of York to Queen Mother, 12 April 1926, RA QM/PRIV/CC11/86.

189　"a certain line": *The Times,* 22 April 1926.

PART THREE: THE ROAD TO THE CROWN
SIXTEEN: Tremendous Joy

193　"Such relief": Queen Mary, diary, 20 April 1926, RA QM/PRIV/QMD/1926: "We were awakened (21st) at 4 A.M."

193　an odd coincidence: Queen Mary, diary, 21 April 1926, RA QM/PRIV/QMD/1926.

193　"I have a feeling": Channon II, p. 211.

193　"tremendous joy": Duke of York to Queen Mary, 22 April 1926, RA QM/PRIV/CC11/87.

194   **"I was very"**: Duke of York to King George V, 27 April 1926, RA GV/
       PRIV/AA61/310.

194   **"I am sure"**: Ibid.

194   **"I quite approve"**: King George V to Duke of York, 28 April 1926, RA
       GV/PRIV/1161/311.

194   **"Little 'Lilibet'"**: King George V, diary, 5 May 1928, GV/PRIV/
       GVD/1928.

194   **It was a nickname**: "Liliebeth is her own name for herself," Anne Ring
       [pseudonym for Beryl Poignand], *The Story of Princess Elizabeth Told
       with the Sanction of Her Parents* (London: John Murray, 1930), p. 61;
       "Lilibet walk self," "Lilibet thut door self," Asquith II, p. 170.

194   **"unconditionally"**: King George V, diary, 12 May 1926, GV/PRIV/
       GVD.

195   **"Of course poor baby"**: Queen Mary, diary, 29 April 1926, RA QM/
       PRIV/QMD/1926.

195   **"The First Member"**: *The Illustrated London News,* 26 June 1926.

195   **"aroused the greatest"**: Ibid.

195   **"Now I know"**: Greig, *King Maker,* p. 205.

195   **"practicing and"**: Ibid., p. 204.

195   **"lashing out"**: Ibid., p. 5.

195   **"Try the other"**: Ibid.

196   **ran a photograph**: *The Times,* 26 June 1926.

196   **"mission of first-rate"**: Wheeler-Bennett, *George VI,* p. 212.

196   **he had been seated**: Duchess of York, diary, 11 October 1923, RA
       QEQM/PRIV/DIARY/3.

196   **"appalled"**: Wheeler-Bennett, *George VI,* p. 212.

196   **"secret dread"**: Ibid.

197   **"just one more try"**: Ibid., p. 213.

197   **"He must come here"**: Mark Logue and Peter Conradi, *The King's
       Speech: How One Man Saved the British Monarchy* (London: Sterling,
       2010), p. 63.

197   **"slim quiet man"**: Ibid., p. 67.

197   **"acute nervous"**: Ibid.

197   **"struck dumb"**: Pound, *Harley Street,* p. 155.

197   **"but it will need"**: Logue and Conradi, *King's Speech,* p. 67.

197   **"you could see"**: Ibid., p. 68.

197   **"on equal terms"**: Ibid.

198   **"In spite of yr new"**: Queen Mary to Duke of York, 2 July 1926, RA
       GVI/PRIV/RF/11/361.

198   **"There are possibilities"**: Queen Mary, diary, 7 July 1926, RA QM/
       PRIV/QMD/1926.

198   **"psychological error"**: Logue and Conradi, *King's Speech,* p. 72.

199   **"She is going to be"**: Duchess of York to Lady Strathmore, 28 October
       1926, Glamis Archives, RA, Shawcross, *QEQM Letters,* pp. 149–50.

199   **"a million times"**: Ibid.

199 “We shall not see”: Duchess of York, diary, 2 January 1927, RA QEQM/PRIV/DIARY/7.

199 “this horrible trip”: Duchess of York to Mrs. Beevers, 5 October 1926, Beevers Papers, Shawcross, *QEQM Letters,* p. 148.

199 James Stuart, who: Duchess of York, diary, 4 January 1927, RA QEQM/PRIV/DIARY/7.

199 “I did the Charleston”: Duchess of York, diary, 4 January 1927, RA QEQM/PRIV/DIARY/7.

SEVENTEEN: Eager to Do Well

201 “very miserable”: Duchess of York, diary, 6 January 1927, RA QEQM/PRIV/DIARY/7.

201 “terrible pang”: Duke of York to Queen Mary, 10 January 1927, RA QM/PRIV/CC11/96.

202 “It is clear that”: Patrick Hodgson to Queen Mary, 11 February 1927, RA QM/PRIV/CC11/102.

202 She was the mother: Author interviews with Jane FitzGerald, granddaughter of Tortor Gilmour.

202 “much liked”: Patrick Hodgson to Queen Mary, 20 January 1927, RA QM/PRIV/CC11/98.

202 “I feel it is better”: Patrick Hodgson to Queen Mary, 11 April 1927, RA QM/PRIV/CC11/108.

203 Bertie sometimes: Duchess of York, diary, 13 January 1927, RA QEQM/PRIV/DIARY/7.

203 “natural tendency”: Patrick Hodgson to Queen Mary, 20 January 1927, RA QM/PRIV/CC/11/98.

203 “I have not been”: Logue and Conradi, *King's Speech,* p. 73.

203 “though perhaps”: Ibid.

203 “I miss the baby”: Duchess of York, diary, 5 February 1927, RA QEQM/PRIV/DIARY/7.

203 “I miss her quite”: Duchess of York to Queen Mary, 9 February 1927, RA QM/PRIV/CC11/101.

203 “Yight!”: Dr. George F. Still to Duchess of York, 20 April and 9 May 1927, RA QEQM/PRIV/PAL, Shawcross, *QEQM,* p. 289.

204 “funny little noises”: Queen Mary to Duke of York, 30 March and 6 April 1927, RA GVI/PRIV/RF/11, Shawcross, *QEQM,* pp. 285–86.

204 “begged me to see”: Lady Strathmore to Beryl Poignand, 10 January 1927, Glamis Archives, 270/3/18.

204 “Here comes the Bambina!”: Ring, *Story of Princess Elizabeth,* p. 31.

204 “determined to make”: Patrick Hodgson to Queen Mary, 14 February 1927, RA QM/PRIV/CC/11/102.

204 “both sensitive”: Lord Cavan to Clive Wigram, 13 January 1927, RA AEC/GG/6/2/2, Shawcross, *QEQM,* p. 272.

205 “with affectionate”: Wheeler-Bennett, *George VI,* p. 218.

205 "I cannot thank": Clive Wigram to Lord Cavan, 23 February 1927, RA AEC/GG/6/2/2, Shawcross, *QEQM*, p. 272.

205 "the New Zealand": Duke of York to Queen Mary, 22 February 1927, RA QM/PRIV/CC11/103.

205 "thinking every": Duchess of York to Queen Mary, 8 March 1927, RA QM/PRIV/CC11/104.

205 "Take care": *The Times*, 9 March 1927.

205 "really pleased": Duke of York to Queen Mary, 22 February and 27 February 1927, RA QM/PRIV/CC11/103.

206 "was simply ghastly": Duchess of York to May Elphinstone, 17 March 1927, RA QEQM/OUT/ELPHINSTONE.

206 "In his innate": Wheeler-Bennett, *George VI*, p. 220.

206 "he met nothing": *The Times*, 14 March 1927.

207 "all I wanted": Duchess of York to Duke of York, 15 March 1927, RA GVI/PRIV/RF/26/67.

207 "such a failure": Ibid.

207 "my own little": Duke of York to Duchess of York, 18 March 1927, Ian Shapiro Collection, Shawcross, *QEQM*, p. 283.

207 "looked unpleasant": Wheeler-Bennett, *George VI*, p. 221.

207 "I am delighted": King George V to Duke of York, 12 March 1927, RA GV/PRIV/AA62/14.

207 "crushed and jostled": *The Times*, 28 March 1927.

208 "traditions of loyalty": *The Times*, 26 April 1927.

208 "ragged": *The Times*, 28 April 1927.

208 "The Smile That": *The Illustrated London News*, 7 May 1927.

209 "the language of the eye": Duchess of York to Prince of Wales, 25 January 1927, RA EDW/PRIV/MAIN/B/81, Shawcross, *QEQM*, p. 274.

209 "The strange thing": Shawcross, *QEQM*, p. 289.

209 "tends to get": Patrick Hodgson to Queen Mary, 11 April 1927, RA QM/PRIV/CC/11/103.

209 "Though we are working": Duchess of York to Lady Strathmore, 10 April 1927, Glamis Archives, RA, Shawcross, *QEQM Letters*, p. 158.

209 "gives one quite": Duchess of York to Queen Mary, 8 March 1927, RA QM/PRIV/CC11/104.

209 "Britain's most popular": *The Illustrated London News*, 16 April 1927.

210 "I have missed her all": Duchess of York to King George V, 12 June 1927, RA GV/PRIV/AA62/32, Shawcross, *QEQM*, p. 295.

210 "just a nip in the air": *The Times*, 10 May 1927.

210 "One feels the stirrings": Wheeler-Bennett, *George VI*, pp. 227–28.

210 "perfectly admirable": Ibid., p. 229.

210 "was not a very easy": Duke of York to King George V, 12 May 1927, RA GV/PRIV/AA62/30.

211 "We will not embrace": Wheeler-Bennett, *George VI*, p. 232.

211 "There's Mother!": Asquith I, p. 227.

211   "Elizabeth held": King George V, diary, 27 June 1927, RA GV/PRIV/GVD/1927.
211   "waved her hand": *The Times,* 28 June 1927.
212   "Bertie has been": Duchess of York to Queen Mary, 20 April 1927, RA QM/PRIV/CC11/109.
212   "done wonders": Duke of York to King George V, 12 May 1927, RA GV/PRIV/AA62/30.

EIGHTEEN: Family Crises

215   "the work, the anxiety": *The Times,* 16 July 1927.
216   "affection for the Mother": Ibid.
216   "pleasantly, smoothly": Logue and Conradi, *King's Speech,* p 77.
216   "reach out and squeeze": Ibid., p. 78.
216   "unusual charm": Windsor I, p. 241.
217   "some choice pieces": Prince of Wales and Prince George to Duchess of York, 4 August 1927, RA QEQM/PRIV/RF.
217   felt so disillusioned: Lascelles II, p. 50.
217   One evening the Baldwins: Donaldson I, p. 145.
217   "I told him directly": Lascelles II, p. 50.
218   "practically the only": Ibid., p. 62.
218   "the cold fact": Ibid., p. 71.
218   "the palace with": Asquith II, p. 212.
218   "cosy": Airlie, *Thatched with Gold,* p. 203.
219   "Hullo Jimmie": Vickers, *Elizabeth the Queen Mother,* p. 107.
219   In addition to her: Duchess of York to D'Arcy Osborne, 24 November 1928, RA QEQM/OUT/OSBORNE.
219   could never start: Asquith II, p. 187.
220   liked to pretend: Ibid., p. 197.
220   "She has been with": King George V, diary, 24 January 1928, RA GV/PRIV/GVD/1928.
220   "I don't think you": Queen Mary to Duke of York, 26 September 1928, RA GV/PRIV/RF/11.
221   "curing himself": *Leeds Mercury,* 25 October 1929.
221   "immediately fell": Lady Cynthia Asquith, *Haply I May Remember* (New York: Scribner, 1950), p. 192.
221   "every word": Ibid., p. 193.
221   "whatever she undertakes": Asquith I, p. 153.
221   "though she can express": Ibid., p. 159.
222   "Formerly Attached": Ring, *Story of Princess Elizabeth,* title page.
222   "I have not altered": Duchess of York to Beryl Poignand, 14 August 1929, Glamis Archives (CH).
222   "It is a very harmless": Duchess of York to Beryl Poignand, 22 July 1930, Glamis Archives (CH).

222 "who may some day": *The New York Times,* 3 August 1931.

222 "mania": Lascelles II, p. 130.

223 "last and most urgent": Ibid., p. 109.

223 "incredibly callous": Ibid.

224 "sensational dash": Channon II, p. 345.

224 "greatly changed": Windsor I, p. 226.

224 "At 10:30 David": Queen Mary, diary, 11 December 1928, RA QM/PRIV/QMD/1928.

225 "clearer": Queen Mary, diary, 24 December 1928, RA QM/PRIV/QMD/1928.

225 "for the sea air": Ibid., 22 January 1929.

225 "most favoured": *The Illustrated London News,* 6 July 1929.

225 "She is looking forward": Duke of York to Queen Mary, 12 March 1929, RA QM/PRIV/CC11/130.

225 "I played with Lilibet": Queen Mary, diary, 14 March 1929, RA QM/PRIV/QMD/1929.

226 "P'incess Lilybet": *Time,* 29 April 1929.

226 "When the King was": Rose I, p. 575.

226 "You'll see, your brother": Queen Elizabeth, conversations with Eric Anderson, 1994–95, Shawcross, *QEQM,* p. 308.

226 "might have been": Lascelles III, p. 110.

226 "both vulgar and": Ibid., p. 104.

226 "no comprehension": Ibid., p. 109.

226 "exactly what I": Lascelles II, pp. 119–20.

226 "took Tommy's scolding": Nicolson, diary, 14 December 1936, Balliol.

226 "I suppose the fact": Lascelles II, p. 120.

227 "Whether what I said": Ibid.

227 "take care of Beryl": John Van der Kiste, *George V's Children* (Stroud, Gloucestershire: Sutton, 1991), p. 78.

228 "girl with the silver": Pope-Hennessy II, p. 235.

229 saw his youngest son: King George V, diary, 17 July 1929, RA GV/PRIV/GVD/1929.

229 "Saw David twice": Ibid., 26 July 1929.

229 "not at all an easy": Ibid., 4 November 1929.

229 "Georgie" just once: Queen Mary, diary, 16 August 1929.

229 "tricky and critical": n.d. [probably August 1929], Dudley Ward Papers, Ziegler II, p. 175.

230 "It really is a terrible": Prince of Wales to King George V, 16 January 1930, Ziegler II, p. 175.

230 "Looking after him": King George V to Prince of Wales, 10 February 1930, Ziegler II, p. 176.

230 "I had not seen him": King George V, diary, 22 February 1930, RA GV/PRIV/GVD/1930.

NINETEEN: Interlude

233   "It seems very hard": Duchess of York to Beryl Poignand, 15 February 1930, Glamis Archives (CH).

233   "Your poor Mother": Queen Mary to Duchess of York, 9 February 1930, RA QEQM/PRIV/RF.

233   "My instinct is": Duchess of York to Queen Mary, 14 April 1930, RA QM/PRIV/CC11/154.

233   "clever": Queen Mary to Duchess of York, 15 April 1930, RA QEQM/PRIV/RF.

234   "to try to talk": Logue and Conradi, *King's Speech,* p. 96.

234   "I find I get": Duke of York to Queen Mary, 5 August 1930, RA QM/PRIV/CC11/160.

234   "I do hope you have": Duchess of York to Beryl Poignand, 22 July 1930, Glamis Archives (CH).

234   "The more he hovers": Duchess of York to Queen Mary, 31 July 1930, RA QM/PRIV/CC11/159.

234   "a dear old thing": Dr. Frank Neon Reynolds, letters to his wife, Reynolds Papers, Shawcross, *QEQM,* p. 315.

235   "Give him a glass": Rose I, p. 261.

235   "narrow winding": *Dundee Courier,* 23 August 1930.

235   "a fine chubby-faced": Ibid.

235   "A very nice baby": Dr. Reynolds to Mrs. Reynolds, [21] August 1930, Reynolds Papers, Shawcross, *QEQM,* p. 316.

235   "she stole softly": *The Scotsman,* 23 August 1930.

235   "the mighty beacon": Ibid.

235   In her room: *Dundee Courier,* 23 August 1930.

236   "said he was glad": Clive Wigram to Lady Wigram, 22 August 1930, RA AEC/GG/6, Shawcross, *QEQM,* p. 316.

236   "How I hated": Duke of York to Duchess of York, 25 August 1930, RA QEQM/PRIV/RF.

236   "E looking very": Queen Mary, diary, 30 August 1930, RA QM/PRIV/QMD/1930.

236   "showed us round": King George V, diary, 30 August 1930, RA GV/PRIV/GVD/1930.

236   "Lilibet seemed": Queen Mary, diary, 30 August 1930, RA QM/PRIV/QMD/1930.

236   "Bertie and I have": Duchess of York to Queen Mary, 6 September 1930, RA QM/PRIV/CC11/16.

236   "Scottish Name": *The Scotsman,* 23 September 1930.

236   "I am getting on": Duchess of York to Queen Mary, 6 September 1930, RA QM/PRIV/CC11/16.

237   "She has got large": Duchess of York to Most Rev. Cosmo Lang, 10 September 1930, Lambeth Palace Library, Lang Papers, 318f., 186, Shawcross, *QEQM Letters,* p. 181.

238   "bear equitable": *The Illustrated London News,* 12 September 1931.

238   "down to bedrock": Duchess of York to Queen Mary, 16 September 1931, RA QM/PRIV/CC11/184.

239   "Mrs. 'Fether' cannot": Queen Mary to Duke of York, 19 August 1931, RA GVI/PRIV/RF/11/407.

239   "dilapidation": Wheeler-Bennett, *George VI,* p. 259.

239   "I think we shall": Duchess of York to Queen Mary, 21 September 1931, RA QM/PRIV/CC11/186.

239   "I think it will suit": Wheeler-Bennett, *George VI,* p. 257.

240   "in the cloak rm": Queen Mary to Duke of York, 11 September 1931, RA GVI/PRIV/RF/AA/408.

240   "arranging pictures": Duchess of York to Queen Mary, 19 January 1933, RA QM/PRIV/CC11/209.

240   "I hope & trust": Duchess of York to Queen Mary, 30 January 1933, RA QM/PRIV/CC11/210.

240   "or they will all": Duchess of York to Queen Mary, 6 August 1934, RA QM/PRIV/CC11/225.

240   "we are really very": Ibid.

240   "There really was": Duchess of York to Queen Mary, 14 September 1936, RA QM/PRIV/CC11/31.

240   "shop for 3 months": Queen Mary to Duchess of York, 5 February 1933, RA QEQM/PRIV/RF.

241   "The Duke of Y has": Channon II, p. 386.

241   "considerable mansion": Wheeler-Bennett, *George VI,* p. 259.

241   "the most up-to-date": Crawford, *Little Princesses,* p. 12.

241   "with lemon pleatings": Ibid., p. 16.

241   "wilderness": W. E. Shewell-Cooper, *The Royal Gardeners: King George VI and His Queen* (London: Cassell, 1952), pp. 46–47.

242   "pure Queen Anne": Ibid., p. 28.

242   Ponsonby was one: Nicolson, diary, 21 July 1948, Balliol.

242   "With all yr expenses": Queen Mary to Duke of York, 19 May 1932, RA GVI/PRIV/RF/11/413.

242   "Papa has arranged": Queen Mary to Duke of York, 24 May 1932, RA GVI/PRIV/RF/11/414.

242   "They are very happy": King George V, diary, 24 August 1932, RA GV/PRIV/GVD/1932.

243   "most helpful": Duchess of York to D'Arcy Osborne, 10 October 1932, RA QEQM/OUT/OSBORNE.

TWENTY: A Certain Person

247   "my darling Angel": Edward, Prince of Wales to Freda Dudley Ward, 5 February 1930, Max Reed Papers, Rachel Trethewey, *Before Wallis: Edward VIII's Other Women* (Stroud, Gloucestershire: History Press, 2018), p. 153.

247   "a good looking": Channon II, p. 388.

247   "beautiful dark": Anne Sebba, *That Woman: The Life of Wallis Simpson, Duchess of Windsor* (New York: St. Martin's Press, 2011), p. 37.

247   "chaperones": The Duchess of Windsor, *The Heart Has Its Reasons: The Memoirs of the Duchess of Windsor* (London: David McKay, 1956), p. 154.

247   "I had hoped": Windsor I, p. 257.

248   "the grace of her": Ibid.

248   "small but charming": Ibid., p. 258.

248   "gay, lively and informed": Ibid.

248   "worshipped": Lord Wigram memorandum, 3 March 1932, RA PS/PSO/GVI/6/019/269, Trethewey, *Before Wallis,* p. 158.

249   "navigate around": Gloria Vanderbilt and Lady Thelma Furness, *Double Exposure: A Twin Autobiography* (San Francisco: Papamoa Press, 2017), p. 296.

249   "We have been skating": Patrick Howarth, *George VI: A New Biography* (London: Hutchinson, 1987), p. 54.

249   "Papa one day": Duchess of York to Queen Mary, 1 August 1933, RA QM/PRIV/CC11/214.

249   "Of course Papa": Queen Mary to Duchess of York, 20 August 1933, RA QEQM/PRIV/RF.

250   "look after": Vanderbilt and Furness, *Double Exposure,* p. 306.

250   "Darling, is it": Ibid., p. 314.

250   "I have orders": Trethewey, *Before Wallis,* p. 177.

250   "artificial nonsense": Edward, Prince of Wales to Freda Dudley Ward, 31 February 1930, Max Reed Papers, Trethewey, *Before Wallis,* p. 153.

250   "hunger marchers": *The Illustrated London News,* 29 October 1932.

251   "the sad & lean": Duchess of York to Queen Mary, 21 October 1932, RA QM/PRIV/CC11/204.

251   "I am feeling very": Duchess of York to D'Arcy Osborne, 30 November and 20 December 1932, RA QEQM/OUT/OSBORNE.

251   "two most popular": *The Illustrated London News,* 27 February 1932.

251   "she seems destined": *Vanity Fair,* November 1932.

252   At age four: Queen Mary, diary, 15 December 1930, RA QM/PRIV/QMD/1930.

252   At seven, she: King George V, diary, 29 March 1934, RA GV/PRIV/GVD/1934.

252   the only child: Queen Mary, diary, 3 September 1935, RA QM/PRIV/QMD/1935.

253   "make good wives": Airlie, *Thatched with Gold,* p. 195.

253   "suitable marriage": Channon II, p. 362.

253   the very next day: King George V, diary, 9 May 1934, RA GV/PRIV/GVD/1934.

253   "I was glad that": Duchess of York to Queen Mary, 6 August 1934, RA QM/PRIV/CC11/225.

253   "This girl is": Airlie, *Thatched with Gold,* p. 195.
253   diamond tiara: Sebba, *That Woman,* p. 102.
253   "That woman": Ibid.
254   "great ovation": King George V, diary, 29 November 1934, RA GV/
      PRIV/GVD/1934.
254   "hopeless old maid": Channon II, p. 465.
254   "a kind of pre-beatnik": *The Telegraph,* 13 December 2001.
254   sold her paintings: The Duchess of Gloucester, *The Memoirs of
      Princess Alice, Duchess of Gloucester* (London: Collins, 1983), p. 91.
255   maharajah of Jaipur's: Ibid., p. 101.
255   "muttered it": Ibid., p. 104.
255   "it was time I did": Ibid.
255   "charming and nice looking": King George V, diary, 31 August 1935,
      RA GV/PRIV/GVD/1935.
255   "We like her": Queen Mary, diary, 2 September 1935, RA QM/PRIV/
      QMD/1935.
255   "All the children": King George V, diary, 6 November 1935, RA GV/
      PRIV/GVD/1935.

              TWENTY-ONE: The Sunset of Death

257   In the preceding: King George V, diary, 9 January 1935, 11 January
      1935, 21 February 1935, RA GV/PRIV/GVD/1935.
258   "fully informed": Pope-Hennessy I, p. 553.
258   "would not tolerate": Francis Watson, "The Death of George V,"
      History Today 36 (December 1986).
258   "*maitresse-en-titre*": Channon II, p. 410.
258   "to take stock": Associated Press, "The King's Jubilee," Movietone
      Newsreel.
258   "white and silvery": Channon II, p. 434.
258   "quiet dignity": *The Illustrated London News,* 11 May 1935.
259   "waved again": Ibid.
259   Twice George V: King George V, diary, 12 May 1935 and 26 May
      1935, RA GV/PRIV/GVD/1935.
259   "long talk": King George V, diary, 10 May 1935, RA GV/PRIV/
      GVD/1935.
259   "It was a fine sight": King George V, diary, 14 May 1935, RA GV/
      PRIV/GVD/1935.
259   "I thought I felt": Duchess of Windsor, *Heart Has Its Reasons,* p. 207.
260   "dripped in new jewels": Sebba, *That Woman,* p. 103.
260   the King had been told: Ibid., p. 104.
260   Emerald Cunard introduced: Ibid., p. 438.
261   "much gossip": Ibid., p. 433.
261   "Splendid": King George V, diary, 15 November 1935, RA GV/PRIV/
      GVD/1935.

261 **Bertie brought Lilibet:** King George V, diary, 27 September 1935, RA GV/PRIV/GVD/1935.

261 **"sad loss":** King George V, diary, 21 October 1935, RA GV/PRIV/GVD/1935.

262 **"in splendid health":** Lascelles II, p. 189.

262 **"perhaps the first":** Wheeler-Bennett, *George VI*, p. 264.

262 **"a further depressive":** Francis Watson, *Dawson of Penn* (London: Chatto and Windus, 1950), p. 274.

262 **Queen Mary's annoyance:** Queen Mary, diary, 24 December 1935, RA QM/PRIV/QMD/1935.

263 **"miserable":** Duchess of York to Queen Mary, 27 December 1935, RA QM/PRIV/CC12/18.

263 **"get rid of that":** Bill Husselby, email, 23 April 2019, quoting Penelope Maffey Atiken.

263 **The Prince of Wales left:** Queen Mary, diary, 29 December 1935, RA QM/PRIV/QMD/1935.

263 **back-to-back discussions:** King George V, diary, 6 January and 7 January 1936, RA GV/PRIV/GVD/1936.

263 **"King George had said":** Airlie, *Thatched with Gold,* p. 197.

263 **"sleepiness":** Watson, "Death of George V."

263 **"Walking by the head":** Frederick John Corbitt, *My Twenty Years in Buckingham Palace: A Book of Intimate Memoirs* (New York: David McKay, 1956), p. 192.

263 **"felt rotten":** King George V, diary, 15 January 1936, RA GV/PRIV/GVD/1936.

263 **"Didn't feel very":** King George V, diary, 16 January 1936, RA GV/PRIV/GVD/1936.

263 **"Most worrying":** Queen Mary, diary, 16 January 1936, RA QM/PRIV/QMD/1936.

264 **"in the highest":** *Duff Cooper Diaries,* p. 255.

264 **"burst into my":** Lascelles II, p. 196.

264 **"very amiable":** Ibid., p. 193.

264 **"Only half of each lung":** Ibid.

264 **"bronchial catarrh":***The Times,* 18 January 1936.

264 **kidneys were barely:** Lascelles II, p. 194.

264 **"you and Papa":** Duchess of York to Queen Mary, 18 January 1936, RA QM/PRIV/CC12/22.

265 **He blessed the King:** Watson, "Death of George V."

265 **"very much disturbed":** *Duff Cooper Diaries,* p. 226.

265 **"approved":** Catherine Black, *King's Nurse, Beggar's Nurse* (London: Hurt and Blackett, 1939), pp. 178–79.

265 **"He was unable":** Queen Mary, diary, 20 January 1936, RA QM/PRIV/QMD/1936.

265 **"nodded and smiled":** Lascelles II, p. 198.

265 **At around nine P.M.:** Watson, "Death of George V."

265 "The King's life": *The New York Times,* 28 November 1986.

265 "becoming weaker": Queen Mary, diary, 20 January 1936, RA QM/ PRIV/QMD/1936.

266 "Am brokenhearted": Ibid.

266 "convenience killing": J. H. Rolland Ramsay, "A King, a Doctor, and a Convenient Death," *British Medical Journal* 308, no. 6941 (28 May 1994): 1445.

266 "last stage might": Watson, "Death of George V."

266 "a mission of mercy": *The New York Times,* 28 November 1986.

266 "distended jugular vein": Watson, "Death of George V."

266 Dawson asked his wife: Ibid.

266 "life passed so quietly": Ibid.

267 "death came peacefully": *The Times,* 21 January 1936.

267 "became hysterical": "Memo by Wigram," 20 January 1936, Ziegler II, p. 209.

267 "frantic and unreasonable": Hardinge, *Loyal to Three Kings,* p. 61.

267 "After I am dead": Donaldson II, p. 49.

TWENTY-TWO: Tears of Destiny

269 "debonair, self-possessed": Wheeler-Bennett, *George VI,* p. 286.

269 "causes so much": *Duff Cooper Diaries,* p. 277.

269 "did business": Queen Mary, diary, 22 January 1936, RA QM/PRIV/ QMD/1936.

270 "'Where do I come in'": Watson, "Death of George V."

270 "nice surplus": Ibid.

270 "His Majesty continued": Ibid.

270 "with a face blacker": Lascelles III, p. 107.

271 "A most terrible omen": Nicolson, diary, 23 January 1936, Balliol; Nicolson I, p. 241.

271 "wonderful crowds of sorrowing people": Queen Mary, diary, 28 January 1936, RA QM/PRIV/QMD/1936.

272 "passionate grief": Airlie, *Thatched with Gold,* p. 196.

272 "he is the most obstinate": Ibid., p. 198.

272 "this little obstinate man": Nicolson I, p. 247.

273 "a remarkable example": Wheeler-Bennett, *George VI,* p. 272.

273 "I am religiously going": Duchess of York to Beryl Poignand, 9 March 1936, Glamis Archives (CH).

273 "surprised to find": Twenty-seventh Earl of Crawford to Lord Tweedsmuir, 5 February 1936, John Buchan Fonds.

274 "he could not bear": Papers of Walter Turner Monckton, First Viscount Monckton of Brenchley, Balliol, p. 9.

274 "breaks precedents": Lord Crawford to Lord Tweedsmuir, 9 May 1936, John Buchan Fonds.

274 "nobody would ever": Nicolson, diary, 14 December 1936, Balliol.

274 **rings left by cocktail:** Sebba, *That Woman,* p. 123.
274 **"he shut himself up":** Nicolson, diary, 14 December 1936, Balliol.
274 **"strange hours":** Helen Hardinge, diary, Hon. Lady Murray Papers, Shawcross, *QEQM,* p. 359.
274 **bringing luminaries:** Queen Mary, diary, 30 April and 22 May 1936, RA QM/PRIV/QMD/1936.
275 **"much spoilt":** Queen Mary, diary, 26 May 1936, RA QM/PRIV/QMD/1936.
275 **published the guest list:** *The Times,* 28 May 1936.
275 **"He gives Mrs. Simpson":** Airlie, *Thatched with Gold,* p. 198.
275 **"The unfortunate":** Nicolson, diary, 13 July 1936, Balliol.
276 **"justly famous charm":** Duchess of Windsor, *Heart Has Its Reasons,* p. 216.
276 **"impression that":** Ibid.
276 **"What a pity":** Queen Mary to Duke of York, 13 August 1936, RA GVI/PRIV/11/428.
276 **"She stared at him":** Ziegler I, p. 177.
276 **Only *Cavalcade*:** Sir Alexander Hardinge to Lord Tweedsmuir, 15 October 1936, John Buchan Fonds.
276 **"One must not forget":** Alan Lascelles to Joan Lascelles, 8 September 1936, LASL, CAC.
277 **"loves this place":** Duchess of York to Queen Mary, 14 September 1936, RA QM/PRIV/CC11/31.
277 **"David only told me":** Duke of York to Queen Mary, 13 October 1936, RA QM/PRIV/CC12/35.
277 **"secretly rather":** Duchess of York to Queen Mary, 19 September 1936, RA QM/PRIV/CC12/32.
278 **"surprise visit":** Ziegler II, p. 250.
278 **"It is quite true":** Lady Londonderry to Lord Tweedsmuir, 14 December 1936, John Buchan Fonds.
278 **"The whole of the gold":** Ibid.
278 **"I came to dine":** Sebba, *That Woman,* p. 144.
278 **"a nightmare":** Wheeler-Bennett, *George VI,* p. 276.
279 **"David does not seem":** Duchess of York to Queen Mary, 11 October 1936, RA QM/PRIV/CC12/34.
279 **"Darling David":** Duchess of York to King Edward VIII, 29 October 1936, RA EDW/MAIN/A/3024.
279 **"King's Moll Renoed":** Victor Cazalet, diaries, October 1936, Cazalet Archive, Eton College.
279 **"devastating revelation":** Lord Crawford to Lord Tweedsmuir, 23 September 1936, John Buchan Fonds.
279 **"beneath the surface":** Sir Alexander Hardinge to Lord Tweedsmuir, 15 October 1936, John Buchan Fonds.
280 **"dragging the name":** Ibid.

280 "post bag": Stanley Baldwin to Lord Tweedsmuir, 26 October 1926, John Buchan Fonds.

280 "I spoke plainly": Ibid.

280 "I am beginning to": Windsor I, p. 320.

281 "How unsatisfactory": Queen Mary to Duke of York, 22 October 1936, RA GVI/PRIV/RF/11.

281 "recoiled from it": Wheeler-Bennett, *George VI,* p. 277.

281 "very difficult to see": Duke of York to Queen Mary, 6 November 1936, RA QM/PRIV/CC12/38.

281 "certainly look better": Queen Mary to Duke of York, 8 November 1936, RA GVI/PRIV/RF/11/431.

281 "the silence of the British": Wheeler-Bennett, *George VI,* p. 280.

282 "she almost fled": Windsor I, p. 334.

282 "He was in a great state": *Memoirs of Princess Alice,* pp. 113–14.

282 "They comprehended": Windsor I, p. 334.

282 "understand what she": Ibid., p. 335.

282 "extremely outspoken": Queen Mary to Clive Wigram, 15 July 1938, Ziegler II, p. 281.

283 "true sympathy": Queen Mary to King Edward VIII, 17 November 1936, Ziegler II, p. 281.

283 "I feel so happy": King Edward VIII to Queen Mary, 20 November 1936, Ziegler II, p. 281.

283 "I am more worried": Queen Mary to Duchess of York, 17 November 1936, RA QEQM/PRIV/RF.

283 "was so taken aback": Windsor I, p. 335.

283 "Bertie has just told": Duchess of York to Queen Mary, n.d. [17 November 1936], RA EDW/ADD/ABD/1.

284 "deep compassion": *The Illustrated London News,* 28 November 1936.

284 "These works brought": Ibid.

284 "it was known": Victor Cazalet to John Stone, 30 December 1936, Cazalet Archive, Eton College.

284 "I do hope": Duke of York to King Edward VIII, 23 November 1936, RA EDW/MAIN/A/3035.

284 "For God's sake": Duchess of York to King Edward VIII, 23 November 1936, RA EDW/PRIV/MAIN/B/111.

285 "worst": Wheeler-Bennett, *George VI,* p. 283.

285 "a great strain": Duchess of York to Queen Mary, 20 November 1936, RA EDW/ADD/ABD/1, Shawcross, *QEQM,* p. 374.

285 "It is not only the law": House of Commons Debate on Abdication, 10 December 1936, *Hansard,* vol. 318.

286 he had lowered: Monckton Papers, p. 22, Balliol.

286 "If Mrs. Simpson is": Duchess of York to May Elphinstone, 6 December 1936, RA QEQM/OUT/ELPHINSTONE.

286 "automatically have": Nicolson, diary, 4 December 1936, Balliol.

286 "a shudder of horror": Ibid.

287 "prayer and self-dedication": *The Illustrated London News*, 12 December 1936.

287 "the whole matter": Wheeler-Bennett, *George VI,* p. 285, quoting Duke of York's Abdication Chronicle.

287 "nervous exhaustion": Channon II, p. 600.

287 "damn politicians": Ibid., p. 598.

288 "was in a great": Wheeler-Bennett, *George VI,* p. 285.

288 "dreadful announcement": Ibid.

288 "I feel so terribly sad": Duke of York to Queen Mary, 5 December 1936, RA EDW/ADD/ABD/1.

288 "Three or four times": Papers of the Earl of Halifax, 7, 8, 6, and 11 December 1940, Borthwick Institute of Historical Research, Bradford, *Reluctant King,* p. 192, citing King George VI's confidential conversation with Lord Halifax.

288 "all the King's official": *The Illustrated London News,* 12 December 1936.

288 "like a petulant": Channon II, p. 601.

288 "lost all control": Ibid.

288 "The last days": Lord Crawford to Lord Tweedsmuir, 21 December 1936, John Buchan Fonds.

289 "He had two marked": Keith Middlemas and John Barnes, *Baldwin: A Biography* (London: Weidenfeld and Nicolson, 1969), pp. 1009–10, cited in Denis Judd, *George VI* (1982; London: Tauris, 2012), p. 141.

289 "disorganized": Monckton Papers, p. 27, Balliol.

289 after walking to: *The Illustrated London News,* 12 December 1936.

289 "The strain is terrific": Duchess of York to May Elphinstone, 6 December 1936, RA QEQM/OUT/ELPHINSTONE.

289 "over fatigue": Lady Strathmore to Beryl Poignand, 12 December 1936, Glamis Archives, 270/3/42.

289 "that at this most": Duchess of York to Queen Mary, 10 December 1936, RA EDW/ADD/ABD/1, Shawcross, *QEQM Letters,* pp. 229–30.

289 "No, I will come": Wheeler-Bennett, Duke of York's Abdication Chronicle, p. 285.

290 "trying by every means": Channon II, p. 612.

290 "to withdraw forthwith": Monckton Papers, p. 35, Balliol.

290 David had approved: Ibid.

290 "final & irrevocable": Wheeler-Bennett, Duke of York's Abdication Chronicle, p. 286.

290 "tour de force": Monckton Papers, pp. 35–36, Balliol.

291 "the Throne of this Empire": Queen Mary, diary, 9 December 1936, RA QM/PRIV/QMD/1936.

291 "I broke down": Wheeler-Bennett, Duke of York's Abdication Chronicle, p. 286.

291 "The whole abdication": Nicolson, diary, 21 March 1949, Balliol.

291   "dreadful moment": Wheeler-Bennett, Duke of York's Abdication Chronicle, p. 287.

291   "great faith in Bertie": Duchess of York to Queen Mary, 10 December 1936, RA EDW/ADD/ABD/1, Shawcross *QEQM Letters,* pp. 229–30.

291   "There is no moment": Nicolson, diary, 10 December 1936, Balliol.

291   "The man is mad": Ibid.

291   "the tension was": Wheeler-Bennett, Duke of York's Abdication Chronicle, p. 287.

291   "remarkable scenes": *The Times,* 11 December 1936.

292   "overwhelmed": Wheeler-Bennett, Duke of York's Abdication Chronicle, p. 287.

292   "Wildly indiscreet": Channon II, p. 601.

292   "He will call himself": Ibid., p. 606.

292   "the royal birth he shared": Monckton Papers, pp. 43–44, Balliol.

292   "That's *Mummy* now": Judd, *George VI,* p. 150.

293   "You are not going to": Windsor I, p. 407.

293   "By the way": Ibid., p. 408.

293   "passed pleasantly": Ibid., p. 410.

293   "might have been": Van der Kiste, *George V's Children,* p. 120.

293   "vastly improved": Monckton Papers, p. 45, Balliol.

293   against the advice: Ibid., p. 7.

293   "good & dignified": Queen Mary, diary, 11 December 1936, RA QM/PRIV/QMD/1936.

293   "the dreadful goodbye": Ibid.

293   "For God's sake, don't": Channon II, p. 630.

294   "of all subjects": Monckton Papers, p. 49, Balliol.

294   "Thank you, Sir": Leo Amery to Lord Tweedsmuir, 29 December 1936, John Buchan Fonds.

294   "God bless you, *sir*": Channon II, p. 630.

294   "It is all right": Leo Amery to Lord Tweedsmuir, 29 December 1936, John Buchan Fonds.

294   "I wanted so much": Queen Elizabeth to Duke of Windsor, 11 December 1936, RA EDW/PRIV/MAIN/A3068.

PART FOUR: A ROYAL BEGINNING

TWENTY-THREE: Upright Bearing and Grave Dignity

299   "in a low, clear": Wheeler-Bennett, *George VI,* p. 288.

299   "With My wife": *The Times,* 14 December 1936.

300   "He stood for": Crawford, *Little Princesses,* p. 64.

300   "the gay figures": *The Illustrated London News,* 19 December 1936.

300   "a mild attack": *The Times,* 14 December 1936.

300   "the coincidence": Queen Elizabeth to Queen Mary, 14 December 1936, RA QM/PRIV/CC12/40.

301   "gratitude and affection": Wheeler-Bennett, *George VI,* pp. 296–97.

301   "quite unprepared": Ibid., p. 294.

301   "At first he had been": Ibid., p. 296.

301   "a heavy blow": Queen Elizabeth to the Most Rev. Cosmo Lang, Archbishop of Canterbury, 14 January 1937, Lambeth Palace Library, Lang 318, ff. 181–83, Shawcross, *QEQM Letters*, p. 235.

301   "the curious thing": Queen Elizabeth to the Most Rev. Cosmo Lang, 12 December 1936, Lambeth Palace Library, Lang 318, ff. 177–80, Shawcross, *QEQM Letters*, pp. 231–32.

301   "distress which fills": Queen Mary, Message to the Nation, 12 December 1936, RA QM/PRIV/CC49/99.

302   "craving for private": *The Times,* 14 December 1936.

302   "complained bitterly": Channon II, p. 624.

302   "felt he said": Rhodes James I, p. 189.

302   "smilingly": *The Times,* 23 December 1936.

302   "emotionally and": Wheeler-Bennett, *George VI,* p. 297.

302   "At dinner I nearly": Queen Mary, diary, 24 December 1936, RA QM/PRIV/QMD/1936.

302   "very nearly killed": Rhodes James I, p. 189.

303   a luncheon of: *The Times,* 28 December 1936.

303   Three days later: Ibid., 29 December 1936.

303   "When his people": Ibid., 14 December 1936.

303   Lionel Logue was: Logue and Conradi, *King's Speech,* p. 117.

303   "so stunned": Joseph P. Kennedy, diary, 21 July 1939, *Hostage to Fortune: The Letters of Joseph P. Kennedy,* ed. Amanda Smith (New York: Penguin, 2002), p. 353.

304   "It was a complicated": Author interview with anonymous source, 13 June 2018.

304   After receiving: *Hansard,* 24 May 1937; Civil List Act 1936.

304   "terrible lawyer": Wheeler-Bennett, Duke of York's Abdication Chronicle, p. 297.

304   He said his assets: Ziegler II, p. 283.

304   "I understood from": Ibid., p. 303.

304   "The fact remains": *The Guardian,* 30 January 2003.

305   Walter Monckton worked: Ziegler II, p. 305.

305   "Don't ever let": Channon II, p. 637.

305   "You can't have": Queen Elizabeth, conversations with Eric Anderson, 1994–95, Shawcross, *QEQM,* p. 423.

305   "unfair and intolerable": *The Guardian,* 30 January 2003.

305   resume his life: Donaldson I, p. 309, citing Sir Edward Peacock's notes.

306   "Rat Week": Osbert Sitwell, "Rat Week" (original typed text), Glamis Archives, 270/8/1–40.

306   "The spirit I might": Lord Crawford to Lord Tweedsmuir, 20 January 1937, John Buchan Fonds.

306   "I must tell you": Queen Elizabeth to Osbert Sitwell, 19 February 1937, RA QEQM/OUT/SITWELL.

306 "camping in a museum": Crawford, *Little Princesses,* p. 64.

307 Lilibet wondered: Bolitho, *Their Majesties,* p. 60.

307 "delighted with the wide": Queen Mary, diary, 22 February 1937, RA QM/PRIV/QMD/1937.

307 "the little feminine": Airlie, *Thatched with Gold,* p. 203.

307 "nice and comfortable": Queen Mary, diary, 29 April 1937, RA QM/PRIV/QMD/1937.

307 "show in action": *The Times,* 13 February 1937.

307 "peculiarly close": Ibid.

308 "Nothing could": Nicolson I, p. 298.

308 "I really like": Sir Alan Lascelles to Joan Lascelles, 4 January 1937, LASL, CAC.

308 "We have had": Lord Crawford to Lord Tweedsmuir, 8 March 1937, John Buchan Fonds.

309 "elaborate ritual": *The Times,* 13 May 1937.

309 After having been: Logue and Conradi, *King's Speech,* p. 123.

309 "tone formation": Robert Wood, *A World in Your Ear: The Broadcasting of an Era* (London: Macmillan, 1979), p. 103.

309 "He is indeed": Logue and Conradi, *King's Speech,* p. 126.

309 "He is a good fellow": Ibid., p. 125.

310 "had a sinking": Wheeler-Bennett, quoting the King's Memorandum of the Coronation, 12 May 1937, p. 312.

310 "There were tears": Wheeler-Bennett, *George VI,* p. 311.

310 "the temple and shrine": "Coronation Record Number," *The Illustrated London News.*

310 She chipped in: Queen Mary, diary, 25 February and 9 April 1937, RA QM/PRIV/QMD/1937.

310 She attended: Queen Mary, diary, 9 May 1937, RA QM/PRIV/QMD/1937.

310 "nerve-wracking": Wheeler-Bennett, King's Memorandum of the Coronation, p. 312.

311 "The size and magnificence": *The Times,* 13 May 1937.

311 "small figures": Ibid.

311 "golden radiance": Ibid.

312 "a vitrine of bosoms": Channon II, p. 679.

312 "the containment of": *The Times,* 13 May 1937.

312 "Grannie looked": Queen Elizabeth II, "The Coronation, 12th May 1937, To Mummy and Papa, in Memory of Their Coronation, from Lilibet, by Herself," in *A Birthday Souvenir Album* (London: Royal Collection, 2006), p. 16.

312 "two eager little faces": Henrietta Bell, "How I Saw the Coronation in Westminster Abbey, 12 May 1937," Bell Papers, Lambeth Palace Library, Vickers, *Elizabeth the Queen Mother,* p. 158.

313 "I am willing": *The Times,* 13 May 1937.

313 he could be seen: *The Coronation,* Pathé News, 12 May 1937.

313 "the ink got": King George VI to Lionel Logue, 17 May 1937, BBC News, 23 July 2020.

313 "The things which": *The Times,* 13 May 1937.

313 "though quiet": Ibid.

313 "Not a moment's": King George VI to Lionel Logue, 17 May 1937, BBC News, 23 July 2020.

314 "a curiously slight": *The Times,* 13 May 1937.

314 that would be edited: *Daily Mail,* Hugo Vickers, 12 May 2012.

314 "King over the Peoples": *The Times,* 13 May 1937.

314 "had not my Groom": Wheeler-Bennett, King's Memorandum of the Coronation, p. 312.

314 "a great sapphire": *The Coronation,* Pathé News, 12 May 1937.

314 "the supreme moment": Wheeler-Bennett, King's Memorandum of the Coronation, p. 313.

315 "the arches and beams": Queen Elizabeth II, "The Coronation, from Lilibet," p. 16.

315 "liege man": *The Times,* 13 May 1937.

316 "like swans": Ibid.

316 "the arms disappeared": Queen Elizabeth II, "The Coronation, from Lilibet," p. 16.

316 "crowned, sceptered": *The Times,* 13 May 1937.

316 "with upright bearing": Ibid.

317 "millions": Queen Elizabeth II, "The Coronation, from Lilibet," p. 16.

317 "It's not for me": Bolitho, *Their Majesties,* p. 58.

317 not sat, as reported: Logue and Conradi, *King's Speech,* p. 126.

317 "It is with a very full": *The Times,* 13 May 1937.

317 "dramatic effect": Vickers, *Elizabeth the Queen Mother,* p. 159.

317 "a triumph": Logue and Conradi, *King's Speech,* p. 131.

317 "Bertie and E looked": Queen Mary, diary, 12 May 1937, RA QM/PRIV/QMD/1937.

318 "Papa's spirit was near": Queen Mary to King George VI, 12 May 1937, GVI/PRIV/RF/11/441.

318 "great sense of offering": Robert Beaken, *Cosmo Lang: Archbishop in War and Crisis* (London: I. B. Tauris, 2012), p. 135.

318 "I was not conscious": Queen Elizabeth to Most Rev. Cosmo Lang, 15 May 1937, Lambeth Palace Library, Lang Papers 318, ff. 184–86, Shawcross, *QEQM,* p. 404.

318 "I felt I was being helped": Beaken, *Cosmo Lang,* pp. 134–35.

318 "unaware what was": Nicolson, diary, 27 May 1937, Balliol.

318 One close observer: Bradford, *Reluctant King,* p. 212.

318 "a great sense": Lord Crawford to Lord Tweedsmuir, 13 May 1937, John Buchan Fonds.

318 "Neither Edward": Leo Amery to Lord Tweedsmuir, 29 May 1937, John Buchan Fonds.

TWENTY-FOUR: His Brother's Shadow

321 "during frequent": Donaldson I, pp. 209–10.

322 "all his mature life": Channon II, p. 628.

322 "occasional and momentary": Bradford, *Reluctant King*, p. 260.

322 "there was very little": *Duff Cooper Diaries*, p. 250.

323 "intimate": Nicolson, diary, 26 February 1953, Balliol.

323 "were inclined to be bossy": Ibid.

323 "overloaded": Logue and Conradi, *King's Speech*, p. 132.

324 "People liked to see": Crawford, *Little Princesses*, p. 88.

324 "immense natural": *The Illustrated London News*, 10 July 1937.

324 "over the water": Channon II, p. 680.

324 "unfortunate": Queen Mary to King George VI, 4 February 1937, RA GVI/PRIV/RF/11/434.

325 not a "fit and proper": Shawcross, *QEQM*, p. 422.

325 "The question of": Alan Lascelles to Joan Lascelles, 30 May 1937, LASL, CAC.

325 "None of us can go": Queen Mary to King George VI, 10 April 1937, RA GVI/PRIV/RF/11/436.

326 "It must be too": Queen Elizabeth to Queen Mary, 21 May 1937, RA QM/PRIV/CC12/49.

326 "hurt me very deeply": Queen Mary to Queen Elizabeth, 21 May 1937, RA QEQM/PRIV/RF.

326 including James: Alan Lascelles to Joan Lascelles, 26 August 1937, LASL, CAC.

326 "homely family regime": Lord Crawford to Lord Tweedsmuir, 23 September 1937, John Buchan Fonds.

327 "Elizabethan times": Shawcross, *QEQM*, p. 419.

327 "King and Queen jigged": Cecil Beaton, *The Wandering Years: Diaries, 1922–1939* (London: Weidenfeld and Nicolson, 1961), p. 318.

327 "very domestic & friendly": Alan Lascelles to Joan Lascelles, 21 August 1937, LASL, CAC.

327 "masterful": Wheeler-Bennett, *George VI*, p. 319.

328 "getting over his": King George VI to Queen Mary, 30 August 1937, RA QM/PRIV/CC12/55.

328 "The world is in": King George VI to Queen Mary, 4 October 1937, QM/PRIV/CC12/60.

328 "The solitude": Lord Crawford to Lord Tweedsmuir, 28 October 1937, John Buchan Fonds.

328 "a bombshell": George VI to Walter Monckton, 5 October 1937, RA GVI/OUT/MONCKTON, Shawcross, *QEQM*, p. 425.

328 "I now quit": Duke of Windsor broadcast, 11 December 1936.

328 "private stunts": Sir Alexander Hardinge to Sir Robert Vansittart, 1 October 1937, FO 954/33/61, Bradford, *Reluctant King*, p. 251.

328   "**behaving abominably**": *The Crawford Papers: The Journals of David Lindsay, 27th Earl of Crawford,* ed. John Vincent (Dover, N.H.: Manchester University Press, 1984), pp. 582, Bradford, *Reluctant King,* p. 254.

328   "**She was backing up**": Ibid.

329   "**like the medieval**": Ibid.

329   "**only thinks of his**": Queen Mary to Queen Elizabeth, 30 September 1937, RA QEQM/PRIV/RF.

329   **tying his £25,000 yearly**: *The Guardian,* 30 January 2003.

329   "**Heil Edward!**": *The Illustrated London News,* 16 October 1937.

329   "**Heil Hitler!**": Van der Kiste, *George V's Children,* p. 137.

329   "**an alliance would**": Deborah Cadbury, *Princes at War: The Bitter Battle Inside Britain's Royal Family in the Darkest Days of WWII* (New York: Public Affairs, 2015), p. 118.

330   **who read press**: Ibid., p. 117.

330   "**knowledge poured**": Marion Crawford to Queen Mary, 23 February 1941, Lambeth Palace Library, Lang Papers, 317, ff. 67–69, Shawcross, *QEQM,* p. 535.

330   "**odd distractions**": Marion Crawford to Lady Cynthia Colville, n.d. [8 November 1937], RA QM/PRIV/CC14/62a.

331   "**History and**": Ibid.

331   **The range of**: Bolitho, *Their Majesties,* p. 50.

332   **Queen Mary also**: Queen Mary, diary, 26 October, 1 November, and 29 November 1937, RA QM/PRIV/QMD/1937.

332   "**so absorbed**": *The Illustrated London News,* 4 December 1937.

332   **On other days**: Queen Mary, diary, 6 December 1937, RA QM/PRIV/QMD/1937.

332   "**inferiority complex**": Logue and Conradi, *King's Speech,* p. 133.

332   "**His voice was beautiful**": Ibid.

332   "**truly fine rich**": Nicolson, diary, 17 May 1945, Balliol.

333   "**a very pretty sight**": Queen Mary, diary, 26 October 1937, RA QM/PRIV/QMD/1937.

333   "**the first to make**": *The Illustrated London News,* 30 October 1937.

333   "**toying with**": Channon II, p. 768.

333   "**very very nervous**": Queen Elizabeth to Queen Mary, 26 October 1937, RA QM/PRIV/CC12/61.

333   "**in slow**": Channon II, p. 768.

333   "**Indeed the words**": Logue and Conradi, *King's Speech,* p. 134.

333   "**could not keep**": Ibid.

333   "**I speak now**": Jane Ridley, *George V: Never a Dull Moment* (New York: HarperCollins, 2021), p. 392.

334   **Logue remembered**: Ibid., p. 137.

334   "**The King always**": Wood, *World in Your Ear,* p. 115.

334   "**pulling himself up**": Logue and Conradi, *King's Speech,* p. 139.

334   "**leaning against**": Ibid.

334 "Was all this done": Ibid.

335 "Look at him now": Ibid., p. 140.

TWENTY-FIVE: Simplicity and Dignity

338 She then stepped: *The Illustrated London News,* 30 July 1938.

338 "the most dangerous": Van der Kiste, *George V's Children,* p. 140.

338 "splendid health": Sir Alexander Hardinge to Lord Tweedsmuir, 21 January 1938, John Buchan Fonds.

339 "a German family": Wheeler-Bennett, *George VI,* p. 337.

339 "strong political convictions": *The Illustrated London News,* 26 February 1938.

339 "nothing undone": Sir Alexander Hardinge to Lord Tweedsmuir, 18 June 1938, John Buchan Fonds.

340 by the bedside: *The Times,* 25 June 1938.

340 Thousands of people: *The Times,* 27 June 1938.

340 "exquisite in its simplicity": Queen Elizabeth to Queen Mary, 28 June 1938, RA QM/PRIV/CC12/73.

340 "bare-headed": *The Times,* 28 June 1938.

340 the noise of the wind: Ibid.

341 "They are so nice": Queen Elizabeth to Arthur Penn, 30 June 1938, Penn Papers, Shawcross, *QEQM Letters,* p. 256.

341 "lessened the strain": Queen Elizabeth to Queen Mary, 28 June 1938, RA QM/PRIV/CC12/73.

341 "family mourning": *The Times,* 24 June 1938.

342 The King had inspired: Norman Hartnell, *Silver and Gold* (London: Evans Brothers, 1955), p. 94.

342 as acceptable in court: Ibid., p. 96.

342 "gastric influenza": *The Times,* 11 July 1938.

342 "in case of infection": Queen Elizabeth to Queen Mary, 13 July 1938, RA QM/PRIV/CC12/75.

342 "decided to set aside": *The Times,* 12 July 1938.

342 "astonishing self-control": Longford, *Queen Mother,* p. 169.

343 "have learned to face": *The Manchester Guardian,* 25 July 1938.

343 "spoke well": Harvey I, p.165.

343 "Our entente has lost nothing": *The Times,* 21 July 1938.

344 "modern military might": Ibid.

344 "most elaborate": *The Illustrated London News,* 30 July 1938.

344 "thirteen glasses": Diana Cooper, *Light of Common Day,* p. 221.

344 "To the French": Ibid.

344 "a great personal triumph": *The Illustrated London News,* 30 July 1938.

344 "should make the dictators": Harvey I, p. 179.

345 "horrified at his voice": Queen Mary to King George VI, 15 September 1938, RA GVI/PRIV/11/481.

346 "because of a quarrel": Wheeler-Bennett, *George VI,* p. 408.

346 "the desire of our two peoples": Shawcross, *QEQM,* p. 442.

346 "in a maze": King George VI to Alan Lascelles, 17 September 1938, Wheeler-Bennett, *George VI,* p. 350.

346 "You will see": King George VI to Queen Elizabeth, 19 September 1938, RA QEQM/PRIV/RF.

347 "terribly anxious and worrying": Queen Elizabeth to May Elphinstone, 24 September 1938, RA QEQM/OUT/ELPHINSTONE.

347 "the greatest engineering feat": *The Times,* 27 September 1938.

347 "rang out clearly": *The Times,* 28 September 1938.

347 "bids the people": Ibid.

348 "listened to every word": King George VI to May Elphinstone, 29 September 1938, RA QEQM/OUT/ELPHINSTONE.

348 "a prelude to a larger settlement": *The Times,* 1 October 1938.

348 "peace with honour": Andrew Roberts, *Churchill: Walking with Destiny* (New York: Viking, 2018), p. 454.

348 "We want Neville": *The Times,* 1 October 1938.

348 "magnificent efforts": *The Illustrated London News,* 6 October 1938.

348 "great day": King George VI to Queen Mary, 1 October 1938, RA QM/PRIV/CC/12/82.

348 "I am sure that": Queen Elizabeth to Queen Mary, 2 October 1938, RA QM/PRIV/CC/12/84.

349 "You & Bertie must": Queen Mary to Queen Elizabeth, 5 October 1938, RA QEQM/PRIV/RF.

349 "the balcony appearance": Shawcross interview with D. R. Thorpe, Shawcross, *QEQM,* p. 443.

349 "one year to re-arm": Queen Elizabeth, conversations with Eric Anderson, 1994–95, Shawcross, *QEQM Letters,* p. 258.

TWENTY-SIX: Transatlantic Triumph

351 "practical expression": *The Manchester Guardian,* 1 January 1939.

351 "My Dear King George": Wheeler-Bennett, *George VI,* p. 372.

351 "that we all might": Eleanor Roosevelt, *This I Remember* (New York: Harper, 1949), pp. 183–84.

352 "As I said to": Franklin D. Roosevelt to Lord Tweedsmuir, 3 November 1938, John Buchan Fonds.

352 "The liberty that we": Wheeler-Bennett, *George VI,* p. 364.

352 "deep distress": Ibid.

352 Lilibet sat: "Court Circular," *The Times,* 6 April 1939.

353 Elizabeth told her friend: Crawford, *Little Princesses,* p. 84.

353 "Piles of books": Ibid.

353 Under Marten's: Bolitho, *Their Majesties,* p. 51.

353 "Try and learn": Queen Elizabeth to Princess Elizabeth, 13 May 1939, RA QEII/PRIV/RF, Shawcross, *QEQM Letters,* p. 265.

353 "as big as Glamis": Ibid., p. 264.

353 "the twang": Queen Elizabeth to Queen Mary, 15 May 1939, RA QM/PRIV/CC12/54.

353 "sensation of being": Alan Lascelles to Joan Lascelles, 14 May 1939, LASL, CAC.

354 "very soap-box": Queen Elizabeth to Queen Mary, 8 May 1939, RA QM/PRIV/CC12/93.

354 "I do not advise": Queen Elizabeth to Lord Halifax, 15 November 1939, Hickleton Papers A2/278/26A 1, Shawcross, *QEQM*, p. 490.

354 "the only really": Alan Lascelles to Joan Lascelles, 15 May 1939, LASL, CAC.

354 "his first real": Ibid., 16 May 1939.

354 "*our* King and Queen": Wheeler-Bennett, *George VI*, p. 381.

354 dropped to her knees: Bradford, *Reluctant King*, p. 288.

355 "genteel of Ottawa": Lord Tweedsmuir to Sir Alexander Hardinge, 22 May 1939, John Buchan Fonds.

355 "must go down": Lord Tweedsmuir to his sister Nan [Anna Buchan, who wrote thrillers under the pseudonym O. Douglas], 22 May 1939, John Buchan Fonds.

355 "perfect bodyguard": Lord Tweedsmuir to Stair Gillon, 26 May 1939, John Buchan Fonds.

355 "simply staggered": Ibid.

355 "a people's king": Ibid.

355 "face these gigantic": Lord Tweedsmuir to Anna Buchan, 22 May 1939, John Buchan Fonds.

355 "really very nice": Queen Elizabeth to Queen Mary, 1 June 1939, RA QM/PRIV/CC12/99.

355 "what a wonderful": Lord Tweedsmuir to Stair Gillon, 26 May 1939, John Buchan Fonds.

355 "very deep respect": Lord Tweedsmuir to Anna Buchan, 22 May 1939, John Buchan Fonds.

356 "simply a genius": Ibid.

356 "I was quite impressed": Mackenzie King, diary, 19 May 1939, LAC/BAC/Mg26-J13, Shawcross *QEQM*, pp. 465–66.

356 The task of filling: Lady Tweedsmuir to Lord Tweedsmuir, 9 May 1939, John Buchan Fonds.

356 "great joy": Queen Elizabeth to Lady Tweedsmuir, 28 July 1939, RA QEQM/OUT/MISC, Shawcross, *QEQM Letters*, p. 274.

356 "the pine trees": Queen Elizabeth to Princess Elizabeth, 27 May 1939, RA QEII/PRIV/RF, Shawcross, *QEQM Letters*, p. 267.

356 "I am sure": Ibid., p. 268.

356 "very hard work": Ibid., p. 267.

357 Logue had also coached: Logue and Conradi, *King's Speech*, p. 151.

357 "rather nerve-wracking": Alan Lascelles to Joan Lascelles, 25 May 1939, LASL, CAC.

357 "tremendous success": Logue and Conradi, *King's Speech,* p. 151.
357 "splendid impression": Franklin D. Roosevelt to Lord Tweedsmuir, 24 May 1939, John Buchan Fonds.
357 "two burning": Queen Elizabeth to Princess Elizabeth, 11 June 1939, RA QEII/PRIV/RF, Shawcross, *QEQM Letters,* p. 272.
357 "In the course of": Roosevelt Archives, Mrs. Roosevelt's Diary, June 9, 1939, President's Secretary's File, Box 44, Wheeler-Bennett, *George VI,* p. 383.
358 "eyes a snapping blue": *Time,* 29 May 1939.
358 "set her in the people's": *The Times,* 9 June 1939.
358 A cushion equipped: Bradford, *Reluctant King,* p. 292.
358 "many of them felt": Ibid.
358 "There are quite a lot": *The Times,* 10 June 1939.
358 "keen sense": Ibid.
359 "gracious, informed": Rhodes James II, p.163.
359 "never seen a hotter": Joseph P. Kennedy, diary, 21 July 1939, Kennedy, *Hostage to Fortune,* p. 350.
359 lay on the floor: Ibid.
359 "with a swifter": Washington press reports, 9 June 1939 RA F&V/VISOV/CAN/1939/Press cuttings/Vol. III, pp. 83–85; Journal of Their Majesties' Tour, 10 June 1939, RA PS/PSO/GVI/C/251/01, Shawcross, *QEQM,* p. 475.
359 "Victorian picture frock": *The Times,* 10 June 1939.
360 "very good & very interesting": Queen Elizabeth to Queen Mary, 11 June 1939, RA QM/PRIV/CC12/101.
360 His temper had flared: Will Swift, *The Roosevelts and the Royals* (Hoboken, N.J.: John Wiley and Sons, 2004), p. 238.
360 One newspaperwoman: Bradford, *Reluctant King,* p. 294.
360 "the King's cheek muscles": Lord Crawford to Lord Tweedsmuir, 19 June 1939, John Buchan Fonds.
360 "was Squire, not President": Wheeler-Bennett, *George VI,* p. 386.
361 "the greatest affection": Queen Elizabeth to Queen Mary, 11 June 1939, RA QM/PRIV/CC12/101.
361 "as would any two": *The Times,* 10 June 1939.
361 "He is so easy": Wheeler-Bennett, *George VI,* p. 388.
361 "frank & friendly": Ibid., p. 390.
361 "vitality oxygenates": Lord Tweedsmuir report on trip to Washington, D.C., 1 April 1937, John Buchan Fonds.
362 "something could be done": Wheeler-Bennett, *George VI,* p. 391.
362 "Young man": Ibid., p. 389.
362 "Why don't my": Ibid.
362 "was completely natural": Swift, *Roosevelts and the Royals,* p. 266.
362 "firm & trusted": Wheeler-Bennett, *George VI,* p. 391.
362 "If he saw": Ibid.
362 "If London was": Ibid.

362 "F.D.R.'s ideas": Ibid., p. 392.

362 "what Roosevelt had": Mackenzie King, *The Mackenzie King Record*, vol. 1, *1939–1944*, ed. J. W. Pickersgill (Chicago: University of Chicago Press, 1960), p. 256.

363 "We saw a large": Queen Elizabeth the Queen Mother to Sir Antony Acland, 24 June 1989, Acland Papers, Shawcross, *QEQM Letters*, p. 596.

363 "He was conversing": Queen Elizabeth to Queen Mary, 11 June 1939, RA QM/PRIV/CC12/101.

363 served on silver: *The New York Times*, 12 June 1989.

363 invited "all his own": Queen Elizabeth to Queen Mary, 11 June 1939, RA QM/PRIV/CC12/101.

363 "all our food on one": Queen Elizabeth to Princess Elizabeth, 11 June 1939, RA QEII/PRIV/RF, Shawcross, *QEQM Letters*, pp. 272–73.

363 "with gusto": *The New York Times*, 12 June 1989.

363 "<u>Mrs.</u> R's own": Queen Elizabeth to Queen Mary, 11 June 1939, RA QM/PRIV/CC12/101.

363 "It was deliciously": Queen Elizabeth to Princess Elizabeth, 11 June 1939, RA QEII/PRIV/RF, Shawcross, *QEQM Letters*, pp. 272–73.

364 "Good luck": Bradford, *Reluctant King*, p. 298.

364 "standing on the rear": Shawcross, *QEQM*, p. 478.

364 "It is unbelievable": Lord Tweedsmuir to Stair Gillon, 22 June 1939, John Buchan Fonds.

364 "The King especially": Lord Tweedsmuir to Franklin D. Roosevelt, 17 June 1939, John Buchan Fonds.

364 "found it easier": Bradford, *Reluctant King*, p. 298.

364 "The King has a remarkable": Lord Tweedsmuir to Stanley Baldwin, 19 June 1939, John Buchan Fonds.

364 "He is profoundly": Lord Tweedsmuir to Neville Chamberlain, 19 June 1939, John Buchan Fonds.

364 "I nearly cried": Wheeler-Bennett, *George VI*, p. 392.

364 "the tiny figures": Lord Tweedsmuir to Anna Buchan, 19 June 1939, John Buchan Fonds.

364 "we have all fallen": Ibid.

365 "What a piece of luck": Lord Tweedsmuir to Lord Crawford, 6 July 1939, John Buchan Fonds.

TWENTY-SEVEN: We Shall Prevail

367 "Hullo!": *The Times*, 23 June 1939.

367 "kissed them": Crawford, *Little Princesses*, p. 96.

367 the King tossed: *The Times*, 23 June 1939.

368 "long talk": Ibid.

368 "We lost all": Nicolson I, p. 405.

368 "The roar could be": *Daily Mirror,* 23 June 1939.

368 "hurricane of cheers": *The Times,* 23 June 1939.

368 "the greatest of all": *Daily Mirror,* 23 June 1939.

368 "a little nervous": Logue and Conradi, King's Speech, p. 156.

368 "had been written": Sir Alan Lascelles to Lord Tweedsmuir, 28 May 1939; King George VI to Lord Tweedsmuir, 5 July 1939, John Buchan Fonds.

368 "deep gratitude": *The Times,* 24 June 1939.

369 "Even in this age": Ibid.

369 "admirable and shapely": Logue and Conradi, *King's Speech,* p. 158.

369 "never heard the King": Wheeler-Bennett, *George VI,* p. 304.

369 "everyone was pleased": Logue and Conradi, *King's Speech,* p. 156.

369 "was a change": Greig, *King Maker,* p. 261.

369 "all the help you": King George VI to Lord Tweedsmuir, 5 July 1939, John Buchan Fonds.

369 "made us": King, *Mackenzie King Record,* 1:255.

369 "have been struck": Neville Chamberlain to Lord Tweedsmuir, 7 July 1939, John Buchan Fonds.

369 "everybody here": King George VI to Lord Tweedsmuir, 5 July 1939, John Buchan Fonds.

370 "a mere symbol": Lord Tweedsmuir to Leo Amery, 6 July 1939, John Buchan Fonds.

370 "to trust his own": Wheeler-Bennett, *George VI,* p. 393.

370 "high-hat business": Ibid.

370 "perfect genius": Lord Tweedsmuir to Stair Gillon, 26 May 1939, John Buchan Fonds.

370 "daring innovation": Beaton, *Wandering Years,* p. 372.

370 "blue haze": Ibid., p. 374.

371 "monkey-like frenzy": Ibid., p. 375.

371 "porcelain doll": [28] July 1939, Cecil Beaton Papers, St. John's College, Cambridge, Vickers, *Elizabeth the Queen Mother,* p. 194.

371 "sweated with the effort": Beaton, *Wandering Years,* p. 375.

371 "Piccadilly were on": Ibid., p. 377.

371 "in a brilliant & penetrating": Vickers, *Elizabeth the Queen Mother,* p. 206.

371 "out of the royal": Channon II, 30 November 1936.

372 "noble work": Elizabeth, Queen Consort to King George VI, *The Queen's Book of the Red Cross* (London: Hodder and Stoughton, 1939).

372 "the great work": Ibid.

372 more portraits: *The Times,* 5 December 1939.

372 "H.M. the Queen": *The Tatler,* 6 December 1939.

372 in a downpour: Wheeler-Bennett, *George VI,* p. 396.

373 "never took her eyes": Crawford, *Little Princesses,* p. 101.

373 "You were so shy": Alexandra, Queen of Yugoslavia, *Prince Philip: A Family Portrait* (Indianapolis: Bobbs Merrill, 1959), p. 73.

373 "mischievous, enquiring": Queen Elizabeth II, Christmas Broadcast, 25 December 2021.

373 "was not allowed to stay": Crawford, *Little Princesses,* p. 101.

373 "pink-faced": Ibid., p. 102.

373 "huge flotilla": *The Times,* 24 July 1939.

373 "rowing away": Crawford, *Little Princesses,* p. 101.

373 "The young fool": Ibid.

373 "the King's Camp": *The Times,* 2 August 1939.

374 When the campers: *The Times,* 8 August 1939.

374 "we got to know": Letter from a Bryanston schoolboy, n.d., RA GVI/ PRIV/CAMP.

374 To set a casual tone: *The Times,* 8 August 1939.

374 "wonderful how happily": Queen Elizabeth to Queen Mary, 8 August 1939, RA QM/PRIV/CC12/105.

374 "pointed out": Captain J. G. Paterson, n.d., Wheeler-Bennett, *George VI,* p. 398.

375 "We talked to the King": Letter from a Bryanston schoolboy, n.d., RA GVI/PRIV/CAMP.

375 "His Majesty is": "A Cadby Boy and His King," *The Lyons Mail* 24, no. 5 (September 1939), RA GVI/PRIV/CAMP.

375 "without any forewarning": Sir Alan Lascelles to Lord Tweedsmuir, 8 August 1939, John Buchan Fonds.

375 They met at: *The Times,* 14 August 1939.

375 When they left: "A Cadby Boy and His King," *The Lyons Mail* 24, no. 5 (September 1939), RA GVI/PRIV/CAMP.

376 "No one any longer": Sir Alexander Hardinge to Lord Tweedsmuir, 31 August 1939, John Buchan Fonds.

376 "All hope is not gone": King George VI to Queen Elizabeth, 25 August 1939, RA QEQM/PRIV/RF.

376 "very calm": Queen Elizabeth to Queen Mary, 31 August 1939, RA QM/PRIV/CC12/110.

376 "as a citizen of the world": Monckton Papers, p. 81, Balliol.

376 "one of the minor calamities": Joseph P. Kennedy, diary, 27 September 1938, Kennedy, *Hostage to Fortune,* p. 287.

376 "speaking constantly": Monckton Papers, p. 81, Balliol.

377 "unless he was promised": Ibid., p. 82.

377 "What are we going": Queen Elizabeth to Queen Mary, 31 August 1939, RA QM/PRIV/CC12/110.

377 "We went to bed": Queen Elizabeth notes, 4 September 1939, RA QEQM/PRIV/PERS, Shawcross, *QEQM,* p. 488.

377 "he was so worried": Logue and Conradi, *King's Speech,* p. 166.

377 "We only have": Queen Elizabeth notes, 4 September 1939, RA QEQM/PRIV/PERS, Shawcross, *QEQM,* p. 488.

377 "I had a certain feeling": King George VI, diary, 3 September 1939, RA GVI/PRIV/DIARY.

377   "He spoke so quietly": Queen Elizabeth notes, 4 September 1939, RA QEQM/PRIV/PERS, Shawcross, *QEQM*, p. 488.

378   "the country is calm": King George VI, diary, 3 September 1939, RA GVI/PRIV/DIARY.

378   "ghastly, horrible": Queen Elizabeth notes, 4 September 1939, RA QEQM/PRIV/PERS, Shawcross, *QEQM*, p. 488.

378   "very well trained": King George VI, diary, 3 September 1939, RA GVI/PRIV/DIARY.

378   "We prayed with": Queen Elizabeth notes, 4 September 1939, RA QEQM/PRIV/PERS, Shawcross, *QEQM*, p. 488.

378   Logue marked pauses: Logue and Conradi, *King's Speech*, p. 164.

378   "In this grave hour": Ibid., pp. 165–66.

378   "That was good": Ibid.

378   "came through very well": Queen Mary to King George VI, 3 September 1939, RA GVI/PRIV/RF/11/511.

379   "try my very best": Lady Granville to Queen Elizabeth, 6 September 1939, RA QEQM/PRIV/BL.

379   When Henry Marten: Crawford, *Little Princesses*, p. 107.

379   "Stick to the usual": Ibid., p. 106.

379   from "the Gorbals": Queen Elizabeth to Queen Mary, 26 September 1939, RA QM/PRIV/CC12/113.

379   "handed round": Crawford, *Little Princesses*, p. 109.

380   "The children were terrified": Ibid., p. 108.

380   "swimming over": Queen Elizabeth to Prince Paul of Yugoslavia, 2 October 1939, RA QEQ/OUT/PAUY, Shawcross, *QEQM Letters*, p. 281.

380   "gold plate" was: Corbitt, *My Twenty Years in Buckingham Palace*, p. 165.

380   Unmarked cars: Andrew Stewart, *The King's Private Army: Protecting the British Royal Family During the Second World War* (Solihull, West Midlands: Helion, 2015), p. 23.

380   "to wrench the major": Sir Owen Morshead, *Windsor Castle* (London: Phaidon, 1971), quoted in Stewart, *King's Private Army*, p. 23.

380   "until the raids": King George VI to Queen Mary, 6 September 1939, QM/PRIV/CC12/111.

381   The day after: Pope-Hennessy I, p. 596.

381   "quite a fleet": Queen Mary, diary, 4 September 1939, RA QM/PRIV/QMD/1939.

381   immediately displaced: Osbert Sitwell, *Queen Mary and Others* (New York: John Day, 1975), p. 33.

381   "I run Badminton": Queen Mary to Duke of Windsor, 18 October 1942, RA EDW/PRIV/MAIN/B/161.

381   Once ensconced: Sitwell, *Queen Mary and Others*, p. 34.

381   horror of anything: Ibid., p. 36.

381   "unprofitable crusade": Ibid.

381 **she enlisted:** Pope-Hennessy I, p. 601; Queen Mary, diary, 3 April 1940, QM/PRIV QMD/1939.

381 **she handed out:** Pope-Hennessy I, p. 603.

381 **"salvage scheme":** Ibid., p. 602.

381 **"she used every":** Sitwell, *Queen Mary and Others,* p. 49.

382 **"discovered democracy":** Pope-Hennessy II, p. 142.

382 **"Their surprise":** Lady Cynthia Colville, *Crowded Life* (London: Evans Brothers, 1963), pp. 193–94.

382 **high armless chair:** Sitwell, *Queen Mary and Others,* p. 41.

382 **"Her personality":** Ibid., p. 40.

382 **"She lived in all":** Hugh Montgomery-Massingberd and Christopher Simon Sykes, *Great Houses of England & Wales* (London: Laurence King, 1994), p. 228.

382 **"by excluding women":** Monckton Papers, p. 86, Balliol.

382 **"no recriminations":** King George VI, diary, 14 September 1939, RA GVI/PRIV/DIARY.

382 **"agreeably weak":** J. Bryan III and Charles J. V. Murphy, *The Windsor Story* (New York: Morrow, 1979), p. 436.

383 **"I touched on":** King George VI, diary, 14 September 1939, RA GVI/PRIV//DIARY.

383 **"the sooner he went":** King George VI, diary, 15 September 1939, RA GVI/PRIV/DIARY.

383 **"did not want D attached":** King George VI, diary, 16 September 1939, RA GVI/PRIV/DIARY.

383 **"is not only alive":** Bryan and Murphy, *Windsor Story,* p. 437.

383 **"put it very strongly":** King George VI, diary, 16 September 1939, RA GVI/PRIV/DIARY.

383 **"precaution":** Queen Elizabeth to Prince Paul, 2 October 1939, RA QEQM/OUT/PAUY, Shawcross, *QEQM Letters,* p. 280.

383 **"he did not ask":** King George VI, diary, 14 September 1939, RA GVI/PRIV/DIARY.

383 **"no intention":** King George VI, diary, 15 September 1939, RA GVI/PRIV/DIARY.

383 **"kept away":** Queen Elizabeth to Prince Paul, 2 October 1939, 2 October 1939, RA QEQM/OUT/PAUY, Shawcross, *QEQM Letters,* p. 280.

384 **"would be difficult":** King George VI, diary, 14 September 1939, RA GVI/PRIV/DIARY.

384 **"It is all an amazing":** King George VI, diary, 25 September 1939, RA GVI/PRIV/DIARY.

384 **"a man of great vigour":** King George VI, diary, 12 October 1939, RA GVI/PRIV/DIARY.

384 **"very pleased to be":** King George VI, diary, 5 September 1939, RA GVI/PRIV/DIARY.

384 **"Winston is difficult":** King George VI, diary, 9 October 1939, RA GVI/PRIV/DIARY.

385 **"a fine head"**: Joseph P. Kennedy, diary, 9 April 1938, Kennedy, *Hostage to Fortune,* p. 251.

385 **"geography"**: Ibid., p. 252.

385 **"financial and material"**: Wheeler-Bennett, *George VI,* p. 419.

385 **"three really free"**: King George VI to Joseph P. Kennedy, 12 September 1939, Wheeler-Bennett, *George VI,* p. 419.

386 **"to help England"**: Joseph P. Kennedy to King George VI, 14 September 1939, Kennedy, *Hostage to Fortune,* p. 377.

386 **"stern simplicity"**: *The Times,* 29 November 1939.

386 **"deep significance"**: Ibid.

386 **"didn't look very well"**: Joseph P. Kennedy, diary, 28 November 1939, Kennedy, *Hostage to Fortune,* p. 402.

386 **"cowardly and conceited"**: Nicolson, diary, 18 October 1940, Balliol.

387 **"contempt"**: Ibid.

387 **"always the shrewd"**: King George VI, diary, 11 October 1940, RA GVI/PRIV/DIARY.

387 **"a very disappointed"**: King George VI, diary, 17 October 1940, RA GVI/PRIV/DIARY.

387 **"I feel that it is so important"**: Queen Elizabeth to Prince Paul of Yugoslavia, 6 December 1939, RA QEQM/OUT/PAUY, Shawcross, *QEQM Letters,* p. 285.

387 **"speak words of comfort"**: Lord Tweedsmuir to Sir Alexander Hardinge, 2 October 1939, John Buchan Fonds.

387 **"skeleton"**: Queen Elizabeth to the Most Rev. Cosmo Lang, Archbishop of Canterbury, 6 November 1939, Lambeth Palace Library, Lang 318, ff. 199–200, Shawcross, *QEQM Letters,* p. 281.

387 **As Bertie listened**: *The Times,* 13 November 1939.

388 **"It went off"**: King George VI, diary, 11 November 1939, RA GVI/PRIV/DIARY.

388 **"one of the best"**: Shawcross, *QEQM,* p. 498.

388 **Listeners as far away**: *The Times,* 13 November 1939.

388 **"very much enjoyed"**: Sir Alexander Hardinge to Lord Tweedsmuir, 21 December 1939, John Buchan Fonds.

388 **"Lovely undulating"**: King George VI, diary, 9 December 1939, RA GVI/PRIV/DIARY.

388 **He marveled at**: King George VI, diary, 9 December 1939, RA GVI/PRIV/DIARY.

389 **"very impressive"**: Sir Alexander Hardinge to Lord Tweedsmuir, 21 December 1939, John Buchan Fonds.

389 **"a bit awkward"**: Field Marshal Lord Alanbrooke, *War Diaries 1939–1945* (Berkeley: University of California Press, 2001), p. 23.

389 **"if all goes well"**: King George VI, diary, 23 November 1939, RA GVI/PRIV/DIARY.

389 **"They are waiting"**: King George VI, Christmas Broadcast, 25 December 1939.

389 his peroration: Shawcross, *QEQM*, p. 502.

390 "This is always": King George VI, diary, 25 December 1939, RA GVI/
     PRIV/DIARY.

390 "At their age": King George VI, diary, 20 January 1940, RA GVI/PRIV/
     DIARY.

390 hosting Monday-night: King George VI, diary, 22 January 1940, RA
     GVI/PRIV/DIARY.

390 "They go with": King George VI, diary, 5 February 1940, RA GVI/
     PRIV/DIARY.

390 "blizzard of snow": King George VI, diary, 14 March 1940, RA GVI/
     PRIV/DIARY.

390 He stepped out: *The Times*, 15 March 1940.

390 "new blood": King George VI, diary, 2 April 1940, RA GVI/PRIV/
     DIARY.

391 "amusing": King George VI, diary, 28 February 1940, RA GVI/PRIV/
     DIARY.

391 "his usual calm self": King George VI, diary, 20 March 1940, RA
     GVI/PRIV/DIARY.

391 "very angry": King George VI, diary, 13 March 1940, RA GVI/PRIV/
     DIARY.

391 "a shadow or a ghost": King George VI, diary, 10 May 1940, RA GVI/
     PRIV/DIARY.

391 "only person": King George VI, diary, 10 May 1940, RA GVI/PRIV/
     DIARY.

391 "full of fire": King George VI, diary, 10 May 1940, RA GVI/PRIV/
     DIARY.

391 "support and comfort": Queen Elizabeth to Neville Chamberlain,
     17 May 1940, BUA NC1/23/81A, Cadbury Research Library, Special
     Collections, University of Birmingham, Shawcross, *QEQM Letters*,
     pp. 290–91.

391 "I cried, mummy": Ibid, p. 291.

PART FIVE: THE WAR YEARS
TWENTY-EIGHT: Sharing the Suffering

395 "The French command": King George VI, diary, 21 May 1940, RA
     GVI/PRIV/DIARY.

395 "an impossible place": King George VI, diary, 22 May 1940, RA GVI/
     PRIV/DIARY.

395 Churchill had predicted: Roberts, *Churchill*, p. 456.

396 "guns, tanks": King George VI, diary, 23 May 1940, RA GVI/PRIV/
     DIARY.

396 "to practise": Logue and Conradi, *King's Speech*, p. 176.

396 "hitherto impossible": Ibid., p. 177.

396 "grand": Ibid.

396 **"It was easily"**: King George VI, diary, 24 May 1940, RA GVI/PRIV/DIARY.
396 **"an epic for history"**: King George VI, diary, 31 December 1940, RA GVI/PRIV/DIARY.
397 **"We shall go on"**: Roberts, *Churchill,* p. 552.
397 **"go on fighting"**: King George VI, diary, 4 June 1940, RA GVI/PRIV/DIARY.
397 **"I cannot yet think"**: King George VI, diary, 11 May 1940, RA GVI/PRIV/DIARY.
397 **"superbly prepared"**: Roberts, *Churchill,* p. 517.
398 **"a defeatist"**: King George VI, diary, 12 June 1940, RA GVI/PRIV/DIARY.
398 **"Personally, I feel"**: King George VI to Queen Mary, 27 June 1940, RA QM/PRIV/CC12/129.
398 **"the survival of"**: Roberts, *Churchill,* p. 563.
399 **"very upset & had"**: King George VI, diary, 13 May 1940, RA GVI/PRIV/DIARY.
399 **"One very seldom"**: King George VI, diary, 15 May 1940, RA GVI/PRIV/DIARY.
399 **had entertained**: Queen Mary, diary, 13 September 1935, RA QM/PRIV/QMD/1935.
399 **respectfully stood**: Queen Mary, diary, 15 May 1940, RA QM/PRIV/QMD/1940.
399 **"very calm"**: Queen Mary, diary, 16 May 1940, RA QM/PRIV/QMD/1940.
399 **"a remarkable woman"**: King George VI, diary, 17 May 1940, RA GVI/PRIV/DIARY.
399 **"sensible black hat"**: Crawford, *Little Princesses,* p. 116.
400 **"Uncle Charles"**: King George VI, diary, 9 June 1940, RA GVI/PRIV/DIARY.
400 **the King welcomed**: King George VI, diary, 10 June 1940, RA GVI/PRIV/DIARY.
400 **"depleted"**: Queen Elizabeth to Queen Mary, 24 July 1940, RA QM/PRIV/CC12/131.
401 **"We must guard"**: King George VI, diary, 25 June 1940, RA GVI/PRIV/DIARY.
401 **"he could only"**: King George VI, diary, 29 June and 30 June 1940, RA GVI/PRIV/DIARY.
401 **"appalling gloom"**: Nicolson, diary, 1 October 1940, Balliol.
401 **"He is going to be"**: King George VI, diary, 29 June and 30 June 1940, RA GVI/PRIV/DIARY.
401 **"firm supporter"**: Robert Hutton on newly released British government documents from 1940, Bloomberg News, 20 July 2017.
401 **"accommodate any"**: Ribbentrop message in *Documents on German*

Foreign Policy, series D, 10, no. 2 (1957), quoted in Bradford, *Reluctant King,* p. 437.

402 **"movement for peace"**: Nicolson, diary, 1 October 1940, Balliol.

402 **"activities"**: Winston Churchill to Prime Ministers, 4 July 1940, CHAR 29/9A/34 (CAC), cited by Andrew Lownie, *Traitor King: The Scandalous Exile of the Duke and Duchess of Windsor* (London: Blink, 2021), pp. 113–14. Lownie notes the eventual version: "The position of the Duke and Duchess of Windsor on the Continent in recent months has been causing HM and HMG embarrassment as though his loyalties are unimpeachable; there is always a backwash of Nazi intrigue which seeks to make trouble about him."

402 **"I did not see"**: King George VI, diary, 3 July 1940, RA GVI/PRIV/DIARY.

402 **"W. suggested his"**: King George VI, diary, 3 July 1940, RA GVI/PRIV/DIARY. This diary entry shows clearly that the idea for shipping the Duke and Duchess of Windsor to the Bahamas was from Churchill, not the King.

402 **George VI initially**: King George VI, diary, 3 July 1940, RA GVI/PRIV/DIARY.

402 **"most annoying"**: King George VI, diary, 3 July 1940, RA GVI/PRIV/DIARY.

402 **"D. must leave"**: King George VI, diary, 5 July 1940, RA GVI/PRIV/DIARY.

402 **The duke promptly**: King George VI, diary, 4 July 1940, RA GVI/PRIV/DIARY.

402 **"this arrangement"**: King George VI, diary, 5 July 1940, RA GVI/PRIV/DIARY.

402 **"I am sure D could"**: King George VI, diary, 6 and 7 July 1940, RA GVI/PRIV/DIARY.

402 **"must have a job"**: King George VI to Queen Mary, 7 July 1940, RA QM/PRIV/CC12/130.

403 **"three husbands"**: Queen Elizabeth notes, 6 July 1940 (copy), Shawcross, *QEQM,* pp. 519–20. Shawcross writes that the original notes were enclosed in a letter from Sir Alexander Hardinge to Lord Lloyd, CAC GLLD/21/7A/1, and that Lloyd burned the Queen's "original handwritten memorandum" but retained a typed copy in Lloyd Papers at CAC.

403 **"the lesser of two"**: Sir Alexander Hardinge to Queen Elizabeth, 7 July 1940, RA QEQM/PRIV/OFF, Shawcross, *QEQM,* p. 520.

403 **According to Cadogan**: Cadbury, *Princes at War,* pp. 285–86, reproducing the original report to Cadogan, 7 July 1940, and writing "he passed it up the line and it reached the palace that same day."

403 **"telling them that they"**: King George VI, diary, 16 July 1940, RA GVI/PRIV/DIARY.

403 **"preposterous"**: King George VI, diary, 18 July 1940, RA GVI/PRIV/DIARY.

403 **"D has got to obey"**: King George VI, diary, 18 July 1940, RA GVI/PRIV/DIARY.

403 **persuade the Windsors**: King George VI to Queen Mary, 22 August 1940, RA QM/PRIV/CC12/133: "It was Monckton who really made him leave Europe. Of course the Germans would have used him in their propaganda."

403 **"remain in continuing"**: Bradford, *Reluctant King,* p. 438, quoting Huene message to Ribbentrop on 2 August 1940 mentioning the Duke's intention to communicate using a code word.

403 **"D. had different ideas"**: King George VI, diary, 6 August 1940, RA GVI/PRIV/DIARY.

404 **"twenty little silver"**: Nicolson, diary, 18 August 1940, Balliol.

404 **"talked with people"**: King George VI, diary, 1 August 1940, RA GVI/PRIV/DIARY.

404 **"Air Activity"**: King George VI, diary, 10 August 1940, RA GVI/PRIV/DIARY.

404 **"This looks like"**: King George VI, diary, 13 August 1940, RA GVI/PRIV/DIARY.

405 **He pledged retaliation**: Roberts, *Churchill,* pp. 584–85.

405 **"the enemy dropped"**: Roberts, *Churchill,* p. 588.

405 **"descend into the"**: Queen Elizabeth to Queen Mary, 20 August 1940, RA QM/PRIV/CC12/132.

405 **Between August 24**: Roberts, *Churchill,* p. 588.

405 **"major strategic"**: Roberts, *Churchill,* p. 592.

406 **"wiser for us"**: King George VI, diary, 9 September 1940, RA GVI/PRIV/DIARY.

406 **fourteen months later**: King George VI, diary, 27 November 1941, RA GVI/PRIV/DIARY.

406 **Haakon and Olav**: King George VI, diary, 9 September 1940, RA GVI/PRIV/DIARY.

406 **"really intense"**: King George VI, diary, 10 September 1940, RA GVI/PRIV/DIARY.

406 **spent three hours**: David Euan Wallace, diary (typescript copy), Bodleian Library, University of Oxford, 9 September 1940.

407 **"Are we downhearted?"**: *The Times,* 10 September 1940.

407 **"all and sundry"**: David Euan Wallace, diary (typescript copy), Bodleian Library, University of Oxford, 9 September 1940.

407 **"We felt the concussion"**: King George VI, diary, 9 September 1940, RA GVI/PRIV/DIARY.

407 **Its force catapulted**: *The Times,* 12 September 1940.

407 **"I had been sitting"**: King George VI, diary, 10 September 1940, RA GVI/PRIV/DIARY.

407 **They also hosted the first**: King George VI, diary, 10 September

1940, RA GVI/PRIV/DIARY; Winston S. Churchill, *The Second World War: Their Finest Hour* (Boston: Houghton Mifflin, 1949), p. 379.

407   **They helped themselves:** Corbitt, *My Twenty Years in Buckingham Palace,* p. 151.

408   **"gracious intimacy":** Roberts, *Churchill,* p. 594.

408   **"does tell me":** King George VI, diary, 20 January 1941, RA GVI/PRIV/DIARY.

408   **"our weekly luncheons":** Churchill to King George VI, 5 January 1941, RA PS/PSO/GVI/C/069/07, Shawcross, *QEQM,* p. 537.

408   **"many things both":** King George VI, diary, 22 October 1940, RA GVI/PRIV/DIARY.

408   **"told me everything":** Queen Elizabeth, conversations with Eric Anderson, 1994–95, Shawcross *QEQM,* p. 560.

408   **"It will make a fine":** Nicolson, diary, 11 September 1940, Balliol.

408   **The trio stood:** *The Times,* 12 September 1940.

409   **"The usual collapsed":** King George VI, diary, 11 September 1940, RA GVI/PRIV/DIARY.

409   **entered the dimly:** Ibid., *The Illustrated London News,* 21 September 1940.

409   **"I think we must":** Queen Elizabeth, conversations with Eric Anderson, 1994–95, Shawcross, *QEQM,* p. 529.

409   **"heard an aircraft":** King George VI, diary, 13 September 1940, RA GVI/PRIV/DIARY.

409   **"the noise of aircraft":** Queen Elizabeth to Queen Mary, 13 September 1940, RA QM/PRIV/CC12/135.

410   **"looked foolishly":** Ibid.

410   **"We all wondered":** King George VI, diary, 13 September 1940, RA GVI/PRIV/DIARY.

410   **"Had the windows":** Churchill, *Second World War,* 2:379.

410   **"They have just":** Nicolson, diary, 13 September 1940, Balliol.

410   **eyewitness accounts:** *The Times,* 14 September 1940.

410   **"calmly making":** Crawford, *Little Princesses,* p. 146.

410   **The shelter:** *The Illustrated London News,* 21 September 1940.

411   **"had developed an unreasonable dislike":** Queen Elizabeth, conversations with Eric Anderson 1994–95, Shawcross, *QEQM,* p. 517.

411   **"made their reception":** David Euan Wallace, diary (typescript copy), 13 September 1940, Bodleian Library, University of Oxford.

411   **"Their Majesties appeared":** *The Times,* 14 September 1940.

411   **"a dead city":** Queen Elizabeth to Queen Mary, 13 September 1940, RA QM/PRIV/CC12/135.

411   **"a ghastly experience":** King George VI, diary, 13 September 1940, RA GVI/PRIV/DIARY.

412   **"I should not put":** King George VI, diary, 19 September 1940, RA GVI/PRIV/DIARY.

412   **during air raids:** David Euan Wallace, diary (typescript copy), 27

September 1940, Bodleian Library, University of Oxford: "The sirens went as we were on our way to the first rendezvous and while we were still there a considerable air battle developed not very far away."

412   "with whom they are": *The Times,* 20 September 1940.

412   "unite the King": Roberts, *Churchill,* p. 597.

412   "Like so many other": *The Times,* 14 September 1940.

412   "we have both found": King George VI to Queen Mary, 14 October 1940, RA QM/PRIV/CC12/138.

412   "I'm glad we've been bombed": Betty Spencer Shew, *Queen Elizabeth, the Queen Mother* (London: Hodder and Stoughton, 1955), p. 76, cited in Wheeler-Bennett, *George VI,* p. 470.

412   "were booed": Nicolson, diary, 17 September 1940, Balliol.

413   She dispatched sixty: Longford, *Queen Mother,* p. 85.

413   "a liability": King George VI, diary, 18 June 1940, RA GVI/PRIV/DIARY. On 20 May 1940, the King had written in his diary "E & I had a talk with Mr. Chamberlain . . . about the childrens' safety. He advised us to wait for the time being, before making any plans for their future." King George VI, diary, 20 May 1940, RA GVI/PRIV/DIARY.

413   "The children could": Shawcross, *QEQM,* p. 516.

413   "personal patriotism": Nicolson II, p. 100.

413   "Brontosaurus": King George VI, diary, 29 December 1940, RA GVI/PRIV/DIARY.

413   fitted out: Stewart, *King's Private Army,* p. 74.

413   "always felt that": King George VI, diary, 12 December 1941, RA GVI/PRIV/DIARY.

413   "We are not going": Nicolson, diary, 10 July 1940, Balliol.

414   "mobile column": King George VI, diary, 2 July 1940, RA GVI/PRIV/DIARY.

414   "saloon cars": Stewart, *King's Private Army,* p. 76.

414   "great stuff": Marion Crawford to Queen Mary, 23 February 1941, Lambeth Palace Library, Lang Papers, 318, ff. 67–69, Shawcross, *QEQM,* p. 534.

414   would never sing: Confidential interview with author, March 2019.

414   "She is so sweet": Alathea Fitzalan Howard, *The Windsor Diaries, 1940–1945: My Childhood with the Princesses Elizabeth and Margaret,* ed. Celestria Noel (London: Hodder and Stoughton, 2020), p. 69.

414   "four people who": Ibid., p. 152.

415   "very hurried moment": Queen Elizabeth to Queen Mary, 17 July 1944, RA QM/PRIV/CC13/95.

415   "right combination": Richard Hough, *Louis and Victoria: The Family History of the Mountbattens,* 2nd ed. (London: Weidenfeld and Nicolson, 1984), p. 354.

415   At their mother's: Longford, *Queen Mother,* p. 83.

415   the latter included: Fitzalan Howard, *Windsor Diaries,* p. 43.

415   "making conversation": Ibid., p. 65.

415 "Lilibet herself put": Crawford, *Little Princesses*, p. 130.

416 "She was not at all": King George VI to Queen Mary, 14 October 1940, RA QM/PRIV/CC12/138.

416 "I feel so much": *The Times*, 14 October 1940.

416 "thousands of children": Ibid.

416 "most admirably": Ibid.

416 "certainly showed": King George VI, diary, 31 December 1940, RA GVI/PRIV/DIARY.

417 "hot blitz": Nicolson, diary, 16 April 1941, Balliol.

417 "gale of fire": Ibid.

417 "shrieks and jabbers": Ibid.

417 "architectural and historic": *The Illustrated London News*, 4 January 1941.

417 "It really makes": Queen Elizabeth to Queen Mary, 19 October 1940, RA QM/PRIV/CC12/139.

417 "vandalism": King George VI, diary, 29 December 1940, RA GVI/PRIV/DIARY.

417 "a mass of tangled": King George VI, diary, 14 May 1941, RA GVI/PRIV/DIARY.

417 "It is just four": King George VI, diary, 14 May 1941, RA GVI/PRIV/DIARY.

418 "horrified": King George VI, diary, 16 November 1940, RA GVI/PRIV/DIARY.

418 "he had done much": Nicolson, diary, 20 November 1940, RA GVI/PRIV/DIARY.

418 "to alleviate": King George VI, diary, 16 November 1940, RA GVI/PRIV/DIARY.

418 "terribly difficult": Queen Elizabeth to Queen Mary, 19 October 1940, RA QM/PRIV/CC12/139.

418 "so depressing": King George VI, diary, 22 November 1940, RA GVI/PRIV/DIARY.

418 "the journey to London": King George VI, diary, 22 November 1940, RA GVI/PRIV/DIARY.

418 "I would much rather": King George VI, diary, 27 and 28 July 1940, RA GVI/PRIV/DIARY.

419 "Palace on Wheels": *The Illustrated London News*, 17 July 1937.

419 armored the train: King George VI, diary, 20 May 1940, RA GVI/PRIV/DIARY.

419 The only specific: Corbitt, *My Twenty Years in Buckingham Palace*, p. 75.

419 "Some clothes do not": Longford, *Queen Mother*, p. 85.

419 "gentle colours": Hartnell, *Silver and Gold*, p. 101.

419 "If the poor people": Longford, *Queen Mother*, p. 86.

420 Lilibet's pet chameleon: Fitzalan Howard, *Windsor Diaries*, p. 84.

420 *Royal Road*: *The Illustrated London News*, 20 September 1941.

420 **"very dirty child"**: Papers of Frederick James Marquis, first Earl of Woolton, diaries, Bodleian Library, University of Oxford, 11 October 1940.

420 **"Tell me about it"**: Shawcross, *QEQM,* p. 533.

420 **Lord Woolton once**: Woolton, diary, Bodleian Library, University of Oxford, 11 October 1940.

420 **She told Queen Mary**: Queen Elizabeth to Queen Mary, 19 October 1940, RA QM/PRIV/CC12/139.

420 **"<u>loathe</u>" visiting**: Queen Elizabeth to May Elphinstone, 25 October 1940, RA QEQM/OUT/ELPHINSTONE.

421 **"I am still"**: Queen Elizabeth to Elizabeth Elphinstone, 7 February 1941, RA QEQM/OUT/ELPHINSTONE.

421 **"Nashvilles"**: Lascelles III, p. 169.

421 **"always conscious"**: Sir Alan Lascelles to Joan Lascelles, 20 January 1941, LASL, CAC.

421 **"partly epileptic"**: Oliver Woods interview with Sir Alan Lascelles, 14 November 1972, McMaster University Archive, Hamilton, Ontario, Canada.

421 **"never knew how"**: Rose II, p. 103.

421 **"threw her fork"**: Oliver Woods interview with Sir Alan Lascelles, 14 November 1972, McMaster University Archive, Hamilton, Ontario, Canada.

422 **"We heard the 'swish'"**: King George VI, diary, 22 October 1940, RA GVI/PRIV/DIARY.

422 **"It was the first time"**: Queen Elizabeth to May Elphinstone, 25 October 1940, RA QEQM/OUT/ELPHINSTONE.

422 **designed to look**: Crawford, *Little Princesses,* p. 136.

422 **"remarkably well"**: King George VI, diary, 21 and 22 December 1940, RA GVI/PRIV/DIARY.

422 **"were absolutely amazed"**: Crawford, *Little Princesses,* p. 138.

422 **"I wept through"**: King George VI, diary, 21 and 22 December 1940, RA GVI/PRIV/DIARY.

422 **"a past master"**: King George VI, diary, 23 December 1940, RA GVI/PRIV/DIARY.

422 **"a frozen mass"**: Logue and Conradi, *King's Speech,* p. 181.

422 **"firm and deliberate"**: *The Times,* 27 December 1940.

423 **"hope and sober confidence"**: Ibid.; King George VI, diary, 25 December 1940, RA GVI/PRIV/DIARY: "I also stressed . . . that this spirit of fellowship which is growing in war must continue after the war is won. I feel this so strongly."

TWENTY-NINE: American Friends

425 **"a little rest"**: King George VI, diary, 27 December 1940, RA GVI/PRIV/DIARY.

425 "well camouflaged": King George VI, diary, 27 December 1940, RA GVI/PRIV/DIARY.

425 "surrounded completely": Queen Elizabeth to the Duke of Kent, 14 January 1941, RA QEQM/OUT/GDK, Shawcross, *QEQM Letters*, pp. 303–4.

425 "It is warm": King George VI, diary, 27 December 1940, RA GVI/PRIV/DIARY.

426 snowball fights: Stewart, *King's Private Army*, p. 94.

426 "The children are": Queen Elizabeth to Queen Mary, 7 January 1941, RA QM/PRIV/CC12/147.

426 "The fresh air": King George VI, diary, 1, 2, 3, and 4 January 1941, RA GVI/PRIV/DIARY.

426 "all wrong being": King George VI, diary, 31 December 1940, RA GVI/PRIV/DIARY.

426 "The damage to": King George VI, diary, 6 January 1941, RA GVI/PRIV/DIARY.

426 "The effect of": Nicolson, diary, 6 January 1941, Balliol.

426 "When the car stops": Nicolson II, p. 137.

426 "quality of making": Ibid.

426 "clear, soft voice": James Lees-Milne, *Diaries, 1942–1954*, ed. Michael Bloch (London: John Murray, 2006), p. 373.

427 "It is very much": *The Times*, 27 January 1941.

427 "asked innumerable": King George VI, diary, 26, 27, and 28 January 1941, RA GVI/PRIV/DIARY.

427 "The former are": Ibid.

427 "I find that they": King George VI, diary, 5 April 1941, RA GVI/PRIV/DIARY.

427 "new mark of honour": Wheeler-Bennett, *George VI*, p. 472.

428 "The spirit of the": United Press, 23 September 1940.

428 "untimely death": King George VI, diary, 31 December 1940, RA GVI/PRIV/DIARY.

428 "by all means short": Wheeler-Bennett, *George VI*, p. 504.

429 "magnificent": Ibid., p. 512.

429 "I often think": Ibid., p. 525.

429 "with deep interest": Ibid., p. 518.

429 "delighted & thankful": King George VI to Franklin D. Roosevelt, 11 November 1940, Wheeler-Bennett, *George VI*, pp. 516–17.

429 "doing everything": Franklin D. Roosevelt to King George VI, 22 November 1940, Wheeler-Bennett, *George VI*, pp. 517–18.

429 "meant every word": King George VI, diary, 12 January 1941, RA GVI/PRIV/DIARY.

430 "glorious conception": Wheeler-Bennett, *George VI*, p. 522.

430 "as there was": King George VI, diary, 30 January 1941, RA GVI/PRIV/DIARY.

430 "much impressed": King George VI, diary, 29 January 1941, RA GVI/ PRIV/DIARY.

430 "rather tired": King George VI, diary, 30 January 1941, RA GVI/PRIV/ DIARY.

430 "intimate knowledge": Harry Hopkins, diary, 30 January 1941, Harry Hopkins Papers at Georgetown University, Washington, D.C.

431 "to send us more": King George VI, diary, 30 January 1941, RA GVI/ PRIV/DIARY.

431 "very helpful": Queen Elizabeth to Queen Mary, 4 February 1941, RA QM/PRIV/CC12/151.

431 "victory in the long": Hopkins, diary, 30 January 1941.

431 "If ever two people": Ibid.

431 "the newspapers were": Nicolson, diary, 25 January 1941, Balliol.

431 "a gesture which I": King George VI to Franklin D. Roosevelt, 14 February 1941, Wheeler-Bennett, *George VI,* pp. 520–21.

432 "return the compliment": King George VI, diary, 1 March 1941, RA GVI/PRIV/DIARY.

432 "completely informed": John Gilbert Winant, *Letter from Grosvenor Square: An Account of Stewardship* (Boston: Houghton Mifflin, 1947), p. 29.

432 "I have a lot to read": King George VI, diary, 5, 6, and 7 April 1941, RA GVI/PRIV/DIARY.

432 "If only those idiotic": Queen Elizabeth to Queen Mary, 17 February 1941, RA QM/PRIV/CC12/153.

433 "was definitely": King George VI, diary, 22 June 1941, RA GVI/PRIV/ DIARY.

433 "Poor Paul has": King George VI, diary, 24 September 1941, RA GVI/ PRIV/DIARY.

433 "Nobody wants him": King George VI, diary, 3 May 1941, RA GVI/ PRIV/DIARY.

434 "on the verge of": King George VI, diary, 19 February 1943, RA GVI/ PRIV/DIARY.

434 "He has made such": Queen Elizabeth to Queen Mary 13 April 1941, RA QEQM/PRIV/CC12/161.

434 "I am sure": Queen Elizabeth to Lord Halifax, 23 April 1941, BIUY, Hickleton Papers, A2/278/26A 1–6, Shawcross *QEQM Letters,* pp. 310–11.

434 "grave defeat": Nicolson, diary, 1 June 1941.

434 "bitter blow": Wheeler-Bennett, *George VI,* pp. 498–99.

434 "we have been left": King George VI, diary, 14, 15, 16 June 1941, RA GVI/PRIV/DIARY.

434 "no ultimatum": King George VI, diary, 22 June 1941, RA GVI/PRIV/ DIARY.

435 "When Winston has": King George VI, diary, 24 June 1941, RA GVI/ PRIV/DIARY.

435   "this war with Russia": King George VI, diary, 25 June 1941, RA GVI/
       PRIV/DIARY.

435   "bright-eyed and": *The Illustrated London News*, 8 November 1941.

435   "it was so nice going": Queen Elizabeth to Queen Mary, 20 July
       1942, RA QM/PRIV/CC13/20.

436   "I fear it is not": Queen Elizabeth to Winston Churchill, 2 August
       1941, CAC/CHAR/20/20/32, Shawcross, *QEQM*, p. 539.

436   "working in factory": *The Times*, 12 August 1941.

436   "quiet eloquence": Ibid.

436   "her radio address": Franklin D. Roosevelt to King George VI,
       11 August 1941, Wheeler-Bennett, *George VI*, p. 530.

437   "I am sure you will": King George VI to Franklin D. Roosevelt, n.d.,
       delivered 9 August 1941, Wheeler-Bennett, *George VI*, p. 527.

437   "an admission by": *The Illustrated London News*, 21 August 1941.

437   "at the moment": King George VI, diary, 19 August 1941, RA GVI/
       PRIV/DIARY.

437   "America is not": King George VI, diary, 15, 16, and 17 November
       1941, RA GVI/PRIV/DIARY.

438   "He's called Prince": Fitzalan Howard, *Windsor Diaries*, p. 71.

438   "But she's only": Alexandra, Queen of Yugoslavia, *Prince Philip*,
       p. 83.

438   "enormous chest": Fitzalan Howard, *Windsor Diaries*, p. 67.

438   "outward calm": Ibid., pp. 144, 214–15.

438   Lilibet's first dance: King George VI, diary, 23 July 1941, RA GVI/
       PRIV/DIARY; Fitzalan Howard, *Windsor Diaries*, pp. 87–88.

438   "real change": King George VI, diary, 19 August 1941, RA GVI/PRIV/
       DIARY.

438   "a great deal": King George VI, diary, 8, 9, and 10 August 1941, RA
       GVI/PRIV/DIARY.

438   "ten times better": Queen Elizabeth to Queen Mary, 5 September
       1941, RA QM/PRIV/CC12/174.

439   a simple meal: King, *Mackenzie King Record*, 1:254.

439   "feels as I do": King George VI, diary, 20 to 24 August 1941, RA GVI/
       PRIV/DIARY.

439   "very natural": King, *Mackenzie King Record*, 1:257.

439   hosted Prince Philip: King George VI, diary, 18, 19, and 20 October
       1941, RA GVI/PRIV/DIARY.

439   "alertness and": Philip Eade, *Prince Philip: The Turbulent Early Life of
       the Man Who Married Queen Elizabeth II* (New York: Henry Holt,
       2011), p. 282.

439   "She said he's very funny": Fitzalan Howard, *Windsor Diaries*, p. 96.

440   "We felt we had to": King George VI, diary, 27 November 1941, RA
       GVI/PRIV/DIARY.

440   "a bomb shell": King George VI, diary, 7 December 1941, RA GVI/
       PRIV/DIARY.

440 **The Queen heard:** Queen Elizabeth, conversations with Eric Anderson, 1994–95, Shawcross, *QEQM,* p. 541.

440 **"Japan would remain":** King George VI, diary, 19 August 1941, RA GVI/PRIV/DIARY.

440 **"so that the Japanese":** King George VI, diary, 6, 7, and 8 December 1941, RA GVI/PRIV/DIARY.

440 **"We are proud":** King George VI to Franklin D. Roosevelt, 10 December 1941, Wheeler-Bennett, *George VI,* p. 533.

440 **"not well armed":** Queen Elizabeth to Queen Mary, 9 December 1941, RA QM/PRIV/CC12/179.

441 **"warm-hearted":** *The Times,* 27 December 1941.

441 **"All very good":** King George VI, diary, 18 and 19 December 1941, RA GVI/PRIV/DIARY.

441 **"uneasy moment":** Wood, *World in Your Ear,* p. 149.

441 **"the boys and girls":** *The Times,* 27 December 1941.

442 **"confident now":** King George VI, diary, 19 January 1942, RA GVI/PRIV/DIARY.

442 **"Bertie & I have":** Queen Elizabeth to Queen Mary, 14 February 1942, RA QM/PRIV/CC13/5.

442 **"heroism and":** King George VI, diary, 16 April 1942, RA GVI/PRIV/DIARY.

442 **"aircraft works":** King George VI, diary, 24 April 1942, RA GVI/PRIV/DIARY.

443 **"There are no war":** Ibid.

443 **"A great many":** King George VI, diary, 2 May 1942, RA GVI/PRIV/DIARY.

443 **"Devon people are":** King George VI, diary, 8 May 1942, RA GVI/PRIV/DIARY.

443 **"nearly wept":** King George VI, diary, 11 October 1940, RA GVI/PRIV/DIARY.

443 **"know-it-all":** King George VI, diary, 11 February 1940, RA GVI/PRIV/DIARY.

443 **"is very good":** King George VI, diary, 20 April 1942, RA GVI/PRIV/DIARY.

443 **"much more intelligible":** King George VI, diary, 3 April 1942, RA GVI/PRIV/DIARY.

443 **"studied the way":** King George VI to Queen Mary, 1 February 1943, RA QM/PRIV/CC13/38.

444 **"so straightforward":** Queen Elizabeth to Queen Mary, 10 April 1942, RA QM/PRIV/CC13/10.

444 **"I can do all things":** Airlie, *Thatched with Gold,* pp. 219–20.

444 **"a grave little face":** Ibid.

444 **"There we can be":** King George VI, diary, 2 to 5 April 1942, RA GVI/PRIV/DIARY.

444   "It was so nice to be": Queen Elizabeth to Queen Mary, 10 April
       1942, RA QM/PRIV/CC13/10.

445   "so pointedly nice": Fitzalan Howard, *Windsor Diaries,* p. 131.

445   "Everyone's talking": Ibid., p. 140.

445   "scribbled on a piece": Ibid., p.147.

445   "like a brother": Queen Elizabeth to Osbert Sitwell, 13 September
       1942, Sitwell Papers (Weston), Shawcross, *QEQM Letters,* p. 324.

445   "a great affection": Wheeler-Bennett, *George VI,* p. 547.

445   "filthy": King George VI, diary, 25 August 1942, RA GVI/PRIV/DIARY.

446   "Darling, What": King George VI to Queen Elizabeth, 25 August
       1942, RA QEQM/PRIV/RF.

446   They assumed: *Memoirs of Princess Alice, Duchess of Gloucester,*
       p. 128.

446   "No, Ma'am": Colville, *Crowded Life,* p. 131.

446   "My most precious": Queen Mary, diary, 25 August 1942, RA QM/
       PRIV/QMD/1942.

446   "never really recovered": Airlie, *Thatched with Gold,* p. 220.

446   "We were a comfort": Queen Mary, diary, 26 August 1942, RA QM/
       PRIV/QMD/1942.

447   the duke's funeral: *The Times,* 31 August 1942.

447   "terrible loss": Queen Elizabeth to Osbert Sitwell, 13 September
       1942, Sitwell Papers (Weston), Shawcross, *QEQM Letters,* p. 324.

447   "I have attended": King George VI, diary, 29 August 1942, RA GVI/
       PRIV/DIARY.

447   "the remains": King George VI, diary, 14 September 1942, RA GVI/
       PRIV/DIARY.

447   "Marina is still": King George VI, diary, 18 to 21 September 1942, RA
       GVI/PRIV/DIARY.

447   "all my loving": Queen Mary, diary, 30 August 1942, with telegram
       from Duke of Windsor inserted, RA QM/PRIV/QMD/1942.

447   "knowing how": Queen Mary to Duke of Windsor, 31 August 1942,
       RA EDW/PRIV/MAIN/B/156, Shawcross, *QEQM,* p. 552.

448   "was not compromising": Queen Mary to King George VI, 1 Septem-
       ber 1942, RA GVI/PRIV/11/666.

448   "this irreparable loss": Duke of Windsor to King George VI, 15 Sep-
       tember 1942, RA GVI/PRIV/0102/16.

448   "ice has at last been broken": Queen Mary to King George VI,
       15 October 1942, RA GVI/PRIV/F/11/652.

448   "it is a good thing to": Queen Elizabeth to Queen Mary, 19 October
       1942, RA QM/PRIV/CC13/26.

448   "restored": King George VI to Queen Mary, 4 December 1942, RA
       QM/PRIV/CC13/30: "You will see that he once again asks that the
       title H.R.H. should be 'restored' to his wife."

449   "This worry coming": Ibid.

449　**"D. should bother you"**: Queen Mary to King George VI, 4 December 1942, RA GVI/PRIV/RF/11/659.

THIRTY: The Tide Turns

451　**"his remedies"**: King George VI, diary, 24 to 28 September 1942, RA GVI/PRIV/DIARY.

451　**"eats up the bad"**: Queen Elizabeth to Queen Mary, 23 August 1943, RA QM/PRIV/CC13/62.

451　**"I want you and"**: President Roosevelt to King George VI, 17 October 1942, Wheeler-Bennett, *George VI,* p. 550.

451　**"dirty and dark"**: Queen Elizabeth to Queen Mary, 19 October 1942, RA QM/PRIV/CC13/26.

452　**"windowless"**: Ibid.

452　**"quite serious"**: Bradford, *Reluctant King,* p. 348.

452　**"young and charming"**: Roosevelt, *This I Remember,* p. 264.

452　**"they were anxious"**: Ibid.

452　**gold and silver**: Bradford, *Reluctant King,* p. 348.

452　**His cocktail**: Corbitt, *My Twenty Years in Buckingham Palace,* p. 66.

452　**"gin and orange"**: Ibid. Later the Queen would switch to gin and Dubonnet as her favored aperitif, a cocktail her daughter, Queen Elizabeth II, would also prefer.

452　**"cat on hot bricks"**: Lascelles III, p. 66.

453　**"I was the only man"**: King George VI, diary, 24 October 1942, RA GVI/PRIV/DIARY.

453　**"an appalling mess"**: Lascelles III, p. 67.

453　**the blitzed East End**: *The Times,* 26 October 1942.

453　**"They both gave"**: King George VI, diary, 24 October 1942, RA GVI/PRIV/DIARY.

453　**"very egotistical"**: King George VI, diary, 24 October 1940, RA GVI/PRIV/DIARY.

453　**"strong man"**: King George VI, diary, 28 May 1940, RA GVI/PRIV/DIARY.

453　**"got on like"**: Lascelles III, p. 68.

453　**"charming guest"**: Queen Elizabeth to Queen Mary, 2 November 1942, RA QM/PRIV/CC13/28.

454　**"much impressed"**: King George VI, diary, 13 November 1942, RA GVI/PRIV/DIARY.

454　**"flagrantly gate-crashing"**: Lascelles III, p. 82.

454　**"personality in her own"**: *The Times,* 24 October 1942.

454　**"publicize themselves"**: Lascelles III, p. 83.

454　**"enormous pride"**: Eleanor Roosevelt Press Conference, 18 November 1942, RA PS/PSO/GVI/PS/MAIN/06093.

454　**"quite a good"**: Queen Elizabeth to Sir Alan Lascelles, 13 December 1942, RA PS/PSO/GVI/PS/MAIN/06093.

454   "I bring you victory": King George VI, diary, 3 November 1942, RA
       GVI/PRIV/DIARY.
455   "'Is he going mad?'": Queen Elizabeth, conversations with Eric
       Anderson, 1994–95, Shawcross, *QEQM*, p. 559.
455   "a very depressing": King George VI, diary, 3 November 1942, RA
       GVI/PRIV/DIARY.
455   "Yes! Yes! Well": Logue and Conradi, *King's Speech*, p. 183.
455   "after 12 days": King George VI, diary, 4 November 1942, RA GVI/
       PRIV/DIARY.
455   "The enemy is in full": Logue and Conradi, *King's Speech*, p. 183.
455   "Well . . . that's grand": Ibid.
455   "A Victory at last": King George VI, diary, 4 November 1942, RA GVI/
       PRIV/DIARY.
455   "many arduous": King George VI to Winston Churchill, 5 November
       1942, Wheeler-Bennett, *George VI*, pp. 553–54.
455   "It is some 4 months": King George VI, diary, 8 November 1942, RA
       GVI/PRIV/DIARY.
456   "relief of Malta": King George VI, diary, 10 November 1942, RA GVI/
       PRIV/DIARY.
456   This was the first: Mary Soames, *A Daughter's Tale: The Memoir of
       Winston and Clementine Churchill's Youngest Child* (London: Double-
       day, 2011), p. 250.
456   stood in the Grand Hall: *The Times,* 27 November 1942.
456   "a very nice-looking": Memorandum on Thanksgiving Day, 26
       November 1942, U.S. Naval History and Heritage Command, Royal
       Collection.
456   "good at trying": James Lees-Milne, *Ancestral Voices* (New York:
       Scribner, 1975), p. 131.
456   "Everybody felt": Memorandum on Thanksgiving Day, 26 November
       1942, U.S. Naval History and Heritage Command, Royal Collection.
456   "very good manners": King George VI, diary, 26 November 1942, RA
       GVI/PRIV/DIARY.
456   "the study of a country": *The Times,* 28 December 1942.
456   With Churchill: King George VI, diary, 22 December 1942, RA GVI/
       PRIV/DIARY.
456   "the First and Eighth": *The Times,* 28 December 1942.
457   "unspeakable Huns": Queen Elizabeth to David Bowes Lyon, 14 Feb-
       ruary 1943, Bowes Lyon Papers (SPW), Shawcross, *QEQM Letters,*
       p. 340.
457   "impressed by": King George VI, diary, 7 and 8 April 1943, RA GVI/
       PRIV/DIARY.
457   "One would like to": Queen Elizabeth to Sir Alexander Hardinge,
       19 March 1943, Lady Murray Papers, Shawcross, *QEQM Letters,*
       p. 343.
457   "very rough draft": Queen Elizabeth to Winston Churchill, 6 April

1943, CAC, CHAR 20/98 A/54, Shawcross, *QEQM Letters*, pp. 344–45.

457 **He added only ten lines:** Lascelles III, p. 121.

457 **"own words and feelings":** Winston Churchill to Queen Elizabeth, 8 April 1943, CAC, CHAR 20/93B/125, Vickers, *Elizabeth the Queen Mother*, p. 238.

457 **"just as you wrote":** Queen Elizabeth to Winston Churchill, 13 April 1943, CAC, CHAR 20/98A/56, Shawcross, *QEQM Letters*, p. 348.

457 **"You understand what":** Queen Elizabeth to Sir Alan Lascelles, 11 April 1943, RA PS/PSO/AL/BoxB, Shawcross, *QEQM Letters*, p. 345.

458 **"the grey & narrow":** Ibid.

458 **"my fellow countrywomen":** *The Times*, 12 April 1943.

458 **bicycling around:** King George VI, diary, 26 April 1943, RA GVI/PRIV/DIARY.

459 **the King was pleased:** King George VI, diary, 15 to 17 May 1943, RA GVI/PRIV/DIARY.

459 **they took Lilibet:** King George VI, diary, 2 June 1943, RA GVI/PRIV/DIARY.

459 **they went behind:** *The Times*, 3 June 1943.

459 **gave a dance:** Fitzalan Howard, *Windsor Diaries*, p. 184.

459 **"did so enjoy it":** King George VI, diary, 25 March 1943, RA GVI/PRIV/DIARY.

459 **"the whole royal":** Lascelles III, p. 118.

459 **"It is an overwhelming":** King George VI, diary, 13 May 1943, RA GVI/PRIV/DIARY.

459 **"the King remains":** *The Times*, 18 May 1943.

460 **"how to prepare":** King George VI, diary, 12, 13, and 14 December 1942, RA GVI/PRIV/DIARY.

460 **He had set up:** Corbitt, *My Twenty Years in Buckingham Palace*, p. 165.

460 **"help in the war effort":** King George VI, diary, 12, 13, and 14 December 1942, RA GVI/PRIV/DIARY.

460 **"Secrecy is all important":** King George VI, diary, 4 to 7 June 1943, RA GVI/PRIV/DIARY.

460 **"take the entire charge":** King George VI, Instructions to Queen Elizabeth, 9 June 1943, RA QEQM/PRIV/RF, Shawcross, *QEQM*, p. 568.

460 **"discussed matters":** King George VI, diary, 10 June 1943, RA GVI/PRIV/DIARY.

461 **"an anxious few hours":** Queen Elizabeth to Queen Mary, 12 June 1943, RA QM/PRIV/CC13/54.

461 **they had spent:** King George VI, diary, 8 July 1942, RA GVI/PRIV/DIARY.

461 **"most personable":** Harry C. Butcher, *My Three Years with Eisen-*

hower: The Personal Diary of Captain Harry C. Butcher (New York: Simon and Schuster, 1946), p. 17.

461   "one very tall": Ibid., p. 18.

462   "fond of the King": Ibid., p. 151.

462   "soberly and with": Ibid., p. 334.

462   Several days later: King George VI, diary, 19 June 1943, RA GVI/PRIV/DIARY.

462   "the smiles on their": King George VI, diary, 17 June 1943, RA GVI/PRIV/DIARY.

462   "grease & a lotion": King George VI, diary, 17 June 1943, RA GVI/PRIV/DIARY.

462   "A lovely sunny": King George VI, diary, 20 June 1943, RA GVI/PRIV/DIARY.

462   "brought a lump into": King George VI to Queen Mary, 28 June 1943, RA QM/PRIV/CC13/56.

463   "by sea and by night": Ibid.

463   "But I have been": Wheeler-Bennett, *George VI*, p. 578.

463   her first investiture: Lascelles III, p. 135.

463   "obviously enjoyed": Ibid.

463   "Please don't get": Queen Elizabeth to King George VI, 17 June 1943, RA GVI/PRIV/RF/26/79.

463   "he looks very thin": Queen Elizabeth to Queen Mary, 24 June 1943, RA QM/PRIV/CC13/55.

463   "internal trouble": King George VI, diary, 21 June 1943, RA GVI/PRIV/DIARY.

463   he had lost: King George VI, diary, 25 June 1943, RA GVI/PRIV/DIARY.

463   "I found Elizabeth": King George VI, diary, 25 June 1943, RA GVI/PRIV/DIARY.

464   "has not been well": King George VI, diary, 14 to 19 February 1943, RA GVI/PRIV/DIARY.

464   "great secrecy": King George VI, diary, 6 July 1943, RA GVI/PRIV/DIARY.

464   "flat refusal": Lascelles III, pp. 138–39.

464   "he could no longer": King George VI, diary, 6 July 1943, RA GVI/PRIV/DIARY.

464   "at once": Lascelles III, p. 140.

464   "had always found": King George VI, diary, 6 July 1943, RA GVI/PRIV/DIARY.

465   "unwilling target": Lascelles III, p. 138.

465   "kindness & support": Queen Elizabeth to Sir Alan Lascelles, 26 June 1943, RA PS/PSO/AL/Box B.

465   "a serious thing": Harvey II, p. 275.

466   "very angry at me": Helen Hardinge, diary, 8 July 1943, Hon. Lady Murray Papers, Shawcross, *QEQM*, p. 573.

466 "simply grand": Lascelles III, p. 141.

466 "extended knowledge": Lady Airlie to Sir Alan Lascelles, 3 August 1943, British Library, Airlie Papers.

466 "rather wearily": Lascelles III, p. 141.

THIRTY-ONE: Overlord

470 "The more one goes": King George VI, diary, 3 February 1944, RA GVI/PRIV/DIARY.

470 she also saw her patronage: Susan Owens, *Watercolours and Drawings from the Collection of Queen Elizabeth the Queen Mother* (London: Royal Collection, 2005), p. 17.

470 "romantic": Sir Kenneth Clark to Queen Elizabeth, 9 August 1941, RA QEQM/PRIV/PIC, Owens, *Watercolours and Drawings,* p. 34.

470 "really exquisite": Queen Elizabeth to Sir Kenneth Clark, 11 February 1944, Clark Papers, Shawcross, *QEQM Letters,* p. 358.

470 "covered with wisteria": Owens, *Watercolours and Drawings,* p. 37.

471 "You seem to have": James Lees-Milne, *Prophesying Peace* (London: Chatto and Windus, 1977), p. 212.

471 The King watched: King George VI, diary, 10 to 14 December 1943, RA GVI/PRIV/DIARY.

471 "I can't hear a word": Crawford, *Little Princesses,* p. 141.

471 The presence of: King George VI, diary, 18 to 20 October 1943, RA GVI/PRIV/DIARY.

471 "It was admirably": Lascelles III, p. 186.

471 "I have never known": Crawford, *Little Princesses,* p. 150.

471 "seems so suited": Fitzalan Howard, *Windsor Diaries,* p. 217.

471 "They rolled back": Lascelles III, p. 189.

471 "we had a very gay": Princess Elizabeth to Marion Crawford, 1 January 1944, RA QEII/OUT/BUTHLAY, Shawcross, *QEQM,* p. 578.

472 "behaviour did not": Prince Philip to Queen Elizabeth, 31 December 1943, RA QEQM/PRIV/RF, Shawcross, *QEQM,* p. 578.

472 King and the general: King George VI, diary, 10 to 17 January 1944, RA GVI/PRIV/DIARY.

472 "From now on I shall": King George VI, diary, 24 to 31 January 1944, RA GVI/PRIV/DIARY.

472 he saw Prince Philip: King George VI, diary, 12 May 1944, RA GVI/PRIV/DIARY.

472 "a wonderful sight": King George VI, diary, 19 May 1944, RA GVI/PRIV/DIARY.

472 "family matter": King George VI, diary, 8 February 1944, RA GVI/PRIV/DIARY.

472 "How could I create": King George VI to Queen Mary, 20 February 1944, Wheeler-Bennett, *George VI,* pp. 591–92.

473 "any change": Wheeler-Bennett, *George VI,* p. 591.

473   "liked it very much": Robert Barrington-Ward, diary, 16 February 1944, collection of Mark Barrington-Ward.

473   "beginning to move": *The Times,* 17 April 1944.

473   uniform she wore: *The Times,* 19 April 1944.

473   "<u>fascinated</u> her": Fitzalan Howard, *Windsor Diaries,* p. 228.

473   "her life is becoming": Ibid.

473   now she was "Ma'am": Ibid., p. 240.

473   "lovely hot day": King George VI, diary, 21 April 1944, RA GVI/PRIV/DIARY.

473   The Grenadiers did: *The Times,* 22 April 1944.

474   very small air raid shelter: King George VI, diary, 14 March 1944, RA GVI/PRIV/DIARY.

474   From Eisenhower on: King George VI, diary, 15 May 1944, RA GVI/PRIV/DIARY.

474   "astonishment": Lascelles III, p. 219.

474   "This is the biggest": Wheeler-Bennett, *George VI,* p. 600.

474   "capture some villas": Butcher, *My Three Years with Eisenhower,* p. 539.

475   "cafeteria style": Ibid., p. 550.

475   "bombarding ships": King George VI, diary, 30 May 1944, RA GVI/PRIV/DIARY.

475   "I told Elizabeth": Ibid.

475   "shook the King": Lascelles III, p. 224.

475   "not right": King George VI, diary, 31 May 1944, RA GVI/PRIV/DIARY.

475   "As I thought he": King George VI, diary, 1 June 1944, RA GVI/PRIV/DIARY.

476   "I have been very": King George VI, diary, 2 June 1944, RA GVI/PRIV/DIARY.

476   "in deference to": Lascelles III, p. 228.

476   the King diverted: King George V, diary, 2 June 1944, RA GVI/PRIV/DIARY.

476   "very cramped": King George VI, diary, 4 to 5 June 1944, RA GVI/PRIV/DIARY.

476   "spent almost": Fitzalan Howard, *Windsor Diaries,* p. 244.

477   "Bertie's message": Queen Mary to Queen Elizabeth, 18 May 1944, RA QEQM/PRIV/RF.

477   worked with Lionel: Logue and Conradi, *King's Speech,* pp. 194–95.

477   Bishop of Lichfield: King George VI to Queen Mary, 10 June 1944, RA QM/PRIV/CC13/90.

477   "a great opportunity": Ibid.

477   "very fierce": King George VI, diary, 9 June 1944, RA GVI/PRIV/DIARY.

477   viewed models: King George VI, diary, 8 June 1944, RA GVI/PRIV/DIARY.

477   "waddled": Lascelles III, p. 234.

477   Camembert: Ibid.

477   "would not hear": Ibid., p. 235.

477   "elaborately staged": Ibid., p. 234.

477   "most encouraging": King George VI, diary, 16 June 1944, RA GVI/
      PRIV/DIARY.

478   Elizabeth told him: Ibid.

478   "It looks as if": Ibid.

478   "a great shock": King George VI, diary, 17 to 19 June 1944, RA GVI/
      PRIV/DIARY.

478   "felt the concussion": King George VI, diary, 20 June 1944, RA GVI/
      PRIV/DIARY.

478   burst some windows: Queen Elizabeth to Queen Mary, 8 July 1944,
      RA QM/PRIV/CC13/93.

478   "our normal life": King George VI, diary, 4 July 1944, RA GVI/PRIV/
      DIARY.

479   "much worse": Queen Elizabeth to Queen Mary, 8 July 1944, RA
      QM/PRIV/CC13/93.

479   "constantly on": Queen Elizabeth to Queen Mary, 17 July 1944, RA
      QM/PRIV/CC13/95.

479   "You can't take": Queen Elizabeth to David Bowes Lyon, 14 Novem-
      ber 1944, Bowes Lyon Papers (SPW), Shawcross, *QEQM Letters*,
      p. 377.

479   "in case I get": Queen Elizabeth to Princess Elizabeth, 27 June
      1944, RA QEQM/OUT/CHILD, Shawcross *QEQM Letters*,
      pp. 365–66.

479   "put in the shade": King George VI, diary, 3 August 1944, RA GVI/
      PRIV/DIARY.

479   "intense anxiety": Queen Elizabeth to Queen Mary, 26 July 1944, RA
      QM/PRIV/CC13/96.

480   "strenuous eleven days": King George VI, diary, 3 August 1944, RA
      GVI/PRIV/DIARY.

480   "darling Angel": King George VI to Queen Elizabeth, 22 July 1944,
      RA QEQM/PRIV/RF, Shawcross, *QEQM*, p. 585.

480   "It was nearly dark": Queen Elizabeth to Queen Mary, 26 July 1944,
      RA QM/PRIV/CC13/96.

480   "It looked as big": Lascelles III, p. 247.

480   "nice little kitchen": Queen Elizabeth to Queen Mary, 26 July 1944,
      RA QM/PRIV/CC13/96.

480   "I have only been": King George VI to Queen Elizabeth, 29 July 1944,
      RA QEQM/PRIV/RF.

480   "I got to know him": King George VI, diary, 3 August 1944, RA GVI/
      PRIV/DIARY.

481   own rubber bathtub: Field-Marshal Earl Alexander of Tunis, *The
      Alexander Memoirs 1940–1945* (London: Cassell, 1962), pp. 129–30.

481   "panorama of": King George VI, diary, 25 July 1944, RA GVI/PRIV/ DIARY.

481   "very well": Lascelles III, p. 249.

481   "longing to get": Queen Elizabeth to Queen Mary, 4 August 1944, RA QM/PRIV/CC13/97.

481   "most important": King George VI, diary, 12 August 1944, RA GVI/ PRIV/DIARY.

481   "that training": King George VI, diary, 21 to 23 August 1944, RA GVI/ PRIV/DIARY.

482   "very bright eyes": Queen Elizabeth to Queen Mary, 19 August 1944, RA QM/PRIV/CC13/98.

482   her first salmon: Lascelles III, p. 257.

482   "peace and beauty": Queen Elizabeth to Queen Mary, 4 August 1944, RA QM/PRIV/CC13/97.

482   "Germany first": King George VI, diary, 17 July 1942, RA GVI/PRIV/ DIARY: "Americans don't seem to understand that we (USA and UK) have got to beat the Germans in Europe. Japan can wait for her defeat."

482   "admiration for": King George VI, diary, 23 to 25 September 1944, RA GVI/PRIV/DIARY.

482   Monty's dogs: Lascelles III, p. 262.

482   "I found out that": King George VI, diary, 15 October 1944, RA GVI/ PRIV/DIARY.

483   "I have got to know": King George VI, diary, 15 October 1944, RA GVI/PRIV/DIARY.

483   "I had not seen": King George VI, diary, 17 October 1944, RA GVI/ PRIV/DIARY.

483   died in his sleep: King George VI, diary, 7 November 1944, RA GVI/ PRIV/DIARY.

483   "active & virile": Queen Elizabeth to Queen Mary, 6 November 1944, RA QM/PRIV/CC13/109.

483   "great position": *The Times,* 8 November 1944.

483   "very grateful": Queen Elizabeth to Winston Churchill, 14 November 1944, CAC, CHAR 1/380/52, Shawcross, *QEQM Letters,* p. 377.

483   echoed the austere: *The Times,* 11 November 1944.

484   "He seems to really": Queen Elizabeth to David Bowes Lyon, 14 November 1944, Bowes Lyon Papers (SPW), Shawcross, *QEQM Letters,* p. 376.

484   "danced round": Fitzalan Howard, *Windsor Diaries,* p. 282.

484   "laughed v. loudly": Ibid., p. 247.

484   "the simple enjoyment": Prince Philip to Queen Elizabeth, 23 July [1944], RA QEQM/PRIV/RF, Shawcross, *QEQM,* p. 578.

484   "learnt quite a lot": Queen Elizabeth to Queen Mary, 26 January 1945, RA QM/PRIV/CC13/117.

484   "the greatest": *The Times,* 2 December 1944.

484   "ceremony of national significance": Ibid.

485   "I think it will": Queen Elizabeth to Queen Mary, 26 January 1945, RA QM/PRIV/CC13/117.

485   "new and utterly": Fitzalan Howard, *Windsor Diaires*, p. 287.

485   "I've never worked": Sarah Bradford, *Elizabeth: A Biography of Britain's Queen* (New York: Riverhead, 1997), p. 108.

485   "has become very": King George VI, diary, 20 February 1945, RA GVI/PRIV/DIARY.

485   "a very great man": King George VI, diary, 13 April 1945, RA GVI/PRIV/DIARY.

486   "Internment Camp": *The Times,* 19 April 1945.

486   "Camp of Death": Ibid., 16 April 1945.

486   "persecution and": Nicolson, diary, 9 December 1942, Balliol.

486   "barbarous and": Ibid., 17 December 1942.

486   "Tens of thousands": King George VI, diary, 19 April 1945, RA GVI/PRIV/DIARY.

486   "the German people": King George VI, diary, 19 April 1945, RA GVI/PRIV/DIARY.

486   "Events are moving": King George VI, diary, 28 to 30 April 1945, RA GVI/PRIV/DIARY.

486   "A great victory": King George VI, diary, 2 May 1945, RA GVI/PRIV/DIARY.

487   "No more fear": King George VI, diary, V-E Day, Tuesday, 8 May 1945, RA GVI/PRIV/DIARY.

487   "evil doers": Nicolson, diary, 8 May 1945, Balliol.

487   first of eight: *The Times,* 9 May 1945.

487   "Speaking from": Ibid.

487   had been practicing: Logue and Conradi, *King's Speech,* pp. 206–7.

488   "The words are": Nicolson, diary, 8 May 1945, Balliol.

488   "and it showed": Logue and Conradi, *King's Speech,* p. 208.

488   "Embankment": Rhodes, *Final Curtsey,* p. 69.

488   "Poor darlings": King George VI, diary, 8 May 1945, RA GVI/PRIV/DIARY.

489   "great ovation": King George VI, diary, 9 May 1945, RA GVI/PRIV/DIARY.

489   "what this country": King George VI, diary, 17 May 1945, RA GVI/PRIV/DIARY.

489   "a dignity": Lascelles III, pp. 325–26.

489   "with his sense": Nicolson II, p. 462.

PART SIX: AN INDELIBLE LEGACY
THIRTY-TWO: Changing of the Guard

493   international mission: King George VI, diary, 12 March 1940, RA GVI/PRIV/DIARY.

493 **Ernest Bevin had:** King George VI, diary, 18 July 1940, RA GVI/PRIV/DIARY.

493 **"must stick together":** King George VI, diary, 16 October 1940, RA GVI/PRIV/DIARY.

494 **"must get rid of":** King George VI, diary, 11 to 15 March 1942, RA GVI/PRIV.DIARY.

494 **"done gradually":** King George VI, diary, 27 February 1941, RA GVI/PRIV/DIARY.

494 **"Parliament is ten":** King George VI, diary, 28 May 1945, RA GVI/PRIV/DIARY.

494 **predicted to the King:** King George VI, diary, 25 July 1945, RA GVI/PRIV/DIARY.

494 **"the people's reaction":** Lascelles III, p. 342.

495 **"gross inequalities":** Wheeler-Bennett, *George VI,* p. 655.

495 **"with great calm":** Lascelles III, p. 343.

495 **"The change of Govt":** King George VI, diary, 26 July 1945, RA GVI/PRIV/DIARY.

495 **"would help":** King George VI, diary, 28 July 1945, RA GVI/PRIV/DIARY.

495 **"It was a very sad":** King George VI, diary, 26 July 1945, RA GVI/PRIV/DIARY.

495 **"in recognition":** King George VI, diary, 28 July 1945, RA GVI/PRIV/DIARY.

495 **"after the rebuff":** Lascelles III, p. 344.

495 **"could remain in":** King George VI, diary, 26 July 1945, RA GVI/PRIV/DIARY.

495 **"obviously in a state":** Lascelles III, p. 344.

495 **"found he was":** King George VI, diary, 26 July 1945, RA GVI/PRIV/DIARY.

495 **"shy & reserved":** King George VI, diary, 24 October 1939, RA GVI/PRIV/DIARY.

495 **"as usual was":** King George VI, diary, 13 February 1945, RA GVI/PRIV/DIARY.

495 **"Clem the Clam":** Mackenzie King, *The Mackenzie King Record,* vol. 3, *1945–1946,* ed. J. W. Pickersgill and D. F. Forster (Toronto: University of Toronto Press, 1970), p. 240.

496 **"anarchist son":** Nicolson, diary, 14 April 1949, Balliol.

496 **"I did not tell":** King George VI, diary, 4 March 1942, RA GVI/PRIV/DIARY.

496 **"the most important subject":** King George VI, diary, 26 July 1945, RA GVI/PRIV/DIARY.

496 **"HM begged":** Lascelles III, p. 344.

496 **"insisted":** Wheeler-Bennett, *George VI,* p. 638.

496 **"everything that":** King George VI to Duke of Gloucester, 21 January 1946, Wheeler-Bennett, *George VI,* p. 654.

496   "long talk": King George VI to Queen Mary, 2 September 1945, RA QM/PRIV/CC13/130.

497   "had learnt": King George VI, diary, 2 August 1945, RA GVI/PRIV/DIARY.

497   "impressed with": Wheeler-Bennett, *George VI*, p. 644.

497   "a great talker": King George VI, diary, 2 August 1945, RA GVI/PRIV/DIARY.

497   "informality": Wheeler-Bennett, *George VI*, p. 645.

497   "Tube Alloy experiment": King George VI, diary, 25 July 1945, RA GVI/PRIV/DIARY.

497   "horrified": Nicolson, diary, 8 August 1945, Balliol.

497   "so secret": Lascelles III, p. 347.

497   "I think, Mr. Byrnes": Nicolson, diary, 8 August 1945, Balliol.

497   "million American": Roberts, *Churchill*, p. 890.

498   "We did not want": King George VI, diary, 15 August 1945, RA GVI/PRIV/DIARY.

498   "public ownership": *The Times*, 16 August 1945.

498   "courage and devotion": Ibid.

499   Churchill arrived on his own: King George VI, diary, 15 August 1945, RA GVI/PRIV/DIARY.

499   "Victory Talk": *The Times*, 16 August 1945.

499   "with a vast crowd": Lascelles III, pp. 351–52.

499   "We want the King": *The Times*, 16 August 1945.

499   "I wish he could": King George VI, diary, 15 August 1945, RA GVI/PRIV/DIARY.

500   "informed the crowds": *The Times*, 16 August 1945.

500   "walked miles": Rhodes, *Final Curtsey*, p. 69.

500   "stifle all private": King George VI, diary, 20 November 1945, RA GVI/PRIV/DIARY.

500   "He was a very hard": Judd, *George VI*, p. 224.

500   "He was essentially": Wheeler-Bennett, *George VI*, p. 796.

500   "very depressing": Queen Elizabeth to Queen Mary, 26 July 1945, RA QM/PRIV/CC13/128.

500   "wouldn't strike one": Queen Elizabeth, conversations with Eric Anderson, 1994–95, Shawcross, *QEQM*, p. 602.

501   "How refreshing": King George VI, diary, 21 November 1945, RA GVI/PRIV/DIARY.

501   When the King needed: Lord Moran, *Winston Churchill: The Struggle for Survival 1940–1965* (London: Sphere Books, 1968), p. 338.

501   "very much": King, *Mackenzie King Record*, 3:240.

501   he also asked: Lascelles III, p. 355. On October 5, 1945, when the Duke of Windsor arrived in London to ask for the ambassadorial post, Tommy Lascelles briefed the King and Attlee on why they should reject his request.

501   "personal and secret": Ibid., pp. 222–24, memo written 30 May
       1944.
502   "purely private matter": Ibid., pp. 269–70.
502   "same conditions": King George VI, diary, 12 November 1944, RA
       GVI/PRIV/DIARY.
502   signed a brief: Lascelles III, p. 271.
502   "constant harping": Ibid., p. 270.
502   "substratum of truth": Lascelles III, p. 351.
502   shared the telegrams: Ibid., p. 352.
503   "dreading": Queen Mary to King George VI, 25 September 1945, RA
       GVI/PRIV/RF/11/785.
503   "After some moments": King George VI, diary, 5 to 6 October 1945,
       RA GVI/PRIV/DIARY.
503   "discussed the whole": King George VI, diary, 5 to 6 October 1945,
       RA GVI/PRIV/DIARY.
503   "a job under the Crown": King George VI, diary, 5 to 6 October 1945,
       RA GVI/PRIV/DIARY.
503   had convinced his brother: Lascelles III, p. 356.
503   "a real truthful statement": King George VI, diary, 5 to 6 October
       1945, RA GVI/PRIV/DIARY.
504   become "shriller": Lascelles III, p. 358.
504   "characteristically": Ibid., p. 361.
504   "silken thread": Ibid., p. 371.
504   Finally, early in 1946: Ibid., p. 381.
505   "chief hobby": Ibid., p. 337.
505   "he never mentioned": King George VI, diary, 16 October 1946, RA
       GVI/PRIV/DIARY.
505   "ice-veined bitches": Bradford, *Reluctant King*, p. 448.
505   "had one of his violent": Queen Elizabeth to Princess Elizabeth,
       21 December 1949, RA QEII/PRIV/RF, Shawcross, *QEQM Letters*,
       p. 421.
505   "burnt out:" King George VI to Duke of Gloucester, 21 January 1946,
       Wheeler-Bennett, *George VI*, p. 654.
505   "sandy-coloured hair": *Time*, 1 July 1946.
506   "a new man": Lascelles III, p. 363.
506   "congregated round": Airlie, *Thatched with Gold*, pp. 223–25.

THIRTY-THREE: Romance in the Air

509   "hatless" and "always in": Crawford, *Little Princesses*, pp. 198–99.
510   "get back to his": King George VI, diary, 10 March 1944, RA GVI/
       PRIV/DIARY.
511   "very handsome": Airlie, *Thatched with Gold*, p. 227.
511   "has a good sense": King George VI to Queen Mary, 17 March 1944,
       RA QM/PRIV/CC13/84, Shawcross, *QEQM*, p. 579.

511 **"P. sounds extremely"**: Queen Mary to King George VI, 20 March 1944, RA GVI/PRIV/RF/11, Shawcross, *QEQM,* p. 579.

511 **"They have been"**: Airlie, *Thatched with Gold,* p. 227.

511 **"would always know"**: Ibid., p. 228.

512 **"I defy anyone"**: Crawford, *Little Princesses,* p. 163.

512 **"monumental cheek"**: Prince Philip to Queen Elizabeth, 12 June 1946, RA QEQM/PRIV/RF, Shawcross, *QEQM,* p. 624.

512 **"You certainly can"**: Queen Elizabeth to Prince Philip, 3 March 1950, Duke of Edinburgh, Personal Archives, Buckingham Palace, Shawcross, *QEQM Letters,* p. 424.

512 **"We have had"**: King George VI, diary, 8 August to 22 September 1946, RA GVI/PRIV/DIARY.

512 **"a rather heated"**: Prince Philip to Queen Elizabeth, 3 December [1946], RA QEQM/PRIV/RF, Shawcross, *QEQM,* p. 625.

512 **"had always played"**: Queen Elizabeth to Prince Philip, 1 December 1947, Duke of Edinburgh Personal Archives, Buckingham Palace, Shawcross, *QEQM Letters,* p. 406.

513 **"fallen in love"**: Prince Philip to Queen Elizabeth, 14 September 1946, RA QEQM/PRIV/RF, Shawcross, *QEQM,* p. 625.

513 **that pleased George VI**: Wheeler-Bennett, *George VI,* p. 751.

513 **"Serving Officer"**: *London Gazette,* 18 March 1947.

513 **two "distinct white races"**: Wheeler-Bennett, George VI, p. 688.

513 **"real friend"**: King George VI, diary, 14 October 1942, RA GVI/PRIV/ DIARY.

514 **"discussed everything"**: King George VI, diary, 29 January 1947, RA GVI/PRIV/DIARY.

514 **"dawn lightened"**: Queen Elizabeth to Queen Mary, 1 February 1947, RA QM/PRIV/CC13/162.

514 **"like being stroked"**: Peter Townsend, *Time and Chance: An Autobiography* (London: Methuen, 1978), p. 168.

514 **"it would only make"**: Queen Elizabeth to Queen Mary, 9 March 1947, Wheeler-Bennett, *George VI,* p. 687.

516 **"In 30 years of public"**: Sir Alan Lascelles to Joan Lascelles, 18 February 1947, LASL, CAC.

516 **"staggering amounts"**: Queen Elizabeth to Queen Mary, 21 February 1947, RA QM/PRIV/CC13/169.

516 **"in full force"**: *The Times,* 22 February 1947.

516 **"repeated spasms"**: Sir Alan Lascelles to Joan Lascelles, 22 February 1947, LASL, CAC.

517 **"the basses coming in"**: *Diary of the Royal Visit to South Africa 1947,* 1 March 1947, RA F&V/VISOV/SA/1947-Tour Diary of South Africa.

517 **"lest the King"**: Ibid., 5 March 1947.

517 **tribal dances with sticks**: Ibid., 19 March 1947.

517 **"even the old Boer"**: Queen Elizabeth to the Hon. Elizabeth Elphinstone, 23 March 1947, RA QEQM/OUT/ELPHINSTONE.

517   "astounded": Sir Alan Lascelles to John Lascelles ("my dear Wool"),
       10 March 1947, LASL, CAC.

517   a clandestine visit: Graham Viney, *The Last Hurrah: The 1947 Royal
       Tour of Southern Africa and the End of Empire* (London: Robinson,
       2019), pp. 241–47.

518   "Olga very pretty": King George VI to Queen Mary, 6 April 1947, RA
       QM/PRIV/CC13/174.

518   "deep happiness": Duchess of Kent to Queen Elizabeth, 20 April
       1947, RA QEQM/PRIV/RF.

518   "lavished much care": Sir Alan Lascelles to Joan Lascelles, 23 April
       1947, LASL, CAC.

518   spent two hours huddled: Viney, *Last Hurrah,* pp. 270–76. Viney
       writes that in Victoria Falls, the speech was "prerecorded and filmed."
       The discs "were sent to London lest the unreliable radio beam be-
       tween Cape Town and London prove faulty on the night. . . . The
       broadcast went out 'live' from Government House after all, as the
       beam radio service behaved well. . . . It was only later admitted that a
       prerecorded version had existed 'in case.'"

519   "at home": *The Times,* 22 April 1947.

519   "perfect": Queen Mary to Queen Elizabeth, 22 April 1947, RA
       QEQM/PRIV/RF.

519   "of course I wept": Ibid.

519   "delicate control": Enid Bagnold to Lady Diana Cooper, Lady Diana
       Cooper Papers, Eton College Archive.

519   "quite sucked dry": Queen Elizabeth to May Elphinstone, 26 April
       1947, RA QEQM/OUT/ELPHINSTONE.

519   "internal storms": Sir Alan Lascelles to Joan Lascelles, 2 March 1947,
       LASL, CAC.

520   "incessant tirade": Townsend, *Time and Chance,* pp. 177–78.

520   "to convince": Sir Alan Lascelles to Joan Lascelles, 30 April 1947,
       LASL, CAC.

520   "given me a new": Wheeler-Bennett, *George VI,* p. 692.

520   "it is such a complex": Queen Elizabeth to May Elphinstone, 26 April
       1947, RA QEQM/OUT/ELPHINSTONE.

520   "remarkable development": Sir Alan Lascelles to Joan Lascelles,
       30 April 1947, LASL, CAC.

THIRTY-FOUR: Sunlight and Clouds

523   "crowned a decade": *The Times,* 12 May 1947.

523   "slight chill": Tour Diary of South Africa, 5 May 1947, RA F&V/
       VISOV/SA/1947.

523   "getting fatter": King George VI to Queen Mary, 6 April 1947, RA
       QM/PRIV/CC13/174.

523   "We are all glad": *The Times,* 13 May 1947.

524   "showing the scars": Ibid., 16 May 1947.
524   written by Tommy: Sir Alan Lascelles to Joan Lascelles, 30 April
      1947, LASL, CAC.
524   "miserable ordeal": *The Times*, 16 May 1947.
524   "constantly": Crawford, *Little Princesses*, p. 185.
524   Writing to the Queen: Prince Philip to Queen Elizabeth, 11 June
      [1947], RA QEQM/PRIV/RF, Shawcross, *QEQM*, p. 626.
524   "This is one line": Queen Elizabeth to May Elphinstone, 7 July 1947,
      RA QEQM/OUT/ELPHINSTONE.
525   "with the greatest": *The Times*, 10 July 1947.
525   "so lovely to know": Queen Elizabeth to Prince Philip, 9 July 1947,
      Duke of Edinburgh Personal Archives, Buckingham Palace, Shawcross,
      QEQM Letters, p. 401.
525   "flushed and radiant": Airlie, *Thatched with Gold*, p. 228.
525   The five thousand guests: *The Times*, 11 July 1947.
525   "Everybody is straining": Nicolson III, p. 102.
525   "the whole party": *The Times*, 11 July 1947.
526   The following week: *The Times*, 16 to 22 July 1947, Pathé News.
526   "I have put our names": *The Times*, 22 July 1947.
526   "He is so nice": King George VI to Queen Mary, 18 August 1947, RA
      QM/PRIV/CC13/181.
526   "a flash of colour": Martin Gilbert, *Winston S. Churchill*, vol. 8,
      Never Despair 1945–1964 (Boston: Houghton Mifflin, 1988), p. 359.
527   "Whenever I come": King George VI to Queen Mary, 18 August 1947,
      RA QM/PRIV/CC13/181.
527   "I do wish one": King George VI to Queen Mary, 14 September 1947,
      RA QM/PRIV/CC13/183.
527   "statesmanlike": King George VI, diary, 12 March 1946, RA GVI/
      PRIV/DIARY.
527   Churchill told him: King George VI, diary, 22 to 28 April 1946, RA
      GVI/PRIV/DIARY.
527   benefited India: King George VI, diary, 1 August 1941, RA GVI/PRIV/
      DIARY.
527   "many Indians still": King George VI, diary, 2 March 1942, RA GVI/
      PRIV/DIARY.
528   "humbug": King George VI, diary, 28 October 1943, RA GVI/PRIV/
      DIARY.
528   "wants us out": King George VI, diary, 8 August and 9 August 1942,
      RA GVI/PRIV/DIARY.
528   "We cannot leave": King George VI, diary, 1 December 1943, RA
      GVI/PRIV/DIARY.
528   "considered pink": Author interview with Patricia Knatchbull, second
      Countess Mountbatten of Burma, 13 June 2008.
528   "You've got to do": Author interview with Lady Pamela Hicks, 13 Feb-
      ruary 2018.

529 "The first time": King George VI to Queen Mary, 18 August 1947, RA QM/PRIV/CC13/181.

529 "very much": King George VI to Lord Mountbatten, 12 October 1948, Wheeler-Bennett, *George VI*, p. 720.

529 "the symbol of": Wheeler-Bennett, *George VI*, p. 730.

529 "The Southern Irish": King George VI, diary, 11 December 1940, RA GVI/PRIV/DIARY.

529 his condolences: Lascelles III, p. 320.

530 "Why leave": Nicolson, diary, 27 October 1948, Balliol.

530 "I mustn't miss": Eileen Parker, *Step Aside for Royalty: Treasured Memories of the Royal Household* (n.p.: Eileen Parker and Christopher Moore, 2017), p. 19.

530 "having a quiet": Ibid., p. 20.

530 more than one thousand: *The Times*, 19 November 1947.

531 twenty-one diamonds: Ibid.

531 "here, is the Queen": Nicolson, diary, 14 February 1950, Balliol.

531 "Presently all the royalties": *Duff Cooper Diaries*, p. 453.

531 "a marvellous": Parker, *Step Aside for Royalty*, p. 22.

531 "I know Philip": King George VI to Queen Mary, 6 November 1947, Wheeler-Bennett, *George VI*, p. 753.

532 gave a salute: *The Times*, 21 April 1947.

532 "exactly the same": Ibid.

532 "miracle of wireless": Ibid.

532 "Colour came back": Ibid.

532 "leaders to whom": Ibid.

533 "looking quite miserable": Alexandra, Queen of Yugoslavia, *Prince Philip*, p. 65.

533 "My mouth, my eyes": Princess Elizabeth to Queen Elizabeth, 22 November 1947, RA QEQM/PRIV/RF, Shawcross, *QEQM*, p. 629.

533 "deep-throated roar": *The Times*, 21 November 1947.

534 "It is a far more": King George VI to Archbishop of Canterbury, Lambeth Palace Library, Fisher Papers, vol. 276, ff. 1–11, Bradford, *Elizabeth*, p. 130.

534 "but when I handed": Wheeler-Bennett, *George VI*, pp. 754–55.

534 "Papa & I are happy": Queen Elizabeth to Princess Elizabeth, 24 November 1947, RA QEII/PRIV/RF, Shawcross, *QEQM Letters*, pp. 403–4.

534 "cherish and look after": Queen Elizabeth to Prince Philip, 1 December 1947, Duke of Edinburgh, Personal Archives, Buckingham Palace, Shawcross, *QEQM Letters*, pp. 405–6.

534 arranged for Winston: Conversation with Sarah Churchill on 7 December 1947 in James Lees-Milne, *Caves of Ice: Diaries: 1946–1947* (London: Chatto and Windus, 1983), p. 254.

534 "rough, ill-mannered": Nicolson, diary, 12 June 1955, Balliol.

535 "The young man came": Nicolson, diary, 8 June 1948, Balliol.

535   "concealed the wounds": *The Times,* 27 April 1948.

535   **topped by a silver bowl:** *The Illustrated London News,* 1 May 1948.

536   "remembered how": *The Times,* 27 April 1948.

536   "memorable and": *The Illustrated London News,* 1 May 1948.

536   "beloved country": *The Times,* 27 April 1948.

536   "We were both": King George VI to Queen Mary, 3 May 1948, RA QM/PRIV/CC13/198.

536   **The pain began:** "King George VI Memorial Number," *The Sphere,* 16 February 1952.

536   **began keeping track:** Wheeler-Bennett, *George VI,* p. 762.

537   "'What's the matter'": Townsend, *Time and Chance,* p. 182.

537   "a real break": Queen Elizabeth to Sir Alan Lascelles, 28 October 1948, RA PS/PSO/AL/Box B.

537   **legs in clamps:** Shawcross, *QEQM,* p. 638.

538   "beaming with": Major Thomas Harvey, Private Secretary to Queen Elizabeth, "Notes on the Birth of Prince Charles," Harvey private collection, 14 November 1948.

538   "only recently": Wheeler-Bennett, *George VI,* p. 765.

538   "to do this treatment": Queen Elizabeth to Queen Mary, 12 December 1948, RA QM/PRIV/CC13/216.

538   "try and make it": Ibid.

539   "take up his life": Queen Elizabeth to Prince Paul of Yugoslavia, 5 January 1949, RA QEQM/OUT/PAUY, Shawcross, *QEQM Letters,* p. 413.

539   **He shot rabbits:** Queen Elizabeth to Queen Mary, 13 February 1949, RA QM/PRIV/CC13/219.

539   "recognized invalid": Nicolson, diary, 15 February 1949, Balliol.

539   "cover to cover": Howarth, *George VI,* p. 234.

539   "So our treatment": Wheeler-Bennett, *George VI,* p. 766.

540   **The princess confidently:** *The Times,* 10 June 1949.

540   "both psychological and physical": Wheeler-Bennett, *George VI,* p. 768.

540   "I've only got to": Ibid.

540   "Let's take the plates": Parker, *Step Aside for Royalty,* p. 124.

540   "lovely & warm": King George VI to Queen Mary, 24 August 1949, RA QM/PRIV/CC13/236.

541   "plunged into": Queen Elizabeth to Duke of Edinburgh, 21 December 1949, Duke of Edinburgh, Personal Archives, Buckingham Palace, Shawcross, *QEQM Letters,* pp. 422–23.

541   "to have achieved": Princess Elizabeth to Major Thomas Harvey, Harvey private collection, 31 August 1950.

541   "those heavenly: Queen Elizabeth to Princess Elizabeth, 7 April 1951, RA QEII/PRIV/RF, Shawcross, *QEQM Letters,* pp. 436–37.

542   "short vulgar": Queen Elizabeth to Princess Elizabeth, 29 December 1950, RA QEII/PRIV/RF, Shawcross, *QEQM Letters,* p. 433.

542   "bumped his leg": Queen Elizabeth to Princess Elizabeth, 31 January
       1951, RA QEII/PRIV/RF, Shawcross, *QEQM Letters*, p. 435.

542   "You will have to see": Queen Elizabeth to Princess Elizabeth, 29 De-
       cember 1950, RA QEII/PRIV/RF, Shawcross, *QEQM Letters*, p. 433.

542   "They cheer us up": Queen Elizabeth to Princess Elizabeth, 7 April
       1951, RA QEII/PRIV/RF, Shawcross, *QEQM Letters*, pp. 436–37.

542   "I do hope the Americans": King George VI to Queen Mary, 22 Janu-
       ary 1951, RA QM/PRIV/CC14/17.

542   "to think before": Queen Elizabeth to Princess Elizabeth, 31 January
       1951, RA QEII/PRIV/RF, Shawcross, *QEQM Letters*, p. 436.

543   "here prices": Ibid.

543   "positions of confidence": Queen Elizabeth to Marion Crawford,
       4 April 1949, Papers of Bruce and Beatrice Blackmar Gould, Manu-
       scripts Division, Department of Rare Books and Special Collections,
       Princeton University, Vickers, *Elizabeth the Queen Mother*, p. 283.

543   "Old Miss Poignand": Queen Elizabeth to Duke of Edinburgh,
       15 July 1949, Duke of Edinburgh, Personal Archives, Buckingham
       Palace, Shawcross, *QEQM Letters*, p. 417.

544   "You must resist": Queen Elizabeth to Marion Crawford, 4 April
       1949, Vickers, *Elizabeth the Queen Mother*, p. 283.

544   thirteen offensive passages: Vickers, *Elizabeth the Queen Mother*,
       p. 286.

544   "true & trustworthy": Queen Elizabeth to Marion Crawford, 1
       January 1949, RA QEII/OUT/BUTHLAY, Shawcross, *QEQM*, p. 641.

THIRTY-FIVE: Farewell, with Love

547   "curious air of mystery": Sitwell, *Queen Mary and Others*, p. 42.

547   "heavily made up": Nicolson, diary, 14 March 1950, Balliol.

548   "It was remarked": Wheeler-Bennett, *George VI*, p. 785.

548   "got him very down": Queen Elizabeth to Princess Elizabeth, 7 April
       1951, RA QEII/PRIV/RF, Shawcross, *QEQM Letters*, p. 437.

548   "I feel now": King George VI to Queen Mary, 12 June 1951, RA QM/
       PRIV/CC14/30.

548   "chuck out the bug": Wheeler-Bennett, *George VI*, p. 787.

548   began reading cabinet: Howarth, *George VI*, p. 243.

549   "strong enough": Queen Elizabeth to Queen Mary, 10 July 1951, RA
       QM/PRIV/CC14/32.

549   moving slowly: Townsend, *Time and Chance*, p. 190.

549   "flaming and dancing": Princess Margaret to Major Thomas Harvey,
       Harvey private collection, 25 September 1951.

549   "lonely forlorn figure": Townsend, *Time and Chance*, p. 190.

550   Among the family party: *The Times*, 17 September 1951.

550   "sand table-model": Aubrey Buxton, *The King in His Country* (Wood-
       stock, Vt.: Countryman Press, 1956), p. 132.

550   "Royal shooting ceased": Ibid., p. 133.

551   "structural changes": *The Times*, 19 September 1951.

551   "Because they were": Lord Moran, *Winston Churchill*, pp. 364–65.

551   "scarring and narrowing": *The Times*, 22 September 1951.

551   "Poor fellow": Lord Moran, *Winston Churchill*, p. 366.

551   "drastic surgery": *Time*, 8 October 1951.

551   "If it's going to help": Wheeler-Bennett, *George VI*, p. 788.

551   "so wonderfully brave": Queen Elizabeth to Queen Mary, 21 September 1951, RA QM/PRIV/CC14/37.

551   "Winston said to me": Sir Alan Lascelles to Queen Elizabeth, 23 September 1951, RA QEQM/PRIV/PAL.

551   "long hell": Queen Elizabeth to Queen Mary, 23 September 1951, RA QM/PRIV/CC14/38.

552   "Thank goodness": King George VI to Queen Mary, 14 October 1951, Wheeler-Bennett, *George VI*, p. 790.

552   "making steady progress": Queen Elizabeth to May Elphinstone, 5 October 1951, RA QEQM/OUT/ELPHINSTONE.

552   "You can imagine": Queen Elizabeth to Sir Alan Lascelles, 23 September 1951, RA PS/PSO/AL/Box B.

553   front-page article: *The Times*, 28 September 1951.

553   "continued anxiety": *The Times*, 1 October 1951.

553   "bury that hatchet": Queen Mary to King George VI, RA GVI/PRIV/RF/11, Shawcross, *QEQM*, p. 649.

552   "smiling confidence": *The Times*, 3 November 1951.

553   "beginning to take": Queen Elizabeth to Princess Elizabeth, 15 October 1951, RA QEII/PRIV/RF, Shawcross, *QEQM Letters*, pp. 440–42.

553   "enough to keep": *The Times*, 27 October 1951.

554   "twinkle of merriment": Buxton, *King in His Country*, p. 133.

554   "FINISHED": Nicolson, diary, 11 January 1952, Balliol.

554   "to get up & do": Wheeler-Bennett, *George VI*, p. 790.

554   "As we drove": Ibid., p. 798.

554   "remarkable recovery": King George VI to Lionel Logue, 15 December 1951, Logue and Conradi, *King's Speech*, p. 224.

555   "undue fatigue": *The Times*, 6 November 1951.

555   A landline was set: *The Times*, 30 October 1951.

555   "up the greater part": *The Times*, 6 November 1951.

555   "liable to be a little": *The Times*, 22 December 1951.

555   "It took a very": Wood, *World in Your Ear*, p. 165.

555   "in the best of health": Princess Margaret to Major Thomas Harvey, Harvey private collection, 9 February 1952.

556   "both familiar": Logue and Conradi, *King's Speech*, p. 221.

556   "Not only by the grace": *The Times*, 26 December 1951.

556   vigorous enough: *The Times*, 27 December 1951.

556   "I shot with the King": Gavan Naden and Maxine Riddington, *Lilac*

Days: The True Story of the Secret Love Affair That Altered the Course of History (London: HarperCollins, 2005), p. 264.

556   **"well satisfied"**: Wheeler-Bennett, *George VI*, p. 802.

556   **His activity that day**: "Court Circular," *The Times*, 30 January 1952.

557   **The skies were gray**: *The Times*, 1 February 1952.

557   **"gay and even jaunty"**: Lord Moran, *Winston Churchill*, p. 397.

557   **"could not help"**: Queen Elizabeth to Princess Elizabeth, 2 February 1952, RA QEII/PRIV/RF, Shawcross, *QEQM Letters*, p. 443.

557   **"I do hope that"**: Ibid.

557   **"various remedies"**: King George VI to Sir John Weir, 3 February 1952, RA QEQM/PRIV/PAL.

558   **informal day**: Buxton, *King in His Country*, p. 138; Lord Moran, *Winston Churchill*, p. 397.

558   **stand to stand**: *The Times*, 28 December 1951.

558   **heated waistcoat**: Naden and Riddington, *Lilac Days*, p. 265.

558   **"It was one of"**: *The Sphere*, 16 February 1952.

558   **"had not meant"**: Naden and Riddington, *Lilac Days*, p. 265.

558   **"didn't complain"**: Ibid., p. 266.

558   **"full speed"**: Buxton, *King in His Country*, p. 138.

558   **"enchanted with"**: Queen Elizabeth to Edward Seago (extract), n.d. [February 1952], RA QEQMH/PS/GEN/1989/Seago, Shawcross, *QEQM*, p. 653.

558   **played the piano**: Naden and Riddington, *Lilac Days*, p. 265.

558   **listened to the radio**: Ibid.

558   **"With his customary"**: Wheeler-Bennett, *George VI*, p. 803.

559   **"said good night"**: *The Sphere*, 16 February 1952.

559   **"I flew to his"**: Queen Elizabeth to Queen Mary, 6 February 1952, RA QM/PRIV/CC14/44.

559   **"in a perch"**: Nicolson, diary, 6 February 1952, Balliol.

559   **"in wonderful form"**: Queen Elizabeth to Queen Mary, 6 February 1952, RA QM/PRIV/CC14/44.

560   **"great affection"**: Queen Mary to Queen Elizabeth, 7 February 1952, RA QEQM/PRIV/RF.

560   **"ardent & controlled"**: Queen Elizabeth to Duke of Edinburgh, 3 March 1950, Duke of Edinburgh, Personal Archives, Buckingham Palace, Shawcross, *QEQM Letters*, p. 425.

560   **"at this most tragic"**: Queen Mary to Queen Elizabeth, 7 February 1952, RA QEQM/PRIV/RF.

560   **"this beautiful young"**: Author interview with Jane Portal Williams, 21 May 2018.

560   **"remained completely"**: Ibid.

560   **"Her old Grannie"**: Pope-Hennessy I, p. 620.

561   **"they looked well"**: Queen Mary, diary, 7 February 1952, RA QM/PRIV/QMD/1952.

561   **"moment of serenity"**: *The Times*, 8 February 1952.

561   "with befitting pomp": *The Times,* 9 February 1952.

561   "Darling Papa": *The Sphere,* 16 February 1952.

562   "Poured in sheets": Queen Mary, diary, 11 February 1952, RA QM/PRIV/QMD/1952.

562   "We had a few": Ibid.

563   "rode like a ship": *The Times,* 16 February 1952.

563   "Here *he* is": Airlie, *Thatched with Gold,* p. 236.

563   In their carriage: *The Times,* 16 February 1952. The Duchess of Windsor, who had not been invited to the funeral, remained in a hotel suite in New York City.

563   draped in black and purple: Ibid.

564   "Very slight": Ibid.

564   "noble, lovely": Ibid.

564   "our brother": Ibid.

564   "King walked": Roberts, *Churchill,* p. 929.

564   "It was his fate": C. R. Attlee, *As It Happened* (London: Heinemann, 1954), p. 242.

565   "Yr. Majesty's": Winston Churchill to Queen Elizabeth, 14 February 1952, RA QEQM/PRIV/DEATH/GVI.

ILLUSTRATION CREDITS

Page 268: King Edward VIII with Wallis Simpson and Katherine Rogers during their cruise on the *Nahlin*, August 1936. Central Press/Getty Images.

Page 296: Coronation of King George VI and Queen Elizabeth at Westminster Abbey with Queen Mary and Princesses Elizabeth and Margaret in the royal box behind, May 12, 1937. © Illustrated London News Ltd./Mary Evans Picture Library.

Page 298: Queen Elizabeth, Princess Elizabeth, Queen Mary, Princess Margaret, and King George VI on the balcony at Buckingham Palace after the coronation, May 12, 1937. © Hulton Deutsch Collection/Corbis/Getty Images.

Page 320: Adolf Hitler greeting the Duke and Duchess of Windsor, Germany, 1937. PA Images/Alamy Stock Photo.

Page 336: King George VI and Queen Elizabeth with the president of France, Albert Lebrun, at a garden party, Château de Bagatelle, in the Bois de Boulogne, France, July 1938. TopFoto.

Page 350: King George VI with President Franklin D. Roosevelt and Queen Elizabeth with Mrs. Roosevelt driving to the White House, Washington, D.C., June 8, 1939. © Illustrated London News Ltd./Mary Evans Picture Library.

Page 366: King George VI addresses the people of Britain and the British Empire over the BBC, the day of Britain's declaration of war on Nazi Germany, September 3, 1939. © Hulton Deutsch Collection/Corbis/Getty Images.

Page 392: King George VI and Queen Elizabeth visit a munitions factory in the Midlands, April 1940. AFP via Getty Images.

Page 394: King George VI, Queen Elizabeth, and Winston Churchill inspect bomb damage to Buckingham Palace following German air raids over London, September 1940. Popperfoto/Getty Images.

Page 424: President Franklin D. Roosevelt and Prime Minister Winston Churchill after a religious service aboard the HMS *Prince of Wales*, off the coast of Newfoundland, August 10, 1941. Photo by Lieutenant L. C. Priest/Imperial War Museums/Getty Images.

Page 450: King George VI arriving in Malta aboard the HMS *Aurora*, June 1943. Military Images/Alamy Stock Photo.

Page 468: King George VI, Queen Elizabeth, and Princesses Elizabeth and Margaret with Prime Minister Winston Churchill on V-E Day, May 8, 1945. Associated Press.

Page 490: King George VI and Princess Elizabeth at Windsor Castle, July 1946. Lisa Sheridan/Studio Lisa/Hulton Archive/Getty Images.

Page 492: King George VI meets with new prime minister Clement Attlee at Buckingham Palace, July 28, 1945. Fox Photos/Getty Images.

Page 508: King George VI and Queen Elizabeth with Princesses Elizabeth and Margaret, Cape Town, South Africa, February 1947. Sport and General Press Agency Limited/AFP/Getty Images.

Page 522: Princess Elizabeth and the Duke of Edinburgh after their marriage, November 20, 1947. © Hulton Deutsch Collection/Corbis/Getty Images.

Page 546: Substituting for King George VI, Princess Elizabeth leads the Trooping the Colour ceremony, London, June 7, 1951. Ullstein Bild/Getty Images.

First Insert

Page 1, top: Prince Albert, Princess Mary, and Prince Edward, circa 1900. Popperfoto/Getty Images.

Page 1, bottom: Elizabeth Bowes Lyon and brother David Bowes Lyon, 1904. Classic Image/Alamy Stock Photo.

Page 2: Elizabeth Bowes Lyon and her mother, Lady Strathmore, with wounded soldiers, Glamis Castle, World War I. World History Archive/Alamy Stock Photo.

Page 3: The Princess of Wales, later Queen Mary, with sons Prince Edward and Prince Albert, circa 1905. Popperfoto/Getty Images.

Page 4, top: Lady Elizabeth Bowes Lyon and the Duke of York, Glamis Castle, September 1920. Image by courtesy of the Earl of Strathmore and Kinghorne, Glamis Castle.

Page 4, bottom: Lady Elizabeth Bowes Lyon and the Duke of York with shooting party, Glamis Castle, September 1921. Image by courtesy of the Earl of Strathmore and Kinghorne, Glamis Castle.

Page 5, top: The Duke and Duchess of York after their wedding, April 26, 1923. Photo 12/Alamy Stock Photo.

Page 5, bottom: The Prince of Wales, the Duchess of York, and her sister, Lady Rose Leveson-Gower, followed by the Duke of York at a shooting party on the moors, Glamis, Scotland, 1923. © Illustrated London News Ltd./Mary Evans Picture Library.

Page 6: Christening of Princess Elizabeth at Buckingham Palace, 1926. Bettmann/Getty Images.

Page 7, top: The Duke of York and Wing Commander Louis Greig playing doubles at Wimbledon, 1926. Hulton Archive/Getty Images.

Page 7, bottom: King George V, Queen Mary, and the Duke and Duchess of York with baby Princess Elizabeth on the balcony of Buckingham Palace, 1927. © Illustrated London News Ltd./Mary Evans Picture Library.

Page 8: The Duchess of York and Princess Elizabeth greeting a disabled soldier, 1929. PA Images/Alamy Stock Photo.

Page 9: Wedding portrait of Prince George, Duke of Kent, and Princess Marina of Greece, November 29, 1934. Historia/Shutterstock.

Page 10: King George V with three sons, the Duke of Kent, the Prince of Wales, and the Duke of York, 1935. SuperStock/Alamy Stock Photo.

Page 11: King George VI and Queen Elizabeth with Princesses Elizabeth and Margaret at Windsor Castle, June 1936. Lisa Sheridan/Studio Lisa/Hulton Archive/Getty Images.

Page 12, top: King Edward VIII and Wallis Simpson at Balmoral, 1936. Popperfoto/Getty Images.

Page 12, bottom: King George VI leaving for the Accession Council, 1936. Antiqua Print Gallery/Alamy Stock Photo.

Page 13: Funeral cortege for Lady Strathmore, the mother of Queen Elizabeth, Glamis Castle, Scotland, June 27, 1938. © Illustrated London News Ltd./Mary Evans Picture Library.

Page 14: Queen Elizabeth placing a poppy on the Australian war memorial in France, July 1938. © Illustrated London News Ltd./Mary Evans Picture Library.

Page 15, top: King George VI and Queen Elizabeth celebrate the signing of the Munich Agreement with Prime Minister Neville Chamberlain and his wife on the Buckingham Palace balcony, 1938. © Illustrated London News Ltd./Mary Evans Picture Library.

Page 15, bottom: King George VI riding with Princesses Elizabeth and Margaret on Princess Elizabeth's thirteenth birthday, Windsor Great Park, April 21, 1939. Popperfoto/Getty Images.

Page 16, top: King George VI and Queen Elizabeth with war veterans in Ottawa, Canada, May 1939, RCIN 2941061. Royal Collection Trust/ All Rights Reserved.

Page 16, bottom: President Franklin D. Roosevelt and Mrs. Roosevelt bid farewell to King George VI and Queen Elizabeth, Hyde Park, New York, 1939. Smith Archive/Alamy Stock Photo.

Second Insert

Page 1: Luncheon for King George VI and Queen Elizabeth after their trip to North America, the Guildhall, London, 1939. SuperStock/Alamy Stock Photo.

Page 2: Queen Elizabeth by Cecil Beaton, Buckingham Palace, 1939. © Cecil Beaton/Victoria and Albert Museum, London.

Page 3: King George VI, Queen Elizabeth, and Princesses Elizabeth and Margaret at the boys' camp singing "Under the Spreading Chestnut Tree," Abergeldie Castle at Balmoral, Scotland, August 1939. Associated Press.

Page 4, top: Queen Elizabeth Armistice Day broadcast to women from Buckingham Palace, November 11, 1939. Bettmann/Getty Images.

Page 4, bottom: King George VI inspecting the troops during a visit to the western front in France, December 1939. Associated Press.

Page 5: King George VI and Queen Elizabeth with exiled members of

European royal families and Allied heads of governments, Buckingham Palace, 1941. Bettmann/Getty Images.

Page 6, top: King George VI, Queen Elizabeth, and Winston Churchill after inspecting bomb damage to Buckingham Palace following German air raids over London, September 1940. George Rinhart/Corbis/Getty Images.

Page 6, bottom: Bomb shelter beneath Buckingham Palace for King George VI and Queen Elizabeth, drawing by James Gardner, 1940. © Illustrated London News Ltd./Mary Evans Picture Library.

Page 7: King George VI and Queen Elizabeth speaking to a workman in bomb-damaged London, October 1940. Central Press/Getty Images.

Page 8, top: Princess Elizabeth, with Princess Margaret by her side, making a broadcast to the children of the empire and the United States, October 1940. Topical Press Agency/Getty Images.

Page 8, bottom: Queen Elizabeth exits the royal armored car, named "Brontosaurus," 1940. © Illustrated London News Ltd./Mary Evans Picture Library.

Page 9, top: King George VI greets new American ambassador John Winant as he arrives in Windsor, 1941. Trinity Mirror/Mirrorpix/Alamy Stock Photo.

Page 9, bottom: King George VI visits British troops in North Africa, 1943. Mary Evans Picture Library.

Page 10, top: Princesses Elizabeth and Margaret performing the *Aladdin* pantomime, Windsor Castle, 1943. Getty Images.

Page 10, bottom: Princess Elizabeth and family celebrate her eighteenth birthday, April 21, 1944. Associated Press.

Page 11, top: King George VI visits troops with Field Marshal Montgomery, Holland, October 1944. Gamma-Keystone/Getty Images.

Page 11, bottom: King George VI with President Harry Truman on board the HMS *Renown,* Plymouth, England, August 1945. Popperfoto/Getty Images.

Page 12, top: King George VI and Queen Elizabeth take part in victory procession on V-J Day, August 15, 1945. AP/Shutterstock.

Page 12, bottom: King George VI with Princesses Elizabeth and Margaret, Royal Lodge, Windsor, July 1946. Lisa Sheridan/Studio Lisa/Hulton Archive/Getty Images.

Page 13, top: King George VI and Princess Elizabeth arriving at Westminster Abbey for her wedding to the Duke of Edinburgh, November 20, 1947. Trinity Mirror/Mirrorpix/Alamy Stock Photo.

Page 13, bottom: King George VI and Queen Elizabeth during a service to commemorate their silver wedding anniversary, St. Paul's Cathedral, London, 1948. Central Press/Getty Images.

Page 14: King George VI and Queen Elizabeth with their grandchildren Prince Charles and Princess Anne. Keystone Press/Alamy Stock Photo.

Page 15: Princess Elizabeth and the Duke of Edinburgh leave for a
    Commonwealth tour of Africa, Australia, and New Zealand, cut short
    by the death of King George VI, January 31, 1952. SuperStock/Alamy
    Stock Photo.
Page 16: Queen Elizabeth the Queen Mother at the funeral of King
    George VI, February 1952. Popperfoto/Getty Images.

INDEX

References to people whose names change over time are grouped together under the name most commonly used by today's readers (for example, Elizabeth II rather than Lilibet), both in main entries and subentries. Please see "A Note on Royal Names" on page xi for a guide to the various name changes.

Page numbers in *italics* refer to photographs or their captions.